RICHMOND
ENGLISH
DICTIONARY

Published by Peter Haddock Ltd.

Published by Peter Haddock

Bridlington, England

Ⓒ BBJF London

Printed in Poland

ISBN NO 07105 0346 6

ABBREVIATIONS
USED IN THIS BOOK

a.	adjective.
adv.	adverb.
n.	noun.
n.m.	noun masculine.
n.f.	noun feminine.
fem.	feminine.
v.t.	verb transitive.
v.i.	verb intransitive.
v. refl.	reflexive verb.
v. aux.	auxiliary verb.
pron.	pronoun.
prep.	preposition.
p.p.	past participle.
pres. p.	present participle.
conj.	conjunction.
interj.	interjection.
sl.	slang.
q.v.	which see.
v.i.	see below.
v.s.	see above.
esp.	especially.
cp.	compare.
Syn.	Synonym.
Ant.	Antonym.

DICTIONARY

OF THE ENGLISH LANGUAGE

A, an *a.* one ; any.

Ab'aca (-ka) *n.* Manila hemp.

Aback' *adv.* backwards, reversed.

Ab'acus *n.* a flat piece at the top of a column ; a frame with parallel wires on which slide beads for counting.

Abaft' *adv.* and *prep.* behind.

Abalo'ne (-ō-nē) *n.* a shellfish, used as food in the East, which yields mother-of-pearl.

Aban'don *v.t.* to give up altogether.—**aban'donod** *pp.* and *a.* given up, *esp.* to evil. —**aban'donment** *n.*
  Syn. to yield, surrender, cede, relinquish, renounce. *Ant.* to keep, retain, adhere to, cherish.

Abase' *v.t.* to lower, humiliate. —**abase'ment** *n.*

Abash' *v.t.* to confuse, make ashamed.

Abate' *v.t.* to lessen.—*v.i.* to become less.—**abate'ment** *n.*

Ab'atis, ab'attis *n.* a barricade of felled trees for defence.

Abattoir' *n.* slaughter-house.

Abb'ot *n.* the head of a monastery.—**abb'ess** *n. fem.* —**abb'ey** *n.* a monastery.— **abb'acy** *n.* the office of abbot.

Abbre'viate *v.t.* to shorten.— **abbrevia'tion** *n.*

Ab'dicate *v.t.* to give up formally.—*v.i.* to give up power.—**abdica'tion** *n.*

Abdo'men *n.* belly.—**abdom'-inal** *a.*

Abduce' *v.t. Anat.* to draw to a different part.—**abducent** (ab-dū'-sent) *a.* drawing away.

Abduct' *v.t.* to carry off, kidnap.—**abduc'tion** *n.*

Abeam' *adv.* abreast, in line.

Abed' *adv.* in bed.

Aberra'tion *n.* wandering, *esp.* mental disorder, " wandering of wits."—**aber'rant** *a.*

Abet' *v.t.* to help in something bad.—**abett'er, abett'or** *n.*

Abey'ance *n.* condition of not being in use or action.

Abhor' *v.t.* to dislike very strongly, loathe.—**abhor'-rence** *n.*—**abhor'rent** *a.*

Abide' *v.i.* to stay, reside.— *v.t.* to endure, put up with.

Ab'ject *a.* mean, despicable.

Abjure' *v.t.* to give up by oath, renounce.—**abjura'tion** *n.*

Ab'lative *a.* and *n.* a Latin case of nouns, primarily meaning " away from."

Ablaze' *a.* burning.

A'ble *a.* capable, clever, having power.—**a'bly** *adv.*—**abil'ity** *n.*

Ablu'tion *n.* washing.

Ab'negate *v.t.* to give up, renounce.—abnega'tion *n.*

Abnorm'al *a.* irregular; not usual.—abnorm'ally *adv.*—abnormal'ity *n.*

Aboard' *adv.* on board, on a ship or train.—*prep.* on board of.

Abode' *n.* home; dwelling.

Abol'ish *v.t.* to do away with.—aboli'tion *n.*—aboli'tionist *n.* one who wishes to do away with, *esp.* an evil, e.g. slavery.

Abom'inate *v.t.* to hate strongly.—abom'inable *a.*—abom'inably *adv.*—abomina'tion *n.*

Aborig'ines (-ji-nēz) *n.pl.* the original inhabitants of a country.—aborig'inal *a.*

Abort' *v.i.* to miscarry.—abor'tion *n.* something misshapen or unnatural.—abor'tive *a.*—abor'tively *adv.*

Abound' *v.i.* to be plentiful.

About' *adv.* on all sides; nearly; up and down; out, astir.—*prep.* round; near; dealing with.

Above' *adv.* in a higher place.—*prep.* on top of; higher, more than.

Abrade' *v.t.* to rub off, scrape away.—abra'sion *n.*

Abreac'tion *n.* in psychoanalysis, elimination of a morbid complex by expression through conscious association with the original cause.

Abreast' *adv.* side by side.

Abridge' *v.t.* to cut short, abbreviate.—abridg'ment *n.*

Abroad' *adv.* out of house or country; at large.

Ab'rogate *v.t.* to cancel, put an end to.—abroga'tion *n.*
    Syn. to abolish, set aside, recall. *Ant.* maintain, continue, enforce.

Abrupt' *a.* hasty; steep; sudden; blunt.—abrupt'ness *n.*—abrupt'ly *adv.*

Ab'scess (-ses) *n.* a collection of pus.

Abscind' (sind) *v.t.* to cut off, pare away.—abscis'sion *n.*

Abscis'sa (-sis-) *n.* *maths.* the distance of a point from the axis o ordinates.

Abscond' (-sk-) *v.i.* to withdraw, decamp.

Ab'sent *a.* away; not attentive.—absent' *v.t.* to keep away.—ab'sence *n.*—ab'sently *adv.*—absentee' *n.* one away, one who habitually stays away—absentee'ism *n.* the practice of a landlord living away from his estate.

Absinthe' *n.* wormwood; liqueur flavoured with wormwood.

Absolve' *v.t.* to free from, pardon. —absolu'tion *n.*—ab'solute *a.* not limited, unconditional; entire, pure (as *absolute alcohol*).—ab'soluteness *n.*—ab'solutely *adv.*

Ab'sonant *a.* discordant, inharmonious.

Absorb' *v.t.* to suck up, drink in.—absorp'tion *n.*—absorb'ent *n.* and *a.*—absorp'tive *a.*
    Syn. to engross, swallow up, imbibe, engulf. *Ant.* reject, throw away, bore.

Abstain' *v.i.* to keep from, refrain, *esp.* from strong drink. abstain'er *n.*—absten'tion *n.*—ab'stinence *n.*—ab'stinent *a.*

Abste'mious *a.* sparing in food or *esp.* drink.—abste'miousness *n.*—abste'miously *adv.*

Absterge' *v.t.* to clean by wiping.—abster'gent *a.*—abster'sion *n.*

Ab'stract *a.* separate; existing only in the mind; not concrete.—*n.* a summary, abridgment.—abstract' *v.t.* to draw from, remove.—abstrac'tion *n.*—abstract'ed *a.* absent-minded. — abstract'ly *adv.*

Abstruse' *a.* obscure, hard to understand.—abstruse'ly *adv.*

Absurd' *a.* silly, contrary to reason.—absurd'ity *n.*—absurd'ly *adv.*

Abu'lia, aboulia (-bŏŏ'-) *n.* loss or lack of will.

Abun'dance *n.* great, plenty. —abun'dant *a.*—abun'dantly *adv.*

Abuse' (-būz) *v.t.* to misuse; miscall, address in rude language.—abuse' (-būs) *n.*—abu'sive *a.*—abu'sively *adv.*—abu'siveness *n.*

Abut' *v.i.* to end on, border on. —abut'ment *n.* a support, *esp.* for the end of a bridge.

Abyss' *n.* a very deep gulf or pit.—abys'mal (-z-) *a.*—abys'mally *adv.*

Abyssin'ian *a.* of or pert. to Abyssinia.—abyssinian gold, an alloy of copper and zinc, thinly plated with gold.

Aca'cia (akāsha) *n.* a thorny tropical shrub.

Acad'emy *n.* a higher school; a society to advance arts or sciences.—academi'cian *n.*—academ'ic, academ'ical *a.* of an academy; theoretical.—academ'ically *adv.*

Acan'thus *n.* a prickly plant, the "bear's breech"; an architectural ornament like this leaf.

Accede' (aks-) *v.i.* to enter on an office; agree, consent.—acces'sion (ak-se'-shn).

Accel'erate (aks-) *v.t.* and *i.* to quicken motion, increase speed.—accelera'tion *n.*—accel'erative *a.*—accel'erator *n.* mechanism to increase speed, *esp.* in a motor-car.
  Syn. to speed, hasten, quicken, expedite, despatch. *Ant.* retard, check, linger.

Ac'cent (aks-) *n.* a stress of the voice; a mark to show such stress; a manner of speech peculiar to a district or individual.—accent' *v.t.*—accen'tuate *v.t.*—accentua'tion *n.* —accen'tual *a.*

Accept' (aks-) *v.t.* to take, receive; admit, believe; agree to.—accep'table *a.*—accept'ably *adv.*—acceptabil'ity.—accep'tance.—accepta'tion.—accep'ter *ns.*

Ac'cess (-ks-) *n.* admission; entrance; attack.—access'ible *a.* easy to approach.—accessibil'ity *n.*—access'ibly *adv.*—access'ary *n.* a helper, *esp.* in a crime.—access'ory *n.* something helping or additional.

Ac'cidence (-ks-) *n.* the part of grammar dealing with changes in the form of words, e.g. plurals, etc.

Ac'cident (-ks-) *n.* something happening by chance; a mishap; a quality not essential.

—acciden'tal *a.*—acciden'tal-ly *adv.*

Acclaim' *v.t.* to applaud, receive with applause.—acclama'tion *n.*—acclam'atory *a.*

Accli'matize *v.t.* to accustom to a new climate.—acclimatiza'tion *n.*

Accliv'ity *n.* a slope up.

Accolade' *n.* part of the ceremony of conferring knighthood, a light stroke with the flat of a sword.

Accomm'odate *v.t.* to fit; harmonize; supply. — accomm'odating *a.* obliging.—accommoda'tion *n.* lodgings; a loan.

Accom'pany *v.t.* to go with; join with.—accom'paniment *n.* something which accompanies, *esp.* in *music*, the part which goes with other music, e.g. solos.—accom'panist *n.* one who plays an accompaniment.

Accom'plice *n.* a companion in evil deeds.

Accom'plish *v.t.* to carry out; finish. — accom'plished *a.* complete, perfect.—accom'plishment *n.* completion; a personal ability.

Syn. to ach.eve, effect, execute, fulfil, realise, perfect. *Ant.* fail in, leave unfinished or incomplete, spoil.

Accord' *v.t.* to compose, settle.—*v.i.* to agree.—*n.* agreement, harmony.—accord'ant *a.*—accord'ance *n.*—accord'ing *adv.*—accord'ingly *adv.* as the 'circumstances suggest.

Accord'ion *n.* a wind instrument worked by a bellows in the hands, a concertina.

Accost' *v.t.* to speak to, approach.

Account' *v.t.* to reckon, judge.—*v.i.* to give a reason; make a statement of money.—*n.* a statement of monies; a report, description.—account'able *a.* responsible.—accountabil'ity *n.*—accoun'tant *n.* a professional reckoner, one skilled in accounts.

Accou'tre (-ōō-) *v.t.* to equip.—accout'rements *n.pl.* equipment, *esp.* military.

Accred'it *v.t.* to recommend; vouch for.

Accre'tion *n.* growth; something added on.

Accrue' (-ōō-) *v.i.* to result; come as an addition.

Accu'mulate *v.t.* to amass.—*v.i.* to grow into a mass, increase.—accumula'tion *n.*—accu'mulator *n.* an electrical storage battery.

Acc'urate *a.* exact, correct.—acc'urately *adv.*—acc'uracy *n.*

Accurs'ed, accurst' *a.* under a curse, hateful.

Accuse' *v.t.* to charge with wrong doing; blame.—accu'ser *n.*—accusa'tion *n.*—accu'satory *a.*—accu'sative *n.* a Latin case of nouns indicating an object.

Accus'tom *v.t.* to make used to, familiarise.—accus'tomed *a.*

Ace *n.* the one at dice, cards, dominoes; a single point; (*slang*) a very success.ul fighting airman.

Acen'tric (-sen'-) *a.* not central; away from the centre.

Acerb'ity n. sour bitterness.

Ace'tic a. derived from or having the nature of vinegar. —ac'etous (as-) a.

Ac'etone (as'-) n. a highly inflammable gas obtained from acetates.

Acet'ylene n. a gas, made from calcium carbide and water, burning with a bright flame.

Ache (āk) n. a continuous pain.—v.i. to be in pain.—ach'ing a.

Achieve' v.t. to finish, accomplish, perform successfully. —achieve'ment n. something accomplished; a coat of arms.

Achromat'ic a. free from or not showing colour, as of a lens.

Ac'id a. sharp, sour.—n. a sour substance; chem. one of a class of compounds which combine with bases (alkalis, oxides, etc.) to form salts.— acid'ify v.t.—acid'ity n.— acid'ulous a.—acid'ulate v.t. to make slightly acid.—acid test, final conclusive test of value.

A'cierate (ă'-sĕ-) v.t. to change into, to render like, steel.

Ackemm'a n. army signallers' name for A.M. of time, popularised during the Great War.

Acknowl'edge (ak-nol'ij) v.t. to admit, own, recognise.—acknowl'edgment n.

Ac'me n. highest point.

Ac'olyte n. a lesser church officer, an attendant on a priest.

Ac'onite n. a poisonous plant, wolf's-bane or monk's-hood.

A'corn (āk-) n. the fruit of the oak.

Acous'tic a. pertaining to hearing.—acous'tics n.pl. the science of sounds.

Acquaint' v.t. to make to know, inform. — acquaint'ance n. personal knowledge; a person known. — acquai 'tanceship n.

Acquiesce' v.i. to agree in silence; consent.—acquies'-cence n.—acquies'cent a.

Acquire' vt. to gain, get.— acquire'ment n.—acquisi'tion n. act of getting; a material gain.—acquis'itive a. desirous of gaining.—acquis'itiveness n.

Acquit' v.t. to settle, discharge, as a debt; behave (one's self); declare innocent.—acquitt'al n. act of declaring innocent in a court.—acquitt'ance n. discharge of a debt.

A'cre (-her) n. a measure of land, 4840 square yards; pl. lands, estates.—a'creage n. the number of acres in a piece of land.

Ac'rid a. bitter and hot; irritating.—acrid'ity n.—ac'-ridness n.

Ac'rimony n. bitterness of feelings or language.—acrimo'nious a.

Syn. harshness, animosity, asperity. Ant. love, concord, sympathy, benevolence.

Ac'robat n. a rope-dancer; tumbler.—acrobat'ic a.

Across' adv. and prep. crosswise; from side to side.

Acros'tic n. a poem in which the first or last letters of the lines, in order, spell a word or words.

Act. n. a thing done, a deed;

process of doing; law or decree; a section of a play.—*v.t.* to perform, as in a play.—*v.i.* to exert force; work, as a mechanism; behave.—**ac'ting** *n.* performance of a part; working.—**ac'tion** *n.* activity; operation; gesture; a battle; a lawsuit.—**ac'tionable** *a.* subject to a lawsuit.—**ac'tive** *a.* brisk, energetic.—**ac'tively** *adv.*—**activ'ity** *n.*—**ac'tor** *n.* a performer in plays (*fem.* **ac'tress**).

Ac'tinism *n.* the chemical action of the sun's rays.—**actin'ic** *a.* — **actinother'apy** *n.* treatment of disease by light, *esp.* sunshine.

Actin'ium *n.* a radio-active substance found in pitch-blende.

Ac'tual *a.* real; existing in the present.—**actual'ity** *n.*—**ac'tually** *adv.*

Ac'tuary *n.* a registrar; one who makes calculations for insurance companies. — **actua'rial** *a.*

Ac'tuate *v.t.* to move, impel.

Acu'men *n.* sharpness of wit.

Acute' *a.* sharp; sensitive; keen, shrewd; critical.—**acute'ly** *adv.*—**acute'ness** *n.* *Syn.* sagacious, subtle, penetrating. *Ant.* obtuse, dull, stupid.

Ad'age *n.* an old saying, a proverb.

Ada'gio *a.* and *adv.* (*music*) slowly.

Ad'amant *n.* a very hard stone; diamond.—**adaman'tine** *a.*

Adam's ap'ple *n.* the projecting part of a man's throat.

Adapt' *v.t.* to fit; to alter for a new use.—**adapta'tion** *n.*—**adapt'able** *a.*—**adaptabil'ity** *n.*

Add *v.t.* and *i.* to join; to put something on; to say further. —**addi'tion** *n.*—**addi'tional** *a.* —**adden'dum** (*pl.* **-a**) something to be added.

Add'er *n.* a small poisonous snake.

Add'ict *n.* one given up to something, usually an evil, e.g. *a drug-addict.*—**addict'ed** *a.*—**addic'tion** *n.*

Ad'dle *v.t.* and *i.* to make or become rotten, muddled.

Address' *v.t.* to speak to; direct; dispatch; to mark a destination, as on an envelope.—*n.* skill; a speech; the direction on a letter.—**addressee'** *n.* person addressed. — **address'es** *n.pl.* courtship.

Adduce' *v.t.* to bring forward, allege.—**addu'cible** *a.*—**adduc'tion** *n.*

Ad'enoids *n.pl.* small growths at the back of the nose.

Adept' *a.* skilled.—*n.* an expert.

Ad'equate *a.* sufficient, suitable.—**ad'equacy** *n.*—**ad'equately** *adv.*

Adhere' *v.i.* to stick to; to become or remain firm, in an opinion, etc.—**adhe'rent** *n.* and *a.*—**adhe'sion** *n.*—**adhe'sive** *a.*

Adhib'it *v.t.* to use or apply; to attach.

Adieu' (adū) *int.* farewell.—*n.* act of taking leave.

Ad'ipose *a.* fatty.

Ad'it *n.* a horizontal entrance into a pit.

Adja'cent *a.* lying close to.—**adja'cency** *n.*

Ad'jective *n.* a word added to a noun to show quality or circumstance.—**adjecti'val** *a.*

Adjoin' *v.t.* and *i.* to add; to be next to.—**adjoin'ing** *a.* next to, near.

Adjourn' (a-jẹrn) *v.t.* and *i.* to put off, postpone; to end a meeting; to move to another place.—**adjourn'ment** *n.*

Adjudge' *v.t.* to decide; award.

Adju'dicate *v.t.* and *i.* to try, judge; to sit in judgment.—**adjudica'tion** *n.*—**adju'dicator** *n.*

Adj'unct *a.* joined, added.—*n.* a person or thing added.

Adjure' *v.t.* to beg, entreat.—**adjura'tion** *n.*

Adjust' *v.t.* to set right; make exact or suitable.—**adjust'ment** *n.*—**adjust'able** *a.*

Ad'jutant *n.* a military officer who assists a superior officer.—**ad'jutancy** *n.*

Ad'juvant (or ad-ōō'-) *n.* one who, or that which assists; in medicine, something added to a prescription to aid the effects of the chief ingredient.

Admin'ister *v.t.* to manage, look after; dispense, as justice, etc. ; supply.—**administra'tion** *n.*—**admin'istrative** *a.*—**admin'istrator** *n.*

Ad'miral *n.* a naval officer of highest rank.—**ad'miralty** *n.* the board which controls the navy ; the buildings of that board.

Admire' *v.t.* to look on with wonder and pleasure ; respect highly.—**ad'mirable** *a.*—**ad'mirably** *adv.*—**admira'-tion** *n.*—**admir'er** *n.*—**admir'ingly** *adv.*

Admit' *v.t.* to let in ; allow ; accept as true ; grant.—**admiss'ible** *a.*—**admiss'ion** *n.*—**admitt'ance** *n.*—**admissibil'ity** *n.*—**admiss'ibly** *adv.*

Syn. to permit, suffer, tolerate, receive, acknowledge. *Ant.* refuse, reject, persist in, adhere to, keep out, exclude.

Admix'ture *n.* the act of mixing ; a blend, alloy, or compound.

Admon'ish *v.t.* to warn ; reprove gently ; advise.—**admoni'tion** *n.*—**admon'itory** *a.*

Ado' (a-dōō) *n.* fuss.

Ado'be (-bi) *n.* sun-dried brick.

Adoles'cent *a.* growing to manhood.—*n.* a youth—**adoles'cence** *n.*

Adopt' *v.t.* to take into relationship, *esp.* as one's child ; to take up, as a principle, a resolution.—**adop'tion** *n.*—**adop'tive** *a.* that adopts or is adopted.

Adore' *v.t.* and *i.* to worship ; love intensely.—**ador'able** *a.*—**adora'tion** *n.*—**ador'er** *n.*

Syn. to revere, reverence, venerate. *Ant.* despise, abominate, hate.

Adorn' *v.t.* to beautify, embellish, deck.—**adorn'ment** *n.*

Adre'nalin *n.* extract of the adrenal glands, a powerful astringent used in medicine.—**adrenal glands**, also known as **suprarenal glands**, two ductless glands situated close to the kidneys.

Adrift' *a.* and *adv.* floating free ; loose.

Adroit' *a.* skilful, expert,

clever. — **adroit'ly** *adv.*—
adroit'ness *n.*

Adula'tion *n.* flattery.—**ad'-
ulatory** *a.*—**ad'ulate** *v.t.*—**ad'-
ulator** *n.*

Adult' *a.* grown-up, mature.—
n. a grown-up person.

Adul'terate *v.t.* to corrupt;
make impure by mixture.—
adul'terated *a.*—**adul'terant**
n.—**adul'teration** *n.*—**adul'-
terator** *n.*

Adul'tery *n.* sexual intercourse
of two persons, either of
whom is married to a third.
—**adul'terer** *n.m.*—**adul'ter-
ess** *n.f.*—**adul'terous** *a.*

Ad'umbrate *v.t.* to outline;
give 'an indication of.—**ad-
umbra'tion** *n.*—**adum'brant,
adum'brative** *a.*

Advance' *v.t.* to bring forward;
promote; encourage; pay
beforehand.—*v.i.* to go forward ; improve in rank or
value.—*n.* movement for-
ward; promotion; improve-
ment; a loan.—**advance'-
ment** *n.*

Advan'tage *n.* gain ; superiority.—**advanta'geous** *a.*—**advanta'geously** *adv.*

Ad'vent *n.* a coming, arrival;
the coming of Christ; the
season of four weeks before
Christmas.—**adven'tual** *a.*

Adventi'tious (-shus) *a.* added;
accidental.

Adven'ture *n.* a remarkable
happening; enterprise; risk;
bold exploit; a commercial
speculation.—*v.t.* and *i.* to
risk; take a risk.—**adven'-
turer** *n.m.*—**adven'turess** *n.f.*
one who seeks adventures;
one who lives on his wits.—

adven turous *a.*—**adven'tur-
ously** *adv.*—**adven'turousness**
n.

Ad'verb *n.* a word added to a
verb, adjective, or other adverb to modify the meaning.
—**adverb'ial** *a.*—**adverb'ially**
adv.

Ad'verse *a.* opposed to; hostile; contrary to desire.—
ad'versely *adv.*—**ad'versary**
n. an enemy.—**advers'ity** *n.*
distress, misfortune.—**advers'ative** *a.*

Advert' *v.i.* to turn the mind
or attention to; refer.—**advert'ence** *n.*—**advert'ency** *n.*
—**advert'ent** *a.*—**advert'ently**
adv.

Ad'vertise *v.t.* to make known;
give notice of, *esp.* in newspapers, bills, etc.—**ad'ver-
tiser** *n.*—**advert'isement** *n.*—
ad'vertising *a.*
Syn. to announce, publish,
proclaim, promulgate, ap-
prise. *Ant.* conceal, withdraw, withhold.

Advice' *n.* opinion given;
counsel; information, news
(*esp.* in *pl.*).

Advise' *v.t.* to give an opinion
to; recommend a line of
conduct; inform.—**advis'-
able** *a.* expedient.—**advised'**
(-zd) *a.* considered, deliberate, as in *well-advised*.—**advi'sedly** *adv.*—**advi'ser** *n.*—
advi'sory *a.*

Ad'vocate *n.* a defender; one
who pleads the cause of another, *esp.* in a court of law;
a barrister.—*v.t.* to uphold,
recommend.—**ad'vocacy** *n.*—
advoca'tion *n.*

Advow'son *n* the right of

patronage or presentation to a church benefice.—**advow'ee** *n.* one who has that right.

Adze (adz) *n.* a carpenter's tool, like an axe, but with a curved blade set with the edge at right angles to the handle.

Ae'gis *n.* a shield given by Zeus; anything that protects.

Ae'grotat *n.* a certificate, in an English university, of illness preventing attendance at class or examination.

Aeo'lian *a.* acted on by the wind, as Aeolian harp.

Ae'on *n.* an age, period of time; eternity.

A'erate *v.t.* to expose to air; charge with carbonic acid or other gas.—**a'erator** *n.* an apparatus to do this.—**aera'tion** *n.*

Aer'ial *a.* belonging to the air. —*n.* a wire to send out or receive radio signals.

A'erie, a'ery, ey'ry *n.* the nest of a bird of prey, *esp.* an eagle.

A'ero- *prefix* having to do with air or aircraft.—**aerobat'ics** *n.* "stunts" in aircraft. **a'erobomb** *n.*—**a'erodart** *n.*—**a'erodrome** *n.* an aircraft station.—**aerodynam'ics** *n.*—**a'erofoil** *n.* wing of an aeroplane.—**a'erogram** *n.* wireless message.—**aerohy'droplane** *n.*—**a'erolite** *n.* a meteoric stone.—**aerolit'ic** *a.*—**a'eromotor** *n.*—**a'eronaut** *n.* an "air-sailor".—**aerol'ogy** *n.*—**aerom'etry** *n.*—**a'erophyte** *n.* a plant which feeds on air.—**a'eroplane** *n.* a heavier-

than-air flying machine.—**a'erostat** *n.* a balloon.—**aerosta'tion** *n.* the art of raising balloons.—**aerostat'ics** *n.*

Aesthet'ic (ĕs-) *a.* relating to the principles of beauty and taste, and of art.—**aesthet'ics** *n.*—**aes'thete** *n.* one who affects an extravagant love of art.—**aesthet'icism** *n.*—**aesthet'ically** *adv.*

Aes'tival *a.* of or in the summer.—**aestiva'tion** *n.* act of remaining dormant in summer, opposite of hibernation. —**aes'tivate** *v.i.*

Ae'ther, see ETHER.

Aetiol'ogy *n.* the study of causes, *esp.* the inquiry into the origin of a disease.—**aetiolo'gical** *a.*

Afar' *adv.* from, at, or to, a distance.

Aff'able *a.* easy to speak to, polite and friendly.—**aff'ably** *adv.*—**affabil'ity** *n.*

Syn. courteous, civil, benign, complaisant, condescending. *Ant.* surly, rude, uncongenial.

Affair' *n.* a business operation; any small matter; *pl.* matters in general, public business.

Affect' *v.t.* to act on, influence; move the feelings; make a show of, make pretence; assume; have a liking for. —**affecta'tion** *n.* show, pretence.—**affec'ted** *a.* making a pretence.—**affec'tedly** *adv.* —**affec'tion** *n.* fondness, love. —**affec'tionate** *a.*—**affec'tionately** *adv.*—**affec'ting** *a.* moving the feelings, pathetic.— **affec'tingly** *adv.*

Aff'erent *a.* bringing to, *esp.* describing nerves which carry sensation to the brain.

Affi'ance *v.t.* to betroth.

Affida'vit *n.* a written statement on oath.

Affil'iate *v.t.* to adopt; to attach, as a society to a federation, etc.; to attribute to, father on.—**affilia'tion** *n.*

Affin'ity *n.* relationship; resemblance; attraction, *esp.* chemical attraction.—**affin'itive** *a.*

Affirm' *v.t.* to assert positively; to maintain a statement.— *v.i.* to make a solemn declaration, *esp.* without oath in a court of law.—**affirma'tion** *n.* —**affirm'ative** *a.* asserting.— *n.* word of assent.—**affirm'atively** *adv.*

Affix' *v.t.* to fasten to, attach. —**aff'ix** *n.* an addition, *esp.* to a word, as a suffix·or prefix.

Affla'tus *n.* inspiration, as of poet, orator; religious inspiration, *the divine afflatus.*

Afflict' *v.t.* to give pain or grief; vex.—**afflic'tion** *n.*— **afflic'tive** *a.*

Aff'luent *a.* wealthy.—*n.* a tributary stream.—**aff'luence** *n.* wealth.

Afford' *v.t.* to be able to buy; produce, yield.

Affor'est *v.t.* to turn land into forest, plant trees.—**afforesta tion** *n.*

Affray' *n.* a fight brawl.

Affright' *v.t.* to terrify.   *Syn.* to alarm, intimidate, daunt, dismay. *Ant.* calm, quiet, pacify, soothe, encourage, hearten.

Affront' *v.t.* insult openly; meet face to face.—*n.* an insult; contemptuous treatment.

Afield' *adv.* in or on the field.

Afire' *adv.* on fire.

Aflame' *adv.* burning.

Afloat' *adv.* floating ; at sea.

Afoot' *adv.* on foot; astir.

Afore' *prep.* and *adv.* before. Usually in compounds, as **afore'said, afore'thought, afore'time.**

Afraid' *a.* in fear; timid.

Afresh' *adv.* again, anew.

Aft (àft) *adv.* towards or near the stern of a ship.

Af'ter (àft-) *adv.* behind: later. —*prep.* like or in imitation of; behind; later than.—*a.* behind; later; nearer to the stern of a ship.

Af'ter (àft-) as prefix makes compounds, as **af'terbirth** *n.* membrane expelled after a birth.—**af'terclap** *n.*—**af'tercrop** *n.*—**af'ter-damp** *n.* gas left after an explosion in a coal-mine. — **af'terglow** *n.* light after sunset.—**af'termath** *n.* second mowing of grass.—**afternoon'** *n.*—**af'terthought** *n.*

Af'terwards (àft-) **af'terward** *adv.* later.

A'ga (à'-) *n.* Turkish civil or military officer of high rank; a Turkish title of respect.

Again' *adv.* once more; back, in return; besides.

Against' *prep.* opposite; in opposition to; in contact with; in exchange for.

Ag'aric *n.* a name of various fungi, including the common mushroom.—*a.* fungoid.

Ag'ate *n.* a precious stone composed of layers of quartz in different colours.

Age *n.* the length of time a person or thing has existed; a period of time; periods of history; maturity; a long time.—*v.t.* to make old.—*v.i.* to grow old.—**a'ged** *a.* old.—*n.pl* old people.—**age'-less** *a.*—**age'long** *a.*

Agen'da *n.* things to be done; the programme of a business meeting.

A'gent *n.* a person or thing producing an effect; a cause; a natural force; a person authorised to carry on business or affairs for another.—**a'gency** *n.* instrumentality; the business or place of business of an agent.

Agglom'erate *v.t.* and *i.* to gather into a mass.—**agglom'erate, agglom'erated** *a.* —**agglom'erate** *n.* rock consisting of volcanic fragments. —**agglomera'tion** *n.* — **agglom'erative** *a.*

Agg'randize *v.t.* to make greater in size, power, or rank.—**aggran'dizement** *n.*

Agg'ravate *v.t.* to make worse. —**aggrava'tion** *n.*—**agg'ravating** *a.*
Syn. to exaggerate, magnify, exasperate, irritate. *Ant.* allay, alleviate, soothe, placate, minimise, diminish.

Agg'regate *v.t.* to gather into a mass.—*n.* mass, sum total. —**aggrega'tion** *n.*—**agg'regative** *a.*

Aggres'sion *n.* an unprovoked attack.—**aggress'ive** *a.*—**aggress'iveness** *n.*—**aggress'or** *n.*—**aggress'** *v.*

Aggrieve' *v.t.* to pain or injure.

Aghast' *a.* struck with horror.

Ag'ile (-j-) *a.* active. nimble. -**ag'ilely** *adv.*—**agil'ity** *n.*

Ag'itate (-j-) *v.t.* to keep in motion; disturb, excite; keep in discussion.—**agita'tion** *n.* —**ag'itator** *n.*

Agnos'tic *n.* one who holds that we know nothing of things outside the material world.—**agnos'ticism** *n.*

Ago' *adv.* gone; since.

Agog' *a.* and *adv.* eager, astir.

Ag'ony *n.* extreme suffering; a violent struggle; death struggle.—**ag'onize** *v.i.* to suffer great pain or sorrow. —**ag'onizing** *a.*

Agra'rian *a.* relating to land or its management.—**agra'rianism** *n.* a political movement to change the conditions of land ownership.

Agree' *v.i.* to be of one mind; consent; harmonise; determine, settle; suit.—**agree'able** *a.*—**agree'ably** *adv.*—**agree'ment** *n.*—**agree'ableness** *n.*—**agreeabil'ity** *n.*

Ag'riculture *n.* the art or practice of cultivating the ground.—**agricul'tural** *a.*—**agricul'turist** *n.*

Ag'rimony *n.* a plant of the rose group, with small yellow flowers and bitter taste.

Agrimo'tor *n.* a motor vehicle or tractor used for agricultural purposes.

Aground' *adv.* stranded.

A'gue *n.* a fever in periodic fits, with shivering; quaking.

Ahead' *adv.* in front of.

Māte, mēte, mīte, mōte, mūte, bōōt.

Ahoy' *interj.* a shout used at sea for hailing, calling attention.

Aid *v.t.* to help.—*n.* help, support.

Syn. to assist, succour, support, relieve. *Ant.* hinder, obstruct, embarrass.

Aide-de-camp (ā-de-kon') *n.* (*pl.* **aides-de-camp**) an officer who attends a general, conveys his orders, etc.

Aigrette' *n.* a tuft of feathers; an ornament of jewellery, spray-shāped.

Ail *v.t.* to trouble, disturb.—*v.i.* to be ill.—**ail'ing** *a.*—**ail'ment** *n.*

Ai'leron (ā'-) *n.* a part of the plane of an aeroplane that serves to balance and steer the machine.

Aim *t.* and *i.* to direct effort towards, try to; to give direction to a weapon; strike or throw.—*n.* a direction; endeavour; object, purpose.—**aim'less** *a.* without object.

Air *n.* the mixture of gases we breathe, the atmosphere; breeze; a tune; a manner; affected manner—*pl.* affected manners.—*v.t.* to expose; to dry or warm.—**air'y** *a.*—**air'ily** *adv.*—**air'iness** *n.*—**air'ing** *n.* a trip into the open.—**air'less** *a.*

Air- used as prefix makes compounds denoting things in, of, or having to do with the air. As **air'-balloon'** *n.*—**air'-base** *n.*—**air'-bath** *n.*—**air'-bed** *n.*—**air'-brake** *n.*—**air'-cell** *n.*—**air'-cham'ber** *n.*—**air' chief-mar'shal'** *n.*—**air' comm'odore** *n.*—**air'craft** *n.*

—**air'-cushion** *n.* a pillow which can be inflated.—**air'-duct** *n.*—**air'-force** *n.* the strength of a country in aircraft.—**air'-funnel** *n.*—**air'-gas** *n.*—**air'-gun** *n.* a gun discharged by force of compressed air.—**air'-hole** *n.*—**air'-line** *n.* a bee-line; an aircraft route.—**air'-lock** *n.*—**air'man** *n.*—**air'-mechan'ic** *n.* a "private" in the R.A.F.; an artificer working on aircraft.—**air'-pilot** *n.* a man who steers and controls the machinery of an aeroplane.—**air'-pock'et** *n.* a part of the air where an aeroplane drops suddenly.—**air'-port** *n.* a station for passenger aircraft.—**air'-power** *n.*—**air'-pump** *n.* a machine to draw out the air from a vessel.—**air'-raid** *n.* an attack by aircraft.—**air'-scout'** *n.*—**air'-screw** *n.* the propeller of any aircraft.—**air'-shaft** *n.*—**air'-ship** *n.*—**air'stone** *n.* a meteorite.—**air'tight** *a.* not allowing the passage of air.—**air'-trap** *n.*—**air'-valve** *n.*—**air vice-mar'shal** *n.*—**air'way** *n.* a regular aircraft route.—**air'worthy** *a.* fit for service in the air.—**airwor'thiness** *n.*

Aire'dale *n.* a large terrier dog.

Aisle (īl) *n.* the wing of a church, or lateral division of any part of a church; a walk between seats in a church.

Ait *n.* a small flat island in a river.

Aitch'bone *n.* the bone of the rump; the cut of beef over this bone.

Ajar' *adv.* partly open.

Akim'bo *adv.* with arm bent and hand on hip.

Akin' *a.* related by blood; like, having the same qualities.

Al'abaster *n.* a soft, white, semi-transparent stone.

Alack' *interj.* a cry of sorrow. —**alack-a-day** *interj.*

Alac'rity *n.* quickness, briskness.

Alarm' *n.* notice of danger; sudden fright; call to arms. —*v.t.* to warn of danger; frighten.—**alarm'ing** *a.*—**alarm'ist** *n.* one given to prophesying danger.—**alarum** (**alarm'**) *n.* a variant of alarm, now mainly used in **alarum-clock**, a clock which rings a bell at a set hour to give warning of the time.

Alas' *interj.* a cry of grief.

Al'batross *n.* a large, long-winged sea-bird, remarkable for its flying powers.

Albi'no (-ē-) *n.* a person or animal with unusually white skin and hair, and pink eyes, due to lack of colouring matter in the skin.—**al'binism** *n.*

Al'bum *n.* a book of blank leaves, for collecting portraits, stamps, autographs, etc.

Albu'men *n.* a constituent of animal and vegetable matter, found nearly pure in white of egg.—**albu'minous** *a.*

Al'chemy *n.* the earlier stage of chemistry, in which the main aims were the turning of base metals into gold and the finding of an elixir of life. —**al'chemist** *n.*

Al'cohol *n.* a liquid made in fermenting sugar, etc., and forming the intoxicating part of fermented drinks.—**alcohol'ic** *a.*—**al'coholism** *n.* a disease, alcohol poisoning.—**al'coholise** *v.t.*—**alcoholisa'tion** *n.*

Al'cove *n.* a recess.

Al'dehyde *n.* a liquid produced by the oxidation of alcohol.

Al'der (awl-) *n.* a tree related to the birch.

Al'derman (awl-) *n.* a member of the council of a city or town, but appointed for life or a long period and not elected like the ordinary councillors. The aldermen rank next to the mayor, in the order of citizens.—**alderman'ic** *a.*

Ale *n.* fermented malt liquor, beer.—**ale'-house** *n.*

Alert' *a.* watchful, brisk.—*n.* a sudden attack or surprise. —**alert'ness** *n.* *Syn.* active, smart, quick. *Ant.* sluggish, somnolent, inactive, lazy.

Alfal'fa *n.* a plant used as fodder, lucerne.

Al'gebra *n.* a method of calculating, using letters to represent the numbers and signs to show relations between them, making a kind of abstract arithmetic.—**algebra'ic, algebra'ical** *a.*—**al'gebraist** *n.*

A'lias *adv.* otherwise.—*n.* an assumed name.

Al'ibi *n.* a plea that a person charged with a crime was somewhere else when it was committed.

A'lien *a.* foreign; different in nature; adverse.—*n.* a foreigner.—**a'lienate** *v.t.* to transfer; estrange.—**a'lienable** *a.* capable of being transferred, as property not entailed.—**alienabil'ity** *n.*—**aliena'tion** *n.*—**a'lienism** *n.*—**a'lienist** *n.* a doctor who specialises in treatment of mental disease.

Alight' *v.i.* to get down.

Alight' *a.* on fire.

Align', **aline'** *v.t.* to bring into line.—**align'ment**, **aline'ment** *n.*

Alike' *a.* like, similar.

Al'iment *n.* food.—*v.t.* to feed; support. — **alimen'tary** *a.*—**alimenta'tion** *n.*

Al'imony *n.* an income allowed to a wife legally separated from her husband.

Al'iquot *a.* such part of a number as will divide it without remainder.

Alive' *a.* living; in life or activity.

Aliz'arine *n.* the red colouring matter of madder.

Al'kali *n.* substance which combines with acid and neutralises it, forming a salt. Potash, soda, etc., are alkalis. —**al'kaline** *a.*—**alkalin'ity** *n.*—**al'kaloid** *n.* and *a.*—**al'kalise** *v.t.*

All (awl) *a.* the whole of, every one of.—*adv.* wholly, entirely. — *n.* the whole, everything.

Allay' *v.t.* to lighten, relieve, calm.

Syn. to soothe, tranquillise.

Ant. irritate, arouse inflame.

Allege' *v.t.* and *i.* to plead, bring forward as an argument; assert.—**allega'tion** *n.*

Alle'giance *n.* the duty of a subject to his sovereign; loyalty.

All'egory *n.* a story with a meaning other than the literal one, a description of one thing under the image of another.—**allego'rical** *a.*—**all'egorise** *v.t.*—**allego'rically** *adv.*—**all'egorist** *n.*

Alleg'ro (-lā-) *adv.* (*music*) briskly.

Alle'viate *v.t.* to make light, ease, lessen.—**allevia'tion** *n.* —**alle'viator** *n.*

All'ey *n.* a walk, path; a narrow passage, less than a street; an enclosure for playing skittles.—*pl.* **alleys.**

All'ey *n.* a fine marble (in the game).

All'igator *n.* an animal of the crocodile family found in America.

Allitera'tion *n.* the beginning of two or more words in close succession with the same sound, as e.g. *Sing a Song of Sixpence.*—**allit'erative** *a.*—**allit'erate** *v.i.*

All'ocate *v.t.* to place; to assign as a share.—**alloca'tion** *n.*

All'ocution *n.* a formal speech or address.—**all'ocute** *v.i.*

Allo-ero'tism (-rŏ'-) *n.* in psycho-analysis, object-love; concentration upon some external person or thing.—**allo-erotic** *a.*

Allomor'phism *n.* the power

of changing form without change of composition.

Allop'athy *n.* the orthodox practice of medicine, applying treatment to produce a condition incompatible with the disease; opposite of *homeopathy.*

Allot' *v.t.* to give out; distribute as shares.—**allot'ment** *n.* distribution; a portion of a field divided among many holders for vegetable gardens, etc.

Allot'ropy *n.* the property of some elements of existing in more than one form, as e.g. carbon in the form of coal, diamond, and charcoal.—**allotrop'ic** *a.*—**allot'ropism** *n.*

Allow' *v.t.* to acknowledge; permit; give.—**allow'able** *a.* —**allow'ance** *n.*—**allow'ably** *adv.*

Syn. to grant, concede, admit, tolerate. *Ant.* disallow, refuse, reject.

Alloy' *n.* a mixture of two or more metals.—*v.t.* to mix metals, debase.—**alloy'age** *n.*

All'spice (awl-) *n.* Pimento or Jamaica pepper, supposed to combine the flavours of various spices.

Allude' *v.i.* to mention lightly, make indirect reference to; refer to.—**allu'sion** *n.*—**allu'sive** *a.*—**allu'sively** *adv.*

Allure' *v.t.* to entice, win over. —**allur'ing** *a.* charming, seductive.—**allur'ingly** *adv.*— **allure'ment** *n.*

Alluv'ial (-ōōv-) *a.* deposited by rivers. — **alluv'ium** *n.* water-borne matter deposited on lower lands.—**alluv'-**

ion *n.* land formed by washed-up earth and sand.

Ally' *v.t.* to join in relationship by treaty, marriage, or friendship.—**allied'** *a.*—**all'y** *n.* a confederate; a state or sovereign bound to another by treaty.—*pl.* **allies.**

Al'manac (awl-) *n.* a table of days and months, etc.

Almi'ghty (awl-mī'ti) *a.* having all power.—**The Almighty** *n.* God.

Alm'ond (ahm-) *n.* the kernel of the fruit of a tree related to the peach; that tree.

Al'most (āwl-) *adv.* nearly, all but.

Alms (ämz) *n.* gifts to the poor.—**alm'oner** *n.* a distributer of alms.—**alm'onry** *n.* place of distribution of alms. —**alms'-house** *n.* a house endowed for poor persons to live in.

Al'oe *n.* a genus of plants of medicinal value; *pl.* the bitter drug made from the plant.

Aloft' *adv.* on high; overhead; at the masthead of a ship.

Alone' *a.* single, solitary.— *adv.* separately.

Along' *adv.* lengthwise; forward; together (with).

Aloof' *adv.* at a distance; apart.

Aloud' *adv.* with loud voice.

Alp *n.* a high mountain; *pl.* **Alps,** *esp.* the mountains of Switzerland. — **al'pine** *a.* — **al'pinist** *n.* a mountain climber.

Alpac'a *n.* the Peruvian sheep; cloth made from its wool.

Al'phabet *n.* the set of letters

used in writing a language.
—alphabet'ic, alphabet'ical *a.*
in the order of the letters.—
alphabet'ically *adv.*

Alread'y (awl-red'i) *adv.* be-
ore, previously.

Alsa'tian (al-sā'shan) *a.* from
Alsatia, i.e. Alsace.—*n.* a
large dog of a breed like a
wolf.

Al'so (awl-) *adv.* further, too.

Al'tar (awl-) *n.* a raised place,
a stone, etc., on which sacrifice may be offered; in a
Christian church, the table
on which the priest conse-
crates the eucharist.—Forms
compounds, as al'tar-cloth *n.*
—al'tar-piece *n.*—al'tar-rails
n. etc.

Al'ter (awl-) *v.t.* to change,
make different.—*v.i.* to become different.—al'terable *a.*
—alterabil'ity *n.*—al'terably
adv.—altera'tion *n.*—al'tera-
tive *a.*
  Syn. to transform, vary,
modify. *Ant.* maintain, persist, remain.

Alterca'tion (awl-) *n.* dispute,
wrangling.—al'tercate *v.i.*—
al'tercative *a.*

Al'ternate *v.t.* to cause to occur
by turns.—*v.i.* to happen by
turns.—alter'nate *a.* one after
the other, by turns.—alter'-
nately *adv.*—alterna'tion *n.*—
alter'native *a.* and *n.*—alter'-
natively *adv.*

Alterna'tor (-nā'-) *n.* an electric generator for producing
alternating current.—alternating current, an electrical
current flowing in a circuit
first in one direction, then
in the opposite.

Although' (awl-THŌ') *conj* admitting that, notwithstand-
ing that.

Altim'eter *n.* an instrument
for measuring heights.

Al'titude *n.* height.
  Syn. eminence, elevation,
loftiness. *Ant.* depression,
depth, lowness.

Al'to *n. music,* the male voice
of highest pitch; the part
written for it.

Altogeth'er (awl-) *adv.* entirely.

Al'truism *n.* the principle of
living and acting for the
good of others.—altruis'tic *a.*
—altruis'tically *adv.*

Al'um *n.* a mineral salt,
double sulphate of alumina
and potash.

Alumin'ium *n.* a metal resembling silver, very light.

Alum'nus *n.* a pupil; a gradu-
ate of a college.

Al'ways (awl-) *adv.* at all
times; for ever.—also alway.

Amal'gam *n.* a compound of
mercury and another metal;
a soft mixture; a combination of elements.—amal'ga-
mate *v.t.* to mix mercury
with another metal; com-
pound.—*v.i.* to unite; blend;
esp. to unite two companies,
societies, etc.—amalgama'-
tion *n.*

Amanuen'sis *n.* one who
writes to dictation; a copyist, secretary.

Amass' *v.t.* to collect in quantity.—amass'able *a.*

Am'ateur (-tẹr) *n.* one who
carries on an art, study,
game, etc., for the love of it,
not for money.—am'ateur,

amateur′ish *a.* imperfect, like the work of an amateur, not a professional hand.— **amateur′ishly** *adv.* — **amateur′ism** *n.*

Am′atory *a.* relating to or causing love.

Amaze′ *v.t.* to surprise greatly, astound.—**amaze′ment** *n.*— **ama′zing** *a.* — **ama′zingly** *adv.*

Am′azon *n.* a female warrior; a masculine woman.—**amazo′nian** *a.*

Ambass′ador *n.* a representative of the highest rank sent by one state to another.— **ambass′adress** *n. fem.*—**ambassador′ial** *a.*—**ambass′adorship** *n.*—**am′bassage** now usually **em′bassage** *n.*

Am′ber *n.* a yellowish fossil resin.—*a.* made of, or coloured like, amber.

Am′bergris *n.* a gray, fragrant substance, found on the seashore, and in the spermaceti whale.

Ambidex′ter, ambidex′trous *a.* able to use both hands with equal ease.—**ambidexter′ity** *n.*

Ambig′uous *a.* of double meaning, doubtful.—**ambig′uously** *adv.*—**ambigu′ity** *n.*

Am′bit *n.* a circuit; space round.

Ambi′tion (bi′-shun) *n.* desire of power, fame, honour; the object of that desire.—**ambi′tious** *a.*—**ambi′tiously** *adv.*—**ambi′tiousness** *n.*

Am′ble *v.i.* of a horse, to move with both legs together one side, then both the other side; to move at an easy pace;—*n.* this movement.— **am′bler** *n.*

Ambro′sia *n.* the food of the gods.—**ambro′sial** *a.*

Am′bulance *n.* a special carriage for the sick or wounded; a movable hospital.

Ambuscade′ *n.* a hiding to attack by surprise, an ambush.

Am′bush *n.* a lying in wait.— *v.t.* to waylay, attack from hiding.

Ame′liorate *v.t.* and *i.* to make better, improve.— **ameliora′tion** *n.*—**ame′liorative** *a.*

Amen′ (ä-, ā-) *interj.* surely, so let it be.

Ame′nable *a.* easy to be led or controlled; subject to.— **amenabil′ity, ame′nableness** *n.*—**ame′nably** *adv.*

Amend′ *v.i.* to grow better— *v.t.* to make better, improve; alter in detail, as a bill in parliament, etc.—**amend′ment** *n.*—**amends′** *n.pl.* reparation.

Ame′nity *n.* pleasantness; *pl.* pleasant ways, civilities.

Am′ethyst *n.* a bluish-violet precious stone.

A′miable *a.* friendly, kindly. —**a′miably** *adv.*—**amiabil′ity, a′miableness** *n.*
Syn. lovely, lovable, charming, pleasing. *Ant.* offensive, revolting, hateful.

Am′icable *a.* friendly.—**am′icably** *adv.*—**amicabil′ity** *n.*

Amid′, amidst′ *prep.* in the middle of, among.

Amid′ships *adv.* half-way between stem and stern of a ship.

Amiss' *a.* wrong.—*adv.* faultily.

Am'ity *n.* friendship.
Syn. friendliness, goodwill, harmony. *Ant.* discord, unfriendliness, illwill.

Amm'onal *n.* a high explosive containing aluminium, charcoal and ammonium nitrate.

Ammo'nia *n.* a pungent alkaline gas.—**ammo'niac, ammo'nical** *a.*—**ammo'niated** *a.*—**ammo'nium** *n.* the hypothetical base of ammonia.

Ammuni'tion *n.* cartridges, powder, etc., for firearms; formerly, all military stores, as now adjectively in **ammunition boots**, etc.

Amne'sia *n.* loss of memory.

Am'nesty *n.* a general pardon.

Amœb'a *n.* the simplest microscopic animal, a unit mass which constantly changes its shape.

Amok' *see* AMUCK.

Among' (-mu-) **amongst'** *prep.* mixed with, of the number of.

Am'orous *a.* easily moved to love; in love.—**am'orously** *adv.*—**am'orousness** *n.*

Amorph'ous *a.* shapeless.—**amorph'ism** *n.*
Syn. formless, heterogeneous, irregular. *Ant.* crystalline, regular, shapely.

Amount' *v.i.* to come to, be equal to.—*n.* sum total.

Amour' (-ōō-) *n.* a love intrigue or illicit love affair.—**amour propre** *n.* self-esteem.

Am'pere *n.* unit of current of electricity, the amount one volt can send through one ohm.

Amphib'ious *a.* living both on land and in water.—**amphib'ian** *n.*

Amphithe'atre *n.* a building with tiers of seats round an arena.

Am'ple *a.* big enough, full, spacious.—**am'ply** *adv.*—**am'pleness** *n.*—**am'plify** *v.t.* to make bigger, louder, etc.—**amplifica'tion** *n.*—**am'plitude** *n.* spaciousness, width.—**amplifica'tory** *a.*—**am'plifier** *n.*

Am'putate *v.t.* to cut off (a limb, etc.)—**amputa'tion** *n.*

Amuck', amok' *adv.* (*only in phrase,* to run amuck) in murderous frenzy, running to murder indiscriminately.

Am'ulet *n.* something carried, worn as a charm.

Amuse' *v.t.* to divert; occupy pleasantly; excite a sense of fun.—**amu'sing** *a.*—**amu'singly** *adv.*—**amu'sement** *n.*

Am'yl *n.* hypothetical radicle thought to exist in many chemical compounds, as amylic alcohol, etc.—**amyl nitrate**, an amber-coloured fluid with a pleasant odour.

Anabap'tist *n.* one who holds that baptism should be adult only, and that those baptised in infancy should be baptised again.

Anac'hronism (-k-) *n.* a mistake of time, by which something is put in the wrong period; something out of keeping with the time.—**anac'hronise** *v.t.*—**anachronis'tic** *a.*

Anacoluth'on n. a sentence or words faulty in grammatical sequence.

Anacon'da n. a large water-snake, found in South America.

Anæm'ia n. lack of blood.—**anæm'ic** a.

Anæsthet'ic a. causing insensibility.—n. a drug that does this.—**anæsthe'sia** n. state of insensibility. — **anæsthet'ically** adv.—**anæs'thetise** v.t.—**anæs'thetist** n.

An'agram n. a word or sentence made by arranging in different order the letters of another word or sentence; e.g. ant from tan.—**anagrammat'ic, -al,** a.—**anagramm'atise** v.t.—**anagramm'atist** n.

Anal'ogy n. agreement or likeness in certain respects; correspondence.—**analo'gical** a.—**analo'gically** adv.—**anal'ogise** v.t.—**anal'ogist** n.—**anal'ogous** a. having similarity or correspondence.—**anal'ogously** adv.

Anal'ysis n. a separation or breaking up of anything into its elements or component parts.—pl. **anal'yses.**—**an'alyse** v.t.—**an'alyst** n.—**analyt'ic, -al** a.—**analyt'ically** adv.

An'archy n. lack of government in a state; lawlessness; confusion.—**anarc'hic, -al,** a.—**anarc'hically** adv.—**an'archism** n. the system of certain revolutionaries aiming at a society in which there should be no government, each man being a law unto himself.—**an'archist** n.

Anath'ema n. a solemn curse; anything accursed.—**anath'ematize** v.t.

Anat'omy n. the dissection of a body; the science of the structure of the body; a detailed analysis or examination.—**anatom'ical** a.—**anatom'ically** adv.—**anat'omise** v.t.—**anat'omist** n.

An'cestor n. a forefather.—**ances'tral** a.—**an'cestry** n.

Anc'hor (-k-) n. an implement for chaining a ship to the bottom of the sea.—v.t. to fasten by an anchor.—v.i. to cast anchor.—**anc'horage** n. a suitable place for anchoring.

Anc'horite, anc'horet (-k-) n. one who has retired from the world, esp. for religion; a hermit.

Ancho'vy (-ch-) n. a small fish of the herring family.

An'cient (ān-shent) a. old; belonging to a former age; time-worn;—n. an old man; one who lived in an earlier age (esp. in pl.).—**an'ciently** adv.

An'cillary a. subordinate, subservient.

Anco'na n. a breed of domestic fowl, usually speckled black and white.

And conj. is a connecting word, used to join words and sentences, to introduce a consequence, etc.

Andalu'sian n. a native of Andalusia; a breed of fowls, blue in colour.

Andan'te adv. (music) moderately slow.

An'diron n. an iron bar or

bracket for supporting logs in a wood fire.

An'ecdote n. a very short story dealing with a single incident.—**an'ecdotal** a.—**an'ecdotage** n. a collection of anecdotes; chattering old age.

Anele', **aneal'** v.t. to give extreme unction. (*Archaic*, see *Hamlet* I. v.)

Anelec'tric (-lek'-) a. nonelectric;—n. a body that does not become electric; a conductor of electricity.

Anem'ograph n. an instrument for recording automatically the force and direction of the wind.

Anemom'eter n. an instrument to measure the strength of wind, a wind-gauge.—**anemomet'ric** a.—**anemom'etry** n.

Anem'one (-ni) n. the windflower.—**sea-anem'one** n. a plant-like animal living in the sea.

An'eroid a. denoting a barometer which measures atmospheric pressure without the use of mercury or other liquid.

An'eurism n. a swelling out of a part of an artery.

Anew' adv. afresh.

An'gel (ānj-) n. a divine messenger; a ministering or attendant spirit; a person with the qualities of such a spirit, as gentleness, purity, etc.—**angel'ic** a.—**angel'ically** adv.

Ang'er n. wrath, a strong emotion including a sense of injury and a desire to retaliate.—v.t. to rouse this emotion in.—**ang'ry** a.—**ang'rily** adv.

Ang'le (ang'gl) v.i. to fish.—n. a hook.—**ang'ler** n.—**ang'ling** n.

Ang'l n. a corner; the meeting of two lines.—**ang'ular** a.—**angular'ity** n.

Ang'lican a. of the Church of England.—**Ang'licanism** n.

Ang'licise v.t. to express in English, turn into English form.—**ang'licism** n. an English idiom or peculiarity.

Ang'lo- *prefix* English; as Anglo-American, Anglo-Catholic, Anglo-Indian, Anglo-Saxon, etc.—**anglopho'bia** n. dislike of England.

Angor'a n. a goat with long white silky hair; a cat with long silky fur; a rabbit with long white fine fur; cloth or wool made from the hair of the goat or rabbit.

Ang'uish (-nggw-) n. great pain, mental or bodily. *Syn.* agony, suffering, pang. *Ant.* pleasure, happiness, ecstasy.

Anhy'drous a. free from water (of chemical substances).

An'iline n. a product of coal-tar which yields dyestuffs.

Animadvert' v.i. to criticise, pass censure.—**animadver'sion** n.

An'imal n. a being having life, feeling the power of voluntary motion; a beast.—a. of or belonging to animals; sensual.—**an'imalism** n.—**an'imally** adv.

Animal'cule n. a very small animal, *esp.* one which cannot be seen by the naked eye.—**animal'culer** *a.*

An'imate *v.t.* to give life to; enliven; actuate.—**an'imated** *a.* lively.—**anima'tion** *n.*

An'imism *n.* primitive religion, a belief that natural effects are due to spirits, that inanimate things have spirits. —**animis'tic** *a.*

Animos'ity *n.* hatred, enmity. —**an'imus** *n.* actuating spirit; enmity.

Syn. acrimony, asperity, harshness. *Ant.* love, friendship, amity.

An'ion *n.* an electro-negative ion; and therefore set free at the positive plate or anode.

An'ise *n.* a plant with aromatic seeds, which are used for flavouring.—**an'iseed** *n.* a liqueur or preparation of the seeds.

An'ker *n.* a measure of liquids, a cask. The quantity varies; a Rotterdam anker is $8\frac{1}{2}$ gallons.

An'kle (ang'kl) *n.* the joint between the foot and the leg.—**ank'let** *n.* an ornament or ring for the ankle.

Ann'a *n.* an Indian coin, the sixteenth part of a rupee.

Ann'als *n.pl.* records of events set down year by year.—**ann'alist** *n.*

Anneal' *v.t.* to toughen metal or glass by heating and slow cooling.—**anneal'ing** *n.*

Annex' *v.t.* to add, attach; take possession of, *esp.* territory.—**ann'exe** *n.* something added; a supplementary building.—**annexa'tion** *n.*

Syn. to affix, unite, bind to,

join. *Ant.* separate, disunite, sever.

Anni'hilate (-nī-i-) *v.t.* to reduce to nothing, destroy.— **annihila'tion** *n.*—**anni'hilator** *n.*—**anni'hilative** *a.*

Anniver'sary *a.* yearly.—*n.* the day on which an event happened or is celebrated.

Ann'otate *v.t.* to make notes upon.—**annota'tion** *n.*—**ann'otator** *n.*

Announce' *v.t.* to make known, proclaim.—**announce'ment** *n.* —**announ'cer** *n.*

Annoy' *v.t.* to trouble, vex; tease.—**annoy'ance** *n.*

Ann'ual *a.* yearly.—*n.* a plant which lives only a year; a book published every year. —**ann'ually** *adv.*

Annu'ity *n.* a sum paid every year.—**annu'itant** *n.* one who receives such a sum.

Annul' *v.t.* to reduce to nothing, abolish.—**annul'ment** *n.*

Ann'ular *a.* ring-shaped.— **ann'ulated** *a.* formed in rings. —**annula'tion** *n.*—**ann'ulet** *n.* a ring or fillet.

Annuncia'tion *n.* an announcing ; the angel's announcement to the Virgin Mary.

An'ode *n. in electricity,* the positive pole, or point of entry of a current.—**anode rays**, in wireless, rays of positively charged particles emanating from the heated anode (plate) of a thermionic valve.

An'odyne *a.* relieving pain.— *n.* a drug with the power of allaying pain.

Anoint' *v.t.* to smear with oil or ointment; to consecrate with oil.—anoint'ment *n.*—the Anointed *n.* the Messiah.

Anom'alous *a.* irregular.—anom'aly *n.* irregularity; something showing irregularity.

Anon' *adv.* in a short time; now and then.

Anon'ymous *a.* nameless; *esp.* without an author's name.—anonym'ity *n.* — anon'ymously *adv.*

Anoth'er (-u-) *pron.* one other; a different one.

An'swer (ản-sẹr) *v.t.* to reply to; pay, meet; satisfy, suit. —*v.i.* to reply; succeed.—*n.* a reply; a solution.—an'swerable *a.*—an'swerer *n.*

Ant' *n.* a small social insect, proverbial for industry.—ant'-eater *n.* a South American animal which feeds on ants by means of a long, sticky tongue.—ant'-hill *n.* the mound raised by ants in building their home.

Ant- *prefix* for anti before a vowel. *see* words in ANTI-.

Antag'onist *n.* an opponent. —antag'onism*n.*—antag'onise *v.t.*—antagonis'tic *a.*—antagonis'tically *adv.*

Antarc'tic *a.* of the south polar regions.—*n.* these regions.

Ante- *prefix* found in compound words as antece'dent *a.* or *n.* going before.—an'techamber *n.*—an'techapel *n.*—antedate' *v.t.*—antedilu'vian *a.* before the flood.—antemerid'ian *a.*—antemun'dane *a.*—antena'tal *a.*—anteni'cene *a.*—antenup'tial *a.*—

antepenult' *n.*—antepenultimate *a.*—an'teroom *n.*

An'telope *n.* a deer-like ruminant animal, remarkable for grace and speed.

Antenn'a *n.* (*pl.* antenn'æ) an insect's feeler; *in wireless*, an aerial.

Ante'rior *a.* before; earlier. *Syn.* antecedent, prior, precedent, previous. *Ant.* succeeding, following, subsequent, later.

An'them *n.* a piece of Scripture set to music for singing in churches; a piece of sacred music (originally sung in alternate parts by two choirs).

An'ther *n.* the top of the pollen-bearing stamen in a flower.

Anthol'ogy *n.* a collection of choice poems, literary extracts, etc.—anthol'ogist *n.* a maker of such.

An'thracite *n.* a hard coal burning almost without flame or smoke.

An'thropoid *a.* like man (of certain apes).

Anthropol'ogy *n.* the scientific study of the human race.—anthropolog'ical *a.*—anthropol'ogist *n.*

Anthropomorph'ism *n.* the ascription of human form and qualities to the Deity.

Anti- *prefix* against; ant- before a vowel. Makes compounds as anti-air'craft *a.*—anti-body *n.* a substance in, or introduced into, blood serum which is antagonistic to a toxin or poison injurious to the animal

organisation. — anticath'olic
a.—An'tichrist n.—anticli'-
max n.—anticli'nal a.—
anticy'clone n.—an'tidote n.
a counter poison.—antilog'-
arithm n.—antimacas'sar n.
a cover to protect chairs
from *macassar oil*.—an'ti-
masque n.—antimonarc'hical
a.—antiphlogis'tic a.—an'ti-
pope n. a pope elected in
opposition to the one regularly chosen.—antirachit'ic
a.—antiscorbu'tic n.—anti-
semit'ic a.—antisep'tic a. and
n.—antispasmod'ic a. and n.
—antitox'in n.—an'titrade n.
—etc.

An'tic a. odd, grotesque.—n.
a grotesque figure or movement, an odd trick.

Anti'cipate v.t. to be beforehand; to take or consider
before the due time; foresee;
enjoy in advance; expect.—
anticipa'tion n.—anti'cipa-
tive, anti'cipatory a.

An'timony n. a brittle, bluish-
white metal.

Antip'athy n. dislike.—anti-
pathet'ic a.
   Syn. hatred, enmity. *Ant.*
liking, sympathy, esteem,
affinity.

Antip'odes n.pl. a region of the
globe exactly opposite ours.
—antip'odal a.

Antique' (-ĕk) a. ancient; old-
fashioned.—n. a relic of
former times.—Antiq'uity n.
great age; former times.—
an'tiquary, antiqua'rian n. a
student or collector of old
things.—an'tiquated a.

Antirrhi'num (-rī-) n. snap-
dragon.

Antith'esis n. contrast; direct
opposite; opposition of ideas.
—antithet'ical a.—antithet'-
ically adv.

Ant'ler n. a deer's horn; a
branch of that horn.—ant'-
lered a.

An'tonym n. a word of which
the meaning is the opposite
of another, e.g. *cold* is an
antonym of *hot*.

A'nus (ā-) n. the lower opening
of the bowels.

An'vil n. an iron block on
which a smith hammers
metal.

Anx'ious (angk'shus) a. troubled, uneasy, *esp.* about
something doubtful or in the
future. — anx'iously adv. —
anxi'ety n.

An'y (en'i) a. and pron. one
indefinitely; some.—an'y-
body n.—an'ything n.—an'y-
how, an'yway, an'ywhere adv.

An'zac a. of the Australian
army in the War of 1914-18.
—n. a soldier of that army.

Aort'a n. the great artery
which rises from the left
ventricle of the heart and
sends its branches all through
the body.—aort'al a.

Apace' adv. swiftly.

Apache' (-ăsh) n. a desperado,
esp. a Parisian one.

Apart' adv. separately; aside.

Apart'ment n. a room; pl.
lodgings, rooms rented.

Ap'athy n. want of feeling;
indifference.—apathet'ic a.—
apathet'ically adv.
   Syn. insensibility, unconcern, supineness. *Ant.* concern, interest, solicitude.

Ape' n. a monkey; a monkey

with no tail; one who plays the ape, an imitator.—*v.t.* to imitate.—a′pish *a.*—a′pishly *adv.*

Apep′sia, apep′sy *n.* indigestion; dyspepsia.

Apercu (-sū) *n.* a rapid survey of a subject; an outline; a sketch.

Ape′rient *a.* opening; mildly laxative.—*n.* any such medicine.

Ap′erture *n.* an opening.

A′pex (ā-) *n.* (*pl.* **a′pexes, a′pices**) top or peak of anything.

Apha′sia *n.* dumbness due to disease of the brain.

Aphe′lion *n.* the point of a planet's orbit farthest from the sun.

A′phis *n.* (*pl.* **a′phides**) a family of small insects found as parasites on roots, leaves, etc., of plants.

Aph′orism *n.* a maxim, a pithy saying.—aphoris′tic *a.*—aph′orist *n.*

Aphrodis′iac *a.* exciting to sexual intercourse.—*n.* that which so excites.

A′piary (ā-) *n.* a place where bees are kept.—a′piarist *n.* a bee-keeper.—apiar′ian, a′pian *a.*—a′piculture *n.*

Apiece′ *adv.* for each.

Aplanat′ic *a.* in optics, without aberration.

Aplomb′ *n.* self-possession, coolness.

Apoc′alypse *n.* the Revelation of St. John; any revelation.—apocalyp′tic *a.*—apocalyp′tically *adv.*

Apoc′rypha *n.* a religious writing of doubtful authenticity, or excluded from the Canon; *esp.* the fourteen books or parts of books known as the Apocrypha of the Old Testament, found in the Septuagint but not in the Hebrew Canon.—apoc′ryphal *a.*

Apod′osis *n. in grammar,* the consequent clause in a conditional sentence, as distinct from the *protasis,* or *if* clause.

Ap′ogee *n.* the point of the sun's or moon's orbit farthest from the earth.

Ap′ologue *a* moral fable or parable.

Apol′ogy *n.* something spoken in defence; acknowledgment of an offence and expression of regret; a poor substitute (with *for*).—apol′ogise *v.i.*—apol′ogist *n.*—apologet′ic *a.*—apologet′ically *adv.*—apologet′ics *n.* the branch of theology charged with the *defence* of Christianity.

Ap′ophthegm, apothegm (-o-them) *n.* a terse saying.

Ap′oplexy *n.* a sudden stroke, causing loss of sensation and motion, usually through hæmorrhage in the brain.—apoplec′tic *a.*

Apos′tasy *n.* abandonment of one's religious or other faith.—apos′tate *n.*

Apos′tle (-sl) *n.* one sent to preach the Gospel, *esp.* one of the first disciples of Jesus; the founder of the Christian church in a country; the chief champion of any new system.—apos′tleship *n.*—apostol′ic, apostol′ical *a.*—apostolic′ity *n.*

Apos′trophe *n.* a turning away

from the subject of a speech to address some person present or absent; a mark (') showing the omission of a letter or letters in a word.— apos'trophise *v.t*

Apoth'ecary *n.* old name for one who prepares and sells drugs, now druggist.

Apothegm *see* APOPHTHEGM.

Apotheo'sis *n.* deification, the act of raising any person or thing into a god.

Appal' (-awl) *v.t.* to dismay, terrify.—appall'ing *a.*
Syn. overwhelm, daunt, scare, frighten. *Ant.* assure, reassure, encourage, embolden.

App'anage, apanage *n.* an allowance for bread and other victuals; lands assigned by a prince for the maintenance of his younger sons.

Appara'tus *n.* equipment, instruments, for performing any experiment or operation.

Appa'rel (-a-) *v.t.* to clothe.— *n.* clothing.

Appa'rent *a.* seeming; obvious.—appa'rently *adv.*

Appari'tion (-i-shun) *n.* an appearance, *esp.* of a ghost or other remarkable thing.

Appeal' *v.i.* to call upon, make earnest request; refer to, have recourse to ; refer to a higher court.—*n.* a request, reference, supplication.—appeal'ing *a.*—appeal'ingly *adv.* —appeal'able *a.*—appell'ant *n.* one who appeals to a higher court.—appell'ate *a.*

Appear' *v.i.* to become visible; to come before; to seem, be plain.—appear'ance *n.*

Appease' *v.t.* to pacify, quiet, allay.—appease'able *a.*—appease'ment *n.*

Appell'ant *see* APPEAL.

Appella'tion *n.* a name.—appell'ative *a.*

Append' *v.t.* to join on, add.— appen'dage *n.*—appen'dix (*pl.* appen'dices, -ixes) *n.*—appendici'tis *n.* inflammation of the vermiform appendix, a prolongation of the intestine.
Syn. to fasten to, subjoin, annex. *Ant.* detach, remove, take from.

Appertain' *v.i.* to belong, relate to.

App'etite *n.* desire, inclination; *esp.* desire for food.— appet'itive *a.*—app'etise *v.t.*— app'etiser *n.*—app'etising *a.* —app'etisingly *adv.*

Applaud' *v.t.* to praise by handclapping; to praise loudly.—applaud'er *n.*—applause' *n.*—applaud'ing *a.*— applaud'ingly *adv.*

Ap'ple *n.* a familiar round, firm, fleshy fruit; the tree bearing it.

Apply' *v.t.* to lay or place on; administer, bring into operation; devote, employ.—appli'ance *n.*—app'licable *a.*— applicabil'ity *n.*—app'licably *adv.*—app'licant *n.*—applica'tion *n.*

Appoint' *v.t* to fix, settle; name to an office; equip.— appoint'men *n.*

Apport (ap-or *n.* in spiritualism, the alleged moving of material objects without material agency *esp.* at seances.

Appor'tion *v.t.* to divide out in shares.—**appor'tionment** *n.*

App'osite *a.* suitable, apt.—**app'ositely** *adv.*—**app'ositeness** *n.*—**apposi'tion** *n.* proximity; the placing of one word beside another in explanation.—**appos'itive** *a.*

Appraise' *v.t.* to set a price on, value.—**apprais'able** *a.*—**appraise'ment** *n.*—**apprais'al** *n.*—**apprais'er** *n.*

Appre'ciate (-shi-) *v.t.* to estimate justly; to be sensible of good qualities in the thing judged.—*v.i.* to rise in price.—**appre'ciable** *a.*—**appre'ciably** *adv.*—**apprecia'tion** *n.*—**appre'ciative** *a.*—**appre'ciator** *n.*

Apprehend' *v.t.* to take hold of; seize by authority; recognise, understand; fear.—**apprehen'sible** *a.*—**apprehensibil'ity** *n.*—**apprehen'sion** *n.*—**apprehen'sive** *a.*—**apprehen'siveness** *n.*

Appren'tice *n.* one bound to a master to learn an art or trade; a novice.—*v.t.* to bind as an apprentice.—**appren'ticeship** *n.*

Apprise' *v.t.* to inform.

Approach *v.i.* to draw near; come near in quality, condition, etc.—*v.t.* to come near to.—*n.* a drawing near; a means of reaching; approximation.—**approach'able** *a.*—**approachabil'ity** *n.*

Approba'tion *n.* sanction, approval.

Appro'priate *v.t.* to take to oneself.—*a.* suitable, fitting.—**appro'priately** *adv.*—**appro'priateness** *n.*—**appropria'tion** *n.*—**appro'priator** *n.*—**appro'priative** *a.*

Syn. to claim, annex, assume, usurp, arrogate. *Ant.* to give up, surrender, yield.

Approve' (-ōōv) *v.t.* to think well of, commend.—**approv'al** *n.*—**approv'er** *n.*—**approv'ingly** *adv.*

Approx'imate *a.* nearly resembling; nearing correctness.—*v.t.* to bring close.—*v.i.* to come near.—**approx'imately** *adv.*—**approxima'tion** *n.*—**approx'imative** *a.*

Appurt'enance *n.* a thing which appertains to; an accessory.

A'pricot (ā-) *n.* an orange-coloured stone-fruit of the plum kind.—*a.* of the colour of the fruit.

A'pril (ā-) *n.* the fourth month of the year.

A'pron (ā-) *n.* a cloth, piece of leather, etc., worn in front to protect the clothes, or as part of an official dress.

Apropos (-pō) *adv.* or *a.* to the purpose; seasonably.

Apse *n.* an arched recess at the end of a church.—**ap'sidal** *a.*

Apsy'chic (a-si'-kik) *a.* not controlled by, or connected with, mind.

Apt *a.* suitable; prompt, quick-witted; likely.—**ap''ly** *adv.*—**apt'ness** *n.*—**apt'itude** *n.*

Aquamarine' *n.* a precious stone, the beryl.—*a.* blue, sea-coloured.

Aq'uaplane (ak'-wa-) *n.* a plank or boat towed by a fast motor-boat.—*v.i.* to ride on an aquaplane.—**aquaplaning** n.

Aquar′ium (pl. **aquar′iums**, **aquar′ia**) n. a tank or pond for keeping water animals or plants.

Aquat′ic a. living or growing in water, or having to do with water.—**aquat′ics** n.pl. water-sports.

Aq′ueduct n. an artificial channel for water, esp. a bridge to carry water across a valley, a canal across an obstacle, etc.

A′queous a. watery.

Aq′uiline a. relating to an eagle ; hooked like an eagle's beak.

Ar′ab (a-) n. a native of Arabia; an Arabian horse.—**street arab′** a neglected, homeless child.—**Ar′abic** n. the language of the Arabs.

Arabesque′ n. a painted or carved ornament of Arabian design.—a. in the style of that design, fantastic.

Ar′able (a-) a. fit for ploughing
Syn. cultivable, agricultural. Ant. barren, uncultivable.

Arb′alest, arb′last n. a strong crossbow.

Arb′iter n. a judge, umpire.—**arb′itress** fem.—**arbit′rament** n.—**arb′itrate** v.i. to act as umpire, to decide a dispute. —v.t. to submit a dispute to an umpire.—**arbitra′tion** n.—**arb′itrator** n.—**arb′itrary** a. not bound by rules, despotic.—**arb′itrarily** adv.

Arbor′eal, arbor′eous a. relating to trees.—**arbore′tum** n. a place for cultivating specimens of trees.—**arb′oriculture** n. forestry, the cultivation of trees.

Arb′our n. a garden seat enclosed by branches, plants; a shaded walk.

Arc n. part of a circle or other curve.

Arcade′ n. a row of arches on pillars; a covered walk or avenue.

Arca′num (pl. **arca′na**) n. a secret, a mystery.

Arch n. a curved structure in building, supporting itself over an open space by the pressure of the stones one against the other.—v.t. to give, or make into. an arch. —**arch′ed** a.—**arch way** n.

Arch a. chief; roguish, sly.—**arch′ly** adv.—**arch′ness** n.— arch prefix chief, e.g. **arch-an′gel** (-k-) n. **archbish′op** n.—**arch-en′emy** n.—**arch-he′retic** n.—**arch-rogue′** n.

Archæol′ogy (-k-) n. the study of ancient times from remains of art, implements, etc.—**archæolo′gical** a.—**archæol′ogist** n.

Archa′ic (-k-) a. old, primitive.—**archa′ically** adv.—**archa′ism** n. an obsolete word or phrase.

Archbish′op n. a chief bishop. —**archbish′opric** n.

Archdeac′on n. a chief deacon, the clergyman next in rank to a bishop.—**archdeac′onry** n. — **archdeac′onate** n. — **archidiac′onal** a.

Arch′duke n. a duke of specially high rank.—**arch-**

duch'ess *fem.*—archdu'cal *a.*
—arch'duchy *n.*

Arch'er *n.* one who shoots with a bow.—arch'ery *n.*

Arc'hetype (-ki-) *n.* an original pattern or model.—arc'hetypal *a.*

Archiepis'copal (-k-) *a.* relating to an archbishop.—archiepis'copate *n.*—archiepis'copacy *n.*

Archipel'ago *n.* a sea full of small islands; a group of islands.—archipel'agoes *pl.*—archipela'gic *a.*

Arc'hitect (-k-) *n.* a master-builder, one who designs buildings ; any maker or contriver.—architecton'ic *a.*—arc'hitecture *n.*—architec'tural *a.*

Arc'hives (-kīvz) *n.* the place where government records are kept; *pl.* public records.—arc'hival *a.*—arc'hivist *n.*

Arc'tic *a.* of northern polar regions; extremely cold.—*n.* the region round the north pole.

Ard'ent *a.* fiery; passionate.—ard'ently *adv.*—ard'our, ard'ency *n.*

Syn. Intense, fierce, vehement, zealous, earnest. *Ant.* indifferent, cool, calm, temperate.

Ard'uous *a.* laborious, hard to accomplish.—ard'uously *adv.*—ard'uousness *n.*

Are (ār, år) *n.* a unit of square measure containing 100 square metres, or 1076.44 square feet.

Ar'ea (èr-) *n.* an open space; a sunken yard round the basement of a house; the

superficial contents of a figure; extent, scope.

Are'na *n.* the space in the middle of an amphitheatre; a place of public contest; a battlefield.

Arête (-rāt) *n.* a sharp mountain ridge, a rocky spur.

Ar'gent *n.* silver.—*a.* silver, silvery-white,*esp.* in heraldry.

Arg'on *n.* a gas forming part of the air.

Arg'osy *n.* a richly-laden merchant-ship.

Arg'ot (-ō) *n.* slang.

Arg'ue *v.i.* to prove; offer reasons; dispute.—*v.t.* prove by reasoning; discuss.—arg'uable *a.*—arg'uer *n.*—arg'ument *n.*—argumenta'tion *n.*—argumen'tative *a.*

Ar'ia *n.* an air or rhythmical song in a cantata, opera, etc.

Ar'id *a.* parched, dry; empty, uninteresting.—arid'ity *n.*

Aright' *adv.* rightly.

Arise' *v.i.* to come up; spring up; ascend, rise up.

Aristoc'racy *n.* government by the best in birth or fortune; the nobility or chief persons of a state; upper classes generally.—ar'istocrat *n.*—aristocrat'ic *a.*—aristocrat'ically *adv.*

Arith'metic *n.* the science of numbers; the art of reckoning by figures.—arithmet'ical *a.*—arithmet'ically *adv.*—arithmeti'cian *n.*

Ark *n.* a box, chest; Noah's vessel; a place of refuge; a ship.

Arm *n.* the limb extending from the shoulder to the wrist; anything projecting from the main body, as a branch of the sea, the supporting rail of a chair, etc.—*v.t.* to give an arm to.—Compounds as arm'chair *n.*—arm'ful *n.*—arm'-hole *n.* etc.

Arm. *n.* a weapon; a branch of the army.—*pl.* weapons; war; the military profession.—*v.t.* to supply with weapons.—*v.i.* to take up arms.—armed' *a.*—arm'ament *n.*

Armad'a (-ad-) *n.* a fleet of armed ships.

Armadill'o *n.* a small American animal protected by bands of bony plates.

Arm'ature *n.* apparatus for defence; a piece of iron across the ends of a magnet; the revolving part of a dynamo or motor.

Arm'istice *n.* a truce, suspension of fighting.

Arm'our *n.* defensive covering or dress; plating of warships.—arm'ourer *n.*—arm'oury, arm'ory *n.*—armor'ial *a.* relating to heraldic arms.

Arm'y *n.* a large body of men armed for warfare and under military command; a host; a great number.

Ar'nica *n.* in botany, a genus of the compositæ. A tincture of *arnica montana* is used for wounds and bruises.

Aro'ma *n.* a sweet smell; a peculiar charm.—aromat'ic *a.*—arom'atise *v.t.*

Around' *adv.* on every side; in a circle.—*prep.* on all sides of.

Arouse' *v.t.* to awaken.

Arpe'ggio (-j-) *n.* a chord of which the notes are sounded

in quick succession, not together.

Arraign' (-ān) *v.t.* to accuse, indict, put on trial.—arraign'er *n.*—arraign'ment *n.*

Arrange' *v.t.* to set in order; settle, adjust; plan.—*v.i.* to make agreement.—arrange'ment *n.*

   Syn. to adapt, dispose, determine. *Ant.* derange, disarrange, misplace, disorganise, muddle, dislocate.

Ar'rant *a.* downright, notorious.—ar'rantly *adv.*

Ar'ras *n.* tapestry.

Array' *v.t.* to set in order; dress, equip, adorn.—*n.* order, *esp.* military order; dress.

Arrear' *n.* state of being behindhand; anything unpaid or undone (usually in *pl.*).

Arrest' *v.t.* to stop; catch the attention; apprehend by legal authority.—*n.* seizure by warrant; making prisoner.

Arrive' *v.i.* to reach a destination; (with *at*) to attain an object.—arri'val *n.*

Ar'rogate *v.t.* to claim as one's own; to claim proudly or unjustly.—ar'rogance *n.* aggressive conceit.—ar'rogant *a.*—ar'rogantly *adv.*

Ar'row *n.* a pointed weapon to be shot with a bow.—ar'rowy *a.*—ar'row-head *n.* the metal part of an arrow.

Ar'rowroot *n.* a West-Indian plant from which is prepared a nutritious starch, used as a food *esp.* for children and invalids.

Ars'enal *n.* a magazine of stores

---

for warfare, guns, ammunition, etc.

Ars'enic n. one of the chemical elements, a soft, gray metal; its oxide, a powerful poison. —**ars'enate** n.—**arsen'ical** a. —**arse'nious** a.

Ars'on n. the crime of intentionally setting on fire houses, ships or other property.

Art n. skill; human skill as opposed to nature; skill applied to music, painting, poetry, etc.; any of the subjects of this skill; a system of rules; a profession or craft; contrivance, cunning, trick; pl. certain branches of learning, languages, history, etc., as distinct from natural science.— **art'ful** a.—**art'fully** adv.— **art'fulness** n.—**art'less** a.— **art'lessly** adv.—**art'lessness** n. —**art'ist** n. one who practises a fine art, esp. painting; one who makes his craft a fine art.—**artis'tic** a.—**artis'tically** adv.—**art'istry** n.— **art'iste** n. a professional singer or other entertainer —**art silk**, see ARTIFICIAL SILK.
Syn. knowledge, adroitness, dexterity. Ant. unskilfulness, incompetence, unproficiency, maladministration.

Art'ery n. a tube or vessel carrying blood from the heart; any main channel of communications.—**arte'rial** a.

Arte'sian a. describes a well bored down until water is reached which rises by itself.

Arthri'tis n. inflammation of a joint; gout.—**arthrit'ic** a.

Art'ichoke n. a thistle-like, perennial, eatable plant.— **Jerusalem artichoke**, a different plant, a sunflower with tubers like the potato.

Art'icle n. a clause, head, para raph, section; a literary composition in a journal, etc.; rule or condition; a commodity or object.—v.t. to indict; to bind as an apprentice.

Artic'ulate v.t. to joint; utter distinctly.—v.t. to speak.— a. jointed; of speech, clear, distinct.—**artic'ulately** adv.— **articula'tion** n.—**artic'ulateness** n.

Art'ifice n. a contrivance, trick; cunning, skill.—**artif'icer** n. a craftsman.—**artifi'cial** a.— **artifi'cially** adv.—**artificial'ity** n.—**artificial silk**, yarn, resembling natural silk in appearance, produced industrially by a synthetic process.

Artill'ery n. cannon; the troops who use them.

Artisan' n. a craftsman, mechanic.

Ar'yan (ẽr-) a. relating to the family of nations and languages otherwise called Indo-European.

As adv., conj. in that degree, so far, since, because, when, while. in like manner.

Asafœt'ida n. a medicinal resin, with an offensive smell.

Asbes'tos n. a fibrous mineral which does not burn.

Ascend' v.i. to climb, mount up; rise; go back in time.— v.t. to walk, climb, mount up. —**ascen'sion** n.—**ascent'** n. rise.—**ascen'dancy** n. control,

---

Māte, mēte, mīte, mōte, mūte, bōōt.

domination.—**ascen'dant** *a.* rising.

Ascertain' *v.t.* and *i.* to get to know, find out.—**ascertain'able** *a.*—**ascertain'ment** *n.*

Ascet'ic *n.* a strict hermit; one who denies himself pleasures for the sake of conscience or religion.—*a.* rigidly abstinent, austere.—**ascet'ically** *adv.*—**ascet'icism** *n.*

Ascribe' *v.t.* to attribute, assign.—**ascri'bable** *a.*—**ascrip'tion** *n.*

Asep'tic (ă-) *a.* not liable to decay, or to blood-poisoning.—**asep'sis** *n.*

Ash *n.* a familiar timber tree; its wood.—**ash'en** *a.*

Ash *n.* the dust or remains of anything burnt; (*pl.*) a dead body.—**ash'y** *a.*

Ashamed' (-ămd) *a.* affected with shame.

Ash'lar *n.* a hewn or squared stone for building.

Ashore' *adv.* on shore.

Aside' *adv.* to, or on one side; privately.—*n.* words spoken in an undertone not to be heard by some person present.

As'inine *a.* of or like an ass.—**asinin'ity** *n.*

Ask *v.t.* to request, require, question, invite.—*v.i.* to make inquiry.

Askance' *adv.* sideways, awry; with a side look or meaning.—**to look askance**, to look at with suspicion.

Aska'ri *n.* a native soldier employed in the service of a European power in East Africa.

Askew' *adv.* aside, awry.

Aslant (-ănt) *adv.* on the slant, obliquely.

Asleep' *a.* and *adv.* sleeping; at rest.
  Syn. dead, dormant, benumbed, inactive. *Ant.* awake, unwearied, indefatigable, industrious, diligent.

Asp *n.* a small venomous snake.

Aspar'agus *n.* a plant cultivated for its young shoots, esteemed as a delicacy.

As'pect *n.* look, view, appearance.

As'pen *n.* the trembling poplar tree.—*a.* tremulous.

Asper'ity *n.* roughness; harshness; coldness.
  Syn. tartness, acrimony, sharpness, crabbedness. *Ant.* smoothness, softness, calm, good temper, sweetness.

Asperse' *v.t.* to besprinkle; to slander, calumniate.—**asper'sion** *n.*

As'phalt, asphal'tum *n.* a black, hard bituminous substance, a mineral pitch, used for paving, etc.—**asphal'tic** *a.*

Asphyx'ia *n.* suffocation.—**asphyx'iate** *v.t.*—**asphyx'iated** *a.*—**asphyxia'tion** *n.*

As'pic *n.* the asp; a piece of ordnance; a jelly containing meat, eggs, fish, etc.; in botany, the great lavender.

Aspire' *v.i.* to desire eagerly; aim at high things; tower up.—**as'pirant** *n.* one who aspires; a candidate.—**aspira'tion** *n.*—**aspi'ring** *a.*—**aspi'ringly** *adv.*—**as'pirate** *v.t.* to pronounce with full breathing, as "h."

As'pirin *n.* a drug used to relieve rheumatic and neuralgic pains.

Ass *n.* a familiar quadruped of the horse family; a stupid fellow.

Ass'agai, assegai *n.* a slender spear used by South African tribes.

Assail' *v.t.* to attack, assault. —**assail'ant** *n.*

Assass'in *n.* one who kills by treacherous violence, usually for reward.—**assass'inate** *v.t.* —**assassina'tion** *n.*

Assault' *n.* a sudden attack; an attack of any kind.—*v.t.* to make an attack on.

Assay' *v.t.* to test the proportions of metals in an alloy or ore; a test of the fineness of a metal, etc.—**assay'er** *n.*— **assay'ing** *n.*

Assegai *see* ASSAGAI.

Assem'ble *v.t.* to bring together, collect; put together, as machinery.—*v.i.* to meet together.—**assem'blage** *n.*— **assem'bly** *n.*

Assent' *v.i.* to concur, agree.— *n.* acquiescence, agreement.

Assert' *v.t.* to declare strongly, insist upon.—**asser'tion** *n.*— **asser'tive** *a.* — **asser'tively** *adv.*

Assess' *v.t.* to fix the amount (of a tax or fine); to tax or fine; to fix the value, estimate, *esp.* for taxation.—**assess'able** *a.*—**assess'ment** *n.*— **assess'or** *n.*

Ass'ets *n.pl.* property available to pay debts, *esp.* of an insolvent debtor; *sing.* an item of such property; a thing of value.,

Assev'erate *v.t.* and *i.* to assert positively, solemnly.—**assevera'tion** *n.*

Assid'uous *a.* persevering.— **assid'uously** *adv.*—**assidu'ity** *n.*

Assign' (-in) *v.t.* to allot, apportion, fix; transfer; ascribe. —**assign'able** *a.*—**assigna'tion** (-ig-nā-) *n.* an appointment to meet; tryst.—**assignee'** (-ĭ-nĕ), **assign'** *n.*—**assign'or** *n.*—**assign'ment** *n.*

Assim'ilate *v.t* to make similar; to convert into like substance, absorb into the system.—**assim'ilable** *a.*—**assimila'tion** *n.* — **assim'ilative** *a.*

Assist' *v.t.* to help.—*v.i.* to be present.—**assis'tance** *n.*—**assis'tant** *n.*

Assize' *n.* regulation of price; standard; *pl.* sittings of a court held in counties periodically for civil and criminal cases, tried by a judge of the High Court and a jury.

Asso'ciate *v.t.* to join with, unite.—*v.i.* to combine, unite. —*n.* a companion, partner, ally, friend.—*a.* joined, connected.—**associa'tion** *n.*

Ass'onance *n.* likeness in sound.—**ass'onant** *a.*

Assort' *v.t.* to classify, arrange. —*v.i.* to match, agree with. —**assort'ed** *a.*—**assort'ment** *n.*

Assuage' (-sw-) *v.t.* to soften, allay.—**assuage'ment** *n.*

Syn. to alleviate, appease, mitigate, soothe, relieve. *Ant.* to aggravate, provoke, irritate, magnify.

Assume' *v.t.* to take for granted; put on; claim, arrogate; pretend.—*v.t.* to

be arrogant.—**assump'tive** *a.*
—**assump'tion** *n.*

Assure' *v.t.* to make safe; to insure; tell positively; give confidence.—**assur'ed** *a.*—**assur'edly** *adv.*—**assur'ance** *n.*

Astat'ic *a.* in physics, having no tendency to take a fixed position.—**astatic coil,** in wireless, an inductance with a limited external field.

As'ter *n.* a plant with star-like flowers; the Michaelmas daisy.

As'terisk *n.* a star (*) used in printing.

Astern' *adv.* at the stern; behind.

As'teroid *n.* a small planet.

Asth'ma (-sm-) *n.* a disease entailing difficulty of breathing, wheezing and tightness in the chest, etc.—**asthmat'ic** *a.*—**asthmat'ically** *adv.*

Astig'matism *n.* a defect of the eye in which the rays are not brought to a proper focus at one point.—**astigmat'ic** *a.*

Astir' *adv.* on the move; out; in excitement.

Aston'ish, astound' *v.t.* to amaze, surprise greatly.—**aston'ishing** *a.*—**aston'ishment** *n.*

Astound' *see* ASTONISH.

Ast'rakhan *n.* lambskin with curled wool from the Caspian region.

As'tral *a.* of the stars, starry.

Astray' *adv.* out of the right way.

Astride' *adv.* with the legs apart.

Astrin'gent *a.* binding, contracting.—*n.* a binding medicine.—**astrin'gency** *n.*

Astrol'ogy *n.* the pretended art of fortune-telling by the stars, out of which grew astronomy.—**astrol'oger** *n.*—**astrolo'gical** *a.*

Astron'omy *n.* the study of the heavenly bodies.—**astron'omer** *n.*—**astronom'ical** *a.*

Astute' *a.* crafty, cunning.—**astute'ly** *adv.*—**astute'ness** *n.* *Syn.* wily, sly, subtle, keen. *Ant.* dull, slow-witted, apathetic, stupid.

Asun'der *adv.* apart, in pieces.

Asy'lum *n.* a refuge, sanctuary; a home for the care of the unfortunate, *esp.* lunatics.

As'ymptote *n.* a straight line that continually approaches a curve, but never meets it within a finite distance.

Asyn'deton *n.* a figure of style in which the conjunctions are omitted.

At *prep.* near to, by, in; engaged on; in the direction of.

At'avism *n.* appearance of ancestral, not parental, characteristics in an animal or plant.—**atavis'tic** *a.*

Atelier' (-el-yā) *n.* a workshop, *esp.* an artist's studio.

A'theism (ā-) *n.* disbelief in the existence of a god.—**a'theist** *n.*—**atheis'tic, atheis'tical** *a.*

Athirst' *a.* thirsty.

Ath'lete *n.* one trained to physical exercises, feats or contests of strength.—**athlet'ic** *a.*—**athlet'ics** *n.pl.* sports of running, wrestling, etc.—**athlet'icism** *n.*—**athlet'ically** *adv.*

Athwart' *prep.* across.—*adv.* across, *esp.* obliquely.

At'las *n.* a volume of maps.

At'mosphere n. the mass of gas surrounding a heavenly body, *esp.* the earth.—**atmospher'ic** a.—**atmospher'ics** n.pl. noises in wireless reception due to electrical disturbances from the atmosphere.

Atoll' n. a ring-shaped coral island.

At'om n. the smallest particle of matter which enters into chemical combination; any very small particle.—**atom'ic** a.

Atone' v.i. to give satisfaction or make reparation.—**atone'-ment** n.

Atrabil'ious, **atrabil'iar** a. melancholy.

Atro'cious (-shus) a. extremely cruel or wicked.—**atro'ciously** adv.—**atro'city** n.

At'rophy n. wasting away in a living body, with lessening of size and strength.—v.i. to waste away, become useless.—**at'rophied** a.

Attach' v.t. to fasten, seize, connect, join to.—v.i. to adhere.—**attach'ment** n.

Attach'é (a-tash'ā) n. a member of an ambassador's suite.—**attach'é-case** n. a small rectangular handbag for papers.

Attack' v.t. to fall upon violently; assault, assail; affect (of a disease).—n. an assault, seizure.

Attain' v.t. to arrive at, reach, gain by effort.—**attain'able** a.—**attainabil'ity** n.—**attain'-ment** n. esp. a personal accomplishment.

Attain'der n. loss of rights through conviction of high treason.—**attaint'** v.t. to convict; deprive of rights; accuse; stain.

Att'ar n. a very fragrant oil made in the East, chiefly from roses.

Attempt' v.t. to try, endeavour, make an effort or attack on;—n. a trial, effort.

Attend' v.t. to wait upon, accompany; wait for.—v.i. to give the mind (to).—**atten'-dance** n.—**atten'dant** n.—**atten'tion** n.—**atten'tive** a.—**atten'tively** adv.—**atten'tive-ness** n.

Syn. to serve, heed, mind, regard, listen, escort. Ant. to ignore, disregard, slight, be inattentive.

Atten'uate v.t. to make thin or slender; weaken, reduce.—v.i. to become weak or slender.—**atten'uated** a.—**attenua'tion** n.

Attest' v.t. to bear witness to, certify.—**attesta'tion** n.

Att'ic n. a low story above the cornice of a building; a room in the roof.—a. of Athens; elegant.

Attire v.t. to dress, array.—n. dress.

Att'itude n. posture, position; behaviour, relation of persons expressing thought, feeling, etc.—**attitu'dinise** v.i.

Attor'ney (-ter-) n. a solicitor; one appointed to act 'or another.

Attract' v.t. to draw towards, literally or figuratively; entice; cause to approach.—**attrac'tion** n.—**attrac'tive** a.—**attrac'tively** adv.—**attrac'-tiveness** n.

Syn. to fascinate, charm, allure, arrest. *Ant.* revolt, disgust, offend, nauseate, appal, shock.

Attrib'ute *v.t.* to ascribe, assign, refer to.—**att'ribute** *n.* a quality, property or characteristic of anything.—**attrib'-utable** *a.*—**attribu'tion** *n.*—**attrib'utive** *a.*—**attrib'utively** *adv.*

Attri'tion (-i-shun) *n.* rubbing away, wearing down.

Attune' *v.t.* to put in tune, harmonise.

Atyp'ic *a.* without distinct typical characters.

Auberge (ō-bārzh) *n.* an inn; a place of entertainment for travellers.

Aub'urn *a.* reddish brown.

Auc'tion *n.* a public sale in which the bidder offers increase of price over another and what is sold goes to who bids highest.—**auctioneer'** *n.* —**auc'tion-bridge** *n.* a card game.—Dutch auction, selling in which the seller starts at a high price and comes down until he meets a bidder.

Auda'cious *a.* bold, daring.—**auda'city** *n.*

Aud'ible *a.* able to be heard. —**aud'ibly** *adv.* — **audibil'ity** *n.*

Aud'ience *n.* act of hearing; judicial hearing; formal interview; an assembly of hearers.

Aud'it *n.* a formal examination of accounts; a periodical settlement.—*v.t.* to examine (accounts).

Audi'tion *n.* sense of hearing; a hearing.—**auditor'ium** *n.* a place for hearing, a hall.—**aud'itory** *a.*

Aug'er *n.* a carpenter's tool for boring holes.

Aught *n.* anything.—*adv.* to any extent.

Augment' *v.t.* and *i.* to increase, enlarge.—**aug'ment** *n.* increase.—**augmenta'tion** *n.*—**augmen'tative** *a.*

Aug'ur *n.* among the Romans one who predicted the future by observations of birds, etc —**aug'ury** *n.*

August' *a.* majestic, dignified. —**Aug'ust** *n.* the eighth month.—**Augus'tan** *a.* of Augustus, the Roman Emperor; hence classic, distinguished, as applied to a period of literature.

Auk *n.* a northern sea-bird with short wings used only as paddles.

Aunt (ánt) *n.* a father's, or a mother's sister; an uncle's wife.

Au'ra (aw'-) *n.* a subtle emanation from the body; atmosphere; character; a peculiar sensation, as of a current of air rising to the head, preceding an attack of epilepsy or hysteria; a gentle breeze.

Aur'al *a.* of the ear.—**aur'ally** *adv.*

Aure'ola, aur'eole *n.* gold colour or illumination painted round the head or figure of holy persons in Christian art; a halo.

Aur'icle *n.* the outside ear; *pl* the upper cavities of the heart.—**auric'ular** *a.* of the ear; known by ear, told in the ear, *esp.* of confession

Aurif′erous *a.* bearing or yielding gold.

Aur′ist *n.* an ear-doctor.—**aur′iscope** *n.* an instrument for examining the ear.

Auror′a *n.* lights in the atmosphere to be seen radiating from the regions of the poles. The northern is called *aurora borealis* and the southern *aurora australis*.

Ausculta′tion *n.* listening to the movement of the heart and lungs with a stethoscope.—**ausculta′tor** *n.*—**auscul′tatory** *a.*

Aus′pice *n.* an omen drawn from the observation of birds (usually in *pl.*).—**auspi′cious** *a.* of good omen, favourable.—**auspi′ciously** *adv.*

Austere′ *a.* harsh, strict, severe.—**austere′ly** *adv.*—**auste′rity** *n.*
  Syn. rigid, rough, unrelenting, stern. *Ant.* kindly, engaging, tender, sweet.

Aus′tin *a.* a contraction of *Augustine*, as, añ *Austin* friar.

Aus′tral *a.* southern.

Authen′tic *a.* trustworthy, real, genuine, true.—**authen′-tically** *adv.*—**authen′ticate** *v.t.*—**authentica′tion**n.—**authen-ti′city** *n.*

Auth′or *n.* an originator, constructor; the writer of a book.—**auth′oress** *fem.*—**auth′orship** *n.*

Author′ity *n.* legal power or right; delegated power; influence; permission; a book, person, etc., settling a question, entitled to be believed; a body or board in control, *esp.* in *pl.*—**author′itative** *a.*—**author′itatively** *adv.*—**auth′orize** *v.t.*—**authoriza′-tion** *n.*

Au′to-anal′ysis *n.* psychoanalysis, self-applied.

Autobiog′raphy *n.* the biography or life of a person written by himself.—**autobiog′rapher** *n.*—**autobiograph′ical**a.—**autobiograph′i-cally** *adv.*

Aut′ocrat *n.* an absolute ruler.—**autoc′racy** *n.*—**autocrat′ic** *a.*—**autocrat′ically** *adv.*

Auto-da-fé *n.* public judgment and punishment by the Inquisition in Spain and Portugal, *esp.* the burning of heretics.

Au′to-er′otism *n.* in psychoanalysis, self-love, with satisfaction of desire.

Autogi′ro (-ji′-) *n.* aeroplane using horizontal airscrew for vertical ascent and descent.

Aut′ograph *n.* one's own handwriting; a signature.—**autograph′ic** *a.*

Autom′aton *n.* a self-acting machine, *esp.* one simulating a human being; *fig.* a human being who acts by routine, without intelligence.—**automat′ic** *a.*—**automat′ically** *adv.*—**autom′atism** *n.*

Automo′bile *n.* a motor-car.—**automo′bilism** *n.*—**automo′-bilist** *n.*

Auton′omyn. self-government.—**auton′omous** *a.*

Autop′sy *n.* personal inspection; post-mortem examination.

Au′to-sugges′tion *n.* a process of influencing the mind (towards health, future action, etc.), conducted by the subject himself.

Aut'umn n. the third season of the year.—**autum'nal** a.—**autum'nally** adv.

Auxil'iary a. helping, subsidiary.—n. a helper; something subsidiary, as troops; a verb used to form tenses of other verbs.

Avail' v.i. to be of value, of use.—v.t. to benefit, help; **to avail oneself of**, to make use of.—n. benefit, as *to be of little avail*, etc.—**avail'able** a.—**availabil'ity** n.
Syn. of n. advantage, profit, utility. Ant. uselessness, futility, inutility, detriment.

Av'alanche n. a mass of snow and ice sliding down a mountain.

Av'arice n. greediness of wealth.— **avari'cious** a.— **avari'ciously** adv.

Avast' interj. (naut.) enough ! stop !

Avatar' n. descent of a Hindu god in visible form; incarnation.

Avaunt' interj. away.

Avenge' v.t. to take vengeance on behalf of (a person) or on account of (a thing).—**aven'ger** n.

Av'enue n. an approach; a double row of trees, with or without a road; a handsome street

Aver' v.t. to declare true; assert.—**aver'ment** n.

Av'erage n. the mean value or quantity of a number of values or quantities (formerly meant charge over and above

freight at sea; loss from damage, etc.).—a. medium, ordinary.—v.t. to fix or calculate a mean.—v.i. to exist in or form a mean.

Avert' v.t. to turn away, ward off.—**averse'** a. disinclined, unwilling.—**aver'sion** n. dislike.

A'viary n. a place for keeping birds.—**a'viarist** n.

Avia'tion (ā-) n. the art of flying by mechanical means.—**a'viator** n.

Avid'ity n. eagerness, greediness.—**av'id** a.

Avoca'tion n. employment, business. (Formerly distraction from business, diversion.)

Avoid' v.t. to keep clear of, escape. — **avoid'able** a. — **avoid'ance** n.

Avoirdupois' (av-er-dū-poiz) n. or a. the British system of weights.

Avow' v.t. to own, acknowledge.—**avow'al** n. — **avow'able** a.—**avowed'** a.—**avow'edly** adv.
Syn. to confess, aver, profess, recognise, admit. Ant. deny, conceal, refute.

Await' v.t. to wait or stay for ; to be in store for.

Awake', **awa'ken** v.t. to rouse from sleep; stir up.—v.i. to cease from sleep; bestir oneself.—a. not sleeping.—**awa'kening** n.

Award' v.t. to adjudge.—n. judgment, final decision.

Aware' a. informed, conscious.—**aware'ness** n.

Awash' adv. level with the surface of water.

Away' *adv.* absent, apart, at a distance.

Awe *n.* dread mingled with reverence.—**awe'some** *a.*—**awful** *a.*—**aw'fully** *adv.*

Awhile' *adv.* for a short time.

Awk'ward *a.* clumsy, ungainly; difficult to deal with; embarrassed. — **awk'wardly** *adv.*—**awk'wardness** *n.*

Awl *n.* a pointed tool for boring small holes, *esp.* in leather

Awn *n.* beard of corn, etc.

Awn'ing *n.* a covering of canvas, etc., to shelter from the sun.

Awry' (a-rī') *adv.* crookedly, perversely;—*a.* crooked, distorted; wrong.

Axe *n.* a tool with a blade in line with the handle, for hewing or chopping.

Ax'iom *n.* a self-evident truth; a received principle.—**axiomat'ic** *a.*

Ax'is *n.* a straight line round which a body revolves ; a line or column about which parts are arranged.—**ax'ial** *a.*—**ax'ially** *adv.*

Ax'le (ak'sl), **ax'le-tree** *n.* the rod on which a wheel turns.

Ay, aye *adv.* ever.

Aye *adv.* yes.—*n.* an affirmative answer or vote; *pl.* those voting for a motion.

Aza'lea *n.* a genus of shrubby plants, with fine white, yellow, or red flowers, allied to the rhododendron.

Az'ure (a'-zhur, ā'-zhur) *a.* clear blue, sky-coloured.—*n.* a delicate blue; the sky.

B

Bab'ble *v.i.* to speak like a baby; talk idly.—*v.t.* to utter idly.—*n.* chatter, idle talk.—**bab'bling, bab'blement** *n.*—**bab'bler** *n.*

Babe *n.* an infant, a child.—**ba'by** *n.*—**ba'byish** *a.*—**ba'byhood** *n.*

Ba'bel *n.* a confusion of sounds; a scene of confusion.

Baboon' *n.* a species of large monkey, with long face and dog-like tusks.—**baboon'ish** *a.*

Ba'by *see* BABE.

Bacc'arat (-rà) *n.* a game of cards.

Bacc'hanal (-ka-) *n.* a worshipper of Bacchus; a reveller.—**bacchana'lian** *a.*

Bach'elor *n.* an unmarried man; one who has taken his first degree at a university; a young knight.—**bach'elorship, bach'elorhood** *n.*

Bacill'us *n.* (bacill'i *pl.*) a microbe, a minute organism causing disease.—**bacill'iform** *a.*

Back *n.* the hinder part.—*a.* situated behind.—*v.t.* to support; to make recede.—*v.i.* to move away, to the rear.—*adv.* to the rear; to a former condition; in return.—**back'bite** *v.t.* to slander an absent person. — **back'biter** *n.* — **back'biting** *n.*—**back'blocks** *n.* the interior of Australia.—**back'bone** *n.* spinal column.—**back'er** *n.* one who supports another, *esp.* in a contest.—**backfire'** *v.i.* to ignite wrongly, as a gas-burner, etc.—*n.* in internal combustion engines, explosion in cylinder occurring before piston has reached top of stroke.—**backgamm'on** *n.* a game played with draughtsmen and dice.—**back'ground** *n.* space at the back; space behind the chief figures of a picture, etc.—**back'hand** *n.* a stroke with the hand turned backward; writing that slopes to the left.—**back'ing** *n.* support.—**backslide** *v.i.* to fall back in faith or morals. —**back'stays** *n.pl.* ropes to strengthen the mast of a ship. —**back'wards, back'ward** *adv.* to the rear, to the past, from a better to a worse state.— **back'ward** *a.* lagging, behind-hand.—**back'wardness** *n.*

Ba'con *n.* cured pig's flesh.

Bacte'rium *n.* a microbe, a disease-germ.—**bacte'ria** *pl.* —**bacte'rial** *a.*—**bacteriol'ogy** *n.*—**bacteriol'ogist** *n.*

Bad *a.* no good; evil, wicked; faulty.—**bad'ly** *adv.*—**bad'ness.** *n.*
  Syn. vile, unwholesome, naughty, vicious, sinful, corrupt, hurtful. *Ant.* good, virtuous, moral, wholesome, innocuous.

Badge *n.* a mark or sign.

Badg'er *n.* a burrowing night animal, about the size of a fox.—*v.t.* to hunt eagerly, to worry, as dogs, a badger.

Bad'inage (-àzh) *n.* playful talk, banter, chaff.

Bad'minton *n.* a game like lawn-tennis, but played with shuttlecocks.

Baf'fle *v.t.* to check, frustrate.
  Syn. to balk, defeat, elude, confuse, perplex. *Ant.* help, aid, assist, encourage.

Bag *n.* a sack, pouch; a measure of quantity.—*v.i.* to swell out.—*v.t.* to put in a bag; to kill, seize, as game, etc.—**bagg'ing** *n.* cloth.— **bagg'y** *a.*—**bag'man** *n.* a commercial traveller.

Bagasse' (-gas') *n.* the refuse of the sugar-cane, after crushing.

Bagatelle' *n.* a trifle; a game played with nine balls and cue on a board.

Bagg'age *n.* the luggage of an army; any luggage; a saucy or worthless woman.

Bag'pipe *n.* a musical wind-instrument, consisting of a leather wind-bag and pipes. —**bag'piper** *n.*

Bail *n.* (*law*) security given for a person's reappearance in court; one giving such security.—*v.t.* to release on security.

Bail *n.* a pole separating horses in a stable; a crosspiece on the wicket at cricket.

Bail, bale *v.t.* to empty out water from a boat.

Bail'iff *n.* a sheriff's officer; a land-steward.—**bail'iwick** *n.* the jurisdiction of a bailiff.

Bait *n.* food put on a hook to entice fish; any lure or enticement; refreshment on a journey.—*v.t.* to set a lure; to feed and water; to annoy, persecute.—*v.i.* to take refreshment on a journey.

Baize *n.* coarse woollen cloth.

Bake *v.t.* to cook or harden by

dry heat.—*v.i.* to make bread; to become scorched. ba'king *n.*—ba'ker *n.*—ba'kery, bake'house *n.*

Bake'lite *n.* a hard strong synthetic resin, used as insulating material, and in many varieties of coloured ware.

Balalai'ka (-li'-) *n.* an old Slavic musical instrument, resembling a guitar.

Bal'ance *n.* a pair of scales; equilibrium; surplus; sum due on an account; difference of two sums.—*v.t.* to weigh; bring to equilibrium; adjust.—*v.i.* to have equal weight; to be in equilibrium. —bal'ance-wheel *n.* the regulating wheel of a watch.

Bal'cony *n.* a platform projecting from the wall of a building; a gallery of a theatre.

Bald (bawld) *a.* hairless; plain, meagre.—bald'ly *adv.*—bald'ness *n.*—bald'head *n.*

Bal'derdash (bawl-) *n.* idle, senseless talk.

Bal'dric (bawl-) *n.* a shoulder-belt.

Bale *n.* a bundle or package.—*v.t.* to make into bundles.

Bale *v.t. see* BAIL.

Bale *n.* evil, mischief, woe.—bale'ful *a.*—bale'fully *adv.*—bale'fulness *n.*

Balk, baulk (bawk) *n.* a strip of land left unploughed; a squared timber, a beam; a hindrance.—*v.t.* to thwart, hinder.—*v.i.* to swerve, pull up.

Ball (bawl) *n.* anything round; a glove, sphere; bullet.—*v.i.* to clog, gather into a mass.

Ball (bawl) *n.* an assembly for dancing.

Ball'ad *n.* a simple spirited narrative poem; a simple song.

Ballade' (-ád) *n.* a form of poem.

Ball'ast *n.* heavy material put in a ship to give steadiness by added weight.—*v.t.* to load thus.

Ball'et (-ā) *n.* a theatrical dance.

Balloon' *n.* a large bag filled with gas to make it rise in the air.—*v.i.* to go up in a balloon; to puff out.—balloon'ist *n.*

Ball'ot *n.* a method of voting secretly by putting balls or tickets into a box.—*v.i.* to vote by this method.—ball'ot-box *n.*

Balm (bàm) *n.* an aromatic substance; a healing or soothing ointment; anything soothing.—balm'y *a.*—balm'iness *n.*

Bal'sam (bawl-) *n.* a resinous aromatic substance. — balsam'ic *a.*—Canada balsam *n.* a kind of turpentine.

Bal'uster *n.* a short pillar.—balustrade' *n.* a row of short pillars surmounted by a rail.

Bamboo' *n.* a large Indian reed, with hard, hollow stem.

Ban *n.* a denunciation, curse; proclamation.—*v.t.* to curse, forbid, outlaw.—banns *n.pl.* proclamation of marriage.

Syn. censure, prohibition, outlawry, interdict. *Ant.* permission, grant, sanction, licence, approval.

Banal' *a.* commonplace, trivial.
—banal'ity *n.*

Bana'na (-nä-) *n.* a tropical or sub-tropical tree; its fruit.

Band *n.* a strip used to bind; a bond.—ban'dage *n.* a strip of cloth used by surgeons for binding.

Band *n.* a company, troop; a company of musicians.—*v.t.* and *i.* to join into a band.—band'master *n.*—bands'man *n.*—band'stand *n.*

Bandann'a *n.* a patterned, coloured silk or cotton handkerchief.

Band'box *n.* a light box for hats, etc.

Ban'dit *n.* (bandits', banditt'i *pl.*) an outlaw; robber.

Bandolier, bandoleer (-ĕr) *n.* a shoulder-belt with pockets for cartridges.

Ban'dy *n.* a game like hockey. —*v.t.* to beat to and fro, toss from one to another. —ban'dy, ban'dy-legged *a.* having crooked legs.

Bane *n.* ruin, destruction; poison.—bane'ful *a.*—bane'fully *adv.*—bane'fulness *n.*

Bang *n.* a heavy blow; a sudden loud noise, an explosion.—*v.t.* to beat; strike violently, slam; make a loud noise.

Bangle (bang'gl) *n.* a ring worn on arm or leg.

Ban'ish *v.t.* to condemn to exile; drive away.—ban'ishment *n.*
Syn. to expatriate, transport, expel. *Ant.* to welcome, invite, summon.

Ban'ister *n.* corrupt. of baluster.

Ban'jo *n.* a musical instrument, having a body like a flat drum, a long neck and strings played with the fingers.—ban'joist *n.*

Bank *n.* a mound or ridge of earth; margin of a river, lake, etc.; rising ground in the sea. —*v.t.* and *i.* to enclose with a ridge; to pile up; of an aeroplane, to tilt inwards in turning.

Bank *n.* an establishment for keeping, lending, exchanging, etc., money.—*v.t.* to put in a bank.—*v.i.* to keep or deal with a bank.—bank'er *n.*—ban'ing *n.*

Bank *n.* a bench in a galley; a row or rank.

Bank'rupt *n.* one who fails in business, cannot pay his debts.—bank'ruptcy *n.*

Bann'er *n.* a flag bearing a device.

Banns *n. see* BAN.

Banq'uet (hang'-kwet) *n.* a feast.—*v.i.* to feast.—*v.t.* to treat with a feast.—banq'ueter *n.*

Ban'tam *n.* a dwarf variety of domestic fowl; a boxing weight.

Ban'ter *v.t.* to make fun of.— *n.* raillery in fun.

Ban'tingism *n.* a diet, mainly of lean meat, prescribed as a remedy for corpulence.

Ban'tling *n.* a child; brat.

Baptize' (-īz) to immerse in, or sprinkle with water ceremoniously; to christen.— bap'tism *n.*—bap'tist *n.* a believer in baptism by immersion only. — baptis'mal (-z-) *a.*—baptis'mally *adv.*

Bar *n.* a rod of any substance;

an obstacle; a bank of sand at the mouth of a river; a rail in a law-court; a body of lawyers; a counter in a public-house.—*v.t.* to make fast; obstruct; except.—*prep.* except.—**barr'ing** *prep.* excepting.—**bar'maid** *n.*

Ba'rad *n.* unit of pressure.

Barb *n.* the curved jag on the point of a spear, fish-hook, etc.—*v.t.* to furnish with such jags.

Bar'barous *a.* savage, brutal, uncivilised.—**barba'rian** (-è-) *n.*—**barbar'ic** *a.*—**barbar'ity** *n.*—**bar'barism** *n.*—**bar'barously** *adv.*
   Syn. rude, wild, cruel, brutal, ferocious, untutored, ignorant. *Ant.* civilised tame, gentle, cultured, polished, kind, humane.

Barb'er *n.* one who shaves beards and cuts hair.

Bard *n.* a poet, minstrel.—**bard'ic** *a.*

Bare *a.* uncovered; naked; poor, scanty.—*v.t.* to make bare.—**bare'ly** *adv.*—**bare'ness** *n.*—**bare'faced** *a.* impudent.

Barg'ain (-gin) *n.* a contract or agreement; a favourable purchase.—*v i.* to make a bargain; to chaffer.

Barge *n.* a flat-bottomed freight boat; a state or pleasure boat.—**barge'man, bargee'** *n.*

Bar'itone *n.* a voice between tenor and bass.—*a.* having such a voice; written for this voice.

Ba'rium (-è-) *n.* a metal element.

Bark *n.* the rind of a tree.—*v.t.* to strip the bark from; to rub off (skin).

Bark, barque *n.* a small ship; a three-masted vessel with fore and main masts square-rigged and mizzen mast fore-and-aft rigged.—**barq'nentine** *n.* a ship like a barque, but with main mast also fore-and-aft rigged.

Bark *v.i.* to utter a sharp cry, *esp.* of a dog.—*n.* the cry of a dog, etc.

Bar'ley *n.* a hardy grain used for food and for making malt liquors and spirits.—**bar'leycorn** *n.* a grain of barley.—**bar'ley-sugar** *n.* a sweetmeat made with barley.

Barm *n.* yeast.

Barn *n.* a building to store grain, hay, etc.—**barn'door, barn'yard** *a.* rustic.

Bar'nacle *n.* a shellfish which sticks to rocks and bottoms of ships.—**bar'nacle-goose** *n.* a species of wild goose.

Barom'eter *n.* an instrument to measure the weight or pressure of the atmosphere. —**baromet'ric** *a.*—**bar'ograph** *n.* a recording barometer.

Bar'on *n.* a peer of the lowest rank.—**bar'oness** *fem.*—**bar'onage** *n.*—**baro'nial** *a.*—**bar'ony** *n.*

Bar'onet *n.* the lowest hereditary title in the United Kingdom.—**bar'onetage** *n.*—**bar'onetcy** *n.*

Baroque' (-k) *a.* extravagantly ornamented (in art).

Barouche (-ōōsh) *n.* a four-wheeled carriage with folding top.

Barque *n.* **barq'uentine** *see* BARK.

Barr ack *n.* a building for soldiers; a huge bare building.

Barr'ack *v.t.* and *i.* to jeer at, *esp.* on a cricket field.

Barr'age (-ăzh) *n.* a dam built across a river; a curtain of shellfire to cover an attack, etc.

Barr'atry *n.* fraudulent breach of duty by the master of a ship; vexatious encouragement of law suits.—**barr'ator** *n.*—**barr'atrous** *a.*

Barr'el *n.* a round wooden vessel, made of curved staves bound with hoops; the quantity held by such a vessel; anything long and hollow, as the tube of a gun, etc.—*v.t.* to put in a barrel.—**barr'elled** *a.*

Barr'en *a.* unfruitful, sterile; unprofitable.—**barr'enness** *n.* *Syn.* unproductive, unfertile, unprolific, scanty, empty. *Ant.* prolific, plentiful, rich, plenteous, abundant, fecund.

Barricade' *n.* an improvised fortification against an enemy.—*v.t.* to obstruct, fortify.

Barr'ier *n.* a fence, obstruction.

Barr'ister *n.* an advocate in the higher law courts.

Barr'ow *n.* a small wheeled hand-carriage.

Barr'ow *n.* a burial mound.

Bart'er *v.i.* to traffic by exchange of things.—*v.t.* to give (one thing) in exchange for another.—*n.* traffic by exchange.

Bar'ytone *n. see* BARITONE.

Bas'alt (-sawlt) *n.* a dark-coloured, hard, igneous rock.—**basalt'ic** *a.*

Base *n.* a bottom, foundation; starting-point; fixed point.—*v.t.* to found, establish.—**base'less** *a.*—**base'ment** *n.* lowest story of a building.

Base low, mean; despicable.—**base'ly** *adv.*—**base'ness** *n.*—**base'-born** *a.*—**base-mind'-ed** *a.* *Syn.* vile, ignoble, plebeian, vulgar, contemptible, worthless. *Ant.* high, praiseworthy, eminent, honourable, exalted, lofty.

Base'-ball *n.* an American game, developed from rounders.

Bash *v.t.* to smash in.

Bash'ful *a.* shy modest, wanting confidence.—**bash'fully** *adv.*—**bash'fulness** *n.*

Bas'il (baz'-) *n.* a fragrant aromatic plant; slope of the cutting edge of a tool; the tanned skin of a sheep.

Bas'ilisk (-z-) *n.* a fabulous small fire-breathing dragon.

Ba'sin *n.* a deep circular dish; a dock; the land drained by a river.

Ba'sis *n.* foundation, groundwork.

Bask (-à-) *v.i.* to lie in warmth and sunshine.

Bas'ket (bàs-) *n.* a vessel made of plaited twigs, rushes, etc.

Bas-relief' *n.* sculpture in which the figures do not stand out much.

Bass (bā-) *n.* the lowest part in music; the lowest man's voice; one having such a voice.—*a.* low in the scale, deep.

Bass (bas) *n.* fish of the perch family.

Bassinet' *n.* a baby-carriage or cradle.

Bassoon' *n.* a wood wind instrument.—**bassoon'ist** *n.*

Bast *n.* the inner bark of trees; fibre; matting.

Bas'tard *n.* a child born of parents not married.—*a.* illegitimate; not genuine.—**bas'tardy** *n.*

Baste *v.t.* to beat with a stick.—**ba'sting** *n.*

Baste *v.t.* to drop melted fat over roasting meat.

Baste *v.t.* to sew together loosely.

Bastina'do *n.* a beating with a stick, *esp.* on the soles of the feet (in the East).—*v.t.* to beat so.

Bas'tion *n.* a projecting part of a fortification.

Bat *n.* a heavy stick; a flat club, *esp.* as used in cricket.—*v.i.* to use the bat in cricket.—**bats'man** *n.*—**batt'ing** *n.*

Bat *n.* a mouse-like flying animal.

Batch *n.* quantity of bread baked at one time; any quantity or number; a set.

Bate *v.* same as ABATE.

Bath (bâth) *n.* water to plunge the body in; act of bathing; a vessel for bathing.—*v.t.* to wash.

Bathe (-TH-) *v.t.* and *i.* to wash. **ba'ther** *n.*—**ba'thing** *n.*

Ba'thonism (bā'-) *n.* an evolution tendency to develop along divergent lines.

Ba'thos (-TH-) *n.* a ludicrous descent from the elevated to the mean in writing or speech.

Ba'tik (bȧ-tēk) *n.* a process of dyeing with several colours; a fabric so treated; a design so produced.

Bat'man *n.* an officer's servant, or groom.

Bat'on *n.* staff, *esp.* of a policeman, a conductor, or a marshal.

Batra'chian (-trā'-ki-) *n.* an animal of the frog order.

Battal'ion (-yon) *n.* a division of a regiment of soldiers; troops in battle array.

Batt'er *v.t.* to strike continuously. — *n.* ingredients beaten up with liquid into a paste.

Batt'ery *n.* a number of cannon; the place where they are mounted; a unit of artillery, men, horses, and guns; (*law*) assault by beating.

Bat'tle *n.* a fight between armies.—*v.i.* to fight.

Bat'tledore *n.* a bat for striking a shuttlecock.

Bat'tlement *n.* a wall on a fortification with openings or embrasures.

Bau'ble *n.* a jester's stick; a trifle.

Baulk *see* BALK.

Bawl *v.i.* to shout.—*n.* a shout.

Bay *a.* reddish-brown.

Bay *n.* a wide inlet of the sea.

Bay *n.* space between two columns; a recess.—**bay'-window** *n.*

Bay *n.* the laureltree; *pl.* an honorary crown of victory.

Bay n. bark; cry of hounds in pursuit.—v.i. to bark.—v.t. to bark at.

Bay'onet n. a stabbing weapon fixed to a rifle.—v.t. to stab with a bayonet.

Bazaar' (-zàr) n. an Eastern market; a fancy fair.

Be v.i. to live; exist; to have a state or quality.

Beach n. the shore of the sea. —v.t. to run on the shore.

Beac'on n. a signal-fire; a sea-mark.

Bead n. a little ball pierced for threading on a string; a narrow moulding.—bead'y a. —bead'ed a.—bead'ing n.

Bea'dle n. a mace-bearer; a parish-officer.

Bea'gle n. a small hound.

Beak n. the bill of a bird; anything pointed or projecting; in Australia, a magistrate.

Beak'er n. a large drinking-cup; a glass vessel used by chemists.

Beam n. a long squared piece of wood; the bar of a balance; a shaft of light.— v.t. to emit in rays.—v.i. to shine.—a. (of wireless transmission) in a controlled direction.

Bean n. any of various kinds of leguminous plants and their seeds.

Bear (bèr) v.t. to carry; support; produce; press (upon).

Bear (bèr) n. a heavy, partly-carnivorous quadruped; a rough fellow; a speculator for a fall in stocks.

Beard n. the hair on the chin; a similar growth in plants.— v.t. to defy.

Beast n. an animal; a four-footed animal; a brutal man. —beast'ly a.—beast'liness n.

Beat v.t. to strike repeatedly; to overcome.—v.i. to throb; to sail against the wind.—n. a stroke; a pulsation; a regularly-trodden course.

Beat'ify (bē-at'-) v.t. to make happy; to pronounce in eternal happiness (the first step in canonisation).—beat-if'ic a.—beatifica'tion n.— beat'itude n.

Beaune (bōn) n. a red wine of Burgundy.

Beaut'y (bū-) n. loveliness, grace; a beautiful person or thing.—beaut'iful a.—beaut'-eous a.—beaut'ifully adv.— beaut'ify v.t.
Syn. of "beautify," to adorn, deck, embellish, decorate, grace. Ant. to mar, tarnish, sully, blemish.

Beav'er n. an amphibious rodent quadruped; its fur; a hat made of the fur.

Becalm' (-kám) v.t. to make calm; deprive of wind.

Because' adv. and conj. by reason of.

Bêche'-de-mer (bāsh'-de-màr) n. the sea slug, or trepang, a food-fish highly prized by the Chinese.

Beck n. a sign, gesture.

Beck n. a brook.

Beck'on v.i. to make a silent signal.—v.t. to call by a nod.

Become' (-kum) v.i. to come to be.—v.t. to suit.—becom'ing a. suitable to; graceful.

Bed n. a couch or place to sleep on; the place in which anything rests, in architecture, etc.; the bottom of a river; a layer, stratum; a garden plot.—*v.t.* to lay in a bed; to plant.—bedd'ing *n.* —bed'ridden *a.*—bed'rock *n.* —bed'room *n.*—bed'stead *n.*

Bedi'zen (-iz'n *or* -i'zn) *v.t.* to dress gaudily.—bedi'zened *a.*

Bed'lam *n.* a place of uproar; a lunatic asylum.—bed'lamite *n.*

Bee *n.* an insect that makes honey.—bee'hive *n.*—bee'line *n.* shortest route.—bees'wax *n.*

Beech *n.* a common tree with smooth silvery bark and small nuts.—beech'en *a.*—beech'mast *n.* beech nuts.

Beef *n.* the flesh of an ox, or cow.—beef'y *a.* fleshy, stolid.

Beef'eater *n.* a yeoman of the guard; a warder of the Tower of London.

Beer *n.* fermented alcoholic liquor made from malt and hops.—beer'house *n.*—beer'y *a.*

Beet *n.* a plant with a carrot-shaped root, edible and used for extraction of sugar.

Bee'tle *n.* a coleopterous insect.—bee'tle-browed *a.* with prominent brows.

Bee'tle *n.* a heavy wooden mallet.

Befall' (-awl) *v.i.* to happen.— *v.t.* to happen to.

Befit' *v.t.* to be suitable to.— befitt'ing *a.*—befitt'ingly *adv.*

Before' *prep.* in front of; in presence of; in preference to; earlier than.—*adv.* ahead; earlier; in front.—*conj.* sooner than.

Befoul' (-owl) *v.t.* to make dirty.

Befriend' (-rend) *v.t.* help.

Beg *v.t.* to ask earnestly, beseech; to take for granted, *esp.* in *to beg the question,* to take for granted what ought to have been proved.—*v.i.* to ask for or live on alms.— begg'ar *n.*—begg'ary *n.*— begg'arly *a.*

Beget' *v.t.* to produce, generate.—begett'er *n.*

Begin' *v.i.* to take rise; to commence.—*v.t.* to enter on, originate.—beginn'ing *n.*— beginn'er *n.*
  Syn. of "beginning," rise, origin, original. *Ant.* end, finish, termination, close, conclusion.

Begrudge' *v.t.* to grudge, envy any one the possession of something; give unwillingly.

Beguile' (-gīl) *v.t.* to cheat; wile away.—beguile'ment *n.* —beguil'er *n.*

Behalf' (-háf) *n.* favour, benefit (in phrases such as *on behalf of*).

Behave' *v.i.* to bear, carry, conduct (*esp.* oneself.)—beha'viour (-yer) *n.* conduct.

Behead' *v.t.* to cut off the head.

Behest' *n.* charge, command.

Behind (-hī-) *prep.* in the rear of.—*adv.* in the rear.—behind'hand *adv.*; *a.* in arrears, tardy.

Behold' (-hō-) *v.t.* to watch, see.—behold'en *a.* bound in gratitude.—behold'er *n.*

Behoof' *n.* use, benefit.—behove' *v.i.* to be fit, right, necessary; (only impersonal).

Beige (bāzh) *n.* woollen cloth

made of undyed wool; hence the colour or unbleached wool.

Bela'bour *v.t.* to beat soundly.

Bela'ted *a.* overtaken by night; late.

Belay' *v.t.* to fasten a running rope by coiling it round a cleat.

Belch *v.i.* to void wind by the mouth.—*v.t.* to eject violently; cast up.—*n.* emission of wind, etc.

Bel'dam *n.* an old woman, *esp.* an ugly one; a hag.

Beleag'uer (-er) *v.t.* to besiege.

Bel'fry *n.* a bell-tower.

Belie' (-lī) *v.t.* to falsify; counterfeit; speak falsely of.

Believe' *v.t.* to regard as true.—*v.i.* to have faith.—**belief'** *n.*—**believ'er** *n.*—**believ'ing** *a.*—**believ'able** *a.*
  Syn. to credit, think, suppose, trust in, understand. *Ant.* to suspect, doubt, distrust, question, dispute.

Belit'tle *v.t.* to cause to appear small; to make small.—**belit'tlement** *n.*

Bell *n.* a hollow metal vessel to give a ringing sound when struck; anything shaped like a bell.

Bell'icose *a.* war-like.

Belli'gerent (-ij'-) *a.* waging war.—*n.* a nation or person taking part in war.

Bell'ow *v.i.* to roar like a bull; shout.—*n.* the roar of a bull; any deep cry or shout.

Bell'ows *n.* an instrument for making a blast of air (to blow up a fire, etc.).

Bell'y *n.* the part of the body which contains the bowels; the stomach.—*v.t.* and *i.* to swell out.

Belong' *v.i.* to be the property or attribute of; to be connected with.

Belov'ed (-luv-) *a.* much loved.

Below' (-ō) *adv.* beneath.—*prep.* lower than.

Belt *n.* a band; girdle.—*v.t.* to furnish, surround, or mark, with a band.

Bench *n.* a long seat; a seat or body of judges, etc.—*v.t.* to place on a bench.—**bench'er** *n.* a senior member of an inn of court.

Bend *v.t.* to curve or bow.—*v.i.* to take a curved shape.—*n.* a curve.

Beneath' *prep.* under, lower than.—*adv.* in a lower position.

Benedic'tion *n.* an invocation of the divine blessing.

Ben'efit *n.* advantage, favour, profit, good.—*v.t.* to do good to.—*v.i.* to receive good.—**benefac'tion** *n.*—**ben'efactor** *n.*—**ben'efactress** *fem.*—**benef'icent** *a.*—**benef'icently** *adv.*—**benef'icence** *n.*—**benefi'cial** *a.*—**benefi'cially** *adv.*—**ben'efice** *n.* an ecclesiastical living.—**benefi'ciary** *n.*

Benev'olent *a.* kindly, charitable.—**benev'olently** *adv.*—**benev'olence** *n.*

Benight'ed (-nīt-) *a.* overtaken by night; in mental or moral darkness.

Benign' (-īn) *a.* kindly, mild, gentle.—**benign'ly** *adv.*—**benig'nant** *a.*—**benig'nantly** *adv.*—**benig'nity** *n.*—**benig'nancy** *n.*
  Syn. gracious, generous,

liberal, propitious, favourable. *Ant.* unsympathetic, hard, cruel, severe.

Bent *n.* a wiry grass.

Bent *n.* inclination, turn of mind.

Benumb' (-m) *v.t.* to deaden, stupefy.

Ben'zene *n.* a tarry liquid distilled from oil; a by-product of coal-tar.—**ben'zine** (-ĕn) *n.* a distillate of American petroleum.—**ben'zol** *n.* benzene.—**ben'zoline** *n.* impure benzene or benzine.—**ben'zoin** *n.* an aromatic gum.

Bequeath (-th) *v.t.* to leave by will.—**bequest'** *n.* act of bequeathing; a legacy.

Bereave' *v.t.* to rob of.—**bereave'ment** *n.*

Beret, berret (-rā, -ret) *n.* a soft, round, tight-fitting cap worn by the Basque peasantry; similar or modified cap worn generally.

Berr'y *n.* a small stoneless fruit.

Berth *n.* a ship's anchoring place; a place to sleep in a ship; an employment situation.—*v.t.* to moor.

Ber'yl *n.* a green precious stone.

Beseech' *v.t.* to entreat, implore.

Beset' *v.t.* assail, invest.

Beside' *prep.* by the side of, near; distinct from.—**besides'** *adv.* and *prep.* in addition, otherwise.

Besiege' *v.t.* to invest, beset with armed forces; throng round.

Be'som (bĕz-) *n.* a broom, usually of twigs.

Bespeak' *v.t.* engage beforehand.

Best *a., adv.* *superlative* of good or well.—*v.t.* to defeat.

Bes'tial *a.* like a beast.—**bestial'ity** *n.*
   Syn. brutish, brutal, beastly, carnal, sensual, vile. *Ant.* humane, considerate, intellectual, spiritual, pure, immaculate.

Bestir' *v.t.* rouse to lively action.

Bestow' *v.t.* to give; put away.—**bestow'al** *n.*

Bestride' *v.t.* to sit or stand over with legs apart.

Bet *n.* a wager.—*v.t.* and *i.* to wager.

Be'tel (bĕ'-tl) *n.* a species of pepper, the leaves of which are prepared as a stimulant and chewed by the inhabitants of India.—**betel-nut,** the nut of the areca palm.

Betide' *v.i.* to happen.

Betimes' *adv.* early.

Betray' *v.t.* to give up treacherously; to be disloyal to; mislead; reveal, show signs of.—**betray'al** *n.*—**betray'er** *n.*

Betroth' (-ŏth) *v.t.* to bind to marry. — **betroth'al** *n.*—**betrothed'** *n.* and *a.*

Bett'er *a.* and *adv.* comparative of good and well.—*v.t.* and *i.* to improve.

Between', betwixt' *prep.* in the middle of two, of space, time, etc.; in the middle or intermediate space. — *adv.* midway.

Bev'el *n.* a slant, diagonal surface; a tool for setting off angles.—*a.* slanted.—*v.t.* to cut away to a slope.

Bev'erage n. a liquor for drinking.

Bev'y n. a flock of birds, esp. quails; a company, esp. of ladies.

Bewail' v.t. to lament.

Beware' v.i. to be on one's guard.

Bewil'der v.t. to puzzle, lead astray.—bewil'derment n.—bewil'dering a. — bewil'deringly adv.

Bewitch' v.t. to affect by witchcraft; to charm, fascinate. — bewitch'ing a. — bewitch'ingly adv.

Bewray' (bi-rā) v.t. to reveal unintentionally.

Beyond' adv. farther away.—prep. on the farther side of; later than; surpassing, out of reach of.

Bez'el n. the part of a setting which holds a precious stone.

Bi'as n. a slant; a one-sided inclination; leaning, bent; swaying impulse.—v.t. to influence, affect.—bi'ased a. prejudiced.

Bib n. a cloth put under a child's chin.

Bi'ble n. the sacred writings of the Christian Church.—bib'lical a.

Bibliog'raphy n. history and description of books.—bibliograph'ical a.—bibliog'rapher n.

Bib'ulous a. given to drinking.

Bi'ceps n. a two - headed muscle, esp. the muscle of the upper arm.

Bick'er v.i. to brawl; to quiver, flash.—bick'ering n.

Bi'cycle n. a vehicle with two wheels one in front of the other, propelled by the rider.—bi'cyclist n.

Bid v.t. to offer; command.—n. an offer, esp. of a price.—bidd'er n.—bidd'ing n.
Syn. to call, invite, summon, order. Ant. forbid, prohibit, disallow.

Bide v.i. to remain.—v.t. to await.

Bienn'ial (bī-en-) a. happening every two years; lasting two years.—n. a plant which lives two years.—bienn'ially adv.

Bier n. a frame of wood for bearing the dead to the grave.

Big a. large, great; pregnant; haughty.—big'ness n.

Big'amy n. the crime of having two husbands or two wives at once.—big'amist n.

Bight (bīt) n. the loop of a rope; a bend or curve; a bay.

Big'ot n. one blindly and obstinately devoted to a party or creed.—big'oted a.—big'otry n.

Bilat'eral (bī-) a. two-sided.

Bil'berry n. the whortleberry, a plant with blue berries.

Bile n. the fluid secreted by the liver; anger, bitter temper.—bil'ious a.—bil'iousness n.

Bilge n. the bottom of a ship's hull; the foulness collecting there.—v.i. to spring a leak.—bilge'-water n.

Biling'ual (bī-) a. having or written in two languages.—biling'ualism n.

Bill n. a tool for pruning; an old weapon.

Bill n. a bird's beak.—v.i. to join bills, as doves; to caress.

Bill *n.* a note of charges; the draft of an Act of Parliament; an advertisement; a commercial document.—*v.t.* to announce by advertisement.

Bill'et *n.* a note; civilian quarters for troops; a resting-place.—*v.t.* to quarter, as troops.

Bill'et *n.* a short thick stick.

Bill'iards (-ly-) *n.* a game played on a table with balls and cues.

Bill'ion *n.* a million millions (in U.S.A. and France, a thousand millions).

Bill'ow *n.* a great swelling wave.—*v.i.* to rise in waves.

Bimonth'ly (bī-) *adv.* and *a.* every two months; twice a month.

Bin *n.* a receptacle for storing corn, wine, etc.

Bind (-ī-) *v.t.* to tie fast; to tie round, gird, tie together; unite; put (a book) into a cover.—bind'ing *a.*—bind'er *n.*—bind'ery *n.*—bind'ing *n.* cover of book.—bind'weed *n.* *Syn.* to oblige, compel, coerce. *Ant.* excuse, exonerate, relinquish, untie, release.

Binn'acle *n.* the box in which a ship's compass is kept.

Binoc'ular *a.* adapted to both eyes.—*n.* a telescope made for two eyes; (usually in *pl.*).

Bio- (bī-ō) *prefix* meaning life. Forms compounds as biodynam'ics *n.*—biogen'esis *n.*—biom'etry *n.*—bi'oplasm *n.*, etc., for which see the simple word.

Biog'raphy *n.* the story of a man's life.—biog'rapher *n.*—biograph'ical *a.*—biograph'ically *adv.*

Biol'ogy *n.* the science of life. —biol'ogist *n.* — biolo'gical (-oj) *a.*—biolo'gically *adv.*

Bi'oscope *n.* a kinematograph. also bi'ograph.

Bi'ped (bī-) *n.* a two-footed animal.

Bi'plane (bī-) *n.* an aeroplane with two planes in each wing.

Birch *n.* a tree with smooth white bark; a rod for punishment, made of birch twigs.—*v.t.* to flog.

Bird *n.* a feathered animal.

Birth *n.* the bearing or the being born of offspring; parentage.

Bis'cuit (-kit) *n.* a hard, dry bread in small cakes.

Bisect' (bī-) *v.t.* to cut in equal halves.—bisect'or *n.*

Bish'op *n.* a clergyman in charge of a diocese.—bish'opric *n.*

Bis'muth *n.* a reddish-white metal.

Bi'son (bī-) *n.* a large wild ox.

Bissex'tile *n.* the leap-year.

Bit *n.* a fragment, piece.

Bit *n.* the biting part of a tool; the mouthpiece of a horse's bridle.—*v.t.* to put the bit in.

Bitch *n.* female dog.

Bite *v.t.* to cut into with the teeth; to cut into generally; to corrode.—*n.* act of biting; wound made by biting; a mouthful.—bi'ter *n.*

Bitt'er *a.* sharp tasting; sharp, painful; stinging.—bitt'erly *adv.*—bitt'erness *n.*—bitt'ers *n.pl.* bitter medicines or essences.

Bitt'ern *n.* a bird like a heron.

Bit'umen *n.* any of various inflammable mineral substances, e.g. petroleum, asphalt, etc.—**bitu'minous** *a.*

Bi'valve (bī-) *a.* having a double shell.—*n.* a mollusc with such a shell.

Biv'ouac *n.* a temporary resting-place of troops, without tents.—*v.i.* to pass the night in the open.

Bizarre' *a.* quaint, fantastic.

Black *a.* without light; dark; of the darkest colour.—*n.* darkest colour; black paint or fabric.—**black'en** *v.t.* and *i.*—**black'ing** *n.*—**black'bird** *n.*—**black'berry** *n.*—**black'-lead** *n.*—**black'letter** *n.*

Black'guard (blag'-ard) *n.* a scoundrel.—*a.* scoundrelly.—*v.t.* to revile.—**black'guardly** *a.*—**black'guardism** *n.*

Black'mail *n.* money extorted by threats.—*v.t.* to extort thus.

Black'shirt *n.* the original uniform of a fascist; a fascist.

Black'smith *n.* a smith who works in iron, black metal.

Bladd'er *n.* a membraneous bag to contain liquid, *esp.* as part of the body.

Blade *n.* a leaf; a loaf-like part of anything; the edge of a tool; a sword; a dashing fellow; flat of an oar.

Blame *v.t.* to find fault with; censure.—*n.* censure, culpability.—**blame'able**, **blam'able** *a.*—**blame'worthy** *a.*—**blame'less** *a.*

Bland *a.* smooth in manner.—**bland'ish** *v.t.*—**bland'ishment** *n.*

Syn. soft, kind, affectionate. *Ant.* harsh, rough, rude. uncongenial.

Blank *a.* without marks or writing; empty; vacant, confused; (verse) without rhyme.—*n.* an empty space; a lottery ticket not drawing a prize; a void.—**blank'ly** *adv.*

Blank'et *n.* a woollen covering for a bed.—*v.t.* to cover with a blanket; to cover.

Blare (-ėr) *v.i.* to roar; to trumpet.—*n.* a trumpet sound, roar.

Blaspheme' *v.i.* to talk profanely.—*v.t.* to speak irreverently of.—**blas'phemy** *n.*—**blasphe'mer** *n.*—**blas'phemous** *a.*—**blas'phemously** *adv.*

Blast (-àst) *n.* a current of air; a gust of wind; an explosion.—*v.t.* to blow up; to blight; to ruin.

Bla'tant *a.* noisy, clamorous, loud.

Blaze *n.* a bright flame of fire; brightness; an outburst.—*v.i.* to burn fiercely, brightly; to burn with passion, etc.

Blaze *v.t.* to proclaim, publish; (as with trumpet).

Bla'zon *n.* a coat of arms.—*v.t.* to describe or depict (arms); to make public.

Bleach *v.t.* to whiten.—*v.i.* to become white.

Bleak *a.* cold and cheerless; exposed. originally *pale.*

Syn. chilly, raw, bare, desolate, unsheltered. *Ant.* warm mild, comforting, unexposed, congenial.

Blear *a.* sore or inflamed.—**blear'-eyed** *a.*

Bleat v.i. and t. to cry, as a sheep.—n. the sheep's cry.

Bleed v.i. to lose blood.—v.t. to draw blood from; to extort money from.

Blem'ish v.t. to mar, spoil.—n. a disfigurement, stain, defect.

Blench v.i. to start back.

Blend v.t. to mix.—n. a mixture.—**blend'er** n.

Bless v.t. to consecrate; give thanks to; invoke happiness on; make happy.—**bless'ing** n.—**bless'edness** n.

Blight (blīt) n. mildew; a baneful influence.—v.t. to affect with blight; spoil.

Bligh'ty (blīt'-i) n. soldier's name for Britain, or for a wound involving a return to Britain.

Blind (-ī-) a. lacking sight; heedless, random; dim; closed at one end —v.t. to deprive of sight.—n. something cutting off light; a screen for a window; a pretext.—**blind'ly** adv.—**blind'ness** n.—**blind'fold** v. and a.—**blind'worm** n.—**blind'-man's buff** n. game in which one player is blindfolded.

Blink v.i. to look with half-closed eyes; to wink; to shine unsteadily.—v.t. to shut the eyes to, shirk.—n. a gleam.—**blin'kers** n.pl. leather covers to prevent a horse from seeing in any direction but straight forward.

Bliss n. perfect happiness.—**bliss'ful** a.—**bliss'fully** adv.—**bliss'fulness** n.

Blis'ter n. a bubble on the skin; a plaster to produce one.—v.t. to raise a blister.

Blithe a. happy, gay.—**blithe'ly** adv.—**blithe'ness** n.—**blithe'some** a.

Blizz'ard n. a blinding storm of wind and snow.

Bloat'ed a. swollen.

Bloc n. a combination of two or more political or economic parties for the purpose of obstructing legislative action, or fostering special interests.

Block n. a solid piece of wood, a stump; any compact mass; an obstacle; a stoppage; a pulley with frame; a group of houses; a stupid person.—v.t. to obstruct, stop up; to shape on a block; to sketch.—**blockade'** n. shutting of a place by siege.—v.t. to close by siege.—**block'ish** a.—**block'head** n.

Blonde a. light golden-brown; fair.—n. one who is fair.

Blood (blud) n. the red fluid in the veins of men and animals; race, kindred; good parentage; temperament; passion.—v.t. to draw blood from; to harden to bloodshed.—**blood'y** a.—**blood'ily** adv.—**blood'less** a.—**blood'-guilty** a.—**blood'guiltiness** n.—**blood'heat** n.—**blood'horse** n.—**blood'hound** n.—**blood'money** n.—**blood'-poisoning** n. — **blood'-relation** n. — **blood'shed** n.—**blood'shot** a. - **blood'-thirsty** a.—**blood'-vessel** n.

Bloom n. flower of a plant; blossoming; prime, perfection; glow; powdery deposit on fruit.—*v.i.* to be in flower; to flourish.—**bloom'ing** *a.*

Bloss'om *n.* a flower; a flower-bud.—*v.i.* to flower.

Blot *n.* a spot, stain; blemish; disgrace.—*v.t.* to spot, stain; to obliterate; to dry with blotting-paper *n.*—**blott'ing-pad** *n.*

Blotch *n.* a dark spot on the skin.—*v.t.* to make spotted. —**blotch'y** *a.*

Blouse (-ow-) *n.* a light, loose upper garment, belted.

Blow (blō) *v.i.* to make a current of air; to pant; to sound a blast.—*v.t.* to drive air upon or into; to drive by current of air; to sound; to spout (of whales); to boast; to fan.—*n.* a blast.—**blow'er** *n.*—**blow'fly** *n.*—**blow'hole** *n.* —**blow'pipe** *n.*

Blow (blō) *v.i.* to blossom.

Blow (blō) *n.* a stroke or knock.

Syn. knock, thump, rap, disaster, affliction, misfortune, loss.

Blubb'er *n.* the fat of whales. —*v.i.* to weep.

Bludg'eon (bluj'n) *n.* a short thick club.—*v.t.* to strike with such club.

Blue *a.* of the colour of the sky or shades of that colour; livid; depressed.—*n.* the colour; paint, clothing, etc., of that colour.—*v.t.* to make blue; to dip in blue liquid. —**blu'ish** *a.*—**blue'bell** *n.*—**blue'book** *n.*—**blue'bottle** *n.* blowdy. — **blue'grass** *n.* — **blue'jacket** *n.*—**blue-pen'cil** *v.t.* to correct or edit.—**blue-print** *n.* a copy of a drawing

made by the action of light on sensitized paper, in which the lines are white on a blue ground.—and many other compounds.—**The Blues** *n.* the Royal Horse Guards.— **a blue** *n.* one chosen to represent Oxford or Cambridge University at various games or sports.

Bluff *a.* steep; abrupt; rough and hearty; blunt.—*n.* a cliff, a high steep bank.

Bluff *v.t.* to deceive by pretence of strength.

Syn. boisterous, downright, blunt. *Ant.* gentle, tactful, considerate.

Blun'der *v.i.* to flounder; make a stupid mistake.—*n.* a gross mistake.

Blun'derbuss *n.* a short gun with wide bore.

Blunt *a.* having dull edge or poin ; abrupt of speech.— *v.t.* to dull.—**blunt'ly** *adv.*— **blunt'ness** *n.*—**bluntwitt'ed** *a.*

Blur *n.* a spot, stain.—*v.t.* to stain; to obscure, dim.

Blurt *v.t.* to utter suddenly or unadvisedly.

Blush *v.i.* to become red in the face; to be ashamed; to redden.—*n.* a red glow on the face; a flush of colour.

Blus'ter *v.i.* of wind, to blow boisterously; to swagger.— *n.* a blast.

Bo'a *n.* a genus of snakes without poison fangs; a long coil of fur worn round the neck by ladies.

Boar *n.* the male of the swine. —**boar'spear** *n.*

Board *n.* a broad, flat piece of wood; a table, meals; an authorised body of men; thick, stiff paper; *pl.* the theatre, stage.—**on board**, in or into a ship.—*v.t.* to cover with planks; to supply food daily; to enter ship; to attack.—*v.i.* to take daily meals.—**board'er** *n.*—**board'-ing-house** *n.*—**board'ing-pike** *n.* — **board'ing-school** *n.* — **board'-school** *n.* — **board'-wages** *n.* money allowed to servants in pla e of food.

Boast *n.* a brag, vaunt.—*v.i.* to brag.—*v.t.* to brag of; to have to show.—**boast'er** *n.*—**boast'ful** *a.*—**boast'fully** *adv.* —**boast'fulness** *n.*

Boat *n.* a small open vessel; a ship generally.—*v.i.* to sail about in a boat.—**boat'ing** *n.* — **boat'-hook** *n.* — **boat'-house** *n.* — **boat'man** *n.* — **boat'swain** (bōs'n) *n.* a ship's officer in charge of boats, sails, etc.—**boat'er** *n.* a flat straw hat.

Bob *n.* a pendant; a slight blow; a knot of hair, ribbon etc.; the weight of a plumb-line, etc.—*v.i.* to move up and down.—*v.t.* to move jerkily; to cut (women's) hair short.—**bobbed'** *a.*

Bobb'in *n.* a small round stick on which thread is wound.

Bode *v.t.* to portend, prophesy.

Bod'ice (-is) *n.* the upper part of a woman's dress.

Bod'kin *n.* a small dagger; a tool for piercing holes; a blunt needle.

Bod'y *n.* the whole frame of a man or animal; the main part of such frame; the main part of anything; substance; a mass; a person; a number of persons united or organ-ised; matter, opposed to spirit.—*v.t.* to give form to. —**bod'iless** *a.*—**bod'ily** *a.* and *adv.*—**bod'yguard** *n.*—**bod'y-servant** *n.*—**bod'y-snatcher** *n.*

Boer (boor) *n.* a Dutch farmer of S. Africa; a person of Dutch descent.

Bog *n.* wet, soft ground.—*v.t.* to entangle in such ground. —**bogg'y** *a.*

Bog'gle (bog'l) *v.i.* to stop at, hesitate; make difficulties; bungle, fumble.—**bogg'ler** *n.*

Bo'gle *n.* a spectre.

Bo'gie *n.* a low truck on four wheels; a revolving under-carriage, as on a railway-engine.

Bo'gus *a.* sham.

Bo'gey *n* a goblin, a bugbear.

Boil *n.* an inflamed swelling.

Boil *v.i.* to bubble up from the action of heat; to be agi-tated, seethe; to be cooked by boiling.—*v.t.* to cause to bubble up; cook by boiling. —**boil'er** *n.* a vessel.—**boil'-ing-point** *n.*

Bois'terous *a.* wild; noisy; turbulent.—**bois'terously** *adv.* —**bois'terousness** *n.*

Syn. stormy, tempestuous, tumultuous. *Ant.* quiet, calm, gentle, mild.

Bold *a.* daring, fearless; pre-sumptuous; well-marked, prominent.—**bold'ly** *adv.*— **bold'ness** *n.*

Bole *n.* the trunk of a tree.

Bol'shevik *n.* a revolutionary.

Bol'ster *n.* a long pillow; a pad, support.—*v.t.* to sup-port, uphold.

Bolt (bō-) *n.* a bar or pin; an arrow; a rush, running away; a discharge of lightning.—*v.t.* to fasten with a bolt; to swallow hastily.—*v.i.* to rush away; break from control.

Bo'lus *n.* a rounded mass of medicine; a large pill.

Bo'ma (bōma) *n.* a fenced enclosure.

Bomb (bom) *n.* an explosive projectile, a grenade.—*v.t.* to attack with bombs.—**bombard'** *v.t.* to shell.—**bombard'ment** *n.*—**bombardier'** *n.* an artillery non-commissioned officer.

Bom'bast *n.* inflated language.—**bombas'tic** *a.*

Bom'bic (-bik) *a.* of or pertaining to the silkworm.—**bomby'cinous** *a.* silken; of the colour of the silkworm.

Bo'na fi'des *adv.* or *a.* good faith.

Bond *n.* that which binds; link, union; written promise to pay money or carry out a contract.—*v.t.* to bind; to store goods until duty is paid on them.

Bond'age *n.* slavery.—**bond'man** *n.*—**bond'servant** *n.*

Bone *n.* hard substance forming the skeleton of animals; a piece of this.—*v.t.* to take out bone.—**bo'ny** *a.*—**bone'less** *a.*—**bone'-black** *n.*—**bone'meal** *n.*

Bon'fire *n.* an open-air fire to express joy, burn rubbish, etc.

Bonn'et *n.* a hat or cap.—*v.t.* to put a hat on; to crush a man's hat over his eyes.

Bonn'y *a.* beautiful, handsome.—**bonn'ily** *adv.*

Bont *a.* in South Africa, many-coloured, motley.

Bo'nus *n.* an extra payment.

Boob'y *n.* a dunce.—**boob'y-prize** *n.*—**boob'y-trap** *n.*

Book *n.* a collection of sheets of paper bound together; a literary work; a main division of a work.—*v.t.* to enter in a book.—**book'ish** *a.*—**book'let** *n.*—**book'binder** *n.*—**book'binding** *n.*—**book'case** *n.*, and other compounds.

Boom *n.* a long spar; a barrier.

Boom *v.i.* to hum, roar.—*n.* a hum or roar.

Boom *n.* sudden commercial activity; prosperity.—*v.i.* to become active, prosperous —*v.t.* to push into prominence.

Boon. *n.* a favour; a thing asked for.

Boor *n.* a rustic; a rude fellow.—**boor'ish** *a.*

Boot *n.* a covering for the foot and lower leg.—**boot'ed** *a.*—**boot'lace** *n.*—**boot'-last** *n.*—**boot'-tree** *n.*—**boots** *n. sing.* an inn servant.

Boot *n.* profit, use.—**to boot.** in addition.—**boot'less** *a.*

Booth (-TH-) *n.* a hut or stall.

Boot'legger *n.* (U.S. *sl.*) a smuggler, *esp.* an illicit importer of alcoholic liquor into U.S.A.—*v.t.* to smuggle.

Boot'y *n.* plunder, spoil.

Bord'er *n.* margin; frontier; limit, boundary; strip of garden.—*v.t.* to put on a margin, edging; to adjoin.—*v.i.* to resemble (with *on*);

to be adjacent (with *upon*). —bord'erer *n*.

Syn. boundary, bounds, confines, frontier, verge, precinct, margin.

Bore *v.t.* to pierce, making a hole; to weary.—*n*. a hole; the size or cavity of a gun; a wearisome person.—**bore'-dom** *n*.—**bor'er** *n*.

Bore *n*. a tidal wave in a river.

Bo'rough (bu'rō) *n*. a town with a corporation.

Bor'row *v.t.* to obtain on loan or trust; to adopt from abroad.—**bor'rower** *n*.

Bors'tal *a*. in *Borstal system*, a reformatory treatment for young criminals.

Bo'som (booz-) *n*. human breast; dress covering it; the seat of the passions and feelings.

Boss *n*. a knob or stud.—*v.t.* to ornament with bosses.

Bot'any *n*. the science of plants.—**bot'anist** *n*.—**botan'ic, botan'ical** *a*.—**bot'anize** *v.i.*

Botch *v.t.* to patch or put together clumsily; to bungle. —*n*. a clumsy patch; a bungled piece of work.—**botch'er** *n*.

Both (bō-) *a*. the two.—*adv*. and *conj*. as well.

Both'er (-TH-) *v.t.* to pester; perplex.—*v.i.* to fuss, be troublesome. — *n*. trouble, fuss.

Bot'tle *n*. a vessel for holding liquids; the contents of such vessel.—*v.t.* to put into a bottle.

Bot'tle *n*. a bundle of hay.

Bott'om *n*. the lowest part of anything; the bed of a sea, river, etc.; the sitting part of the human body; a ship; staying power.—*v.t.* to put a bottom to; base (upon); get to the bottom of.—**bott'omless** *a*.—**bott'omry** *n*. a loan on the security of a ship.

Syn. foundation, base. *Ant*. top, apex, summit, head, crown.

Bough (bow) *n*. a branch of a tree.

Boul'der (bōl-) *n*. a large stone rounded by action of water.

Bounce *v.i.* to bound, like a ball; to throw oneself about; to boast, exaggerate.—*n*. a leap, spring, rebound; boast. —**bounc'er** *n*.—**bounc'ing** *a*. large; swaggering.

Bound *n*. a limit, boundary. —*v.t.* to limit, close in.—**bound'ary** *n*.—**bound'less** *a*. —**bound'ed** *a*.

Bound *v.i.* to spring, leap.—*n*. a spring or leap.—**bound'er** *n*. a boisterous, vulgar fellow.

Bound *a*. ready to go, as "outward bound," etc.

Boun'ty *n*. liberality; a gift; a premium. — **boun'teous, boun'tiful** *a*. — **boun'tifully** *adv*.

Syn. generosity, munificence, kindness, benevolence.

Bouquet' (boo-kā') *n*. a bunch of flowers; perfume of wine.

Bout *n*. a turn, a round; attempt; contest.

Bo'vine *a*. of the ox ; oxlike.

Bow (bō) *n*. a bend, bent line; rainbow; weapon for shooting arrows; ornamental knot of ribbon, etc.; implement

---

Māte, mēte, mīte, mōte, mūte, bōōt.

for playing a violin.—**bow'-window** n.

Bow (bow) v.i. to bend the body in respect, assent, etc.; to submit.—v t. to bend downwards; to cause to stoop; crush.—n. an inclination in respect.

Bow (bow) n. the fore end of a ship.

Bow'el (-ow-) n. an intestine; pl. pity, feeling.

Bow'er (-ow-) n. a shady retreat; an inner room.

Bow'er (-ow-) n. an anchor at the bow of a ship.

Bowl (-ō-) n. a round vessel, a deep basin; a drinking-cup; the hollow part of anything.

Bowl (-ō-) n. a wooden ball.—v.t. and i. to roll or throw a ball in various ways.—**bowls** n. a game.—**bowl'er** n.—**bowl'ing-green** n.

Bow'sprit (-ow-) n. a spar projecting from the bow of a ship.

Box n. a tree yielding hard smooth wood; its wood: a case, generally with a lid; the contents of such case; a small house or lodge; a driver's seat; a compartment.—v.t. to put in a box; to confine; to box the compass, name the thirty-two points in order and backwards, make a complete turn round.—**box'-iron** n.—**box'-pleat** n.—**box'wood** n.

Box n. a blow.—v.t. to cuff; in Australia, to mix together sheep that ought to be separate;—v.i. to fight with the fists, esp. with gloves on.

Boy n. a male child; a lad; a young man; a native servant.

Boy'cott v.t. to refuse to deal with.—n. a concerted refusal to deal with.

Brace n. a clasp, clamp; a pair, couple; a strut, support; a carpenter's tool for turning boring instruments; pl. trouser-suspenders.—v.t. to stretch, strain, string up, support, make firm.—**bra'cing** a.

Brace'let n. an ornament for the arm.

Brack'en n. fern.

Bracket n. a support for a shelf; a pipe with a gas burner; pl. in printing, the marks [ ] used to enclose words.—v.t. to enclose in brackets; to couple, connect; (artillery) to range by dropping shells nearer and farther than a mark.

Brack'ish a. saltish.

Brad n. a small nail.—**brad'awl** n. a tool to pierce holes.

Brag v.i. to boast, bluster. — n. boastful language. — **bragg'art** n. — **braggado'cio** (-shy-o) n.

Braid v.t. to plait; to trim with braid.—n. plaited cord; a woven band.

Braille (bral) n. a system of printing books to be read by the blind; the letters used, consisting of raised dots.

Brain n. the nervous matter in the skull; the intellect.—v.t. to dash out the brain.—**brain'y** a.—**brain'less** a.

Braise (-āz) v.t. to stew with

vegetables, etc., and then bake.

Brake *n.* a fern; a place overgrown with ferns; a thicket.

Brake *n.* an instrument for retarding the motion of a wheel.—*v.t.* to apply a brake to.—**brake′van** *n.*

Bram′ble *n.* a prickly shrub; the blackberry.—**bram′bly** *a.*

Bran *n.* sifted husks of corn.

Branch (-à-) *n.* a limb of a tree; anything like a limb; a subdivision, section; a subordinate department of a business.—*v.i.* to bear branches; to divide into branches; to diverge. — **branch′y** *a.*

Brand *n.* a burning piece of wood; a mark made by a hot iron; a trade-mark; a sword; a class of goods; a mark of infamy.—*v.t.* to burn with an iron; to mark.

Bran′dish *v.t.* to flourish.

Bran′dy *n.* a spirit distilled from wine.—**bran′dysnap** *n.* a biscuit.

Brass *n.* an alloy of copper and zinc; impudence. — **brass′y** *a.*—**bra′zen** *a.*—**bra′zier** *n.*

Brass′ard *n.* a badge for the arm; armour for the upper part of the arm.

Brat *n.* a contemptuous name for a child.

Brava′do (-và-) *n.* a display of boldness.

Brave *a.* bold, courageous; splendid; finely dressed.— *n.* a warrior.—*v.t.* to defy, meet boldly.—**brave′ly** *adv.* —**bra′very** *n.*

Syn. fearless, valiant, valorous, intrepid, gallant, undaunted, excellent. *Ant.* cowardly, timid.

Brawl *v.i.* to quarrel noisily; to flow noisily.—*n.* a noisy quarrel.—**brawl′er** *n.*

Brawn *n.* muscle; thick flesh; strength; a preparation of chopped meat.—**brawn′y** *a.*

Bray′ *n.* the ass's cry.—*v.i.* to utter that cry; to give out harsh shounds.

Braze *v.t.* to solder with alloy of brass.

Bra′zier *n.* a pan for burning charcoal.

Breach *n.* a break, opening; a breaking of rule, duty etc.; a quarrel.—*v.t.* to make a gap in.

Bread (-ed) *n.* food made of flour or meal baked; food; livelihood.

Breadth (-edth) *n.* extent across, width; largeness of view, mind.

Break (brāk) *v.t.* to part by force; to shatter, crush, bruise, burst, destroy, frustrate; make bankrupt; discard; loosen, dissolve; tell with care; in the Colonies, to plough virgin soil.—*v.i.* to become broken, shattered, divided; open, appear; crack, give way; part, fall out.— *n.* fracture; a gap, opening; dawn; separation, interruption.—**break′age** *n.*—**break′er** *n.*—**break′down** *n.*—**break′fast** *n.*—**break′water** *n.*

Breast (brest) *n.* the human chest; a woman's mammary gland; the affections; any protuberance.—*v.t.* to face, oppose; mount. — **breast′plate** *n.*

Breath (breth) *n.* the air taken into and put out from the lungs; life; power of breathing; a slight breeze. — **breathe** (brēth) *v.i.* to inhale and exhale air from the lungs; to live; to pause, rest. — *v.t.* to inhale and exhale; to utter softly; to exercise. — **breath'less** *a.* — **brea'ther** (-TH-) *n.* — **brea'thing** (-TH-) *n.*

Breech *n.* the lower part of the body behind; the hinder part of anything, *esp.* of a gun. — **breech'es** *pl.* trousers. — **breech** *v.t.* to put into breeches. — **breech-load'er** *n.*

Breed *v.t.* to generate, bring forth; give rise to; rear. — *v.i.* to be produced; to be with young. — *n.* offspring produced; race, kind. — **breed'er** *n.* — **breed'ing** *n.* *Syn.* to propagate, procreate, engender. *Ant.* annihilate.

Breeze *n.* a gentle wind; a wind; a rumour; a quarrel. — **breez'y** *a.* — **breez'ily** *adv.*

Brent'ing *n.* a form of wandering minstrelsy carried out by Boy Scouts, hikers, etc.

Bre'viary *n.* a book of daily prayers of the Catholic Church.

Brev'ity *n.* shortness.

Brew (-ōō) *v.t.* to prepare a liquor, as beer from malt, etc.; to plot, contrive. — *v.i.* to be in preparation. — **brew'age** *n.* — **brew'er** *n.* — **brew'ing** *n.* — **brew'ery** *n.*

Bri'ar *n. see* BRIER.

Bri'ar *a.* only in *briar pipe*, one made of a heather root.

Bribe *n.* a gift to corrupt; allurement. — *v.t.* to influence by a bribe; to win over. — **bri'ber** *n.* — **bri'bery** *n.*

Brick *n.* an oblong mass of hardened clay; any oblong block. — *v.t.* to lay or pave with bricks.

Bri'dal *n.* a wedding. — *a.* belonging to a wedding.

Bride *n.* a woman about to be, or just, married. — **bride'groom** *n.* a man about to be, or just, married. — **brides'maid** *n.*

Bridge *n.* a structure for crossing a river, etc.; a raised narrow platform on a ship; the upper part of the nose; the part of a violin supporting the strings. — *v.t.* to make a bridge over.

Bridge *n.* a card game.

Bri'dle *n.* the headgear of horse-harness; a curb or restraint. — *v.t.* to put on a bridle; to restrain. — *v.i.* to throw up the head. — **bri'dlepath** *n.*

Brief *a.* short; concise. — *n.* a summary of a case for the use of counsel; a papal letter. — **brief'less** *a.* — **brief'ly** *adv.* — **brief ness** *n.*

Brief'je (brē-fē) *n.* in South Africa, a note or letter, particularly one giving permission to a native.

Bri'er, bri'ar *n.* a prickly shrub, *esp.* the wild rose.

Brig *n.* a two-masted, square-rigged ship.

Brigade' *n.* a division of an army, two or more regiments together under a general; an organised band. — *v.t.* to join units into a brigade.—brig-ade'-ma'jor n. — brigadier', brigadier-gen'eral n.

Brig'and n. robber.—brig'andage n.

Brig'antine n. a two-masted vessel, with square-rigged foremast and fore-and-aft mainmast.

Bright (brīt) a. shining; full of light; cheerful; clever.—bright'en v.t. and i.—bright'-ly adv.—bright'ness n.

Syn. clear, illustrious, glorious, vivid, luminous, quick, keen, lustrous. Ant. dull, thick, stupid, slow.

Brill'iant (-lya-) a. shining; sparkling; splendid.—brill'-iantly adv.—brill'iance, brill'-iancy n.

Brim n. the margin or edge, sp of a river, cup, hat.—brimm'ing a.—brim'less a.

Brim tone n. sulphur.

Br.n'dled, brin'ded a. spotted and streaked.

Brine n. salt water.—bri'ny a.

Bring v.t. to fetch; carry with one; to cause to come.

Brink n. the edge of a steep place; the very edge of anything.

Briquette' n. a block of compressed coal-dust.

Brisk a. active, lively, sharp.—v.t. to enliven.—v.i. to cheer up.—brisk'ly adv.—brisk'ness n.

Bris'tle (-is'l) n. a short, stiff hair.—v.i. to stand erect.—v.t. to erect like bristles.—bris'tly a.—bris'tliness n.

Brit'tle a. easily broken, fragile.—brit'tleness n.

Broach n. a boring tool; a spit.—v.t. to pierce (a cask); to open, begin.

Broad (-awd) a. wide, ample, open; outspoken; coarse; general; tolerant; of pronunciation, dialectal.—broad'en v.t. and i.—broad'ly adv.—broad-ar'row n. a Government mark (♦).—broad'cast a. scattered freely.—v.t. to scatter, as seed; to send out wireless messages, music, etc for general reception.—broad'cloth n.—broad'-gauge n. and a.—broad'ness n.—broad'side n. a discharge of all guns on one side; a sheet printed on one side.—broad'-sword n.

Syn. extensive, large, com prehensive, gross. Ant. narrow, intensive.

Brocade' n. silk stuff wrought with figures.—broc'aded a.

Brochure' (-shoor) n. a pamphlet.

Brogue (-ōg) n. a stout shoe.

Brogue (-ōg) n. a dialectal pronunciation, esp. the Irish pronunciation of English.

Broil n. a noisy quarrel.

Broil v.t. to cook over hot coals; to grill;—v.i. to be heated.

Bro'ker n. one employed to buy and sell for others; a dealer; one who values goods distrained for rent.—bro'-kerage n. the payment to a broker.

Bro'mine n. a gaseous element, allied to chlorine.—bro'mide n.—bro'mate n.—bro'mic a.

Bron'chi (-ngk-) n.pl. the branches of the windpipe.—bronch'ial a.—bronchi'tis n.

Bronc'o n. a half-tamed horse.

Bronze n. an alloy of copper and tin.—a. made of, or coloured like, bronze.—v.t. to give the appearance of bronze to.—**bronzed** coated with bronze; sunburnt.

Brooch (-ō-) n. an ornamental pin or fastening.

Brood (-ōō-) n. a family of young, esp. of birds; a tribe, race.—v.t. to sit, as a hen on eggs; to meditate, think anxiously about.—**brood'** a.

Brook (-oo-) n. a small stream.—**brook'let** n.

Brook (-oo-) v.t. to put up with, endure.

Broom (-ōō-) n. a yellow-flowered shrub; a brush for sweeping (originally of twigs).—**broom'stick** n.

Brose (-z) n. a Scottish dish made of oat or ease meal.

Broth n. a decoction of meat, usually with vegetables.

Broth'el n. a house of prostitutes.

Broth'er (-uth-) n. a son of the same parents; any one closely united with another.—**broth'erhood** n. relationship; a fraternity company.—**broth'er-in-law** n. the brother of a husband or wife; the husband of a sister—**broth'erly** a.—**broth'erliness** n.

Brow n. the ridge over the eyes; the forehead; the edge of a hill.—**brow'beat** v.t. to bully.

Brown a. of a dark colour inclining to red or yellow.—n. the colour.—v.t. or i. to make or become brown.

Browse v.i. to feed on shoots and leaves; to study desultorily, as books.

Bruise (-ōōz) v.t. to injure by a blow or pounding; oppress.—n. a contusion, a discoloured lump raised on the body by a blow.—**bruis'er** n. a boxer, prize-fighter.

Bruit (-ōō-) n. noise; rumour.—v.t. to noise abroad.

Brumal (-ōō) a. belonging to the winter.

Brunch n. late breakfast and early lunch combined.

Brunette' n. a woman of dark complexion.

Brunt' n. the shock of an attack; the chief stress of anything.

Brush n. small shrubs; a utensil for sweeping; a tool of hair used by painters; a bushy tail; a skirmish, fight; a bundle of wires, or anything like a broom.—v.t. to remove dust, clean with a brush; to touch lightly.—v.i. to move lightly.—**brush'-wood** n.—**brush'y** a.

Brusque (-sk) a. rough in manner.

Syn. rough, blunt. Ant. sensitive, polished, kind, gentle.

Brute (-ōō-) n. one of the lower animals; a man like such animal.—a. animal; sensual; stupid.—**bru'tal** a.—**bru'tish** a.—**bru'tally** adv.—**brutal'ity** n.—**bru'talise** v.t.

Bry (-ī) v.t. in South Africa, to roast meat in hot ashes or toast it on a fork.

Bub'ble n. a hollow globe of liquid, blown out with air;

anything empty; a swindle.
—*v.i.* to form bubbles, rise
in bubbles.—bubb'ly *a*.

Buccaneer' *n.* a pirate.—buccaneer'ing *n*.

Buck *n.* a male deer, or other
male animal; a dandy.—
v.i. of a horse, to attempt
to throw a rider by jumping
upwards.—buck'jumper *n*.—
buck'shot *n*.—buck'skin *n*.

Buck'et *n.* a vessel, usually
round with an arched handle,
for water, etc.—buck'etful *n*.

Buc'kle *n.* a metal instrument
with a rim and tongue, for
fastening straps, bands, etc.
—*v.t.* to fasten with a buckle.
—*v.i.* to warp, bend.—buck'-
ler *n.* a shield.

Buck'ram *n.* a coarse cloth
stiffened with size.

Bucol'ic (bū-) *a.* rustic.

Bud *n.* the first shoot of a
plant, leaf, etc.—*v.i.* to begin
to grow.—*v.t.* to graft.

Budge *v.i.* to move, stir.

Budg'et *n.* a bag and its contents; an annual financial
statement; a collection of
things.—*v.i.* to prepare a
financial statement.

Buff *n.* leather made from
buffalo or ox hide; a light
yellow colour; the bare skin.

Buff'alo *n.* any of several
species of large oxen.

Buff'er *n.* a contrivance to
lessen the shock of concus-
sion.—buff'er-state *n.* a neu-
tral country between two
others which may not be
friendly.

Buff'et *n.* a blow, slap.—*v.t.*
to strike with the fist; to contend against.—buff'eting *n*.

Buff'et (boo-fā) *n.* a sideboard;
a refreshment bar.

Buffoon' *n.* a clown; a fool.—
buffoon'ery *n*.

Bug *n.* a small blood-sucking
insect.

Bug'bear *n.* an object of terror,
generally needless terror.

Bu'gle *n.* a hunting-horn; an
instrument like a trumpet.
—bu'gler *n*.

Bu'gle *n.* a glass bead, usually
black.

Build (bild) *v.t.* to erect, as a
house, bridge, etc.; to form,
construct.—*v.i.* to depend
(on). — *n.* make, form.—
build'er *n*.—build'ing *n*.
    Syn. to fabricate. *Ant.* to
rase.

Bulb *n.* the rounded stem or
shoot of the onion and other
plants; anything resembling
this.—*v.i.* to form bulbs.—
bulb'ous *a*.

Bulge *n.* a swelling, protuberance.—*v.i.* to swell out.—
bulg'y *a.* bulg'iness *n*.

Bulk *n.* size; volume; the
greater part; a cargo.—*v.i.*
to be of weight or impor-
tance.—bulk'y *a*.—bulk'iness
n.
    Syn. magnitude, dimen-
sions, mass. *Ant.* part,
single, individual.

Bulk'head *n.* a partition in
the interior of a ship.

Bull (-oo-) *n.* the male of
cattle; the male of various
other animals; a speculator
for a rise in stocks.—bull's-
eye' *n.* a boss in glass; a lantern; the middle part of a
target.—bull'ock *n.* a castrated bull.

Bull (-oo-) *n.* a Papal edict.

Bull (-oo-) *n.* a laughable inconsistency in language.

Bull′et (-oo-) *n.* the metal ball discharged from a rifle, pistol, etc.

Bull′etin (-oo-) *n.* an official report.

Bull′ion (bool′yon) *n.* uncoined gold or silver, in mass.

Bully (-oo-) *n.* a rough, overbearing fellow.—*v.t.* to intimidate, overawe; ill-treat.

Bul′rush (-oo-) *n.* a tall, strong rush.

Bulse *n.* a bag for holding diamonds, etc., a measure of diamonds.

Bult *n. pl.* **bults, bulties,** in South Africa, a hillock or ridge.

Bul′wark (-oo-) *n.* the raised side of a ship; a breakwater; a rampart; any defence or means of security.—*v.t.* to protect.

Bum′ble-bee *n.* a large bee; a humble-bee.

Bump *n.* a heavy blow, dull in sound; a swelling caused by a blow; a protuberance. —*v.t.* to strike against.— **bump′er** *n.* a full glass.—*a.* full, abundant.

Bump′kin *n.* a rustic.

Bump′tious (-shus) *a.* self-assertive and self-conceited to an offensive degree.

Bun *n.* a small sweet cake; a round mass of hair.

Bunch *n.* a number of things tied or growing together; a cluster; a tuft, knot.—*v.t.* to put together in a bunch. —*v.i.* to draw together into a cluster.—**bunch′y** *a.*

Bun′dle *n.* a package; a number of things tied together. —*v.t.* to tie in a bundle; to send (off) without ceremony.

Bung *n.* a stopper for a cask; a large cork.—*v.t.* to stop up. —**bung′-hole** *n.*

Bung′alow (bung′ga-lō) *n.* a one-storied house.

Bung′le (bung′gl) *v.t.* to do badly for lack of skill, to manage awkwardly.—*v.i.* to act clumsily, awkwardly.— *n.* a blunder, muddle.— **bung′ler** *n.*—**bung′led** *a.*— **bung′ling** *a.*

Bun′ion *n.* an inflamed swelling on the foot.

Bunk *n.* a box or recess for sleeping in, *esp.* in a ship's cabin.

Bunk′er *n.* a receptacle for coal, *esp.* in a ship; a sandy hollow on a golf-course.

Bunk′um *n.* claptrap oratory, bombastic speechmaking.

Bun′ting *n.* a bird allied to the lark.

Bun′ting *n.* material for flags.

Buoy (boi) *n.* a floating mark anchored in the sea; something to keep a person afloat. —*v.t.* to mark with a buoy; keep from sinking; support. —**buoy′ant** *a.*—**buoy′ancy** *n.*

Bur, burr *n.* a prickly head of a plant; a rough ridge or edge; a north-country accent.

Burd′en, burth′en (-TH-) *n.* a load; weight; cargo; anything difficult to bear.—*v.t.* to load, encumber.

Burd′en *n.* the chorus of a song; the chief theme.

Bu′rean (-rō) *n.* a writing-desk; an office, *esp.* for public business. — **bureau'cracy** (-ok'-) *n.* government by officials; a body of officials.—**bu'reaucrat** *n.*—**bureaucrat'ic** *a.*

Bur'gee (-je) *n.* a swallow-tailed flag; small coal for furnaces.

Bur'gess *n.* an inhabitant of a borough, *esp.* a citizen with full municipal rights.

Bur'glar *n.* one who breaks into a house by night.—**bur'glary** *n.*—**burglar'ious** *a.*—**burglar'iously** *adv.*

Burlesque' (-esk) *n.* a travesty, a grotesque imitation, mockery.—*v.t.* to caricature.—*a.* mocking, derisively imitative.

    Syn. humour, wit, sarcasm, farce, caricature, parody, lampoon.

Bur'ly *a.* sturdy, stout.—**bur'liness** *n.*

Burn *n.* a small stream.

Burn *v.t.* to destroy or injure by fire.—*v.i.* to be on fire, literally or figuratively; to shine; to be consumed by fire.—*n.* an injury or mark caused by fire.—**burn'ing** *a.*—**burn'er** *n.*

Burn'ish *v.t.* to make bright by rubbing, polish.—**burn'isher** *n.*

Bu'rrow (-rō) *n.* the hole of a rabbit, etc.—*v.t.* to make holes in the ground, as a rabbit; to bore; conceal oneself.

Burs'ar *n.* a treasurer, *esp.* of a college; one who holds a bursary or scholarship.—**burs'ary** *n.*

Burst *v.i.* to fly asunder; break into pieces; break open violently; to break suddenly into some expression of feeling.—*v.t.* to shatter, break violently.—*n.* a bursting; an explosion; an outbreak, spurt.

Bur'y (ber'i) *v.t.* to put underground; put in a grave.—**bur'ial** *n.*

Bus'by (-z-) *n.* a fur hat worn by hussars.

Bush (-oo-) *n.* a shrub; woodland, thicket.—**bush'y** *a.*

Bush'el (-oo-) *n.* a dry measure of eight gallons.

Bust *n.* a sculpture representing the head and shoulders of the human body; the upper part of the body.

Bus'tle (-sl) *v.i.* to be noisily busy; to be active.—*n.* fuss, stir.—**bus'tler** *n.*

Bus'y (biz'i) *a.* actively employed; diligent; meddling.—*v.t.* to occupy.—**bus'ily** *adv.* **bus'ybody** *n.* a meddler.—**bus'iness** (biz'nis) *n.* affairs, work, occupation.—**bus'yness** *n.*

    Syn. occupied, active, energetic, fussy. *Ant.* disengaged, unoccupied, inactive.

But *prep.* and *conj.* without; except; only; yet; still; besides.

Butch'er (-oo-) *n.* one who kills animals for food, or sells meat; a bloody or savage man.—*v.t.* to slaughter, murder.—**butch'ery** *n.*

But'ler *a.* a servant in charge of the wine-cellar; a chief servant.

Butt *n.* a large cask.

Butt *n.* a target; an object of ridicule.

Butt *n.* the thick end of anything.

Butt *v.t.* and *i.* to strike with the head; to push.—*n.* a blow with the head, as of a sheep.

Butt'er *n.* the oily substance got from cream by churning. —*v.t.* to spread with butter; to flatter grossly.—butt'ery *a.*—butt'ercup *n.*—butt'erfly *n.*—butt'ermilk *n.*—butt'erscotch *n.*

Butt'ock *n.* the rump, protruding hinder part. (usually in *pl.*).

Butt'on *n.* a knob or stud. *esp.* for fastening dress; a bud.—*v.t.* to fasten with buttons.

Butt'ress *n.* a structure to support a wall. a prop.—*v.t.* to support.

Bux'om *a.* full of health, gay, lively.

Buy (bī) *v.t.* to get by payment; obtain in exchange for something; bribe.—buy'er *n.*

Buzz *v.i.* to make a humming sound.—*n.* a humming; the sound of bees.—buzz'er *n.*

Buzz'ard *n.* a bird of prey of the falcon family.

By *prep.* near; beside; with; through.—*adv.* near. close, out of the way; beyond.—by and by, soon.

By'law, bye'law *n.* a local law made by a subordinate authority.

By'-pass *n.* a road for diversion of traffic from crowded centres; tube in internal-combustion engine; in wireless, a diversion of undesired frequencies.

Byre *n.* a cow-shed.

C

Cab *n.* a public carriage.—cab'man, cabb'y *n.*

Cabal' *n.* a secret plot; a small body of people engaged in one.—*v.i.* to plot, intrigue.—caball'er *n.*

Syn. conspiracy, faction, junto.

Cab'aret *n.* a small tavern; a restaurant entertainment.

Cabb'age *n.* a green vegetable.

Cab'in *n.* a hut; a small room, *esp.* in a ship.—*v.t.* to shut up, confine.—cab'in-boy *n.*

Cab'inet *n.* a case of drawers for things of value; a small room or private apartment; a committee of politicians governing a country.— cab'inet-maker *n.*

Ca'ble *n.* a strong rope; a submarine telegraph line; a message sent by such line.—*v.t.* and *i.* to telegraph by cable.—ca'blegram *n.*

Ca'bre (ka-brā) *v.i.* to fly upside down.—cabring *n.*

Cac'kle *v.i.* to make a chattering noise, as a hen.—*n.* cackling noise; empty chatter.—cac'kler *n.*

Cacoph'ony *n.* a disagreeable sound, a discord of sounds.—cacoph'onous *a.*

Cac'tus *n.* a prickly plant.

Cadav'erous *a.* corpse-like; sickly-looking.

Cadd'ie *n.* golfer's attendant;

Māte, mēte, mīte, mōte, mūte, bōōt.

in Australia, a slouch-hat or wide-awake.

Cadd'y n. a small box for tea.

Ca'dence n. a fall or modulation of voice, music, or verses.

Cadet' n. younger son or brother; student in a naval or military college.

Cadge (kaj) v.i. to hawk goods.

Ca'dre (kā'der) n. a nucleus or framework, esp. the permanent skeleton of a regiment.

Caf'é (kaf'ā) n. a restaurant.

Cafete'ria n. a restaurant where the patrons serve themselves from a counter.

Caff'eine n. an alkaloid in tea and coffee.

Cage n. a place of confinement; a box with bars, esp. for keeping animals or birds.— v.t. to put in a cage, confine. —cage'bird n.

Cairn n. a heap of stones, esp. as a monument or landmark.

Caiss'on n. an ammunition wagon; a box for working under water; an apparatus for lifting a vessel out of the water.

Cait'iff n. a mean, despicable fellow.

Cajole' v.t. to cheat by flattery. —cajole'ment n.—cajo'ler n. —cajo'lery n.

Cake n. a piece of dough baked; fancy bread; a flattened hard mass.—v.t. and i. to make into a cake.

Calam'ity n. a great misfortune; . deep distress, disaster.—calam'itous a.

Calca'reous a. containing lime.

Calcif'erol n. vitamin D in pure crystalline form.

Cal'cine v.t. to reduce to lime; to burn to ashes.

Cal'culate v.t. to reckon, compute.—v.i. to make reckonings.—cal'culating a.—calcula'tion n.—cal'culable a.— cal'culator n.—cal'culus n. a stone in the body; a method of calculation.

Caldron see CAULDRON.

Cal'endar n. a table of months and days; a list of documents, a register.

Cal'ender n. a machine with rollers for smoothing cloth, paper, etc.—v.t. to smooth or finish in such machine.

Calf (käf) n. the young of the cow, also of various other animals; leather made of calf's skin.—calves (kävz) pl. —calve v.i. to give birth to a calf.

Calf (käf) n. the fleshy hinder part of the leg below the knee.

Cal'ibre n. the size of the bore of a gun; capacity, character. —cal'ibrate v.t.—calibra'tion n.

Cal'ico n. cotton cloth.

Calk see CAULK.

Call (kawl) v.t. to announce; name; summon.—v.i. to shout; to pay a short visit. —n. a shout; an animal's cry; a visit; an invitation, as to be pastor of a church, etc.—call'er n.—call'ing n.

Callig'raphy n. handwriting; penmanship.

Cal'ipers n. an instrument for measuring diameters.

Callisthen'ics (kal-is-then-iks)

n. light gymnastic exercises.
—**callisthen'ic** *a.* pertaining to callisthenics.

Call'ous *a.* hardened, unfeeling.—**call'ously** *adv.*—**call'ousness** *n.*—**callos'ity** *n.* hard lump.

Syn. hard, obdurate, indurated, unsusceptible. *Ant.* kind, susceptible, sentimental.

Call'ow *a.* unfledged; raw, inexperienced.

Calm (kăm) *n.* stillness, want of wind.—*a.* still, quiet.—*v.t.* and *i.* to become, make, still or quiet.—**calm'ly** *adv.*—**calm'ness** *n.*

Cal'orie *n.* a unit of heat.—**calorif'ic** *a.* heat-making.—**calorim'eter** *n.*

Cal'umny *n.* a slander.—**calum'niate** *v.t.*—**calumnia'tion** *n.*—**calum'niator** *n.*—**calum'nious** *a.*

Ca'lyx *n.* covering of a bud.

Cam *n.* a device to change a rotary motion to a reciprocating one.

Cam'ber *n.* convexity upon an upper surface; curvature of aeroplane wing.

Cam'bric (kā-) *n.* fine white linen.

Cam'el *n.* an animal of Asia and Africa, with a hump on its back, used as a beast of burden.

Cam'eo *n.* a stone of two layers cut in ornamental relief.

Cam'era *n.* an apparatus used to make photographs; a judge's private room.

Cam'ion (-i-un) *n.* heavy motor lorry used in military transport.

Cam'isole *n.* an under-bodice.

Cam'omile *n.* an aromatic creeping plant.

Cam'ouflage (-ăzh) *n.* disguise; means of deceiving enemy observation.—*v.t.* to disguise.

Camp *n.* the tents of an army; military quarters; travellers' resting-place.—*v.i.* to form or lodge in a camp.—**camp'ing** *n.*—**camp'er** *n.*

Campaign' (-păn) *n.* the time in which an army keeps the field; a series of operations.—*v.i.* to serve in a war.—**campaign'er** *n.*

Cam'phor *n.* a solid essential oil with aromatic taste and smell.—**cam'phorated** *a.*

Cam'shaft *n.* in motoring, a rotating shaft to which cams are fixed to lift the valves.

Can *v.i.* to be able; to have the power; to be allowed.

Can *n.* a vessel for holding liquids, usually of metal.—*v.t.* to put, or preserve, in a tin.

Canal' *n.* an artificial watercourse; a duct in the body.—**can'alise** *v.t.*—**canalisa'tion** *n.*

Canar'y (-ĕr-) *n.* a yellow singing-bird; a light wine.

Can'cel *v.t.* to cross out; to annul, abolish, suppress.—**cancella'tion** *n.*

Can'cer *n.* a malignant growth or tumour.

Can'did *a.* frank, open, impartial. — **can'didly** *adv.*—**can'didness** *n.*

Syn. sincere, cordial, hearty, just, ingenuous. *Ant.* secretive, reticent, insincere.

Can'didate *n.* one who seeks an office appointment, privilege, etc.

Can'dle n. a stick of wax with a wick; a light.—can dle-stick n.—can'dlemas n.—can'dle-power n.

Can'dour n. candidness (q.v.).

Can'dy n. crystallised sugar.—v.t. to preserve with sugar.—v.i. to become encrusted with sugar.—can'died a.

Cane n. stem of a small palm or large grass; a walking-stick.—v.t. to beat with a cane.

Ca'nine a. like or pertaining to the dog.

Can'ister n. a box or case, usually of tin.

Cank'er n. an eating sore, anything that eats away, destroys, corrupts.—v.t. to infect, corrupt.—v.i. to become cankered.—cank'er-worm n.

Cann'ibal n. one who eats human flesh.—a. relating to this practice.—cann'ibalism n.

Cann'on n. a large gun.—cannonade' n. and v.—cann'on-ball n.—cann'on-bone n. a horse's leg-bone.

Cann'on n. a billiard stroke, hitting both object balls with one's own.—v.t. to make this stroke.—v.i. to rebound.

Cann'y a. shrewd; cautious; crafty. — cann'ily adv.—cann'iness n.

Canoe' (-nōō) n. a boat made of a hollow trunk or of bark or skins; a light boat.—canoe'ist n.

Can'on n. a law or rule, esp. of the church; a standard; a body of books accepted as genuine; the list of saints.—can'onise v.t.—canonisa'tion n.

Can'on n. a church dignitary, a member of a cathedral chapter.—canon'ical a.

Can'opy n. a covering over a throne, bed, etc.—v.t. to cover with a canopy.

Cant n. hypocritical speech; whining; the language of a sect; technical jargon, slang, esp. of thieves.—v.i. to use such language.

Canteen' n. a small tin vessel; a shop or tavern in a camp or barracks; a case of cutlery, etc.

Can'ter n. an easy galloping pace.—v.i. to move at this pace.—v.t. to make to canter.

Can'ticle n. a hymn.

Can'to n. a division of a poem.

Can'vas n. a coarse cloth of hemp, used for sails, painting on, etc.; the sails of a ship; a picture.—can'vass v.t. to sift, discuss, examine; to solicit votes, contributions, etc.—n. a solicitation.

Cap n. a covering for the head; a lid, top, or other covering.—v.t. to put a cap on; to outdo; to raise the cap in respect.

Ca'pable a. able, gifted; having the capacity, power.—capabil'ity n.
   Syn. fitted, efficient, qualified. Ant. incompetent, unfit, impotent, incapable.

Capa'city (-as'-) n. power of holding or grasping; room; volume; character; ability, power of mind.—capa'cious (-ā-) a. roomy.

Cape n. a covering for the shoulders.

Cape n. a point of land running into the sea.

Ca'per n. a pickled flower-bud of a shrub growing in Sicily.

Ca'per v.i. to skip or dance.—n. a frolic; a freak.

Capias n. a writ authorising a person or his goods to be laid hold of.

Capill'ary a. hair-like.—n. a tube with very small bore, esp. a small vein.

Cap'ital n. a headpiece of a column; a chief town; a large-sized letter; money, stock, funds.—a. affecting life; serious; chief, leading; excellent.—cap'itally adv.—capita'tion n. and a.—cap'italist n.—cap'italise v.t.—cap'italism n.

Capita'tion n. a census; a tax or grant per head.

Capit'ulate v.i. to surrender on terms.—capitula'tion n.

Ca'pon n. a castrated cock.—ca'ponise v.t.

Caprice' (-ēs) n. a whim, freak.—capri'cious a.—capri'ciousness n.

Capsize' v.t. to upset.—v.i. to be upset, overturned.

Cap'stan n. a machine turned by spokes to wind a cable, esp. to hoist an anchor on board ship.

Cap'sule n. a seed vessel of a plant; a gelatine case for a dose of medicine.

Cap'tain (-tin) n. a leader, chief; the commander of a vessel, company of soldiers.

Cap'tion n. title, of an article, picture, etc.

Cap'tious (-shus) a. ready to catch at faults; critical; peevish.—cap'tiously adv.—cap'tiousness n.

Cap'tive n. one taken prisoner, kept in bondage. a. taken, imprisoned. — cap'tivate v.t. to fascinate.—captiv'ity n.—cap'tivating a

Cap'ture n. seizure, taking.—v.t. to seize, catch, make prisoner.—cap'tor n.

Car n. a wheeled vehicle; a tramway carriage; a motor-car.

Car'amel n. burnt sugar.

Car'at n. a small weight used for gold, diamonds, etc.; a proportional measure of twenty-fourths used to state the fineness of gold.

Car'avan n. a company of merchants, etc., travelling together, esp. in the East; a covered van or house on wheels.—caravan'serai n. an Eastern inn for the reception of caravans; a large hotel.

Carb'ide n. compound of carbon with an element, esp. calcium carbide.

Carb'ine n. a short rifle.—carabineer' n.

Carbol'ic a'cid n. an acid made from coal-tar and used as a disinfectant.

Carb'on n. a non-metallic element. the substance of pure charcoal, found in all organic matter.—carbon'ic a.—carb'onise v.t. — carb'onate n.—carbonif'erous a.

Car'boy n. a large glass bottle protected by a wicker casing.

Carb'uncle n. a fiery-red

precious stone; an inflamed ulcer or umour.

Carb'urettor n. an apparatus for mixing oil-vapour and air in an engine.

Carc'ass n. a dead body, originally skeleton.

Card n. pasteboard; a small piece of pasteboard with a figure for playing games, or with a name and address etc.; the dial of a compass. —**card'board** n. pasteboa d.

Card n. an instrument for combing wool, etc.—v.t. to comb.—**card'er** n.

Card'iac a. pertaining to the heart.

Card'igan n a knitted woollen jacket, waistcoat.

Card'inal a. chief, principal.— n. one of the seventy princes of the Church composing the Pope's council.—**card'inalate** n.

Care n. anxiety; pains, heed; charge, oversight.—v.i. to e anxious; to be disposed (to); to have regard or king (for). —**care'ful** a.—**care'less** a.— **care'fully** adv.—**care'fulness** n.—**care'lessness** n.

Syn. solicitude, regard, management, caution, direction, attention. *Ant.* carelessness, negligence, inattention, heedlessness, disregard.

Careen' v.t. to lay a ship over on her side for cleaning.— v.i. to lie over.

Career' n. course through life; course of action, height of activity; course, running.— v.i. to run or move at full speed.

Caress' v.t. to fondle, embrace, treat with affection.—n. an act or expression of affection.

Car'go n. a ship's load.—**car'-go-plane** n. aeroplane designed to carry goods.

Car'icature n. a likeness exaggerated or distorted to appear ridiculous.—v.t. to portray in this way.

Car'illon n. a set peal of bells of different tones.

arn'age n. slaughter.

Carn'al a. fleshly, sensual; wo dly.—**carn'ally** adv.— **carnal'ity** n.

Carna tion n. flesh colour; a cultivated flower, a double-flowering variety of the clove pink.

Carn'ival n. a revel; the season of revelry before Lent.

Carniv'orous a. flesh-eating.— **carn'ivore** n.—**carniv'ora** n.pl.

Car'ol n. a song of joy or praise.—v.i. to sing or warble. —v.t. to sing.—**car'olling** n.

Carouse' n. a drinking-bout. —v.i. to hold a drinking-bout.—**carous'al** n.—**carous'-er** n.

Carp n. a freshwater fish.

Carp v.i. to catch at small faults or errors.—**carp'er** n. —**carp'ing** a.—**carp'ingly** adv.

Carp enter n. a worker in timber as in building, etc.— **carp'entry** n.

Carp'et n. a cloth for covering a floor.—v.t. to cover a floor. —**carp'et-bag** n.—**c a r p e t-bagg'er** n. a political adventurer.—**carp'et-sweeper** n.

Car'riage n. act or cost of carrying; a vehicle; bearing, conduct.—**car'riage-horse** n.

Car'rion n. rotting dead flesh. —car'rion-crow n.

Car'rom (-om) n. a cannon at billiards.

Car'rot n. a plant with a reddish, eatable root.—car'roty a. red.

Car'ry v.t. to convey, transport; capture; effect, behave.—v.i. to reach, of a projectile.—n. range.—car'rier n.

Cart n. a two-wheeled vehicle without springs.—v.t. to convey in such vehicle; to carry. — cart'age n. — cart'er n.— cart'wright n.

Cart'ilage n. firm elastic tissue in the body; gristle.— cartila'ginous (-aj-) a.

Car'ton n. thin pasteboard.

Cartoon' n. a design for a painting; an illustration in a journal, esp. relating to current events.—cartoon'ist n.

Cart'ridge n. a case containing the charge for a gun.

Carve v.t. to cut; hew, sculpture; engrave; cut up (meat). —carv'er n.—carv'ing n.

Cascade' n. a waterfall; anything resembling this.—v.i. to fall in cascades.

Case n. an instance; state of affairs; condition; lawsuit; grounds for a suit.—case'-law n.

Case n. a box, sheath, covering; any receptacle; a box and its contents.—v.t. to put in a case.—case'-harden v.t. —case'-hardening n.

Case'mate (-sm-) n. a bombproof vault.

Case'ment (-sm-) n. a window frame; a window opening on hinges.

Cash n. money, coin.—v.t. to turn into or exchange for money. — cash'book n. — cashier' n.—cash'-register n. a recording till.

Cash'mere n. a shawl; a fabric.

Casi'no (-sē-) n. a public assembly-room, esp. one in which gambling is carried on.

Cask n. a barrel.

Cask'et n. a small case or box for jewels, etc.

Cass'ock n. a long tunic worn by clergymen.

Cast (-á-) v.t. to throw or fling; to shed; to throw down; to allot, as parts in a play; to found, as metal.—v.i. to cast about, to look round.—n. a throw; the thing thrown; the distance thrown; a squint; a mould; the shape received from a mould; manner, quality, tinge, colour, degree; set of actors.—cast'-away n. —cast'ing n.—cast'ing-vote.

Caste n. a section of society in India; social rank.

Cas'tigate v.t. to chastise; punish or rebuke severely.— cas'tigator n.—castiga'tion n.

Cas'tle (kásl) n. a fortress; a country mansion.

Cast'or (-á-) n a beaver; a hat made of beaver fur.

Cast'or-oil (-á-) n. a vegetable medicinal oil.

Cast'or (-á-) n. a small vessel with a perforated top; a small wheel.

Cas'trate v.t. to remove the testicles, deprive of the power of generation.—castra'tion n.

Cas'ual (-z-) *a.* accidental; unforeseen; occasional; unmethodical.—cas'ually *adv.*—cas'ualty *n.* an accident; a loss in war.

Syn. fortuitous, occasional, unexpected. *Ant.* expected, organised.

Cas'uist *n.* one who studies and solves cases of conscience; quibbler.—casuis'tical *a.*—cas'uistry *n.*

Cat *n.* a tame or wild animal of the genus *Felis*; a spiteful woman; a piece of wood tapered at both ends; a ninelashed whip.—*v.t.* to raise an anchor to the cathead.—catt'y *a.*—cat'gut *n.* cord made of intestines of animals other than cats.—cat'head *n.* a beam at the bow of a ship.—cat'kin *n.* a spike of flowers.—cat's'-paw *n.* a dupe; a breath of wind.—cat's'-whisker *n.* a fine wire used in a crystal wireless set.

Cat'aclysm *n.* an upheaval.

Cat'acomb *n.* an underground gallery for burial.

Cat'alogue (-og) *n.* a descriptive list.—*v.t.* to make such a list of; to enter in a catalogue.

Cat'apult *n.* a small forked stick with an elastic sling used by boys for throwing stones; formerly an engine of war for hurling arrows, stones, etc.

Cat'aract *n.* a waterfall; a defect in an eye.

Catarrh' *n.* a discharge from the nose, a cold.—catar'rhal *a.*

Catas'trophe (-fi) *n.* the culmination of a tragedy; a great disaster.

Catch *v.t.* to take hold of, seize, understand.—*v.i.* to be contagious; to get entangled.—*n.* a seizure; anything that holds stops, etc.; that which is caught; a form of musical composition; an advantage taken or to be gained.—catch'ing *a.*—catch'er *n.*—catch'ment-basin *n.*—catch'penny *a.*—catch'word *n.*

Syn. to grasp, gripe, arrest, charm. *Ant.* to loose, set free, disgust.

Cat'echise (-k-) *v.t.* to instruct by question and answer; to question.—cat'echism *n.*—cat'echist *n.*—catechet'ic *a.*—catechu'men *n.* one under instruction in Christianity.

Cat'egory *n.* a class of order, a division.—categor'ical *a.* positive; what may be affirmed of a class.—categor'ically *adv.*—cat'egorise *v.t.*

Catena'tion *n.* a chain or series like the links of a chain.

Ca'ter *v.i.* to provide food, entertainment etc.—ca'terer *n.*—ca'tering *n.*

Cat'erpillar *n.* the hairy grub of a moth or butterfly.—cat'erpillar-wheel' *n.* an endless band instead of a wheel for vehicles crossing rough ground.

Cathe'dral *n.* the principal church of a diocese.—*a.* pertaining to a cathedral.

Cath'ode *n.* the negative pole of an electric current; in wireless, the filament of a thermionic valve.

Cath'olic *a.* universal; including the whole body of Christians; relating to the

Roman Catholic Church.—*n.* an adherent of the R.C. Church.—**cathol'icise** *v.t.*—**cathol'icism** *n.*—**catholi'city** *n.*

Cat'tle *n.* beasts of pasture, *esp.* oxen, cows; sometimes horses, sheep also.—**cat'tleman** *n.*—**cat'tle show** *n.*

Cau'cus (kaw-) *n.* an electioneering political committee.

Caul'dron, cal'dron *n.* a large kettle or boiler.

Caul'iflower (kol-) *n.* a cabbage with an eatable white flowerhead.

Caulk, calk (kawk) *v.t.* to press oakum into the seams of a ship, to make it watertight. —**caulk'er** *n.*—**caulk'ing** *n.*—**caulk'ing-iron** *n.*

Cause (-z-) *n.* that which produces an effect; reason, origin; motive, purpose; a lawsuit.—*v.t.* to bring about, make to exist.—**caus'al** *a.*—**causal'ity** *n.*—**causa'tion** *n.*—**cause'less** *a.*

Cause'way, caus'ey (-z-) *n.* a raised way, a paved street.

Caus'tic *a.* burning; bitter, severe.—*n.* a corrosive substance.—**caus'tically** *adv.*

Syn. pungent, stinging, corrosive, severe, sharp, mordant.

Caut'erise *v.t.* to burn with a caustic or hot iron. — **cauterisa'tion** *n.*

Cau'tion *n.* heedfulness, care; a warning.—*v.t.* to warn.—**cau'tious** *a.*—**cau'tiously** *adv.* —**cau'tioner** *n.*—**cau'tionary** *a.*—**cau'tiousness** *n.*

Syn. watchfulness, circumspection, forethought. *Ant.*

carelessness, imprudence, rashness.

Cavalcade' *n.* a column or procession of persons on horseback.—**cavalier'** *n.* a horseman; a courtly gentleman; an adherent of the King in the Civil War.—*a.* careless, disdainful.—**cavalier'ly** *adv.* —**cav'alry** *n.* mounted troops.

Cave *n.* a hollow place in the earth; a den.—**cav'ern** *n.* a deep cave.—**cav'ernous** *a.*—**cav'ernously** *adv.*—**cav'ity** *n.* a hollow, an opening.

Cave in *v.i.* to fall in; to submit.

Caviare', caviar' *n.* salted sturgeon roe; *fig.* something too fine for the vulgar taste.

Cav'il *v.i.* to find fault without sufficient reason, make trifling objections.—**cav'illing** *n.* —**cav'iller** *n.*

Syn. to carp, wrangle.

Caw *n.* the crow's cry.—*v.i.* to cry as a crow.

Cayenne', cayenne'-pep'per *n.* a very pungent red pepper.

Cease *v.i.* to stop, give over.— *v.t.* discontinue.—**cease'less** *a.* —**cease'lessly** *adv.*

Ce'dar *n.* a large evergreen tree; its wood.

Cede *v.t.* to yield, give up, *esp.* of territory.

ceil'ing (sel-) *n.* an inner roof. —**ceil'** *v.t.*

Cel'andine *n.* a yellow flower, swallow-wort.

Cel'ebrate *v.t.* to make famous; to mark by ceremony as an event or festival; to perform with proper rites.—**cel'ebrant** *n.* — **celebra'tion** *n.* — **cel'ebrated** *a.* famous.—**celeb'rity**

n. fame; a famous person. *Syn.* to honour, distinguish, solemnise. *Ant.* to dishonour.

Celer'ity *n.* swiftness.

Cel'ery *n.* a vegetable with long white eatable stalks.

Celes'tial *a.* heavenly, divine.

Cel'ibacy *n.* single life. unmarried state.—**cel'ibate** *n.*

Cell *n.* a small room; a small cavity; a unit-mass of living matter.—**cell'ular** *a.*—**cell'ule** *n.*—**cell'uloid** *n.* imitation ivory.—**cell'ulose** *n.*

Cell'ar *n.* an underground room for storage.—**cell'arage** *n.*—**cell'arer** *n.*—**celi'aret** *n.* a case for bottles.

Cement' *n.* mortar; anything used for sticking two bodies together.—*v.t.* to unite with cement; to join firmly.

Cem'etery *n.* a burying-ground.

Cen'otaph *n.* an empty tomb, a monument to some one buried elsewhere.

Cen'ser *n.* a pan in which incense is burned.

Cen'sor *n.* a supervisor of morals; one who examines plays, books, news, etc., before publication.—**censor'ial** *a.*—**censor'ious** *a.* fault-finding.—**censor'lously** *adv.*—**censor'iousness** *n.*—**cen'sorship** *n.*

Cen'sure *n.* blame; reproof.—*v.t.* to blame; reprove.—**cen'surable** *a.*—**cen'surably** *adv.*

Cen'sus *n.* an official counting of the inhabitants of a country; any official counting.

Cent *n.* a hundred; the hundredth part of a dollar.—per **cent**, in, to, by each hundred.

Cente'nary *n.* a hundred years; a celebration of a hundredth anniversary.—*a.* pertaining to a hundred.—**centena'rian** *n.* one a hundred years old.—**centenn'ial** *a.* lasting a, or happening every, hundred years.—**cen'tury** *n.* a hundred years; a hundred.

Cen'tigrade *a.* having a hundred degrees.

Centill'ion (-yun) *n.* the hundredth power of a million.

Cen'tipede *n.* a small segmented animal with many legs.

Cen'tre *n.* the mid-point of anything; pivot, axis; a point to which or from which things move or are drawn.—**cen'tral** *a.*—**cen'tric** *a.*—**cen'tralise** *v.t.*—**centralisa'tion** *n.*—**central'ity** *n.*—**cen'trally** *adv.*—**centrif'ugal** *a.* tending from a centre.—**centrip'etal** *a.* tending towards a centre.

Centu'rion *n.* a commander of a hundred men.

Cen'tury *see* CENTENARY.

Ce'real *a.* pertaining to corn.—*n.* grain used as food (usually *pl.*).

Cer'ebal *a.* pertaining to the brain.—**cerebra'tion** *n.* brain action.—**cer'ebro-spi'nal** *a.*

Cer'emony *n.* a sacred rite; formal observance; usage of courtesy; formality.—**ceremon'ial** *a.* and *n.* — **ceremo'nious** *a.*—**ceremo'nially, ceremo'niously** *adv.*—**ceremo'niousness** *n.*

Cert'ain *a.* sure, settled, fixed, inevitable; some, one; of moderate (quantity, degree, etc.).—cert′ainly *adv.* — cert′ainty *n.*—cert′itude *n.*

Syn. real, regular, constant, unfailing. *Ant.* uncertain, doubtful.

Cert′ify *v.t.* to make known as certain; to declare formally. —cert′ifier *n.*—certif′icate *n.* a written declaration.—*v.t.* to give a written declaration. —certifica′tion *n.*

Ceru′lean *a.* skyblue.

Cessa′tion *n.* ceasing or stopping.

Cess′ion *n.* a yielding up.

Cess′pool *n.* a pit in which filthy water collects, a receptacle for sewage.

Chafe *v.t.* to make hot by rubbing; to fret or wear by rubbing; to vex, irritate. —cha′fing-dish *n.*—cha′fing-gear *n.*

Cha′fer *n.* beetle.

Chaff (-àf) *n.* husks of corn; worthless matter; banter, making fun.

chaff′er *v.i.* to haggle, bargain. —*n.* bargaining.—chaff′erer *n.*

Cha′fing-dish *n.* a vessel holding live coal or charcoal, used to keep dishes warm.

Chag′rin (sha-grin′) *n.* vexation, disappointment.—*v.t.* to vex.

Chain *n.* a series of links or rings each passing through the next; a fetter; anything that binds; a connected series of things or events; a surveyor's measure.—*v.t.* to fasten with a chain; confine. —makes compound nouns as chain-arm′our, chain′-mail,

chain′-shot, chain′-stitch, etc.

Chair *n.* a movable seat; a seat of authority; a professor's seat, or his office; an iron support for a rail on a railway.—*v.t.* to carry in triumph.—chair′man *n.* one who presides.—chair′manship *n.*

Chaise (shāz) *n.* a light carriage.

Chal′dron (kawl-) *n.* a measure for coals, 36 bushels.

Chal′ice *n.* a cup or bowl; a communion-cup.

Chalk (chawk) *n.* a white substance, a carbonate of lime. —*v.t.* to rub or mark with chalk.—*v.i.* to mark with chalk; to keep a reckoning. —chalk′y *a.*—chalk′iness *n.*

Chall′enge *v.t.* to call to fight; call to account; dispute; claim; object to.—chall′enger *n.*—chall′engeable *a.*

Chalyb′eate (ka-lib′i-at) *a.* containing iron.

Cha′mber *n.* a room; a room for an assembly; an assembly or body of men; a compartment; a cavity.—cha′mberlain *n.* an officer appointed by a king, etc., for domestic and ceremonial duties.— cha′mber-maid *n.* a servant with care of bedrooms.— cha′mber-pot, cha′mber *n.* a vessel for urine.

Chame′leon (ka-) *n.* a small lizard famous for its power of changing colour.

Cham′fer *v.t.* to groove; to bevel.—*n.* a groove.

Cham′ois (sham′wà) *n.* a goat-like mountain animal; a soft leather.

Cham′pion n. one who fights for another; one who defends a cause; in sport, etc., one who excels all others; a hero.—v.t. to fight for, maintain.—**cham′pionship** n.

Chance (-á-) n. that which happens: fortune; risk; opportunity; possibility; probability.—v.t. to risk.—v.i. to happen.—a. casual, unexpected.

Syn. hazard, probability, possibility, fate, casualty. *Ant.* cause, plan, design.

Chan′cel n. the eastern part of a church.

Chan′cellor n. a high officer of state; the head of a university.—**chan′cellorship** n. —**chan′cellery** n.

Chan′cery n. a division of the High Court of Justice.

Chand′ler n. a retail dealer.— **chandelier′** (sh-) n. a frame with branches for holding lights.

Change v.t. to alter or make different; put or give for another; exchange, interchange.—v.i. to alter; to put on different clothes.—n. alteration, variation; variety; conversion of money; small money; balance received on payment.—**change′able** a.— **change′ably** adv.—**changeabil′ity** n.—**change′ableness** n.—**change′ful** a.—**change′less** a.—**change′ling** n. a child substituted for another by fairies.

Syn. to vary, to substitute, to exchange. *Ant.* to maintain, keep, retain.

Chann′el n. the bed of a stream; the deeper part of a strait, bay, harbour; a groove; a means of passing or conveying.—v.t. to groove, furrow.

Chant (-á-) v.t. and i. to sing. —n. a song; a church melody. —**chant′er** n.—**chant′ry** n. an endowment or chapel for singing masses.— **chan′ty** (sh-) n. a sailor's song.

Chan′ticleer n. a cock.

Cha′os (kā-) n. disorder, confusion; state of the universe before the Creation.

Chap v.t. to crack; to strike.— v.i. to fissure.—n. a crack in the skin.—**chapp′ed** a.

Chaps n.pl. jaws. (*see* CHOP).

Chap′el n. a subordinate place of worship, as one attached to a garr.son, house, prison, etc., and not a cathedral or parish church; a division of a church with its own altar; a Dissenters′ or Nonconformists′ place of worship; an association of printers.

Chap′eron (sh-) n. one who attends a young unmarried lady in public as a protector.—v.t. to attend in this way.

Chap′lain n. the clergyman attached to a chapel, regiment, ship of war, institution. etc.—**chap′laincy** n.

Chap′man n. one that buys or sells.

Chap′ter n. a division of a book; a section, heading; an assembly of the clergy of a cathedral, etc.; an organised branch of a society, fraternity.—**chap′ter-house** n.

Char v.t. to scorch, burn, reduce to charcoal.—**charr'ed** a.

Char'-a-banc (-bang) n. a long, open coach with transverse seats.

Char'acter (ka-) n. a letter, sign, or any distinctive mark; an essential feature; nature; the total of qualities making up an individuality; moral qualities; the reputation of possessing them; a statement of the qualities of a person who has been in one's service; a person noted for eccentricity; a personality in a play or novel.—**characteris'tic** a.—**characteris'tically** adv.—**char'acterise** v.t.—**characterisa'tion** n.—**char'acterless** a.

Charade' (shar-ád') n. a riddle, often acted, on the syllables of a word.

Charc'oal n. the black residue of wood, bones, etc., by smothered burning; charred wood.—**char'coal-burner** n.

Chare, chore n. a turn of work, an odd job.—v.i. to do odd jobs (also CHAR).—**char'-woman** n.

Charge v.t. to fill: load; lay a task on, command; deliver an injunction; bring an accusation against; ask as a price; fill with electricity.—v.i. to make an onset.—n. that which is laid on; cost, price; load for a gun, etc.; command, exhortation; accusation; an accumulation of electricity; pl. expenses.—**charge'able** a.—**char'ger** n. an officer's horse.

Cha'riot (cha-) n. a state car; a war-car.—**charioteer'** n.

Cha'rity (cha-) n. love, kindness; disposition to think kindly of others; practical kindliness, alms-giving. — **cha'ritable** a. — **cha'ritably** adv.

Syn. benevolence, affection, tenderness, indulgence, alms. Ant. malevolence, lack of affection.

Charl'atan (sh-) n. a quack.—**charl'atanry** n.

Charm n. a magic spell; a thing worn to avert evil; anything that fascinates; attractiveness.—v.t. to bewitch; to delight, attract.—**charm'ed** a.—**charm'ing** a.—**charm'ingly** adv.—**charm'er** n.

Charn'el-house n. a place where the bones of the dead are put.

Chart n. a map of the sea; a diagram or tabulated statement.—**chart'-house** n.

Chart'er n. a writing in evidence of a grant of privileges, etc.; a patent.—v.t. to establish by charter; to let or hire.

Char'y (-ě-) a. cautious, sparing.—**char'ily** adv.—**char'iness** n.

Chase' v.t. to hunt, pursue; to drive from, into, etc.—n. a pursuit, hunting; the thing hunted; hunting-ground.

Chase v.t. to decorate with engraving.—**cha'sing** n.—**cha'ser** n.

Chasm (kazm) n. a deep cleft, an abyss.

Chas'sé (chas'-ā) n. a gliding step used in dancing.—v.i. to perform the step.

Chassis (shas'ē) n. the framework, wheels and machinery of a motor-car; the under-frame of an aeroplane.

Chaste *a.* pure; modest; virtuous.—**chaste′ly** *adv.*—**chas′tity** *n.*—**cha′sten** *v.t.* to free from faults by punishment; to restrain, moderate.—**cha′stened** *a.*—**chastise′** *v.t.* to inflict punishment on to reduce to order.—**chas′tisement** *n.*

Chat *v.i.* to talk idly, or familiarly.—*n.* familiar talk; idle talk.—**chatt′y** *a.*—**chatt′ily** *adv.*

Chatoy′ment (sha-toi-) *n.* play of colours.—**chatoy′ant** *a.* possessing a changeable lustre.

Chatt′el *n.* any movable property (usually in *pl.*).

Chatt′er *v.i.* to talk idly or rapidly; to rattle the teeth.—*n.* idle talk.—**chatt′erer** *n.*—**chatt′ering** *n.*—**chatt′erbox** *n.*

Chat′wood *n.* little sticks for burning.

Chauffeur (shō-fẹr′) *n.* a motor-car driver.

Cheap *a.* low in price; supplying at a low price; easily obtained; of little value or estimation.—**cheap′ly** *adv.*—**cheap′ness** *n.*—**cheap′en** *v.t.*

Cheat *v.t.* to deprive of by deceit, defraud, impose upon.—*v.i.* to practise deceit.—*n.* a fraud.

Check *v.t.* to stop; restrain; hinder; repress; control; examine.—*n.* a threatening the king at chess; a repulse; stoppage; restraint; a token, ticket; an order for money

(usually *cheque*).—**check′er** *n*—**checkmate′** *n.* in chess, the final winning move; any overthrow, defeat.—*v.t.* to make the movement ending the game; to defeat.

Syn. to curb, hinder, chide. *Ant.* to help, encourage.

Checker *see* CHEQUER

Cheek *n.* the side of the face below the eye; impudence.—*v.t.* to address impudently.—**cheek′y** *a.*—**cheek′ily** *adv.*

Cheer *n.* mood; mirth, joy; food; shout of approval.—*v.t.* to comfort; gladden; encourage, *esp.* by shouts.—*v.i.* to shout applause.—**cheer′ful** *a.*—**cheer′fully** *adv.*—**cheer′fulness** *n.*—**cheer′y** *a.*—**cheer′ily** *adv.*—**cheer′less** *a.*—**cheer′lessness** *n.*

Cheese *n.* curd of milk coagulated, separated from the whey and pressed.—**chees′y** *a.*—**chees′iness** *n.*—**cheese′monger** *n.*—**cheese′paring** *a.* mean.

Chem′istry (k-) *n.* the science which treats of the properties of substances and their combinations and reactions.—**chem′ist** *n.*—**chem′ical** *n.* and *a.*—**chem′ically** *adv.*

Chenille′ (she-nĕl) *n.* a soft cord of silk or worsted.

Cheque (-ek) *n.* an order on a banker.—**cheque′-book** *n.*

Che′quer (-ek-ẹr) *n.* marking like a chessboard; *pl.* squares like those of a chessboard.—*v.t.* to mark in squares; to variegate. — **che′quered** *a.* marked in squares; uneven, varied.

Cher′ish *v.t.* to treat with

affection; protect; encourage.

Cheroot' (sh-) *n.* an open-ended cigar.

Cher'ry *n.* a small red stone-fruit; the tree.—*a.* ruddy.

Cher'ub *n.* a winged creature with a human face; an angel. —cher'ubs, cher'ubim *pl.*—cheru'bic *a.*

Chess *n.* a game of skill played by two persons with 32 "pieces" on a board of 64 squares.—chess'men *n.pl.* the pieces used in chess.—chess'-board *n.*

Chest *n.* a box; coffer; the upper part of the trunk of the body.

Ches'terfield *n.* a long overcoat; a heavily padded sofa.

Chest'nut (-sn-) *n.* a large reddish-brown nut growing in a prickly husk; the tree bearing it.—*a.* reddish-brown.

Chev'ron (sh-) *a.* V-shaped band of braid or lace, used as badge in the Forces.

Chew (-ōō) *v.t.* to grind with the teeth.—chew'ing-gum *n.*

Chiaroscu'ro (kya-ros-koo-rō) *n.* the reproduction of light and shade in a picture.

Chicane', **chica'nery** *n.* quibbling; trick, artifice.—chicane' *v.t.* to quibble, use tricks.

Chick short for **chick'en** *n.* the young of birds, *esp.* of the hen.—chick'en-heart'ed *a.*—chick'en-pox *n.* a fever.

Chic'ory *n.* a salad plant of which the root is ground and mixed with coffee.

Chide *v.t.* to scold, reprove. *Syn.* to blame, reproach,

censure, reprove. *Ant.* approve, commend.

Chief *n.* a head or principal person.—*a.* principal, foremost, leading.—chief'ly *adv.*

Chief'tain *n.* a leader or chief of a clan or tribe.

Chil'blain *n.* an inflamed sore due to cold.

Child' (-ī-) *n.* an infant; a boy or girl; a son or daughter.—child'ren (-i-) *pl.*—child'ish (-ī-) *a.*—child'ishly *adv.*—child'hood *n.*—child'birth *n.*—child'bed *n.* the state of a woman giving birth to a child.—child'like *a.*—child'less *a.*

Chill *n.* coldness; a cold with shivering; anything that damps, discourages.—chilled' *a.*—chill'y *a.*—chill'iness *n.*—chill'ing *a.*

Chime *n.* the sound of bells in harmony; a set of bells.—*v.i.* to ring harmoniously; to agree; to chime in, to come into a conversation with agreement.—*v.t.* to strike (bells).

Chime'ra, **chima'ra** (kī-mĕr-a) *n.* a fabled monster, made up of parts of various animals; a wild fancy.—chimer'ic, -al *a.* fanciful.

Chim'ney *n.* a passage for smoke.

Chin *n.* the part of the face below the mouth.

Chi'na *n.* fine earthenware.

Chink *n.* a cleft, crack.

Chink *n.* the sound of pieces of metal knocking together.—*v.i.* to make this sound.—*v.t.* to cause to do so.

Chintz *n.* cotton cloth printed in coloured designs.

Chip v.t. to chop or cut into small pieces; to break little pieces from; to shape by cutting off pieces.—v.i. to break off.—n. a small piece broken off.

Chirog´raphy (ki-rog-ra-fi) n. the art of writing; handwriting.

Chirp. chirr´up n. a short, sharp cry of a bird.—v.i. to make this sound.

Chis´el (-zl) n. a cutting tool, usually a bar of steel with an edge across the main axis.—v.t. to cut or carve with a chisel.

Chiv´alry (sh-) n. bravery and courtesy; the feudal system of knighthood.—chiv´alrous a.—chiv´alrously adv.

Chlor´ine (kl-) n. a yellowish-green gas, an element, with a suffocating action on the lungs.—chlor´ide n.—chlor´-ate n.—chlor´inate v.t.

Chlor´oform (kl-) n. a liquid used as an anæsthetic.—v.t. to put to sleep with this drug.

Chlor´ophyll (kl-) n. the colouring matter of plants.

Choc´olate n. a paste made from the seeds of the cacao tree; a drink made from this paste.—a. dark brown.

Choice n. act or power of choosing; an alternative; something chosen.—a. select, fine. worthy of being chosen.—choice´ly adv.

Choir (kwīr) n. a band of singers, esp. in a church; the part of a church set aside for them.

Choke v.t. to throttle; stop up; smother, stifle; obstruct.—

v.i. to suffer choking.—n. the act or noise of choking.—choked a.—choke´-bore n. a gun narrowed towards the muzzle, to concentrate the shot.—choke´damp n. carbonic gas in coal-mines.

Chol´er (k-) n. bile; anger.—chol´eric a.

Chol´era (k-) n. a deadly disease marked by vomiting and purging.

Chondrom´eter n. a steelyard for weighing grain.

Choose v.t. to take one thing rather than another; select,—v.i. to will, think fit.—choos´er n.

Chop v.t. to cut with a blow; to cut in pieces.—n. a hewing blow; a slice of meat containing a rib.—chop´-house n.—chopp´er n.

Chop v.t. to exchange, bandy, e.g. to chop logic, to chop and change.

Chop, chap n. the jaw (usually in pl.).—chop´-fallen a. dejected.

Chord (k-) n. a string of a musical instrument; a straight line joining the ends of an arc.

Chord (k-) n. a union of musical notes.

Chore see CHARE.

Chor´us (k-) n. a band of singers; combination of voices singing together; a refrain.—v.t. to sing or say together.—chor´ic a.—chor´al a.—chor´ister n.

Chris´tian (kris´tyan) n. a follower of Christ.—a. following Christ; relating to Christ or His religion —Christian name, the name given at christening, the individual name.—Christian Science, a religious system founded by Mrs. Eddy, in America.—christ'en (kri'sn) v.t. to baptize, give a name to.—Christian'ity n. the religion of Christ.—chris'tianise v.t.—Chris'tendom n. all Christian countries.—Chris'tmas n. the festival of the birth of Christ.—Christmas-card n.—Christmas-box n.

Chromat'ic (k-) a. relating to colour; (music) of a scale proceeding by semi-tones.

Chron'ic (k-) a. lasting a long time.—chron'icle n. a record of events in order of time.—v.t. to record.—chron'icler n.—chronol'ogy n. science of dates.—chronolo'gical a.—chronolo'gically adv.—chronol'ogist n.—chronom'eter n. an instrument for measuring time exactly; a watch.—chronom'etry n.—chronomet'rical a.

Chrys'alis (k-) n. the resting state of an insect between grub and fly; the case from which it emerges.

Chub n. a river fish.—chubb'y a. plump.

Chuck v.t. to tap, as under the chin; to throw.—n. a tap; a throw.

Chuc'kle v.t. to laugh in a quiet manner.—n. such laugh.

Chukk'er n. one of the periods into which the game of polo is divided.

Church n. a building for Christian worship; the whole body of Christians; the clergy; a body or sect of Christians.—v.t. to give thanks on behalf of (a woman) after childbirth, etc.—church'man n.—churchward'en n.—church'woman n.—church'yard n.

Churl n. a rustic; an ill-bred fellow.—churl'ish a.—churlishly adv.—churl'ishness n.

Churn n. a vessel for making butter.—v.t. to shake up (a liquid).

Chy'ak v.t. in Australia, to tease; chaff; make game of.

Cicero'ne (chē-chā-rō-nā) n. a guide.

Ci'der n. a drink made from apples.

Cigar' n. a roll of tobacco-leaves for smoking.—cigarette' n. finely-cut tobacco rolled in paper for smoking.

Cin'der n. a piece of glowing coal; a partly-burnt coal.

Cinemat'ograph n. an apparatus for throwing moving pictures on a screen by means of light.—cinematograph'ic a.—cinematog'raphy n.

Cinn'amon n. the spicy bark of a tree in Ceylon; the tree.—a. of a light brown colour.

Ci'pher, cy'pher n. the arithmetical symbol 0; a figure; a person of no importance; a monogram; a secret writing.—v.i. to work at arithmetic.

Cir'cle (ser'kl) n. a perfectly round figure; a ring; a company of persons gathered round another, or round an object of interest; a class or division of society.—v.t. to surround.—*v.i.* to move round.—**circ'ular** *a.* round; moving round.—*n.* a letter sent to several (a circle of) persons.—**circ'ulate** *v.i.* to move round; to pass from place to place; to come to readers.—*v.t.* to send round. —**circula'tion** *n.*

Circ'uit (-kit) *n.* a moving round; area; a round of visitation, *esp.* of judges; a district; the path of an electric current.—**circu'itous** *a.*—**circu'itously** *adv.*

Circ'umcise *v.t.* to cut off the foreskin of.—**circumcis'ion** *n.*

Circum'ference *n.* the boundary line. *esp.* of a circle.

Circumlocu'tion *n.* roundabout speech.

   Syn. periprasis, verbosity, diffuseness. *Ant.* concise, pithy.

Circumnav'igate *v.t.* to sail round.—**circumnaviga'tion** *n.* —**circumnav'igator** *n.*

Circ'umscribe *v.t.* to confine, bound, limit, hamper.

Circ'umspect *a.* watchful, cautious, prudent.—**circ'umspectly** *adv.*—**circumspec'tion** *n.*

Circ'umstance *n.* a detail; an event, matter of fact; *pl.* state of affairs; condition in life; the surroundings or things accompanying an action.—**circ'umstanced** *a.* situated.—**circumstan'tial** *a.* depending on details; particular as to details; indirect.— **circumstan'tially** *adv.*—**circumstantial'ity** *n.*—**circumstan'tiate** *v.t.* to prove by details; to describe exactly.

Circumvent' *v.t.* to outwit.— **circumven'tion** *n.*

Circ'us *n.* a circular building for public shows; an entertainment of horse-riding, clowning, etc.; a group of houses built in a circle.

Ci'rrus *n.* a high fleecy cloud.

Cis'tern *n.* a water-tank.

Cit'adel *n.* a fortress in, near, or commanding a city.

Cite *v.t.* to summon; quote; bring forward as proof.— **cita'tion** *n.*

Cit'izen *n.* an inhabitant of a city; a townsman; a member of a state.—**cit'izenship** *n.*

Cit'ron *n.* a fruit like a lemon; the tree.—**cit'ric** *a.* of the acid of the lemon and citron.

Cit'y *n.* a large town.

Civ'ic *a.* pertaining to a city or citizen.—**civ'ics** *n.* the science of municipal and national life, or service.

Civ'il *a.* relating to citizens or the state; refined, polite, not barbarous; not military.— (*law*) not criminal.—**civ'illy** *adv.*—**civil'ity** *n.* politeness. —**civil'ian** *n.* a non-military person.—**civ'ilise** *v.t.* to refine, bring out of barbarism. —**civilisa'tion** *n.*—**civ'ilised** *a.*

   Syn. political, civilised, urbane, courteous, well-bred, refined. *Ant.* military, rude, churlish, brusque.

Clach'an (klak-) *n.* a hamlet.

Claim *v.t.* to call for; demand as a right.—*n.* a demand for a thing supposed due; a right; the thing claimed.— **claim'ant** *n.*—**clam'ant** *a.* demanding attention.

Clairvoyance (klăr-voi-ans) *n.* the alleged power of seeing things not present to the senses.—**clairvoyant** *n.* one that claims this power.

Clam'ber *v.i.* to climb with hands and feet, with difficulty.

Clamm'y *a.* moist and sticky. —**clamm'iness** *n.*

Clam'our *n.* loud shouting, outcry, noise.—*v.i.* to shout; to call noisily (for).—**clam'orous** *a.*—**clam'orously** *adv.*

Clamp *n.* a tool for holding or compressing.—*v.t.* to fasten with clamps.

Clan *n.* a tribe or collection of families under a chief and of supposed common ancestry; a sect, group.—**clann'ish** *a.*—**clann'ishly** *adv.* —**clann'ishness** *n.*

Clandes'tine *a.* secret; sly.— **clandes'tinely** *adv.* secretly.

Clang *n.* a loud ringing sound. —*v.i.* to make such sound.— *v.t.* to strike together with a clang.—**clang'our** *n.*

Clank' *n.* a short sound as of pieces of metal struck together.—*v.t.* and *i.* to cause, or move with, such a sound.

Clap *n.* a hard, explosive sound; a slap.—*v.i.* to strike with noise; to strike the open hands together; applaud.—*v.t.* to strike together; to pat; to applaud; thrust suddenly, impose abruptly. —**clapp'er** *n.*—**clapp'ing** *n.*— **clap'trap** *n.* empty words.

Clar'et *n.* red Bordeaux wine.

Clar'ify *v.t.* to make clear; purify.—**clarifica'tion** *n.*

Clar'ion *n.* a clear-sounding trumpet.—**clarionet'**, **clar'inet** *n.* a wood wind instrument.

Clash *n.* a loud noise, as of weapons striking together; conflict, collision.—*v.i.* to make a clash; to come into conflict.—*v.t.* to strike together to make a clash.

Clasp *n.* a hook or other means of fastening; an embrace; a military decoration. —*v.t.* to fasten; embrace, grasp.

Class (-á-) *n.* a rank of society; a division of pupils; a division by merit, quality; any division, order, kind, sort. —*v.t.* to assign to the proper division.—**class'ify** *v.t.* to arrange methodically in classes. —**classifica'tion** *n.*

Class'ic, **class'ical** *a.* of the first rank of Greek and Roman authors; of the highest rank generally, but *esp.* of literature; resembling in style the Greek writers; refined, chaste; famous.—**class'ically** *adv.*— **class'icism** *n.*—**classi'cist** *n.*

Clatt'er *n.* a rattling noise; noisy conversation.—*v.i.* to make a rattling noise; to chatter. — *v.t.* to make rattle.

Clause (-z) *n.* a part of a sentence; an article in a formal document.
Syn. subdivision, paragraph, article.

Clav'ichord (-k-) *n.* an obsolete musical instrument like a spinet.

Claviform *a.* club-shaped.

Claw *n.* the hooked nail of a bird of beast; the foot of an animal with hooked nails; anything like a claw.—*v.t.* to tear with claws; to grip.

Clay *n.* a stiff viscous earth; earth generally; the human body.—**clay'ey** *a.*

Clay'more *n.* a Highland sword.

Clean *a.* free from dirt, stain, or any defilement; pure; guiltless; trim, shapely.— *adv.* so as to leave no dirt; entirely.—*v.t.* to free from dirt.—**clean'ness** *n.*—**clean'er**—**clean'ly** (klĕn-) *adv.*—**clean'liness**(klen-)*n.*—**clean'ly** (klen-) *a.*—**cleanse** (klenz) *v.t.*

Clear *a.* free from cloud; pure, undimmed, bright; free from obstruction or difficulty; plain, distinct; without defect or drawback; transparent.—*adv.* brightly; wholly, quite.—*v.t.* to make clear; acquit; pass over or through; to make as profit; to free from cloud, obstruction, difficulty; to free by payment of dues.—*v.i.* to become clear, bright, free, transparent. — **clear'ly** *adv.* — **clear'ance** *n.*—**clear'ness** *n.* —**clear'ing** *n.* — **clear'ing-house** *n.* a place where cheques are exchanged.— **clear'ing-station** *n.* a place from which wounded are removed.—**clear-sight'ed** *a.* —**clear-starch'ing** *n.*

Syn. manifest, patent, unclouded. *Ant.* dim, dingy, obscure.

Cleat *n.* a piece of wood or iron with two projecting ends, round which ropes are made fast; a porcelain insulator.

Cleave *v.t.* to split asunder.— *v.i.* to crack, part asunder. — **cleav'age** *n.*— **cleav'er** *n.*

Cleek *n.* an iron hook; a golf-club with an iron head.

Clef *n.* a mark to show the pitch in music.

Cleft *n.* an opening made by cleaving; a crack, fissure.

Clem'atis *n.* a flowering, climbing perennial plant.

Clem'ent *a.* merciful; gentle; kind. — **clem'ently** *adv.* — **clem'ency** *n.*

Clench *v.t.* to make fast; set firmly together: grasp; drive home.

Clere'story (klērs-) *n.* an upper part of a church with a row of windows.

Cler'gy *n.* the appointed ministers of the Christian church. —**cler'gyman** *n.*

Cler'ic *a.* belonging to the clergy.—*n.* a clergyman.— **cler'ical** *a.*—**cler'icalism** *n.*

Clerk (-ark) *n.* a clergyman or priest; one who leads the responses in church; an officer in charge of records, correspondence, etc., of a department or corporation; a subordinate in an office.— **clerk'ly** *a.*—**clerk'ship** *n.*

Clev'er *a.* able, skilful, adroit. —**clev'erly** *adv.*—**clev'erness** *n.*

Syn. dexterous, talented, sharp, smart. *Ant.* stupid, dull, unintelligent, clumsy, awkward.

Clew *see* CLUE.

Cli'ché (clē-shā) *n.* a stereotyped hackneyed phrase.

Click n. a short, sharp sound, as of a latch in a door.—v.t. to make this sound.

Cli'ent n. a customer; one who employs a professional man.—cli'entele n. a body of clients.

Cliff n. a steep rock face.—cliff'y a.

Climacter'ic n. a critical period in human life.

Cli'mate n. the condition of a country with regard to weather.—climat'ic a.

Cli'max n. a highest point, culmination; arrangement of language to rise in dignity and force; the point of greatest excitement, tension, in a play, story, etc.

Climb (klīm) v.t. and i. to mount by clutching, grasping, pulling; to creep up, mount, ascend.—climb'er n.—climb'ing n.

Clime n. climate. q.v.

Clinch v. clench. q.v.

Cling v.i. to stick fast, attach; remain by.

Clin'ic a. relating to practical instruction in medicine in hospitals.—n. a place or meeting for medical examination or teaching (also clinique).—clin'ical a.—clin'ically adv.—a clinical thermometer is used for taking the temperature of patients.

Clink n. a sharp metallic sound.—v.t. and i. to make or cause to make such sound.

Clink'er n. hard slag.

Clip v.t. to grip, clutch, hug. —n. a device for gripping.

Clip v.t. to cut with scissors or shears; to cut short.—n.

the wool shorn at a place or in a season.—clipp'er n.

Clipp'er n. a fast sailing ship.

Clique (-ēk) n. a small exclusive set; a faction, gang.

Cloak n. a loose outer garment; a disguise, pretext. —v.t. to cover with a cloak; disguise, conceal. — cloak'room n. a place for keeping coats, hats, luggage, etc.

Clock n. an instrument for measuring time; an ornament on the side of a stocking.

Clod n. a lump of earth; a blockhead.

Clog n. an obstruction, impediment, a wooden-soled shoe.—v.t. to gather in a mass and cause stoppage; choke up.—clog'-dance n.

Clois'ter n. a covered arcade; a convent.—v.t. to confine in a cloister, or within walls. —clois'tral a.—clois'tered a.

Close (-s) a. shut up; confined; secret; unventilated, stifling; reticent; niggardly; compact; crowded; strict, searching.—adv. nearly, tightly.— n. a shut-in place; the precinct of a cathedral.—close'ly adv.—close'ness n.—close'corpora'tion n.—close'-fisted a.—close'-sea'son n.

Syn. retired, secret, secretive, cautious, taciturn, reticent, familiar. *Ant.* open, generous, indiscreet, distant, far.

Close (-z) v.t. to shut; stop up; finish.—v.i. to come together; grapple.—n. end.

Clos'et (-z-) n. a small private

room.—*v.t.* to shut up in a closet; conceal.

Clo'sure (-z-) *n.* the ending of a debate by vote or other authority.

Clot *n.* a mass or lump.—*v.t.* to form into lumps.

Cloth (-th) *n.* woven fabric.—clothes (-TH-) *n.pl.* dress; bed-coverings.—clo'thing *n.* —clothe *v.t.* to put clothes on.—clo'thier *n.*

Cloud *n.* vapour floating in the air; a state of gloom; a great number or mass.—*v.t.* to overshadow, dim, darken. —*v.i.* to become cloudy.—cloud'y *a.*—cloud'less *a.*

Clout *n.* a piece of cloth.—*v.t.* to patch.

Clove *n.* a dried flower-bud of an Eastern tree, used as a spice.

Clo'ver *n.* a forage plant, trefoil.

Clown *n.* a rustic; a jester.—clown'ish *a.*

Cloy *v.t.* to weary by sweetness, sameness, etc.

Club *n.* a thick stick; a bat; one of the suits at cards; an association for a common object.—*v.t.* to strike with a club; to put together.—*v.i.* to join for a common object.

Cluck *n.* the noise of a hen.—*v.i.* to make that noise

Clue, clew (-ōō) *n.* a ball of thread; a thread used as a guidance, trail; an indication, *esp.* of the solution of a mystery.

Clump *n.* a cluster of trees or plants; a compact mass.

Clum'sy (-z-) *a.* awkward, un-wieldy, badly made or arranged. — clums'ily *adv.*—clums'iness *n.*

Clus'ter *n.* a group, bunch.—*v.t.* and *i.* to gather or grow in a cluster.

Clutch *v.t.* to grasp eagerly, snatch — *v.i.* to make a snatch at.—*n.* a grasp, tight grip.

Coach *n.* a large four-wheeled carriage; a railway carriage; a tutor.—*v.i.* to ride in a coach.—*v.t.* to tutor.—coach'man *n.*

Coadju'tor *n.* an assistant; an associate destined to be a successor.

Coag'ulate *v.t.* and *i.* to curdle, form into a mass.—coagula'tion *n.*

Coal *n.* a glowing ember; a mineral consisting of carbonised vegetable matter, used as fuel.—*v.t.* to supply with coal.—*v.i.* to take in coal.

Coalesce' (-es) *v.i.* to unite. —coales'cence *n.*—coalition *n.* an alliance, *esp.* of parties.

Coarse *a.* rough, harsh; unrefined, indecent.—coarse'ly *adv.*—coarse'ness *n.* *Syn.* rude, gross, unpolished, indelicate. *Ant.* fine, refined, tasteful, dainty.

Coast *n.* sea-shore.—*v.i.* and *t.* to sail by the coast.—coast'er *n.*

Coat *n.* an outer garment; an animal's fur or feathers; a covering; a layer.—*v.t.* to clothe; cover with a layer.

Coax *v.t.* to wheedle, cajole. persuade.

Cob *n.* a short-legged stout horse; a lump.

Cob'ble *v.t.* to patch roughly, *esp.* to mend shoes.—**cob'bler** *n.*

Cob'ble *n.* a round stone. [dim. of *cob.*]

Cob'web *n.* a spider's web.

Cocaine' *n.* an alkaloid drug used as an anæsthetic.

Coch'ineal *n.* a scarlet dye got from a Mexican insect.

Cock *n.* a male bird; a tap for liquids; the hammer of a gun; its position drawn back; an upward turn.—*v.t.* to set or turn assertively; to draw back (gun hammer).—**cock-ade'** *n.* a knot of ribbon, a badge.

Cock *n.* a conical heap, *esp.* of hay.—*v.t.* to put up in heaps.

Cockatoo' *n.* a crested parrot.

Cock'boat *n.* a small ship's boat.

Cock'chafer *n.* a humming beetle.

Cock'ie *n.* in Australia, a small farmer.

Coc'kle *n.* a shell-fish.

Cock'ney (-ni) *n.* a native of London.

Cock'roach *n.* a blackbeetle.

Co'co *n.* a tropical palm.—**co'conut, cok'ernut, co'coa-nut** *n.* a very large, hard nut from the coco.

Co'coa *n.* a powder made from the seed of the cacao, a tropical tree; a drink made from the powder.

Cocoon' *n.* the sheath of an insect in the chrysalis stage.

Cod *n.* a large sea fish.

Cod'dle *v.t.* to nurse exces-sively, take too great care of.

Code *n.* a collection of laws; a system of signals.—**cod'ify** *v.t.*—**codifica'tion** *n.*

Co'dex (-deks) *n. pl.* **codices** a manuscript volume.

Cod'icil *n.* an addition to a will.

Co-educa'tion *n.* education of boys and girls together.

Coeffi'cient *n.* a joint agent or factor.

Coerce' *v.t.* to force.—**coer'cive** *a.*—**coer'cion** *n.*

Coe'val *a.* equally old; lasting to the same time.

Coexist' *v.i.* to exist together — **coexis'tent** *a.* — **coexis'-tence** *n.*

Coff'ee *n.* the seeds of a shrub originally from Arabia; a drink made from these seeds.

Coff'er *n.* a chest for valuables.

Coff'in *n.* a box for a dead body.—*v.t.* to put into a coffin.

Cog *n.* one of a series of teeth on a wheel.

Co'gent *a.* forcible, convin-cing.—**co'gently** *adv.* — **co'-gency** *n.*

Cog'itate (koj-) *v.i.* to think, reflect.—*v.t.* to plan.—**cogi-ta'tion** *n.*

Cog'nate *a.* of the same stock, elated.

Cogni'tion *n.* perception; act or faculty of knowing.

Cog'nisance, cog'nizance (*or* kon-) *n.* knowledge, aware-ness, observation.—**cog'nis-able** (*or* kon-) *a.*—**cog'nisant** (*or* kon-) *a.*

Cogno'men *n.* a surname.

Cohab'it *v.i.* to live together as husband and wife.

Cohere' *v.i.* to stick together; to be consistent.—**cohe'rent** *a.* sticking together, making sense.—**cohe'rence** *n.*—**cohe'rently** *adv.*—**cohe'sion** *n.*

Syn. to coalesce, amalgamate, adhere, cleave. *Ant.* disintegrate, dis-unite, separate.

Co'hort *n.* a troop; a tenth of a legion.

Coil *v.t.* to lay in rings; to twist into a winding shape; in motoring and aviation, a device to transform low tension current to higher voltage.—*v.i.* to twist, take up a winding shape; a series of rings.

Coin *n.* a piece of money; money.—*v.t.* to make into money, stamp; to invent.—**coin'age** *n.*

Coincide' (kō-in-) *v.i.* to happen together; to agree exactly.—**coin'cident** *a.*—**coin'cidence** *n.*

Coke *n.* the residue left from the distillation of coal.

Col'ander *n.* a sieve.

Cold *a.* lacking heat; indifferent, apathetic; dispiritin .—*n.* lack of heat; an illness, marked by running at the nose, etc.—**cold'ly** *adv.*—**cold'ness** *n.*

Col'ic *n.* severe pains in the intestines.

Collab'orate *v.i.* to work with another, *esp* in literature.—**collab'orator** *n.*—**collabora'tion** *n.*

Collapse' *v.i.* to fall together, give way; lose strength, fail.

—*n.* the act of collapsing.—**collaps'ible** *a.*

Coll'ar *n.* a band worn round the neck.—*v.t.* to seize, capture.

Collate' *v.t.* to compare carefully; to appoint to a benefice.—**colla'tion** *n.*

Collat'eral *a.* accompanying; subordinate; of the same stock but a different line.—*n.* a kinsman.

Coll'eague *n.* an associate, companion in an office, employment.

Collect' *v.t.* to gather, bring together.—*v.i.* to come together.—**collect'ed** *a.* gathered; calm.—**collect'ive** *a.*—**collect'ively** *adv.*—**collect'ivism** *n.* the theory that the State should own all means of production.—**collec'tion** *n.*—**collec'tor** *n.*—**coll'ect** *n.* a short prayer.

Syn. to muster, assemble, aggregate, amass. *Ant.* scatter, distribute, separate, spread.

Collége *n.* a society of scholars; a place of higher education; an association.—**colle'giate** *a.* — **colle'gian.** *n.*

Coll'et *n.* a collar; the rim in which a jewel is set.

Collide *v.i.* to strike or dash together; come into conflict.—**colli'sion** *n.*

Coll'ier *n.* a coal-miner; a coal-ship.—**coll'iery** *n.* a coal mine.

Coll'oquy *n.* a conversation.—**collo'quial** *a.* conversational, informal.—**collo'quialism** *n.*

Collu'sion *n.* arrangement,

action in secret with another. —collu′sive a.

Co′lon n. a mark (:) indicating a break in a sentence.

Colonel (kur′nel) n. the commander of a regiment, the highest regimental officer.— colonelcy (kūr-) n.

Colonnade′ n. a row of columns.

Col′ony n. a body of people who settle in a new country; the country so settled.— colo′nial a.—col′onist n.— col′onise v.t.—colonisa′tion n.

Coloss′us n. a huge statue; a very big man.—coloss′al a. huge.

Col′our (kul′ẹr) n. hue, tint; complexion; paint or anything giving colour; pl. flags. —v.t. to stain, dye, paint, give colour to; disguise; misrepresent.—v.i. to become coloured; blush.

Colt n. the young of the horse.

Col′umn n. a long vertical cylinder, a pillar; a division of a page; a body of troops; anything like these.—colum′- nar a.

Co′ma n. stupor, unnatural sleep.—co′matose a.

Comb (kōm) n. a toothed instrument for arranging hair, or ornamenting it; a cock's crest; a mass of honey-cells. —v.t. to apply a comb to.

Com′bat v.t. to fight.—n. a fight.—com′batant n.—com′- bative a.

Combine′ v.t. and i. to join together; ally.—combina′- tion n.—com′bine n.

Syn. to agree, unite, connect, coalesce, confederate.

Ant. separate, disagree, sunder, withdraw.

Combus′tion n. burning.— combus′tible a.—combustibil′ity n.

Come (kum) v.i. to approach, arrive, move towards; reach; happen (to); originate (from); get to be, become; turn out to be.

Com′edy n. drama dealing with the lighter side of life, ending happily, or treating its subject humorously; a play of this kind.—come′dian n. a player in comedy.

Come′ly (kum′-) a. fair, pretty; seemly.—come′liness n.

Com′et n. a heavenly body like a star or planet with a tail of light.—com′etary a.

Com′fit (kum-) n. a sweetmeat.

Com′fort (kum-) v.t. to console, cheer, gladden.—n. consolation; well-being, ease; a means of consolation, ease, or satisfaction.—com′fortable a.—com′fortably adv.—com′- forter n.

Com′ic a. relating to comedy; funny, laughable.—com′ical a.—com′ically adv.

Com′ity n. courtesy, friendliness.

Comm′a n. a mark (,) separating short parts of a sentence.

Command′ v.t. to order; rule; compel; have in one's power; overlook, dominate.—v.i. to exercise rule.—n. an order; rule; power of controlling, ruling, dominating, overlooking; the post of one commanding; his district.— command′er n.—command-

ant′ n.—command′ment n.
—commandeer′ v.t. to seize
for military service.

Comman′do (-dō) n. a military expedition undertaken
by private persons.

Commem′orate v.t. to celebrate, keep in memory by
ceremony. — commem′orative a.—commemora′tion n.

Commence′ v.t. and i. to begin.
—commence′ment n.

Commend′ v.t. to praise; to
commit, entrust. — commend′able a.—commend′ably
adv.—commenda′tion n. —
commen′datory a.

Commen′sal n. an animal or
plant that lives as a tenant
of another.

Commen′surate a. in proportion, adequate; equal in size
or length of time.

Comm′ent v.i. to make remarks, notes, criticisms.—
n. a note, collection of notes,
explanation, remark, criticism.—comm′entator n.

Comm′erce n. buying and selling; dealings, intercourse.—
commer′cial a.

Commina′tion n. threatening
with divine wrath.

Commis′erate (-z-) v.t. to pity,
condole with.—commisera′tion n.

Comm′issar (-sar) n. one of
the heads of a Soviet government department.

Commissar′iat n. the military
department in charge of
supplies and transport.

Commis′sion n. a doing, committing; something entrusted to be done; payment by
a percentage for doing something; delegated authority;
a warrant, esp. a royal warrant, giving authority; a
body entrusted with some
special duty.—v.t. to give an
order for; to authorise, give
power to.

Commissionaire′ n. a messenger, doorkeeper (usually uniformed).

Commit′ v.t. to entrust, give
in charge; to perpetrate, be
guilty of; to compromise,
entangle.—commit′ment n.
—committ′al n.
  Syn. to consign, confide,
perform, do, post. Ant. redeem, ransom, release, omit.

Committ′ee n. a body appointed or elected for some
special business, usually from
som larger body.

Commode′ n. a chest of drawers; a stool containing a
chamber-pot.—commo′dious
a. roomy, convenient. —
commo′diously adv.—commod′ity n. an article of trade,
anything meeting a need.

Comm′odore n. a naval officer,
a senior captain; the president of a yacht club.

Comm′on a. shared by or belonging to all, or to several;
public, general; ordinary,
usual, frequent; inferior,
vulgar.—n. land belonging
to a community, unenclosed
land not belonging to a
private owner; pl. ordinary
people; the lower House of
Parliament; rations, food
provided daily.—comm′only
adv.—comm′onalty n. the
general body of people.—
comm′oner n. — comm′on-

wealth *n.* a state.—**comm'on- place** *n.* anything ordinary, trivial.

Commo'tion *n.* stir, disturbance, tumult.

Commune' *v.i.* to have intimate intercourse.—**commu'nicate** *v.t.* to impart, give a share.—*v.i.* to give or exchange information; to receive Communion.—**commu'nicant** *n.* one who receives Communion. — **commu'nicable** *a.*—**communica'tion** *n.* act of giving, *esp.* information; information, letter, message; passage (road, railway etc.), or means of exchanging messages (telegraph, post, etc.) between places; connection between military base and front.—**commu'nicative** *a.* free with information.—**commu'nion** *n.* fellowship; a body with a common faith; sharing.—**Commu'nion** *n.* participation in the sacrament of the Lord's Supper; that sacrament, Eucharist.

Commu'nity *n.* a state; a body of people with something in common, e.g. district of residence, religion, etc.; joint ownership.—**community singing**, conducted but unpractised singing by large crowds. —**comm'unism** *n.* the doctrine that all goods, means of production, etc., should be the property of the community.—**comm'unist** *n.*

Commute' *v.t.* to exchange; to change (a punishment, etc.) into something less; to change (a duty, etc.) for a moneypayment.—**commuta'tion** *n.*

Com'pact *n.* an agreement, covenant.

Compact' *a.* neatly arranged or packed; solid, concentrated; terse. — **compact'ly** *adv.*—**compact'ness** *n.*

Compa'ges *n.* a system or structure of many united parts.

Compan'ion *n.* a mate, fellow, comrade, associate.—**compan'ionable** *a.*—**compan'ionship** *n.*

Compan'ion *n.* a raised cover over a staircase from the deck to the cabin of a ship; a deck skylight.

Com'pany *n.* a gathering of persons; guests; an association for business; a troop under a captain.

Compare' *v.t.* to notice or point out the likenesses and differences of anything; to liken or contrast; to make the comparative and superlative of an adjective or adverb.—*v.i.* to be like; to compete with.—**com'parable** *a.*—**compar'ative** *a.* that may be compared; not absolute; relative, partial.—**compar'atively** *adv.*—**compar'ison** *n.*

Compart'ment *n.* a division or part divided off, a section.

Com'pass (kum-) *n.* an instrument for showing the north; an instrument for describing circles (usually in *pl.*); a circumference, measurement round; space, area, scope, reach.—*v.t.* to contrive; surround; attain.

Compas'sion (-shn) *n.* pity,

sympathy. — compas'sionate a.—compas'sionately adv.

Compat'ible a. consistent, a-greeing with.—compat'ibly adv.—compatibil'ity n.

Compat'riot n. a fellow-countryman.

Compel' v.t. to force, oblige, bring about by force.—compul'sion n.—compul'sory a.

Compen'dium n. an abridgement or summary.—compen'dious a. brief but inclusive. —compen'diously adv.

Com'pensate v.t. to make up for.—compensa'tion n.

Compete' v.i. to strive, vie (with). — competi'tion n.—compet'itive a.—compet'itor n.

Com'petent a. able, skilful; properly qualified; proper, due, legitimate, suitable, sufficient.—com'petently adv. —com'petence, com'petency n.

Compile' v.t. to make up (e.g. a book) from various sources or materials; to put together.—compi'ler n.—compila'tion n.

Compla'cent a. self-satisfied. —compla'cently adv.—compla'cence, compla'cency n.—com'plaisant (-liz-) a. obliging, willing to please.—com'plaisance (-liz-) n.

Complain' v.t. to grumble; bring a charge, make known a grievance; (with of) to make known that one is suffering from.—complaint' n. a statement of a wrong, a grievance; an illness.—complain'ant n.

Syn.—to murmur, regret, repine, bewail, deplore. Ant. to endure, tolerate, overlook, rejoice, be glad for.

Com'plaisance see COMPLACENT.

Complete' a. full, finished, ended, perfect.—v.t. to finish; make whole, full, perfect.—complete'ly adv.—complete'ness n.—comple'tion n.—com'plement n. something making up a whole; a full allowance, equipment, etc.—complemen'tary a.

Syn. entire, whole, total, absolute, integral. Ant. incomplete, imperfect, defective, faulty.

Compesce' (-pes) v.t. to hold in check; to restrain.

Com'plex a. intricate, compound, involved.—n. a psychological abnormality, an obsession.—complex'ity n.

Complex'ion (-ek'shn) n. look, colour, esp. of the skin.

compli'ant see COMPLY.

Com'plicate v.t. to make intricate, involved, difficult.—complica'tion n.

Compli'city n. partnership in wrong-doing.

Com'pliment n. a remark neatly expressing praise; in pl. expression of courtesy, formal greetings.—v.t. to praise, congratulate.—complimen'tary a.

Comply' v.i. to consent, yield, do as asked.—compli'ant a. —compli'ance n.

Compo'nent n. a part element.—a. composing, making up.

Compose' v.t. to make up; write, invent; arrange, put in order; settle, adjust;

calm. —compos d' *a.* calm.—
compo'ser *n.*—com'posite *a.*
compound, not simple.—
composi'tion *n.*—compo'sure
n. calmness.—compos'itor *n.*
a type-setter, one who arranges type for printing.

Syn. to confirm, form,
fashion, tranquillise, soothe.
Ant. unsettle, disarrange,
irritate, excite.

Compound' *v.t.* to mix, make
up, put together; to com-
promise, make a settlement
of debt by partial payment;
to condone.—*v.i.* to come to
an arrangement, make terms.
—com'pound *a.* not simple;
composite, mixed.—*n.* a mixture, joining; a substance,
word, etc., made up of
parts.

Com'pound *n.* in the East, an
enclosure containing houses.

Comprehend' *v.t.* to understand, take in; to include,
comprise.—comprehen'sion *n.*
—comprehen'sive *a.*—com-
prehen'sively *adv.*—comprehen'siveness *n.*—comprehen'-
sible *a.*

Compress' *v.t.* to squeeze
together; to make smaller
in size, bulk.—com'press *n.*
a pad of wet lint, etc., applied
to a wound, inflamed part,
etc.—compres'sion (-shn) *n.*
—compress'ible *a.*

Comprise' *v.t.* to include, contain.

Com'promise (-iz) *n.* a meeting
half-way, a coming to terms
by giving up part of a claim.
—*v.t.* to expose to risk or
suspicion.—*v.i.* to come to
terms.

Comptroll'er (kon-trō'-) *n.* con-
troller (in some titles).

Compul'sion *n.* act of com-
pelling; an irresistible impulse.—compulsory *a.*—compulsorily *adv.*

Compunc'tion *n.* regret for
wrong-doing.

Compute' *v.t.* to reckon, estimate.—computa'tion *n.*

Com'rade (kom'rid *or* kum'rid)
n. a mate, companion, friend.
—com'radeship *n.*

Con *v.t.* to learn, pore over.

Con *v.t.* to direct the steering
of a ship.—conn'ing-tower *n.*

Concat'enate *v.t.* to link together.

Con'cave *a.* hollow, rounded
inwards.—concav'ity *n.*

Conceal' *v.t.* to hide, keep
secret.—conceal'ment *n.*

Concede' *v.t.* to admit, grant;
yield.—conces'sion (-shn) *n.*
—conces'sive *a.*

Con'cept *n.* an abstract notion.

Conceit' (-sēt) *n.* vanity, over-
weening opinion of oneself;
a far-fetched comparison.—
conceit'ed *a.*

Conceive' (-sēv) *v.t.* to become
pregnant with; to take into
the mind, think of, imagine;
understand.—conceiv'able *a.*
—conceiv'ably *adv.*—con'cept
n. an idea, notion.

Con'centrate *v.t.* to reduce to
small space; increase in
strength; gather to one
point.—*v.i.* to come to-
gether; devote all attention.
—concentra'tion *n.*—concen'-
tric *a.* having a common
sense.

Concern' *v.t.* to be the business
of.—*v.i. in passive,* to be in-

terested, affected, troubled, involved.—*n.* affair, importance, business, establishment. —**concern'ing** *prep.* respecting.

Concert' *v.t.* to arrange, plan together.—**concert'** *n.* a musical entertainment; harmony, agreement. — **concert'ed** *a.* mutually arranged. — **concert'o** (-chẹr-) *n.* a musical composition for solo instrument and orchestra.—**concerti'na** (-tĕ-) *n.* a musical instrument with bellows and keys.

Conces'sion *see* CONCEDE.

Conchol'ogy (-sh-) *n.* the science of shells and shell-fish.

Concil'iate *v.t.* to pacify, gain friendship.—**concilia'tion** *n.* —**concil'iatory** *a.*

Concise' *a.* brief, in few words. —**concise'ly** *adv.*—**concise'ness** *n.*—**conci'sion** (-sizn) *n.* *Syn.* succinct, condensed, comprehensive, short. *Ant.* wordy, discursive, longwinded, diffuse, verbose.

Con'clave *n.* a private meeting; the assembly for the election of a Pope.

Conclude' (-ōōd) *v.t.* to end, finish; settle.—*v.i.* to come to an end; infer, deduce; decide.—**conclu'sion** (-ōō'zhn) *n.*—**conclu'sive** *a.* decisive, convincing. — **conclu'sively** *adv.*

Concoct' *v.t.* to make a mixture, prepare with various ingredients; make up.—**concoc'tion** *n.*

Concom'itant *a.* accompanying.

Conc'ord *n.* agreement.—**concord'ance** *n.* agreement; an index to the words of a book. —**concord'ant** *a.*

Conc'ourse *n.* a crowd; a flocking together.

Conc'rete *a.* solid; consisting of matter, facts, practice, etc.; not abstract.—*n.* a mixture of sand, cement, etc., used in building.—**concrete'ly** *adv.*

Conc'ubine *n.* a woman living with a man as his wife, but not married to him.—**concu'binage** *n.*

Concu'piscence *n.* lust.

Concur' *v.i.* to agree, express agreement; happen together. —**concur'rence** *n.*—**concur'rent** *a.*—**concur'rently** *adv.* *Syn.* to assent, co-operate, coincide, combine, conspire. *Ant.* disagree, dissent, oppose.

Concus'sion (-shn) *n.* violent shock; injury by blow, fall, etc.

Condemn' *v.t.* to blame; find guilty; doom; find unfit for use.—**condemna'tory** *a.*—**condemna'tion** *n.*

Condense' *v.t.* to concentrate, make more solid; turn from gas into liquid; pack into few words.—*v.i.* to turn from gas to liquid.—**condensa'tion** *n.*—**condenser** *n.* in electricity an arrangement for storing electrical energy. —**condenser microphone** *n.* a microphone consisting of two plates of a condenser.

Condescend' *v.i.* to stoop, deign; to be gracious; to patronise.—**condescen'sion** *n.*

Condign' (-ĭn) *a.* adequate, sufficient; deserved.

Con'diment n. relish, seasoning.

Condi'tion n. a thing on which a statement or happening or existing depends; a stipulation; state or circumstances of anything.—v.t. to be essential to the happening or existence of; stipulate.—**condi'tional** a.

Condole' v.i. to grieve with, offer sympathy.—**condo'lence** n.

Condomin'ium n. joint rule.

Condone' v.t. overlook, forgive, treat as not existing.

Conduce' v.i. to help, to promote.

Conduct' v.t. to lead, direct, manage.—**con'duct** n. behaviour; management.—**conduc'tor** n.—**conduc'tion** n.—**conduc'tive** a.—**conductiv'ity** n.

Con'duit (-dit) n. a channel or pipe for water.

Cone n. a solid figure with a circular base and tapering to a point; the fruit of the pine, fir, etc.—**con'ic, con'ical** a.—**co'nifer** n. a tree bearing cones.—**conif'erous** a.

Confec'tion n. prepared delicacy, sweetmeat; made-up millinery, etc.—**confec'tioner** n. a dealer in cake, pastry, sweets, etc.—**confec'tionery** n.

Confed'erate n. an ally; accomplice.—v.t. and i. to unite.—**confed'eracy** n.—**confedera'tion** n.

Confer' v.t. to grant, give.—v.i. to talk with, take advice.—**confer'ment** n.—**con'ference** n.

Confess' v.t. to admit, own, acknowledge, declare; (of a priest) to hear the sins of.—v.i. to acknowledge; to declare one's sins orally to a priest.—**confes'sion** n.—**confes'sional** n. a confessor's stall or box. **confes'sor** n. a priest who hears confessions; a person who keeps his faith under persecution but without martyrdom; one who confesses.

Confet'ti n. small bits of paper for throwing at carnivals and weddings.

Confide' v.i. to trust (in).—v.t. to entrust.—**confidant'** n. one entrusted with secrets.—**con'fidence** n. trust; boldness, assurance; intimacy.—**con'fident** a.—**con'fidently** adv.

Configura'tion n. shape, aspect.

Confine' v.t. to shut up, imprison; keep within bounds; keep in house, bed.—**con'fines** n.pl. boundaries.—**confine'ment** n.

Syn. to enclose, limit, bound, environ, circumscribe, restrain. Ant. extend, diffuse, liberate, release, unloose.

Confirm' v.t. to make strong, settle; make valid, ratify; make sure, verify; administer confirmation to.—**confirma'tion** n. a making strong, valid, certain, etc.; a rite administered by a bishop to confirm baptized persons in the vows made for them at baptism.—**confirm'ative, confirm'atory** a.

Confis'cate v.t. to seize by

authority.—confisca'tion *n.* —con'fiscatory *a.*

Con'fiture *n.* a sweetmeat; a confection.

Conflagra'tion *n.* a great fire.

Con'flict *n.* a struggle, trial of strength; variance.—conflict' *v.t.* to be at odds with, inconsistent with; clash.

Con'fluence *n.* a union of streams; a meeting place.—con'fluent *a.*

Conform' *v.t.* and *i.* to comply, adapt to rule, pattern, custom, etc.—conform'able *a.*—conform'ably *adv.*—conforma'tion *n.* structure; adaptation.—conform'ity *n.*

Confound' *v.t.* to baffle, bring to confusion, defeat; mix up.

Confront' (-unt) *v.t.* to face; bring face to face with.—confronta'tion *n.*

Confuse' *v.t.* to disorder; mix mentally.—confu'sion *n.* *Syn.* to confuse, baffle, perplex, disconcert, astonish. *Ant.* help, clear, enlighten.

Confute' *v.t.* prove wrong.—confuta'tion *n.*

Congeal' (-j-) *v.t.* and *i.* to solidify by freezing or otherwise.—congela'tion *n.*

Con'gener (-j-) *n.* a thing or person of the same kind.

Conge'nial (-jĕ-) *a.* suitable, to one's liking; of kindred disposition.—conge'nially *adv.*—congenial'ity *n.*

Congen'ital (-je-) *a.* born with one, dating from birth.

Cong'er (kong'-ger) *n.* a large sea eel.

Conge'ries *n.* a collection or mass.

Conges'tion (-jes'chn) *n.* abnormal accumulation of blood, population, etc.; overcrowding.—conges'ted *a.*

Conglom'erate *a.* gathered into a mass.—*v.t.* to gather into a round body.—*n.* puddingstone.

Congrat'ulate (-n-g-) *v.t.* to felicitate, offer expression of pleasure at another's good fortune, success, etc.—congratula'tion *n.*—congrat'ulatory *a.*

Con'gregate (-ng-g-) *v.i.* to flock together; assemble.—congrega'tion *n.* an assembly, *esp.* for religious worship.—congrega'tional *a.* relating to a congregation or Congregationalism.— Congrega'tionalism *n.* a system in which each separate church is self-governing.—Congrega'tionalist *n.*

Cong'ress (-ng-g-) *n.* a meeting; a formal assembly for discussion; a legislative body.—congres'sional *a.*

Cong'ruent (-ng-groo-) *a.* fitting together; suitable, accordant.—cong'ruence *n.*—cong'ruous *a.*—congru'ity *n.*

Con'ic, co'nifer *see* CONE.

Conjec'ture *n.* a guess.—*v.t.* and *i.* to guess.—conjec'tural *a.*

Con'jugal *a.* relating to marriage; between married persons.—conjugal'ity *n.*

Con'jugate *v.t.* to inflect a verb in its various forms (past, present, etc.).—conjuga'tion *n.*

Conjunc'tion *n.* a part of speech joining words, phrases, etc.; a union; simultaneous happening.—conjunc'tive *a.* —conjunc'ture *n.*

Conjure' (-oor) *v.t.* to implore solemnly.—con'jure (kun'jer) *v.t.* and *i.* to produce magic effects by secret natural means; to invoke devils.—conjura'tion *n.* — con'jurer, con'juror *n.*

Connect' *v.t.* and *i.* to join together, unite; associate in the mind.—connec'tion, con-ne'xion *n.*—connec'tive *a.*

Conn'ing-tower *n. see* CON.

Connive' *v.i.* to wink at, to refrain from preventing, or forbidding, an offence.—con-ni'vance *n.*

Connoisseur' (kon-a-sur') *n.* a critical expert in matters of taste.

Connote' *v.t.* to imply, mean in addition to the chief mean-ing.—connota'tion *n.*

Connu'bial *a.* connected with marriage.

Conq'uer (-ker) *v.t.* to win by war; overcome, defeat.—*v.i.* to be victorious.—conq'ueror (-ke-) *n.*—conq'uest *n.*

Consanguin'ity *n.* kinship.—consanguin'eous *a.*

Con'science (-shens) *n.* mental sense of right and wrong.—conscien'tious *a.*—conscien'-tiously *adv.*

Con'scious (-shus) *a.* aware, awake to one's surroundings and identity, in one's senses.—con'sciously *adv.*—con'-sciousness *n.*

Con'script *n.* one compulsorily enlisted for military service.—conscrip'tion *n.*

Con'secrate *v.t.* to make sacred.—consecra'tion *n.*

Consec'utive *a.* orderly; in un-broken succession; express-ing consequence.—consec'u-tively *adv.*

Consent' *v.i.* to agree to, comply.—*n.* agreement, ac-quiescence.

    Syn. accord, assent, con-currence, permission. *Ant.* dissent, dissention, discord, dispute, refusal.

Con'sequence *n.* result, effect, what follows on a cause.—con'sequent *a.*—consequen'-tial *a.* self-important.—con'-sequently *adv.*

Conservatoire' *n.* a school for teaching music.

Conserve' *v.t.* to keep from change or decay.—conserva'-tion *n.*—conserv'ative *a.* and *n.*—conserv'atism *n.*—con-serv'atory *n.* a greenhouse.

Con'shy *n.* a conscientious objector.

Consid'er *v.t.* to think over; examine; make allowance for; esteem; be of opinion that.—considera'tion *n.*—consid'erable *a.* important; somewhat large.—consid'er-ably *adv.*—consid'erate *a.* thoughtful for others; care-ful.—consid'erately *adv.*

Consign' (in) *v.t.* to commit or hand over to; entrust to a carrier.—consign'or *n.*—con-signee' *n.*—consign'ment *n.*

Consist' *v.i.* to be composed of; to agree with, be com-patible.—consist'ent *a.* agree-ing (with); constant.—con-sist'ently *adv.*—consist'ency *n.*—consist'ence *n.* degree of density.—con'sistory *n.* an ecclesiastical court or council, *esp.* of the Pope and Cardinals.

Console' *v.t.* to comfort in distress.—consola'tion *n.*—consol'atory *a.*

Consol'idate *v.t.* to make firm; to combine into a connected whole.—consolida'tion *n.*—con'sols *n.* short for Consolidated Annuities, i.e. British Government securities.

Con'sols *n.pl.* funded stocks of the British National Debt.

Con'sonant *n.* a sound making a syllable only with a vowel, a non-vowel.—*a.* agreeing with, in accord.—con'sonance *n.*

Con'sort *n.* a ship sailing with another; a husband or wife, *esp.* of a queen or king.—consort' *v.i.* to associate, keep company with.

Conspic'uous *a.* striking to the eye, very noticeable; eminent.—conspic'uously *adv.*

Conspire' *v.i.* to combine for an evil purpose, to plot.—conspir'ator *n.*—conspir'acy *n.*—conspirator'ial *a.*

Con'stable (kun'-) *n.* a policeman; an officer of the peace; the governor of a royal fortress.—constab'ulary *n.* a police force.—special constable *n.* a person sworn in as a constable on emergency.

Con'stant *a.* fixed, unchanging; steadfast; always duly happening or continuing.—con'stantly *adv.*—con'stancy *n.*

Syn. invariable, unshaken, permanent, resolute. *Ant.* inconstant, changing, fickle, impermanent.

Constella'tion *n.* a group of stars.

Consterna'tion *n.* a terrifying sense of disaster.

Constipa'tion *n.* difficulty in emptying the bowels.—con'-stipate *v.t.* to affect with this disorder.

Con'stitute *v.t.* to set up, establish, make into, found, give form to.—constitu'tion *n.* make, composition; health; character; disposition; the body of principles on which a state is governed.—constitu'tional *a.* relating to a constitution; in harmony with a political constitution. constitu'tionally *adv.*—constit'uent *a.* going towards making up a whole; electing a representative.—*n.* a component part; an elector.—constit'uency *n.* a body of electors, a parliamentary division.

Constrain' *v.t.* to force, compel.—constraint' *n.* compulsion, restraint.

Constric'tion *n.* compression, squeezing together.—constrict' *v.t.*—constrict'ive *a.*

Construct' *v.t.* to make, build, form, put together.—construc'tion *n.*—construc'tive *a.* —construc'tively *adv.*—construe' *v.t.* to interpret, analyse grammatically.

Con'sul *n.* a state agent residing in a foreign town; in ancient Rome, one of the chief magistrates.—con'sular *a.*—con'sulate *n.*—con'sulship *n.*

Consult' *v.t.* and *i.* to seek counsel, advice, information (from).—consulta'tion *n.*

Māte, mēte, mīte, mōte, mūte, bōōt.

Consume' *v.t.* make away with; use up; eat or drink up; destroy. — **consump'tion** *n.* using up; destruction; wasting of the body by phthisis. —**consump'tive** *a.*

Con'summate *v.t.* to complete, finish.—**consumm'ate** *a.* of the greatest perfection or completeness. — **consumm'ately** *adv.*—**consumma'tion** *n.*

Con'tact *n.* a touching; a being in touch.—**conta'gion** (-jn) *n.* passing on of disease by touch, contact; physical or moral pestilence.—**conta'gious** *a.*

Contain' *v.t.* to hold; have room for; include; restrain (oneself).—**contain'er** *n.*

Contam'inate *v.t.* to stain, sully, infect.—**contamina'tion** *n.*

Contang'o *n.* the charge made by a stockbroker for carrying over a bargain to the next settling day.

Contemn' *v.t.* to scorn, despise.—**contempt'** *n.* scorn; disgrace.—**contemp'tible** *a.* —**contemp'tibly** *adv.*—**contemp'tuous** *a.*—**contemp'tuously** *adv.*

Syn. to disdain, spurn, slight, underrate, neglect. *Ant.* to esteem, respect, admire.

Con'template *v.t.* to gaze upon; meditate on; intend, purpose. — **contempla'tion** *n.*—**contem'plative** *a.*

Contem'porary *a.* existing at, or lasting, the same time; of the same age.—*n.* one existing at the same time as another.— **contempora'neous** *a.*—**contempora'neously** *adv.*

Contend' *v.i.* to strive, fight, dispute.—**conten'tion** *n.* — **conten'tious** *a.*—**conten'tiously** *adv.*

Content' *a.* satisfied.—*v.t.* to satisfy.—*n.* satisfaction.— **con'tent** *n.* holding capacity; *pl.* that contained.—**content'ment** *n.*

Contest' *v.t.* to dispute, debate, fight for.—**con'test** *n.* debate; conflict, strife; competition. —**contes'tant** *n.*—**contes'table** *a.*

Con'text *n.* what comes before and after a passage, words, *esp.* as fixing meaning.

Contig'uous *a.* touching, neighbouring.—**contigu'ity** *n.*

Con'tinent *a.* self-restraining; sexually chaste.—**con'tinence** *n.*

Con'tinent *n.* a large continuous mass of land, one of the main divisions of the earth.—**continen'tal** *a.*

Contin'gent (-j-) *a.* uncertain; depending for occurrence (on); accidental.—*n.* a quota of troops supplied by an ally, an organisation, etc.—**contin'gently** *adv.*—**contin'gency** *n.*

Contin'ue *v.t.* and *i.* to go on, carry on, last, remain, keep in existence prolong, resume. —**contin'ual** *a.*—**contin'nally** *adv.*—**contin'nance** *n.*—**continua'tion** *n.*—**continu'ity** *n.* — **contin'uous** *a.*—**contin'uously** *adv.*

Syn. to stay, remain, abide, extend, protract, endure, persist. *Ant.* to cease, desist, half, stop, pass, vanish, suspend.

Contort' v.t. to twist out of normal shape.—**contor'tion** n.

Con'tour (-oor) n. outline or shape of anything, esp. mountains, coast, etc.—**contour** (line) n. a line on a map showing uniform elevation.

Con'traband n. forbidden traffic; smuggling; smuggled goods.—**con'trabandist** n.

Con'tract n. a bargain, agreement; formal writing recording an agreement; an agreement enforceable by law.—**contract'** v.i. to enter into an agreement; to become smaller; to agree upon; to incur, become involved in; to make smaller; shorten.—**contrac'tile** a.—**contrac'tion** n.—**contrac'tor** n. one making a contract, esp. a builder working to a contract.

Contradict' v.t. to deny; be at variance with. — **contradic'tory** a.—**contradic'tion** n.

Contral'to n. the voice, or part, next above alto; a singer of that voice.

Con'trary a. opposed; the opposite, other.—n. something the exact opposite of another.—adv. in opposition.—**con'trarily** adv.—**contrari'ety** n.—**con'trariwise** adv.

Contrast' (-à-) v.t. to bring out differences; set in opposition for comparison. — v.i. to show great difference.—**con'trast** n. a striking difference; something showing a marked difference; placing, comparison, to bring out differences.

Contravene' v.t. to transgress, infringe; conflict with, contradict.—**contraven'tion** n.

Contrib'ute v.t. to give or pay to a common fund; help to a common result.—v.i. to give or pay or help in a common fund or effort.—**contribu'tion** n.—**contri utor** n.—**contrib'utory** a.—**contrib'utive** a.

Con'trite a. sorrowing for wrong-doing.—**contri'tion** n.—**con'tritely** adv.

Contrive' v.t. to devise, invent, design; succeed in bringing about.—**contri'ver** n.—**contri'vance** n.

Control' (-ōl) v.t. to command, dominate; regulate; direct; check, test.—n. domination; restraint; direction; check.—**controll'able** a.—**controll'er** n.—**control room** n. room in a wireless broadcasting station in which microphone currents are controlled before being passed to the transmitter.—**control-surface** n. rudder or stabiliser in an aeroplane.—**control-wire** n. any wire from a movable part of an aeroplane to the cockpit.

Con'troversy n. dispute, debate, esp. a dispute in the press and of some duration.—**controvert'** v.t.—**controver'sial** a.—**controver'sialist** n.—**controvert'ible** a.

Con'tumacy (-tū-) n. stubborn disobedience. — **contuma'cious** a.

Con'tumely (-e-li) n. insulting language or treatment; disgrace.—**contume'lious** a.

Syn. scorn, contempt, disrespect. *Ant.* deference, esteem, respect, regard.

Contuse' (-ūz) *v.t.* to bruise.—**contu'sion** *n.*

Conun'drum *n.* a riddle, *esp.* one with a punning answer.

Convales'cent *a.* recovering from illness.—*n.* a person recovering from sickness.—**convales'cence** *n.*

Convec'tion *n.* act of transmission, *esp.* of heat, by means of currents in liquids or gases.

Convene' *v.t.* to call together.—**conven'tion** *n.* a calling together; an assembly; a treaty, agreement; a rule or practice based on agreement; an accepted usage, *esp.* one grown quite formal, deadening.—**conven'tional** *a.*—**conven'tionally** *adv.*—**conventional'ity** *n.*—**con'vent** *n.* a community of monks or nuns; their building.—**conven'tual** *a.*—**conven'ticle** *n.* a meeting-house, *esp.* of dissenters when dissent was illegal.

Conve'nient *a.* handy; favourable to needs, comfort; well-adapted to one's purpose.—**conve'niently** *adv.*—**conve'nience** *n.*

Converge' *v.i.* to approach, tend to meet.—**conver'gent** *a.*—**conver'gence** *n.*

Converse' *v.i.* to talk (with).—**con'verse** *n.* talk.—**conversa'tion** *n.*—**conversa'tional** *a.*—**con'versant** *a.* familiar with, versed in.

Con'verse *a.* opposite, turned round.—*n.* the opposite, a statement with the terms of another interchanged or turned round.

Convert' *v.t.* to apply to another purpose; to change, transform; to cause to adopt a religion, an opinion.—**con'vert** *n.* a converted person.—**convert'ible** *a. Syn.* to change, turn, alter, appropriate, transform, transmute. *Ant.* to maintain, keep, perpetuate.

Con'vex *a.* curved outwards like any part of the surface of an egg; opposite of concave.—**convex'ity** *n.*

Convey' *v.t.* to carry, transport; impart, communicate; make over, transfer.—**convey'ance** *n.*—**convey'ancer** *n.* one skilled in legal forms of transferring property.—**convey'ancing** *n.*

Convict' *v.t.* to prove or declare guilty.—**con'vict** *n.* a criminal undergoing penal servitude.—**convic'tion** *n.* a convicting, verdict of guilty; a being convinced, firm belief, state of being sure.—**convince'** *v.t.* to bring to a belief, satisfy by evidence or argument.

Conviv'ial *a.* festive, jovial.—**convivial'ity** *n. Syn.* gay, mirthful, merry. *Ant.* sad, mournful, gloomy.

Convoke' *v.t.* to call together.—**convoca'tion** *n.* a calling together; an assembly, *esp.* an assembly of clergy, university graduates, etc.

Convolu'tion *n.* state of being coiled; a turn of a coil or spiral.—**convolu'ted** *a.* spiral, rolled.—**convol'vulus** *n.* a genus of plants with twining stems, *esp.* bindweed.

Convoy' *v.t.* to escort for protection, as ships, war supplies, etc.—**con'voy** *n.* a party (of ships, troops, etc.) convoying or convoyed.

Convulse' *v.t.* to shake violently; affect with violent involuntary contractions of the muscles.—**convuls'ive** *a.* —**convuls'ively** *adv.* — **convul'sion** *n.*

Co'ny, co'ney *n.* a rock-badger; rabbit.

Coo *n.* the cry of doves.—*v.i.* to make such cry.

Coo'ee *n.* cry used at long-distance by Australians.—*v.i.* to make this cry.

Cook *n.* one wh prepares food for the table.—*v.i.* to act as cook; to ndergo cooking.—*v.t.* to prepare (food) for the table, *esp.* by heat; *slang* to falsify accounts, etc.—**cook'ery** *n.*—**cook'er** *n.*

Cool *a.* moderately cold; unexcited, calm; lacking friendliness or interest.—*v.t.* and *i.* to make or become cool.—*n.* cool time, place, etc.—**cool'ness** *n.*—**cool'er** *n.*

Cool'ie *n.* a native labourer in India or China.

Coom *n.* refuse matter, as that in the boxes of carriage-wheels; coal-dust.

Coomb *n.* a dry measure of four bushels; a small wooded valley.

Coop *n.* a cage or pen for fowls. —*v.t.* to shut up in a coop; to confine.—**coop'er** *n.* one who makes casks.—**coop'erage** *n.*

Co-op'erate *v.i.* to work together. — **co-opera'tion** *n.* working together; production or distribution by co-operators who share the profits.—**co-op'erative** *a.*—**co-op'erator** *n.*

Co-opt' *v.t.* to bring on (a committee, etc.) as a member, colleague, without election by the larger body choosing the first members.

Co-ord'inate *a.* equal in degree, status, etc.—*v.t.* to place in the same rank; to bring into order as parts of a whole.—*n.* a co-ordinate thing.—**co-ordina'tion** *n.*

Coot *n.* a small black water-fowl of the genus Fulica.

Cope *n.* an ecclesiastical vestment like a long cloak.—*v.t.* to cover the top of a wall.—**co'ping** *n.* the top course of a wall, usually sloping to throw off rain.

Cope' *v.i.* to contend, deal with.

Co'per *n.* a dealer (chiefly in *horse-coper*).

Co'pious *a* plentiful, full, abundant.—**co'piously** *adv.*—**co'piousness** *n.* *Syn.* ample, plenteous full, diffuse. *Ant.* insufficient, scarce, rare, niggardly.

Copp'er *n.* a reddish malleable ductile metal; bronze money, a bronze coin; a large vessel for boiling clothes.—*v.t.* to cover with copper.—**copp'erplate** *n.* a plate or copper for engraving or etching; a print from such plate; copybook writing.—**copp'ersmith** *n.* one who works in copper.

Copp'ice, copse n. a small wood of small trees grown for periodical cutting.

Cop'ra n. dried coconut kernels.

Cop'ula n. a word acting as a connecting link in a sentence; a connection.—**cop'ulate** v.i. to unite sexually.—**copula'tion** n.—**cop'ulative** a.

Cop'y n. an imitation; a single specimen of a book; a piece of writing for a learner to imitate; matter for printing.—v.t. to make a copy of, to imitate.—**cop'yhold** n. a form of land-tenure with *copy* of the manor court-roll as title.—**cop'yright** n. legal exclusive right to print and publish a book, article, work of art, etc.—a. protected by copyright.—v.t. to protect by copyright.—**cop'yist** n.

Coquette' (-ket) n. a woman who plays with men's affections.—**coquett'ish** a.—**coquet'** v.i.—**co'quetry** n.

Cor'acle n. a boat of wicker covered with skins.

Cor'al n. a hard substance made by sea polyps and forming pink or red or white growths, islands, reefs; an ornament or toy of coral.—**cor'alline** a.

Corb'el n. a stone or timber projection from a wall to support something.

Cord n. thin rope or thick string; a rib on cloth, a ribbed fabric; a measure of cut wood, usually 128 cub. ft.—v.t. to fasten or bind with cord.—**cord'age** n.—**cord'uroy** n. a ribbed cotton stuff.

Cord'ial a. hearty, sincere, warm.—n. a stimulating medicine or drink.—**cord'ially** adv.—**cordial'ity** n.

Cord'on n. a chain of troops or police; an ornamental cord; a fruit-tree grown as a single stem.

Cor'duroy (-doo-) n. a thick cotton stuff, corded or ribbed on the surface.

Core n. the horny seed-case of the apple and other fruits; central or innermost part of anything.

Co-respon'dent n. a person proceeded against together with the respondent in a divorce suit.

Corin'thian (-th-) a. of Corinth; of the Corinthian order of architecture, ornate Greek.—n. a native of Corinth; a man of fashion.

Cork n. the bark of the cork-oak; a piece of it, *esp.* a round piece used as a stopper.—v.t. to stop up with a cork; to stop up generally.—**cork'y** a. light, buoyant.—**cork'screw** n. a tool for pulling out corks.—**cork'age** n. a charge for opening bottles.

Cor'morant n. a large and voracious sea-bird.

Corn n. grain, fruit of cereals; a grain.—v.t. to preserve (meat) with salt.—**corn'crake** n. a bird, the landrail.—**corn'flower** n. a blue flower growing in cornfields.

Corn n. a horny growth on foot or toe.

Corn'ea n. the horny membrane covering the front of the eye.

Corn'er n. the part of a room where two sides meet; a remote or humble place; the point where two walls, streets, etc., meet; an angle, projection; a buying up of the whole existing stock of a commodity.—v.t. to drive into a position of difficulty, or leaving no escape; to establish a monopoly.

Corn'et n. a trumpet with valves.

Corn'ice n. a projecting source near the top of a wall; an ornamental moulding.

Cornuco'pia n. a symbol of plenty, consisting of a goat's horn overflowing with fruit and flowers.

Coroll'a n. a flower's inner envelope of petals.

Coroll'ary n. a proposition that follows without proof from another proved; a natural consequence.

Coro'na n. the flat projecting part of a cornice; a halo around a heavenly body; in wireless, blue luminous discharge from transmitting aerial working at high voltage.

Corona'tion n. the ceremony of crowning a sovereign.

Cor'oner n. an officer who holds inquests on bodies of persons supposed killed by violence, accident, etc.—cor'onership n.

Cor'onet n. a small crown.

Corp'oral n. a non-commissioned officer below a sergeant.

Corp'oral a. of the body. Syn. corporeal, physical, bodily.

Ant. incorporeal, spiritual, ghostly, immaterial, mental.

Corpora'tion n. a body of persons legally authorised to act as an individual; authorities of a town or city.—corp'orate a.

Corpor'eal a. of the body, material.

Corps (kor) n. a military force, body of troops.—**Corpse** n. dead body of man.

Corp'ulent a. bulky of body, fat.—corp'ulence n.

Corp'uscle (-usl) n. a minute organism or particle, esp. the red and white corpuscles of the blood.

Correct' v.t. to set right; rebuke, punish; counteract, neutralise.—a. right, exact, accurate, in accordance with facts or a standard.—correct'ly adv.—correc'tion n.—correc'tive n. and a.—correct'ness n. Syn. amend, rectify, reform, chastise, reprove, discipline. Ant. falsify, distort, impair.

Cor'relate v.t. to bring into mutua relation.—n. either of two things or words necessarily implying the other.—correla'tion n.

Correspond' v.i. to exchange letters; to answer or agree with in some respect.—correspond'ence n.—correspon'dent n.

Cor'ridor n. a passage in a building, railway-train, etc.

Corrigen'dum n. a thing to be corrected.—pl. corrigen'da.

Corrob'orate v.t. to confirm, support (a statement, etc.).—

corrobora'tion n.—corrob'or-ative a.

Corrode' v.t. to eat away, eat into the surface of (by chemical action, disease, etc.).—corro'sive a.—corro'sion n.

Cor'rugated a. wrinkled, bent into ridges.—corruga'tion n.

Corrupt' v.t. to make rotten; pervert, make evil; bribe.—v.i. to rot.—a. tainted with vice or sin; influenced by bribery; spoilt, by mistakes, altered for the worse (of words, literary passages etc.).—corrupt'ly adv.—corrupt'-ible a.—corruptibil'ity n.—corrup'tion n. Syn. to defile, pollute, debase, vitiate, pervert, contaminate, deprave, rot, spoil. Ant. purify, cleanse, refine.

Cors'air n. a pirate.

Corse n. poet. corpse.

Cors'et n. a stiffened inner bodice; stays.

Cors'let n. a piece of armour to cover the trunk.

Cortège (tazh) n. a train of attendants; a procession.

Cor'uscate v.i. to sparkle.—corusca'tion n.

Coseis'mal, coseis'mic (kō-sīz'-) a. experiencing an earthquake shock simultaneously at all points.

Cosmet'ic n. a preparation to beautify the skin.

Cos'mic (koz'-) a. relating to the universe; of the vastness of the universe.—cosmog'-ony n. a theory of the universe and its creation.—cosmol'ogy n. the science or study of the universe.—cosmolo'gical a.—cosmol'ogist n.

—cosmog'raphy n. the description or mapping of the universe.—cosmog'rapher n.—cosmograph'ic a.—cosmopol'itan a. relating to all parts of the world; having the world as one's country; free from national prejudice.—n. a cosmopolitan person.—cosmopol'itanism n.—cosmop'-olite n.—cos'mos n. the universe; ordered system, as opposed to chaos.

Coss'et v.t. to pamper, pet.

Cost v.t. to entail the payment, or loss, or sacrifice of; have as price.—n. price; expenditure of time, labour, etc.—pl. expenses of a lawsuit.—cost'ing n. the system of calculating cost of production.—cost'ly a. of great price or value; involving much expenditure, loss, etc.—cost'liness n.

Cos'tard n. a large ribbed apple.

Cos'ter, cos'termonger n. one who sells fruit, fish, etc., in the street from a barrow.

Cos'tive a. constipated.

Cos'tume n. style of dress; outer clothes; set of outer clothes for a woman; theatrical clothes.—costu'mier n.

Co'sy (-z-) a. snug, comfortable, sheltered.—n. a covering to keep a teapot hot.—co'sily adv.

Cot n. a small house.—cott'ar n.

Cot n. a child's bed; a swinging bed on board ship; a light or folding bed.

Cote n. a shelter for animals.

Co'terie n. a set or circle of persons; a clique.

Cotill'ion, cotill'on (-lyon) n. a dance.

Cott'age n. a small house.—**cott'ager** n.

Cott'on n. a plant; the white downy fibrous covering of its seeds; thread or cloth made of this fibre.

Cotyle'don n. primary leaf of plant embryos.

Couch v.t. to put into (words); to lower (a lance) for action; to cause to lie down.—v.i. to lie down, crouch.—n. a piece of furniture for reclining on by day, a sofa; a bed, or what serves for one.

Cough (kof) v.i. to expel air from the lungs with sudden effort and noise, often to remove an obstruction.—n. an act of coughing; an ailment or affection of coughing.

Couloir' (kōōl-wor') n. a dredging machine; a deep gorge.

Coun'cil n. any deliberative or administrative body; one of its meetings.—**coun'cillor** n.

Coun'sel n. deliberation or debate; advice; intentions; a barrister or barristers.—v.t. to advise, recommend.—**coun'sellor** n.

Count v.t. to reckon, calculate, number; to include; to consider to be.—v.i. to be reckoned in; to depend or rely (on); to be of importance.—n. a reckoning; an item in a list of charges or indictment; an act of counting.—**count'less** a.—**count'ing-house** n. a room or building for book-keeping.

Count n. a foreign nobleman of rank corresponding to British earl.—**count'ess** n. fem. the wife or widow of a count or earl.

Count'enance n. the face; its expression; support, patronage.—v.t. to give support. Syn. to sanction, approve, encourage. Ant. to discountenance, disapprove, discourage.

Count'er n. the table of a bank, shop, etc., on which money is paid, etc.; a disc or other object used for counting, esp. in card games; a token.

Count'er n. the curved part of the stern of a ship.

Count'er adv. in the opposite direction; contrary.—v.t. to oppose, contradict.

Count'er n. fencing, etc., a parry.—v.t. and i. to parry.

Counter- prefix used to make compounds with meaning of reversed, opposite, rival, retaliatory. — **counteract'** v.t. neutralise or hinder.—**counterac'tion** n.—**count'er-attack** v.t. and i. and n. attack after an enemy's advance.—**count'erattrac'tion** n. — **counterbal'ance** n. a weight balancing or neutralising another.—**count'erblast** n. energetic declaration in answer.—**count'erclaim** n.—**count'erclock wise** adv. and a.—**count'er-irr'itant** n.—**count'ermarch** v.i.—**count'ermine** v.i.—**count'erplot** n.—**count'er-reforma'tion** n.—**count'er-revolut'ion** n., etc. etc.

Māte, mēte, mīte, mōte, mūte, bōōt.

Count′erfeit (fēt) *a.* sham, forged, false.—*n.* an imitation, forgery.—*v.t.* to imitate with intent to deceive; forge. —**count′erfeiter** *n.* *Syn.* of *a.*, false, imitated, sham, hypocritical. *Ant.* true, genuine, original, sincere.

Count′erfoil *n.* part of a cheque, receipt, etc., kept as a record. *see* FOIL.

Countermand *v.t.* to cancel (an rder).

Count′erpane *n.* a coverlet or quilt or a bed.

Count′erpart *n.* something so like another as to be mistaken for it; something complementary or correlative of another.

Count′erpoint *n.* melody added as accompaniment to a given melody; the art of so adding melodies.

Count′ersign (-sīn) *n.* a signal or password used in answer to another.—*v.t.* to sign a document already signed by another, to ratify.

Count′ess *n.* *see* COUNT.

Coun′try (kun′-) *n.* a region, district; the territory of a nation; land of birth, residence, etc.; rural districts as opposed to town; a nation. —**coun′tryside** *n.* any rural district or its inhabitants.— **coun′trified** *a.* rural in manner or appearance.

Coun′ty *n.* a division of a country or state.

Coup (kōō) *n.* a successful stroke.

Coupé (koo-) *n.* two-seater motor - car with enclosed body.

Coup′le (kup′l) *n.* two, a pair; a leash for two hounds.—*v.t.* to tie (hounds) together; to connect, fasten together; to associate, connect in the mind.—*v.i.* to join, associate. —**coup′ler** *n.*—**coup′ling** *n.*— **coup′let** *n.* a pair of lines of verse, *esp.* rhyming and of equal length.

Cou′pon (kōō-) *n.* a detachable ticket entitling the holder to something, e.g. to a periodical payment of interest, to entrance to a competition, etc.

Cou′rage (ku-) *n.* bravery, boldness.—**coura′geous** (kurā′jus) *a.*—**coura′geously** *adv.* *Syn.* daring, hardihood, intrepidity;—of "courageous," valiant, intrepid, valorous. *Ant.* cowardice, timidity;— of *a.*, cowardly, timid, fainthearted, craven.

Cou′rier (koo-) *n.* an express messenger; an attendant on travellers.

Course (kors) *n.* movement or run in space or time; direction of movement; successive development, sequence; line of conduct or action; series of lectures, exercises, etc.; any of the successive parts of a dinner; a continuous line of masonry at a level in a building a match between greyhounds pursuing a hare.—*v.t.* to hunt. *v.i.* to run swiftly, gallop about.—**cours′er** *n.* a swift horse.

Court (kort) *n.* a space enclosed by buildings, a yard; a number of houses enclosing a yard opening on to a street;

a section of a museum, etc.; an area marked off or enclosed for playing various games; the retinue and establishment of a sovereign; an assembly held by a sovereign; a body with judicial powers, the place where they sit, one of their sittings; attention, homage, flattery.—*v.t.* to seek; woo, try to win or attract.—**cour'teous** (kur-) *a.* polite.—**cour'teously** *adv.*—**cour'tier** *n.* one who frequents a royal court.—**court'ly** *a.* ceremoniously polite; characteristic of a court. — **court'liness** *n.* — **court-mar'tial** *n.* a court of naval or military officers for trying naval or military offences.—**courts-mar'tial** *pl.*—**court'ship** *n.* wooing.—**court'yard** *n.* space enclosed by buildings. — **courtesan'** (kor-ti-zan') *n.* a prostitute, *esp.* highly-placed or refined.

Court'-card *n.* a king, queen, or knave at cards.

Cour'tesy (kur'-) *n.* politeness of manners; an act of civility.—courtesy title, a title to which one has no valid claim. *Syn.* urbanity, affability, courteousness. *Ant.* incivility, impoliteness, disrespect, rudeness.

Cous'in (kuz-) *n.* the son or daughter of an uncle or aunt; person related to another by descent from one ancestor through two of his or her children.

Cove *n.* a small inlet of coast, a sheltered small bay.

Cov'enant (ku-) *n.* a contract, a mutual agreement: a compact.—*v.t.* to agree to by a covenant.—*v.i.* to enter into a covenant.—**cov'enanter** *n.*

Cov'er (ku-) *v.t.* to be over the whole top of; enclose, include; shield; protect, screen; counterbalance. — *n.* lid, wrapper, envelope, binding, screen, anything which covers.—**cov'ert** *a.* secret, veiled.—*n.* a thicket, a place sheltering game.—**cov'ertly,** *adv. Syn.* to conceal, hide, cloak, veil. *Ant.* to strip, lay bare, expose, disclose, reveal.

Cov'erlet (ku-) *n.* the top covering of a bed.

Cov'et (ku-) *v.t.* to long to possess, *esp.* what belongs to another.—**co'vetous** *a.*—**co'vetousness** *n.*

Cov'ey (ku-) *n.* a brood of partridges or quail, *esp.* flying together.

Cov'in (kuv') *Law,* an arrangement between persons to prejudice another.

Cow *n.* female ox; female of elephant, whale, etc.—**cow'-pox** *n.* a disease of cows, the source of vaccine.

Cow *v.t.* to frighten into submission, overawe.

Cow'ard *n.* one given to fear or faint-hearted.—**cow'ardly** *a.*—**cow'ardice** *n. Syn.* of "cowardly," timorous, mean, pusillanimous, craven. *Ant.* courageous, valiant, bold, intrepid.

Cow'er *v.i.* to crouch, shrinking, in fear or cold.

Cowl *n.* a monk's hooded cloak; its hood; a hooded top for a chimney.

Cow'rie *n.* a small shell used as money in parts of Africa and Asia.

Cow'slip *n.* a species of primrose.

Cox'comb *n.* one given to showing off.

Cox'swain (kok'sn), **cox** *n.* the steersman of a boat, *esp.* one in permanent charge of a boat.—**cox** *v.t.* and *i.* to act as coxswain.

Coy *a.* shy; slow to respond, *esp.* to love-making.—**coy'ly** *adv.*—**coy'ness** *n.*

Coyo'te (-ō-ti) *n.* the N. American prairie-wolf.

Coz'en (ku-) *v.t.* to cheat.—**coz'enage** *n.*

Crab *n.* an eatable crustacean with ten legs, of which the front pair are armed with strong pincers, noted for sidelong and backward walk.—**crabb'ed** *a.* perverse; bad-tempered, irritable; of writing, hard to read.

Crab *n.* a wild apple of sour taste.

Crack *v.t.* to break, split partially; to break with sharp noise; to cause to make a sharp noise, as of whip, rifle, etc.—*v.i.* to make a sharp noise; to split, fissure; of the voice, to lose clearness when changing from boy's to man's.—*n.* a sharp explosive noise; a split, fissure; a flaw.—*a.* special, smart, of great reputation for skill or fashion.—**crack'er** *n.* an explosive firework: a thin dry biscuit.—**crac'kle** *n.* and *v.i.* sound of repeated small cracks, e.g. of distant rifle-fire, crumpled stiff paper, etc.—*v.i.* to make this sound.—**crack'ling** *n.* crackle; the crisp skin of roast pork.—**crack'nel** *n.* a crisp biscuit.

Cra'dle *n.* an infant's bed on rockers; *fig.* earliest resting-place or home; a supporting framework.—*v.t.* to lay in, or as in, a cradle; to cherish in early stages.

Craft *n.* skill, cunning; a manual art; a skilled trade; the members of a trade.—**crafts'man** *n.*—**crafts manship** *n.*—**craft'y** *a.* cunning.—**craf'tily** *adv.* *Syn* of "crafty," subtle, artful, deceitful, shrewd. *Ant* sincere, frank, honest, candid.

Craft *n.* a vessel of any kind for carriage by water or air; a ship; ships collectively.

Crag *n.* a steep rugged rock.—**cragg'y** *a.*—**crags'man** *n.* a rock-climber.

Cram *v.t.* to fill quite full; stuff, force; pack tightly; feed to excess; prepare quickly for examination.—*n.* a close-packed state; rapid preparation for examination; information so got.—**cramm'er** *n.*

Cramp' *n.* painful muscular contraction; a clamp for holding masonry, timber, etc., together.—*v.t.* to hem in, keep within too narrow limits.

Cran *n.* a measure of herrings, holding about 750 fish; hence a basket, *esp.* for fish and soft fruit.

Cran'berry *n.* the red berry of a dwarf shrub.

Crane n. a large wading bird with long legs, neck, and bill; a machine for moving heavy weights.—v.i. to stretch the neck for better seeing.

Cra'nium n. the skull.—**cra'nial** a.

Crank n an arm at right angles to an axis, for turning a main shaft, changing reciprocal into rotary motion, etc.; a fanciful turn of speech; a fad; a faddist.—v.t. and i. to turn, wind. — **crank'y** a. shaky; crotchety.

Crank a. of a ship, easily capsized; rickety, needing care.

Crann'y n. a small opening, a chink.—**crann'ied** a.

Crape n. gauzy wrinkled fabric, usually of black silk for mourning.

Crash n. a violent fall or impact with loud noise; a burst of mixed loud sound, e.g. of thunder, breaking crockery; sudden collapse or downfall. —v.i. to make a crash; fall, come with, strike with, a crash; to collapse; of an aeroplane, to come to earth by, or with, an accident.

Crash n. coarse linen for towels.

Crass a. grossly stupid; gross.

Crate' n. an open-work case of wooden bars or wicker.

Cra'ter n. the mouth of a volcano; a bowl-shaped cavity, esp. one made by the explosion of a large shell, a mine, etc.

Cravat' n. a neckcloth; a necktie.

Crave v.t. and i. to have a very strong desire for, long for; to ask.—**cra'ving** n.

Cra'ven a. cowardly, abject — n. a coward.

Crawl v.i. to move along the ground on the belly or on the hands and knees; to move very slowly; to move stealthily or abjectly; to swim with the crawl-stroke.—n. a crawling motion; a very slow walk; a racing stroke at swimming.—**crawl'er** n.

Cray'fish, craw'fish n. a crustacean like a small lobster.

Cray'on n. a stick or pencil of coloured chalk; a picture made with crayons.

Cra'zy a. rickety, falling to pieces; full of cracks; insane, extremely foolish; madly eager (for).—**craze** v.t. to make crazy.—n. ε general or individual mania.—**crazy pavement**, a path, usually a garden walk, surfaced with flat irregularly shaped slabs of stone.

Creak n. a harsh grating noise —v.i. to make a creak.

Cream n. the oily part of milk; the best part of anything.— v.i. to form cream.—v.t. to take cream from; to take the best part from.—**cream'y** a.—**cream'ery** n. a butter and cheese factory; a shop for milk and cream.

Crease (-s) n. a line made by folding; a wrinkle.—v.t. and i. to make, develop, creases.

Create' (krē-āt') v.t. to bring into being; give rise to; make.—**crea'tion** (-ē-ā-) n.— **crea'tive** (-ē-ā-) a.—**crea'tor** (-ē-ā) n.—**crea'ture** (krē'tyer) *n.* anything created a living being; a dependant, tool.

Crèche (krāsh) *n.* a public nursery for babies.

Cre'dence *n.* belief, credit; a side-table for the elements of the eucharist before consecration. — **creden'tials** *n.pl.* letters of introduction, *esp.* those given to an ambassador.

Cred'it *n.* belief, trust; good name; influence or honour or power based on the trust of others; trust in another's ability to pay; allowing customers to take goods for later payment; money at one's disposal in a bank, etc.; the side of a book on which such sums are entered.—*v.t.* to believe; to put on the credit side of an account; to attribute, believe that a person has.—**cred'itable** *a.* bringing honour. — **cred'itably** *adv.*—**cred'itor** *n.* one to whom a debt is due.

Creed *n.* a system of religious belief; a summary of Christian doctrine; a system of beliefs, opinions, principles, etc.

Creek *n.* a narrow inlet on the sea-coast.

Creel *n.* an osier basket; an angler's basket.

Creep *v.i.* to make way along the ground, as a snake; to move with stealthy, slow movements; to go about abjectly; of skin or flesh, to feel a shrinking, shivering sensation, due to fear, or repugnance.—**creep'er** *n.* a creeping or climbing plant.—

creep'y *a.* uncanny, unpleasant, causing the flesh to creep.

Crema'tion *n.* burning as a means of disposing of corpses; an act of this.—**cremate'** *v.t.*—**cremator'ium** *n.* a place for cremation.

Cremo'na (krē-) *n.* a superior kind of violin.

Cre'ole *n.* a native of the West Indies or Sp. America descended from European ancestors.

Cre'osote *n.* an oily antiseptic liquid distilled from coal-tar.—*v.t.* to coat or impregnate with creosote.

Crêpe (krāp) *n.* a fabric with a rough surface. — **crêpe-de-chine'** *n.* fine silk crape.— **crêpe rubb'er** *n.* rough-surfaced rubber for soles of shoes, etc.

Crep'itate *v.i.* to crackle.— **crepita'tion** *n.*

Crepus'cular *a.* pertaining to twilight

Crescen'do (-sh-) *a., adv.,* and *n.* increase of loudness.

Cres'cent *n.* the moon as seen on the first or last quarter; any figure of this shape; a row of houses on a curve.—*a.* growing, increasing.

Cress *n.* various plants with eatable pungent leaves.

Cress'et *n.* a fire-basket slung as a beacon.

Crest *n.* comb or tuft on an animal's head; plume or top of a helmet; top of mountain, ridge, wave, etc.; a badge above the shield of a coat of arms, also used separately on sea, plate, etc.—*v.t.*

to crown.—*v.t.* to reach the top of.—crest'fallen *a.* cast down by defeat or failure.

Creta'ceous (-shus) *a.* chalky.

Cret'in *n.* a deformed idiot.— cret'inism *n.*—cret'inous *a.*

Cretonne' *n.* unglazed cotton cloth printed in colours.

Crev'ice (-is) *n.* a cleft, fissure. —crevassé *n.* a deep open chasm in a glacier.

Crew (-ōō) *n.* a ship's or boat's company, excluding passengers; a gang or set.

Crib *n.* a barred rack for fodder; a child's bed with barred sides; the cards thrown out at cribbage; a plagiarism; a translation.— *v.t.* to confine in small space; to copy unfairly.—cribb'age *n.* a card game.

Crick *n.* a spasm or cramp, *esp.* in the neck.

Crick'et *n.* a chirping insect.

Crick'et *n.* an open-air game played with bats, ball, and wickets.—crick'eter *n.*

Crime *n.* a violation of the law (usually of a serious offence); a wicked or forbidden act; *military*, an offence against regulations.—*v.t.* to charge (in army) with an offence against the regulations.— crim'inal *a.* and *n.*—crim'inally *adv.*—criminal'ity *n.*— criminol'ogy *n.* study of crime and criminals.

Crimp *v.t.* to pinch with tiny parallel pleats.

Crimp *n.* an agent who procures men for service as sailors or soldiers by decoying or force.

Crim'son (-z-) *a.* of rich deep red.—*n.* the colour.—*v.t.* and *i.* to turn crimson.

Cringe *v.i.* to shrink, cower; behave obsequiously.

Crin'kle (kring'kl) *v.t.* to wrinkle, make a series of bends, windings or twists in a line or surface.—*v.i.* to wrinkle.—*n.* a wrinkle, winding.

Crin'oline (-lēn) *n.* a hooped petticoat.

Crip'ple *n.* one not having the normal use of the limbs, a disabled or deformed person. —*v.t.* to maim or disable; diminish the resources of.

Cri'sis *n.* turning point or decisive moment, *esp.* in illness; time of acute danger or suspense.

Crisp *a.* brittle but of firm consistence; brisk, decided; clear-cut; crackling; of hair, curly.

Crite'rion (kri-) *n.* a standard of judgment.

Crit'ical *a.* skilled in, or given to, judging; fault-finding; of great importance, decisive.— crit'ic *n.* one who passes judgment; a writer expert in judging works of literature, art, etc.—crit'icism *n.*—crit'ically *adv.*—crit'icise *v.t.*— critique' (-ēk) *n.* a critical essay, a carefully written criticism. *Syn.* exact, captious, censorious. *Ant.* vague, indefinite, loose, uncritical, laudatory.

Croak *v.i.* to utter a deep hoarse cry, as a raven, frog; to talk dismally.—*n.* such cry.—croak'er *n.*

Cro'chet (-shā) *n.* a kind of

knitting done with a hooked needle.—*v.t.* and *i.* to do such work.

Crock *n.* an earthenware jar or pot; a broken piece of earthenware; an old broken-down horse.—**crock'ery** *n.* earthenware.

Croc'odile (krok-) *n.* a large amphibious reptile.—**croc'-odile-tears**, hypocritical pretence of grief, the crocodile being fabled to shed tears while devouring human victims.

Cro'cus *n.* a small bulbous plant with yellow or purple flowers.

Croft *n.* a small piece of arable land; a small-holding, *esp.* in Scotland.—**crof'ter** *n.*

Crom'lech (-lek) *n.* a prehistoric structure of a flat stone resting on two upright ones.

Crone *n.* a withered old woman.

Cronk *a.* in Australia, of race-horses, ill, unfit to race; doped.

Cro'ny *n.* an intimate friend.

Crook *n.* a hooked staff; any hook, bend, sharp turn.—*v.t.* to bend into a hook or curve. —**crook'ed** *a.* bent, twisted; deformed; dishonest.

Croon *n.* a long continued murmuring.—*v.t.* and *i.* to sing softly.

Crop *n.* year's produce of cultivation of any plant or plants, in a farm, field, country, etc.; a harvest, *lit.* or *fig.*; a pouch in a bird's gullet; stock of a whip; a hunting whip; a cutting of the hair short, a closely-cut head of hair.—*v.t.* and *i.* to poll or clip; to bite or eat down; to raise produce or occupy land with it.—**crop'-eared** *a.* with clipped ears; with hair short to show the ears.—**cropp'er** *n.* a fall on the head; a heavy fall.

Cro'quet (-kā) *n.* a lawn game played with balls, mallets and hoops.

Croquette' (-ket') *n.* a fried ball of minced meat, fish, etc.

Cro'sier, cro'zier (-zhyer) *n.* a bishop's staff.

Cross *n.* a stake with a transverse bar, used for crucifixion.—**the Cross**, that on which Christ suffered; a model or picture of this; the symbol of the Christian faith; an affliction, misfortune, annoyance; any thing or mark in the shape of a cross; an intermixture of breeds, a hybrid.—*v.t.* to place so as to intersect; to make the sign of the cross on or over; to pass across, over; to meet and pass; to mark with lines across; to thwart; oppose; to modify breed of animals or plants by intermixture.— *v.i.* to intersect; pass over.— *a.* transverse; intersecting; contrary; adverse; out of temper. — **cross'ly** *adv.*— **cross'-bill** *n.* a bird whose mandibles cross when closed. —**cross'bow** *n.* a bow fixed across a wooden shoulder-stock.—**cross-exam'ine** *v.t.* to examine a witness already examined by the other side. —**cross'ing** *n.* an intersection of roads, rails, etc.; a part of street kept clean for foot passengers to cross.—**cross'-ing-sweeper** n. a person who cleaned a crossing in a street. —**cross'wise** adv — **cross'-word puzzle** n. a puzzle built up of intersecting words, of which some letters are common to two or more words, the words being indicated by clues.

Crotch'et n. a musical symbol; a fad.—**crotch'ety** a.

Crouch v.i. to bend low for hiding, or to spring, or servilely.

Croup (-ōō-) n. a throat-disease of children.

Croup (-ōō-) n. the hind-quarters of a horse.

Croup'ier (-ōō-) n. a raker-in of the money on a gaming-table; the vice-chairman of a dinner.

Crow (-ō) n. a large black carrion-eating bird.

Crow (-ō), **crow'bar** n. an iron bar, usually beaked at one end, for levering.

Crow (-ō) v.i. to utter the cock's cry; to utter joyful sounds; to exult.—n. the cry of the cock.

Crow v.t. in South Africa to dig holes in the ground with a sharp-pointed stick.

Crowd v.i. to flock together.—v.t. to cram, force, thrust, pack; fill with people.—**crowd out**, exclude by excess already in.—n. a throng, large number, mass.

Crown n. a monarch's head-dress; a wreath for the head; royal power; an English coin of five shillings; various foreign coins; the top of the head; a summit or topmost part; completion or perfection of anything.—v.t. to put a crown on.

Cru'cial (krōō'shl) a. decisive, critical.

Cru'cible n. a melting-pot.

Cru'cify v.t. to put to death on a cross.—**crucifix'ion** n.—**cru'cifix** n. an image of Christ on the cross.

Crude (-ōō-) a. in the natural or raw state; rough, unfinished, rude.—**crude'ly** adv.—**cru'dity** n.

Cru'el (-ōō-) a. delighting in or callous to others' pain; merciless.—**cru'elty** n.—**cru'elly** adv. Syn barbarous, severe, unmerciful. Ant. kind, gentle, merciful, humane.

Cru'et (-ōō-) n. a small stoppered bottle for vinegar, oil, etc.; a stand holding such bottles, mustard-pots, etc.

Cruise (-ōōz) v.i. to sail about without precise destination.—n. a cruising voyage.—**cruis'er** n. a warship of less weight and greater speed than a battleship.

Crumb (-m) n. a small particle, a fragment; the soft part of bread.—v.t. to reduce to, or cover with crumbs.

Crum'ble v.t. and i. to break into small fragments; decay. Syn. to crush, moulder, perish. Ant. to consolidate, flourish, endure.

Crum'pet n. a flat soft batter-cake, eaten with much butter.

Crum'ple v.t. and i. to make or become crushed, wrinkled, creased.—**crum'pled** a. crushed, creased; bent, curled.

Crunch *n.* sound made by chewing crisp food, treading on gravel, hard snow, etc.—*v.t.* and *i.* to chew, tread, etc., with this sound.

Crupp'er *n.* a strap holding back a saddle by passing round a horse's tail; a horse's croup.

Cru'ral *a.* belonging to the leg; shaped like a leg.

Crusade' *n.* a mediæval Christian war to recover the Holy Land; a campaign against an evil.—*v.i.* to engage in a crusade.—**crusa'der** *n.*

Cruse (-ööz) *n.* a small earthen pot.

Crush *v.t.* to compress so as to break, bruise, crumple; break to small pieces; defeat utterly, overthrow.—*n.* an act of crushing; a crowded mass of persons, etc.

Crust *n.* the hard outer part of bread; a similar hard outer casing on anything.—*v.t.* and *i.* to cover with or form a crust.—**crust'y** *a.* having or like a crust; short-tempered. —**crust'ily** *adv.*—**crusta'cean** (-shn) *n.* a hard-shelled animal, e.g. crab, lobster, shrimp.—**crusta'ceous** (-shus) *a.*

Crutch *n.* a staff with a crosspiece to go under the armpit for the use of cripples; a forked support.

Cry *v.i.* to utter a call; shout; weep, wail.—*v.t.* to utter oudly, pro'claim.—*n.* a loud utterance; a scream, wail, shout; the characteristic call of an animal; a watchword; a fit of weeping.

Crypt *n.* a vault, *esp.* under a church.—**cryp'tic** *a.* secret, mysterious.—**cryp'togram** *n.* a piece of cipher-writing.

Crys'tal *n.* a clear transparent mineral; very clear glass; cut-glass vessels; a form assumed by many substances with a definite internal structure and external shape of symmetrically arranged plane surfaces. — **crys'talline** *a.*— **crys'tallize** *v.t.* and *i.* to form into crystals; to become definite.—**crystallisa'tion** *n.*— **crystal detector**, in wireless, a crystal arranged in a circuit so that the current passes in one direction only through the telephones.

Cub *n.* the young of the fox and other animals.—**Wolf Cub**, a junior Boy Scout.— *v.t.* and *i.* to bring forth (cubs).

Cube (kū-) *n.* a regular solid figure contained by six equal squares; a cube-shaped block; the product obtained by multiplying a number by itself twice.—*v.t.* to multiply thus.—**cu'bic, cu'bical** *a.*— **cu'bism** *n.* a style of art in which objects are presented to give the appearance of an assemblage of geometrical shapes.—**cu'bist** *n.*

Cu'bicle (kū-) *n.* a small separate sleeping compartment in a dormitory.

Cu'bism *n.* modern movement in art. It lays much stress on the third dimension.—**cubist** *n.*

Cu'bit (kū-) an old measure of length, about 18 inches.

Cu'ckoo (koo'kōō) *n.* a migratory bird named from its call.

Cu'cumber (kū-) *n.* a creeping plant with long fleshy green fruit, usually eaten as salad; the fruit.

Cud *n.* the food which a ruminant animal brings back into its mouth to chew.

Cud'dle *v.t.* to hug.—*v.i.* to lie close and snug, to nestle.

Cud'dy *n.* the cabin of a half-decked boat.

Cud'gel *n.* a short thick stick. —*v.t.* to beat with a cudgel.

Cue (kū) *n.* a pigtail; the long tapering stick used by a billiard player.—**cue'ist** *n.*

Cue (kū) *n.* last words of an actor's speech as signal to another to act or speak; a hint or example for action.

Cuff *n.* the ending of a sleeve; a wrist-band.

Cuff *v.t.* to strike with the hand.—*n.* a blow with the hand.

Cuirass' (kwi-) *n.* metal or leather armour of breastplate and backplate.

Cul'inary *a.* of or for cooking.

Cull *v.t.* to gather, select.

Cul'minate *v.i.* to reach the highest point; come to a climax.—**culmina'tion** *n.*

Cul'pable *a.* blameworthy.—**culpabil'ity** *n.*—**cul'pably** *adv.* —**cul'prit** *n.* an offender, one guilty of an offence.

Cult *n.* a system of religious worship; a pursuit of, or devotion to, some object.

Cul'tivate *v.t.* to raise (crops) on land; to develop, improve, refine; devote attention to, practise, frequent.—**cultiva'-tion** *n.*—**cul'tivator** *n.*—**cul'ture** *n.* a cultivating; a state of manners, taste, and intellectual development at a time or place.—**cul'tured** *a.* refined, showing culture.—**cul'tural** *a.* *Syn.* of "cultivated," civilised, educated, refined. *Ant.* uncultivated, uncivilised, illiterate, vulgar.

Cul'vert *n.* a tunnelled drain for the passage of water, under a road, etc.

Cum'ber *v.t.* to block up, be in the way of, hamper.—**cum'bersome, cum'brous** *a.*

Cu'mulative (-iv) *a.* representing the sum of many items; of shares, entitled to arrears of interest before other shares receive current interest.—**cu'mulus** *n.* a cloud shaped in rounded white masses.—**cu'muli** *pl.*

Cune'iform (kū-nĕ'-ĭ-) *a.* wedge-shaped, *esp.* of ancient Persian and Assyrian writing.

Cunn'ing *n.* skill, dexterity; selfish cleverness; skill in deceit or evasion.—*a.* having such qualities, crafty, sly.—**cunn'ingly** *adv.* *Syn.* artful, wily, subtle, ingenious, clever. *Ant.* artless, frank, plain, sincere, candid.

Cup *n.* a small drinking vessel of china or earthenware with a handle at one side; any small drinking vessel; the contents of a cup; various cup-shaped formations, cavities, sockets, etc.; a prize in the shape of a cup of gold or other precious material; a portion or lot; an iced drink of wine and other ingredients.

—*v.t.* to bleed surgically.—
cup'ful *n.*—cup'board (kub'-erd) *n.* a closed cabinet, recess, or case with shelves, *esp.* one for crockery or provisions.

Cupid'ity (kū-) *n.* greed of gain.

Cu'pola (kū-) *n.* a dome.

Cu'preous (kū-), cu'pric, cu'prous *a.* of or containing copper.

Cur *n.* a worthless dog; a surly, ill-bred, or cowardly, selfish fellow.—curr'ish *a.*

Cur'ate (kūr'at) *n.* a clergyman who is a parish priest's appointed assistant.—cur'acy *n.*

Cur'ative (kū-) *a.* tending to cure disease.

Cura'tor *n.* person in charge of something, *esp.* a museum, library, etc.—cura'torship *n.*

Curb *n.* a chain or strap passing under a horse's lower jaw and giving powerful control with reins; any check or means of restraint; a stone edging to a footpath or sidewalk.—*v.t.* to apply a curb to (a horse); to restrain.—curb'stone *n.*

Curd *n.* coagulated milk.—curd'le *v.t.* and *i.* to turn into curd, coagulate; of blood, to shrink with horror, etc.—curd'y *a.*

Cure *v.t.* to heal, restore to health; to remedy; to preserve (fish, skins, etc.).—*n.* a remedy; course of medical treatment; successful treatment, restoration to health. —cure of souls, care of a parish or congregation.—cu'rable *a.*—curabil'ity *n.*—cu'rative *a.*

Curé (koo-rā) *n.* a parish priest in France; a clergyman.

Cur'few *n.* a ringing of a bell at a fixed evening hour, originally as a signal to put out fires, now, under martial law, to mark the time after which inhabitants may be out of doors.

Cu'rious (kū-) *a.* eager to know, inquisitive; prying; puzzling, strange, odd; minutely accurate.—cu'riously *adv.*—curios'ity *n.* eagerness to know; inquisitiveness; a strange or rare thing.—cu'rio *n.* a curiosity of the kind sought for collections.

Curl *v.t.* to bend into spiral or curved shape.—*v.i.* to take spiral or curved shape or path.—*n.* a spiral lock of hair; a spiral or curved state or form or motion —cur'ly *a.* —curl'ing *n.* a game like bowls played with large rounded stones on ice.

Curl'ew *n.* a long-billed wading bird.

Curmudg'eon (-jn) *n.* a miser or churlish fellow.

Curr'ach, curr'agh (kur'-aн) *n.* a coracle; a wicker boat covered with tarred canvas.

Curr'ant *n.* dried fruit of a Levantine grape; the fruit of various plants allied to the gooseberry; the plants.

Curr'ent *a.* in circulation or general use going on, not yet superseded; fluent, running.—*n.* a body of water or air in motion; the flow of a river, etc.; tendency, drift; transmission of electricity through a conductor.—curr'ently *adv.*—curr'ency *n.* time during which anything is current; money in use; state of being in use.—**curr'ency-note** *n.* a treasury note, a £1 or 10-shilling note.

Curric'ulum (ku-rik'-) *n.* a specified course of study.

Curr'y *v.t.* to rub down (a horse) with a comb; to dress (leather); curry fa'vour, orig. to *curry "favel," "the* fawn-coloured horse," a type of hypocrisy in an old allegory, hence to try to win favour unworthily, to ingratiate oneself.—**curr'ier** *n.* a leather dresser.

Curr'y *n.* a preparation of turmeric; a dish flavoured with it.—*v.t.* to prepare a dish with curry.

Curse *n.* an utterance intended to send a person or thing to destruction or punishment; an expletive in the form of a curse; an affliction, bane, scourge.—*v.t.* and *i.* to utter a curse, swear at, afflict.

Curs'ive *a.* written in running script.—**curs'ory** *a.* rapid, hasty, without attention to details.—**curs'orily** *adv.*

Curt *a.* short, brief; rudely brief.—**curt'ness** *n.*—**curt'ly** *adv.*—**curtail'** *v.t.* to cut short, diminish.—**curtail'ment** *n.*

Curt'ain (-tin) *n.* a cloth hung as a screen; screen separating audience and stage in a theatre; an end to an act or scene.—*v.t.* to provide or cover with a curtain.—**curt'ain-raiser** *n.* a short play coming before the main one. —**curt'ain-fire** *n.* a barrage.

Curt'ilage *n.* area of ground attached to a dwelling-house.

Curt'sy *n.* a woman's bow or respectful gesture made by bending the knees and lowering the body.

Curve *n.* a line of which no part is straight, a bent line.—*v.t.* to bend into a curve.—*v.i.* to have or assume a curved form or direction.—**curv'ature** *n.* a bending; a bent shape.—**curvet'** *n.* a horse's trained movement like a short leap over nothing.—*v.i.* to make this movement.—**curvilin'ear** *a.* of bent lines.

Cu'shion (koo'shn) *n.* a bag filled with soft stuffing or air, to support or ease the body; a pad; the elastic lining of the sides of a billiard-table. —*v.t.* to provide or protect with a cushion.

Cu'shy (koo'-) *a. slang*, soft, comfortable, pleasant, light, and well-paid.

Cus'tard *n.* a preparation of eggs and milk flavoured and cooked.

Cus'tody *n.* safe - keeping, guardianship, imprisonment. —**custo'dian** *n.* a keeper, caretaker, curator.

Cus'tom *n.* a fashion, usage, habit; business patronage; *pl.* duties levied on imports. —**cus'tomary** *a.*—**cus'tomarily** *adv.*—**cus'tomer** *n.* one who enters a shop to buy, *esp.* one who deals regularly with it. *Syn.* fashion, usage, manner, habit. *Ant.* desuetude, disuse.

Cut *v.t.* to sever or penetrate or wound or divide or separate with pressure of an edge or edged instrument; to pain or detach or trim or shape by cutting; to divide; intersect; reduce, abridge; to ignore (a person); to strike (with a whip, etc.); to hit a cricket ball to point's left.— *n.* an act of cutting; a stroke, blow (of knife, whip, etc.); a fashion, shape; an incision; an engraving; a piece cut off; a division.—to draw cuts, to draw lots.—cutt'er *n.* one who or that which cuts; a warship's rowing and sailing boat; a small sloop-rigged vessel with straight running bowsprit.—cutt'ing *n.* an act of cutting or a thing cut off or out; *esp.* an excavation (for a road, canal, etc.) through high ground; a piece cut from a newspaper, etc.— cut-in *n.* in motoring, to overtake a vehicle in face of an on-coming one.—cut-out *n.* a device by which part of an electric circuit may be shut off; in motoring, a device for allowing the exhaust gases to escape.

Cuta'neous (kū-) *a.* of the skin.—cu'ticle *n.* the outer skin.

Cut'lass *n.* a sailor's short broad-bladed sword.—cut'ler *n.* one who makes, repairs or deals in knives and cutting implements. — cut'lery *n.* knives, scissors, cutler's wares.

Cut'let *n.* a small piece of meat broiled or fried.

Cutt'er *see* CUT.

Cut'tle, cut'tle-fish *n.* a ten-armed sea mollusc which ejects an inky fluid when pursued.

Cy'cle (sī-) *n.* a recurrent series or period; rotation of events; complete series or period; development following a course of stages; a series of poems, etc.; a bicycle.—*v.i.* to move in cycles; to use a bicycle. — cy'clic, cy'clical *a.* — cy'clist *n.* a bicycle-rider. — cy'cle - car *n.* a small light motor - car.— cyclom'eter *n.* an instrument for measuring circles or recording distance travelled by a wheel, *esp.* of a bicycle.— cy'clone *n.* a system of winds moving round a centre of low pressure; a circular storm.— cyclon'ic *a.*—cy'clostyle *n.* a duplicating apparatus with stencil paper written on by a *style* ending in a minute toothed wheel.—*v.t.* to reproduce thus.

Cyclopæd'ia *see* ENCYCLOPEDIA

Cyg'net (sig'-) *n.* a young swan.

Cyl'inder (sil'-) *n.* a roller-shaped solid or hollow body, of uniform diameter; a piston-chamber of an engine. —cylin'drical *a.*

Cym'bal (sim'-) *n.* one of a pair of cymbals; *pl.* a musical instrument consisting of two round brass plates struck together to produce a ringing or clashing sound.

Cymom'eter *n.* an instrument for measuring the frequency of electric oscillations.

Cyn'ic (sin'-) *n.* one of a sect of Greek philosophers affecting contempt of luxury and bluntness of speech; a cynical person —**cyn′ical** a. sceptical of or sneering at goodness; given to showing up human weakness, seeing the more unworthy motive in others; shameless in showing or admitting motives more commonly concealed.—**cyn′icism** n.

Cyn′osure (sĭn′o-shoor) n. a centre of attraction.

Cy′pher see CIPHER.

Cy′press n. a coniferous tree with very dark foliage; its wood; its foliage as a symbol of mourning.

Cyst (si-) n. a bladder or sac containing liquid secretion or morbid matter or embryos.

Czar, Tzar, Tsar (zàr) n. emperor or king, esp. of Russia 1547-1917, or of Bulgaria in the Middle Ages and since 1908.—**Czarit′sa, Ts-, Tz-** n. fem. the wife of a Russian Czar. — **Tsar′evitch, Ce-** n. the heir apparent of a Russian Czar.

D

Dab v.t. to strike feebly; apply with momentary pressure, esp. anything wet and soft. —n. a slight blow or tap; a smear; a small flat roundish mass; a small flat fish.

Dab′ble v.i. to splash about; to be a desultory student or amateur (in).—**dab′bler** n.

Dab′chick n. a small diving bird.

Dace n. a freshwater fish.

Dachs′hund (daks′hoont) n. a short-legged long-bodied dog.

Dacoit′ n. a Burmese bandit. —**dacoit′y** n.

Da′do n. the lower part of a room wall when lined or painted separately.

Daff′odil n. a yellow narcissus.

Daft (-à-) a. foolish, crazy.

Dagg′er n. a short, edged, stabbing weapon.

Da′go n. a Spaniard, Portuguese, or other Latin.

Dague′rreotype (-gèro-) n. an early photographic process; a portrait by it.

Dahl′ia (dăl-) n. a garden plant.

Dail′y a. done, occurring, published, etc., every day.—adv. every day, constantly.—n. a daily newspaper.

Dain′ty a. choice, delicate; pretty and neat; hard to please, fastidious.—**dain′tily** adv.—**dain′tiness** n. Syn. delicious, nice, fastidious, scrupulous, affected. Ant. coarse, nasty, common, nauseous

Dair′y (dèr-) n. a place for dealing with milk and its products.—**dair′yman** n.—**dair′ymaid** n.—**dair′ying** n.

Dais (dās) n. a low platform, usually at one end of a hall.

Dais′y (-z-) n. a flower with yellow centre and white petals.

Dale n. a valley.—**dales′man** n. a hillsman of N. England.

Dall′y v.i. to spend time in idleness or amusement or love-making; loiter.—**dall′iance** n.

Dam n. a mother, usually of animals.

Dam n. a barri̇er to hold back a flow of waters.—v.i. to supply, or hold with a dam.

Dam'age n. injury, harm; pl. sum claimed or adjudged in compensation for harm or injury.—v.t. to do harm to, injure.

Dam'ask n. figured woven material of silk or linen, esp. white table linen with design shown up by the light; the colour of the damask-rose, a velvety red.—a. made of damask; coloured like damask-rose.—v.t. to weave with figured designs. — **damaskeen**, **damascene'** v.t. to decorate (steel, etc.) with inlaid gold or silver.

Dame n. a lady; a rank for a lady in the Order of the British Empire. — **dame'-school** n. an elementary school of the kind formerly kept as private ventures by old women.

Damn (-m) v.t. to condemn to hell; to be the ruin of; to give a hostile reception to.—v.i. to curse.—interj. an expression of annoyance, impatience, etc. — **dam'nable** a. deserving damnation, hateful, annoying.—**damna'tion** n.—**dam'natory** a.

Damp a. moist; slightly moist. —n. diffused moisture; in coal-mines, a dangerous gas. —v.t. to make damp; to deaden, discourage.—**damp'er** n. anything that discourages or depresses: a silencing-pad in a piano; a plate in a flue to control the draught.

Damping' n. in wireless, rate at which an electrical oscillation dies away.

Dam'sel (-z-) n. girl.

Dam'son (-z-) n. a small dark-purple plum; its tree; its colour.

Dance (-à-) v.i. to move with rhythmic steps, leaps, gestures, etc., usually to music; to be in lively movement; to bob up and down.—v.t. to perform (a dance); to cause to dance.—n. a rhythmical movement; an arrangement of such movements; a tune for them; a dancing-party. —**dan'cer** n. — **danseuse'** (dong-sez') n. a female dancer.

Dan'delion n. a yellow-flowered wild plant.

Dan'druff n. dead skin in small scales among the hair.

Dan'dy n. a man who pays excessive attention to dress and fashion, a fop.—**dan'dyism** n.

Dan'ger (dān-j-) n. liability or exposure to injury or harm; risk, peril.—**dan'gerous** a.—**dan'gerously** adv.

Dan'gle (dang'gl) v.t. and i. to hang loosely and swaying.

Dank a. oozy, unwholesomely damp.—**dan'ki** interj. in South Africa, an expression signifying refusal.

Dapp'er a. neat and precise, esp. in dress.

Dap'ple v.t. and i. to mark with rounded spots. — **dap'ple-grey'** a. grey marked with darker spots.

Dare (dèr) v.t. to venture, have the courage (to); defy.—**dar'ing** a. bold.—n. adventurous courage.—**dare'devil**

a. reckless.—*n.* reckless person.

Dark *a.* having little or no light; gloomy; deep in tint; dim, secret; unenlightened; wicked.—*n.* absence of light or colour or knowledge.—**dark'en** *v.t.* and *i.*—**dark'ly** *adv.*—**dark'ness** *n.*—**dark'ling** *a.* and *adv.* in the dark.—**dark'some** *a. Syn.* obscure, mysterious, hidden, ignorant, vile. *Ant.* clear, distinct, open, light.

Dar'ling *n.* one much loved or very lovable.—*a.* beloved or prized.

Darn *v.t.* to mend by filling (hole, etc.) with interwoven yarn.—*n.* a place so mended.—**darn'ing** *n.*

Dart *n.* a light javelin or other pointed missile; a darting motion.—*v.t.* to cast, throw rapidly (a dart, glance, etc.).—*v.i.* to go rapidly or abruptly, like a missile.

Das *n.* in South Africa, a badger.

Dash *v.t.* to smash, throw, thrust, send with violence; cast down; tinge, flavour.—*v.i.* to move or go with great speed or violence.—*n.* a rush, onset; vigour; smartness; a small quantity, tinge; a stroke (—) between words.—**dash'ing** *a.* spirited, showy.—**dash'board** *n.* a mudscreen.

Das'tard *n.* a base coward, *esp.* one who commits a brutal act without danger to himself.—**das'tardly** *a.*

Das'ymeter *n.* an instrument for testing the density of a gas.

Date *n.* a stone-fruit of a palm; the palm.

Date *n.* the statement on a document of its time, or time and place of writing; the time of an occurrence; the period of a work of art, etc.; season, time.—*v.t.* to mark with a date; refer to a date.—*v.i.* to exist (from); to betray time or period of origin.—**date'less** *a.* without date; immemorial. — **date' - stamp** *n.*

Da'tive (-tiv) *n.* a noun-case indicating the indirect object, etc.

Da'tum *n.*, **da'ta** *pl.* a thing given, known, or assumed as the basis for a reckoning, reasoning, etc.

Daub *v.t.* to coat, plaster, paint roughly.—*n.* a smear; rough picture.—**daub'er** *n.* one who daubs; a bad painter.

Daught'er (dawt-) *n.* a female child, female descendant.—**daught'er-in-law** *n.* the wife of a son.—**daught'erly** *a.*

Daunt *v.t.* to frighten, *esp.* into giving up a purpose.—**daunt'less** *a.* not to be daunted.

Dauph'in (dō-fin) *n.* formerly (1349-1830) the eldest son of the King of France.

Dav'enport *n.* a small writing-table with drawers.

Dav'it *n.* a crane, usually one of a pair at a ship's side for lowering boats.

Da'vy-lamp *n.* a miner's safety lamp.

Da'vy Jones's lock'er (-jōn-ziz-) *n.* the sea as a grave.

Daw *n.* a small bird like a crow.

Māte, mēte, mīte, mōte, mūte, bōōt.

Daw'dle v.i. to idle, waste time, loiter.

Dawn v.i. to begin to grow light; to appear, begin.—n. first ight, daybreak, first gleam or beginning of anything.—**dawn'ing** n.

Day n. the time during which the sun is above the horizon; period of 24 hours; a point or unit of time; daylight; time, period.—**dail'y** a., adv., and n. (see in alphabet. place).—**day'-boarder** n. a boy fed but not lodged at school.—**day'book** n. a book in which the sales, etc., of a day are entered for later transfer to ledger.—**day'light** n. natural light, dawn, publicity, enlightenment. — **day'light-sa'ving** n. the system of summer-time. — **day'spring** n. dawn.

Daze v.t. to stupefy, stun, bewilder.—n. stupefied or bewildered state.—**daz'zle** v.t. to blind or confuse or overpower with brightness, light, brilliant display or prospects.—n. a brightness that dazzles the vision.—**daz'zle-painting** n. camouflage-work on a ship.—**daz'zle-lights** n. pl. motor-car headlights of dazzling brightness.

Deac'on n. one in the lowest degree of holy orders; an official of a free church.—**deac'oness** n. fem. a churchwoman appointed to perform charitable works.

Dead (ded) a. no longer alive; benumbed; obsolete; extinguished; lacking lustre or movement or vigour; sure, complete.—n. dead person or persons (gen. in pl., the dead).—**dead of night**, time of greatest stillness and darkness.—adv. utterly.—**dead'en** v.t.—**dead'ly** a. fatal; deathlike.—adv. as if dead.—**dead'-alive** a. dull.—**dead'heat** n. a race in which competitors finish exactly even.—**dead'-eye** n. a pulley.—**dead'head** n. a nonpaying member of audience, or passenger.—**dead let'ter** n. a law no longer observed; a letter which the post office cannot deliver.—**dead'lock** n. a standstill.—**dead-spot**, in wireless, an area of low wave intensity caused by obstacles of great absorbing power (e.g. mountains, large building areas). Syn. lifeless, inanimate, extinct, dull, gloomy. unproductive. Ant. alive, lively, animated, living, existing, effective, useful.

Deaf (def) a. wholly or partly without hearing; unwilling to hear. — **deaf'ness** n.—**deaf'en** v.t.

Deal n. a plank of fir or pine; fir or pine wood.

Deal v.t. to distribute, give out.—v.i. to do business (with, in).—**deal with**, handle, act in regard to.—n. a share; distribution; quantity.—**deal'er** n. one who deals; a trader.

Dean n. the head of a cathedral chapter; a university or college official.—**dean'ery** n. a dean's house or appointment.

Dear a. beloved; costly, expensive.—*n.* beloved one.— *adv.* at a high price.—**dear'ly** *adv.*—**dear'ness** *n.*—**dearth** (durth) *n.* scarcity.

Death (deth) *n.* dying; end of life; end, extinction; annihilation; personified power that annihilates, kills.— **death'less** *a.* immortal or destined to be immortal.— **death'ly** *a.* and *adv.* like death. —**death'watch** *n.* a ticking beetle.

Débâcle (di-bàkl') *n.* utter collapse, rout, disaster.

Debar' *v.t.* to shut out from, stop.

Debase' *v.t.* to lower in value or quality or character; to adulterate the metal in coinage.—**debase'ment** *n.* *Syn.* to humble, lower, disgrace, degrade. *Ant.* exalt, elevate, dignify, honour.

Debate' *v.t.* to discuss, dispute about.—*v.i.* to engage in discussion; consider; reason out (with oneself).—*n.* discussion, controversy. — **deba'table** *a.*—**deba'ter** *n.*

Debauch' (-tsh) *v.t.* to lead away from virtue; spoil, vitiate; seduce.—*n.* a bout of sensual indulgence.—**debauchee'** (-osh-) *n.*—**debauch'ery** *n.*

Deben'ture *n.* a bond of a company or corporation.

Debil'ity *n.* feebleness, *esp.* of health.—**debil'itate** *v.t.* *Syn.* infirmity, feebleness, enervation. *Ant.* strength, vigour, energy.

Deb'it *n.* an entry in an account of a sum owed; the side of the book in which such sums are entered.—*v.t.* to charge, enter as due.

Debonair' *a.* genial, pleasant.

Debouch' *v.i.* to move out from a narrow place to a wider one.—**debouch'ment** *n.*

Deb'ris (-rē) *n* fragments, rubbish.

Debt (det) *n.* what is owed; state of owing—**debt'or** *n.*

Debut' (dā-boo') *n.* first appearance in public.—**de'butant** *n.* (**-ante** *fem.*).

Dec'ade *n.* a period of ten years; a set of ten.

Dec'adent *a.* declining, falling away.—**dec'adence** *n.*

Dec'agon *n.* a figure of ten angles.—**decag'onal** *a.*—**dec'agramme** *n.* ten grammes.— **decahe'dron** *n.* a solid of ten faces.—**decahe'dral** *a.*—**dec'alitre** *n.* ten litres. — **dec'alogue** (-log) *n.* the ten commandments. — **dec'ametre** *n.* ten metres.

Decamp' *v.i.* to make off, abscond.

Dec'anal *a.* relating to a dean or deanery.

Decant' *v.t.* to pour off (liquid, wine, etc.) to leave sediment behind.—**decant'er** *n.* a stoppered bottle for wine or spirits.

Decap'itate *v.t.* to behead.— **decapita'tion** *n.*

Decar'bonise (-niz) *v.t.* to deprive of carbon; to remove a deposit of carbon, as from a motor cylinder —**decar'bonisation** *n.*

Decasyll'able *n.* a word or line of ten syllables.—**decasyllab'ic** *a.*

Decay' *v.t.* and *i.* to rot, de-

compose; fall off, decline.—
n. rotting; a falling away,
break up.

Decease' *n.* death.—*v.i.* to die.
—**deceased'** *a.* dead.—*n.* person lately dead.

Deceive' (-sēv) *v.t.* mislead,
persuade of what is false.—
deceiv'er *n.* — **deceit'** *n.* —
deceit'ful *a.*

Decem'ber *n.* the twelfth
month.

Decenn'ial *a.* of a period of
ten years.—**decenn'ially** *adv.*

De'cent *a.* seemly, not immodest; respectable; passable.—**de'cency** *n.*—**de'cently**
adv. *Syn.* proper, suitable,
decorous, seemly. *Ant.* improper, unsuitable, indecorous, unseemly.

Decep'tion *n.* deceiving; being deceived; a trick.—**decep'tive** *a.* misleading; apt
to mislead.

Decide' *v.t.* to settle, determine,
bring to resolution; give
judgment.—*v.i.* to determine,
resolve.—**deci'ded** *a.* settled;
resolute.—**deci'dedly** *adv.* certainly, undoubtedly.—**deci'sion** (-zhn) *n.*—**deci'sive** *a.*—
deci'sively *adv.*

Decid'uous *a.* of leaves, horns,
etc., falling periodically; of
trees, losing leaves annually.

Dec'imal (des-) *a.* relating to
tenths; proceeding by tens.
—*n.* a decimal fraction.—
—**dec'imal system**, a system
of weights and measures in
which the value of each denomination is ten times the
one below it.—**dec'igramme**
n. a tenth of a gramme.—
dec'ilitre *n.* a tenth of a litre.

—**dec'imetre** *n.* a tenth of a
metre.—**dec'imalise** *v.t.*—**decimalisa'tion** *n.* to convert
into decimal fractions or
system.—**dec'imate** *v.t.* to
kill a tenth or large proportion of.—**decima'tion** *n.*

Deci'pher *v.t.* to turn from
cipher into ordinary writing;
to make out the meaning of.
—**deci'pherable** *a.*

Deck *n.* a platform covering
the whole or part of a ship's
hull.—*v.t.* to array, decorate.

Declaim' *v.i.* and *t.* to speak
in oratorical style.—**declama'-
tion** *n.*—**declam'atory** *a.*

Declare' (-ēr) *v.t.* to announce
formally; state emphatically;
show; name (as liable to customs duty).—*v.i.* to take
sides (for).—**declara'tion** *n.*
—**declar'atory** *a.* *Syn.* to
manifest, proclaim, assert,
announce. *Ant.* to keep
secret, to conceal.

Decline' *v.i.* to slope or bend
or sink downward; to decay;
to refuse; to make the caseendings of nouns.—*n.* a
gradual decay, loss of vigour;
a wasting disease.—**declen'-
sion** *n.* a falling off; a declining; a group of nouns.—
decli'nable *a.*—**declina'tion**
n. downward slope or angle.

Decliv'ity *n.* downward slope.

Declutch' *v.t.* to take the
clutch out of engagement.

Decoc'tion *n.* extraction of an
essence by boiling down; an
essence or whatever results
from a boiling down.—**decoct'** *v.t.*

Decompose' (dē-, -ōz) *v.t.* to
separate into elements.—*v.i.*

to rot.—decomposi'tion *n.*

Dec'orate *v.t.* to beautify by additions; to invest (with an order, medal, etc.).—decora'-tion *n.*—dec'orative *a.*—dec'orator *n. esp.* a tradesman who paints and papers houses.

Decor'um *n.* seemly behaviour, usage required by decency or good manners.—dec'orous *a.* —dec'orously *adv.*

Decoy' *n.* a bird or person trained or used to entrap others; a bait, enticement; a pond with appliances for catching ducks.

Decrease' *v.t.* and *i.* to diminish, make or grow less.—de'crease *n.* a lessening. *Syn.* diminish, lessen, wain, reduce. *Ant.* increase, grow, wax, magnify.

Decree' *n.* an authoritative order; an edict.—*v.t.* to order with authority.

Dec'rement *n.* the act or state of decreasing; the quantity lost by decrease.

Decrep'it *a.* old and feeble.—decrep'itude *n.*

Decrescen'do (-kresh-) *n. Mus.* in a gradually diminishing manner.

Decry *v.t.* to cry down, disparage. *Syn.* to depreciate, disparage, traduce, defame. *Ant.* appreciate, enhance, extol, over-rate.

Ded'icate *v.t.* to devote to God's service; to set aside entirely for some purpose; to inscribe or address (a book, etc.).—dedica'tion *n.* ded'icatory *a.*—ded'icator *n.*

Deduce' *v.t.* to draw as a conclusion from facts.—deduct' *v.t.* to take away, subtract. —deduc'tion *n.* deducting; amount subtracted; deducing; conclusion deduced; an inference from general to particular.—deduc'tive *a.*—deduc'tively *adv.*

Deed *n.* an act: action or fact; a legal document.

Deem *v.t.* to judge, consider, hold to be.—deems'ter *n.* in the Isle of Man, a judge.

Deep *a.* extending far down or in or back; at or of a given depth; far down or back; profound; heartfelt; hard to fathom; cunning; engrossed, immersed; of colour, dark and rich; of sound, low and full.—*n.* a deep place.—*adv.* far down, etc.—deep'en *v.t.* —deep'ly *adv.*

Deer *n.* a family of ruminant animals with deciduous horns in the male.—deer'hound *n.* a large rough-coated greyhound.—deer'stalker *n.* one who stalks deer; a pattern of cloth hat.

Deface' *v.t.* to mar the appearance of; blot out.—deface'-ment *n.*

Defalca'tion *n.* misappropriation of funds; the resulting shortage.—de'falcate *v.i.*—de'falcator *n.*

Defame' *v.t.* speak ill of, dishonour by slander or rumour. —de'famation *n.* — defam'-atory *a.*

Default' *n.* failure to act or appear or pay.—in default of, in the absence of.—*v.t.* and *i.* to fail to pay.—default'er *n. esp.* a soldier punished for failure to comply with regulations.

Defeat' n. overthrow; lost battle or encounter; frustration.—v.t. to overcome.— **defeat'ism** n. conduct tending to bring about acceptance of defeat.—**defeat'ist** n.

Def'ecate v.t. to clear of impurities.—**defeca'tion** n.

Defect' n. lack, falling short, blemish, failing.—**defec'tion** n. abandonment of a leader or cause.—**defect'ive** a. incomplete, faulty, lacking some part.

Defend' v.t. to protect, guard, uphold. — **defence'** n. — **defend'er** n.—**defens'ible** a.— **defensibil'ity** n.—**defens'ive** a. serving for defence.—n. position or attitude of defence.

Defer' v.t. to pull off.—**defer'ment** n. Syn. to procrastinate, prolong. Ant. expedite, quicken.

Defer' v.i. to submit in opinion or judgment (to another).— **def'erence** n. respect for another inclining one to accept his views, etc.—**deferen'tial** (-shl) a.—**deferen'tially** adv.

Defi'cient (-ish'nt) a. wanting or falling short in something, insufficient —**defi'ciency** n.— **def'icit** n. the amount by which a sum of money is too small, excess of liabilities over assets, or expenditure over income.

Defile' n. a narrow pass; a march in file.—v.i. to march in file.

Defile' v.t. to make dirty, pollute.—**defile'ment** n.

Define' v.t. mark out; show clearly the form; lay down clearly, fix; state contents or meaning of.—**defi'nable** a. —**defini'tion** n. — **def'inite** (-it) a. exact, precise, defined.—**def'initely** adv.—**defin'itive** a. conclusive, to be looked on as final.—**defin'itively** adv.

Deflate' v.t. to release air from (something inflated); to remove excess of paper money in circulation.—**defla'tion** n. —**defla'tor** n.

Deflect' v.t. and i. to make to turn, or turn, from a straight course or direction.—**deflec'tion, deflex'ion** n.

Defolia'tion n. the fall of leaves.

Deform' v.t. to spoil the shape of; to make ugly.—**deform'ity** n.—**deforma'tion** n.

Defraud' v.t. to cheat.

Defray' v.t. to provide the money for (expenses, etc.).

Deft a. skilful, neat-handed. —**deft'ly** adv.—**deft'ness** n.

Defunct' a. dead.

Defy' v.t. to set at naught, challenge to do, esp. something beyond expected power; offer insuperable difficulties. —**defi'ance** n.—**defi'ant** a.— **defi'antly** adv.

Degen'erate v.i. to fall away from the qualities proper to race or kind.—a. fallen away in quality.—n. a degenerate person.—**degenera'tion** n.— **degen'eracy** n.

Degrade' v.t. to reduce to a lower rank; dishonour; debase.—**degrada'tion** n.—**degra'ded** a.

Degree' *n.* a step or stage in a process or scale or series; relative rank, order, condition, manner, way; a university rank; a unit of measurement of angles or temperature; a form in the comparison of *a.* and *adv.*

De'ify (dĕ-if-ī) *v.t.* to make a god of, treat as a god.—**deifica'tion** *n.*

Deign (dān) *v.i.* to condescend, think fit.

De'ism *n.* belief in a god but not in revelation.—**de'ist** *n.* —**deis'tic** *a.*—**de'ity** *n.* divine status or attributes, a god.

Deject' *v.t.* to dispirit, cast down.—**deject'ed** *a.*—**dejec'tion** *n.*

Déjeuner (dā-zhe-nā') *n.* a breakfast; an early luncheon.

Delay *v.t.* to postpone, hold back.—*v.i.* to be tardy, linger. —*n.* act of delaying; fact of being delayed.

De'leble *a.* capable of being blotted out.

Delec'table *a.* delightful.— **delecta'tion** *n.*

Del'egate *v.t.* to send as deputy; commit (authority, business, etc.) to a deputy.— **delega'tion** *n.*—**del'egate** *n.* —**del'egacy** *n.*

Delete' *v.t.* to strike out.— **dele'tion** *n.*

Delete'rious (-ĕr-) *a.* harmful. *Syn.* hurtful, noxious, pernicious, injurious, detrimental. *Ant.* wholesome, innocuous, harmless, beneficial.

Delf, delft *n.* a glazed earthenware.

Delib'erate *v.t.* and *i.* to consider, debate.—*a.* done on purpose; well - considered; without haste, slow.—**delib'erately** *adv.* — **delibera'tion** *n.* — **delib'erative** *a.*

Del'icate *a.* dainty; tender; fastidious; exquisite; deft; ticklish; sensitive; modest. —**del'icately** *adv.*—**del'icacy** *n. Syn.* gentle, fastidious, refined, tender. *Ant.* rough, course, clumsy, healthy, strong.

Deli'cious (-ish'us) *a.* very delightful or pleasing.—**deli'ciously** *adv.*

Delight' (-līt) *v.t* to please highly. — *v.i.* to take great pleasure (in).—*n.* great pleasure.—**delight'ful** *a.*

Delimita'tion *n.* assigning of boundaries.

Delin'eate *v.t.* to portray by drawing or description.— **delin'eator** *n.*—**delinea'tion** *n.*

Delin'quent *n.* an offender.— **delin'quency** *n.*

Deliquesce' (-es) *v.i.* to change into liquid form.—**deliques'cence** *n.*—**deliques'cent** *a.*

Delir'ium *n.* disorder of the mind.—**delir'ious** *a.*

Deliv'er *v.t.* to set free; hand over; launch, send in, deal; give forth.—**deliv'ery** *n.*— **deliv'erer** *n.*—**deliv'erance** *n.*

Dell *n.* a wooded hollow.

Del'ta *n.* a tract of alluvial land at the mouth of a river.

Delude' (-ōōd) *v.t.* to deceive. —**delu'sion** *n.*—**delu'sive** *a.*

Del'uge *n.* a flood, great flow, rush, downpour.—*v.t.* to flood.

Delve *v.t.* and *i.* to dig.

Demag'netise *v.t.* to deprive

of magnetic polarity; to free from mesmeric influence.

Dem'agogue (-og) *n.* a mob leader or agitator. — **demagog'ic** *a.* — **dem'agogy** *n.*

Demand' (-à-) *v.t.* to ask as by right, ask as giving an order; to call for as due or right or necessary. — *n.* an urgent request, claim, requirement; a call for (a commodity).

Demarca'tion *n.* boundary line; its marking out.

Demean' (-mēn) *v.* demean oneself, to behave, show specified bearing. — **demean'our** (-ẹr) *n.* conduct, bearing.

Dement'ed *a.* mad; beside oneself.

Demer'it *n.* bad point; undesirable quality.

Demesne' (-ēn) *n.* an estate kept in the owner's hands; possession of land with unrestricted rights; a sovereign's or state's territory; a landed estate.

Dem'i, a prefix signifying *half,* used only in composition.

Dem'igod *n.* a being half divine, half human.

Dem'ijohn *n.* a large wicker-cased bottle.

Demise' (-z) *n.* death; conveyance by will or lease; transfer of sovereignty on death or abdication. — *v.t.* to convey to another.

Demo'bilise *v.t.* to disband (troops). — **demobilisa'tion** *n.*

Democ'racy *n.* government by the people; a state so governed. — **dem'ocrat** *n.* an advocate of democracy. — **demo-**

crat'ic *a.* — **democrat'ically** *adv.* — **democ'ratise** *v.t.* — **democratisa'tion** *n.*

Demol'ish *v.t.* to knock to pieces, destroy, overthrow. — **demoli'tion** *n.*

De'mon *n.* a devil, evil spirit; a person of preternatural cruelty or evil character or energy. — **demo'niac** *n.* one possessed with a devil. — **demoni'acal** *a.* — **demon'ic** *a.* of the nature of a devil, or of genius. — **demonol'ogy** *n.* study of demons.

Dem'onstrate *v.t.* to show by reasoning, prove; to describe or explain by specimens or experiments. — *v.i.* to make exhibition of political sympathy; make a show of armed force. — **demon'strable** *a.* — **demon'strably** *adv.* — **demonstra'tion** *n.* — **dem'onstrator** *n.* — **demon'strative** *a.* conclusive; needing outward expression, unreserved; pointing out.

Demor'alise *v.t.* to deprave morally; deprive of courage and discipline, *morale.* — **demoralisa'tion** *n.*

Demul'cent *a.* softening; soothing.

Demur' (-mẹr) *v.i.* to raise objections, make difficulties. — *n.* raising objection.

Demure' *a.* reserved, quiet, staid; affecting to be grave or decorous. — **demure'ly** *adv.*

Demurr'age *n.* charge for keeping a ship, truck, etc., beyond the time agreed for unloading. — **demurr'er** *n. law,* an exception taken to an opponent's point.

Den n. a cave or hole of a wild beast; a lurking place; a small room.

Dena′ture v.t. to deprive of essential qualities.—**dena′-tured al′cohol**, spirit made undrinkable.

Dene (dēn) n. a little valley.

Deni′al see DENY.

Den′izen n. an inhabitant.

Denom′inate v.t. to give a name to.—**denomina′tion** n. a name, esp. one applicable to each individual of a class; a distinctively named church or sect.—**denomina′tional** a.—**denom′inator** n. the number written below the line in a fraction, the divisor.

Denote′ v.t. to stand for, be the name of; mark, indicate, show.—**denota′tion** n.

Denoue′ment (dā-nōō-mōn) n. the unravelling of a dramatic plot; final solution of a mystery.

Denounce′ v.t. to speak violently against; accuse; give notice to withdraw from (a treaty, etc.).—**denuncia′tion** n.—**denun′ciatory** a.

Dense a. thick, compact; stupid.—**dense′ly** adv.—**dens′-ity** n. Syn. close, heavy, opaque, compact. Ant. sparse, light, clear, quick-witted.

Dent n. hollow or mark left by a blow or pressure.—v.t. to make a dent in.

Dent′al a. of or relating to teeth or dentistry; pronounced by applying the tongue to the teeth.—**dent′ate** a. toothed.—**dent′ifrice** (-is) n. powder, paste, or wash for cleaning the teeth.—**dent′ist**

n. a surgeon who attends to teeth.—**dent′istry** n. the art of a dentist.—**denti′tion** n. teething; arrangement of teeth.—**dent′ure** n. a set of teeth, esp. artificial.

Denude′ v.t. to strip, make bare. — **denuda′tion** n. esp. removal of forest or surface soil by natural agency.

Denuncia′tion see DENOUNCE.

Deny′ v.t. to declare untrue or non-existent; contradict, reject; disown; refuse to give; refuse.—**deni′al** n.—**deni′able** a. Syn. to disavow, repudiate, disclaim, abjure. Ant. to assert, affirm, confess, admit, grant.

Deo′dorize v.t. to rid of smell.—**deodoriza′tion** n. — **deo′-dorizer** n.

Depart′ v.i. to go away; start; die; diverge, stray from.—**depart′ure** n.—**depart′ment** n. a division, branch, province.—**department′al** a.—**department′ally** adv.

Depend′ v.i. to rely entirely; live (on): to be contingent, await settlement or decision (on); to hang down.—**depend′able** a. reliable.—**depend′ant** n. one for whose maintenance another is responsible.—**depend′ent** a.—**depend′ence** n. — **depend′-ency** n. a country or province controlled by another.

Depict′ v.t. give a picture of.—**depic′tion** n. — **depict′or** n.

Depil′atory a. removing hair.—n. a substance that does this.—**depila′tion** n.

Deplete′ v.t. to empty, exhaust,

or nearly. — deple'tion *n.*

Deplore' *v.t.* to lament, regret. —deplor'able *a.*

Deploy' *v.i.* of troops, ships, etc., to spread out from column into line.—deploy'ment *n.*

Depo'larise *v.t* to deprive of polarity.—depolarisation *n.* process by which any substance loses its polarity, as the rays of light.

Depo'nent *n.* one who makes a statement on oath, a deposition.

Depopu'late *v.t.* to deprive of, or reduce, population.—depopula'tion *n.*

Deport' *v.t.* to remove into exile.—deporta'tion *n.*

Deport'ment *n.* behaviour, bearing.—deport' *v. refl.*

Depose' *v.t.* to remove from office, *esp.* of a sovereign.— *v.i.* to make a statement on oath, give evidence.—deposi'tion *n.*

Depos'it (-z-) *v.t.* to set down; give into safe keeping, *esp.* in a bank; pledge for the carrying out of a contract.—*n.* act of depositing; thing deposited.—depos'itor *n.*—depos'itory *n.* a place for safe keeping.—depos'itary *n.* a person with whom a thing is deposited.

Dep'ot (-ō) *n.* a place for stores; headquarters of a regiment; (U.S.) (dē'pō) a railway station.

Deprave' *v.t.* to make bad, corrupt, pervert.—deprav'ity *n.* wickedness.

Dep'recate *v.t.* to express disapproval of; advise against.

—depreca'tion *n.*—dep'recatory *a.*

Depre'ciate (-shi-) *v.t.* to lower the price or value or purchasing power of; belittle.— *v.i.* to fall in value.—deprecia'tion *n.*—depre'ciator *n.* —depre'ciatory *a. Syn.* to detract, traduce, lower, underestimate. *Ant.* appreciate, enhance, extol, overestimate.

Depreda'tion *n.* plundering, ravages. — dep'redator *n.*— dep'redate *v.t.* to plunder, to despoil.

Depress' *v.t.* to lower, in level or activity; affect with low spirits.—depres'sion (-shn) *n.* a depressing; a hollow; a centre of low barometric pressure; low spirits; low state of trade.—depress'ible *a.*

Deprive' *v.t.* to strip, dispossess (of).—depriva'tion *n.*

Depth *n.* deepness; degree of deepness; a deep place, abyss.—depth'-oharge *n.* a bomb for dropping on a submerged submarine, exploding at a set depth.

Depute' *v.t.* to commit to (a substitute); appoint as substitute.—dep'uty *n.* a substitute, delegate.—deputa'tion *n.* persons sent to speak for others. — dep'utise *v.i.* to act for another.

Derail' *v.t.* to make (a train) leave the rails.—derail'ment *n.*

Derange' *v.t.* throw into confusion or disorder; disturb; disorder the mind of.—derange'ment *n.*

Der'elict *a.* abandoned, forsaken, *esp.* of a ship.—*n.* a

thing forsaken, *esp.* a ship.
—derelic'tion *n.* neglect (of duty).

Deride' *v.t.* to laugh to scorn.
—deris'ion *n.*—deris'ive *a.*—deris'ory *a.* futile. *Syn.* to taunt, insult, jeer at. *Ant.* to appreciate, respect, reverence.

Derive' *v.t.* to get from; deduce; show the origin of.—*v.i.* to issue (from), be descended (from).—deriva'tion *n.*—deriv'ative *a.* traceable back to something else.—*n.* a thing or word derived from another.

Derm *n.* the natural covering of an animal; the true skin.

Der'ogate *v.i.* detract (from); degenerate.—deroga'tion *n.*—derog'atory *a.* involving discredit, loss of dignity.

Derr'ick *n.* a hoisting-machine.

Derr'ing-do' *n.* desperate valour.

Derr'inger (-j-) *n.* a small pistol.

Der'vish *n.* a Mohammedan religious beggar.

Des'cant *n.* sung accompaniment to plainsong.—descant' *v.i.* to talk at large; dwell on *esp.* with enthusiasm.

Descend' *v.i.* to come or go down; slope down; swoop on or attack; stoop, condescend; spring from (ancestor, etc.); pass to an heir, be transmitted.—*v.t.* to go or come down.—descend'ant *n.* one descended from another.—descent' *n.*

Describe' *v.t.* to give a detailed account of; to trace out (a geometrical figure, etc.); to pass along (a course, etc.).—descrip'tive *a.*—descrip'tion *n.* a detailed account; a marking out; a kind, sort, species.

Descry' *v.t.* to make out, catch sight of, *esp.* at a distance.

Des'ecrate *v.t.* to violate the sanctity of; to profane; convert to evil uses.—desecra'tion *n.*—des'ecrator *n.*

Desert' (-z-) *n.* (usually *pl.*) conduct or qualities deserving reward or punishment; what is due as reward or punishment; merit, virtue.

Desert' (-z-) *v.t.* to abandon, leave. — *v.i.* to run away from service, *esp.* of soldiers and sailors.—des'ert (-z-) *n.* an uninhabited and barren region.—*a.* barren, uninhabited, desolate. — deser'tion *n.*—desert'er *n.*

Deserve' (-z-) *v.t.* to show oneself worthy of; to have by conduct a claim to.—*v.i.* to be worthy (of reward, etc.).—deserv'edly *adv.*—deserv'ing *a.* meritorious.

Deshabille' (des-a-) *n.* undress; careless toilet for indoors.

Des'iccate *v.t.* to dry up.—desicca'tion *n.*

Desid'erate *v.t.* to feel as missing.—desidera'tum *n.*;—ata *pl.* a felt want.

Design' (-zīn) *v.t.* to plan out; purpose, set apart for a purpose; make working drawings for; sketch.—*n* a project, purpose, mental plan; outline, sketch, working plan; art of making decorative patterns, etc.—design'edly *adv.* on purpose.—de-

sign'ing a. crafty, scheming.
—design'er n. esp. one who draws designs for manufacturers.—des'ignate (dez'-ig-) v.t. name, pick out, appoint to office. — a. appointed but not yet installed in office. —designa'tion n. name.

Desip'ient a. trifling; foolish; playful.

Desire' (-z-) v.t. to wish for, long for; ask for, entreat.—n. longing; expressed wish; wish or felt lack; request; thing wished or requested. —desi'rable a.—desirabil'ity n.—desi'rous a.

Desist' v.i. to cease, give over.

Desk n. a sloped board on which a writer rests his paper, a reader his book; a table or other piece of furniture designed for the use of a writer or reader.

Des'olate a. solitary; neglected, barren, ruinous; dreary, dismal, forlorn.—v.t. to depopulate, lay waste; overwhelm with grief.—desola'tion n.

Despair' v.t. to lose all hope. —n. loss of all hope; something causing complete loss of hope.—des'perate a. leaving no room for hope; hopelessly bad or difficult or dangerous; reckless from despair.—despera'tion n.—des'perately adv.—despera'do (-á-) n. one ready for any lawless deed.

Despatch' see DISPATCH.

Despise' (-z) v.t. to look down on.—des'picable a. base, contemptible, vile.—des'picably adv.—despite' n. scorn; ill-will, malice, spite.—prep. in spite of.—despite'ful a.—despite'fully adv.

Despoil' v.t. plunder, rob, strip of.—despolia'tion n.

Despond' v.i. to lose heart or hope.—despond'ent a.—despond'ency n.—despond'ently adv.

Des'pot n. a tyrant, oppressor. —despot'ic a.—despot'ically adv.—des'potism n.

Des'pumate v.i. to throw off impurities; to form scum.—despuma'tion n. separation of the scum on the surface of liquor.

Des'quamate v.i. to come off in scales.—desquama'tion n.

Dessert' (-z-) n. fruit, etc., served after dinner.

Des'tine (-tin) v.t. to ordain or fix beforehand; set apart, devote.—des'tiny n. the power which foreordains; course of events or person's fate, etc., regarded as fixed by this power.—destina'tion n. place to which a person or thing is bound, intended end of a journey.

Des'titute a. in absolute want, in great need of food, clothing, etc.—destitu'tion n.

Destroy' v.t. to make away with, put an end to, reduce to nothingness or uselessness. —destruct'ible a.—destruc'tion n.—destruc'tive a.—destruc'tively adv.—destruc'tor n. that which destroys, esp. a furnace for destroying refuse. —destroy'er n. one who destroys; a small swift war-vessel using guns and torpedoes; (in full, *torpedo-boat destroyer*, fr. its original purpose, and often abbrev. as T.B.D.). *Syn.* to ruin, overthrow, extirpate, annihilate. *Ant.* to repair, renew, recondition.

Des'uetude (-swi-) *n.* state of disuse.

Des'ultory *a.* off and on, flitting from one thing to another, unmethodical.

Detach' (-tsh) *v.t.* to unfasten, disconnect, separate. — **detach'ed** *a.* standing apart, isolated.—**detach'ment** *n.* detaching; part of a body of troops separated for a special duty.—**detach'able** *a.*

De'tail *n.* treatment of anything item by item; an item or particular; a small or unimportant part; a party or man told off for a duty in the army.—**detail'** *v.t.* to relate with full particulars; to appoint for a duty.

Detain' *v.t.* to keep under restraint; keep from going; keep waiting.—**deten'tion** *n.*

Detect' *v.t.* to find out or discover the existence or presence or nature or identity of. —**detect'or** *n.*—**detec'tion** *n.* —**detect'ive** *a.* employed in or apt for detection. — *n.* a policeman or other person employed in detecting criminals.

Deter' *v.t.* to make, to abstain (from); discourage, frighten. —**deterr'ent** *a.*

Deter'gent *a.* cleansing.—*n.* a purifier.—**deterge** *v.t.* to cleanse.

Dete'riorate *v.i.* and *t.* to become or make worse.—**deteriora'tion** *n.*

Deter'mine *v.t.* to make up one's mind, decide; to fix as known; to bring to decision; to be the deciding factor in; *law,* to end.—*v.i.* to come to an end; come to a decision.— **deter'minable** *a.*—**deter'minant** *a.* and *n.*—**deter'minate** *a.* fixed in scope or nature.— **determina'tion** *n.* a determining; a resolve; firm or resolute conduct or purpose.— **deter'mined** *a.* resolute.—**deter'minism** *n.* the theory that human action is settled by forces independent of the will.—**deter'minist** *n.*

Detest' *v.t.* to hate, loathe.— **detest'able** *a.* — **detest'ably** *adv.*—**detesta'tion** *n.* *Syn.* to dislike extremely, execrate, abominate. abhor. *Ant.* to love, cherish, respect, like, be fond of.

Dethrone' *v.t.* to remove from a throne. — **dethrone'ment** *n.*

Det'onate *v.i.* and *t.* to explode with a loud report; set off an explosive.—**detona'tion** *n.*—**det'onator** *n.* *esp.* a detonating apparatus as a railway fog-signal, part of a bomb, etc.

Detour' (-tōōr) *n.* a course which leaves the main route to rejoin it later.

Detract' *v.t.* and *i.* to take away (a part) from; belittle. —**detrac'tion** *n.*— **detract'or** *n.*

Detrain' *v.i.* and *t.* to alight or make alight from a train.

Det'riment *n.* harm done, loss, damage.—**detriment'al** *a.*— **detriment'ally** *adv.*

Detri'tus n. worn-down matter such as gravel, from wearing of exposed surfaces.

Deuce n. the two at dice, cards, etc.; score of forty all at tennis. — in exclamatory phrases, the devil.

Dev'astate v.t. to lay waste.—**devasta'tion** n.

Devel'op v.t. to bring to maturity; bring forth, bring out; evolve.—v.i. to grow to a maturer state.—**devel'oper** n. esp. photographic chemical; muscle exerciser.—**devel'opment** n.

De'viate v.i to leave the way, turn aside, diverge.—**devia'tion** n.—**de'viator** n.—**de'vious** a.

Device' n. a contrivance, invention; fancy; scheme, plot; a heraldic or emblematic figure or design.

Dev'il n. the personified spirit of evil; a superhuman evil being; a vice; fierceness in fighting; person of great wickedness, cruelty, etc.; one who devils for a lawyer or author; a dish of deviled food. —v.t. to do work that passes for the employer's, as for lawyer or author; to grill with hot condiments.—**dev'ilish** a.—**dev'ilry** n.—**dev'ilment** n.—**dev'il-may-care** a. happy-go-lucky. — **dev'il's ad'vocate** n. one appointed to state the disqualifications of a person whom it is proposed to make a saint.

Devis'cerate v.t. to disembowel.

Devise' (-z) v.t. to plan, frame, contrive; plot; leave by will. —**devi'sor** n.—**devisee'** n.

Devoid' a. empty of, lacking, free from.

Devolve' v.i. to pass or fall (to, upon).—v.t. to throw (a duty, etc.) on to another.—**devolu'tion** n.

Dev'onport n. small writing table; in Australia, a small cake; in the Colonies, a dust storm.

Devote v.t. to set apart, give up exclusively (to a person, purpose, etc.).—**devotee'** n. one devoted, a worshipper.—**devo'ted** a. esp. very loyal or loving. — **devo'tion** n. a setting apart, application; dedication; religious earnestness; pl. prayers, religious exercises.—**devo'tional** a.

Devour' v.t. to eat up, consume, destroy.—**devour'er** n.

Devout' a. earnestly religious; reverent.—**devout'ly** adv.

Dew n. moisture from the air deposited as small drops on cool surfaces between nightfall and morning; any beaded moisture.—v.t. to wet with, or as with, dew.—**dew'y** a.—**dew'iness** n.

Dew'lap n. fold of loose skin hanging from the neck, esp. of cattle.—**dew'claw** n. partly developed inner toe of some dogs.

Dew'pond n. means of collecting water on chalk downs in dry weather, dating from prehistoric times.

Dexter'ity n. manual skill, neatness, adroitness.—**dex'terous** a. neat-handed, skilful. —**dex'ter** a. in heraldry, on the bearer's right-hand of a shield. Syn. expertness, address, cleverness, aptitude, faculty. *Ant.* clumsiness, awkwardness, unskilfulness.

Diabe'tes (-ēz) *n.* a urinary disease.—**diabe'tic** *a.*

Diabol'ic, diabol'ical *a.* devilish.—**diabol'ically** *adv.*—**diab'olism** *n.* devil-worship.—**diab'olo** *n.* a top sent spinning in the air from a string attached to two sticks.

Diac'onal *a.* relating to a deacon.—**diac'onate** *n.* office or rank of deacon; body of deacons.

Di'adem *n.* a crown.

Diaer'esis (dī-èr-) *n.* a mark (¨) placed over a vowel to show that it is sounded separately from a preceding one (e.g. in aërate).

Diagno'sis *n.* art or act of deciding from symptoms the nature of a disease; a guess at the cause of anything.—**diagnose'** *v.t.*—**diagnos'tic** *a.*—**diagnosti'cian** *n.*

Diag'onal *a.* from corner to corner; oblique.—*n.* a line from corner to corner.—**diag'onally** *adv.*

Di'agram *n.* a drawing, a figure in lines, to illustrate something being expounded, as in a geometrical figure, a weather-chart, etc. — **diagrammat'ic** *a.* — **diagrammat'ically** *adv.*

Di'al *n.* a plate marked with graduations on a circle or arc on which something may be recorded (e.g. time on a sundial, dial of a clock, etc.).—*v.t.* to indicate on a dial; to work an automatic telephone.

Di'alect *n.* characteristic speech of a district; a local variety of a language.—**dialect'al** *a.*—**dialect'ic** *n.* the art of arguing.—**dialect'ic, dialect'ical** *a.*—**dialect'ically** *adv.*—**dialecti'cian** *n.*—**di'alogue** *n.* conversation between two or more; literary work representing this; the conversational part of a novel, etc.

Diam'eter *n.* a straight line passing from side to side of a figure or body through its centre; thickness; unit of magnifying power. — **diamet'rical** *a.*—**diamet'rically** *adv.*

Di'amond *n.* a very hard and brilliant precious stone; a lozenge-shaped figure; a card of the suit marked by (red) lozenges or *diamonds*.

Diapa'son (-zn) *n.* one of certain organ-stops; the compass of a voice or instrument; a swelling chorus, burst of harmonious sounds.

Di'aper *n.* a fabric with a small diamond pattern; a pattern of that kind; a towel, etc., made of the fabric.—**di'apered** *a.*

Diaph'anous *a.* transparent. *Syn.* clear, pellucid, transparent. *Ant.* opaque, cloudy, hazy.

Di'aphragm (-am) *n.* the partition dividing the two cavities of the body, the midriff; a plate or disc wholly or partly closing a tube or opening.

Diarrhœ'a (-rē'a) *n.* excessive looseness of the bowels.

Di'ary *n.* a daily record of

events or thoughts; a book for such record.—di′arist n.

Dias′tole (tolē) n. a dilatation of the heart.

Di′atribe n. a bitter speech of criticism, an invective.

Dib′ble n. an implement for making holes in the ground for seeds or plants.—v.t. to prepare (ground) or sow or plant with such implement.

Dice see DIE.

Dick′y, dick′ey n. a detachable false shirt-front; a seat for servants at the back of a carriage, etc.

Dictate′ v.t. and i. to say or read for exact reproduction by another on paper; prescribe, lay down.—dic′tate n. bidding.—dicta′tion n.—dicta′tor n. one with absolute authority, a supreme ruler.—dictator′ial a. despotic; overbearing.—dictator′ially adv. —dic′taphone, dic′tograph n. instrument for recording speech for later writing.—dicta′torship n.

Dic′tion n. choice and use of words.—dic′tionary n. a book setting forth, usually in alphabetical order, the words of a language with meanings, derivations, foreign equivalents, etc.; a book of reference with items in alphabetical order.—dic′tum n. (dic′ta pl.) a. pronouncement, maxim, saying.

Didac′tic a. instructive; meant, or meaning, to teach.—didac′ticism n.

Did′dle v.t. to cheat.—v.i. toddle as a child.

Die (dī) v.i. to cease to live; come to an end.—die′hard n. one who resists (reform, etc.) to the end.

Die (dī) n. a cube with sides marked one to six for games of chance; a small cube of bread, etc.; (pl. dice); a stamp for embossing, etc. (pl. dies). — dice v.i. to gamble with dice.—di′cer n.

Die′sel (dē′-zl) a. pert. to a slow speed type of internal-combustion engine, burning heavy oil.

Di′et n. kind of food lived on; a regulated course of feeding, restricted choice of foods; food.—di′etary n. allowance or character of food, esp. in an institution, etc.—a. relating to diet. — dietet′ic a.—n. pl. the science of diet.

Di′et n. a parliamentary assembly.

Diff′er v.i. to be unlike; disagree.—diff′erence n. unlikeness; degree or point of unlikeness; disagreement; remainder left after subtraction.—diff′erent a. unlike.—diff′erently adv.—differen′tial a. varying with circumstances.—n. the mechanism in a motor-car which allows the back wheels to revolve at different speeds when rounding a corner.—differen′tially adv.—differen′tiate v.t. to make different; develop into unlikeness.—v.i. discriminate.—differentia′tion n.

Diff′iculty n. hardness to be done or understood; a hindrance, obstacle; an obscurity; embarrassment.—diff′i-cult *a.* not easy, hard, obscure.

Diff'ident *a.* timid, shy.— **diff'idently** *adv.*—**diff'idence** *n.* *Syn.* bashful, distrustful, hesitating, dubious. *Ant.* confident, assured, forward, arrogant.

Diffuse' (-z) *v.t.* to spread abroad.—*a.* (-s) loose, verbose, wordy.—**diffu'sion** *n.*— **diffu'sive** *a.*—**diffuse'ly** *adv.*— **diffu'sively** *adv.*

Dig *v.i.* to work with a spade. —*v.t.* to turn up with a spade; hollow out, make a hole in; get by digging; thrust into.—**digg'er** *n.* one who digs; a gold-miner; an Australian.

Digest' *v.t.* to prepare (food) in the stomach, etc., for assimilation; bring into handy form by sorting, tabulating, summarising; reflect on; absorb; endure.—*v.i.* of food, to undergo digestion.—**di'gest** *n.* a methodical summary, *esp.* of laws.—**digest'ible** *a.*—**digest'ive** *a.*—**diges'tion** *n.*

Dig'it (-j-) *n.* any of the numbers 0 to 9; a finger or toe.—**digita'lis** *n.* a drug made from foxglove.

Dig'nity *n.* worthiness, excellence, claim to respect; an honourable office or title; stateliness, gravity.—**dig'nify** *v.t.* give dignity to.—**dig'nified** *a.* stately, majestic.— **dig'nitary** *n.* a holder of high office.

Digress' *v.i.* to go aside from the main course, *esp.* to deviate from the subject in speaking or writing.—**digres'sion** *n.*—**digress'ive** *a.*

Dike, dyke *n.* a ditch; a low wall; an embankment.—*v.t.* to provide with a dike.

Dilap'idated *a.* ruinous, falling into decay. — **dilapida'tion** *n.*

Dilate' (dī-) *v.t.* to widen, expand.—*v.i.* to expand; to talk or write at large (on).— **dilata'tion, dila'tion** *n.* *Syn.* to amplify, swell, expatiate, descant. *Ant.* to contract, shrink, lessen, minimise.

Dil'atory *a.* decaying, slow.— **dil'atorily** *adv.*—**dil'atoriness** *n.*

Dilem'ma *n.* a position in fact or argument offering only choice between two or more unwelcome alternatives.

Dilettan'te (-ti) *n.* a person with taste and knowledge of the fine arts as a pastime; an amateur, dabbler.—*a.* amateur, desultory. — **dilletan'tism** *n.*

Dil'igent *a.* unremitting in effort, industrious. — **dil'igence** *n.*

Dill *n.* a herb with medicinal seeds.

Dilute' *a.* to reduce (a liquid) in strength by adding water or other matter —*a.* weakened thus.—**dilu'tion** *n.*

Dilu'vium *n.* a surface deposit of sand, pebbles, etc., attributable to former floods.— **dilu'vial, dilu'vian** *a.* pert. to a deluge.

Dim *a.* indistinct, faint, not bright.—*v.t.* and *i.* to make or grow dim.—**dim'ly** *adv.*— **dim'ness** *n.*

Dimen'sion *n.* measurement, size.—**dimen'sional** *a.*

Dimin'ish *v.t.* and *i.* to lessen. —**diminu'tion** *n.*—**dimin'u-tive** *a.* very small.—*n.* a derivative word implying smallness. *Syn.* abate, decrease, lessen, reduce. *Ant.* increase, add to, enlarge, extend.

Dim'ity *n.* a cotton fabric.

Dim'mer *n.* in motoring, a device to lessen power of headlamp.

Dim'ple *n.* a small hollow in the surface of the skin, *esp.* of the cheek; any small hollow.—*v.t.* and *i.* to mark with, or break into, dimples.

Din *n.* a continuous roar of confused noises.—*v.t.* to repeat to weariness, ram (fact opinion, etc.) *into.*

Dine *v.i.* to take dinner. — *v.t.* to give dinner to —**di'ning-room** *n.* a room used for meals.—**di'ner** *n.* one who dines; a railway restaurant-car.

Dinghy (ding'-gi) *n.* a small boat.

Ding'le (ding'-gl) *n.* a dell.

Ding'o (-ng-gō) *n.* an Australian wild dog.

Din'gy (-j-) *a.* dirty-looking, dull.—**din'giness** *n.*

Dinn'er *n.* the chief meal of the day.

Dint *n.* a dent.—**by dint of**, by force of.

Di'ocese (dī-o-sēs) *n.* the district or jurisdiction of a bishop.—**dioc'esan** *a.*—*n.* a bishop, or clergyman, or the people of a diocese.

Diox'ide *n.* an oxide with two parts of oxygen to one of the other constituent.

Dip *v.t.* to put partly or for a moment into a liquid; to immerse, involve; to lower and raise again; to take up in a ladle, bucket, etc.—*v.i.* to plunge partially or temporarily; go down, sink; slope downwards.—*n.* an act of dipping; a downward slope; a hollow.—**dipp'er** *n.*

Diphthe'ria *n.* an infectious disease of the throat with membranous growth.—**diphtherit'ic** *a.*

Diph'thong *n.* a union of two vowel sounds in a single compound sound.

Diplo'ma *n.* a document vouching for a person's title to some degree, honour, etc.—**diplo'macy** *n.* the management of international relations; skill in negotiation; tactful or adroit dealing.—**dip'lomat** *n.* one engaged in official diplomacy.—**diplo'matist** *n.* a diplomat; a tactful or crafty person.—**diplomat'ic** *a.*—**diplomat'ically** *adv.*

Dipsoma'nia *n.* inability to keep from alcohol.—**dipsoma'niac** *n.*

Dip'tych *n.* a picture on two boards hinged to close like a book.

Dire *a.* dread, terrible.

Direct' *v.t.* to put in the straight way; address (a letter, etc.); aim, point, turn; control, manage, order.—*a.* straight; going straight to the point; lineal; immediate; frank, straightforward.—**direc'tion** *n.* a directing; a body of directors; address, instruction; aim, course of movement.—direct'ive a.—direct'ly adv. — direct'ness n. — director' or n. one who directs; a member of a board managing a company.—direct'ress fem. —direct'orate n.—direct'orship n.—direct'ory n. a book of names and addresses, streets, etc.

Dirge n. a song of mourning.

Diri'gible (-ij'-) a. that may be steered.—n. a balloon or airship that can be steered.

Dirk n. a dagger.

Dirt'y a unclean; soiled; mean.—dirt n. filth; mud; earth.—dirt'ily adv.—dirt'iness n.

Dis- prefix, indicates negation, opposition, deprivation; in many verbs, it indicates the undoing of the action of the simple verb, e.g. disembark', to come out from what one embarked in; many verbs, nouns and adjectives in dis- mean the exact opposite of the simple word, e.g. disarra'nge, disor'der, disloy'al; some verbs in dis- mean to deprive of the thing indicated by the simple word, e.g. disbow'el. All such words are omitted, and the meaning should be sought by looking up the simple word to which dis- is prefixed.

Disa'ble v.t. to incapacitate; disqualify; cripple.—disabil'ity n.

Disabuse' (-z) v.t. to undeceive.

Disaffect'ed a. ill-disposed, inclined to sedition.—disaffec'tion n.

Disagreement n. lack of agreement.—disagree v.i. to be at variance. Syn. difference, discrepancy, division, dispute, variance. Ant. agreement, concurrence, concord, harmony.

Disappoint' v.t. to fail to fulfil (hope).—disappoint'ment n.

Disas'ter (-ȧ-) n. a calamity, a sudden or great misfortune. —disas'trous a.

Disavow' v.t. to refuse to acknowledge; to deny responsibility.—disavowal n. disclaimer. Syn. repudiate, disown, disclaim, disallow. Ant. avow, acknowledge, allow, affirm.

Disburse' v.t. to pay out money.

Disc see DISK.

Discard' v.t. and i. to reject, or play as worthless (a card); to give up; cast off.

Discern' v.t. to make out; distinguish.—discern'ment n. insight.—discern'ible a.

Discharge' v.t. to unload; fire off; release; dismiss; let go, pay; emit.—n. a discharging; a being discharged; matter emitted; a document certifying release, payment, etc.

Disci'ple n. a follower, one who takes another as teacher and model.—disci'pleship n. —dis'cipline (-in) n. training that produces orderliness, obedience, self-control; result of such training in order, conduct, etc.; a system of rules; maintenance of subordination in an army, school, etc.—v.t. to train; chastise.

—disciplin'arian n.—dis'ciplinary a.

Disclaim' v.t. disavow.—disclaim'er n. act of disavowal.

Disclose' v.t. to unclose; to open; to bring to light; divulge.—disclosure n. act of disclosing.

Discol'our (-kul'-) v.t. to alter the colour of.

Discom'fit (-um-) v.t. to defeat, baffle.—discom'fiture n.

Disconcert' v.t. derange, ruffle, confuse.

Discon'solate a. unhappy, downcast.

Dis'cord n. absence of concord; difference, dissension; disagreement of sounds.—discord'ant a. — discord'antly adv.—discord'ance n.

Discount' v.t. give present value of (a bill of exchange, etc.); detract from, lessen; allow for exaggeration in.—dis'count n. a deduction made on discounting a bill, receiving payment for an account, etc.

Discour'age (-kur-) v.t. to reduce the confidence of; deter from; show disapproval of. —discour'agement n. Syn. dispirit, depress, dissuade, damp. Ant. encourage, persuade, exhort, countenance.

Dis'course n. a speech, treatise, sermon; conversation.—discourse' v.i. to speak, converse.—v.t. to utter.

Discov'er (-kuv-) v.t. to find out, light upon; exhibit, make known.—discov'ery n. —discov'erer n.—discov'erable a.

Discreet' a. prudent, knowing when to be silent.—discreet'ly adv.—discre'tion (-esh'n) n.

Discrep'ant a. not tallying.—discrep'ancy n.

Discrim'inate v.t. and i. to detect or draw distinctions; distinguished from or between.—discrimina'tion n.

Discurs'ive a. passing from subject to subject, not keeping to the main thread.

Discuss' v.t. to exchange opinions on; debate; consume (food or drink).—discus'sion n.

Disdain' n. scorn, contempt.—v.t. to scorn.—disdain'ful a.—disdain'fully adv.

Disease' n. illness; disorder of health.

Disfig'ure (-ger) v.t. to mar the appearance of.—disfig'urement n.—disfigura'tion n.

Disgrace' n. ignominy; a cause of shame; loss of favour.—v.t. to bring shame or discredit upon.—disgrace'ful a. —disgrace'fully adv.

Disguise' (-gīz) v.t. to change the appearance of, make unrecognisable; conceal, cloak; misrepresent.—n. false appearance; dress or device to conceal identity.

Disgust' n. violent distaste, loathing.—v.t. to affect with loathing.

Dish n. a shallow vessel for food; a portion or variety of food; the contents of a dish. —v.t. to put in a dish; serve up.

Dishev'elled a. with disordered hair; ruffled, untidy, disorderly.

Disk, disc, n. a thin circular

plate; anything like this.

Dis'locate v.t. to put out of place, esp. of a bone; to put into disorder.—**disloca'tion** n.

Dis'mal (-z) a. depressing, or depressed; cheerless, dreary. —**dis'mally** adv.

Disman'tle v.t. to deprive of defences, furniture, etc.; remove equipment.

Dismay' v.t. to dishearten, daunt. — n. consternation, horrified amazement.

Dismem'ber v.t. to tear or cut limb from limb; divide, partition.—**dismem'berment** n.

Dismiss' v.t. to send away, disperse, disband; put away from employment, or from the mind.—**dismiss'al** n.

Dispar'age v.t. to speak slightingly of; to bring into disrepute.—**dispar'agement** n.

Dis'parate a. essentially different, not related.—**dispar'ity** n.

Dispatch', **despatch'** v.t. to send off; send to a destination or on an errand; kill; eat up; finish off, get done with speed.—n. a sending off; efficient speed; an official written message.

Dispel' v.t. to clear away. Syn. dissipate, banish, disperse. Ant. to gather up, collect, recall.

Dispense' v.t. to deal out; to make up (a medicine); relax, not insist on; do without.—v.i. to make up medicines.—**dispens'er** n.—**dispens'ary** n. a place where medicine is made up.—**dispensa'tion** n. a licence or exemption. a provision of nature or provi-

dence; an act of dispensing. —**dispens'able** a.

Disperse' v.t. to scatter.—**dispersed'** a. scattered; placed here and there.—**disper'sion** n.

Display' v.t. to spread out for show; to show, expose to view.—n. a displaying; exhibition; show, ostentation.

Displease' v.t. & i.to offend; annoy.—**displeasure** (-plezh-) n.

Dispon'dee n. a double spondee, consisting of four long syllables.

Disport' v. refl. to gambol, move about for enjoyment, esp. in water, sunshine.

Dispose' (-z) v.t. to arrange; to make inclined (to).—v.i. to ordain, appoint.—**dispose of**, sell, get rid of; have authority over.—**dispo'sal** n.—**disposi'tion** n. arrangement; plan; inclination; cast of mind or temper.

Dispropor'tion n. want of proportion.

Dispute' v.i. to debate, discuss. —v.t. to call in question; debate, argue; oppose, contest; try to debar from.—**dis'putable** a.—**dis'putant** n.—**disputa'tion** n.—**disputa'tious** a. Syn. to impugn, controvert, wrangle, altercate. Ant. to accept, agree, be friendly, acquiesce.

Disquisi'tion n. a learned or elaborate treatise or discourse.

Disrupt' v.t. to shatter, break in pieces, split.—**disrup'tion** n. —**disrup'tive** a.

Dissect' v.t. to cut up (a body, organism) for detailed examination; to examine or criticise in detail.—**dissec′tion** n.—**dissec′tor** n.

Dissem′ble v.t. and i. to conceal or disguise (opinions, feelings, etc.); to talk or act hypocritically.—**dissem′bler** n.

Dissem′inate v.t. to spread abroad.—**dissemina′tion** n.—**dissem′inator** n.

Dissent′ v.i. to differ in opinion; to express such difference; disagree with the doctrine, etc., of an established church.—n. such disagreement.—**dissent′er** n.—**dissen′tient** a. and n.—**dissen′sion** n.

Disserta′tion n. a discourse.

Diss′ident a. not in agreement.—**diss′idence** n.

dissim′ulate v.t. and i. to pretend not to have; to practise deceit.—**dissimula′tion** n.

Diss′ipate v.t. to scatter, clear away; waste, squander.—v.i. to disappear; clear away.—**dissipa′tion** n. scattering; frivolous or dissolute way of life.—**diss′ipated** a. corrupted, dissolute.

Disso′ciate v.t. to separate, sever.—**dissocia′tion** n.

Dissolve′ v.t. to absorb or melt in a fluid; break up, put an end to, annul.—v.i. to melt in a fluid; disappear, vanish; break up, scatter.—**dissol′uble** a.—**dissolu′tion** n.—**diss′olute** a. lax in morals, profligate.

Diss′onant a. jarring, discordant in sound.—**diss′onance** n.

Dissuade′ (-sw-) v.t. to advise to refrain, persuade not to.—**dissua′sion** n.—**dissua′sive** a.

Dissyll′able n. a word or metrical foot having two syllables.—**dissyllab′ic** a.

Dissymm′etry n. want of symmetry.

Dis′taff n. a cleft stick to hold wool, etc., for hand-spinning.

Dis′tance n. the amount of space between two things; remoteness; excessive dignity.—v.t. to leave behind, esp. in a race.—**dis′tant** a.—**dis′tantly** adv.

Distem′per n. a disordered state of mind or body; a disease of dogs; a method of painting on plaster without oil; the paint used for this.—v.t. to paint in distemper.

Distend′ v.t. and i. to swell out by pressure from within.—**disten′sible** a.—**disten′sion** n.

Dis′tich (-ik) n. a couplet.

Distil′ v.i. to pass over or condense from a still; to trickle down.—v.t. to obtain (a substance or part of it) in a purified state by evaporating and then condensing it.—**distilla′tion** n.—**distill′er** n. one who distils, esp. a manufacturer of alcoholic spirits.—**distill′ery** n.

Distinct′ a. clear, easily seen, sharp of outline; definite; separate, different. — **distinct′ly** adv.—**distinct′ness** n.—**distinc′tion** n. point of difference; act of distinguishing; eminence, high honour, high quality.—**distinct′ive** a. characteristic. — **disting′uish** (-ng-gw-) v.t. to class; make a difference in; to recognise, make out; to honour; make prominent or honoured (usually *refl.*).—*v.i.* to draw a distinction, grasp a difference.—disting'uishable *a.*

Distort' *v.t.* misrepresent; garble; to put out of shape.—distor'tion *n.*

Distract' *v.t.* turn aside, divert; bewilder, drive mad.—distrac'tion *n.*

Distraint' *n.* legal seizure of goods to enforce payment.—distrain' *v.t.*

Distraught' (-awt) *a.* bewildered, crazy.

Distress' *n.* severe trouble, mental pain; severe pressure of hunger or fatigue or want; *law*, distraint.—*v.t.* to afflict, give mental pain.—distress'ful *a.* *Syn.* calamity, adversity, grief, agony. *Ant.* prosperity, good fortune, benefit, ease.

Distrib'ute *v.t.* to deal out; spread, dispose at intervals; classify.—distrib'utive *a.*—distribu'tion *n.*—distrib'utor *n.*

Dis'trict *n.* a portion of territory; a region.

Distrust' *v.t.* to put no trust in.

Disturb' *v.t.* to trouble, agitate; unsettle, derange.—distur'bance *n.*—distur'ber *n.*

Disunite' *v.t.* to destroy the union of.—*v.i.* to part. *Syn.* to divide, sever, disjoin. *Ant.* to unite, join, associate.

Ditch *n.* a long narrow hollow dug in the ground, usually for drainage.—*v.t.* and *i.* to make or repair ditches.

Dit'to same, aforesaid; (used to avoid repetition in lists, etc.).

Ditt'y *n.* a simple song.

Diuret'ic (dī-ūr-) *a.* exciting discharge of urine.—*n.* a substance with this property.

Diur'nal *a.* daily; in or of daytime; taking a day.

Divaga'tion *n.* wandering, digression.—di'vagate *v.i.*

Di'van *n.* a low seat by a wall; a smoking-room; an oriental council.

Dive *v.i.* to plunge under the surface of water; descend suddenly; disappear; go deep down into.—*n.* an act of diving.—di'ver *n.*

Diverge' *v.i.* to get farther apart, separate.—diver'gent *a.*—diver'gence *n.*

Di'vers (-z) *a.* sundry.—diverse' *a.* different, varied.—divers'ify *v.t.*—diverse'ly *adv.*—diversifica'tion *n.*—divers'ity *n.*

Divert' *v.t.* to turn aside, ward off; cause to turn; amuse, entertain.—diver'sion *n.*

Divest' *v.t.* to unclothe, strip, dispossess.

Divide' *v.t.* to make into two or more parts, split up, separate; classify; cut off; deal out; take or have a share; part into two groups for voting;—**to divide a number by another,** to find out how many times the former contains the latter.—*v.i.* to become divided.—div'idend *n.* a number to be divided by another; a share of profits, of money divided among creditors, etc.—divi'ders *n.pl.* measuring compasses.—divis'ible *a.*—divis'ion *n.* (-vizhn).—divis'ional *a.*—divi'sor *n.*

Divine' *a.* of, pertaining to, proceeding from, God; sacred; godlike, heavenly.—*n.* a theologian; a clergyman.—*v.t.* and *i.* to guess; predict, tell by inspiration or magic.—**divine'ly** *adv.*—**divin'ity** *n.* quality of being divine; a god; theology.—**divina'tion** *n.* divining.—**divi'ner** *n.*—**divi'ning-rod** *n.* a switch for detecting underground water or minerals by dowsing.

Divis'ion (-vizh'-) *n.* act of dividing; part of a whole.

Divorce' *n.* legal dissolution of marriage; complete separation, disunion.—*v.t.* to dissolve a marriage; put away; separate.—**divorcee'** *n.*

Div'ot *n.* a piece of turf.

Divulge' *v.t.* to reveal, let out (a secret).

Dizz'y *a* feeling dazed, unsteady, as if about to fall; causing or fit to cause dizziness, as of speed, etc.—*v.t* to make dizzy.—**dizz'iness** *n.*—**dizz'ily** *aav.*

Do (dōō) *v.t.* to perform, effect, transact, bring about, finish, prepare, cook.—*v.i.* to act, manage, work, fare, serve, suffice.—*v. aux.* makes negative and interrogative sentences and expresses emphasis.

Do'cile *a.* willing to obey; easily taught.—**docil'ity** *n.*

Dock *n.* a coarse weed.

Dock *n.* the solid part of a tail; a cut end, stump.—*v.t.* to cut short, *esp.* a tail; curtail, deprive of.

Dock *n.* a basin with floodgates for loading or repairing ships.—*v.t.* to put in a dock. —*v.i.* to go into dock.—**dock'yard** *n.* an enclosure with docks, for building or repairing ships.—**dock'er** *n.* labourer.

Dock *n.* the enclosure in a criminal court in which the prisoner is placed.

Dock'et *n.* an endorsement showing the contents of a document; a memorandum; a certificate of payment of customs.—*v.t.* to make a memorandum, endorse with a summary.

Doc'tor *n.* one holding a University's highest degree in any faculty; a medical practitioner.—*v.t.* to treat medically; to adulterate, garble. —**doc'torate** *n.*—**doc'toral** *a.* —**doc'trine** *n.* what is taught; the teaching of a church, school, or person; a belief, opinion, dogma.—**doctri'nal** *a.*—**doctrinaire'** *n.* a person who seeks to apply principles or theory without regard for circumstances.

Doc'ument *n.* something written furnishing evidence or information.—*v.t.* to furnish with proofs, illustrations, certificates.—**document'ary** *a.* —**documenta'tion** *n.*

Dodge *v.t.* to swerve, make zig-zag movement, *esp.* to avoid a pursuer or gain an advantage; shuffle, play fast and loose.—*v.t.* to elude by dodging.—*n.* an act of dodging; a trick, artifice; shift, ingenious method.—**dodg'er** *n.*

Do'do *n.* an extinct bird.

Doe (dō) *n*. female of deer, hare, rabbit.

Doff *v.t.* to take off (hat, clothing).

Dog *n*. a familiar domestic quadruped; a person (in contempt, abuse, or playfully). —*v.t.* to follow steadily or closely.—**dogg'ed** *a*. persistent, resolute, tenacious.— **dogg'y** *a*.—**dog'like** *a*.—**dog'- cart** *n*. an open vehicle with crosswise back-to-back seats. —**dog'-days** *n*. hot season of the rising of the dog-star.— **dog'-rose** *n*. wild rose.— **dog's'-ear** *n*. turned-down corner of a page in a book — *v.t.* to turn down corners of pages.—**dog'star** *n*. the star Sirius.—**dog'-watch** *n*. in ships, a short half-watch, 4-6, 6-8 p.m. (See illus. p. 165.)

Dogg'erel *n*. slipshod, unpoetic or trivial verse.

Dog'ma *n*. an article of belief, *esp.* one laid down authoritatively by a church; a body of beliefs.—**dogmat'ic** *a*. relating to dogma or dogmas; asserting opinions with arrogance. —**dogmat'ically** *adv*.—**dog'- matism** *n*. arrogant assertion of opinion.—**dog'matist** *n*.— **dog'matise** *v.i.*

Doi'ly *n*. a small cloth, paper, piece of lace to place under a cake, finger-bowl, etc.

Dol'drums *n.pl.* a region of light winds and calms near the equator; a state of depression, dumps.

Dole *n*. a charitable gift; *slang* a payment under unemployment insurance.—*v.t.* (usually **dole out**) to deal out, *esp.* in niggardly quantities.

Dole *n*. woe.—**dole'ful** *a*.— **dole'fully** *adv*.

Doll *n*. a child's toy image of a human being.

Doll'ar *n*. a coin of Canada, U.S., and other countries.

Doll'y *n*. doll.

Dol'man *n*. a cloak; a hussar jacket.

Dol'our (-ẹr) *n*. grief, sadness. —**dol'orous** *a*.—**dol'orously** *adv*.

Dol'phin *n*. a sea mammal like a porpoise; a fish that changes colour in dying; a figure of a curved, large-headed fish common in decoration and heraldry.

Dolt (-ō-) *n*. a stupid fellow.

Domain' *n*. lands held or ruled over; sphere, field of influence, province.

Dome *n*. a rounded vault forming a roof.

Domes'day (dōōmz'-) *a*. in *Domesday Book*, the record of the survey of the land of England made in 1086.

Domes'tic *a*. of or in the home; of the home country, not foreign; home-keeping; of animals, tamed, kept by man. —**domes'ticate** *v.t.*—**domestica'tion** *n*.—**domestic'ity** *n*. *Syn*. private, internal, tame. *Ant*. public, foreign, wild.

Dom'icile *n*. a person's regular place of living (usually in legal terms).—**domicil'iary** *a*.

Dom'inate *v.i.* to rule, control, sway; of heights, to overlook.—*v.i.* to control, be the most powerful or influential member or part of something.

—dom'inant a.—domina'tion n.—domineer' v.i. to act imperiously, tyrannise.

Domin'ion n. sovereignty, rule; territory of a government; a part of the British Empire having independent self-government.

Dom'ino n. a cloak with a half-mask for masquerading;—pl. a game played with small flat pieces, marked on one side with 0 to 6 spots on each half of the rectangular face.—sing. one of these pieces.

Don v.t. to put on (clothes).

Donate' (dō-) v.t. to give.—dona'tion n.—do'nor n.

Donga (dong'-ga) n. South African name for water channel or gully.

Don'jon see DUNGEON.

Donk'ey n. an ass.—donk'ey-engine n. a small hauling or hoisting engine on a ship.

Doom n. fate, destiny; ruin; judicial sentence, condemnation; the Last Judgment.—v.t. to sentence, condemn; destine to destruction or suffering.—dooms'day n. the day of the Last Judgment.

Door (dor) n. a hinged or sliding barrier to close the entrance to a room, carriage, etc.—door'way n. an entrance provided or capable of being provided with a door.

Dop n. the cup in which the diamond is fixed for polishing; Cape brandy.

Dope n. a kind of varnish; a drug.

Dor'mant a. not acting, in a state of suspension.—dor'-mancy n.—dorm'er n. an up-

right window set in a sloping roof.—dor'mitory n. a sleeping-room with a number of beds; a building containing sleeping quarters.

Dor'mouse n. a small hibernating rodent.

Dor'my a. in golf, as many holes up as there are holes to play.

Dorp (dawp) n. in South Africa, a village.

Dor'sal a. of, or on, the back.

Dose n. an amount (of a drug, etc.) administered at one time.—v.t. to give doses to.

Dot n. a small spot or mark.—v.t. to mark with a dot or dots; to place here and there.

Dote v.i. to be silly or weakminded; to be passionately fond of.—do'tage n. feeble-minded old age.—do'tard n.

Dou'ble (dub-) a. of two parts, layers, etc., folded; twice as much or many; of two kinds; ambiguous; deceitful.—adv. twice; to twice the amount or extent; in a pair.—n. a person or thing exactly like, or mistakable for, another; a quantity twice as much as another; a sharp turn; an evasion or shift.—v.t. and i. to make or become double; to increase twofold; to fold in two; to turn sharply; get round, sail round.—doub'ly adv.—doub'let n. a close-fitting body-garment formerly worn by men.—doub-loon' n. a Spanish gold coin.

Doubt (dowt) v.t. to hesitate to believe, call in question; suspect.—v.i. to be wavering or uncertain in belief or opinion.—*n.* a state of uncertainty, a wavering in belief; state of affairs giving cause for uncertainty.— **doubt'er** *n.*—**doubt'ful** *a.*— **doubt'fully** *adv.*—**doubt'less** *adv*

Douche (dōōsh) *n.* a jet or spray of water applied to the body or some part of it.— *v.t.* to give a douche to.

Dough (dō) *n.* flour or meal kneaded with water. — **dough'y** *a.*

Doughty (dowt'i) *a.* valiant.— **dought'ily** *adv.* — **dought'i-ness** *n.*

Dour (dōōr) *a.* grim, stubborn.

Douse *v.t.* to thrust into water.

Dove (duv) *n.* a bird of the pigeon family.—**dove'cot(e)** *n.* a house or hutch for doves.— **dove'tail** *n.* a joint made with a tenon shaped as a spread dove's tail.—*v.t.* and *i.* to fit together by dovetails; to unite or combine neatly or exactly.

Do'ver *n.* in Australia, a clasp knife.

Dow'ager (-j-) *n.* a woman with title or property derived from her late husband.

Dow'dy *a.* lacking smartness; unattractively or shabbily dressed.—*n.* a woman so dressed.

Dow'er *n.* a widow's share for life of her husband's estate; a dowry.—*v.t.* give dowry to; endow.—**dow'ry** *n.* property which a wife brings to her husband; talent.

Down, *n.* an open expanse of high land.

Down *adv.* to, or in, or towards, a lower position; with a current or wind; from the capital, or university; of paying, on the spot.—*prep.* from higher to lower part of; at a lower part of; along, with.—**down'cast** *a.* looking down; dejected.—**down'pour** *n.* a heavy fall of rain.— **down'right** *a.* plain, straightforward.—*adv.* quite thoroughly.—**down'ward** *adv.* and *a.*—**down'wards** *adv.*

down *n.* fluff or fine hair of young birds; anything like this, soft and fluffy.— **down'y** *a.*

Dow'ry *see* DOWER.

Doxol'ogy *n.* a short formula of praise to God.

Doy'en *n.* the senior member of a body.

Doy'ley *see* DOILY.

Doze *v.i.* to sleep drowsily, be half asleep.—*n.* a nap.

Doz'en (duz-) *n.* twelve, a set of twelve.

Drab *a.* of dull light brown; dull, monotonous.—*n.* drab colour.

Drab *n.* slut; prostitute.

Drachm (dram) *n.* a unit of weight, 1/8 of apoth. ounce, 1/16 of avoir. ounce.

Draft (-à-) *n.* a detachment of men, *esp.* troops, reinforcements; a design, sketch; rough copy of a document; an order for money.—*v.t.* to send a detached party; to make a rough copy (of a writing, etc.).—**drafts'man** *n.* one who drafts writings, etc.

Drag *v.t.* to pull along with difficulty or friction; trail, go heavily; sweep with a net or grapnels; protract.—*v.i.* to lag, trail; be tediously protracted.—*n.* a check on progress; checked motion; iron shoe to check a wheel; a vehicle; a lure for hounds to hunt; kinds of harrow, sledge, net, grapnel, rake.—**drag'gle** *v.t.* to make limp or wet or dirty by trailing.

Drag'on *n.* a fabulous fire-breathing monster, like a winged crocodile.—**drag'on-fly** *n.* a long-bodied insect with large gauzy wings.—**dragoon'** *n.* a cavalryman, usually of heavy cavalry.—*v.t.* to subject to military oppression; domineer over, persecute.

Drail *n.* the iron bow of a plough from which the traces draw.

Drain *v.t.* to draw off (liquid) by pipes, ditches, etc.; to dry; drink to the dregs; to empty, exhaust.—*v.i.* to flow off or away; become rid of liquid. — *n.* a channel for removing liquid; a constant outlet, expenditure, strain.—**drain'age** *n.*

Drake *n.* male duck.

Dram *n.* a small draught of strong drink; a drachm.

Dra'ma (drä-) *n.* a stage-play; art or literature of plays; a play-like series of events.—**dramat'ic** *a.*—**dram'atist** *n.*—**dram'atise** *v.t.*—**dramatisa'tion** *n.*

Dram'mock (-ok) *n.* meal and water mixed raw.

Drape *v.t.* to cover, adorn; with cloth, arrange in graceful folds.—**dra'per** *n.* a dealer in cloth, linen, etc.—**dra'pery** *n.*

Dras'tic *a.* strongly effective.

Draught (dráft) *n.* act or action of drawing; act of drinking, quantity drunk at once; one drawing of, or fish taken in, a net; a dose; an inhaling; the depth of water needed to float a ship; a current of air between apertures in a room, etc.; a design, sketch;—*pl.* a game played on a chess-board with flat round "men."—*a.* for drawing; drawn.—*v.t.* to make a sketch or rough design of. — **draughts'man** *n.* — **draughts'manship** *n.*—**draught'y** *a.*

Draw *v.t.* pull, pull along, haul; bend (a bow); inhale; entice, attract; bring (upon, out, etc.); get by lot; of a ship, require (depth of water); take from (a well, barrel, etc.); receive (money); delineate, portray with a pencil, etc.; to frame, compose, draught, write.—*v.i.* to pull; shrink; attract; make or admit a current of air; make pictures with pencil, etc.; write orders for money; come, approach (near).—*n.* an act of drawing; a casting of lots; an unfinished game, a tie. — **draw'back** *n.* a charge paid back; anything that takes away from satisfaction.—**draw'bridge** *n.* a hinged bridge to pull up.—**draw'er** *n.* one or that which draws; a sliding box in a table or chest;—*pl.* two-legged under-garment.—**draw'ing** *n.* the action of the verb; art of depicting in line; a sketch so done.—draw'ing-room n. a reception-room; a room to which ladies retire after dinner; a court reception.

Drawl v.t. and i. to speak slowly in indolence or affectation.—n. such speech.

Dray n. a low cart without sides.

Dread (dred) v.t. to fear greatly. —n. awe, terror.—a. feared, awful, revered.—dread'ful a. —dread'nought n. a large sized modern battleship; a thick heavy coat; a woollen cloth for such coats.

Dream (drēm) n. a vision during sleep; a fancy, reverie, vision of something ideal.—v.i. to have dreams. —v.t. to see or imagine in dreams; think of as possible. —dream'er n.—dream'y a. given to day-dreams, unpractical, vague.—dream'-less a.

Drear'y a. dismal, dull.—drear a.—drear'ily adv.—drear'i-ness n.

Dredge n. machinery, appliance for bringing up mud, objects, etc., from the bottom of sea or river.—v.t. to bring up, or clean, or deepen, with such appliance. —dredg'er n. a ship for dredging.

Dredge v.t. to sprinkle with flour.—dredg'er n. a box with holes in the lid for dredging.

Dree v.i. to endure; to bear the penalty of.

Dregs n.pl. sediment, grounds, worthless part.

Drench v.t. to wet thoroughly, soak; make (an animal) take a dose of medicine.—n. a dose for an animal; a soaking.

Dress v.t. to clothe; array for show, trim, smooth, prepare surface of; draw up (troops) in proper line; prepare (food) for the table; put dressing on.—v.i. to put on one's clothes; to form in proper line.—n. clothing; clothing for ceremonial evening wear; a frock.—dress'er n. one who dresses; a surgeon's assistant: a kitchen sideboard.— dress'ing n. esp. something applied to something else, as ointment to a wound, manure to land, stiffening to linen, etc.—dress'y a. stylish; fond of dress.—dress-cir'cle n. first gallery in a theatre.

Drib'ble v.i. to flow in drops, trickle, run at the mouth; work a ball forward with small touches of the feet.— v.t. to let trickle; work (ball) forward.—n. a trickle, drop. —drib'blet n. a small instalment.

Drift n. a being driven by a current; a slow current or course; deviation from a course; tendency; a speaker's meaning; a wind-heaped mass of snow, sand, etc.; material driven or carried by water; (in S. Africa) a ford. —v.i. to be carried as by current of air, water; to move aimlessly or passively.— drif'ter n. one who drifts; a small fishing-vessel.

Drill n. a boring tool or machine: exercise of soldier

or others in handling of arms and manœuvres; routine teaching.—*v.t.* to bore; exercise in military movements or other routine.—*v.i.* to practise a routine.

Drill *n.* a small furrow for seed; a machine for sowing in drills.—*v.t.* to sow in drills.

Drill *n.* a coarse twilled fabric.

Drink *v.t.* and *i.* to swallow liquid; absorb; to take intoxicating liquor, *esp.* to excess.—*n.* liquid for drinking; a portion of this; act of drinking; intoxicating liquor; excessive use of it.—**drink'er** *n.*—**drink'able** *a.*

Drip *v.t.* and *i.* to fall or let fall in drops.—*n.* a process of dripping; that which falls by dripping.—**drip'stone** *n.* projection over round window or door to stop dripping of water.—**drip'ping** *n.* act of dripping; melted fat that drips from roasting meat.

Drive *v.t.* to force to move in some direction; to make move and steer (a vehicle, animal, etc.), chase; convey in a vehicle, fix by blows, as a nail; urge, impel.—*v.i.* to keep a machine, animal, going, steer it; be conveyed in a vehicle; rush, dash, drift fast.—*n.* act or action of driving; journey in a carriage; a carriage-road, *esp.* leading to a house.—**dri'ver** *n.*

Driv'el *v.i.* to run at the mouth or nose; to talk nonsense.—*n.* silly nonsense.—**driv'eller** *n.*

Driz'zle *v.i.* to rain in fine drops.—*n.* fine rain.

Drogue (drōg) *n.* the drag of

boards, attached to the end of a harpoon line.

Droll (-ō-) *a.* funny, odd, queer.—*n.* a funny fellow.—**drol'ly** *adv.*—**droll'ery** *n.* *Syn.* amusing, comical, facetious. *Ant.* boring, serious, grave.

Drom'edary *n.* a fast camel.

Drone *n.* the male of the honey bee; a lazy idler; a deep humming; bass pipe of bagpipe, or its note.—*v.i.* and *t.* to hum; talk in a monotonous tone.

Droop *v.i.* to hang down as in weariness; languish, flag.—*v.t.* to let hang down.—*n.* drooping condition.

Drop *n.* a globule of liquid; a very small quantity; a fall, descent; a thing that falls, as a gallows platform; distance through which a thing falls.—*v.t.* let fall; let fall in drops; utter casually; discontinue.—*v.i.* to fall; fall in drops; lapse; come or go casually.

Drop'sy *n.* a disease with watery fluid collecting in the body.—**drop'sical** *a.*

Dross *n.* scum of molten metal, impurity, refuse.

Drost'dy *n.* in S. Africa, the official residence of a landdrost, or sheriff.

Drought (-owt) *n.* long-continued dry weather; thirst.

Drove *n.* a herd, flock, crowd, *esp.* in motion.—**dro'ver** *n.* a driver of, or dealer in, cattle.

Drown *v.i.* to be suffocated in water.—*v.t.* to suffocate in water; of sound, etc., to overpower.

Drow'sy (-z-) *a.* half-asleep; lulling; dull; lacking life.—

drow'sily *adv.*—drow'siness *n.* —drowse *v.i.*

Drub *v.t.* thrash, beat.— drubb'ing *n.*

Drudge *v.i.* to work hard at mean or distasteful tasks.— *n.* one who drudges.— drudg'ery *n.*

Drug *n.* a medicinal substance; a commodity not wanted (usually with in the market). —*v.t.* to mix drugs with; to administer a drug to, *esp.* one inducing sleep or unconsciousness.—drugg'ist *n.* a dealer in drugs.

Drugg'et *n.* a coarse woollen stuff.

Dru'id (-ōō-) *n.* an ancient Celtic priest; an Eisteddfod official.—druid'ic, druid'ical *a.*—dru'idism *n.*

Drum *n.* a musical instrument, made of skin stretched over a round hollow frame or hemisphere, and played by beating with sticks; various things shaped like a drum; a part of the ear.—*v.t.* and *i.* to play a drum; to tap or thump continuously.—**drum out**, to expel from a regiment. —drum'fire *n.* heavy continuous rapid artillery fire.— drum'stick *n.* a stick for beating a drum; the lower joint of cooked fowl's leg. — drumm'er *n.*

Drunk *a.* overcome by strong drink; *fig.* under the influence of strong emotion.—drunk'en *a.* drunk; often drunk; caused by or showing intoxication.—drunk'ard *n.* one given to excessive drinking. —drunk'enness *n.*

Dry *a.* without moisture; rainless; not yielding milk, or other liquid; not in, on, or under, water; cold, unfriendly; caustically witty; having prohibition of alcoholic drink; uninteresting; needing effort to study; lacking sweetness.—*v.t.* to remove water, moisture.—*v.i.* to become dry, evaporate.—dri'ly *adv.*—dry'ness *n.*—dry'-nurse *n.* a nurse tending but not suckling a child.—dry' point *n.* a needle for engraving without acid; an engraving so made.—dry rot' *n.* decay in wood not exposed to air.— drysalt'er *n.* a dealer in dyes, gums, oils.—drysalt'ery *n.*

Dry'ad *n.* a wood-nymph.

Du'al (dū-) *a.* twofold; of two, forming a pair.—dual'ity *n.* —du'alism *n.* recognition of two independent powers or principles, as good and evil, mind and matter.

Du'an *n.* a division of a poem.

Dub *v.t.* to confer knighthood on; give a title to; smear with grease, dubbin.—dubb'-in, dubb'ing *n.* grease for making leather supple.

Du'bious *a.* causing doubt, not clear or decided; of suspected character; hesitating.—dubi'ety *n.* *Syn.* undetermined, doubtful, uncertain. *Ant.* determined, certain, unequivocal.

Du'cal *a.* of, or relating to, a duke.

Duc'at (duk-) *n.* a former gold coin of Italy and other countries.

Duch'ess *n.* the wife or widow

of a duke.—**duch'y** n. territory of a duke.

Duck n. a familiar swimming bird.—**drake** n. masc.—**duck'-ling** n.—**duck** v.i. to plunge under water; to bend or bob down.—v.t. to plunge some one under water.

Duck n. a strong linen or cotton fabric;—pl. trousers of it.

Duct n. a channel or tube.—**duct'ile** a. capable of being drawn into wire; flexible and tough; docile.—**ductil'ity** n.—**duct'less** a. (of glands) secreting directly certain substances essential to health.

Dud n. a shell that fails to explode; a futile person or project or thing.

Dudg'eon (-jn) n. anger, indignation.

Duds n.pl. in North America, clothes.

Due a. that is owing; proper to be given, inflicted, etc.; adequate, fitting; usual, ascribable; under engagement to arrive, be present.—adv. (with points of the compass) exactly.—n. a person's fair share; charge, fee, etc. (usually in pl.).—**du'ly** adv.

Du'el n. a fight with deadly weapons between two persons; a keen two-sided contest.—v.i. to fight in a duel or duels.—**du'ellist** n.

Duenn'a n. a Spanish lady-in-waiting; a governess, chaperon.

Duet' n. a piece of music for two performers.

Duff'el, duf'fle n. a coarse woollen cloth.

Duff'er n. a stupid or inefficient person.

Duff'er n. in Australia, a cattle stealer.—to **duff** v.t.

Dug'-out n. a shelter for troops, esp. in trenches, at any depth underground; a hollowed-out tree canoe.

Duke n. a peer of rank next below a prince; a sovereign of a small state called a duchy.—**duke'dom** n.

Dul'cet (-set) a. (of sounds) sweet.

Dul'cimer (-sim-) n. a stringed instrument played with hammers, an ancestor of the piano.

Dull a. stupid; insensible; sluggish; tedious; not keen or clear or bright or sharp or defined; lacking liveliness or variety; gloomy, overcast.—v.t. and i. to make or become dull.—**dul'ly** adv.—**dull'ard** n.—**dull'ness** n. Syn. sluggish, drowsy, gloomy. Ant. bright, sparkling, sunny.

Du'ly see DUE.

Dumb a. incapable of speech; silent. — **dumb'-bell** n. a weight for exercises.—**dumb-found, dumbfound'er** v.t. to confound into silence.—**dumb'-show** n. acting without words.—**dumb'ly** adv.—**dumb'ness** n.—**dumm'y** n. an imaginary card-player; an imitation object.

Dum'dum n. a soft-nosed expanding bullet.

Dump v.t. to throw down in a mass; to send low-priced goods for sale abroad.—n. a rubbish-heap; a temporary depot of stores or munitions. —dump'ling *n.* a small round pudding of dough, often with fruit inside.—dump'y *a.* short and stout.—dumps *n.pl.* low spirits, dejection.—dump *n.* a dumpy object, a small quantity.

Dun *a.* of dull greyish brown. —*n.* this colour; a horse of dun colour.

Dun *v.t.* to make persistent demands, *esp.* for payment of debts.—*n.* one who duns.

Dunce *n.* a dullard, slow learner, blockhead.

Dun'derhead *n.* a blockhead.

Dune *n.* a mound of dry shifting sand on a coast or desert.

Dung *n.* the excrement of animals; manure.—*v.t.* to manure.

Dung'aree (-ng-g-) *n.* coarse calico;—*pl.* overalls of this.

Dung'eon (dun'jn) *n.* an underground cell or vault for prisoners; formerly a tower or keep of a castle.

Duode'cimo (-des-) *n.* the size of a book in which each sheet is folded into twelve leaves; a book of this size.—*a.* of this size.

Dupe *n.* a victim of delusion or sharp practice.—*v.t.* to deceive for an advantage.

Du'plex *a.* two-fold.—du'plicate *v.t.* to make an exact copy of; to double.—*a.* that is an exact copy.—*n.* an exact copy.—duplica'tion *n.*—du'plicator *n.*—dupli'city (-is'-) *n.* deceitfulness, double dealing.

Du'rable *a.* lasting, resisting wear.—durabil'ity *n.*—dura'-tion *n.* the time a thing lasts. —du'rably *adv.* — du'ring *prep.* throughout, in the time of.

Duralu'min *n.* a strong, light alloy of aluminium.

Du'rance *n.* imprisonment.

Dur'bar *n.* a levee of an Indian sovereign, or of an Anglo-Indian governor.

Du'ress *n.* restraint, imprisonment; *law,* illegal compulsion.

Du'ring *prep.* in the time of; throughout.

Dusk *n.* the darker stage of twilight; partial darkness.— dusk'y *a.* dark; dark coloured.—dusk'ily *adv.*

Dust *n.* fine particles, powder, of earth or other matter, lying on a surface or blown along by the wind.—*v.t.* to sprinkle with powder; to rid of dust.—dust'er *n.* a cloth for removing dust.—dust'y *a.*

Du'ty *n.* what one ought to do, moral or legal obligation; office, function, being occupied in these; a tax on goods for the public revenue; respect.—du'tiful *a.*—du'teous *a.*—du'tiable *a.* liable to customs duty.

Dwang *n.* a large bar-wrench for tightening nuts.

Dwarf *n.* a very undersized person.—*a.* unusually small, stunted.—*v.t.* to make stunted; to make seem small by contrast.—dwarf'ish *a.*

Dwell *v.i.* to live, make one's abode (in); fix one's attention, write or speak at length (on).—dwell'ing *n.* house.— dwell'er *n.*

Dwin′dle *v.i.* to grow less, waste away.

Dye (dī) *v.t.* to impregnate (cloth, etc.) with colouring matter; to colour thus.— *n.* colouring matter in solution or which may be dissolved for dyeing; tinge, colour.—**dy′er** *n.*

Dyke *see* DIKE.

Dynam′ics (dī-) *n.pl.* the branch of physics dealing with force as producing or affecting motion; physical or moral forces.—**dynam′ic** *a.* of or relating to motive force, force in operation.—**dynam′-ical** *a.*—**dynam′ically** *adv.*—**dy′namite** *n.* a high explosive of nitro-glycerine.—*v.t.* to blow up with this.—**dy′na-miter** *n.*—**dy′namo** *n.* a machine to convert mechanical into electrical energy, a generator of electricity.—**dyne** *n.* unit of force.—**dyna-mom′eter** *n.* an instrument to measure energy expended.

Dyn′asty (din-) *n.* a line or family of hereditary rulers. —**dyn′ast** *n.*—**dynast′ic** *a.*

Dys′entery (dis-) *n.* a disease of the bowels.

Dyspep′sia *n.* indigestion.— **dyspep′tic** *a.* and *n.*

E

Each *a.* and *pron.* every one taken separately.

Eag′er (ēg-) *a.* full of keen desire; keen, impatient.— **eag′erly** *adv.*—**eag′erness** *n.*

E′ager *n.* a rapid inflow of the tide.

Ea′gle (ē′gl) *n.* a large bird of prey with keen sight and strong flight.—**ea′glet** *n.* a young eagle.

Ean′ling (ēn-) *n.* a lamb just brought forth

Ear *n.* the organ of hearing, *esp.* the external part of it; sensitiveness to musical sounds; attention. — **ear-mark** *n.* owner's mark on ear of sheep, etc.—*v.t.* to mark thus; to assign or reserve for a definite purpose. —**ear′shot** *n.* hearing distance. —**ear′wig** *n.* an insect formerly thought to enter the head through the ear.

Ear *n.* a spike or head of corn.

Earl (erl) *n.* a peer of rank next below a marquis.— **earl′dom** *n.*

Earl′y (erl-) *a.* and *adv.* in the first part, or near or nearer the beginning, of some portion of time.

Earn (ern) *v.t.* to get for labour, merit, etc.

Earn′est (ern-) *a.* serious, ardent, sincere.—*n.* seriousness.—**earn′estly** *adv.*

Earn′est (ern-) *n.* money paid over to bind a bargain; foretaste.

Earth (er-) *n.* the ground, soil; the dry land; the planet or world we live on; mould, soil, mineral; a fox's hole.— *v.t.* to cover with earth; to connect electrically with the earth —**earth′en** (-th-) *a.*— **earth′ly** *a.*—**earth′y** *a.*— **earth′enware** (-th-) *n.* vessels of baked clay.—**earth′quake** *n.* a volcanic convulsion of

the surface of the earth.—
earth'work n. a bank of earth in fortification.

Ease (ēz) n. comfort; freedom from constraint or annoyance or awkwardness or pain or trouble; idleness; informal position or step; relief, alleviation.—v.t. and i. to relieve of pain; reduce burden; give bodily or mental ease to; slacken, relax.—**ease'ful** a.—**ease'ment** n.—**eas'y** a. not difficult; free from bodily or mental pain; complaint; not in much demand; fitting loosely.—**eas'ily** adv.—**eas'y-go'ing** a. not fussy, content with things as they are.

Eas'el (ēz-) n. a frame to support a picture, blackboard, etc.

East n. the part of the horizon where the sun rises; regions towards that.—a. on, or in, or near, the east; coming from the east.—adv. from or to the east.—**east'erly** a. and adv. from or to the east.—**east'ern** a. of or dwelling in the east.—**east'erner** n.—**east'ward** a. and n.—**east'ward(s)** adv.

East'er n. the festival of the resurrection of Christ.

Eas'ting n. distance run by a ship eastward from a given meridian.

Eas'y see EASE.

Eat v.t. and i. chew and swallow; swallow; consume, destroy; gnaw; wear away.—**eat'able** a.

Eaves (ēvz) n.pl. the overhanging edges of a roof.—

eaves'dropper n. one who stands under eaves or elsewhere to overhear.—**eaves'-dropping** n.

Ebb n. the flowing back of the tide; decline, decay.—v.i. to flow back; decline.

Eb'ony n. a hard black wood.—a. made of, or black as, ebony.—**eb'onite** n. vulcanite.

Ebri'ety n. intoxication, drunkenness. — **eb'rious** a. partly intoxicated, inclined to drink to excess.

Ebull'ient a. boiling; exuberant.—**ebull'ience** n.—**ebulli'tion** n. boiling; effervescence; outburst.

Eccen'tric (-ks-) a. not placed, or not having the axis placed, centrally; not circular (in orbit); irregular; odd, whimsical.—n. a mechanical contrivance to change circular into to-and-fro movement; a whimsical person.—**eccen'trically** adv.—**eccentri'city**, n. Syn. singular, peculiar, strange, whimsical, abnormal. Ant. usual, ordinary, normal, commonplace.

Ecclesias'tic (-klez-) a. of or belonging to the church.—n. a clergyman.—**ecclesias'tical** a.—**ecclesiol'ogy** n. the science of church-building and decoration.

Ech'elon (esh-) n. a formation of troops in parallel divisions each with its front clear of the one in front.

Ech'o (ek-) n. a repetition of sounds by reflection; a close imitation.—v.i. to resound or be repeated by echo.—

v.t. to repeat as an echo; imitate opinions.

Éclair' (āk-) *n.* a cake finger filled with cream and iced.

Éclat' (-kla) *n.* splendour, renown, acclamation.

Eclec'tic *a.* borrowing one's philosophy from various sources; catholic in views or taste.—*n.* an eclectic person.—**elec'ticism** *n.*

Eclipse' *n.* a blotting out of the sun, moon, etc., by another body coming between it and the eye or between it and the source of its light; loss of light or brilliance; obscurity.—*v.t.* to cause to suffer eclipse; outshine, surpass.—**eclip'tic** *a.* of an eclipse.—*n.* the apparent path of the sun. (See illus. p. 177.)

Ec'logue (-og) *n.* a short poem, *esp.* a pastoral dialogue.

Econ'omy *n.* management, administration; thrift, frugal use; structure, organisation.—**econom'ic** *a.* on business lines.—**econom'ics** *n.pl.* political economy, the science of the production and distribution of wealth.—**econom'ical** *a.* saving, frugal; of economics.—**econom'ically** *adv.*—**econ'omist** *n.* — **econ'omise** *v.t.* and *i.*

Ecru' (āk-rōō) *n.* and *a.* colour of unbleached linen.

Ec'stasy *n.* exalted state of feeling, rapture; trance; frenzy.—**ecstat'ic** *a.* — **ecstat'ically** *adv. Syn.* madness, transport, enthusiasm. *Ant.* despair, dejection, gloom.

Ec'toplasm *n.* in spiritism, a semiluminous plastic sub-

stance said to exude from the body of the medium.

Ec'zema *n.* a skin disease.

Ed'da *n.* a collection of ancient Icelandic poems.

Edd'y *n.* a small whirl in water, smoke, etc.—*v.i.* to move in whirls.

E'delweiss (ā-dl-vis) *n.* a white Alpine plant growing at a great height.

Edge *n.* the cutting side of a blade; sharpness; a border, boundary.—*v.t.* to sharpen, give an edge or border to; move gradually.—*v.i.* to advance sideways or gradually.—**edge'ways, edge'wise** *adv.*

Ed'ible *a.* eatable.—**edibil'ity** *n.*

E'dict *n.* an order proclaimed by authority, a decree.

Ed'ifice (-fis) *n.* a building, *esp.* a big one.—**ed'ify** *v.t.* to improve morally.—**edifica'tion** *n.*

Ed'it *v.t.* to prepare for publication.—**edi'tion** *n.* the form in which a book is published; the number of copies of a book, newspaper, etc., printed at one time, an issue.—**ed'itor** *n.*—**ed'itress** *fem.*—**editor'ial** *a.* of an editor.—*n.* a newspaper article written or sanctioned by the editor.

Ed'ucate *v.t.* to bring up; train mentally and morally; provide schooling for; train.—**educa'tion** *n.*—**educa'tional** *a.*—**educa'tionally** *adv.*—**ed'ucable** *a.*—**educabil'ity** *n.*—**ed'ucator** *n.*—**educa'tionalist** *n.*—**ed'ucative** *a.*

Educe' *v.t.* to bring out, develop; infer.—**edu'cible** *a.*—**educ'tion** *n.*

Eel *n.* a snake-like fish.

Ee'rie, ee'ry *a.* weird; superstitiously timid.

Efface' *v.t.* wipe or rub out.—**efface'ment** *n.*

Effect' *n.* a result, consequence; impression;—*pl.* property.—*v.t.* to bring about, accomplish.—**effect'ive** *a.*—**effect'ively** *adv.*—**effect'ual** *a*—**effect'ually** *adv.*—**effect'-uate** *v.t.*

Effem'inate *a.* womanish, unmanly.—**effem'inacy** *n.*

Effervesce' (-es) *v.i.* to give off bubbles; issue in bubbles.—**efferves'cent** *a.*—**efferves'-cence** *n.*

Effete' *a.* worn-out, feeble.

Effica'cious *a.* producing or sure to produce a desired result. — **eff'icacy** *n.* — **effi'-cient** *a.* capable, competent, producing effect.—**effi'ciently** *adv.*—**effi'ciency** *n.*

Eff'igy *n.* image, likeness.

Effloresce' (-es) *v.i.* to burst into flower.—**efflores'cent** *a.*—**efflores'cence** *n.*

Eff'luent *a.* flowing out.—*n.* a stream flowing from a larger stream, lake, etc.—**eff'luence** *n.*—**efflu'vium** *n.* (*pl.* **-ia**) something flowing out invisibly, *esp.* affecting lungs or sense of smell.—**eff'lux** *n.*—**efflux'ion** *n.*

Eff'ort *n.* exertion, endeavour.—**eff'ortless** *a.*

Effront'ery (-un-) *n.* brazen impudence. *Syn.* impudence, audacity, hardihood. *Ant.* diffidence, timidity, reserve.

Efful'gent *a.* radiant, shining

brightly. — **efful'gence** *n.*

Effu'sion *n.* a pouring out; a literary composition.—**effu'-sive** *a.* gushing, demonstrative.—**effu'sively** *adv.*—**effu'-siveness** *n.*—**effuse'** *v.t.* to pour out.

Eft *n.* newt.

Egg *n.* the round body produced by the female of birds, etc., *esp.* of domestic fowl, and containing the germ of their young

Egg *v.t.* to egg on, to encourage, urge.

Eg'lantine *n.* sweet briar.

Eg'o *n.* the self; the conscious thinking subject.—**eg'oism** *n.* systematic selfishness; theory that bases morality on self-interest. — **eg'oist** *n.*—**egois'tic, egois'tical** *a.*—**eg'otism** *n.* selfishness; self-conceit.—**eg'otist** *n.*—**egotis'-tic, egotis'tical** *a.*

Egre'gious (-jus) *a.* gross, notable (*esp.* absurdly, as egregious ass, blunder, etc.).

E'gress *n.* way out.

E'gret *n.* the lesser white heron.

Ei'der (ī-) *n.* an Arctic duck.—**ei'derdown** *n.* the breast feathers of the eider.

Ei'doscope *n.* an optical instrument giving great variety of geometrical figures.

Eight (āt) *a.* and *n.* cardinal number one above seven.—**eighth** (āt-th) *a.* ordinal number — **eighth'ly** *adv.*—**eighteen'** *a.* and *n.* eight more than ten. — **eighteenth'** *a.*—**eighteenth'ly** *adv.*—**eight'y** *a.* and *n.* ten times eight.—**eight'ieth** *a.*—**eight'fold** *a.*—

eighteen'fold *a.*—**eight'yfold** *a.*—**eight** *n.* an eight-oared boat; its crew.—**fig'ure-of-eight** *n.* a skating figure; any figure shaped as 8.

Eistedd'fod (ās-teᴛʜ'vod) *n.* a congress of Welsh bards.

Eith'er (-ᴛʜ-) *a.* and *pron.* one or the other; one of two; each.—*adv.* or *conj.* bringing in first of alternatives or strengthening an added negation.

Ejac'ulate *v.t.* and *i.* exclaim, utter suddenly. — **ejacula'tion** *n.*—**ejac'ulatory** *a.*

Eject' *v.t.* to throw out; expel, drive out.—**ejec'tion** *n.*—**eject'or** *n.*—**eject'ment** *n.*

Eke *v.t.* eke out, supply deficiencies of; make with difficulty (a living, etc.).

Elab'orate *v.t.* to work out in detail; produce by labour.—*a.* worked out in details; highly finished; complicated.—**elabora'tion** *n.*

É'lan *n.* dash; ardour.—**elance** *v.t.* to throw out, as a lance.

E'land *n.* a South African antelope.

Elapse' *v.i.* of time, to pass by.

Elas'tic *a.* resuming normal shape after distortion, springy; not unalterable or inflexible.—**elasti'city** (-is'-) *n.*

Ela'tion *n.* high spirits; pride.—**elate'** *v.t.*

El'bow *n.* the outer part of the joint between the upper arm and the forearm.—*v.t.* to thrust, jostle with the elbows.

El'der *n.* a white-flowered tree with much pith.

El'der *a.* older.—*n.* person of greater age; an old person; an official of certain churches.—**el'derly** *a.* growing old.—**el'dest** *a.* oldest.

Eldora'do (-à-) *n.* a fictitious country rich in gold.

Eld'ritch *a.* hideous; weird; haggish.

Elect *v.t.* to choose; choose by vote.—*a.* chosen; select, choice.—**elec'tion** *n.* a choosing, *esp.* by voting.—**electioneer'**, to busy oneself in political elections. — **elect'ive** *a.* appointed, filled, chosen by election.—**elect'or** *n.* — **elect'oral** *a.* — **elect'orate** *n.* a body of electors.

Electri'city (-is'-) *n.* active condition of the molecules of a body or of the ether round it, produced by friction, magnetism, etc.; the force which shows itself in lightning, etc.; the study of this.—**elec'tric** *a.* of, charged with, worked by producing, electricity.—**elec'trical** *a.*—**elec'trically** *adv.* — **elec'trify** *v.t.*—**electrifica'tion** *n.*—**electri'cian** *n.*—**elec'tron** *n.* the smallest known quantity of negative electricity; an essential component of the atom.

Elec'tro- *prefix* makes compounds meaning of, by, caused by, electricity, as **electrodynam'ics** *n.* the dynamics of electricity.—**elec'troscope** *n.* an instrument to show the presence or kind of electricity. — **elec'trocute** *v.t.* to execute (criminals) by electricity;—and many other compound words.

Eleemos'ynary *a.* charitable.

El'egant *a.* graceful, tasteful; refined.—**el'egance** *n.* *Syn.* symmetrical, beautiful, handsome. *Ant.* rude, rough, coarse, indelicate, ugly, uncultured.

El'egy *n.* a lament for the dead; a sad poem.—**elegi'ac** *a.* plaintive.—*n.pl.* elegiac verses.

El'ement *n.* a component part; a substance which cannot be chemically analysed; proper abode or sphere;—*pl.* powers of the atmosphere; rudiments, first principles.——**element'al** *a.* of the powers of nature; tremendous; not compounded. — **element'ary** *a.* rudimentary, simple; primary.

El'ephant *n.* a very big four-footed, thick-skinned animal with ivory tusks and a long trunk.—**elephant'ine** *a.* unwieldly, clumsy, heavily big. **elephanti'asis** *n.* a skin disease.

Eleuthe'rian *a.* liberal, bountiful.—**eleutheroma'nia** *n.* excessive zeal for freedom.

El'evate *v.t.* to raise, lift up.—**eleva'tion** *n.* raising; angle above the horizon, as of a gun; a drawing of one side of a building, etc.—**el'evator** *n.* a lift.

Elev'en *a.* and *n.* the number next above ten, one added to ten; a team of eleven persons.—**elev'enth** *a.* the ordinal number.—**elev'enthly** *adv.*—**elev'enfold** *a.* and *adv.*

Elf *n.* a fairy, a small super-natural being.—**elf'in, elf'-ish, elv'ish** *a.*

Elic'it (-s-) *v.t.* to draw out.

Elide' *v.t.* to omit in pronunciation (a vowel, syllable).—**elis'ion** *n.* (-izh'n).

El'igible *a.* fit or qualified to be chosen; suitable, desirable.—**eligibil'ity** *n.*

Elim'inate *v.t.* to remove, get rid of, set aside.—**elimina'tion** *n.*

Eli'sion *see* ELIDE.

Elite' (ālēt) *n.* the pick of.

Elix'ir *n.* the preparation sought by the alchemists to change base metals into gold, or to prolong life; a sovereign remedy.

Elk *n.* a large deer.

Ell *n.* a measure of length.

Ellipse' *n.* an oval, the figure made by a plane cutting a cone at a smaller angle with the side than the base makes; *gram.* the omission of words needed to complete the grammatical construction or full sense.—**ellip'sis** *n.* *gram.* ellipse.—**ellip'tic, ellip'tical** *a.*—**ellip'tically** *adv.*

Elm *n.* a familiar tree with doubly-serrated leaves; its wood.

Elocu'tion *n.* the art of public speaking, recitation, voice management. — **elocu'tionist** *n.*

E'longate *v.t.* to lengthen.—**elonga'tion** *n.* *Syn.* protract, prolong. *Ant.* curtail, shorten.

Elope' *v.i.* to run away with a lover; escape —**elope'ment** *n.*

El'oquence *n.* fluent and powerful use of language.—**el'o-**

quent *a.* — el'oquently *adv.*

Else *adv.* besides; otherwise. —**elsewhere** *adv.* in or to some other place.

Elu'cidate *v.t.* throw light upon, explain.—elucida'tion *n.*—elu'cidatory *a.*

Elude' *v.t.* escape, slip away from, dodge.—elu'sion *n.*—elu'sive *a.*—elu'sory *a.*—elu'sively *adv.*

Elv'ish *see* ELF.

Em *n.* in printing, the square of any size of type.

Ema'ciate (shi-) *v.t.* to make lean.—emacia'tion *n.*

Em'anate *v.i.* to issue from, originate.—emana'tion *n.*

Eman'cipate *v.t.* to set free.—emancipa'tion *n.*—emancipa'tionist *n.*—eman'cipator *n.*—eman'cipatory *a.*

Emas'culate *v.t.* to castrate; enfeeble, weaken.—emascua'tion *n.* emas'culative *a.*

Embar'go *n.* an order stopping the movement of ships; a suspension of commerce; a ban.—*v.t.* to put under an embargo.

Embark' *v.t.* and *i.* to put, go, on board ship; engage, involve (in).—embarka'tion *n.*

Embarr'ass *v.t.* to perplex, put into difficulty; encumber.—embarr'assment *n. Syn.* to entangle, confuse, disconcert, trouble. *Ant.* to clear, free, smooth, put at ease.

Em'bassy *n.* the office or work or residence of an ambassador; a deputation.

Embed', **imbed'** *v.t.* to fix fast in something solid.

Embell'ish *v.t.* to adorn.—embell'ishment *n.*

Em'ber *n.* a glowing cinder.

Em'ber *a.* Ember-days, days appointed by the Church for fasting, recurring in each of the four seasons.

Embez'zle *v.t.* to divert fraudulently, misappropriate (money in trust, etc.).—embez'zler *n.* —cmbez'zlement *n.*

Embitt'er *v.t.* to make bitter.

Em'blem *n.* a symbol; a heraldic device. — **emblemat'ic** *a.* — emblemat'ically *adv.*

Embod'y *v.t.* to give body, concrete expression, to; represent, be an expression of. —embod'iment *n.*

Em'bolism (-bū-) *n.* intercalation; in medicine, obstruction of an artery by a blood-clot.—embol'ic *a.* inserted, placed between.—em'bolise *v.t.*

Emboss' *v.t.* to mould, stamp or carve in relief.

Embrace' *v.t.* to clasp in the arms; seize, avail oneself of, accept.—*n.* a clasping in the arms.

Embra'sure (-zher) *n.* an opening in a wall for a cannon; the bevelling of a wall at the sides of a window.

Embroca'tion *n.* a lotion for rubbing limbs, etc.

Embroi'der *v.t.* to ornament with needlework; to embellish, exaggerate (a story). —embroi'dery *n.*

Embroil *v.t.* to bring into confusion; involve in hostility. —embroil'ment *n.*

Em'bryo *n.* an unborn or undeveloped offspring, germ; an undeveloped thing.—

Māte, mēte, mīte, mōte, mūte, bŏŏt.

embryon'ic *a.*—**embryol'ogy** *n.*—**embryol'ogist** *n.*

Emend' *v.t.* to remove errors from, correct. — **emenda'tion** *n.*—**e'mendator** *n. Syn.* to improve, mend, reform, rectify. *Ant.* spoil, deteriorate, mar, make worse, debase.

Em'erald *n.* a bright green precious stone.—*a.* of the colour of emerald.

Emerge' *v.i.* to come up, out; rise to notice; come out on inquiry. — **emer'gence** *n.*—**emer'gent** *a.*—**emer'gency** *n.* a sudden unforeseen thing or event needing prompt action.

Emer'itus *a.* retired, honourably discharged.

Em'ery *n.* a hard mineral used for polishing.

Emet'ic *a.* causing vomiting. —*n.* a medicine doing this.

Em'igrate *v.t.* to go and settle in another country.—**emigra'tion** *n.*—**em'igrant** *n.*

Émigré (ā-me-grā) *n.* an emigrant, *esp.* the refugees from France during the Revolution.

Em'inent *a.* distinguished, notable.—**em'inently** *adv.*—**em'inence** *n.* distinction; rising ground. — **Em'inence,** title of cardinal.

Emit' *v.t.* to give out, put forth.—**emitt'er** *n.*—**emis'sion** *n.* — **em'issary** *n.* one sent out on a mission.

Emoll'ient *a.* softening.—*n.* an ointment or other softening application.

Emol'ument *n.* pay, profit.

Emo'tion *n.* mental agitation, excited state of feeling.—**emo'tional** *a.* given to emotion; appealing to the emotions.

Empennage (-azh) *n.* the arrangement of planes at the tail of a dirigible balloon.

Em'peror *n.* the sovereign of an empire. — **em'press** *fem.*—**em'pire** *n.* a large territory, *esp.* an aggregate of states under one supreme ruler; supreme control.

Em'phasis *n.* stress on words; vigour of speech, expression; importance attached.—**em'phasise** *v.t.*—**emphat'ic** *a.* forcible; stressed.—**emphat'ically** *adv.*

Empir'ic *a.* relying on experiment or experience, not on theory.—*n.* an empiric scientist, physician.—**empir'ically** *adv.*—**empir'icism** *n.*

Emplace'ment *n.* a platform or other prepared position for guns.

Employ' *v.t.* to use; use the services of, keep in one's service.—**employ'er** *n.*—**employee'** *n.*—**employ'ment** *n.*

Empor'ium *n.* a centre of commerce, (in affected language) a shop.

Empow'er *v.t.* to enable, authorise.

Em'press *see* EMPEROR.

Emp'ty *a.* containing nothing; unoccupied; senseless; vain, foolish.—*v.t.* and *i.* to make or become empty.—*n.* an empty box, basket, etc.—**emp'tiness** *n. Syn.* void, devoid, vacant, unsubstantial, blank. *Ant.* full, occupied, substantial.

Empyre'an *n.* the sky.

E'mu *n.* a large Australian bird like an ostrich.

Em'ulate *v.t.* to strive to equal or excel; imitate.—**em'ulator** *n.*—**emula'tion** *n.*—**em'ulative** *a.*—**em'ulous** *a.*

Emul'sion *n.* a milky liquid mixture with oily or resinous particles in suspension.—**emul'sive** *a.*—**emul'sify** *v.t.*

En- *prefix* forms verbs with sense of put in, into, on; as **engulf'** *v.t.* swallow up.—**enrage'** *v.t.* to put into rage. Many such words are omitted and the meaning and derivation should be sought under the simple word.

Ena'ble *v.t.* to make able, authorise.

Enact' *v.t.* to make law; play, act.

Enam'el *n.* a glass-like coating applied to metal, etc., to preserve the surface; the coating of the teeth; any hard outer coating.—*v.t.* to cover with enamel; to adorn with colours.

Enam'our (-ẹr) *v.t.* to inspire with love.

Encamp' *v.t.* and *i.* to settle in a camp. — **encamp'ment** *n.*

Encaus'tic *a.* burnt in.—*n.* the art of ornament by burnt-in colours.

Enceinte' *a.* (of a woman) pregnant.—*n.* (in fortification) an enclosure.

Enchant' (-à-) *v.t.* to bewitch, delight.—**enchant'ment** *n.*—**enchant'er** *n.*—**enchant'ress** *fem.*

En'clave *n.* a portion of territory entirely surrounded by foreign land.

Enclit'ic *a.* pronounced as part of (another word).—*n.* an enclitic word.

Enclose' *v.t.* to shut; to place in with something else (in a letter, etc.).—**enclo'sure** (-zhẹr) *n.*

Enco'mium *n.* formal praise; eulogy.—**enco'miast** *n.*—**encomias'tic** *a.*

En'core (ŏn-kor) *interj.* again, once more.—*n.* a call for the repetition of a song, etc.; the repetition.—*v.t.* to call for repetition.

Encount'er *v.t.* to meet in hostility; meet with.—*n.* a hostile or casual meeting.

Encour'age (-kur-) *v.t.* to hearten, inspirit.—**encour'agement** *n. Syn.* to animate, cheer, stimulate, countenance, foster. *Ant.* discourage, depress, dishearten.

Encroach' *v.i.* to intrude (on) as a usurper.—**encroach'ment** *n.*

Encum'ber *v.t.* to hamper; burden.—**encum'brance** *n.*

Encyclopæ'dia (-pĕd-) *n.* a book of information on all subjects, or on every branch of a subject, usually arranged alphabetically. — **encyclopæ'dic** *a.*—**encyclopæ'dist** *n.*

End *n.* a limit; extremity; conclusion, finishing; fragment; latter part; death; event, issue; purpose, aim. —*v.t.* to put an end to.—*v.i.* to come to an end.—**end'ing** *n.*—**end'less** *a.*—**end'ways** *adv.*

Endeav'our (-dev-ẹr) *v.i.* try,

attempt.—*n.* attempt, effort.

Endem'ic *a.* regularly existing or found in a country or district.—*n.* an endemic disease.

End'ive *n.* curly-leaved chicory.

En'docrine (-ēn) *n.* a substance absorbed from the ductless glands into the bloodstream.

Endorse' *v.t.* to write (*esp.* to sign one's name) on the back of.—endorse'ment *n.*

Endow' *v.t.* to provide a permanent income for; furnish.—endow'ment *n.*

Endue' *v.t.* to invest, furnish (with a quality, etc.).

Endure' *v.i.* to last.—*v.t.* to undergo; tolerate, put up with.—endu'rance *n.* power of enduring.—endu'rable *a.*

En'emy *n.* a hostile person, opponent; armed foe; hostile force or ship.

En'ergy *n.* vigour, force, activity.—energet'ic *a.*—energet'ically *adv.* — en'ergise *v.t.*

En'ervate *v.t.* to weaken, deprive of vigour.—enerva'tion *n.*

Enfee'ble *v.t.* to weaken.—enfee'blement *n.*

En'filade *n.* fire from artillery, etc., sweeping a line from end to end.—*v.t.* to subject to enfilade.

Enforce' *v.t.* compel obedience to; impose (action) upon; drive home.—enforce'ment *n.*—enforce'able *a.*

Enfran'chise *v.t.* to give the right of voting for members of parliament; give parliamentary representation to; to set free.—enfran'chisement *n.*

Engage' *v.t.* to bind by contract or promise; hire; order; pledge oneself, undertake; attract; occupy; bring into conflict; interlock.—*v.i.* to begin to fight; employ oneself (in); promise.—engage'ment *n.*

Engen'der *v.t.* to give rise to, beget.

En'gine *n.* a complex mechanical contrivance; a machine; instrument of war.—*v.t.* to supply (a ship) with engines.—engineer' *n.* one who constructs or is in charge of engines, military works, or works of public utility (e.g. bridges, roads).—*v.t.* to construct as an engineer; to contrive.

Eng'lish (ing'gl-) *a.* relating to England.—*n.* the language or people of England.—*v.t.* to translate into English.

Engraft (-à-) *v.t.* to graft in.

Engrain' *v.t.* to dye deep; implant firmly.

Engrave' *v.t.* and *i.* to cut in lines on metal for printing; carve, incise; impress deeply.—engra'ving *n.* a copy of a picture printed from an engraved plate.—engra'ver *n.*

Engross' (-ō-) *v.t.* to write out in large letters or in legal form; to absorb (attention).—engross'ment *n.*

Enhance' *v.t.* to heighten, intensify, raise in price.—enhance'ment *n.* *Syn.* to raise, increase, augment. *Ant.* decrease, deface, lower.

Enig'ma *n.* a riddle; a puzzling thing or person.—enigmat'ic, enigmat'ical a.—enigmat'ically adv.

Enjamb'ment n. in verse, the continuation of a sentence beyond the end of a line.

Enjoin' v.t. command, impose, prescribe.

Enjoy' v.t. to take pleasure in; have the use or benefit of.—v. refl. to be happy.—enjoy'ment n.—enjoy'able a.

Enlarge' v.t. to make bigger; set free.—v.i. to grow bigger; to talk at large.—enlarge'ment, n.

Enlight'en, (-līt-) v.t. instruct, inform.—enlight'enment n.

Enlist' v.t. and i. to engage as a soldier or helper; gain (sympathies, etc.).—enlist'ment n.

Enli'ven v.t. to brighten, make more lively.

En'mity n. ill-will; hostility.

Enno'ble (-n-n-) v.t. to make noble.

En'nui (ōn-wē) n. boredom.

Enoda'tion n the act of untying a knot; the solution of a difficulty.

Enor'mous a. very big, vast.—enor'mity n. a gross offence; great wickedness.

Enough' (i-nuf) a. as much or as many as need be, sufficient.—n. a sufficient quantity.—adv. sufficiently.—enow' a., n., and adv. enough.

Enounce' v.t. to enunciate.

Enrich' v.t. to make rich; add to.—enrich'ment n.

Enrol', enroll (-ō-) v.t. to write the name of on a roll or list; engage, enlist, take in as a member; enter, record. — enroll'ment n.

Ensang'uine v.t. to stain with blood.

Ensconce' v.t. to place snugly, in safety.

En'sign (-sīn) n. a naval or military flag; a badge, emblem; formerly, a commissioned officer of the lowest rank, a sub-lieutenant.

En'silage n. the storing of fodder in a silo; fodder so stored.

Enslave' v.t. to make into a slave.—enslave'ment n.—ensla'ver n.

Ensue' v.i. to follow, happen after.—v.t. strive for.

Ensure' v.t. to make safe, certain to happen.

Entail' v.t. to settle (land, etc.) on persons in succession, none of whom can then dispose of it; to involve as result.—n. such settlement.

Entente' (ōn-tōnt) n. a friendly understanding between nations.

Ent'er v.t. to go or come into; to join (a society, etc.); write in, register.—v.i. to go or come in; join; begin; engage.—en'trance n. going or coming in; right to enter; fee paid for this; door or passage to enter.—en'trant n. one who enters, esp. a contest.—en'try n. entrance; an entering; an item entered, e.g. in an account, list.

Enter'ic n. typhoid fever.—a. typhoid; of or relating to the intestines.

En'terprise n. a design, an undertaking, usually a bold or difficult one; bold spirit.

—en'terprising *a.* prompt to undertake, bold and active in spirit.

Entertain' *v.t.* receive as guest; amuse; maintain; consider favourably, cherish.—entertain'er *n.*—entertain'ment *n.*

Enthu'siasm *n.* ardent eagerness, zeal.—enthu'siast *n.*—enthusias'tic *a.*—enthusias'tically *adv.*—enthuse' *v.i.* (colloq.) to show enthusiasm.

Entice' *v.t.* to allure; attract or entrap adroitly.—entice'ment *n.* *Syn.* to tempt, decoy. *Ant.* repel, repulse.

Entire' *a.* whole, complete, not broken.—entire'ly *adv.*—entire'ty *n.*

Enti'tle *v.t.* to give a title or claim to.

En'tity *n.* a thing's being or existence; a thing having real existence.

Entomol'ogy *n.* the study of insects.—entomol'ogist *n.*—entomolo'gical (-oj'-) *a.*—entomol'ogise *v.i.*

Entourage (ŏn-tŏōr-azh) *n.* surroundings; one's habitual associates.

Entracte' (ŏn-trǎkt) *n.* the interval, or music played between two acts of a play.

En'trails, *n.pl.* bowels, intestines; inner parts.

Entreat' *v.t.* to ask earnestly, beg, implore.—entreat'y *n.*

Entree (ŏn-trǎ) *n.* right of access; a dish served between courses.

Entrust' *v.t.* to confide (to); commit, put in charge.

Entwine' *v.t.* to plait, interweave; wreathe (with).

Enu'merate *v.* to count.—en-umera'tion *n.*—enu'merator *n.*

Enun'ciate *v.t.* to state clearly; proclaim; pronounce.—enuncia'tion *n.* — enun'ciator *n.* —enun'ciative *a.*

Envel'op *v.t.* to wrap up, enclose.—envel'opment *n.*—en'velope *n.* folded, gummed cover of a letter; a covering, wrapper.

Enven'om *v.t.* to put poison in.

Envi'ron *v.t.* to surround.—envi'ronment *n.* surroundings; conditions of life or growth.—envi'rons *n.pl.* the districts round (a town, etc.).

Envis'age (-z-) *v.t.* to view; look at.

En'voy *n.* a messenger; a diplomatic minister of rank below an ambassador.

En'voy *n.* a short concluding stanza of a poem.

En'vy *n.* bitter or longing consideration of another's better fortune or success or qualities; the object of this feeling.—*v.t.* to feel envy of.—en'vious *a.*—en'viable *a.* *Syn.* ill-will, malevolence, jealousy, malignity, hatred. *Ant.* goodwill, benevolence, kindliness.

Ep'aulette *n.* ornamental shoulder-piece of a uniform.

Epergne' (-pern) *n.* an ornament for the middle of a dining-table.

Ephem'eral *a.* short-lived, lasting only for a day, or few days.—ephem'eron, ephem'era *n.* an ephemeral insect or thing.

E'phod *n.* a Jewish priestly vestment.

Ep'ic *a.* telling in continuous story the achievements of a hero or heroes.—*n.* an epic poem.

Ep'icarp *n.* in botany, the outer skin of fruits.

Ep'icene (-sēn) *a.* denoting either sex; for. or having the characteristics of, both sexes.

Ep'icure *n.* one dainty in eating and drinking.—**epicure'an** (-ĕ'-) *a.* of Epicurus, who taught that pleasure, in the shape of practice of virtue, was the highest good; given to refined sensuous enjoyment.—*n.* such a person or philosopher. — **epicure'anism** *n.*

Epidem'ic *a.* prevalent for a time among a community. —*n.* an epidemic disease.

Epider'mis *n.* the outer skin.

Epiglot'tis *n.* a cartilage that covers the opening of the larynx during the act of swallowing.

Ep'igram *n.* a short poem with a witty or satirical ending; a pointed saying.— **epigrammat'ic** *a.*—**epigrammat'ically** *adv.* — **epigram'matist** *n.*

Ep'igraph *n.* an inscription.

Ep'ilepsy *n.* a disease in which the sufferer falls down in a fit, with foaming and spasms. —**epilep'tic** *a.* subject to epilepsy.—*n.* a person who suffers from epilepsy.

Ep'ilogue (-og) *n.* a short speech or poem at the end of a play; the concluding part of a book.

Epiph'any *n.* the festival of the appearance of Christ to the Magi.

Epis'copal *a.* of a bishop; ruled by bishops.—**epis'copacy** *n.* government by bishops; the body of bishops.—**episcopa'lian** *a.* of an episcopal system or church.—*n.* a member or adherent of an Episcopal church.—**epis'copate** *n.* a bishop's office, see, or duration of office; the body of bishops.

Ep'isode *n.* an incident; an incidental narrative or series of events; the part of a Greek tragedy between choric songs.—**episod'ic**, **episod'ical** *a.*

Epis'tle (-sl) *n.* a letter, *esp.* one of the letters of the apostles; a poem in the form of a letter.—**epis'tolary** *a.*

Ep'itaph *n.* an inscription on a tomb.

Ep'ithet *n.* an adjective expressing a quality or attribute; a name full of meaning. —**epithet'ic** *a.*

Epit'ome (-mē) *n.* a summary, abridgment.—**epit'omize** *v.t.* —**epit'omist** *n.*

E'poch (-ok) *n.* the beginning of a period; a period, era, *esp.* one marked by notable events.—**e'pochal** *a.*

Epon'ymous *a.* commemorated by the adoption of the name.

Eq'uable *a.* uniform, not easily disturbed.—**eq'uably** *adv.*—**equabil'ity** *n.* *Syn.* even, cool, calm. *Ant.* unsteady, irritable, excitable.

E'qual *a.* the same in number, size, merit, etc.; fit or

qualified; evenly balanced.
—*n.* one equal to another.—
v.t. to be equal to.—**equal'ity**
(-ol-) *n.*—**e'qually** *adv.*—
e'qualize *v.t.* and *i.*—**equal-
isa'tion** *n.*

Equanim'ity *n.* calmness, even-
ness of mind or temper.

Equate' *v.t.* to state or assume
the equality of.—**equa'tion**
n. a statement of equality
between two mathematical
expressions; a balancing; a
compensation for inaccur-
acy.—**equa'tor** *n.* a great
circle of the earth equidis-
tant from the poles.—
equator'ial *a.*

Eq'uerry *n.* a king's officer in
charge of horses; an officer
in attendance on an English
sovereign.

Eques'trian *a.* of, skilled in,
horse-riding; mounted on a
horse.—*n.* a rider or performer on a horse.

Equi- *prefix*, equal, at equal.
—**equiang'ular** (-ng-g-) *a.*
having equal angles.—**equi-
dis'tant** *a.* at equal distances.
—**equilat'eral** *a.* having equal
sides, etc.

Equilibrium *n.* a state of
balance; balanced mind.—
—**equili'brate** *v.t.* and *i.*—
equil'ibrist *n.* an acrobat,
rope-walker.

Eq'uine *a.* of a horse.

E'quinox *n.* the time at which
the sun crosses the equator
and day and night are equal;
—*pl.* the points at which the
sun crosses the equator.—
equinoc'tial *a.*

Equip' *v.t.* to supply, fit out,
array.—**equip'ment** *n.*—**eq'-**

uipage *n.* a carriage, horses
and attendants; outfit.

Eq'uity *n.* fairness; the use of
the principles of justice to
supplement the law; a
system of law so made.—
eq'uitable *a.* fair, reasonable,
just.—**eq'uitably** *adv.*

Equiv'alent *a.* equal *in* value;
having the same meaning or
result; corresponding.—*n.* an
equivalent thing, amount,
etc. — **equiv'alence, equiv'a-
lency** *n.*

Equiv'ocal *a.* of double or
doubtful meaning; question-
able, liable to suspicion.—
equivocal'ity *n.*—**equiv'ocate**
v.i. to use equivocal words to
hide the truth.—**equivoca'-
tion** *n.*—**equiv'ocator** *n.*—
eq'uivoque, eq'uivoke *n.* a
pun. *Syn.* doubtful, evasive,
double. *Ant.* sure, certain,
unambiguous.

E'ra *n.* a system of time in
which years are numbered
from a particular event; the
time of the event; a memorable date; a period.

Erad'icate *v.t.* to root out.—
eradica'tion *n.*—**erad'icator** *n.*

Erase' *v.t.* to rub out.—**era'sure**
n.

Ere (ĕr) *prep.* and *conj.* before.

Erect' *a.* upright.—*v.t.* to set
up; build.—**erect'ile** *a.*—
erec'tion *n.*—**erect'or** *n.*

Ergoster'ol *n.* a fat, produced
from ergot or sometimes rye
and yeast, from which vitamin D can be produced.

Er'got *n.* a disease of rye and
other plants; the diseased
seed used as a drug.

Er′mine n. an animal like a weasel with fur brown in summer and white, except for black tail-tip, in winter; its fur.

Erode′ v.t. to wear out, eat away. — ero′sion n.—ero′-sive a.

Erot′ic a. relating to, or treating of, sexual love.—erot′-icism, ero′tism n. in psycho-analysis, love of all manifestations, direct, perverted or sublimated.—erotoma′nia n. intense sexual passion.

Err v.i. to make mistakes; to be wrong; to sin.—errat′ic a. irregular in movement, conduct, etc. — erra′tum (-à-) n. erra′ta pl. a mistake noted for correction.—erro′neous a. mistaken, wrong.—err′or n. a mistake; wrong opinion; sin.—err′ant a. wandering in search of adventure; erring. —err′ancy n. erring state or conduct.—err′antry n. state or conduct of a knight errant.

Err′and n. a short journey for a simple business; the business; a purpose.—err′and-boy n.

Erst, erst′while adv. of old.

Eructa′tion n. belching.

Er′udite a. learned.—erudi′-tion n.

Erupt′ v.i. to burst out.—erup′tion n. a bursting out, esp. a volcanic outbreak; a rash.—erupt′ive a.

Erysip′elas n. a disease causing a deep red colouring of the skin.

Escalade′ n. a scaling of walls with ladders.—es′calator n. a moving staircase.

Escall′op see SCALLOP.

Escape′ v.i. to get free; get off safely; go unpunished; find a way out.—v.t. to elude; come out unawares from.—n. an escaping; leakage.—escape′ment n. the mechanism connecting the motive power to the regulator of a clock or watch.—escapade′ n. a flighty exploit. Syn. to flee, shun, avoid, elude, evade. Ant. seek, court.

Escarp′ n. the steep bank under a rampart.—v.t. to cut into a steep slope.—escarp′-ment n.

Eschatol′ogy (-k-) n. doctrine of death, judgment and last things.

Escheat′ n. the lapse of a property to the state on the death of the tenant without proper heirs; an estate so lapsing.—v.t. to make an escheat of; to confiscate.—v.i. to become an escheat.

Eschew′ v.t. to avoid, abstain from.

Es′cort n. an armed guard for a traveller, etc.; a person or persons accompanying another on a journey for protection or courtesy.—escort′ v.t. to act as escort to.

Es′critoire (-twàr) n. a writing-desk with drawers.

Es′culent a. eatable.

Escutch′eon (-chun) n. a shield with a coat of arms.

Esoter′ic (-ō-) a. for the initiated, for a select few.

Espal′ier n. lattice on which trees are trained; a tree so trained.

Espart'o *n.* a rush of which paper is made.

Espe'cial (-esh'l) *a.* pre-eminent, more than ordinary.—**espe'cially** *adv.* *Syn.* particular, essential, exclusive, specific. *Ant.* general, universal, unexacting, ordinary.

Esperan'to *n.* an artificial language meant to be universal. —**Esperan'tist** *n.* one who uses Esperanto.

Es'pionage *n.* spying; the use of spies.

Esplanade' *n.* a level space, *esp.* one used as a public promenade.

Espouse' (-z) *v.t.* to marry; support, attach oneself to (a cause, etc.).—**espous'al** *n.*

Espy' *v.t.* to catch sight of.—**espi'al** *n.*

Esquire' *n.* a title added to a gentleman's name, *esp.* on the address of a letter; formerly, a squire.

Essay' *v.t.* to try, attempt; test.—**ess'ay** *n.* a literary composition, usually short and in prose; an attempt.—**ess'ayist** *n.* a writer of essays.

Ess'ence *n.* an existence, being; absolute being, reality; all that makes a thing what it is; an extract got by distillation, a perfume, scent.—**essen'tial** *a.* of, or constituting, the essence of a thing.—*n.* an indispensable element; a chief point.—**essential'ity** *n.*

Estab'lish *v.t.* to set up; settle; found; prove. — **estab'lishment** *n.* establishing; a church system established by law; a permanent organised body, full number of a regi-

ment, etc.; household; house of business; public institution.

Estaminet (-ā-) *n.* a cheap coffee-house, tap-room, or restaurant where smoking is allowed.

Estate' *n.* a landed property; a person's property; a class as part of a nation; rank, state, condition.

Esteem' *v.t.* to think highly of; consider.—*n.* favourable opinion, regard.

Es'timate *v.t.* to form an approximate idea of (amounts, measurements, etc.); form an opinion of; quote a probable price for.—*n.* an approximate judgment of amounts, etc.; the amount, etc., arrived at; an opinion; a price quoted by a contractor.—**es'timable** *a.* worthy of regard.—**estima'tion** *n.* opinion, judgment, esteem.

Estrange' *v.t.* to make unfriendly, put a stop to affection.—**estrange'ment** *n.*

Es'tuary *n.* the tidal mouth of a river.

Etch *v.t.* to make an engraving by eating away the surface of a metal plate with acids, etc. —*v.i.* to practise this art.—**etch'ing** *n.*—**etch'er** *n.*

Eter'nal *a.* without beginning or end; everlasting; changeless.—**eter'nally** *adv.*—**eter'nity** *n.*

E'ther (-th-) *n.* a substance or fluid supposed to fill all space; the clear sky, region above the clouds; a colourless volatile liquid used as an anæsthetic.—**ethe'real** *a.* light,

airy; heavenly.—~~ethereal'ity~~
n.

Eth'ic, eth'ical *a.* relating to,
or treating of, morals.—
eth'ically *adv.*—**eth'ics** *n.pl.*
the science of morals; moral
principles, rules of conduct.

Eth'nic *a.* of race. — **ethnog'-
raphy** *n.* the description of
races of men.—**ethnograph'ic**
a.—**ethnol'ogy** *n.* the science
of races.—**ethnolo'gical** *a.*

Eth'yl *n.* the radical of
ordinary alcohol and ether;
in motoring, a special type
of petrol (protected trade
name).

E'tiolate *v.t.* to make pale by
shutting out light.—**etiola'-
tion** *n.*

Et'iquette *n.* conventional
rules of manners; court ceremonial; code of conduct for
a profession.

Etymol'ogy *n.* the tracing, or
an account of, a word's formation, origin, development;
the science of this.—**ety-
molo'gical** (-oj'-) *a.*—**ety-
molo'gically** *adv.*—**etymol'-
ogist** *n.*—**et'ymon** *n.* a primitive word from which a derivative comes.

Eucalypt'us *n.* the Australian
gum-tree and allied plants.—
eucalypt'us-oil' *n.* a disinfectant.

Eu'charist (-k-) *n.* the sacrament of the Lord's Supper;
the consecrated elements.—
eucharis'tic *a.*

Eugen'ic *a.* relating to, or
tending towards, the production of fine offspring.—*n.pl.*
the science of this.—**eugen'ist**
n.

Eu'logy *n.* a speech or writing
in praise of a person; praise.
—**eu'logize** *v.t.*—**eu'logist** *n.*—
eulogis'tic *a.*—**eulogis'tically**
adv.

Eu'nuch (-k) *n.* a castrated
man, *esp.* one employed in a
harem.

Eu'phemism *n.* the substitution of a mild word or expression for a blunt one; an instance of this.—**euphemis'tic**
a.—**euphemis'tically** *adv.*—
eu'phemist *n.*

Eu'phony *n.* pleasantness of
sound. — **euphon'ic**, *a.* —**eupho'nious** *a.*—**eupho'nium** *n.*
a bass saxhorn.

Eu'phuism *n.* an affected or
highflown manner of writing,
esp. in imitation of Lyly's
Euphues (1580).—**eu'phuist**
n.—**euphuis'tic** *a.*

Eura'sian *c.* of mixed Euro-
pean and Asiatic descent; of
Europe and Asia.—*n.* a
Eurasian person.

Eure'ka *interj.* "I've found
it" (to announce a dis-
covery, etc.).

Eurhyth'mics *n.pl.* an art of
rhythmical free movement
to music, of expression in
dance movement.—**eurhyth'-
mic** *a.*

Euthana'sia *n.* gentle, easy
death.

Evac'uate *v.t.* to empty; withdraw from; discharge.—
evacua'tion *n.*

Evade' *v.t.* to avoid, escape
from; elude, frustrate.—
eva'sion *n.*—**eva'sive** *a.*—
eva'sively *adv. Syn.* to equi-
vocate, baffle, quibble. *Ant.*
seek, court.

Eval'uate *v.t.* to find or state the value or number of.—evalua'tion *n.*

Evanesce' (-es) *v.i.* to fade away. — evanes'cent *a.*—evanes'cence *n.*

Evan'gel (-j-) *n.* the gospel.—evangel'ical *a.* of, or according to, the gospel teaching; of the Protestant school which maintains salvation by faith.—evangel'icalism *n.*—evan'gelist *n.* a writer of one of the four gospels; a preacher of the gospel; a revivalist.—evan'gelise *v.t.* to preach to; to convert.—evangelisa'tion *n.*

Evap'orate *v.i.* to turn into vapour; pass off in vapour. —*v.t.* to turn into vapour.—evapora'tion *n.*—evap'orator *n.*—evap'orative *a.*

Eva'sion *see* EVADE.

Eve (ēv) *n.* the evening before (a festival, etc.); the time just before (an event, etc.); evening.

E'ven *n.* evening.— e'vensong *n.* evening prayer.

E'ven *a.* flat, smooth; uniform in quality; equal in amount, balanced; divisible by two; impartial.—*v.t.* to make even.—*adv.* invites comparison with something less strong included by implication in the statement: e.g. "*the dog eats even the bones*" (*not just the meat*); or introduces an extreme case: e.g. "*even a worm will turn*"; *archaic*, quite.

E'vening (-vn-) *n.* the close of day.

Event' *n.* the occurrence of a thing; a notable occurrence; issue; result.—event'ful *a.* full of exciting events.—event'ual *a.* that will happen under certain conditions; resulting in the end.—event'ually *adv.*—eventual'ity *n.* a possible event.—event'uate *v.i.* turn out; end.

Ev'er *adv.* always; constantly; at any time; by any chance.

Ev'ery (-vr-) *a.* each of all; all possible. — ev'erybody *n.*—ev'eryday *a.* usual, ordinary. —ev'eryone *n.*—ev'erything *n.*—ev'erywhere *adv.* in all places.

Evict' *v.t.* to expel by legal process, to turn out.—evic'tion *n.*

Ev'ident *a.* plain, obvious.—ev'idently *adv.*—ev'idence *n.* sign, indication; ground for belief, testimony; in evidence, conspicuous.—*v.t.* indicate, prove.—eviden'tial *a.*

E'vil *a.* bad, harmful.—*n.* what is bad or harmful; sin.—e'villy *adv.*

Evince' *v.t.* show, indicate.

Evis'cerate (-vis-er-) *v.t.* to disembowel.—eviscera'tion *n.*

Evoke' *v.t.* to call up.—evoca'tion *n.*

Evolve' *v.t.* to develop; unfold, open out; produce.—*v.i.* to develop, *esp.* by natural process; open out.—evolu'tion *n.* an evolving; development of species from earlier forms; movement of troops or ships; movement in dancing, etc.—evolu'tional *a.*—evolu'tionary *a.*—evolu'tionist *n.*

Ewe (ū) *n.* a female sheep.

Ew'er (ū'-) *n.* a pitcher, water-jug.

Exac'erbate (-as'-) *v.t.* to aggravate, embitter.—**exacerba'tion** *n.*

Exact' (-gz-) *a.* precise, accurate, strictly correct.—*v.t.* to demand, extort; insist upon; enforce.—**exact'ly** *adv.*—**exac'tion** *n.*—**exact'ness** *n.*—**exact'itude** *n.*—**exact'or** *n.*

Exag'gerate (igz-aj'-) *v.t.* to magnify beyond truth, overstate. — **exaggera'tion** *n.*—**exag'gerator** *n.*—**exag'gerative** *a.*

Exalt' (igz-awlt') *v.t.* to raise up; praise; make noble.—**exalta'tion** *n.* an exalting; rapture. *Syn.* to elevate, dignify, extol, aggrandise. *Ant.* degrade, humble.

Exam'ine (-gz-) *v.t.* to investigate; ask questions of; test the knowledge or proficiency of by oral or written questions; inquire into.—**examina'tion** *n.*—**exam'iner** *n.*—**exam'inee** *n.*

Exam'ple (-gz-à-) *n.* a thing illustrating a general rule; a specimen; model, pattern; warning, precedent.

Exas'perate (-gz-) *v.t.* to irritate, enrage; intensify, make worse.—**exaspera'tion** *n. Syn.* to anger, embitter, incense. *Ant.* soothe, calm, pacify.

Excandes'cence *n.* a white of glowing heat.—**excandes'cent** *a.*

Ex'cavate *v.t.* to hollow out; make a hole by digging; unearth.—**excava'tion** *n.*—**ex'cavator** *n.*

Exceed' *v.t.* to be greater than; do more than authorized, go beyond; surpass.—**exceed'ingly** *adv.* very.—**excess'** *n.* an exceeding; the amount by which a thing exceeds; too great an amount; intemperance or immoderate conduct. — **excess'ive** *a.* — **excess'ively** *adv.*

Excel' *v.i.* to be very good, pre-eminent.—*v.t.* to surpass, be better than.—**ex'cellent** *a.* very good.—**ex'cellence** *n.*—**ex'cellency** *n.* a title of ambassadors, etc.

Except' *v.t.* to leave or take out; exclude.—*v.i.* to raise objection.—*prep.* not including; but.—*conj.* unless.—**except'ing** *prep.* not including.—**excep'tion** *n.* an excepting; a thing excepted, not included in a rule; an objection.—**excep'tional** *a.*—**excep'tionally** *adv.*—**excep'tionable** *a.* open to objection.

Ex'cerpt *v.t.* to extract, quote (a passage from a book, etc.). —**ex'cerpt** *n.* a quoted or extracted passage.—**excerp'tion** *n.*

Excess' *see* EXCEED.

Exchange' *v.t.* to give (something) in return for something else.—*v.i.* of an officer, to change posts with another. —*n.* giving one thing and receiving another; giving or receiving coin, bills, etc., of one country for those of another; a thing given for another; a building where merchants meet for business. — **exchange'able** *a.* — **exchangeabil'ity** *n.*

Excheq'uer (-ker) *n.* the government department in charge of the revenue.

Excise' (-z) *n.* duty charged on home goods during manufacture or before sale.—**excise'man** *n.* an officer collecting and enforcing excise. —**exci'sable** *a.* liable to excise.

Excise' *v.t.* to cut out, cut away.—**excis'ion** *n.*

Excite' *v.t.* to rouse up, set in motion; stimulate, move to strong emotion.—**exci'table** *a.* —**exci'tably** *adv.*—**excitabil'ity** *n.*—**excite'ment** *n.*—**excita'tion** *n. Syn.* to stir, inflame, incite, provoke. *Ant.* quench, damp, allay, pacify, check.

Exclaim *v.i.* and *t.* to cry out. —**exclama'tion** *n.*—**exclam'atory** *a.*

Exclude' (-ōōd) *v.t.* to shut out; debar from.—**exclu'sion** *n.*— **exclu'sive** *a.* excluding; inclined to keep out (from society, etc.); sole, only; different from all others.— **exclu'sively** *adv.*

Excog'itate (-koj-) *v.t.* to think out.—**excogita'tion** *n.*

Excommu'nicate *v.t.* to shut off from the sacraments of the church.—**excommunica'tion** *n.* — **excommu'nicative, excommu'nicatory** *a.*

Excor'iate *v.t.* to remove skin from; attack bitterly.—**excoria'tion** *n.*

Ex'crement *n.* waste matter discharged from the bowels, dung.—**excrement'al** *a.*—**excrete'** *v.t.* to discharge from the system.—**excre'tion** *n.*— **excre'tory** *a.*

Excres'cent *a.* growing out of something abnormally; redundant.—**excres'cence** *n.*

Excru'ciate *v.t.* to pain acutely, torture, in body or mind.— **excrucia'tion** *n.*

Ex'culpate *v.t.* to free from blame, clear from a charge.— **exculpa'tion** *n.*—**excul'patory** *a.*

Excur'sion *n.* a journey, ramble, trip, for pleasure.— **excur'sus** *n.* a discussion of a special point, usually at the end of a book.

Excuse' (-z) *v.t.* to try to clear from blame; overlook, forgive; gain exemption; set free, remit.—**excuse'** (-s) *n.* that which serves to excuse; an apology.—**excu'sable** (-z-) *a. Syn.* exculpate, pardon, condone. *Ant.* accuse, blame, charge.

Ex'ecrate *v.t.* to feel or express abhorrence, hatred for; curse. —**execra'tion** *n.*—**ex'ecrable** *a.* abominable, hatefully bad.

Ex'ecute *v.t.* to carry out, perform; sign (a document); kill (criminals).—**execu'tion** *n.*—**execu'tioner** *n.* one employed to kill those sentenced to death by law.—**exec'utant** *n.* a performer, *esp.* of music. —**exec'utive** *a.* carrying into effect, *esp.* of branch of a government enforcing laws, committee carrying on the business of a society, etc.— *n.* an executive body.—**exec'utor** *n.* a person appointed by one making a will to carry out the provisions of the will. —**exec'utrix** *fem.*

Exege'sis (-j-) *n.* explanation,

esp. of Scripture.—**exeget´ic,** **exeget´ical** *a.*

Exem´plar *n.* a model type.— **exemp´lary** *a.* fit to be imitated, serving as an example. —**exemp´larily** *adv.*—**exemp´lify** *v.t.* to serve as an example of; make an attested copy of.—**exemplifica´tion** *n.*

Exempt´ (-gz-) *a.* freed from, not liable.—*v.t.* to free from. —**exemp´tion** *n.*

Exen´terate *v.t.* to disembowel; to eviscerate; to gut.

Ex´equies (-kwĭz) *n.pl.* funeral rites.

Ex´ercise (-z) *n.* employment, use (of limbs, faculty, etc.); use of limbs for health; practice for the sake of training; a task set for training. —*v.t.* to use, employ; give (training, health) exercise to; carry out, discharge; trouble, harass.—*v.i.* to take exercise.

Exert´ (-gz-) *v.t.* to bring into active operation.—**exer´tion** *n.*

Exhale´ *v.t.* to breathe out; give off as vapour.—*v.i.* to breathe out; pass off as vapour.—**exhala´tion** *n.*

Exhaust´ (igz-awst´) *v.t.* to draw off; use up; empty, treat, discuss thoroughly; tire out.—*n.* used steam or fluid from an engine; passage for, or coming out of, this.— **exhaus´tion** *n.*—**exhaust´ive** *a.* —**exhaust´ible** *a.*—**exhaustibil´ity** *n.* *Syn.* weaken, spend, tire. *Ant.* revive, reanimate, replenish, refresh, fill.

Exhib´it (-gz-) *v.t.* to show, display; manifest; show publicly in competition.— *n.* a thing shown, *esp.* in competition or as evidence in a court.—**exhibi´tion** *n.* a display; an act of displaying; a public show (of works of art, etc.); an allowance made to a student, a scholarship.— **exhibi´tioner** *n.* a student holding an exhibition.—**exhib´itor** *n.* one who exhibits, *esp.* in a show.

Exhil´arate (-gz-) *v.t.* to enliven, gladden.—**exhilara´tion** *n.*

Exhort´ (-gz-) *v.t.* to urge, admonish earnestly.—**exhorta´tion** *n.*—**exhort´er** *n.*

Exhume´ *v.t.* to unearth; take out again what has been buried.—**exhuma´tion** *n.*

Ex´igent (-j-) *a.* exacting; urgent.—**ex´igence, ex´igency** *n.* pressing need; emergency.— **ex´igible** *a.* that may be exacted.

Exig´uous *a.* scanty, small.— **exigu´ity** *n.*

Ex´ile *n.* banishment, expulsion from one's own country; long absence abroad; one banished.—*v.t.* to banish.

Exil´ity *n.* thinness; tenuity; fineness; refinement.— **exile** *a.* small; slender; fine.

Exist´ (-gz-) *v.i.* to be, have being, continue to be.—**exist´ence** *n.*—**exist´ent** *a.*

Ex´it *n.* an actor's departure from the stage; a going out; a way out; death.—**ex´it** *v.i. sing.* "goes out."—**ex´eunt** (-i-unt) *plur.* "go out," stage directions, to indicate the going off of a player or players.

Ex´odus *n.* a departure, *esp.*

of a crowd.—**Ex'odus**, the second book of the Old Testament, relating the departure of the Israelites from Egypt.

Exon'erate *v.t.* to free, declare free, from blame; exculpate. —**exoner'ation** *n.*—**exon'erative** *a.* *Syn.* to clear, absolve, acquit. *Ant.* accuse, charge, blame.

Exophthal'mia *n.* excessive prominence of the eye-ball due to disease.—**exophthal'mic goitre** *n.* disease characterised by exophthalmia and enlarged thyroid gland.

Exorb'itant *a.* very excessive, immoderate. — **exorb'itantly** *adv.*—**exorb'itance** *n.*

Ex'orcise (-z) *v.t.* to cast out (evil spirits) by invocation; to free a person of evil spirits. —**ex'orcism** *n.*—**ex'orcist** *n.*

Exord'ium *n.* introductory part of a speech or treatise.

Exoter'ic (-ō-) *a.* understandable by the many; ordinary, popular.

Exot'ic *a.* brought in from abroad, not native.—*n.* an exotic plant, etc.

Expand' *v.t.* and *i.* to spread out; enlarge, increase in bulk, develop.—**expan'sion** *n.*—**expan'sive** *a.*—**expan'sible** *a.*—**expansibil'ity** *n.*—**expanse'** *n.* a wide space; open stretch of land.

Expa'tiate (-shi-) *v.i.* to speak or write at great length (on).

Expat'riate *v.t.* to banish.—**expatria'tion** *n.*

Expect' *v.t.* to look on as likely to happen; to look for as due.—**expect'ant** *a.*—**expect'-** ancy *n.*—**expect'antly** *adv.*—**expecta'tion** *n.*

Expect'orate *v.t.* and *i.* to spit out (phlegm, etc.).—**expectora'tion** *n.*

Expe'dient *a.* fitting, advisable; politic.—*n.* a device, contrivance. — **expe'diently** *adv.*—**expe'diency** *n.*—**ex'pedite** (-īt) *v.t.* to help on, hasten. — **expedi'tion** *n.* promptness; a journey for a definite purpose; a warlike enterprise; a body of men sent on such enterprise.—**expedi'tionary** *a.* — **expedi'tious** *a.* prompt, speedy.

Expel' *v.t.* to drive, cast out.—**expul'sion** *n.*—**expul'sive** *a.*

Expend' *v.t.* to spend, pay out; use up.—**expend'iture** *n.*—**expense'** *n.* spending; cost.—*pl.* charges, outlay incurred. —**expens'ive** *a.* costly.

Expe'rience *n.* observation of facts as a source of knowledge; a being affected consciously by an event; the event; knowledge, skill, gained by contact with facts and events.—*v.t.* to undergo, suffer, meet with.—**experien'tial** *a.*—**exper'iment** *n.* a test, trial; something done in the hope that it may succeed, or to test a theory. —*v.i.* to make an experiment. —**experiment'al** *a.*—**experiment'ally** *adv.*—**experiment'alist** *n.*—**ex'pert** *a.* practised, skilful.—*n.* one expert in something; an authority.

Ex'piate *v.t.* to pay the penalty for; make amends for.—**expia'tion** *n.*—**ex'piator** *n.*—**ex'piatory** *a.*

Expire' v.t. to breathe out.—
v.i. to give out breath; die;
die away; come to an end.—
expira'tion n.—**expi'ratory** a.
—**expi'ry** n. end.

Expis'cate (kāt) v.t. to ascertain by artful means; to
search out.—**expisca'tion** n.
—**ex'piscator** n. — **expis'ca-
tory** a. fitted to get at the
truth of a matter.

Explain' v.t. to make clear,
intelligible; give details of;
account for.—**explana'tion** n.
—**explan'atory** a.

Ex'pletive a. serving only to
fill out a sentence, etc.—n.
an expletive word, esp. an
oath.

Ex'plicable a. explainable.—
ex'plicate v.t. develop, explain.—**ex'plicative** a.—**ex'-
plicatory** a.—**explic'it** (-s-) a.
stated in detail; stated, not
merely implied; outspoken.

Explode' v.i. to go off with a
bang; to burst violently.—
v.t. to make explode; to discredit, expose (a theory, etc.).
— **explo'sion** n.—**explo'sive** a.
and n.

Ex'ploit n. a brilliant feat, a
deed.—v.t. to turn to advantage; make use of for one's
own ends.—**exploita'tion** n.

Explore' v.t. examine (a
country, etc.) by going
through it; investigate.—
explora'tion n.—**explor'atory**
a.—**explor'er** n.

Explo'sion see EXPLODE.

Expo'nent see EXPOUND.

Ex'port v.t. to send (goods) out
of the country.—n. an ex-
ported article.—**exporta'tion**
n.—**export'er** n.

Expose' (-z) v.t. to leave un-
protected; to lay open (to);
exhibit, put up for sale; un-
mask, disclose.—**expo'sure** n.
Syn. reveal, divulge, publish. Ant. conceal, hide,
cloak.

Exposi'tion see EXPOUND.

Expos'tulate v.i. make (esp.
friendly) remonstrances.—
expostula'tion n.—**expos'tula-
tory** a.

Expound' v.t. to explain, interpret.—**expo'nent** n. one
who expounds; an executant;
maths. an index, a symbol
showing the power of a
factor.—**exponen'tial** a.—**exposi'tion** n. an explanation,
description; exhibition of
goods, etc.—**expos'itory** a.—
expos'itor n.

Express' v.t. to put into words;
make known or understood
by words, conduct, etc.;
squeeze out; send by ex-
press.—a. definitely stated;
specially designed; of a
messenger, specially sent off;
of a train, fast and making
few stops.—n. an express
train or messenger.—adv.
specially, on purpose; with
speed.—**express'ly** adv.—**express'ible** a.—**expres'sion** n.
—**express'ive** a.

Expro'priate v.t. to dispossess;
take out of the owner's hands.
—**expropria'tion** n.—**expro'-
priator** n.

Expul'sion see EXPEL.

Expunge' v.t. to strike out,
erase.

Ex'purgate v.t. to remove
objectionable parts (from a
book, etc.).—**expurga'tion** n.

—ex'purgator n.—expurg'a-
tory a.

Ex'quisite (-iz-it) a. of extreme
beauty or delicacy; keen,
acute; keenly sensitive.—n.
a dandy.—ex'quisitely adv.
Syn. delicious, perfect, finished, exact. Ant. unpleasant,
coarse, nasty.

Exsang'uined (-sang-gwind) a.
rendered bloodless, pale, wan.
—exsanguin'eous a. without
blood; anæmic.—exsang'uin-
ous a. destitute of blood, as
an insect.

Exsic'cate v.t. to exhaust or
evaporate moisture from, to
dry up.—ex'siccator n. a
vessel for drying moist substances.

Extant' a. of a document, etc.,
still existing.

Extemp'ore (-ri) a. and adv.
without preparation, off-
hand.—extempora'neous a.—
extemp'orary a. — extemp'o-
rise v.t. to speak without preparation; devise for the
occasion. — extemporisa'tion
n.

Extend' v.t. to stretch out,
lengthen; prolong in duration; widen in area, scope;
accord, grant.—v.i. to reach;
cover an area; have a range
or scope; become larger or
wider.—exten'sible a.—ex-
tensibil'ity n.—exten'sion n.
—extens'ive a. wide, large,
comprehensive.—extent' n.
size, scope; a space, area;
degree.—exten'sile a. that can
be extended.—exten'sor n. a
muscle that straightens a
joint.

Exten'uate v.t. to make less

blameworthy. — extenua'tion
n.

Exte'rior a. outer, outward.—
n. the outside; outward
appearance.

Exterm'inate v.t. to root out,
destroy utterly.—extermina'-
tion n.—exterm'inator n.

Extern'al a. outside.—exter-
n'ally adv.

Exterritor'ial a. free from the
jurisdiction of the territory
one lives in.—exterritorial'ity
n.

Extinct' a. quenched, no longer
burning; having died out or
come to an end.—extinc'tion
n.—exting'uish (-ng-gw-) v.t.
to put out, quench; wipe out.
—exting'uishable a. — ex-
ting'uisher n. that which
extinguishes; a cap to put
out a candle; an apparatus
for putting out a fire.

Ex'tirpate v.t. to root out,
destroy utterly.—extirpa'tion
n.—ex'tirpator n.

Extol' v.t. to praise highly.
Syn. to laud, exalt, glorify.
Ant. abuse, revile, vilify.

Extort' v.t. to get by force or
threats.—extor'tion n.—extor'tionate a. — extor'tioner
n.

Ex'tra a. additional; larger,
better, than usual.—adv.
additionally; more than usually.—n. an extra thing;
something charged as additional.

Extract' v.t. to take out, esp.
by force; obtain against a
person's will; get by pressure,
distillation, etc.; deduce, derive; copy out, quote.—ex'-
tract n. matter got by dis-

tillation; concentrated juice; passage from a book.—**extrac'tion** n. extracting; ancestry.—**extract'or** n.

Extrado'tal a. not forming part of the dowry.

Extradi'tion n. delivery, under a treaty, of a foreign fugitive from justice to the authorities concerned.—**ex'tradite** (-ī-) v.t. to give or obtain such delivery.—**extradi'table** a.

Extra'neous a. added from without, not naturally belonging.

Extraord'inary (-ror-, -ra-or-) a. out of the usual course; additional; unusual, surprising, exceptional.—**extraord'-inarily** adv.

Extraterritor'ial [see EXTERRI-TORIAL.

Extrav'agant a. wild, absurd; wasteful; exorbitant.—**extrav'agantly** adv.—**extrav'a-gance** n.—**extravagan'za** n. a fantastic composition (in music, literature, etc.).

Extrav'asate v.t. to force out (blood, etc.) from its vessel.—v.i. to flow out.—**extrava-sa'tion** n.

Extravert' n. in psychology, one whose emotions express themselves readily in external action.

Extreme' a. at the end, outermost; of a high or the highest degree; severe; going beyond moderation.—n. a thing at one end or the other, the first and last of a series; utmost degree.—**extreme'ly** adv.—**extre'mist** n. an advocate of extreme measures.—**extrem'-ity** n. end.—pl. hands and feet; utmost distress; extreme measures.

Ex'tricate v.t. to disentangle, set free.—**ex'tricable** a.—**extrica'tion** n.

Extrin'sic a. accessory, not belonging, not intrinsic.—**extrin'sically** adv.

Extrude' v.t. to thrust out.—**extru'sion** n.

Exu'berant a. prolific, abundant, luxurious; effusive, high-flown.—**exu'berance** n.—**exu'berantly** adv.

Exude' v.i. to ooze out.—v.t. to give off (moisture).—**exuda'-tion** n.

Exult' v.i. to rejoice, triumph.—**exulta'tion** n. — **exult'ant** a.

Eye (ī) n. the organ of sight; look, glance; attention; various things resembling an eye.—v.t. to look at; observe.—**eye'less** a.—**eye'ball** n. the ball of the eye.—**eye'brow** n. the fringe of hair above the eye.—**eye'glass** n. a glass to assist the sight: monocle.—**eye'lash** n. hair fringing the eyelid.—**eye'lid** n. the lid or cover of the eye.—**eye'opener** n. information that makes one understand what one had failed to see.—**eye'sore** n. an ugly mark, a thing that annoys one to see.—**eye'tooth** n. canine tooth.—**eye'witness** n. one who saw something for himself.—**eye'let** n. a small hole for a rope, etc., to pass through.

Ey'ot n. a small island, esp. in a river.

Eyr'ie see AERIE.

F

Fa'bian *a.* slow and deliberate but persistent.

Fa'ble *n.* a tale; legend; a short story with a moral, *esp.* one with talking animals as characters.—*v.t.* to invent, tell fables about.—**fab'ulist** *n.* a writer of fables.—**fab'ulous** *a.* told of in fables; unhistorical; absurd, unbelievable.

fab'ric *n.* a thing put together, building, frame, structure; a woven stuff; texture.—**fab'ricate** *v.t.* to invent (a lie, etc.); forge (a document).—**fab'ricator** *n.*—**fabrica'tion** *n.*

Façade' *n.* the front of a building.

Face *n.* the front of the head; front, surface, chief side of anything; outward appearance; look, coolness; impudence.—*v.t.* to meet boldly; look or front towards; give a covering surface.—*v.i.* to turn.—**fa'cer** *n.* a blow in the face; a sudden difficulty.—**fac'et** (fas'-) *n.* one side of a many-sided body, *esp.* of a cut gem.—**fa'cial** (fā'shl) *a.*

Face'tious (fas-ē-shus) *a.* waggish, jocose, given to jesting.—**face'tiae** (-sē'shē) *n.pl.* pleasantries, witticisms. *Syn.* jocose, jocular, playful, jesting. *Ant.* serious, grave.

Fac'ile (-sēl) *a.* easy; working easily; easy-going.—**facil'itate** (-sil-) *v.t.* to make easy, help.—**facil'ity** *n.* easiness; dexterity.—*pl.* opportunities, good conditions.—**facilita'tion** *n.*—**facil'itator** *n.*

Facsim'ile (fak-sim'i-li) *n.* an exact copy.

Fact *n.* a thing known to be true or to have occurred.

Fac'tion *n.* a political or other party (*used always in a bad sense*); misguided party spirit.—**fac'tious** *a.*

Facti'tious *a.* artificial, specially got up.

Fac'tor *n.* something contributing to a result; one of numbers which multiplied together give a given number; an agent, one who buys and sells for another.—**fac'tory** *n.* a building where things are manufactured; a trading station in a foreign country.—**facto'tum** *n.* a servant managing affairs, a man-of-all-work.

Fac'ulty *n.* ability, aptitude; an inherent power; a power of the mind; a department of a university; the members of a profession; an authorisation.—**fac'ultative** *a.* optional.

Fad *n.* a pet idea, craze, crotchet.—**fadd'y** *a.*—**fadd'ist** *n.*

Fade *v.i.* to wither; lose colour, grow dim; disappear gradually.—**fade'less** *a.*

Fag *n.* toil; a junior schoolboy who does service to a senior; a cigarette.—*v.t.* to weary; to make act as fag.—*v.i.* to toil; to act as fag.—**fag'-end'** *n.* the last part, an inferior remnant.

Fagg'ot, fag'ot *n.* a bundle of sticks bound together; bundle of steel rods; a dish of baked chopped liver, etc.

—*v.t.* to bind in a faggot.

Fah'renheit (-hĭt) *a.* of the thermometric scale on which the freezing point of water is 32° and the boiling-point 212°.

Fai'ence (fā'-) *n.* glazed earthenware or china.

Fail *v.i.* to be insufficient; run short; lose power; die away; to be wanting at need; be unsuccessful, become bankrupt.—*v.t.* to disappoint, give no help to.—**fail'ure** *n.*

Fain *a.* glad, willing.—*adv.* gladly.

Faint *a.* feeble; dim; pale; weak; inclined to swoon.—*v.i.* to swoon.—*n.* a swoon.—**faint'ly** *adv. Syn.* languid, feeble, timorous, obscure. *Ant.* energetic, strong, clear, distinct.

Fair (fēr) *n.* a periodical gathering for trade, often with amusements added of shows and roundabouts.—**fair'ing** *n.* a present from a fair.

Fair (fēr) *a.* beautiful; ample; blond; unblemished; of moderate quality or amount; just, honest; of weather, favourable.—*adv.* honestly.—**fair'ish** *a.*—**fair'ly** *adv.*—**fair'ness** *n.*

Fairy (fēr-) *n.* a small supernatural being with powers of magic.—*a.* of fairies; like a fairy, beautiful and delicate.—**fair'y-lamp** *n.* a small coloured light used for outdoor illuminations.—**fair'y-land** *n.*—**fair'y-ring** *n.* a circle of darker colour in grass.—**fair'y-tale** *n.*

Faith *n.* trust; belief; belief without proof; religion; promise; loyalty.—**faith'ful** *a.*—**faith'less** *a.*—**faith'fully** *adv.*

Fake *v.t.* to conceal defects of, by artifice.—**fa'kement** *n.* any swindling device.—**fa'ker** *n.* one who deals in fakes; a swindler; a streetvendor; a hanger-on in theatres.

Fak'ir (ēr) *n.* a Mohammedan or Hindu religious beggar.

Fal'chion *n.* a broad curved sword.

Fal'con *n.* a small bird of prey, *esp.* trained in hawking for sport.—**fal'coner** *n.* one who keeps, trains, or hunts with, falcons.—**fal'conry** *n.*

Fall (-aw-) *v.i.* to drop, come down freely; hang down; become lower; come to the ground, cease to stand; perish; collapse; be captured; pass into a condition; become; happen.—*n.* a falling; amount that falls; amount of descent; yielding to temptation; autumn; rope of hoisting tackle.

Fall'acy (fal'-a-si) *n.* a misleading argument; flaw in logic; mistaken belief.—**falla'cious** (-ā'-) *a.*—**fall'ible** *a.* liable to error.—**fall'ibly** *adv.*—**fallibil'ity** *n.*

Fal'-lal *n.* a piece of finery.

Fall'ow (fal'ō) *a.* ploughed and harrowed but left without crop; uncultivated.—*n.* fallow land.—*v.t.* to break up (land).

Fall'ow *a.* pale brown or

reddish yellow.—**fall'ow-deer** n.

False (-aw-) a. wrong, erroneous; deceptive; faithless; sham; artificial.—**false'ly** adv.—**false'hood** n. lie.—**false'ness.**—**fal'sity** n.—**falset'to** n. a forced voice above the natural range.—**fal'sify** v.t. to alter fraudulently; misrepresent; disappoint (hopes, etc.).—**falsifica'tion** n. Syn. unfaithful, feigned, spurious, forged. Ant. true, correct, accurate, precise, faithful, genuine.

Falstaff'ian a. like Shakespeare's Falstaff; corpulent; convivial; boasting.

Fal'ter (-aw-) v.i. to stumble; speak hesitatingly; waver.—v.t. to say hesitatingly.

Fame n. reputation; renown; rumour.—**famed** a.—**fa'mous** a.—**fa'mously** adv.

Famil'iar a. intimate; closely acquainted; well-known, common; unceremonious.—n. a familiar friend or demon.—**famil'iarly** adv.—**familiar'ity** n.—**famil'iarise** v.t.—**familiarisa'tion** n.—**fam'ily** n. household of parents, children, and servants; a group of parents and children, or near relatives; a person's children; all descendants of a common ancestor; a class, group of allied objects.

Fam'ine (-in) n. extreme scarcity of food; starvation.—**fam'ish** v.t. to starve.—v.i. to be very hungry.

Fa'mous see FAME.

Fan n. an instrument for producing a current of air, esp. for cooling the face; a winnowing machine; a thing spread out as a bird's tail; a ventilating machine.—v.t. to winnow, blow, or cool with a fan.—**fan'light** n. fan-shaped window over a door.

Fan n. an enthusiast, particularly for sport.

Fanat'ic a. filled with mistaken enthusiasm, esp. in religion.—n. a fanatic person. — **fanat'ical** a. — **fanat'ically** adv.—**fanat'icism** n.

Fan'cy n. power of imagination; mental image; notion, whim, caprice, liking, inclination; followers of a hobby.—a. ornamental, not plain; of whimsical or arbitrary kind.—v.t. to imagine; be inclined to believe; have or take a liking for.—**fan'cier** n. one with liking and expert knowledge (respecting some specified thing).—**fan'ciful** a.—**fan'cifully** adv.

Fandan'go n. a lively Spanish dance, music for it.

Fane n. a temple.

Fan'fare n. a flourish of trumpets.

Fang n. a long pointed tooth; a snake's poison-tooth; root of a tooth.

Fan'tasy n. power of imagination, esp. extravagant; mental image; a fanciful invention or design.—**fanta'sia** (-z-) n. a fanciful musical composition.—**fantas'tic** a. quaint, grotesque, extremely fanciful.—**fantas'tically** adv.

Far adv. at or to a great distance, or advanced point; by very much.—a. distant.—n.

a great distance or amount.

Farce n. a play meant only to excite laughter; an absurd and futile proceeding.—**far'-cical** a.—**far'cically** adv.

Fare (fèr) n. money paid by a passenger for conveyance; a passenger; food.—v.i. to happen; get on; travel.—**farewell'** interj. good-bye.—n. a leave-taking.

Fari'na n. meal; powder; starch; pollen.—**farina'ceous** a.

Farm n. a tract of cultivated land.—v.t. to pay or take a fixed sum for the proceeds of (a tax, etc.); cultivate.—**farm'stead** (-sted) n.—**farm'house** n.—**farm'yard** n.—**farm'er** n.

Farra'go n. a medley, hotch-potch.

Farr'ier n. a shoeing smith; one who treats diseases of horses.—**farr'iery** n.

Farr'ow n. a litter of pigs.—v.t. and i. to produce this.

Far'ther (-TH-) adv. and a. further.—**far'thest** adv. and a. furthest.

Far'thing (-TH-) n. a quarter of a penny.

Far'thingale (-TH-) n. a hooped petticoat.

Fas'cia n. a long flat surface of wood or stone in a building.

Fas'cinate v.t. to make powerless by look or presence; to charm, attract.—**fascina'tion** n.—**fas'cinator** n. Syn. to disarm, captivate. Ant. repel, disenchant, disgust, offend.

Fas'cist n. a member of an Italian political party aiming at the overthrow of com-munists, radicals, etc., by violence, and strong rule by a dictator.—**fas'cism** n.

Fash'ion (-shun) n. make, style; manner; custom, esp. in dress.—v.t. to shape, make.—**fash'ionable** a.—**fash'ionably** adv.

Fast (-à-) v.i. to go without food, or some kinds of food.—n. an act, or appointed time of fasting.

Fast (-à-) a. firm, fixed, steady, permanent; rapid; ahead of true time; dissipated.—adv. firmly, tightly; rapidly; in a dissipated way.—**fast'en** (-sen) v.t. to attach, fix, secure.—v.i. to seize (upon).—**fast'ness** n. a fast state; a fortress.

Fastid'ious a. hard to please; easily disgusted. Syn. squeamish, disdainful, critical, punctilious. Ant. rough, unrefined, vulgar.

Fat a. plump, thick, solid; containing much fat; fertile.—n. the oily substance of animal bodies; the fat part.—v.t. to feed (animals) for slaughter.—**fatt'en** v.t. and i.—**fat'ness** n.—**fatt'y** a.

Fate n. the power supposed to predetermine events; goddess of destiny; destiny; a person's appointed lot or condition; death or destruction.—v.t. to preordain.—**fate'ful** a. prophetic, fraught with destiny. — **fa'tal** a. deadly, ending in death; destructive; very ill-advised, disastrous; inevitable. —**fa'tally** adv.—**fatal'ity** n. rule of fate; a calamity: death by accident.—**fa'talism** *n.* the belief that everything is pre-determined; submission to fate.—**fa'talist** *n.*—**fatalist'ic** *a.*—**fatalis'tically** *adv.*

Fa'ther (få'TH-) *n.* a male parent; forefather, ancestor; originator, early leader; priest, confessor; oldest member of a society.—*v.t.* to beget; originate; pass as father or author of; act as father to; fix the paternity of —**fa'therhood** *n.*—**fa'ther-in-law** *n.* the father of one's husband or wife.—**fa'therly** *a.*—**fa'therless** *a.*—**fa'therland** *n.* one's country.

Fath'om (få'TH-) *n.* a measure of six feet.—*v.t.* to sound (water); get to the bottom of, understand.—**fath'omless** *a.* too deep to fathom.—**fath'omable** *a.*

Fatid'ic *a.* prophetic; having the power to foretell the future.

Fatigue' (-tēg) *v.t.* to weary.—*n.* weariness; toil; a soldier's non-military duty.

Fat'uous *a.* silly, foolish.—**fatu'ity** *n.*

Fau'cet (faw-set) *n.* a fixture for drawing liquor from a cask or vessel.

Fault *n.* defect; misdeed; blame, culpability; in tennis, a ball wrongly served; in hunting, failure of scent; in geology, a break in strata.—**fault'y** *a.*—**fault'less** *a.*—**fault'ily** *adv.*—**fault'lessly** *adv.*

Faun *n.* a Latin countryside god with tail and horns.

Faun'a *n.* the animals of a region or period.

Fauteuil (fō-te̸'-ye̸) *n.* an arm-chair, usually highly orna-mented; a seat, or member-ship, in the French Academy; a seat in a theatre.

Faux pas (fō på) *n.* a false step; a mistake.

Fa'vour (-ver) *n.* goodwill; approval; partiality; especial kindness; a badge or knot of ribbons.—*v.t.* to regard or treat with favour; oblige; treat with partiality; aid, support. — **fa'vourable** *a.*—**fa'vourably** *adv.*—**fa'vourite** (-it) *n.* a favoured person or thing; a horse, etc., generally expected to win a race.—*a.* chosen, preferred.—**fa'vourit-ism** *n.* the practice of showing undue preference.

Fawn *n.* a young fallow-deer. —*a.* of a light yellowish-brown.

Fawn *v.i.* of a dog, etc., to show affection by wagging the tail and grovelling; of a person, to cringe, court favour in a servile manner.

Fay *n.* a fairy.

Fe'alty *n.* fidelity of a vassal to his lord. *Syn.* fidelity, homage, loyalty. *Ant.* dis-loyalty, infidelity, treachery, treason.

Fear *n.* dread, alarm, the un-pleasant emotion caused by coming evil or danger.—*v.i.* to have this feeling, to be afraid.—*v.t.* to regard with fear; revere; hesitate, shrink from (doing something).—**fear'ful** *a.*—**fear'fully** *adv.*—**fear'some** *a.*—**fear'less** *a.*—**fear'lessly** *adv.*

Feas'ible (-z-) *a.* practicable,

that can be done.—**feas'ibly**
adv.—**feasibil'ity** *n.*

Feast *n.* a banquet, lavish
meal; a religious anniversary to be kept with joy; an
annual village festival.—*v.i.*
to partake of a banquet, fare
sumptuously.—*v.t.* to regale
with a feast.

Feat *n.* a notable deed; a
surprising trick.

Feath'er (fɛTH'-) *n.* one of the
barbed shafts which form
the covering of birds.—*v.t.*
to provide with feathers; to
turn (an oar) edgeways.—*v.i.*
to grow feathers; to turn an
oar.—**feath'ery** *a.*—**feath'er-
weight** *n.* a very light person
or thing.

Feat'ure *n.* a part of the face
(usually *pl.*); a characteristic
or notable part of anything.
—*v.t.* to portray; represent
by cinematograph; give
prominence to.—**feat'ureless**
a.

Feb'rifuge (-j-) *n.* a medicine
to reduce fever.—**feb'rile** *a.*
of fever.

Feb'ruary *n.* the second month.

Feck'less *a.* spiritless; weak;
feeble; worthless.

Fec'ulent *a.* full of sediment,
turbid.—**fec'ulence** *n.*

Fec'und *a.* fertile.—**fecund'ity**
n.—**fec'undate** *v.t.* to fertilise,
impregnate.—**fecunda'tion** *n.*

Fed'eral *a.* of, or like, the
government of states which
are united but retain more or
less independence within
themselves.—**fed'eralism** *n.*—
fed'eralist *n.*—**fed'erate** *v.i.* to
enter into a league, a federal
union.—**federa'tion** *n.* an act
of federating; a federated
society.

Fee *n.* a payment for services,
esp. one due to a public
official or a professional man;
entrance-money.—*v.t.* to pay
a fee to.

Fee'ble *a.* weak.—**fee'bly** *adv.*
Syn. infirm, sickly, faint, de-
bilitated. *Ant.* robust, vigorous, strong, vivid, hardy.

Feed *v.t.* to give food to;
supply, support.—*v.i.* to take
food.—*n.* a feeding; fodder,
pasturage; an allowance of
fodder; material supplied to
a machine; the part of a
machine taking in material.—
feed'er *n.*

Feel *v.t.* to examine, search, by
touch; to perceive, have
knowledge of, by touch or in
emotions.—*v.i.* to use the
sense of touch; grope; to be
consciously; to have, be
affected by (a sentiment);
sympathise, the sense of
touch; an impression on it.
—**feel'er** *n.* the special organ
of touch in some animals; a
proposal put forward to test
others' opinion; that which
feels.—**feel'ing** *n.* sense of
touch; physical sensation;
emotion; sympathy, tenderness; conviction or opinion
not solely based on reason.—
pl. susceptibilities.—*a.* sensitive, sympathetic.

Feet *see* FOOT.

Feign (fān) *v.t.* to pretend,
simulate.—*v.i.* to pretend.

Feint (fānt) *n.* a sham attack
or blow meant to deceive an
opponent.—*v.i.* to make such
move.

Feli'city (-is'-) *n.* great happiness, bliss; appropriateness of wording. — **feli'citous** *a.* apt, well-chosen; happy.— **feli'citate** *v.t.* to congratulate. —**felicita'tion** *n.* (usually in *pl.*).

Fe'line *a.* of cats; catlike.— **felin'ity** *n.*

Fell *n.* a skin or hide with hair; thick matted hair.

Fell *n.* mountain, stretch of moorland, *esp.* in north of England.

Fell *v.t.* to knock down; cut down (a tree).

Fell *a.* fierce, terrible.

Fell'oe (-ō) **fell'y** *n.* the outer part of a wheel; a section of this.

Fell'ow *n.* a comrade, associate; a counterpart, a like thing; member (of certain learned societies, etc.); a person.— *a.* of the same class, associated.—**fell'owship** *n.*

Fel'on *n.* one who has committed a felony.—cruel, fierce.—**fel'ony** *n.* a crime more serious than a misdemeanour. — **felo'nious** *a. Syn.* malefactor, offender, criminal, culprit, convict.

Felt *n.* cloth made by rolling and pressing wool with size; a thing made of this.—*v.t.* to make into, or cover with, felt.

Feluc'ca (-luk) *n.* a boat or vessel with oars and two masts with lateen sails, used in the Mediterranean.

Fe'male *a.* of the sex which bears offspring; relating to this sex or to women.—*n.* one of this sex.

Fem'inine (-in) *a.* of women; womanly; *gram.* of the gender proper to women's names.— **feminin'ity** *n.*—**fem'inism** *n.* influence of women; advocacy of this, of women's political rights, etc.—**fem'inist** *n.*

Fem'oral *a.* of the thigh.

Fen *n.* a tract of marshy land. —**fenn'y** *a.*

Fence *n.* the art of using a sword; a hedge or railing; a receiver of stolen goods.—*v.t.* to put a hedge round, to enclose.—*v.i.* to practise sword-play.—**fen'cible** *n.* a soldier liable only for home defence.

Fend *v.t.* ward off, repel.—*v.i.* provide (for oneself, etc.).— **fend'er** *n.* a faggot, bundle of rope, etc., hung over a ship's side to prevent chafing; a frame round a hearth.

Fenes'tra *n.* in anatomy, a foramen; an opening.— **fenes'tral** *a.* pertaining to a window; in botany, having transparent spots.

Fenn'el *n.* a yellow-flowered fragrant herb.

Fer'ment *n.* leaven, substance causing a thing to ferment; excitement, tumult. — **ferment'** *v.i.* to undergo a chemical change with effervescence, liberation of heat and alteration of properties, e.g. process set up in dough by yeast.—*v.t.* to subject to this process; to stir up, excite.—**fermenta'tion** *n.*

Fern *n.* a plant with feathery fronds. — **fern'y**, *a.* full of ferns. —fern'ery *n.* a place for growing ferns.

Fero'cious (-ō-shus) *a.* fierce, savage, cruel.—fero'city (-s'-) *n.*

Ferr'et *n.* a half-tamed animal like a weasel used to catch rabbits, rats, etc.; —*v.t.* to take or clear with ferrets; to search out.—*v.i.* to search about, rummage.

Ferr'ic *a.*—ferr'ous *a.* containing iron.—ferrif'erous *a.* yielding iron.—ferru'ginous *a.* of iron-rust; reddish-brown.—ferr'o-con'crete *n.* concrete strengthened by a framework of steel or iron.—ferr'otype *n.* a photograph on thin iron plate; the process of making it.

Ferr'ule *n.* a metal band or cap to strengthen the end of a stick (see also FERULE).

Ferr'y *v.t.* and *i.* to carry, pass, by boat across a river, strait, etc.—*n.* a place or a boat for ferrying.—ferr'yman *n.*

Fer'tile *a.* fruitful, producing abundantly.—fertil'ity *n.*—fer'tilise *v.t.* to make fertile. —fer'tiliser *n.*—fertilisa'tion *n.*

Fer'ule *n.* a flat stick or ruler used for punishing boys (see also FERRULE).

Fer'vent *a.* hot, glowing; ardent, intense.—fer'vently *adv.*—fer'vency *n.*—fer'vour (-er) *n.*—fer'vid *a.* ardent, impassioned.—fer'vidly.

Fesse *n.* in heraldry, a horizontal band traversing an escutcheon.

Fes'tal *a.* of a feast; keeping holiday; gay.—fes'tive *a.* of a feast; joyous, gay; jovial. —fes'tival *n.* a festal day; merry-making; a periodical musical celebration.—festiv'ity *n.* gaiety, mirth; an occasion for rejoicing.—*pl.* festive proceedings.

Fes'ter *n.* a suppurating condition, a sore.—*v.i.* to ulcerate, produce matter (in wound); rankle.—*v.t.* to cause to fester.

Festoon' *n.* a chain of flowers, ribbons, etc., hung in a curve between two points.—*v.t.* to make into, or adorn with, festoons.

Fetch *v.t.* to go for and bring; to draw forth; be sold for; charm.—*n.* a trick.—fetch'ing *a.* attractive.

Fet'id *a.* stinking.

Fe'tish *n.* an inanimate object worshipped by savages; anything which is the object of irrational reverence.

Fet'lock *n.* the part of a horse's leg where a tuft of hair grows behind the pastern-joint; the tuft.

Fett'er *n.* a chain or shackle for the feet; check, restraint. —*pl.* captivity.—*v.t.* to chain up; restrain, hamper.

Fet'tle *n.* condition, trim.

Fe'tus *see* FŒTUS.

Feu (fū) *n.* a fief; land held on payment of rent; perpetual possession at a stipulated rent.—*v.t.* to grant or let in feu.—feuar *n.*

Feud (fūd) *n.* bitter and lasting mutual hostility, *esp.* between two families or tribes.

Feud (fūd) *n.* a fief.—feud'al *a.* of a fief.—feud'al system, the mediæval political system based on the holding of land from a superior in return for service.—feud'alism n.

Feuilleton (fẹ-yẹ-tōn) n. a literary article or instalment of a serial, printed on the lower part of a newspaper page.—fe'uilletonism n. superficial and showy qualities in scholarship and literature.

Fe'ver n. a condition of illness with high temperature and waste of tissue; nervous excitement.—v.t. to throw into fever.—fe'verish a.—fe'verishly adv.—fe'verfew n. a herb formerly used as a febrifuge. Syn. heat, excitement, agitation. Ant. tranquillity, coolness, self-possession.

Few a. not many.—n. a small number.—few'ness n.

Fey a. doomed, fated to die; esp. having an unnatural gaiety of spirit foreboding sudden death.

Fez n. a tarbouche, a Turkish cap with a tassel.

Fiancé (fē-ŏn-sā) n. a betrothed man; fem. fiancée.

Fias'co n. a breakdown, ignominious failure.

Fi'at n. a decree; authorisation.

Fib n. a trivial lie.—v.i. to tell a fib.—fibb'er n.

Fi'bre n. a filament forming part of animal or plant tissue; a substance that can be spun.—fi'brous a.

Fich'u (fish-ōō) n. a triangular lace shawl for a woman's shoulders and neck.

Fic'kle a. changeable, inconstant.—fic'kleness n.

Fic'tion n. an invented statement or narrative; novels, stories collectively; a conventionally accepted falsehood.—ficti'tious a. not genuine, imaginary; assumed.

Fid'dle n. a violin; in a ship, a frame to stop things rolling off a table.—v.i. to play the fiddle; to make idle movements, to trifle.—fid'dlestick n. a bow.—pl. nonsense.—fid'dler n.

Fidel'ity n. faithfulness.

Fidg'et v.i. to move restlessly; be uneasy.—n. restless condition with aimless movements; a restless mood; one who fidgets.—fidg'ety a.

Fidu'ciary (-sh-) a. held or given in trust; relating to a trustee.—n. a trustee.

Fief (fēf) n. an estate in land held of a superior in return for service.

Field n. a piece of land tilled or used as pasture; an enclosed piece of land; a battleground; a tract of land rich in a specified product (e.g. goldfield); all the players in a game or sport; all competitors but the favourite; surface of a shield, coin, etc.; range, area of operation.—v.i. and t. at cricket, etc., to stop and return a ball.—field'-day n. a day of manœuvres; an important occasion.—field'-glass n. binoculars for outdoor use.—Field' Marshal n. a general of the highest rank. — field'er n.

Field'fare *n.* a bird related to the thrush.

Fiend *n.* a devil.—**fiend'ish** *a.*

Fierce *a.* savage, wild, raging. — **fierce'ness** *n.* — **fierce'ly** *adv.*

Fi'ery (fī-) *a.* consisting of fire; blazing, glowing; flashing; irritable; spirited.—**fi'erily** *adv. Syn.* ardent, passionate, fierce, impetuous. *Ant.* cool, calm, lethargic, indifferent.

Fife *n.* a shrill flute played with drums in military music.— *v.i.* and *t.* to play on a fife.— **fi'fer** *n.*

Fig *n.* a familiar soft round many-seeded fruit; the tree bearing it.

Fight (fīt) *v.i.* to contend in battle or in single combat.— *v.t.* to contend with; maintain against an opponent; settle by combat; to manœuvre (ships, troops) in battle.—*n.* act of fighting, combat battle; strife.— **fight'er** *n.*

Fig'ment *n.* an invented statement, a purely imaginary thing.

Fig'ure (-er) *n.* form, shape; bodily shape; appearance, *esp.* conspicuous appearance; a space enclosed by lines or surfaces; a diagram, illustration; likeness, image; pattern; a movement in dancing, skating, etc.; a numerical symbol; amount, number; an abnormal form of expression for effect in speech, e.g. a metaphor.— *v.i.* to use numbers; to show, be conspicuous; be estimated.—*v.t.* to calculate, estimate; to represent by picture or diagram; to ornament. — **fig'urative** *a.* metaphorical; full of figures of speech.—**fig'uratively** *adv.*

Fil'ament *n.* a thread-like body.

Fil'bert *n.* the cultivated hazel; its fruit or nut.

Filch *v.t.* to steal.

File *n.* a tool, usually of roughened steel, for smoothing or rubbing down metal or other material.—*v.t.* to apply a file to, to smooth, rub down, polish.—**fi'ling** *n.* action of using a file; a scrap of metal removed by a file.

File *n.* a stiff wire on which papers are threaded; a device for holding papers for reference; papers so arranged.— *v.t.* to place in a file.

File *n.* in formation of soldiers, a front-rank man and the man or men immediately behind him.—in file, arranged in two lines facing to one end of the rank.— single, or Indian file, formation of a single line of men one behind the other.—*v.i.* to march in file.

Fil'ial *a.* of, or befitting, a son or daughter.—**fil'ially** *adv.*

Fil'ibuster *n.* an adventurer in irregular warfare, a privateer; a pirate. — *v.i.* to act as a filibuster.

Fil'igree *n.* fine tracery or open-work of metal, usually gold or silver wire.

Fill *v.t.* to make full; to occupy completely; hold, discharge duties of; stop up; satisfy; fulfil.—*v.i.* to become full.—*n.* a full supply; as much as desired. —fill'er *n.*

Fill'et *n.* a head-band; a strip of meat; a piece of meat or fish boned, rolled and tied. —*v.t.* to encircle with a fillet; to make into fillets.

Fill'ip *n.* the sudden release of a finger bent against the thumb; a flip so given; a stimulus.—*v.t.* to give a fillip to, flip; stimulate.

Fill'y *n.* a female foal.

Film *n.* a very thin skin or layer; a thin sensitised sheet used in photography; a sensitised celluloid roll used in cinematography; a cinematographic picture; dimness on the eyes; a slight haze; a thread.—*v.t.* to photograph or represent by the cinematograph; to cover with a film.—*v.i.* to become covered with a film.—film'y *a.*—film'-star *n.* a popular actor or actress for films.

Fil'ter *n.* a cloth or other apparatus for straining liquids.—*v.t.* and *i.* to pass through a filter.—*v.i.* to make a way through.— filtra'tion *n.*

Filth (-th) *n.* loathsome dirt; garbage; vileness.—filth'y *a.* —filth'ily *adv.*—filth'iness *n.*

Fin *n.* the propelling or steering organ of a fish.

Fi'nal *a.* coming at the end; conclusive.—*n.* a game, heat, examination, etc., coming at the end of a series.— fi'nally *adv.*—final'ity *n.*— fina'le (-à-li) *n.* the closing

part of a musical composition, opera, etc.

Finance' *n.* the management of money.—*pl.* money resources.—*v.t.* to find capital for.—*v.i.* to deal with money. —finan'cial *a.*—finan'cially *adv.*—finan'cier *n.*

Fi'nis *n.* an end; conclusion.

Finch *n.* one of a family of small singing birds.

Find (fī-) *v.t.* to come across, light upon, obtain; recognise; experience, discover; discover by searching; ascertain; declare on inquiry; supply.—*n.* a finding; something found.—find'er *n.*

Fine *n.* a sum fixed as a penalty; a sum paid in consideration of a low rent.—in fine, to sum up.—*v.t.* to punish by a fine.

Fine *a.* choice, pure, of high quality, delicate, subtle; in small particles; slender; excellent; handsome; showy; free from rain; fastidious.— *n.* fine weather.—*adv.* in fine manner.—*v.t.* to make clear or pure; to thin.—*v.i.* to become clear or pure or thinned. —fine'ly *adv.*—fine'ness *n.*— fi'nery *n.* showy dress.— finesse' (fin-) *n.* artfulness. subtle management; at cards, the attempt to take a trick with the lower of two cards not having the intermediate one.—*v.t.* and *i.* to use or attempt finesse.

Fin'ger (-ng-g-) *n.* one of the jointed branches of the hand; various things like this.—*v.t.* to touch or handle with the fingers.—fing'erpost *n.* a

signpost at cross-roads.—
fing′erprint n. an impression
of the tip of a finger. *esp.* as
used for identifying criminals.—**fing′erstall** n. a cover
to protect a finger.

Fin′icking, fin ical, fin′iken a.
fastidious, over-nice; too
delicately wrought.

Fin′gering (-ng-g-) n. wool for
stockings, for knitting.

Fin′ish v.t. to bring to an end,
complete; to perfect; to
kill.—v.i. to come to an end.
—n. end, last stage; decisive
result; completed state;
anything serving to complete
or perfect.—**fin′isher** n.—
fi′nite a. bounded, limited.
Syn. to accomplish, cease,
conclude, perfect. *Ant.*
begin, commence.

Finn′an, finn′an hadd′ock n.
haddock cured with smoke
of green wood, turf, or peat.

Fiord′, fjord (fyord′) n. a narrow inlet of the sea between
cliffs.

Fir n. a coniferous tree; its
wood.

Fire n. state of burning, combustion, flame, glow; a mass
of burning fuel; a destructive burning, conflagration;
ardour, keenness, spirit;
shooting of firearms.—v.t. to
make burn; supply with fuel;
bake; to inspire; to explode;
discharge (a firearm); propel
from a firearm.—v.i. to begin
to burn; to become excited;
to discharge a firearm.—
fire′arm n. a weapon shooting by explosion, a gun,
pistol, cannon—**fire′brand** n.
a burning piece of wood; one

who stirs up strife.—**fire′-
brigade** n. an organised body
of men with appliances to
put out fires and rescue those
in danger from fire.—**fire′-
damp** n. in mines, carburetted
hydrogen; an explosive mixture of this with air.—**fire′-
engine** n. an engine with
apparatus for extinguishing
fires.—**fire′-escape** n. apparatus for escaping from a
burning house.—**fire′fly** n.
an insect giving out a glow
of phosphorescent light.—
fire′-irons n.pl. tongs, poker,
and shovel. — **fire′lock** n. a
musket fired with a spark.—
fire′man n. a member of a
fire-brigade; a stoker, an
assistant to a locomotive
driver. — **fire′new** a. as if
fresh from the furnace.—
fire′place n. a hearth in a
room.—**fire′-plug** n. a connection in a water-main for
a hose.—**fire′-ship** n. a burning vessel sent drifting
against enemy ships.—**fire′-
step** n. a step in a trench on
which a soldier stands to
fire.—**fire′-water** n. strong
spirits, *esp.* when supplied
to savages.—**fire′work** n. a
device to give spectacular
effects by explosions, and
coloured flames.

Firm a. solid, fixed, stable;
steadfast; resolute; settled.
—v.t. to make firm, solidify.—
n. a commercial house, part-
ners carrying on a business.
Syn. stable, unshaken, immovable, robust, sturdy. *Ant.*
unsteady, vacillating, insecure, shaky, irresolute.

Firm'ament *n.* the vault of heaven.

Firn *n.* accumulated snow on the heights of mountain ranges, forming the source of glaciers.

First *a.* earliest in time or order; foremost in rank or position.—*adv.* before others in time, order, etc.—**first'-aid'** *n.* help given to an injured person before the arrival of a doctor.—**first'-ling** *n.* first fruits, the first product, offspring.—**first'ly** *adv.*

Firth, frith *n.* an arm of the sea, an estuary.

Fis'cal *a.* of a state treasury.

Fish *n.* a vertebrate cold-blooded animal with gills, living in water; flesh of fish. —*v.i.* to try to catch fish; to search for.—*v.t.* to try to catch fish in; to draw (up); produce.—**fish'er** *n.*—**fish'-erman** *n.* one who lives by fishing.—**fish'wife** *n.* a woman who sells fish.—**fish'ery** *n.* the business of fishing; a fishing-ground.—**fish'monger** *n.* one who sells fish.—**fish'y** *a.* of, or like, fish; abounding in fish; dubious, open to suspicion. (See illus. p. 213.)

Fish *n.* a piece of wood for strengthening a mast; a metal plate for strengthening a beam.—*v.t.* to mend or join with a fish.—**fish'plate** *n.* a piece of metal for holding rails together.

Fis'sure (-sh-) *n.* a cleft, split. —**fis'sile** *a.* capable of splitting; tending to split.—**fis'sion** *n.* splitting; division of living cells into more cells. —**fissip'arous** *a.* reproducing by fission.

Fist *n.* the clenched hand; handwriting.—*v.t.* to strike with the clenched hand.—**fist'icuffs** *n.pl.* fighting with fists.

Fist'ula *n.* a pipe-like ulcer.

Fit *n.* a sudden passing attack of illness; a seizure with convulsions, spasms, loss of consciousness, etc., as of epilepsy, hysteria, etc.; a sudden and passing state, a mood.—**fit'ful** *a.* spasmodic, capricious.—**fit'fully** *adv.*

Fit *a.* well-suited, worthy; proper, becoming; ready; in good condition.—*v.t.* to be suited to; to be properly adjusted to; to arrange, adjust, apply, insert; supply, furnish.—*v.i.* to be correctly adjusted or adapted, to be of the right size.—*n.* the way a garment fits; its style; adjustment. — **fit'ly** *adv.* — **fit'ness** *n.*—**fitt'er** *n.*—**fit'-ment** *n.* a piece of furniture. —**fitt'ing** *n.* action of fitting; apparatus; fixture.—*a.* that fits; becoming, proper. *Syn.* becoming, applicable, appropriate, meet, qualified. *Ant.* inapt, unsuited, improper, unseemly.

Five *a.* and *n.* the cardinal number next after four.—**fifth** *a.* the ordinal number. —**five'fold** *a.* and *adv.*—**fifteen'** *a.* and *n.* ten and five.—**fifteen'th** *a.*—**fifth'ly** *adv.*—**fifteenth'ly** *adv.*—**fif'ty** *a.* and *n.* five tens.—**fif'tieth** *a.*—**fives** *n.* a ball-game played with the hand or a bat in a court.

Fix *v.t.* to fasten, make firm or stable; to set, establish; appoint, assign, determine; make fast, permanent.—*v.i.* to become firm or solidified; to determine.—*n.* a difficult situation.—fix'ity *n.*—fix'edly *adv.*—fixa'tion *n.*—fix'ative *a.*—fix'ture *n.* a thing fixed in position; a thing annexed to a house; a date for a sporting event; the event.

Fizz *v.i.* to hiss, splutter.—*n.* a hissing noise.—fiz'zle *v.i.* to splutter weakly.—*n.* a fizzling noise; fiasco.

Flabb'ergast *v.t.* to overwhelm with astonishment.

Flabb'y *a.* hanging loose, limp; feeble.—flabb'ily *adv.*—flabb'iness *n.*

Flac'cid (-ks-) *a.* flabby.—flaccid'ity *n.* *Syn.* weak, limber, drooping. *Ant.* firm, steady.

Flag *n.* a water plant with sword-shaped leaves, *esp.* the iris.—flagg'y *a.*

Flag *n.* a flat slab of stone.—*pl.* pavement of flags.—*v.t.* to pave with flags.—flag'stone *n.*

Flag *n.* a banner, a piece of bunting attached to a staff or halyard as a standard or signal.—*v.t.* to inform by flag-signals.—flag'-day *n.* a day on which small flags or emblems are sold in the streets for charity.—flag'-off'icer *n.* an admiral, rear-admiral, or vice-admiral.—flag'ship *n.* a ship with an admiral on board.—flag'-staff *n.* a pole on which a flag is hoisted.

Flag *v.i.* to droop, fade; lose vigour.

Flag'ellate (-j-) *v.t.* to scourge, flog.—flagella'tion *n.*—flag'ellant *n.* one who scourges himself in penance.

Flag'eolet (-j-) *n.* a small wind-instrument with mouthpiece at the end, six holes, and sometimes keys.

Flagit'ious (-jish'us) *a.* deeply criminal or wicked.

Flag'on *n.* a vessel, usually with handle spout and lid, to hold liquor for the table; a large oval bottle.

Fla'grant *a.* glaring, scandalous.—fla'grantly *adv.*—fla'grancy *n.* *Syn.* blatant, notorious. *Ant.* secret, concealed.

Flail *n.* an instrument for threshing corn by hand, a long handle with a short thick stick swinging at the end.

Flake *n.* a light fleecy piece, *esp.* of snow; a thin broad piece, *esp.* split or peeled off; layer.—*v.t.* to break flakes from.—*v.i.* to come off in flakes.—fla'ky *a.*

Flam *n.* a freak; a whim; a falsehood; an illusory pretext.—*a.* lying, false.—*v.t.* to delude; to impose upon.

Flamboy'ant *a.* marked by wavy lines; florid, gorgeous.

Flame *n.* burning gas; a portion of burning gas, *esp.* above a fire; visible burning; passion, *esp.* love; a sweetheart.—*v.i.* to give out flames, to blaze; to burst out in anger, etc.

Flamin'go (-ng-g-) *n.* a large bird with very long neck and legs.

Flaneur *n.* a lounger; a saunterer; a loiterer.

Flange (-anj) *n.* a projecting flat rim, collar, or rib.—*v.t.* to provide with a flange.

Flank *n.* the fleshy part of the side between the hips and ribs; the side of a building or body of troops.—*v.t.* to guard or strengthen on the flank; to attack or take in flank; to be at, or move along, either side of.

Flann'el *n.* a woollen stuff, usually without nap.—*pl.* garments of this, *esp.* trousers for games.—*a.* made of flannel.—**flannelette'** *n.* a cotton fabric imitating flannel.

Flap *v.t.* to strike with something broad, flat and flexible; to move (wings) up and down.—*v.i.* to sway, swing, flutter.—*n.* an act of flapping; a broad piece of anything hanging from a hinge or loosely from one side.—**flapp'er** *n.*—**flapdoo'dle** *n.* nonsense.

Flare (-ër) *v.i.* to blaze with bright unsteady flame.—*n.* act of flaring; a bright unsteady flame.—*n.* act of flaring; a bright unsteady flame; a signal light used at sea.

Flash *v.i.* to break into sudden flame; gleam; burst into view; appear suddenly.—*v.t.* to cause to gleam; to emit (light, etc.) suddenly.—*n.* a sudden burst of light or flame; sudden short access; a ribbon or badge; display.—*a.* showy; sham.—**flash'y** *a.*—**flash'-point** *n.* the temperature at which oil vapour ignites.

Flask (-à-) *n.* a pocket-bottle; a case for gunpowder; an Italian bottle covered with wicker; a long-necked bottle, *esp.* for scientific use.

Flat *a.* level; spread out; at full length; smooth; downright; dull, lifeless; below true pitch.—*n.* what is flat; a simpleton; a note half a tone below the natural pitch. — **flat'ly** *adv.* — **flat'ness** *n.*—**flatt'en** *v.t.* and *i.*

Flat *n.* a storey in a house; a set of rooms on one floor.

Flatt'er *v.t.* to court, fawn on; to praise insincerely; inspire a belief, *esp.* an unfounded one; gratify (senses); represent too favourably.—**flatt'erer** *n.*—**flatt'ery** *n.*

Flat'ulent *a.* generating gases in the intestines; caused by or attended by or troubled with such gases; vain, pretentious. — **flat'ulence** *n.* — **flat'ulency** *n.*

Flaunt *v.t.* and *i.* to wave proudly; show off.

Flaut'ist *n.* a flute-player.

Fla'vour (-vẹr) *n.* a mixed sensation of smell and taste; distinctive taste; an undefinable characteristic quality of anything.—*v.t.* to give a flavour to; season.

Flaw *n.* a crack; defect, blemish.—*v.t.* to make a

flaw in.—*v.t.* to crack.— flaw'less *a.*

Flax *n.* a plant grown for its textile fibre and seeds; its fibres; cloth of this, linen. —flax'seed *n.* linseed.—flax'en *a.* of flax; pale brown.

Flay *v.t.* to strip off skin or hide; to criticise severely.

Flea (-ē) *n.* a small wingless jumping insect which feeds on human and other blood. —flea'bane *n.* a wild plant.— flea'bite *n.* the insect's bite; a trifling injury; a trifle; a small red spot on a horse.— flea'bitten *a.* of a horse, with fleabites on a lighter ground.

Fleck *n.* a spot on the skin, a freckle; a patch of colour; a speck.—*v.t.* to mark with flecks, dapple.

Fledge *v.t.* to provide with feathers or down.—fledge'-ling *n.* a young bird just fledged.

Flee *v.i.* to run away.—*v.t.* to run away from; shun.

Fleece *n.* a sheep's wool.— *v.t.* to rob.—flee'cy *a.*

Fleer *v.i.* to laugh mockingly, jeer.—*n.* a mocking laugh or look.

Fleet *n.* a sea force; a number of ships, boats, etc., sailing in company; a number of cabs, motor-cars, etc., owned by one owner.

Fleet *a.* swift, nimble.

Fleet *v.i.* to glide away; pass quickly; flit, fly.

Flesh *n.* the soft part, the muscular substance, between skin and bone; this as food; of plants, the pulp; fat; the sensual appetites.—

flesh'ings *n.pl.* close-fitting flesh-coloured theatrical garments. — flesh'-pots *n.pl.* high living.—flesh'ly *a.* carnal, material.—flesh'y *a.* plump, pulpy. — flesh'ily *adv.*

Fletch *v.t.* to feather, as an arrow.—fletcher' *n.* a maker of bows and arrows.

Fleur-de-lis (flur-di-lē') *n.* the iris flower; the heraldic lily; the royal arms of France.

Flex'ible *a.* that may be bent without breaking, pliable; manageable; supple.—flexibil'ity *n.*—flex'ibly *adv.*— flex'ion, flec'tion *n.* bending; bent state.—flex *n.* flexible wire for movable electric fittings.—flexure *n.* a bend. *Syn.* bendable, yielding, tractable, manageable. *Ant.* stiff, unyielding, inelastic, rigid.

Flibb'ertigibb'et *n.* a flighty or gossiping person.

Flick *n.* light blow; a jerk.— *v.t.* to strike or move with a flick.

Flick'er *v.i.* to burn or shine unsteadily; to quiver.—*n.* a flickering light or movement.

Flight (-īt) *n.* the act or manner of flying through the air; swift movement or passage; a sally; distance flown; the stairs between two landings; a number flying together, as birds, arrows.

Flight (-īt) *n.* a running away.

Flim'sy (-zi) *a.* frail, easily destroyed; paltry.—*n.* a very thin paper.—flim'sily *adv.*

Flinch v.i. to shrink, draw back.

Fling v.t. to throw.—v.i. to rush, go hastily; kick, plunge.—n. a throw; a hasty attempt; a spell of indulgence; a vigorous dance.

Flint n. a hard stone found in grey lumps with a white crust; a piece of this.—**flint'-lock** n. a ·gun or its lock discharged by a spark struck from flint.—**flint'y** a.—**flint'ily** adv.

Flip n. a flick or fillip, a very light blow.—v.t. to strike or move with a flick.—v.t. to strike or move with a flick.—v.i. to move in jerks.—**flipp'er** n. a limb or fin for swimming.—**flipp'ant** a. treating serious things with unbecoming lightness. —**flipp'antly** adv.—**flipp'ancy** n.

Flirt v.t. to throw with a jerk, give a brisk motion to.—v.i. to play at courtship, pretend to make love.—n. a jerk, sudden throw; one who plays at love-making.—**flirta'tion** n.

Flit v.i. to go away; change dwelling; pass lightly and rapidly; make short flights.

Flitch n. a side of bacon.

Float v.i. to rest or drift on the surface of a liquid; to be suspended freely.—v.t. of a liquid, to support, bear along; in commerce, to get (a company) started.—n. anything small that floats (esp. to support something else, e.g. a fishing net); a low-bodied cart.—**flota'tion** n. an act of floating, esp. floating of a company.

Flock n. a lock or tuft of wool etc.—pl. wool-refuse for stuffing.—**flocc'ulent** (-k-) a. resembling flocks.

Flock n. a number of animals of one kind together; a body of people, a religious congregation.—v.i. to gather in a crowd.

Floe (-ō) n. a sheet of floating ice.

Flog v.t. to beat with a whip, stick, etc.

Flood (flud) n. the flowing of the tide; flowing water; an overflow of water, an inundation.—v.t. to inundate; cover or fill with water.—**flood'-gate** n. a gate for letting water in or out.

Flood'lighting n. artificial lighting of building exteriors.—**flood'light** v.t.—**flood'lit** a.

Floor (flōr) n. the lower surface of a room; a set of rooms on one level; a flat space.—v.t. to supply with a floor; to knock down; to confound.

Flop v.i. to sway about heavily; to move clumsily; to sit or fall with a thump.—v.t. to throw down with a thud.—n. a flopping movement or sound.—adv. with a flop.—**flopp'y** a.—**floppi'ness** n.—**flopp'ily** adv.

Flo'ra (flaw'-) n. the plants of a region; a list of them.—**flo'ral** a. of flowers —**flor'iculture** n. the cultivation of flowers.—**floricul'tural** a.—**floricul'turist** n. — **flores'cence** n. state or time of flowering.—**flor'et** n. a small flower forming part of a composite flower.—**flor'id** a. flowery, ornate; ruddy, high-coloured. — **flor'ist** n. one who deals in, grows, or studies flowers.

Flor'in n. an English silver coin worth two shillings; formerly, a coin of various countries.

Floss n. rough silk on a cocoon; silk for embroidery; fluff.—**floss'y** a. light and downy.

Flota'tion see FLOAT.

Flotill'a n. a fleet of small vessels; a small fleet.

Flot'sam n. floating wreckage.

Flounce v.i. to go, or move abruptly and impatiently. —n. a fling, a jerk of the body or a limb.

Flounce n. an ornamental strip of material on a woman's garment, attached by one edge, and put on full or gathered.—v.t. to adorn with a flounce.

Flound'er n. a flat-fish.

Flound'er v.i. to plunge and struggle, esp. in water or mud; to proceed in bungling or hesitating manner.—n. act of floundering.

Flour n. the sifted finer part of meal; wheat meal; fine soft powder.—v.t. to sprinkle with flour.—**flour'y** a.—**flour'iness** n.

Flour'ish (flur-) v.i. to thrive; be in the prime; to use florid language.—v.t. brandish, display; wave about.—n. an ornamental curve in writing; a florid expression; a waving of hand, weapon, etc.; a fanfare (of trumpets).

Flout v.t. to show contempt for by act or word.—n. a jeer.

Flow (flō) v.i. to glide along as a stream; to hang loose; move easily; move in waves; be ample in form; run full; abound.—n. an act or fact of flowing; quantity that flows; rise of tide; ample supply; outpouring.

Flow'er (flow-) n. the coloured (not green) part of a plant from which the fruit is developed, a bloom, blossom; an ornamentation; the choicest part, the pick.—v.i. to bloom, or blossom.—v.t. ornament with worked flowers. — **flow'eret** n. a small flower.—**flow'ery** a. abounding in flowers; full of fine words. ornamented with figures of speech.—**flow'er-de-luce** n. fleur-de-lis, q.v.

Fluc'tuate v.i. to vary irregularly, rise and fall; waver, be unstable.—**fluctua'tion** n.

Flue (flōō) n. a passage for smoke or hot air, a chimney.

Flu'ent a. flowing, copious and ready (in words); graceful (in movement). — **flu'ently** adv. **flu'ency** n. Syn. voluble, copious, smooth. Ant. halting, hesitating, forced, tongue-tied.

Fluff n. soft feathery stuff; down.—v.t. to make into fluff.

Flu'id a. having the property of flowing easily, not solid. —n. a fluid substance, a gas or liquid.—**fluid'ity** n.

Fluke n. a flat-fish; a parasitic worm.

Fluke n. the flat triangular point of an anchor.

Fluke n. lucky stroke.—v.i. to make a fluke.—**flu'ky** a.

Flumm'ery n. a dish of milk, flour, eggs, etc.; nonsense.

Flunk'ey n. a footman in livery; a toady, snob.

Flu'or n. a mineral containing fluorine. — **fluores'cence** n. luminous state produced in a transparent body by direct action of light, esp. violet and ultra-violet rays; the power of rendering ultra-violet rays visible. — **fluores'cent** a. — **fluoresce'** v.i. — **flu'orine** n. a non-metallic element of the chlorine group.

Flurr'y n. a squall, gust; nervous haste.—v.t. to agitate, bewilder.

Flush v.i. to take wing and fly away.—v.t. to cause to do this.—n. a number of birds flushed at once.

Flush n. a set of cards all of one suit.

Flush v.i. to flow suddenly or violently; of blood, to come with a rush; of the skin, to redden.—v.t. cleanse by rush of water; cause to glow or redden; inflame with pride, etc.—n. a rush of water; excitement; elation; glow of colour; reddening; freshness, vigour.—a. full, in flood; well supplied, esp. with money; level, level with a surrounding surface.

Flus'ter v.t. to flurry, bustle; confuse with drink.—v.i. to be in a flurry.—n. flurry.

Flute n. a musical wind instrument, a wooden pipe with holes stopped by the fingers or keys and a blowhole in the side; a flute-player in a band; a groove or channel.—v.i. to play on a flute.—v.t. to make grooves in.

Flutt'er v.i. to flap wings rapidly without flight or in short flights; to move, come down, quiveringly; to be excited, agitated.—v.t. to flap quickly; to agitate.—n. a fluttering.

Flu'vial a. of rivers.

Flux n. a morbid discharge, as of blood; a flowing; the flow of the tide; a constant succession of changes; a substance mixed with motal to help melting.

Fly n. a two-winged insect.—**fly'-blown** a. tainted.—**fly'-catcher** n. a bird; a trap for flies.

Fly v.i. to move through the air on wings or in aircraft; pass quickly through the air; float loosely, wave; spring, rush; flee, run away. —v.t. to cause to fly; to set flying; to run from.—n. a flying; a one-horse vehicle for hire; flap on a garment or tent; a speed-regulator in a machine.—**fly'-leaf** n. a blank leaf at the beginning or end of a book.—**fly'-wheel** n. a heavy wheel regulating a machine.—**fly'ing-boat** n. an aeroplane fitted with floats instead of landing wheels.—**fly'ing butt'ress** n. a buttress to a wall at a slope with a space between its lower part and the wall. —**fly'ing-fish** *n.* a fish which rises in the air by wing-like fins.

Foal *n.* the young of the horse, ass, or other equine animal. —*v.t.* to bear (a foal).—*v.i.* to bear a foal.

Foam *n.* a collection of small bubbles in a liquid; froth; froth of saliva or perspiration.—*v.i.* to give out, or form into, foam.—**foam'y** *a.*

Fob *n.* a small pocket in the waistband of breeches or trousers.

Fob *v.t.* to cheat; palm (off); only in **fob off** (*a thing on a person*) and **fob off** (*a person with a thing*).

Fo'cus *n.* the point at which rays meet after being reflected or refracted; point of convergence; principal seat or centre.—*v.t.* bring to a focus.—*v.i.* to come to a focus.—**fo'cal** *a.*

Fodd'er *n.* dried food for horses, cattle, etc.

Foe (fō) *n.* enemy. *Syn.* opponent, adversary, antagonist. *Ant.* friend, comrade, ally.

Fœ'tus, fe'tus *n.* the fully-developed young or embryo in womb or egg.

Fog *n.* aftermath.

Fog *n.* thick mist; unusually dark atmosphere.—**fogg'y** *a.* —*v.t.* to cover in fog; puzzle. —**fog'horn** *n.* an instrument to warn ships in fog.

Fo'gey, fo'gy *n.* (usually **old fogey**), an old-fashioned fellow.

Foi'ble *n.* a weak point in character; a quality a person prides himself on mistakenly.

Foil *n.* a small arc or space in the tracery of a window; a thin layer; metal in a thin sheet; a leaf of metal set under a gem; anything which sets off another thing to advantage; a light blunt sword for fencing.

Foil *v.t.* to baffle, defeat. *Syn.* to balk, blunt. *Ant.* aid, facilitate, help forward.

Foist *v.t.* to bring in secretly or unwarrantably; palm (a thing *off* on a person).

Fokk'er *n.* a German type of aeroplane.

Fold (-ō-) *n.* an enclosure for sheep, a pen; a body of believers, a church.—*v.t.* to shut up in a fold.

Fold (-ō-) *v.t.* to double up; bend part of; to clasp (in the arms); to interlace (the arms); wrap up.—*v.i.* to become folded; to be or admit of being folded.—*n.* a folding; space between two thicknesses; coil; winding; line, made by folding, a crease.—**fold'er** *n.*

Fo'liage *n.* leaves collectively.

Fo'lio *n.* a piece of paper numbered only on the front; two pages, or a page, with the opposite sides of an account in a ledger; a number of words as a unit of length; a sheet of printing paper folded once into two leaves or four pages; a book of such sheets.—**in folio**, made of folios.—*a.* made thus.

Folk (fōk) *n.* a race of people; people in general.—**folk'-song** *n.* music originating among a people.—**folk'-lore** *n.* traditions, beliefs popularly held; the study of these.—**folk'-dance** *n.*

Foll'icle *n.* a small sac.—**follic'ular** *a.*

Foll'ow *v.t.* to go or come after; to keep to (a path, etc.); accompany, attend on; take as a guide, conform to; engage in; be consequent on; grasp the meaning of.—*v.i.* to go or come after; to come next; result.—**foll'ower** *n. Syn.* to pursue, chase, attend, succeed, imitate, adopt, observe. *Ant.* to depart from, recant, to move ahead of.

Foll'y *n.* foolishness; a foolish action, idea, etc.

Foment' *v.t.* to bathe with hot lotions; to foster.—**fomenta'tion** *n.*

Fond *a.* tender, loving; credulous; foolish.—**fond of**, having love or great liking for.—**fond'ly** *adv.*—**fond'ness** *n.*—**fon'dle** *v.t.* caress.

Fon'dant *n.* a soft sugar mixture used in making sweets.

Font *n.* a bowl for baptismal water.

Food (-ōō-) *n.* that which is eaten or meant to be; nourishment.

Fool (-ōō-) *n.* a silly or empty-headed person; a simpleton; a jester, clown; dupe.—*v.i.* to act as a fool.—*v.t.* to delude; dupe; make a fool of, mock.—**fool'ish** *a.*—**fool'ishly** *adv.*—**foo'lery** *n.*—**fool'hardy** *a.* foolishly venturesome.—**fool'hard'iness** *n.*—**fools'cap, fool'scap** *n.* a jester's or dunce's cap; this as a water-mark; a size of paper which formerly had this mark.

Fool (-ōō-) *n.* a dish of fruit stewed, crushed and mixed with milk, etc.

Foot (-oo-) *n.* the lowest part of the leg, from the ankle down; lowest part of anything, base, stand; end of a bed, etc.; infantry; a measure of length of twelve inches; a division of a verse.—*v.t.* to set foot to; to put a foot on (a stocking, etc.).—*v.i.* to step, tread, dance.—**foot'ball** *n.* a large blown-up ball; a game played with it.—**foot'baller** *n.*—**foot'brake** *n.* in motoring, brake operated by pressure on foot-pedal.—**foot'ing** *n.* firm standing; relations, conditions.—**foot'-man** *n.* a liveried servant.—**foot'pad** *n.* an unmounted highwayman.—**foot'print** *n.* the mark left by a foot in the ground.

Foo'tle *v.i. slang* to bungle; to be ridiculously incompetent.—**footling** *a.*

Fop *n.* a dandy.—**fopp'ish** *a.*—**fopp'ishly** *adv.*—**fopp'ery** *n.*

For *prep.* because of; instead of; toward; on account of; to prevent or heal; in favour of; respecting; during; in search of; in payment of; in the character of.—*conj.* because.—**forasmuch' as** *conj.* since.

For'age (-ij) *n.* food for cattle and horse, *esp.* of an army.—

v.i. to collect forage; make a roving search.

For′ay *n.* a raid.—*v.i.* to make one.

For′bear (-bér) *n.* ancestor.

Forbear′ (-bér) *v.i.* to refrain; be patient.—*v.t.* to refrain from ; cease.—**forbear′ance** *n.*

Forbid′ *v.t.* to order not to do; refuse to allow; **forbidd′ing** *a.* not inviting.

Force *n.* strength, power; body of troops; body of police; compulsion; mental or moral strength; measurable influence inclining a body to motion.—*v.t.* to constrain, compel; break open; urge, strain; drive; produce by effort; hasten the maturity of. — **for′cible** *a.* — **for′cibly** *adv.* — **force′ful** *a.* — **force′-pump** *n.* a pump driving up water beyond the limit of atmospheric pressure. *Syn.* vigour, energy, efficacy, violence, coercion. *Ant.* weakness, gentleness, to grow naturally.

Force′-meat *n.* meat chopped for stuffing.

For′ceps *n.* surgical pincers.

Ford *n.* a place where a river may be crossed by wading.—**ford′able** *a.*

Fore- *prefix* meaning previous, before, front.

Fore *a.* in front.—*n.* the front part.—**fore-and-aft** *a.* placed in the line from bow to stern of a ship.—**fore′arm** *n.* the arm from wrist to elbow. —**forearm′** *v.t.* to arm beforehand.—**forebode′** *v.t.* to betoken.—**forebo′ding** *n.* a presentiment.—**forecast′** *v.t.* to estimate beforehand, prophesy.—**forecast** *n.* a conjecture, a guess at a future event.—**fore′castle** (fō′ksl) *n.* the forward raised part of a ship; the sailors′ quarters.—**fore′father** *n.* ancestor.—**fore′finger** *n.* the finger next the thumb.—**fore′ground** *n.* the part of a view, *esp.* in a picture, nearest the spectator. —**fore′hand** *n.* the part of a horse before the rider.—*a.* of a stroke in a game, made with the inner side of the wrist leading. — **fore′head** (for′id) *n.* the part of the face above the eyebrows and between the temples.—**fore′man** *n.* one in charge of work; leader of a jury.—**fore′mast** *n.* the mast nearest the bow. —**fore′noon** *n.* the morning. —**fore′runner** *n.* one who goes before, a precursor.— **fore′sail** *n.* the principal sail on a foremast.—**forsee′** *v.t.* to see beforehand.—**foreshad′ow** *v.t.* to figure beforehand, be a type of.—**fore′shore** *n.* the part of the shore between high and low tide marks.— **foreshort′en** *v.t.* to draw (an object) so that it appears shortened.—**fore′sight** *n.* foreseeing; care for the future; the front sight of a gun.— **fore′skin** *n.* the skin that covers the glans penis — **forestall′** *v.t.* to be beforehand with.—**foretell′** *v.t.* to prophesy.—**fore′top** *n.* the ″top″ of the foremast.— **fore′word** *n.* a preface.

Foreclose′ *v.t.* to take away the power of redeeming (a mortgage); to shut out, bar. —foreclo'sure *n.*

Foregath'er *see* FORGATHER.

Forego' *see* FORGO.

For'eign (-in) *a.* not of or in one's own country; introduced from outside; irrelevant; relating to, or connected with other countries. —for'eigner *n.*

Fore'most *a.* most advanced, chief.—*adv.* in the first place.

Foren'sic *a.* of courts of law.

For'est *n.* a large wood; the trees in it; a tract of land mainly occupied by trees, brush and heather; a region kept waste for hunting.— for'ester *n.* one who lives in a forest, or is employed in charge of one.—for'estry *n.* the management of forests.

Forev'er *adv.* always; to eternity, eternally.

For'feit (-fit) *n.* a thing lost by crime or fault; penalty, fine.—*pl.* a game.—*a.* lost by crime or fault.—*v.t.* to lose, have to pay or give up. —for'feiture *n.*

Forfend' *v.t.* avert, turn aside.

Forgath'er, foregath'er (-TH-) *v.i.* to meet, assemble, associate.

Forge *v.t.* to shape (metal) by heating in a fire and hammering; invent; make in fraudulent imitation of a thing, to counterfeit.—*n.* a smithy; a smith's hearth; a workshop for melting or refining metal.—for'ger *n.*— for'gery *n.* a forged document; the making of it.

Forge *v.i.* to advance, make

headway, *esp.* of a boat, usually slowly or with effort.

Forget' *v.t.* to lose memory of, not to remember.—forget'ful *a.*—forget'fully *adv.*—forget'-me-not *n.* a plant with a small blue flower.

Forgive' (giv) *v.t.* to pardon, remit.—forgive'ness *n.* *Syn.* absolve, condone, excuse, overlook. *Ant.* condemn, charge, accuse, blame.

Forgo', forego' *v.t.* to go without; give up.

Fork *n.* a pronged farm tool for digging or lifting; a pronged instrument for holding food in eating or cooking; a division into branches; the point of this division; one of the branches.—*v.i.* to branch.—*v.t.* to make fork-shaped; to dig, lift, or throw with a fork.

Forlorn' *a.* forsaken; desperate. —forlorn hope *n.* a desperate enterprise, *esp.* military; the party trying it.

Form *n.* shape, visible appearance; a visible person or animal; structure; nature; species, kind; a class in a school; customary way of doing a thing; set order of words; a regularly drawn up document, *esp.* a printed one with blanks for particulars; behaviour according to rule; condition, good condition; a long seat without a back, a bench; a hare's nest (also forme); a frame for type (also forme).—*v.t.* to put into shape mould, arrange, organise; train; shape in the mind, conceive; to go to make up, make part of.—*v.i.* to come into existence or shape.— **for'mal** *a.* ceremonial, according to rule; explicit; of outward form or routine; according to a rule that does not matter; precise; stiff.—**for'mally** *adv.* — **formal'ity** *n.*— **for'malism** *n.*—**for'malist** *n.* —**for'mation** *n.* a forming; the thing formed; structure, shape, arrangement.—**for'mative** *a.* serving or tending to form; used in forming.— **for'mat** *n.* size and shape of a book. *Syn.* system, formality, ceremony, propriety, mould, pattern. *Ant.* of *v.* to destroy, to disarrange, to misshape, to deform, disfigure.

For'mer *a.* earlier in time; of past times; first-named.— *pron.* the first-named thing or person or fact.—**for'merly** *adv.*

For'mic *a.* pertaining to ants. — **formicary** *n.* an ant-hill.

For'midable *a.* to be feared; likely to cause difficulty, serious.—**for'midably** *adv.*

For'mula (-ū-) *n.* a set form of words setting forth a principle, or prescribed for an occasion; a recipe; in science, a rule or fact expressed in symbols and figures.—**for'mulary** *n.* a collection of formulas.—**for'mulate** *v.t.* to express in a formula, or systematically.— **formula'tion** *n.*—**for'mulator** *n.*

Fornica'tion *n.* sexual intercourse between unmarried man and woman.—**for'nicate** *v.i.*

Forsake' *v.t.* to abandon, desert; give up.

Forsooth' (-th) *adv.* in truth (only in ironic use).

Forswear' *v.t.* to renounce.— *refl.* perjure.

Fort *n.* a fortified place.

Forte *n.* one's strong point.

Forte (-ti) *adv.* in music, loudly.

Forth (-th) *adv.* onwards, into view; onwards in time.— **forthcom'ing** *a.* about to come; ready when wanted. —**forthwith'** *adv.* at once, immediately.

For'tieth *see* FORTY.

For'tify *v.t.* to strengthen; provide with defensive works. —**fortifica'tion** *n.*—**fortiss'imo** *adv.* in music, very loud.— **for'titude** *n.* courage in adversity or pain.

Fort'night (-nīt) *n.* two weeks. —**fortnight'ly** *adv.* once a fortnight.

Fort'ress *n.* a fortified place, a military stronghold.

Fortu'itous *a.* accidental, due to chance. — **fortu'itously** *adv.*

For'tune *n.* chance; luck; good luck, prosperity; wealth, stock of wealth.—**for'tunate** *a.* lucky, favourable. —**for - tunately** *adv.* — **for'tune-hunter** *n.* a man seeking a rich wife.—**for'tune-teller** *n.* one who predicts a person's future, usually for money. *Syn.* luck, fate, estate, wealth.

For'ty *see* FOUR.

Fo'rum *n.* a public place in Rome where cases were tried and orations delivered; a tribunal.

For'ward a. lying in front of one, onward; prompt; precocious; pert.—n. in football, a player in the first line.—adv. towards the future; towards the front; to the front, into view; at or in the fore part of a ship; onward, so as to make progress.—v.t. to help forward; to send dispatch.—**for'wards** adv. forward.—**for'wardly** adv. pertly.—**for'wardness** n.

Forzand'o (-tsand-) n. in music, with loud and forcible expression.

Fosse n. a ditch or moat.

Foss'icker n. in the Colonies, one who searches for gold or profit.

Foss'il a. preserved in the earth and recognisable as the remains of animals or plants, esp. prehistoric ones; of persons, antiquated.—n. a fossilised thing. — **foss'ilise** v.t. and i. to turn into a fossil.

Fos'ter v.t. encourage; be favourable to; formerly, to tend, cherish. — **fos'ter-brother** n. one related by upbringing not by blood; so, **fos'ter-father, foster-child** n. etc.

Foul a. loathsome, offensive; dirty; charged with harmful matter; clogged, choked; unfair; wet, rough; obscene, disgustingly abusive.—n. a collision; an act of unfair play.—adv. unfairly.—v.i. to become foul.—v.t. to make foul; to jam; to collide with.—**foul'ly** adv.

Foulard' (foo-) n. a thin soft fabric for blouses, ties, etc.

Found v.t. to establish, institute; lay the base of; to base, ground.—**founda'tion** n. a founding; base, lewest part of a building; an endowed institution. — **found'er** n.—**found'ress** fem.

Found v.t. to melt and run into a mould.—**found'er** n.—**found'ry** n. a workshop for founding.

Found'er v.i. of a horse, to fall lame, collapse.—v.t. to cause to do this.

Found'er v.i. of a ship, to sink.

Found'ling n. a deserted infant.

Fount n. fountain.

Fount n. a set of printer's type.

Fount'ain (-in) n. a spring; source of water; jet of water, esp. an ornamental one.

Four (fawr) n. and a. cardinal number next after three.—**fourth** a. the ordinal number.—**fourth'ly** adv.—**four'teen'** n. and a. four and ten.—**fourteenth** a.—**for'ty** n. and a. four tens.—**for'tieth** adv.—**fourteen'fold** adv.—**for'tyfold** adv.—**four'-in-hand** n. a vehicle with four horses all driven by a driver on the vehicle.—**four-post'er** (-ō-) n. a bed with four posts for curtains, etc.—**four'square** a. firm, steady.

Fourchette n. a small forked instrument used to support the tongue in cutting the frenum; the forked piece between glove fingers.

Fowl *n.* a domestic cock or hen; a bird.—*v.i.* to hunt wild birds.—**fowl′er** *n.*—**fowl′ing-piece** *n.* a light gun.

Fox *n.* a red bushy-tailed animal, in many places preserved for hunting; a cunning person.—*v.t.* to discolour (paper) with brown spots.—*v.i.* to act craftily; to sham.—**foxy** *a.*—**fox′-glove** *n.* a tall flowering plant.—**fox′hound** *n.* a dog bred for hunting foxes.—**fox terr′ier** *n.* a small dog now mainly kept as a pet.—**fox′trot** *n.* an American dance.

Foyer *n.* the crucible in a furnace containing molten metal; in theatres, a public-room opening on to the vestibule or stair-case.

Fracas *n.* a noisy quarrel; a disturbance.

Frac′tion *n.* a numerical quantity not an integer; a fragment, piece, small part.—**frac′tional** *a.*—**frac′ture** *n.* a breakage.—*v.t.* and *i.* to break.

Frac′tious *a.* unruly, cross, fretful.

Frag′ile (-j-) *a.* breakable.—fragility *n.* *Syn.* frail, weak, brittle, delicate, *Ant.* sturdy, stout, strong.

Frag′ment *n.* a piece broken off; a small portion; an incomplete part.—**frag′mentary** *a.*

Fra′grant (-ăg-) *a.* sweet-smelling. — **fra′grance** *n.* — **fra′grantly** *adv.*

Frail *a.* easily broken, delicate; morally weak, unchaste.—**frail′ty** *n.*—**frail′ly** *adv.*

Frame *v.t.* to put together, make; adapt; put into words; put into a frame.—*n.* that in which a thing is set, or inserted, as a square of wood round a picture, etc.; structure; constitution; mood.—**frame′work** *n.* a light wooden or other structure; a structure into which completing parts can be fitted.

Franc *n.* a French coin.

Fran′chise *n.* the right of voting; citizenship.

Frank *a.* candid, outspoken; sincere.—*n.* a signature on a letter of a person entitled to send it free of postage charges; a letter with this.—*v.t.* to mark a letter thus.—**frank′ly** *adv.*—**frank′incense** *n.* an aromatic gum resin.

Fran′tic *a.* mad with rage, grief, joy, etc.—**fran′tically** *adv.*—**fran′ticly** *adv.* *Syn.* outrageous, furious, wild, frenzied, *Ant.* calm, unruffled, composed, placid.

Frater′nal *a.* of a brother; brotherly.—**frater′nally** *adv.*—**frater′nity** *n.* brotherliness; a brotherhood.—**frat′ernise** *v.i.* to associate, make friends.—**fraternisa′tion** *n.*—**frat′ricide** *n.* the killing of a brother or sister; the killer.—**frat′ricidal** *a.*

Fraud *n.* criminal deception; a dishonest trick.—**fraud′ulence** *n.*—**fraud′ulent** *a.*

Fraught (-awt) *p.p.* and *a.*—fraught with, laden with, full of.

Fray *n.* fight.

Fray *v.t.* and *i.* to wear through by rubbing, make or become ragged at the edge.

Frazz'le *n.* the act or result of frazzling.—*v.t.* and *v.i.* to fray; reduce to tatters.

Freak *n.* a caprice; prank; monstrosity.—**freak'ish** *a.*

Freck'le *n.* a light brown spot on the skin.—*v.t.* and *i.* to mark or become marked with such spots.

Free *a.* having liberty; not in bondage; not restricted or impeded; released from strict law, literality, tax, obligation, etc.; disengaged; spontaneous; liberal; frank; familiar.—*v.t.* to set at liberty, disengage.—**free'ly** *adv.* —**free'dom** *n.*—**free'-hand** *a.* of drawing, done without guiding instruments.—**free'-hold** *n.* tenure of land without obligation of service or rent; land so held.—**free'-lance** (-å-) *n.* a mediæval mercenary; an unattached journalist; politician independent of party.—**free'-man** *n.* a person not a slave; one with civil rights, admitted a citizen.—**free'-mason** (-å-) *n.* a member of a fraternity, originally of masons, now an institution for social and other purposes. — **free'masonry** *n.* — **free'thinker** *n.* one who rejects authority in religion.

Free'booter *n.* a pirate.

Freeze *v.i.* to become ice; become rigid with cold; feel very cold.—*v.t.* to turn solid by cold; chill; affect with frost. — **freez'ing-point** *n.*

temperature at which a liquid becomes solid.

Freight (-āt) *n.* hire of a ship; a cargo.—*v.t.* to hire or load (a ship).—**freighter** *n.*—**freight'age** *n.*

Fremes'cent *a.* becoming murmurous or noisy.—**fremes'-cence** *n.*

Fren'zy *n.* fury, delirious excitement.—**fren'zied** *a.*

Fre'quency *n.* in electricity, the number of complete cycles per second of an alternating electric current.

Fre'quent *a.* happening often; common; habitual; numerous. — **fre'quently** *adv.* — **fre'quency** *n.*—**frequent'** *v.t.* to go often or habitually to. —**frequent'ative** *a.* expressing repetition.

Fres'co *n.* a method of painting in water-colour on the plaster of a wall before it dries; a painting done thus.

Fresh *a.* new; additional; different; recent; inexperienced; pure; not pickled, salted, etc.; not stale; not faded or dimmed; not tired; of wind, strong. — **fresh'ly** *adv.* — **fresh'ness** *n.*—**fresh'en** *v.i.* and *t.*—**fresh'et** *n.* a rush of water at a river mouth; a flood of river water.— **fresh'man** *n.* a member of a college in his first year. *Syn.* healthy, unfaded, unimpaired, raw, unpractised, unsalted, uncured. *Ant.* old, faded, tarnished, unhealthy, weary, trained, salted, preserved.

Fret *v.t.* and *i.* to chafe, worry.

Māte, mēte, mīte, mōte, mūte, bōōt.

—*n.* irritation.—**fretful** *a.* irritable, easily vexed.

Fret *n.* a pattern of straight lines intersecting; a bar to aid the fingering of a stringed instrument.—*v.t.* to ornament with carved pattern.

Fri'able *a.* easily crumbled.—**friabil'ity** *n.*

Fri'ar *n.* a member of a mendicant religious order.—**fri'ary** *n.* a convent of friars.

Fric'tion *n.* rubbing; resistance met with by a body moving over another.—**fric'tional** *a.*

Friday *n.* the sixth day of the week.—**Good Friday,** the Friday before Easter.

Friend (frend) *n.* one attached to another by affection and esteem; an intimate associate; a supporter; a Quaker.—**friend'less** *a.*—**friend'ly** *a.*—**friend'ship** *n.*—**friend'liness** *n.*

Frieze (frēz) *n.* a coarse woollen cloth.

Frieze (frēz) *n.* a band of decoration.

Frig'ate *n.* a (sailing) warship next in size to a ship of the line.

Fright (frīt) *n.* sudden fear; a grotesque person or thing.—*v.t.* to terrify.—**fright'en** *v.t.* terrify.—**fright'ful** *a.*—**fright'fulness** *n.*

Frig'id (-ij-) *a.* cold; formal; dull.—**frig'idly** *adv.*—**frigid'ity** *n.*

Frill *n.* a fluted strip of fabric gathered at one edge; a similar paper ornament; a fringe.—*v.t.* to make into, or decorate with a frill.

Fringe *n.* an ornamental border of threads, tassels or twists; anything resembling this.—*v.t.* to adorn with, serve as, a fringe.

Fripp'ery *n.* finery.

Frisk *v.i.* to frolic.—*n.* a frolic.—**frisk'y** *a.*—**frisk'ily** *adv.*

Fritt'er *n.* a small pancake.

Fritt'er *v.t.* **fritter away,** to throw away, waste.

Friv'olous *a.* silly, trifling; given to trifling.—**frivol'ity** *n.* *Syn.* vain, foolish, unimportant. *Ant.* serious, important, earnest, grave.

Frizz *v.i.* to sputter in frying.—**frizzle** *v.t.* and *i.* to fry, toast or grill with sputtering noise.

Frizz *v.t.* to crisp, curl up into small curls.—**frizz'le** *v.t.* and *i.* to frizz.—**frizz'y** *a.*

Fro *adv.* away, from; (only in to and fro).

Frock *n.* a woman's dress; a monk's gown.—*v.t.* to invest with the office of priest.—**frock-coat** *n.* a man's long coat not cut away in front.

Froe'belism *n.* the kindergarten system. **frobel'ian** *a.*

Frog *n.* a tailless amphibious animal developed from a tadpole.

Frog *n.* a horny growth in the sole of horse's hoof.

Frog *n.* an attachment to a belt to carry a sword; a military coat-fastening of button and loop.

Frol'ic *a.* sportive.—*v.i.* to gambol, play pranks.—*n.* a prank, merry-making.—**frol'icsome** *a.*

From *prep.* expressing de

parture, moving away, source, distance, cause, change of state, etc.

Frond n. a plant organ consisting of stem and foliage, usually with fruit forms, *esp.* in ferns.

Front (-unt) n. the fore part; forehead.—*v.i.* to look, face. —*v.t.* to face; oppose.—*a.* of or at the front.—**front′age** n.—**front′al** a.—**front′ier** n. the part of a country which borders on another.—**front′ispiece** n. an illustration facing the title-page of a book; the principal face of a building.—**front′let** n. a band for the forehead.

Frost n. act or state of freezing; weather in which the temperature falls below the point at which water turns to ice; frozen dew or mist.—*v.t.* to injure by frost; cover with rime; powder with sugar, etc.; give a slightly roughtened surface; turn (hair) white.—**frost′y** a.—**frost′ily** adv.—**frost′bite** n. inflammation of the skin due to cold.

Froth (-th) n. a collection of small bubbles, foam; scum; idle talk.—*v.i.* and t. to throw up, or cause to throw up, froth. — **froth′y** a.—**froth′ily** adv.

Fro′ward a. perverse, ungovernable.

Frown v.i. to knit the brows, *esp.* in anger or deep thought. —n. a knitting of the brows.

Frow′zy a. ill-smelling; dirty, slatternly.

Fruc′tify v.i. to bear fruit.—

v.t. to make fruitful.—**fructifica′tion** n.

Fru′gal a. sparing, economical, *esp.* in use of food.—**fru′gally** adv.—**frugal′ity** n. *Syn.* parsimonious, saving, temperate. *Ant.* wasteful, extravagant, uneconomical.

Fruit (frōōt) n. a seed and its envelope, *esp.* an eatable one; vegetable products (usually in *pl.*); produce; result, benefit.—*v.i.* to bear fruit. —**fruit′erer** n. a dealer in fruit.—**fruit′ful** a.—**fruit′less** a.—**frui′tion** (-ōō-i-′) n. enjoyment; realisation of hopes.—**fruit′y** a.

Frum′enty, fur′menty n. hulled wheat boiled in milk and sweetened.

Frump n. a dowdy woman.—**frump′ish** a.

Frustrate′ v.t. to baffle, disappoint. — **frustra′tion** n. *Syn.* baffle, defeat, foil. *Ant.* to achieve, help, assist.

Fry n. young fishes.—**small fry**, young or insignificant beings.

Fry v.t. to cook with fat in a shallow pan.—*v.i.* to be cooked thus.—n. fried meat; internal parts of animals usually eaten fried.

Fub v.t. to cheat; to steal.

Fu′chsia (fū′sha) n. an ornamental shrub.

Fud′dle v.t. to intoxicate, confuse.—*v.i.* to tipple.

Fudge int. stuff; nonsense; exclamation of contempt.

Fu′el (fū-) n. material for burning.

Fu′gitive (fū-) a. that runs, or has run, away; fleeting, transient.—*n.* one who flees; an exile, refugee.

Fugue (fūg) *n.* a musical composition in which the themes seem to chase each other.

Ful'crum *n.* **ful'cra** *pl.* the point on which a lever is placed for support. ·

Fulgura'tion *n.* act of lighting; flashing; the sudden brightening of a fused globule of gold or silver.

Fulfil' (fool-) *v.t.* to satisfy; carry out; obey; satisfy the requirements of. — **fulfil'ment** *n.*

Fuli'ginous (-ij-) *a.* sooty.

Full (fool) *a.* holding all it can; containing abundance; ample; complete; plump. —*adv.* very; quite; exactly. —**full'y** *adv.*—**ful'ness, full'ness** *n.*—**ful'some** *a.* offending by excess.

Full'er (fool-) *n.* one who cleans and thickens cloth.— **fuller's earth** *n.* a clay used for this.—**full** *v.t.*

Ful'minate (fool'-) *v.i.* to flash, explode.—*v.t.* and *i.* to thunder out (blame, etc.).—*n.* a chemical compound exploding readily.—**fulmina'tion** *n.*

Fum'ble *v.i.* and *t.* to handle awkwardly, grope about.

Fume *n.* smoke; vapour; exhalation.—*v.i.* to emit fumes; give way to anger, chafe.— **fu'migate** *v.t.* to apply fumes or smoke to, *esp.* for disinfection.—**fumiga'tion** *n.*

Fun *n.* sport, amusement, jest, diversion.—*v.i.* to joke. —**funn'y** *a.* — **funn'ily** *adv.*

Funam'bulate *v.i.* to walk or dance on a rope.—**funambulist** *n.* a rope-walker or dancer.

Func'tion *n.* the work a thing is designed to do; official duty; profession; public occasion or ceremony.—*v.i.* to operate, work.—**func'tional** *a.*—**func'tionary** *n.* an official.

Func'tionalism *n.* modern movement in architecture based on "fitness for purpose."—**func'tionalist** *n.*

Fund *n.* a permanent stock; a stock or sum of money.— *pl.* money resources.—*v.t.* to convert (debt) into permanent form; invest money permanently. — **fund'ament** *n.* the buttocks.—**fundament'al** *a.* essential, primary; of, affecting, or serving as, the base.—*n.* a basic rule, note, etc.—**fundament'alist** *n.* one laying stress on belief in literal and verbal inspiration of the Bible and other traditional creeds. — **fundament'alism** *n.*

Fu'neral *a.* of, or relating to, the burial of the dead.—*n.* the ceremonies at a burial. —**fune'real** (-ēr'-) *a.* fit for a funeral, dismal.

Fun'gus (-ng-g-) *n.* **fun'gi** (-gī) **fun'guses** *pl.* a mushroom or allied plant; a spongy morbid growth.— **fun'gous** *a.* — **fun'gicide** *n.* a substance used to destroy fungus.

Funi'cular *a.* of or worked by a rope.

Funk *n.* fear, panic; a coward. —*v.i.* to show fear.—*v.t.* to be afraid of. — **funk'y** *a.*

Funn'el *n.* a cone-shaped vessel or tube; chimney of locomotive or ship; ventilating shaft.

Funn'y *see* FUN.

Fur *n.* the short soft hair of certain animals; a lining or trimming or garment of dressed skins with such hair; a crust or coating resembling this.—*v.t.* to provide with fur.—**furr'ier** *n.* one who deals in furs.—**furr'y** *a.*

Fur'below *n.* a flounce, trimming.

Fur'bish *v.t.* clean up.

Fur'cate, fur'cated *a.* forked; branching like the prongs of a fork.

Furl *v.t.* to roll up and bind (a sail, an umbrella, etc.).

Fur'long *n.* an eighth of a mile.

Fur'lough (-lō) *n.* leave of absence, *esp.* to soldier.

Fur'menty *see* FRUMENTY.

Fur'nace *n.* an apparatus for applying great heat to metals; a hot place; a closed fireplace for heating a boiler, etc.

Fur'nish *v.t.* to supply, fit up with; fit up a house with furniture; yield. — **fur'niture** *n.* movable contents of a house or room.

Furor'e (fūr-or'i) *n.* a burst of enthusiastic popular admiration.

Furrow (-ō) *n.* the trench made by a plough; a ship's track; a rut, groove.—*v.t.* to make furrows in.

Furry *see* FUR.

Fur'ther (-TH-) *adv.* more; in addition; at or to a greater distance or extént.—*a.* more distant; additional;—*v.t.* to help forward. — **fur'therance** *n.* —**fur'therer** *n.*—**fur'thermore** *adv.* besides.—**fur'thest** *a.* and *adv.* (*superl.*).—**fur'thermost** *a.*

Fur'tive *a.* stealthy, sly.—**fur'tively** *adv.* *Syn.* secret, clandestine. *Ant.* open, frank, undisguised.

Fu'ry (fū-) *n.* wild anger, rage, fierce passion; violence of storm, etc.; a snake-haired avenging deity (usually *pl.*).—**fu'rious** *a.* — **fu'riously** *adv.*

Furze *n.* a prickly shrub.

Fuse (fūz) *n.* a tube containing material for setting light to a bomb, firework, etc.—*v.t.* to fit a fuse to.—**fusee'** *n.* a conical wheel or pulley in a watch or clock; a large-headed match.—**fu'selage** *n.* the spindle-shaped body of an aeroplane.

Fuse (fūz) *v.t.* and *i.* to melt with heat; blend by melting.—**fu'sible** *a.*—**fu'sion** *n.*

Fu'sel (-ūz-) *n.* a mixture of crude alcohols (usually **fusel** oil).

Fu'sil *n.* a light musket.—**fusilier'** *n.* a soldier of certain regiments formerly armed with a fusil.—**fusillade'** *n.* a continuous discharge of firearms.

Fuss *n.* needless bustle or concern.—*v.i.* to make a fuss.—*v.t.* to bustle.—**fuss'y** *a.*—**fuss'ily** *adv.*—**fuss'iness** *n.*

Fus'tian *n.* a thick cotton cloth; inflated language.

Fus'tigate v.t. to cudgel.—**fustiga'tion** n.

Fus'ty a. mouldy; smelling of damp.—**fus'tily** adv.—**fus'tiness** n.

Fu'tile a. useless, ineffectual, frivolous.—**futil'ity** n.

Futt'ock n. one of the timbers in the rib of a vessel.—**futt'ock-plates** n.pl. iron plates on the top of a mast.

Fu'ture a. that will be; of or relating to time to come.—n. time to come; what will happen; tense of a verb indicating this.—**futu'rity** n.—**fu'turism** n. a movement in art marked by complete abandonment of tradition.—**fu'turist** n. and a.—**futurist'ic** a.

Fuze see FUSE.

Fuzz n. fluff.—**fuzz'y** a.—**fuzz'y-wuzz'y** n. a Soudanese warrior.

Fyl'fot (fil-fot) n. the Swastika.

G

Gab n. talk, chatter.—**gift of the gab**, eloquence.—**gab'ble** v.i. and t. to talk, utter inarticulately or too fast.—n. such talk.

Gab'erdine n. a fine hard-laid cloth; a loose upper garment, as of Jews.

Ga'ble n. the triangular upper part of the wall at the end of a ridged roof.

Ga'by n. a simpleton.

Gad v.i. to go about idly.—**gad'about** n. a gadding person.

Gad'-fly n. a cattle-biting fly.

Gadg'et n. a small fitting or contrivance.

Gaff n. a barbed fishing spear; a stick with an iron hook for landing fish; a spar for the top of a fore-and-aft sail.—v.t. to seize (a fish) with a gaff.

Gaff n. formerly, a public fair; a low-class theatrical entertainment (usually **penny-gaff**).

Gag n. a thing thrust into the mouth to prevent speech or hold it open for operation.—v.t. to apply a gag to; to silence.

Gag n. words inserted by an actor in his part.—v.i. of an actor, to put in words not in his part.

Gage n. a pledge, thing given as security, a challenge, or something symbolising one.—v.t. to pledge, stake.

Gaiety see GAY.

Gain v.t. to obtain, secure; obtain as profit; win; earn; persuade; reach.—v.i. increase, improve.—n. profit, increase, improvement. Syn. to arrive at, enrich, acquire, receive. Ant. to depart from, lose, fail.

Gainsay' v.t. to deny, contradict.

Gait n. manner of walking.

Gait'er n. a covering of leather, cloth, etc., for the lower leg.

Gala n. a festive occasion.

Gal'antine (-ēn) n. boned spiced white meat served cold.

Gal'axy n. the Milky Way; a brilliant company.

Gale *n.* a strong wind.

Gal'ilee *n.* a porch or chapel at the entrance of a church.

Gall (gawl) *n.* bile of animals; bitterness; rancour.

Gall (gawl) *n.* a painful swelling, *esp.* on a horse; a sore caused by chafing.—*v.t.* to make sore by rubbing; vex, irritate.

Gall (gawl) *n.* a growth caused by insects on trees, *esp.* the oak.

Gall'ant *a.* fine, stately, brave; chivalrous; (usually **gallant'**) very attentive to women, amatory.—*n.* a man of fashion; a lover, paramour (also **gallant'**). — gall'antly *adv.* (also **gallant'ly**).—gall'antry *n.* *Syn.* heroic, courageous, brave, dignified. *Ant.* ungallant, discourteous, rude, cowardly, timid.

Gall'eon *n.* a large high-built sailing ship of war.

Gall'ery *n.* a raised floor over part of the area of a building, *esp.* a church; the top floor of seats in a theatre; its occupants; a long narrow platform on the outside of a building; a passage in a wall, open to the interior of a building; a covered walk with side openings, a colonnade; a room or rooms for showing works of art; a horizontal passage in mining.

Gall'ey *n.* a one-decked vessel with sails and oars, usually rowed by slaves or criminals; a large rowing-boat, *esp.* that used by the captain of a warship; a ship's kitchen; a printer's tray for set-up type.

—gall'ey-proof *n.* a printer's proof in long slip form.

Gall'igaskins *n.pl.* breeches, leggings.

Gall'ipot *n.* a small earthenware pot.

Gall'on *n.* a liquid measure of four quarts.

Gall'op *v.i.* to go at a gallop.—*v.t.* to cause to move at a gallop.—*n.* a horse's, or other quadruped's, fastest pace with all four feet off the ground together in each stride; a ride at this pace.—gall'oper *n.*

Gall'ows *n.* a structure, usually of two upright beams and a cross-bar, *esp.* for hanging criminals on.

Gal'op *n.* a lively dance.—*v.i.* to dance it.

Galore' *adv.* in plenty.

Galosh', golosh' *n.* an overshoe, usually of rubber.

Gal'vanism *n.* electricity produced by chemical action.—galvan'ic *a.*—gal'vanise *v.t.* to apply galvanism to; stimulate thus; rouse by shock; coat with metal by galvanism.—galvanisa'tion *n.*—galvanom'eter *n.* instrument for measuring galvanism.

Gam'bit *n.* a chess opening involving the sacrifice of a piece.

Gam'ble *v.i.* to play games of chance for money stakes; risk much for great gain.—*n.* a risky undertaking.—gam'bler *n.*

Gamboge' (-ōōzh) *n.* a gum-resin used as yellow pigment.

Gam'bol *n.* a caper, playful

leap.—*v.i.* to caper, leap about.

Game *n.* a diversion, pastime, jest; contest for amusement; scheme, plan of action; animals or birds hunted; their flesh.—*a.* plucky, spirited.—*v.i.* to gamble.—**game'some** *a.* sportive.—**game'ster** *n.* a gambler.—**game'cock** *n.* a fowl bred for fighting.—**game'keeper** *n.* a man employed to breed game, prevent poaching, etc.

Game *a.* of arm or leg, crippled.

Gam'in *n.* a neglected and unruly child in the streets; a city arab.—**gaminesque** *a.* rascally.

Gam'ma-ray *n.* a very penetrative X-ray.

Gam'mon *n.* humbug, nonsense.—*v.t.* to humbug, deceive.

Gamm'on *n.* the bottom piece of a flitch of bacon.

Gamp *n.* a large umbrella.

Gam'ut *n.* the whole series of musical notes; a scale; the compass of a voice.

Gan'der *n.* a male goose.

Gang *n.* a company, band.—**gang'er** *n.* a foreman over a gang of workmen.—**gang'-way** *n.* a bridge from a ship to the shore; anything similar; a passage between rows of seats.

Gang'lion (-ng-gl-) *n.* a knot on a nerve from which nerve fibres spread out; a nerve nucleus.

Gang'rene (-ng-gr-) *n.* mortification, decomposition of a part of the body.—*v.t.* to affect with this.—*v.i.* to be affected with this.—**gang'renous** *a.*

Gang'ster *n.* a member of a criminal gang; a notorious or hardened criminal.

Gann'et *n.* a solan goose, a sea-bird.

Gan'try, gaun'try *n.* a structure to support a crane, railway signals, etc.; a stand for barrels.

Gaol, jail (jāl) *n.* a prison.—**gaol'er, jail'er** *n.* a keeper of a prison.

Gap *n.* a breach, opening; an empty space. *Syn.* hiatus, chasm, interstice, vacuity.

Gape *v.i.* to open the mouth wide; stare; yawn.—*n.* a yawn; a wide opening of the mouth.

Gar'age (-ázh, -ij) *n.* a building to house motor-cars.—*v.t.* to put into a garage.

Garb *n.* dress, fashion of dress. —*v.t.* to dress, clothe.

Garb'age (-ij) *n.* offal; refuse.

Gar'ble *v.t.* to make selections from unfairly, so as to misrepresent.

Garçon *n.* a boy; a waiter.

Gar'den *n.* ground for growing flowers, fruit, or vegetables. —*v.i.* to cultivate a garden. – **gar'dener** *n.*

Gargan'tuan *a.* immense, enormous, incredibly big.

Gar'gle *v.i.* to wash the throat with liquid kept moving by the breath.—*v.t.* to wash (the throat) thus.—*n.* a liquid used for this.

Gar'goyle *n.* a grotesque waterspout.

Gar'ish *a.* showy; glaring.

Gar'land *n.* a wreath of flowers

worn or hung as a decoration.
—*v.t.* to decorate with garlands.

Gar'lic *n.* a plant with a strong smell and taste, used in cooking.

Gar'ment *n.* an article of dress.
—*pl.* clothes.

Garn'er *n.* a granary.—*v.t.* to store up.

Gar'net *n.* a granary.—*v.t.* to store up.

Gar'net *n.* a precious stone.

Gar'nish *v.t.* to adorn, decorate (*esp.* food or literary matter).—*n.* material for this.
—**gar'niture** *n.* furniture, ornaments, trimming. *Syn.* to ornament, beautify. *Ant.* spoil, ruin, strip.

Garr'et *n.* a room on the top floor, an attic.

Garr'ison *n.* troops stationed in a town, fort, etc.—*v.t.* to furnish, or, occupy with a garrison.

Garrotte' *n.* Spanish capital punishment by strangling; apparatus for this; highway robbery by throttling the victim.—*v.t.* to execute, or rob, thus.

Garr'ulous *a.* talkative.—**garrul'ity** *n.*

Gar'ter *n.* a band worn near the knee to keep a stocking up.

Garth *n.* a paddock.

Gas *n.* an elastic fluid such as air, *esp.* one not liquid or solid at ordinary temperatures; such fluid, *esp.* coal-gas, used for heating or lighting; such fluid or a mixture used as poison in warfare, or found as an explosive in mines, or employed as an anæsthetic, etc.—*v.t.* to project gas over; poison with gas.—**gas'eous** *a.*—**gaselier'** *n.* a lamp of several burners for gas.—**gasom'eter** *n.* a tank for storing gas.—**gass'y** *a.* of or like, or full of, gas.

Gash *n.* a long deep cut, a slash.—*v.t.* to make a gash in.

Gasolene' *n.* the American name for petrol.

Gasp (-à-) *v.i.* to catch the breath with open mouth, as in exhaustion or surprise.—*n.* a convulsive catching of the breath.

Gas'tric *a.* of the stomach.—**gastron'omy** *n.* the art of good eating.—**gastronom'ical** *a.* — **gastron'omer, gas'tronome** *n.* a judge of cooking.
—**gas'teropod** *n.* a mollusc, e.g. a snail, with organ of locomotion attached to the ventral surface.

Gate *n.* an opening in a wall which may be closed by a barrier; the barrier for closing it; a contrivance for regulating the flow of water; any entrance or way out.

Gateau *n.* a cake.

Gath'er (-TH-) *v.t.* to bring together; collect; draw together, pucker; deduce.—*v.i.* to come together; collect; form a swelling full of gas.—**gathers** *n.pl.* puckered part of a dress. *Syn.* to assemble. cull, pick, pluck. *Ant.* disperse, scatter, diffuse, distribute.

Gaucherie *n.* an awkward action; clumsiness.

Gaud (gawd) *n.* a showy ornament.—**gaud'y** *a.* showy

without taste.—**gaud'ily** adv.
—**gaud'iness** n.

Gauge, gage (gāj) n. a standard measure, as of diameter of wire, thickness of sheet metal, etc.; distance between rails of a railway; capacity, extent; instruments for measuring such things as size of wire, rainfall, height of water in a boiler, etc.—v.t. to measure, test, estimate.

Gaunt (gaw-) a. lean, haggard.

Gaunt'let (gaw-) n. an armoured glove; a glove covering part of the arm.

Gaunt'let (gaw-) n. **to run the gauntlet,** punishment in which the victim had to run between two lines of men who struck at him with sticks, etc.—fig. to brave criticism.

Gauntry see GANTRY.

Gauze (gawz) n. thin transparent fabric of silk, wire, etc.—**gauz'y** a.

Gav'el n. the mallet of a presiding officer.

Gavotte' n. a lively dance; music written for it.

Gawk n. an awkward or bashful person.—**gawk'y** a.

Gay a. light-hearted; showy; dissolute.—**gai'ly** adv.—**gai'ety** n.

Gaze v.i. to look fixedly.—n. a long intent look.

Gaze'bo (-zē-) n. an outlook turret on roof or wall; a summer-house with wide prospect.

Gazelle' n. a small soft-eyed antelope.

Gazette' n. an official newspaper for announcements of government appointments, bankruptcies, etc.; a title for a newspaper.—v.t. to publish in the official gazette.—**gazetteer'** n. a geographical dictionary; a writer in a gazette.

Gazon' n. pieces of turf used to line parapets and earthworks.

Gear n. apparatus, tackle, tools; set of wheels working together, esp. by engaging cogs; rigging; harness; equipment; clothing; goods, utensils.—v.t. provide with gear; put in gear. Syn. accoutrements, dress, habits, ornaments, possessions.

Gel'atine n. a transparent substance made by stewing skin, tendons, etc.—**gelat'inise** v.t.—**gelat'inous** a.

Geld (g-) v.t. to castrate.—**geld'ing** n. a castrated horse.

Gel'id a. very cold.

Gem n. a precious stone, esp. when cut and polished; a thing of great beauty or worth.—v.t. to adorn with gems.

Gendarme n. an armed policeman in France.

Gen'der n. a classification of nouns, corresponding roughly to sexes and sexlessness (in English).

Geneal'ogy (jē) n. an account of descent from an ancestor or ancestors; pedigree; the study of pedigrees.—**genealog'ical** a.—**geneal'ogist** n.

Gen'eral a. not particular or partial; including or affecting or applicable to all or most; not restricted to one department; usual, prevalent; miscellaneous; dealing with main elements only.—*n.* an officer in the army of rank above colonel.—**generaliss'imo** *n.* a supreme commander.—**general'ity** *n.*—**gen'eralise** *v.t.* to reduce to general laws.—*v.i.* to draw general conclusions. —**generalisa'tion** *n.*—**generally** *adv.*—**gen'eralship** *n.* military skill.

Gen'erate *v.t.* to bring into being; produce.—**genera'tion** *n.* a bringing into being; a step in a pedigree; all persons born about the same time; the average time in which children are ready to replace their parents (about 30 years). —**gen'erative** *a.*—**gen'erator** *n.* a begetter; an apparatus for producing (steam, etc.).

Gener'ic *a.* belonging to, characteristic of, a class or genus.—**gener'ically** *adv.*

Gen'erous *a.* noble-minded; liberal, free in giving; copious; of wine, rich.— **gen'erously** *adv.*—**generos'ity** *n.* *Syn.* magnanimous, high-spirited, bountiful, strong, lively. *Ant.* ungenerous, close-fisted, mean, parsimonious.

Gen'esis *n.* origin; mode of formation.—**Genesis** *n.* the first book of the Old Testament.—**genet'ic** *a.*

Ge'nial *a.* kindly, jovial; sympathetic; mild, conducive to growth.—**ge'nially** *adv.* —**genial'ity** *n.*

Genic'ulated *a.* in botany, bent at an angle like the knee.

Ge'nie *n.* (**ge'nii** *pl.*) a demon.

Gen'ital *a.* pertaining to generation.—*n.pl.* the sexual organs.

Ge'nius *n.* very high power of mind; a person with this; tutelary spirit; prevalent feeling, taste; character, spirit.

Genre *n.* genus; kind; sort; style; a painting of a homely scene.

Genteel' *a.* elegant (usually ironical).—**genteel'ly** *adv.*

Gen'tian *n.* a plant, usually with blue flowers.

Gen'tile *a.* of race other than Jewish;—*n.* a gentile person.

Gen'tle *a.* mild, quiet, not rough or severe; courteous; noble; well-born.—**gentil'ity** *n.* social superiority.—**gen'tleman** *n.* a chivalrous well-bred man; a man of good social position; a man of noble birth; a man (used as a mark of politeness).—**gen'tlemanly, gen'tlemanlike** *a.*—**gen'tlewoman** *n.* **gen'tleness** *n.*—**gent'ly** *adv.*—**gent'ry** *n.* the people next below the nobility. *Syn.* bland, meek, soothing;—of "gentleness," mildness, suavity, meekness, tenderness. *Ant.* ungentle, unkind, rough, rude, wild.

Gen'uflect *v.i.* to bend the knee, *esp.* in worship.— **genuflec'tion, genuflex'ion** *n.*

Gen'uine *a.* real, true, not sham, properly so called.

Ge'nus *n.* (**gen'era** *pl.*) a race, tribe, kind, class.

Geog'raphy *n.* the science of the earth's form, physical features, climate, population,

etc.; a book on this.—
geog′rapher n.—geograph′ical
a.—geograph′ically adv.—
geol′ogy n. the science of the
earth's crust, the rocks,
their strata, etc.—geol′ogist
n.—geolog′ical a.—geolog′-
ically adv.—geol′ogise v.i. to
practise geology.—geom′etry
n. the science of the properties and relations of
magnitudes in space, as
lines, surfaces, etc.—geo-
metri′cian n.—geomet′rical
a.—geomet′rically adv.

Georgette′ (jor-jet) n. a fine
semi-transparent fabric.

Gera′nium n. a genus of
plants with fruit resembling
a crane's bill.

Ge′rant n. the acting partner
or manager of an association,
newspaper establishment.

Germ n. the rudiment of a
new organism, of an animal
or plant; a microbe; an elementary thing. — germ′i-
cide n. a substance for
destroying disease-germs.—
germici′dal a.—germ′inate
v.i. to sprout.—v.t. to cause
to sprout.—germina′tion n.

Ger′man a. of the same
parents, or being a child of a
brother—or sister—german
of either of one's parents
(only in brother-, sister-,
cousin-german).

Germane′ a. relevant, be-
longing to a subject.

Gerryman′der v.t. to arrange
matters for an election,
manipulate a constituency,
so as to give undue influence
to one side.

Gesta′tion n. the carrying of

young in the womb between
conception and birth; this
period.

Gestic′ulate v.i. to use expressive or lively movements
accompanying, or instead
of, speech.—gesticula′tion n.
—ges′ture n. a movement to
convey some meaning.

Get (g-) v.t. to obtain, procure,
earn; cause to go or come;
bring into a position or
state; induce; (in perf. tense)
to be in possession of, to
have (to do).—v.i. to succeed
in coming or going, reach,
attain; become.

Gew′gaw (g-) n. a gaudy toy,
plaything, trifle.

Gey′ser (gīz-, gēz-) n. a hot
spring throwing up a spout
of water from time to time;
an apparatus for heating
water and delivering it from
a tap.

Ghast′ly (gå-) a. horrible,
shocking; death-like, pallid;
grim.—adv. horribly. Syn.
pale, dismal. Ant. healthy,
cheerful, homely, pleasant.

Gher′kin (g-) n. a small
cucumber.

Ghett′o (g-) n. a Jews' quarter.

Ghost (gō-) n. a spirit, a dead
person appearing again, a
spectre; a semblance.—
ghost′ly a.

Ghoul (gōōl) n. in Eastern
tales, a spirit preying on
corpses.—ghoul′ish a.

Gi′ant n. a human being of
superhuman size; a very tall
person, plant, etc.—a. huge.
—gigant′ic a. enormous,
huge.

Gibb′er (j-, g-) v.i. to make

meaningless sounds with the mouth, jabber, chatter like an ape.

Gibb′erish (g-) *n*. meaningless speech.

Gibb′et *n*. a post with an arm on which an executed criminal was hung; death by hanging.—*v.t.* to hang on a gibbet; hold up to contempt.

Gibb′on (g-) *n*. a long-armed ape.

Gibb′ous (g-) *a*. convex; of the moon, with bright part greater than a semi-circle.—**gibbos′ity** *n*.

Gibe, jibe *v.i.* to utter taunts. —*v.t.* to taunt.—*n*. a jeer.

Gib′let *n*. (in *pl*.) the portion of a fowl, goose, etc., removed before cooking.

Gi′bus *n*. a man's opera hat.

Gidd′y (g-) *a*. dizzy, feeling a swimming in the head; liable to cause this feeling; flighty, frivolous.—**gidd′ily** *adv.*— **gidd′iness** *n*. *Syn*. light-headed, gyratory, inconstant, changeable, wild, thoughtless. *Ant*. steady, serious, sober, reliable, trustworthy.

Gift (g-) *n*. a thing given, a present; a faculty, power.— *v.t.* to endow or present (with).—**gift′ed** *a*. talented.

Gig (g-) *n*. a light two-wheeled carriage; a light ship's boat; a rowing boat.

Gigantic (ji-) *see* GIANT.

Gig′gle (g-) *v.i.* to laugh in a half-suppressed way, foolishly or uncontrollably.—*n*. such a laugh.

Gig′olo *n*. a male professional dancing partner.

Gilbert′ian *a*. whimsical, like a Gilbert and Sullivan opera.

Gild (g-) *v.t.* to put a thin layer of gold on.—**gilt** *a*. gilded—*n*. the layer of gold put on.

Gild *see* GUILD.

Gill (j-) *n*. a measure, the fourth of a pint.

Gill (g-) *n*. the breathing organ in fishes; flesh below a person's jaws and ears.

Gill (g-) *n*. a glen.

Gill′ie (g-) *n*. a sportsman's attendant in Scotland.

Gill′yflower *n*. the clove-scented pink; other similar scented flowers, e.g. the wallflower.

Gilt *see* GILD.

Gim′bals *n.pl.* a contrivance of rings, etc., for keeping a thing horizontal at sea.

Gim′crack *a*. flimsy, trumpery. —*n*. a trumpery article.

Gim′let *n*. a boring tool, usually with a screw point.

Gin *n*. a snare, trap; a kind of crane; a machine for separating cotton from seeds.— *v.t.* to snare; to treat (cotton) in a gin.

Gin *n*. a spirit flavoured with juniper.

Gin′ger *n*. a plant with a hot-tasting spicy root used in cooking, etc.; the root; spirit, mettle; light reddish yellow colour.—**gin′gerbread** *n*. cake flavoured with ginger. —**gin′gery** *a*.

Gin′gerly *a*. such as to avoid noise or injury, cautious.— *adv.* in a gingerly manner.

Gip′sy, gyp′sy *n*. one of a wandering race of Hindu

origin, usually living by basket-making, fortune-telling, etc.

Giraffe' *n.* an African ruminant animal, with spotted coat and very long neck and legs.

Gird (g-) *v.t.* to put a belt round; fasten clothes thus; equip with or belt on a sword; encircle.—**gird'er** *n.* a beam supporting joists; an iron or steel beam.—**gir'dle** *n.* a belt.—*v.t.* to surround.—**gird** *v.i.* to gibe.—*n.* a gibe.

Girl (g-) *n.* a female child; a young unmarried woman; a woman.

Girth (g-) *n.* a leather or cloth band put round a horse to hold the saddle, etc.; the measurement round a thing. —*v.t.* to surround, or secure, with a girth.

Gist *n.* substance, essential, point (of remarks, etc.).

Give (g-) *v.t.* to bestow, confer ownership of, make a present of; deliver, impart; assign; yield, supply; make over; cause to have.—*v.i.* to yield, give way.—*n.* yielding, elasticity.

Gizz'ard (g-) *n.* a bird's second stomach for grinding food.

Gla'brous *a.* smooth ; having a surface without hairs or any unevenness.—**gla'brate** *a.* smooth; bald; glabrous with age.

Gla'cé *a.* iced, or with a surface like ice as confectionery; polished, glossy, as leather goods.

Gla'cier (-ā-, -a-) *n.* a river of ice, a slow-moving mass of ice formed by accumulated snow in mountain valleys.— **gla'cial** *a.* of ice, or of glaciers; crystallised.—**gla'ciated** *a.* marked by, or covered by, ice, in glacier form.—**glacia'tion** *n.*—**gla'cis** (-sē) *n.* the outer sloping bank of a fortification.

Glad *a.* pleased; happy, joyous; giving joy.—*v.t.* to make glad.—**glad'den** *v.t.*— **glad'ly** *adv.*—**glad'ness** *n.*— **glad'some** *a.*

Glade *n.* a clear space in a wood or forest.

Glad'iator *n.* a trained fighter in ancient Roman shows.

Gladio'lus *n.* a flowering plant of the iris family, with sword-shaped leaves.

Glad'stone *a.* in **gladstone bag,** a light portmanteau.

Glam'our *n.* magic, enchantment.—**glam'orous** *a.*

Glance *v.i.* to glide off something struck; pass quickly; allude, touch; look rapidly.— *v.t.* direct (the eyes) rapidly. —*n.* brief look; flash; sudden oblique movement or blow.

Gland *n.* an organ separating constituents of the blood, for use or ejection.—**gland'ular** *a.*—**gland'ers** *n.* a contagious disease of horses.

Glare (-ār) *v.i.* to shine with oppressive brightness; look fiercely.—*n.* a dazzling brightness; a fierce look.

Glass (-à-) *n.* a hard transparent substance made by fusing sand with soda, potash, etc.; things made of it collectively; a glass drinking vessel; the contents of this; a lens; a telescope, barometer, or other instrument. — *pl.* spectacles. — glass'y *a.*—glass'ily *adv.*— glass'iness *n.*—glaze *v.t.* to furnish with glass; cover with glassy substance or glaze.— *v.i.* to become glassy.—*n.* a transparent coating; substance used to give this; glossy surface.—gla'zier *n.* one whose trade is to glaze windows.

Gleam *n.* a slight or passing beam of light; a faint or momentary show.—*v.i.* to give out gleams.

Glean *v.t.* and *i.* to gather, pick up, after reapers in a cornfield; pick up (facts, etc.). —glean'er *n.*

Glebe *n.* land forming part of a clergyman's benefice; the soil.

Glee *n.* mirth, merriment; a musical composition for three or more voices.— glee'ful *a.*—glee'fully *adv.*

Glen *n.* a narrow valley, usually wooded and with a stream.

Glengarr'y *n.* a woollen cap woven in one piece, with ribbons hanging down the back.

Glib *a.* fluent; more voluble than sincere.—glib'ly *adv.*— glib'ness *n.*

Glide *v.i.* to pass smoothly and continuously; go stealthily or gradually; of an aeroplane, to move with engines shut off.—*n.* a smooth, silent movement; in music, sounds made in passing from tone

to tone.—glid'er *n.* one or that which glides; an aeroplane for flying without mechanical power.

Glimm'er *v.i.* to shine faintly or with flickering.—*n.* such light.—glimpse *n.* a momentary view; a passing flash or appearance.—*v.t.* to catch a glimpse of.—*v.i.* to glimmer.

Glint *v.i.* and *t.* flash, glitter.— *n.* glitter.

Glissade' *n.* a slide, usually on the feet, down a slope of ice.—*v.i.* to slide thus.

Glis'ten (-is'n) *v.i.* glitter, sparkle.

Glitt'er *v.i.* to shine with bright quivering light, to sparkle.—*n.* such light.

Gloam'ing *n.* evening twilight.

Gloat *v.i.* to feast the eyes, usually with unholy joy.

Globe *n.* a round body, a sphere; a heavenly sphere, *esp.* the earth; a sphere with a map of the earth or the stars; anything of about this shape, as a lamp-shade, fish-bowl, etc.—globe'-trotter *n.* a hasty, sight-seeing traveller.—glob'ule *n.* a small round body; a drop.—glob'ular *a.* globe-shaped.

Gloom *n.* darkness; melancholy, depression.—*v.i.* to look sullen, or dark.—*v.t.* to make dark or dismal.— gloom'y *a.*—gloom'ily *adv.*— gloom'iness *n.* *Syn.* sadness, moroseness, sullenness. *Ant.* joy, happiness, brightness, light.

Glor'y *n.* renown, honourable fame; splendour; heavenly bliss; exalted or prosperous state.—*v.i.* to take pride (in).—**glor'ify** *v.t.* to make glorious, invest with glory.—**glorifica'tion** *n.* — **glor'ious** *a.* — **glor'iously** *adv.* *Syn.* splendour, honour, magnificence, fame, praise. *Ant.* insignificance, obscurity, meanness.

Gloss *n.* a surface shine.—*v.t.* to put a gloss on.—**gloss'y** *a.*—**gloss'iness** *n.*

Gloss *n.* a marginal interpretation of a word; a comment, explanation.—*v.t.* to interpret; comment; explain away.—**gloss'ary** *n.* a collection of glosses; a dictionary or vocabulary of special words.

Glott'is *n.* the opening at the top of the windpipe.

Glove (-uv) *n.* a covering for the hand.—*v.t.* to provide with, or put on, gloves.—**glov'er** *n.* dealer in gloves.

Glow (-ō) *v.t.* to give out light and heat without flames; shine; be, or look, very hot; burn with emotion.—*n.* shining heat; feeling of bodily heat; warmth of colour; ardour.—**glow'-worm** *n.* a female insect which gives out a green light. *Syn.* to brighten, redden.

Glow'er *v.i.* to look angrily.

Gloze *v.t.* to explain away.—*v.i.* use fair words.

Glu'cose *n.* a sugar obtained from grapes and fruits of various kinds.

Glue (-ōō) *n.* a hard substance made from horns, hoofs, etc., and used warm as a cement.—*v.t.* to fasten with glue.—**glu'ey** *a.*

Glum *a.* sullen, frowning, dejected.

Glut *v.t.* to feed, gratify to the full or to excess; overstock.—*n.* excessive supply.

Glutt'on *n.* one who eats too much, a greedy person; one eagerly devouring (books, work, etc.).—**glutt'onous** *a.*—**glutt'ony** *n.*

Gly'cerine, gly'cerin (glis'er-ēn) *n.* a colourless, sweet liquid obtained from oils and used in medicine and the making of explosives.

Gnarled (narld) *a.* of a tree, knobby, rugged, twisted.

Gnash (n-) *v.t.* or *i.* to grind (the teeth) together.

Gnat (n-) *n.* a small two-winged fly.

Gnaw (n-) *v.t.* to bite steadily, wear away by biting; corrode.

Gneiss *n.* a crystalline rock consisting of quartz, feldspar and mica.

Gnome (n-) *n.* a goblin, a fairy living underground.

Gno'mic (nō-) *a.* sententious, pithy.

Gno'mon (nō-) *n.* the pin or rod which casts the shadow on a sundial; an indicator.

Gnos'tic (n-) *a.* of knowledge; having special knowledge.

Gnu (nū) *n.* an antelope like an ox.

Go *v.i.* to move along, make way; be moving; depart; elapse; be kept, put, be able to be put; result; contribute to a result; tend to; become. —*n.* a going; energy, vigour. —**go'er** *n.*

Goad *n.* a spiked stick for driving cattle.—*v.t.* to drive with a goad; urge on; irritate.

Goal *n.* the end of a race; an object of effort; posts through which the ball is to be driven at football.

Go'-ashore *n.* in Australia, an iron cauldron or pot with three feet.

Goat *n.* a four-footed animal with long hair and horns and a beard.—**goat'-herd** *n.* one who tends goats.—**goat'ee** *n.* a beard like a goat's.

Gob *n.* a lump, mouthful.—**gobb'et** *n.* a lump of food.—**gob'ble** *v.t.* to eat hastily and noisily.

Gob'ble *v.i.* of a turkey, to make a gurgling noise in the throat.

Gob'let *n.* a drinking-cup.

Gob'lin *n.* a mischievous and ugly demon.

God *n.* a superhuman being worshipped as having supernatural power; an object of worship, an idol.—**God** *n.* the Supreme Being.—**godd'ess** *fem.*—**god'father** *n.*, **god'mother** *fem.* a sponsor at baptism.—**god'child** *n.* one considered in relation to a **god'parent** *n.*—**god'head** *n.* the divine nature.—**god'-fearing** *a.* religious, good.—**god'less** *a.*—**god'like** *a.*—**god'ly** *a.* religious.—**god'liness** *n.*—**god'-forsaken** *a.* devoid of merit, dismal.

Goff'er, gof'er, goph'er gauff'er (gō-, go-) *v.t.* to make wavy, crimp with hot irons.

Gog'gle *v.i.* to roll the eyes.—*v.t.* to roll about (the eyes).—*a.* rolling, sticking out (only of eyes).—*n.* in *pl.* large spectacles to protect the eyes from glare, dust, etc.

Gold (gō-) *n.* a yellow precious metal; coins of this, wealth; *fig.* beautiful or precious material or thing; the colour of gold.—*a.* of, like, or having the colour of, gold.—**gold'en** *a.*—**gold'finch** *n.* a bird with yellow feathers.—**gold'fish** *n.* a red Chinese carp.—**gold'smith** *n.* a worker in gold.

Golf (golf or gof) *n.* a game in which a small hard ball is struck with clubs.—*v.i.* to play this game.—**golf'er** *n.*

Goll'iwog *n.* a grotesque doll.

Golosh *see* GALOSH

Gon'dola *n.* a Venetian canal-boat; a car suspended from an airship.—**gondolier'** *n.*

Gong *n.* a metal disk with turned rim which resounds as a bell when struck with a soft mallet; anything used in the same way.

Good *a.* commendable; right; proper; excellent; virtuous; kind; safe; adequate; sound; valid.—*n.* that which is good; well-being; profit.—*pl.* property, wares.—**good'ness** *n.*—**good'ly** *a.* handsome; of considerable size.—**good'will** *n.* kindly feeling; heartiness; right of trading as a recognised successor.—**good'y** *n.* a sweetmeat.—*a.* obtrusively or weakly virtuous; (also **good'y-good'y**).

Good-bye' *interj.* farewell.

Goo'gly *n.* in cricket, a ball that "breaks" in an unexpected direction.

Goose *n.* a large web-footed bird; its flesh; a simpleton; a tailor's smoothing iron.—**goose'flesh** *n.* a bristling state of the skin due to cold or fright.—**goose'-step** *n.* a recruit's balancing drill; a formal parade step.

Goose'berry (-z-) *n.* a thorny shrub; its eatable berry; a chaperon to lovers.

Gore *n.* clotted shed blood.—**gor'y** *a.*—**gor'ily** *adv.*

Gore *n.* a triangular piece of cloth inserted to shape a garment.—*v.t.* to shape with one.

Gore *v.t.* to pierce with horns.

Gorge *n.* the inside of the throat; surfeit; narrow opening between hills.—*v.i.* to feed greedily.—*v.t.* to stuff with food; to devour greedily.—**gorg'et** *n.* a piece of armour for the throat.

Gorge'ous (·jus) *a.* splendid, showy, dazzling. *Syn.* grand, imposing, magnificent. *Ant.* sordid, mean, drab, plain.

Gorgonzo'la *n.* a rich cheese.

Gorill'a *n.* an anthropoid ape of the largest kind.

Gor'mandise *v.t.* to eat like a glutton.

Gorse *n.* a prickly shrub.

Gory *see* GORE.

Gos'hawk *n.* a large short-winged hawk.

Gos'ling (-z-) *n.* a young goose.

Gos'pel *n.* the tidings preached by Jesus; the record of His life; any of the four books by the evangelists.

Goss'amer *n.* a filmy substance of spiders web floating in calm air or spread on grass; filmy thing; delicate gauze.—*a.* light, flimsy.

Goss'ip *n.* idle talk about other persons, *esp.* regardless of fact; idle talk or writing; one who talks thus; formerly, a familiar friend.—*v.i.* to talk gossip.

Go'tha (-tǎ) *n.* a large German fighting aeroplane.

Goth'ic *a.* of Goths; barbarous; in architecture, of the pointed arch style common in Europe twelfth-sixteenth cent.; of type, German; black-letter.

Gouge (gowj) *n.* a chisel with a curved cutting edge.—*v.i.* to cut with a gouge, to hollow (out).

Gourd (gord, gŏŏrd) *n.* a trailing or climbing plant; its large fleshy fruit; the rind of this as a vessel.

Gour'mand (gŏŏ-) *a.* greedy.—*n.* a lover of delicate food.—**gour'met** *n.* a connoisseur of wine or food.

Gout (gowt) *n.* a disease with inflammation, *esp.* of the smaller joints; a drop, splash.—**gout'y** *a.*

Gov'ern (guv-) *v.t.* to rule, direct, guide, control; serve as a precedent for; be followed by (a grammatical case, etc.).—**gov'ernable** *a.*—**gov'ernance** *n.*—**gov'ernor** *n.*—**gov'erness** *n.* a woman teacher, *esp.* in a private household.—**gov'ernment** *n.*

—gov'ernmental *a.* *Syn.* to regulate, control, restrain, rule.

Gown *n.* a loose flowing upper garment; a woman's frock; an official robe, as in a university, etc.

Grab *v.t.* to grasp suddenly, snatch.—*n.* a sudden clutch; greedy proceedings.

Grace *n.* charm, attractiveness; easy and refined motion, manners, etc.; ornament, accomplishment; favour; divine favour; a short thanksgiving before or after a meal; a title of a duke or archbishop.—*v.t.* to add grace to, honour.—**grace'ful** *a.*—**grace'less** *a.* shameless, depraved.—**gra'cious** *a.* indulgent, beneficent, condescending.—**grace'fully** *adv.* —**gra'ciously** *adv.* *Syn.* mercy, pardon, salvation, beauty, elegance. *Ant.* severity, inclemency, awkwardness, boorishness.

Grade *n.* a step or stage; degree of rank, etc.; class; slope. — *v.t.* to arrange in classes. — **grada'tion** *n.* series of degrees or steps; each of them; arrangement in steps; insensible passing from one shade, etc., to another.—**gra'dient** *n.* degree of slope.—**grad'ual** *a.* taking place by degrees; moving step by step; slow and steady; not steep.—**grad'ually** *adv.*—**grad'uate** *v.i.* to take a university degree.— *v.t.* to divide into degrees, mark or arrange according to a scale.—*n.* a holder of a university degree.—**gradua'tion** *n.*

Graft *n.* a shoot of a plant set in a stock of another plant; the process.—*v.t.* to insert (a shoot) in another stock; to transplant (living tissue in surgery).

Grail *n.* (usually Holy Grail) the platter or cup used by Jesus at the Last Supper.

Grain *n.* a seed or fruit of a cereal plant; wheat and allied plants; a small hard particle; a unit of weight, 1/7000th of the pound avoirdupois; texture; arrangement of fibres; formerly cochineal, scarlet dye, dye in general.—*v.t.* to paint in imitation of wood grain.— **grainy** *a.*

Gram *see* GRAMME.

Gram'arye *n.* magic.

Graminiv'erous *a.* grass-eating.

Gram'mar *n.* the science of the structure and usages of a language; a book on this; correct use of words.— **grammar'ian** (-ĕr-) *n.*— **grammat'ical** *a.*-**grammat'ically** *adv.*—**gramm'ar-school** *n.* formerly, a school for teaching Latin; a secondary school.

gramme, gram *n.* the unit of weight in the metric system.

Gram'ophone *n.* an instrument for recording and reproducing sounds.

Gram'pus *n.* a blowing and spouting sea-creature of the whale family; a person who breathes heavily.

Gran'ary *n.* a storehouse for grain.

Grand *a.* chief, of chief importance; splendid, magnificent; lofty; imposing; final. —**grand'ly** *adv.*—**grandee'** *n.* a Spanish or Portuguese nobleman.—**grand'eur** (-dyer) *n.* nobility; magnificence; dignity.—**grand'father** *n.*—**grand'mother** *fem.* parents of parents.-**grand'son** *n.*, **grand'- daughter** *fem.*, **grand'child** *n.* children of children.— **grandil'oquent** *a.* pompous in speech.—**grandil'oquently** *adv.*—**grandil'oquence** *n.*— **grand'iose** *a.* imposing; planned on a great scale.

Grange *n.* a granary; a country-house with farm buildings.

Gran'ite (-it) *n.* a hard crystalline rock, used for building.

Grant *v.t.* to consent to fulfil (a request); permit; bestow, give formally; admit.—*n.* a granting; a thing granted.— **grant'or** *n.*—**grant'ee** *n.*

Gran'ule *n.* a small grain.— **gran'ular** *a.* of, or like, grains. —**gran'ulate** *v.t.* to form into grains.—*v.i.* to take the form of grains; of a wound, to begin to grow in small prominences like grains.— **granula'tion** *n.*

Grape *n.* the fruit of the vine. —**grape'shot** *n.* bullets as scattering charge for a cannon.

Graph'ic *a.* of, in, or relating to writing, drawing, painting, etc.; vividly descriptive. —**graph** *n.* a graphic formula, a diagram showing symbolically a series of connections. — **graph'ically** *adv.*—**graphol'ogy** *n.* the study of handwriting.— **graph'ite** *n.* a form of carbon (used in pencils).

Grap'nel *n.* an iron instrument of hooks for seizing, as an enemy ship; a small anchor with several flukes.

Grap'ple *n.* a grapnel; a grip; a contest at close quarters.— *v.t.* to seize with a grapnel; seize firmly.—*v.i.* to contend (with), come to grips.

Grasp (-à-) *v.t.* to seize firmly, clutch; understand.—*v.i.* to clutch (at).—*n.* firm hold; mastery.

Grass (-à) *n.* herbage, plants grown for cattle to eat, to cover lawns, etc.; a plant of this kind.—*v.t.* to cover with turf; to put down on grass.— **grass'hopper** *n.* a jumping, chirping insect. — **grass'- wid'ow** *n.* a wife whose husband is away from her.— **grass'y** *a.*

Grate *n.* a fireplace, a frame of bars for holding fuel; a framework of crossed bars (also **grating** *n.*).

Grate *v.t.* to rub into small bits with something rough.— *v.i.* to rub with harsh noise; to have an irritating effect.— **gra'ter** *n.*

Grate'ful *a.* thankful; pleasing.—**grate'fully** *adv.*—**grat'i- fy** *v.t.* to do a favour to; indulge; pay.—**gratifica'tion** *n.*—**grat'itude** *n.* a sense of being thankful for something received.—**gra'tis** *adv.* and *a.* free, for nothing.—**gratu'i- tous** *a.* given free, done for nothing; uncalled for.— **gratu'itously** *adv.*—**gratu'ity**

n. a gift of money. *Syn.* agreeable, acceptable, delicious. *Ant.* ungrateful, thankless, harsh.

Gratin (grà-tōn) *n.* a method of cooking to form a light crust; a dish so cooked.

Grava'men *n.* the heaviest part (of an accusation); a grievance.

Grave *n.* a hole dug for a dead body; a monument on this; death.

Grave *v.t.* to carve, engrave.

Grave *a.* serious, weighty; dignified, solemn; plain, dark in colour, deep in note.—**grave'ly** *adv.*—**grav'ity** *n.* importance; seriousness; heaviness; the force of attraction of one body for another, *esp.* of objects to the earth.—**grav'itate** *v.i.* to move by gravity; to sink, settle down.—**gravita'tion** *n.* *Syn.* solemn, severe, stern. *Ant.* cheerful, merry, gay, irresponsible.

Grave *v.t.* to clean (a ship's bottom) by burning and tarring.—**gra'ving-dock** *n.* a place for this.

Grav'el *n.* small stones, coarse sand; aggregation of urinary crystals; a disease due to this. —*v.t.* to cover with gravel; puzzle.—**grav'elly** *a.*

Grav'igrade *a.* walking with heavy steps; *n.* an animal that walks heavily.

Gra'vy *n.* juices from meat in cooking; a dressing or sauce for food made from these juices.

Gray, grey *a.* between black and white in colour, as ashes or lead; clouded; dismal; turning white; aged.—*n.* gray colour; a gray horse.—**gray'ling** *n.* a gray fish.

Graze *v.i.* and *t.* to feed on grass.—**gra'zier** *n.* one who feeds cattle for market.

Graze *v.t.* to touch lightly in passing; to abrade the skin thus.—*v.i.* to move so as to touch lightly.—*n.* a grazing.

Grease (-ēs) *n.* soft melted fat of animals; thick oil as a lubricant.—*v.t.* to apply grease to.—**greas'y** *a.*—**greas'ily** *adv.*—**greas'iness** *n.* —**greas'er** *n.*

Great (-āt) *a.* large, big; important; pre-eminent, distinguished.—as *prefix,* indicates a degree further removed in relationship, e.g. **great-grand'father** *n.* the father of a grandfather or grandmother. — **great'-uncle** *n.* the uncle of a parent.— **great'ly** *adv.*—**great'ness** *n.*— **great'coat** *n.* an overcoat, *esp.* military. *Syn.* numerous, superior, commanding, strong, powerful, noble, eminent, weighty. *Ant.* small, insignificant, trivial, unimportant, inconsiderable.

Greave (-ēv) *n.* armour for the leg below the knee.

Grebe *n.* a diving bird.

Gre'cian *a.* Greek.—*n.* one learned in the Greek language.

Grecque (grek) *n.* a vessel having a perforated bottom, fitted into a coffee pot and holding the coffee; a Greek fret.

Greed'y a. gluttonous, over eager for food, wealth, etc.—**greed** n.—**greed'ily** adv.—**greed'iness** n.

Greek n. a native of Greece.— a. of Greece.

Green a. of colour between blue and yellow, coloured like growing grass, emerald, etc.; unripe; inexperienced; easily deceived.—n. the colour; a piece of grass-covered land.—pl. green vegetables. — **green'ery** n. vegetation.—**green'gage** n. a kind of plum.—**green'horn** n. simpleton.—**green'grocer** n. a dealer in vegetables and fruit.—**greengro'cery** n.—**green'house** n. a glass-house for rearing plants.—**green'room** n. a room for actors when not on the stage.—**green'sward** n. turf.—**green'wood** n. woodlands in summer.—**green'ish** a.

Greet v.t. to accost or salute; receive; meet.—**greet'ing** n.

Gregar'ious (-êr-) a. living in flocks; fond of company.

Grenade' n. an explosive shell or bomb, thrown by hand or shot from a rifle.—**grenadier'** n. a soldier of the Grenadier Guards; formerly ,a soldier who threw grenades.

Grey'hound n. a swift slender dog used in coursing and racing.

Grid n. a frame of bars; in motoring, luggage bracket at rear of car; in wireless, the electrode in a thermionic valve.—**the grid**, in electricity, system of main transmission lines.

Grid'iron n. a cooking utensil of metal bars for broiling.—**gridd'le** n. a flat round iron plate for cooking.

Grief (-ĕf) n. a deep sorrow.—**griev'ance** n. a real or imaginary ground of complaint.—**grieve** v.i. to feel grief.—v.t. to cause grief to.—**griev'ous** a. painful, oppressive.

Griff'in, griff'on, gryph'on n. a fabulous monster with eagle's head and wings and lion's body.

Grig n. a cricket; a small eel; a lively creature.

Grill n. a gridiron; food cooked on one.—v.t. and i. to broil on a grill.—**grill'-room** n. place where food is grilled and served.

Grilse n. a young salmon that has only been once to the sea.

Grim a. stern; of stern or harsh aspect; joyless.—**grimly** adv.

Grimace' n. a wry face.—v.i. to make one.

Grime n. soot, dirt.—**gri'my** a.

Grin v.i. to show the teeth.—n. an act of grinning.

Grind (-ī-) v.t. to crush to powder between hard surfaces; oppress; make sharp or smooth; grate.—v.i. to perform the action of grinding; to work (esp. study) hard; grate.—n. action of grinding; hard work.—**grind'-stone** n. a revolving disk of stone for grinding, etc.—**grind'er** n.

Gring'o (gring-gō) n. in America, a contemptuous name for an Englishman.

Grip n. a firm hold, grasp;

grasping power; mastery; a handle.—*v.t.* to grasp or hold tightly.

Gripe *v.t.* to grip; oppress; afflict with pains of colic.—*n.* grip.—*pl.* colic pains. *Syn.* to clutch, compress, squeeze, tighten, pinch, distress. *Ant.* to relax, release, hold or touch lightly.

Grisette' *n.* a gay young Frenchwoman.

Gris'ly (-z-) *a.* grim, causing terror.

Grist *n.* corn to be ground.

Gris'tle (grisl) *n.* cartilage, tough flexible tissue.—**gris'tly** *a.*

Grit *n.* particles of sand; coarse sandstone; courage.—*v.i.* to make a grinding sound.—*v.t.* grind (teeth).—**gritt'y** *a.*—**gritt'iness** *n.*

Grizz'ly *a.* gray-haired. gray. —**grizz'ly bear** *n.* large N. Amer. bear.—**griz'zled** *a.* grizzly.

Groan *v.i.* to make a low deep sound of grief or pain; to be in pain or overburdened.—*n.* the sound.

Groat *n.* a fourpenny piece; formerly, various European coins.

Groats *n.pl.* hulled grain, *esp.* oats.

Gro'cer *n.* a dealer in tea, spices, domestic stores.—**gro'cery** *n.* his trade, or, *pl.* wares.

Grog *n.* spirit (*esp.* rum) and water.—**grogg'y** *a.* unsteady, shaky, weak.

Grog'ram *n.* a coarse fabric of silk, mohair, etc.

Groin *n.* depression between belly and thigh; edge made by intersection of two vaults; a structure of timber, etc., to stop shifting of sand on sea beach.—*v.t.* to build with, or supply with, groins.

Groom *n.* a servant in charge of horses; a bridegroom; an officer in a royal household. —*v.t.* to tend, curry (a horse).—**grooms'man** *n.* a friend attending a bridegroom.

Groove *n.* a channel, hollow, *esp.* cut by a tool as a guide, or to receive a ridge; a rut, routine.—*v.t.* to cut a groove in.—**groov'y** *a.*

Grope *v.i.* to feel about, search blindly.

Gross (-ōs) *a.* rank; overfed; flagrant; total, not net; thick, solid; coarse; indecent.—*n.* twelve dozen. — **gross'ly** *adv.*

Grot *n.* a grotto.

Grotesque' (-esk) *n.* a fantastic decorative painting; a comically distorted figure.—*a.* in grotesque style; distorted; absurd.—**grotesque'ly** *adv.* *Syn.* whimsical, extravagant, ludicrous, antic. *Ant.* normal, ordinary, classical, simple.

Grott'o *n.* a cave.

Ground (-ow-) *n.* the bottom of the sea; reason, motive; surface or coating to work on with paint; surface of the earth; position, area, on this; a special area.—*pl.* dregs; enclosed land round a house. —*v.t.* to establish; instruct (in elementary principles); place on the ground.—*v.i.* to run ashore.—**ground'less** *a.* without reason.

Ground'sel (-ow)- *n.* a weed used as a food for cage-birds.

Group (-ōōp) *n.* a number of persons or things near together, or placed or classified together; a class; two or more figures forming one artistic design.—*v.t.* to arrange in a group.—*v.i.* to fall into a group.

Grouse (-ows) *n.* a game-bird; its flesh.

Grouse *v.i.* to grumble.—**grous'er** *n.*

Grout (-owt) *n.* thin fluid mortar.—*v.t.* to fill with this.

Grove *n.* a small wood.

Grov'el *v.i.* to lie face down; abase oneself.

Grow (-ō) *v.i.* to develop naturally; increase in size, height, etc.; be produced; become by degrees.—*v.t.* produce by cultivation.—**growth** *n.* growing; increase; what has grown or is growing. *Syn.* to extend, thrive, flourish, swell, increase. *Ant.* diminish, shrink, wane, lessen, decrease.

Growl *v.i.* to make a low guttural sound of anger; murmur, complain.—*n.* such sound.

Groyne *see* GROIN.

Grub *v.t.* to dig superficially; root up.—*v.i.* to dig, rummage; plod.—*n.* the larva of an insect.—**grubb'y** *a.* dirty.

Grudge *v.t.* to be unwilling to give or allow.—*n.* a feeling of ill-will.

Gru'el *n.* food of oatmeal,

etc., boiled in milk or water.

Grue'some (grōō-) *a.* fearful, horrible, disgusting.

Gruff *a.* surly, rough in manner or voice.—**gruff'ly** *adv.*

Grum'ble *v.i.* to make growling sounds; murmur, complain. —*n.* a low growl; a complaint.—**grum'bler** *n.*

Grump'y *a.* ill-tempered, surly. — **grump'ily** *adv.* — **grump'i-ness** *n.*

Grunt *v.i.* of a hog, to make its characteristic sound; to utter a sound like this; grumble.—*n.* a hog's sound; a noise like this.

Gru'yère *n.* a Swiss cheese full of holes.

Gua'no (gwä-) *n.* sea-fowl manure.

Guarantee' (ga-) *n.* a giver of guaranty or security; guaranty.—*v.t.* to answer for the fulfilment, or genuineness or permanence of; secure (to) a person; secure (against risk, etc.).—**guar'anty** *n.* a written or other undertaking to answer for performance of obligation; ground or basis of security.—**guar'antor** *n.*

Guard (ga-) *n.* posture of defence; watch; protector; a sentry; soldiers protecting anything; an official in charge of a train; a protection; defence.—*pl.* certain British regiments.—*v.t.* to protect, defend.—*v.i.* to be careful.—**guard'ian** *n.* keeper, protector; person having custody of an infant, etc.—**guard'ianship** *n.*—**guard-room** *n.* a room for a guard, or for prisoners.—guards'man n. a soldier in the Guards.

Gua'va (gwä-) n. a tropical tree with an acid fruit used to make jelly; the fruit.

Gudge'on n. a small freshwater fish.

Guer'don (g-) n. reward.

Guerill'a (g-) n. an irregular war; one engaged in it.

Guern'sey n. a close-fitting knitted woollen shirt.

Guess (ges) v.t. to estimate without calculation or measurement; conjecture, think likely.—v.i. to form conjectures.—n. a rough estimate.

Guest (gest) n. one entertained at another's house; one living in a hotel.

Guffaw' n. a burst of laughter.—v.i. to laugh loudly.

Guide (gīd) n. one who shows the way; an adviser; a book of instruction or information; a contrivance for directing motion.—v.t. to lead, act as guide to; arrange.—guid'ance n.

Guild, gild (g-) n. a society for mutual help, or with common object.

Guile (gīl) n. cunning, treachery, deceit.—guile'ful a.—guile'less a.—guile'fully adv. Syn. artifice, duplicity. Ant. honesty, sincerity, faithfulness.

Guille'mot (gil-i-) n. a sea-bird.

Guill'otine (gil-ōtēn) n. a machine for beheading; a machine for cutting paper.—v.t. to use a guillotine upon.

Guilt (gilt) n. the fact or state of having offended; culpability.—guilt'y a. having committed an offence.—guilt'ily adv.—guilt'less a.—guilt'iness n.

Guin'ea (gin'i) n. a sum of 21 shillings; formerly, a gold coin of this value.—guin'ea-fowl n. a fowl allied to the pheasant.—guin'ea-pig n. a rodent animal originating in S. Amer.

Guise (gīz) n. external appearance, esp. one assumed.

Guitar' (git-) n. a musical instrument with six strings.

Gules n. and a. in heraldry, red.

Gulf n. an enclosed portion of the sea; a chasm, abyss.

Gull n. a long-winged web-footed sea-bird.

Gull n. a dupe, fool.—v.t. to dupe, cheat.—gull'ible a.—gullibil'ity n.

Gull'et n. food-passage from mouth to stomach.

Gull'y n. a channel or ravine worn by water.

Gulp v.t. to swallow.—v.i. to gasp, choke.—n. an act of gulping; an effort to swallow; a large mouthful.

Gum n. the firm flesh in which the teeth are set.—gum'boil n. an abscess in the gum.

Gum n. a sticky substance issuing from certain trees; this prepared for use to stick papers, etc., together.—v.t. to stick with gum.—gumm'y a.—gum'boots n.pl. boots of rubber.

Gump'tion n. capacity; shrewdness.

Gun n. a weapon consisting mainly of a metal tube from

which missiles are thrown by explosion; a cannon, pistol, etc.—gunn′er *n.*—gunn′ery *n.* use of large guns.—gun′boat *n.* a small warship.—gun′-cotton *n.* an explosive of cotton steeped in nitric and sulphuric acids.—gun′-metal *n.* an alloy of copper and tin or zinc, formerly used for guns.—gun′powder *n.* an explosive mixture of saltpetre, sulphur, and charcoal.—gun′room *n.* in a warship. the messroom of junior officers.—gun′shot *n.* the range of a gun.—*a.* caused by missile from a gun.—gun′wale, gunn′el *n.* the upper edge of the side of a boat or ship.

Gur′gle *n.* a bubbling noise.—*v.i.* to make a gurgle.

Gurn′et, gurn′ard *n.* a spiny sea-fish.

Gush *v.i.* to flow out suddenly and copiously.—*n.* a sudden copious flow; effusiveness.—gush′er *n.* a gushing person or oil-well.

Guss′et *n.* a triangle of material let into a garment.—guss′etted *a.*

Gust *n.* a sudden blast of wind; a burst of rain, anger, etc.—gust′y *a.*—gust′ily *adv.*

Gust′o *n.* enjoyment in doing a thing, zest.

Gusto′so *adv.* in music, with taste; elegantly; feelingly.

Gut *n.* in *pl.* entrails, intestines.—*sing.* a material made from guts of animals, as for violin strings, etc.; a narrow passage, strait.—*v.t.* to remove the guts from (fish);

remove or destroy the contents of (a house).

Gutta-perch′a *n.* a horny flexible substance. the hardened juice of a Malayan tree.

Gutt′er *n.* a shallow trough for carrying off water from a roof, from the side of a street.—*v.t.* to make channels in.—*v.i.* flow in streams; of a candle. to melt away by the wax forming channels and running down.—gutt′er press *n.* sensational newspapers.—gutt′er-snipe *n.* a street-arab, a child homeless or living mainly in the streets.

Gutt′ural *a.* of, relating to, or produced in, the throat.—*n.* a guttural sound or letter.

Guy (gī) *n.* a rope or chain to steady or secure something.—*v.t.* to secure with a guy.—guy′-rope *n.*

Guy (gī) *n.* an effigy of Guy Fawkes to be burnt on Nov. 5th; a ridiculously dressed person.—*v.t.* to exhibit in effigy; to ridicule.

Guz′zle *v.t. and i.* to eat or drink greedily.

gybe (jīb) *v.i.* of the boom of a fore-and-aft sail, to swing over to the other side with following wind.—*v.t.* to cause this; to change course thus.

Gymkha′na (jim-, -ä-) *n.* an athletic display; a place for one.

Gymna′sium (jim-) *n.* a place fitted up for muscular exercises, athletic training.—gymnas′tic *a.* of exercise.—*n.* (in *pl.*) muscular exercises, with or without apparatus such as parallel bars, etc.— **gym'nast** *n.* an expert in gymnastics.

Gynæcol'ogy (gĭn-, jĭn-) *n.* the part of medicine dealing with functions and diseases of women.

Gyp'sum (jĭp-) *n.* a mineral, source of plaster of Paris.

Gypsy *see* GIPSY.

Gyrate' (jī) *v.i.* to move in a circle, revolve.—**gyra'tion** *n.* —**gy'ratory** *a.*—**gy'roscope** *n.* a wheel spinning at great speed to preserve equilibrium.

Gyro-stab'iliser *n.* an apparatus using two or more gyroscopes to prevent rolling of a ship or aeroplane.

Gyve (jīv) *n.* (usually in *pl.*) a fetter, *esp.* for the leg.— *v.t.* to shackle.

H

Haar (hår) *n.* a wet mist, sea fog.

Hab'erdasher *n.* a dealer in small articles of dress.— **hab'erdashery** *n.*

Habil'iments *n.pl.* dress.

Hab'it *n.* settled tendency or practice; constitution; dress (*esp.* **riding-habit**).—*v.t.* to dress.—**habit'ual** *a.* that is a habit, customary.—**habit'ually** *adv.*—**habit'uate** *v.t.* to accustom.—**habitua'tion** *n.*— **habit'ué** (-ū-ā) *n.* constant visitor; resident.—**hab'itude** *n.* customary manner of action.

Hab'itable *a.* fit to live in. —**habita'tion** *n.* dwelling.—

hab'itat *n.* natural home of an animal.

Hach'ure (-sh-) *n.* shading on a map to show hills.—*v.t.* to mark with this.

Hacien'da (-thē-) *n.* an isolated farm or farmhouse.

Hack *v.t.* to cut, mangle, gash. —*n.* a notch; bruise.

Hack *n.* a hired horse; a horse for ordinary riding; a drudge. —*v.t.* to hackney.

Hack'le (hak'l) *n.* a comb for flax; the neck feathers of a cock.

Hack'ney *n.* a horse for ordinary riding; a carriage kept for hire.—*v.t.* to make trite or common.

Hadd'ock *n.* a fish like a cod.

Ha'des (-ēz) *n.* the abode of the dead; the lower world.

Hæm'orrhage, hem'orrhage (hem'or-ij) *n.* bleeding.

Hæm'orrhoids, hem'orrhoids *n.* piles.

Haft *n.* handle (*esp.* of knife).

Hag *n.* an ugly old woman; a witch. — **hag'-ridden** *a.* troubled with nightmares.

Hagg'ard *a.* wild-looking.— *n.* an untamed hawk. *Syn.* gaunt, wrinkled. *Ant.* well-conditioned, strapping, sleek.

Hagg'is *n.* a Scottish dish, the pluck of a sheep, chopped with herbs, oatmeal, etc., and boiled in the maw.

Hag'gle *v.i.* dispute terms, chaffer.—*n.* chaffering.

Hagiol'ogy (hag-) *n.* literature of the lives of saints.— **hagiog'rapher** *n.*

Ha-ha *n.* a sunk fence.

Hail *n.* frozen vapour falling in pellets.—*v.i.* it hails, hail falls.—*v.t.* to pour down.— hail'stone *n.*

Hail *interj.* greeting.—*v.t.* to greet; call.—*v.i.* hail from, be arrived from.—*n.* a call.

Hair (hêr) *n.* filament growing from the skin of an animal, as the covering of a man's head; such filaments collectively.—hair'y *a.*—hair'iness *n.*—hair'spring *n.* a fine spring in a watch.—hair'-trigger *n.* a secondary trigger releasing the main one.

Ha'ka *n.* in Australia, a native dance.

Hake *n.* a fish like a cod.

Hal'berd *n.* combined spear and battleaxe.—halberdier'*n.*

Hal'cyon *n.* a bird fabled to calm the sea to breed on a floating nest.—halcyon days, calm days.

Hale *a.* robust, healthy, *esp.* in old age.

Hale *v.t.* to drag.

Half (hâf) *n.* halves (hâvz) *pl.* either of two equal parts of a thing.—*a.* forming a half.—*adv.* to the extent of half.—half'-brother, -sister *n.* a brother (sister) by one parent only.—half'-breed *n.* one of mixed parentage.—half'-caste *n.* a half-breed, *esp.* of European and Asiatic parents.—half-crown' *n.* British coin worth 2*s.* 6*d.*—half-seas-over *a.* half-drunk.—half'-voll'ey *n.* a ball struck the instant it bounces; the striking.—*v.t.* to strike thus. —half'penny (hāp'ni) *n.* a British bronze coin worth half a penny.—halve (hâv) *v.t.* to divide into halves.

Hal'ibut *n.* a large flat eatable fish.

Hall (hawl) *n.* a large room; house of a landed proprietor; building belonging to a guild; an entrance passage.—hall'-mark *n.* mark used (at Goldsmiths' Hall, London) to indicate standard of tested gold and silver.—*v.t.* to stamp with this.

Hallelu'jah (-ya) *n.* and *interj.* an exclamation of praise to God.

Hall'ow (-ō) *v.t.* to make, or honour as, holy.

Hallu'cinate *v.t.* to produce illusion in the mind of.— hallucina'tion *n.* illusion; seeing something that is not present.

Ha'lo *n.* a circle of light round the moon, sun, etc.; a disk of light round a saint's head in a picture; ideal glory attaching to a person.—*v.t.* to surround with a halo; shout.

Halt (hawlt) *a.* lame.—*v.i.* to limp; proceed hesitatingly.

Halt (hawlt) *n.* a stoppage on a march or journey.—*v.i.* to make a halt.—*v.t.* to bring to a halt.

Halt'er (hawlt'-) *n.* a rope or strap with headstall to fasten horses or cattle; a noose for hanging a person. —*v.t.* to fasten with a halter.

Hal'yard, hall'iard *n.* rope for raising a sail, etc.

Ham *n.* the hollow of the knee; the back of the thigh; a hog's thigh salted and dried. —ham'string *n.* a tendon at the back of the knee.—*v.t.* to cripple by cutting this.

Hamadry'ad *n.* a nymph living and dying with the tree she inhabited; an Indian snake.

Ham'let *n.* a small village.

Hamm'er *n.* a tool, usually with a heavy head at the end of a handle, for beating, driving nails, etc.; a machine for the same purposes; a contrivance for exploding the charge of a gun; an auctioneer's mallet.—*v.t.* and *i.* to beat with, or as with, a hammer.

Hamm'ock *n.* a bed of canvas, etc., hung on ropes.

Hamp'er *n.* a large covered basket.

Hamp'er *v.t.* to impede, obstruct the movements of. —*n.* in a ship, cumbrous equipment.

Hamstring *see* HAM.

Hand *n.* the extremity of the arm beyond the wrist; side, quarter, direction; style of writing; cards dealt to a player; a measure of four inches; manual worker; person as a source.—*v.t.* to lead or help with the hand; deliver; pass; hold out.— **hand'bag** *n.* a bag for carrying in the hand.—**hand'bill** *n.* a small printed notice.— **hand'book** *n.* a short treatise. —**hand'cuff** *n.* a fetter for the wrist, usually joined in a pair.—*v.t.* to secure with these.—**hand'ful** *n.* a small quantity.—**hand'icraft** *n.* a manual occupation or skill.— **hand'iwork** *n.* a thing done

by any one in person.— **hand'kerchief** (hang'ker-chif) *n.* a small square of fabric carried in the pocket for wiping the nose, etc., or worn round the neck.— **hand'maiden** *n.* a female servant.—**hand'writing** *n.* the way a person writes.— **hand'y** *a.* convenient; clever with the hands.—**hand'ily** *adv.*

hand'icap *n.* a race or contest in which the competitors' chances are equalised by starts, weights carried, etc.; a condition so imposed; a disability.—*v.t.* to impose such conditions.—**hand'icapper** *n.*

Han'dle *n.* the part of a thing made to hold it by; a fact that may be taken advantage of.—*v.t.* to touch, feel, with the hands; manage, deal with; deal in.

Hand'ley-Page *n.* a type of large aeroplane.

Hand'sel (-ns-) *n.* a gift on beginning something; earnest money; first use.—*v.t.* to give a handsel to; be the first to use.

Hand'some (-ns-) *a.* of fine appearance; generous. — **hand'somely** *adv.* *Syn.* good-looking, graceful, liberal, elegant. *Ant.* unshapely, uncouth, hideous, mean.

Hang *v.t.* to fasten to an object above, suspend; to kill by suspending from gallows; attach or set up (wallpaper, doors, etc.).— *v.i.* to be suspended; cling.— **hangdog** *a.* of sneaking aspect.—**hangman** *n.* an executioner.

Hang'ar (-ng-g-) *n.* shed for aircraft.

Hang'er *n.* a short sword.

Hank *n.* a coil, *esp.* as a measure of yarn.

Hank'er *v.i.* crave.

Hank'y-pank'y *n.* trickery.

Han'som *n.* a two-wheeled cab for two to ride inside with the driver mounted up behind.

Hap *n.* chance.—*v.i.* to happen.—**hap'less** *a.* unlucky.—**haphaz'ard** *a.* random, without design.—*adv.* by chance.—**hap'ly** *adv.* perhaps.—**happ'en** *v.i.* to come about, occur.—**happ'y** *a.* glad, content; lucky, fortunate; apt.—**happ'ily** *adv.*—**happ'iness** *n.*—**happ'y-go-luck'y** *a.* casual.

Ha'ra-ki'ri *n.* an involuntary suicide by disembowelling.

Harangue' (-ang) *n.* a vehement speech.—*v.i.* to make one.—*v.t.* to speak vehemently to.

Harass' *v.t.* to worry, trouble; attack repeatedly. *Syn.* tire, weary, perplex, worry. *Ant.* amuse, comfort enliven.

Harb'inger (-j-) *n.* one who announces another's approach; a forerunner.

Har'bour (-ber) *n.* a place of shelter for ships; a shelter.—*v.t.* to give shelter to.—*v.i.* to take shelter.

Hard *a.* firm, resisting pressure, solid; difficult to understand; harsh, unfeeling; difficult to bear; stingy; heavy; strenuous; of water, not making lather well with soap.—*adv.* vigorously; with difficulty; close.—**hard'en** *v.t.* and *i.*—**hard'ly** *adv.*—**hard'ness** *n.*—**hard'ship** *n.* ill-luck; severe toil or suffering; an instance of this.—**hard'ware** *n.* small ware of metal.

Hard'y *a.* robust, vigorous; bold; of plants, able to grow in the open all the year round. — **hard'ily** *adv.* — **hard'iness** *n.*—**hard'ihood** *n.* extreme boldness.

Hare (hēr) *n.* a rodent with long ears, short tail, and divided upper lip, noted for its speed.—**hare'-and-hounds'** *n.* a paperchase.—**hare'bell** *n.* a round-leaved bell-flower.—**hare'brained** *a.* rash, wild.—**hare'lip** *n.* fissure of the upper lip.

Ha'rem *n.* the women's part of a Mohammedan dwelling.

Har'icot (-kō) *n.* a French bean; a ragout.

Hark *v.i.* to listen.

Har'lequin *n.* in pantomime, a mute character supposed to be invisible to the clown and pantaloon.—**harloquinade'** *n.* harlequin's part.

Har'lot *n.* a prostitute.—**har'lotry** *n.*

Harm *n.* damage, hurt.—**harm'ful** *a.*—**harm'less** *a.*—**harm'fully** *adv.*—**harm'lessly** *adv.*

Har'malin *n.* a vegetable alkaloid from which a valuable dye is made.

Harmattan' *n.* a hot, dry wind blowing along the Guinea Coast from the interior of Africa.

Har'mony n. agreement; combination of musical notes to make chords; melodious sound.—harmo'nious a.—harmo'niously adv. — harmon'ic a. of harmony—n. a tone got by vibration of an aliquot part of a string, etc. —harmo'nium n. a small organ.—harmon'ica n. various musical instruments.—har'monise v.t. to bring into harmony.—v.i. to be in harmony.—har'monist n.—harmonisa'tion n.

Har'ness n. the gear of a draught horse; armour.—v.t. to put harness on.

Harp n. a musical instrument of strings played by the hand.—v.i. to play on a harp; to dwell on continuously.—harp'er n.—harp'ist n. — harp'sichord n. a stringed instrument with keyboard, an ancestor of the piano.

Harpoon' n. a barbed spear with a rope attached for catching whales, etc.—v.t. to strike with a harpoon.—harpoon'er n.—harpoon-gun, gun from which harpoons are discharged in modern whale fishing.

Harp'y n. a monster with body of woman and wings and claws of bird; a rapacious monster.

Harr'idan n. a haggard old woman.

Harr'ier n. hound used in hunting hares; a falcon.

Harr'ow (-ō) n. a frame with iron teeth for breaking up clods. — v.t. to draw a harrow over; to distress greatly.

Harr'y v.t. to ravage.

Harsh a. rough, unpleasing to the touch or taste; severe; unfeeling.—harsh'ly adv.

Hart n. a male deer.—harts'horn n. material made from harts' horns, formerly the chief source of ammonia. —hart's'-tongue n. a fern with long tongue-like fronds.

Hartal' n. Indian equivalent of a strike; literally, a day of mourning.

Ha'rum-sca'rum a. reckless, wild.

Har'vest n. the season for gathering in grain; the gathering; the crop; product of an action.—v.t. to gather in.—har'vester n.

Hash v.t. to cut up small.—n. dish of hashed meat.

Hash'ish, hash'eesh n. the tops of Indian hemp; an intoxicating infusion of this plant.

Hask n. a basket made of rushes or flags.

Hasp n. a clasp passing over a staple for fastening a door, etc.—v.t. to fasten with a hasp.

Hass'ock n. a kneeling-cushion; a tuft of grass.

Has'tate, has'tate. a. in botany, spear-shaped.

Haste (hā-) n. speed quickness; hurry.—v.i. to hasten. —hast'en (-sen) v.i. to come or go quickly or hurriedly.— v.t. to cause to hasten; accelerate.—ha'sty a.—ha'stily adv. Syn. swiftness, eagerness. Ant. slowness, delay, deliberation, sloth.

Hat *n.* a covering for the head, usually with a brim.—**hatt'er** *n.* a dealer in, or maker of, hats.—**hat'-trick** *n.* in cricket, the taking of three wickets with successive balls.

Hatch *n.* the lower half of a divided door; a hatchway; the trapdoor over it.—**hatch'-way** *n.* an opening in the deck of a ship for cargo, etc.

Hatch *v.t.* to bring forth young birds from the shell; incubate.—*v.i.* to come forth from the shell.—*n.* a hatching; the brood hatched.

Hatch *v.t.* to engrave or draw lines on for shading; shade with lines.

Hatch'et *n.* a small axe.

Hate *v.t.* to dislike strongly; bear malice to.—*n.* hatred.—**hate'ful** *a.*—**hate'fully** *adv.*—**ha'tred** *n.* emotion of extreme dislike, active ill-will.

Hatt'er *see* HAT.

Haugh'ty (hawt-i) *a.* proud, arrogant.—**haught'ily** *adv.*—**haught'iness** *n.* *Syn.* lofty, disdainful. *Ant.* humble, meek, submissive.

Haul *v.t.* to pull, drag.—*v.i.* of wind, to shift.—*n.* a hauling; a draught of fishes; an acquisition.—**haul'age** *n.* carrying of loads; the charge of this.

Haulm, halm (hawm) *n.* stalks of beans, etc.; thatch of this.

Haunch (hawnsh) *n.* the part of the body between ribs and thighs; leg and loin of venison, etc.

Haunt *v.t.* to resort to habit-ually; of ghosts, to visit regularly.—*n.* a place of frequent resort.

Haut'boy (ho-boi) *n.* an oboe.

Hauteur' (haw-ter) *n.* haughty spirit.

Havan'a, havann'ah *n.* a fine quality of cigar.

Have (hav) *v.t.* to hold or possess; to be possessed or affected with; to be obliged (to do); to engage in, carry on; obtain; (as auxiliary forms perfect and other tenses).

Ha'ven *n.* a harbour.

Hav'ersack *n.* a soldier's canvas ration-bag; a similar bag for travellers.

Hav'oc *n.* pillage, devastation, ruin.

Haw *n.* the red berry of the hawthorn.—**haw'thorn** *n.* a thorny shrub used for hedges.—**haw'finch** *n.* a small bird.

Haw *n.* a hesitation of speech.—*v.i.* to stop, in speaking, with a haw.—**haw-haw** *v.i.* to laugh boisterously.

Hawk *n.* a bird of prey used in falconry.—*v.t.* and *i.* to hunt with hawks.

Hawk *v.i.* to clear the throat noisily.

Hawk'er *n.* one who carries wares for sale.—**hawk** *v.t.*

Hawse (-z) *n.* the part of a ship's bows with holes for cables.

Haw'ser (-z-) *n.* a large rope or small cable, often of steel.

Hay *n.* grass mown and dried.—**hay'box** *n.* a box filled with hay in which heated food is left to finish cooking.

—hay'cock *n.* a conical heap of hay.—hay'seed *n.* grass seed.—hay'stack *n.* a large pile of hay with ridged or pointed top.

Haz'ard *n.* a game at dice; chance, a chance; risk, danger.—*v.t.* to expose to risk; run the risk of.—haz'ardous *a.* *Syn.* luck, adventure. *Ant.* certainty, safety.

Haze *n.* misty appearance in the air, often due to heat; mental obscurity.—ha'zy *a.* misty.

Haze *v.t.* in North America, to drive an animal in a direction strange to it; to punish or torment by the imposition of excessively heavy or disagreeable tasks, particularly used on sailors; to play jokes on.—haz'ing *n.*

Ha'zel *n.* a bush bearing nuts; the reddish-brown colour of the nuts.—*a.* of this colour.

He *pron.* (the third person masculine pronoun) the person or animal already referred to.

Head (hed) *n.* the upper part of a man's or animal's body, containing mouth, sense organs and brain; the upper part of anything; chief part; leader; progress; section of a chapter; headland.—*v.t.* to provide with a head; get the lead of.—*v.i.* to face, front. —head'ache (-ak) *n.* continuous pain in the head.— head'land *n.* promontory.— head'long *adv.* head foremost, in a rush.—head'ing *n.* title. —head'quarters *n.pl.* residence of commander-in-chief; centre of operations.— head'strong *a.* self-willed.— head'way *n.* progress.— head'er *n.* that or who heads; plunge head foremost; brick laid with end in face of wall. —head'y *a.* impetuous; apt to intoxicate.

Heal *v.t.* to restore to health, make well, cure.—*v.i.* become sound.—**health** (hel'th) *n.* soundness of body; condition of body; a toast drunk in a person's honour.—health'ful *a.* health-giving. –health'y *a.* having, or tending to give, health. — health'ily *adv.* — health'iness *n.*

Heap *n.* a number of things lying one on another; a great quantity.—*v.t.* to pile up; load (with gifts, etc.).

Hear *v.t.* perceive with the ear; listen to; try (a case); get to know.—*v.i.* to perceive sound; learn.—hear'say *n.* rumour.—*a.* not based on personal knowledge —hear'er *n.*

Heark'en (har-) *v.i.* to listen.

Hearse (hers) *n.* a carriage for a coffin.

Heart (hart) *n.* the hollow organ which makes the blood circulate; the seat of the emotions and affections; mind, soul; courage; middle of anything; a playing-card marked with a figure of a heart, one of these marks.— heart'en *v.t.* to inspirit.— heart'less *a.* unfeeling — heart'y *a.* friendly; vigorous; in good health; satisfying the appetite.—heart'ily *adv.*

Hearth (harth) *n.* the place where a fire is made in a house.

Heat *n.* hotness; sensation of this; hot weather or climate; warmth of feeling, anger, etc; sexual excitement in animals; a race (of which there are several) to decide the persons to compete in a deciding course.—*v.t.* to make hot.—*v.i.* to become hot.—**heat′edly** *adv.*

Heath *n.* a tract of waste land; shrubs found on this.

Hea′then(-TH-)*a.* not Christian, Jew, or Mohammedan.—*n.* a heathen person.—**hea′then-ish** *a.*—**hea′thenism** *n.*—**hea′-thendom** *n.*

Heath′er (heTH·er) *n.* a shrub growing on heaths and mountains; heath, ling.—**heath′ery** *a.*

Heave *v.t.* to lift with effort; throw (something heavy); utter (a sigh).—*v.i.* to swell, rise.—*n.* a heaving.

Heav′en (hev-n) *n.* the sky; the abode of God; God; place of bliss.—**heav′enly** *a.*

Heav′y (hev-) *a.* of great weight; striking or falling with force; sluggish; difficult; severe; sorrowful; serious; dull; over compact.—**heav′ily** *adv.*—**heav′iness** *n.* *Syn.* ponderous, oppressive, indolent, tedious. *Ant.* buoyant, porous, flimsy, frivolous.

Hebdom′adal *a.* weekly.

Heb′etude *n.* dullness.—**heb′e-tate** *v.t.* to render obtuse; to blunt.—*a.* dull.

Hec′atomb *n.* a great public sacrifice.

Heck′le (he′ ′l) *n.* a hackle.—*v.t.* to comb with a hackle; to question severely, tease with questions.

Hec′tic *a.* flushed, consumptive.

Hec′tograph *n.* an apparatus for multiplying copies of writings.—**hec′togramme** *n.* one hundred grammes.—**hec′tometre** *n.*—**hec′tolitre** *n.*

Hec′tor *v.t.* and *i.* to bully, bluster.

Hedd′le *n.* in weaving, one of the sets of parallel doubled threads, each having in the middle a loop called a **heddle-eye**, which compose the harness employed to guide the warp threads to the lathe or batten.—*v.i.* to draw warp threads through heddle-eyes.

Hedge *n.* a fence of bushes.—*v.t.* to surround with a hedge.—*v.i.* to make or trim hedges; to bet on both sides; to secure against loss; shift, shuffle.—**hedge′hog** *n.* a small animal covered with spines.—**hedge′row** *n.* bushes forming a hedge.—**hedge′-spar′row** *n.* a small bird.

Hed′onism *n.* the doctrine that pleasure is the chief good.—**hed′onist** *n.*—**hedonist′ic** *a.*

Heed *v.t.* to take notice of, care for.—**heed′ful** *a.*—**heed′less** *a.* *Syn.* to mind, consider. *Ant.* to neglect, disregard.

Heel *n.* the hinder part of the foot; the part of a shoe supporting this.—*v.t.* to supply with a heel; touch ground, or a ball, with the heel.

Heel v.i. of a ship, to lean to one side.—v.t. to cause to do this.—n. a heeling.

Hegem'ony (hĕ-g-) n. leadership, political domination.

Heif'er (hef-) n. a young cow that has not had a calf.

Height (hīt) n. measure from base to top; quality of being high; high position; highest degree; hill-top.—**height'en** v.t. to make higher; intensify. Syn. elevation, intensification, eminence, altitude. Ant. depression, debasement.

Hei'nous (hān) a. atrocious, very bad.

Heir (èr) n. a person legally entitled to succeed to property or rank.—**heir'ess** fem.—**heir'loom** n. a chattel that goes with real estate; a thing that has been in a family for generations.

Hel'ical a. spiral.—**helicop'ter** n. an aeroplane to rise vertically by the pull of an air-screw revolving horizontally.

He'liograph n. an apparatus to signal by reflecting the sun's rays.—**he'liotrope** n. a plant with purple flowers; the colour of the flowers.—**heliotrop'ic** a. turning under the influence of light.—**he'lium** n. a gaseous element, first discovered in the sun.

He'lioscope n. a form of telescope adapted for viewing the sun without dazzling the eyes.

He'liostat n. an instrument for signalling by flashing the sun's rays.

He'liother'apy n. curative treatment by exposure to sunlight.

Hell n. the abode of the damned; place or state of wickedness, or misery, or torture; the abode of the dead generally; a gambling-resort.—**hell'ish** a.

Hell'ebore n. a plant formerly thought to cure madness.

Hellen'ic a. pertaining to the Hellenes or inhabitants of Greece.—**hell'enist** n.

Helm n. a tiller or wheel for turning the rudder of a ship.

Helm n. a helmet.—**helm'et** n. a defensive covering for the head.

Hel'ot n. a serf.

Help v.t. to aid, assist; serve (food, with food); remedy, prevent.—n. aid, assistance; an aid.—**help'er** n.—**help'ful** a.—**help'less** a.—**help'lessly** adv.—**help'mate, help'meet** n. a helpful companion, a husband or wife.

Helt'er-skel'ter adv. in hurry and confusion.

Helve n. the handle of a weapon or tool.

Hem n. the border of a piece of cloth, esp. one made by turning over the edge and sewing it down.—v.t. to sew thus; confine, shut in.—**hem'stitch** n. an ornamental stitch.—v.t. sew with this.

Hem'isphere n. a half sphere; half of the celestial sphere; half of the earth.—**hemispher'ical** a.—**hem'istich** (-ik) n. half a line of verse.

Hem'lock n. a poisonous plant.

Hemp n. an Indian plant of which the fibre is used to

make rope; the fibre.—
hemp'en a.

Hen n. the female of the
domestic fowl and other
birds.—hen'pecked a. domin-
eered over by a wife.

Hence adv. from this point;
for this reason.—hencefor'-
ward adv.—hence'forth adv.

Hench'man n. a squire; a
follower.

Henn'a n. the Egyptian
privet; a dye made from it.

Hep'tagon n. a figure with
seven angles.—heptag'onal
a.—hep'tarchy (-ki) n. rule
by seven; the period of
many kingdoms of Angles
and Saxons. — hep'tateuch
(-tūk) n. the first seven
books of the Old Testament.

Her'ald n. an officer who
makes royal proclamations,
arranges ceremonies, keeps
records of those entitled to
armorial bearings, etc.; a
messenger, envoy.—v.t. to
announce; proclaim the
approach of.—heral'dic a.—
her'aldry n. science of
heraldic bearings.

Herb n. a plant with a soft
stem which dies down after
flowering; a plant of which
parts are used for medicine,
food or scent.—herba'ceous
(-shus) a. of or like a herb.—
herb'age n. herbs; grass,
pasture.—herb'al a. of herbs.
—n. a book on herbs.—
herb'alist n. a writer on
herbs; a dealer in medicinal
herbs.—herbar'ium (-ér) n.
a collection of dried plants.

Herd n. a number of animals
feeding or travelling to-
gether; a large number of
people (in contempt); a herds-
man.—v.i. to go in a herd.—
v.t. to tend (a herd); crowd
together.—herds'man n.

Here adv. in this place; at or
to this point.

Hered'ity n. the tendency of
an organism to transmit its
nature to its descendants.—
hered'itary a. descending by
inheritance; holding office by
inheritance; that can be
transmitted from one generation to another.—hered'it-
arily adv.— heredit'ament n.
something that can be in-
herited.—her'itable a. that
can be inherited.—her'itage
n. that which may be or is
inherited; portion or lot.

Her'esy n. opinion contrary to
the orthodox opinion.—
here'siarch (-k) n. the originator or leader of a heresy.—
her'etic n. the holder of a
heresy.—heret'ical a.—heret'ically adv.

Hermaph'rodite n. a person
or animal with the characteristics of both sexes.

Hermet'ic a. of alchemy.—
hermetic sealing. the airtight closing of a vessel by
melting the edges together,
etc.—hermet'ically adv.

Her'mit n. a person living in
solitude, esp. from religious
motives.—her'mitage n. his
abode.

Hern'ia n. rupture.

He'ro n. an illustrious warrior;
one greatly regarded for
achievements or qualities;
the chief man in a poem,
play or story; a demigod.—

hero'ic *a.*—hero'ically *adv.*—her'oism *n.*—he'ro-worship-per *n.*

Her'oin *n.* trade name for a white crystalline derivative of morphine, used medicin-ally as a nerve sedative and for bronchitis, etc., but also as a habit-forming drug.

Her'on *n.* a long-legged wading bird.—her'onry *n.* a place where herons breed.

Her'pes (hẹr-pēz) *n.* a form of skin disease; shingles.

Herr'ing *n.* a familiar sea-fish.—herr'ingbone *n.* a stitch or pattern of zigzag lines.

Hes'itate (-z-) *v.i.* to hold back, feel, or show indecision; be reluctant. — hes'itant *a.* — hes'itantly *adv.*—hes'itancy *n.*—hesita'tion *n.* *Syn.* doubt, falter, vacillate. *Ant.* determine, decide.

Hest *n.* behest, command.

Het'erodox *a.* not orthodox.—het'erodoxy *n.*—heteroge'-neous *a.* composed of diverse elements.—hetero-gene'ity *n.*

Hew *v.t.* and *i.* to chop or cut with axe or sword.—hew'er *n.*

Hex'agon *n.* a figure with six angles.—hexag'onal *a.*—hex-am'eter *n.* a line of verse of six feet.

Hey'-day *n.* bloom, prime.

Hia'tus (hīā-) *n.* a gap in a series, etc.; break between two vowels, *esp.* in consecu-tive words.

Hi'bernate *v.i.* to pass the winter, *esp.* in a torpid state.—hiberna'tion *n.*—hi'-bernator *n.*

Hic'cough (hik-up) hic'cup *n.* a spasm of the breathing or-gans with an abrupt cough-like sound.—*v.i.* to have this.

Hick *n.* a rustic; country bumpkin; *esp.* applied to the semi-educated class to whom the cinema and other such entertainment chiefly appeal.

Hick'ory *n.* a N. Amer. tree like walnut; its tough wood.

Hidal'go *n.* a Spanish noble-man of the lowest class.

Hide *n.* skin, raw or dressed.

Hide *n.* old measure of land.

Hide *v.t.* to put or keep out of sight; conceal, keep secret.—*v.i.* to conceal one-self.

Hid'eous *a.* repulsive, revolt-ing.—hid'eously *adv.*

Hie *v.i.* and *refl.* to go quickly.

Hi'erarch (-k) *n.* a chief priest.—hi'erarchy *n.* a graded priesthood or other organisation. — hierarch'ical *a.*—hierat'ic *a.* of the priests (*esp.* of old Egyptian writ-ing).—hi'eroglyph *n.* a figure of an object standing for a word or sound, as in ancient Egyptian writing.—hiero-glyph'ic *a.*—hieroglyph'ics *n.pl.*—hi'erophant *n.* an ex-pounder of sacred mysteries.

Hig'gle *v.i.* to dispute about terms; to carry wares for sale.—hig'gler *n.*

Hig'gledy-pig'gledy *adv.* and *a.* in confusion.

High (hī) *a.* of great or specified extent upwards; far up; of great rank, quality or importance; of roads, main; of meat, tainted; of a season, well advanced; of sound, acute in pitch.—*adv.* far up; strongly, to a great extent; at or to a high pitch; at a high rate.—**high'ly** *adv.* —**high'lands** *n. pl.* mountainous country.—**High'lander** *n.*—**high'way** *n.* a main road; an ordinary route.—**high'wayman** *n.* a robber on the road. *esp.* a mounted one.—**high'ness** *n.* quality of being high; title of princes.

Hight (hīt) *a.* named.

Hilar'ity *n.* cheerfulness, boisterous joy.—**hilar'ious** (ēr) *a.*

Hill *n.* a natural elevation, a small mountain; a mound. —**hill'ock** *n.* a little hill.— **hill'y** *a.* —**hill'iness** *n.*

Hilt *n.* the handle of a sword, etc.

Hi'lum *n.* the eye of a bean or other seed.

Hind (hīnd) *n.* a female deer.

Hind (hīnd) *n.* a farm workman, bailiff.

Hind (hīnd) **hind'er** *a.* at the back.

Hin'der *v.t.* to obstruct, impede, delay.—**hin'drance** *n. Syn.* hamper, stop, restrain. *Ant.* aid, help, expedite, hasten.

Hinge (-j) *n.* a movable joint, as that on which a door hangs.—*v.t.* to attach with, or as with, a hinge.—*v.i.* to turn on, depend on.

Hint *n.* a slight indication, a covert suggestion.—*v.t.* to give a hint of.—*v.i.* to make a hint.

Hint'erland *n.* the district

behind that lying along the coast.

Hip *n.* the projecting part of the thigh.

Hip *n.* the fruit of the rose, *esp.* wild.

Hipped *a.* depressed.

Hipp'odrome *n.* a course for chariot races; a circus.— **hippopot'amus** *n.* a large African animal living in rivers.—**hipp'ogriff, hipp'ogryph** *n.* griffin-like creature with horse's body.

Hire *n.* payment for the use of a thing; wages; a hiring or being hired.—*v.t.* to take or give on hire.—**hire'ling** *n.* one who serves for wages (usually *in contempt*).— **hi'rer** *n.*

Hir'sute *a.* hairy.

His'pid *a.* rough with bristles or minute spines; bristly.— **hispid'ity** *n.* the state of being hispid.

Hiss *v.i.* to make a sharp sound of the letter S, *esp.* in disapproval.—*v.t.* to express disapproval of, with hissing. —*n.* the sound.

Hist *int.* hush! be silent! a word commanding silence and attention.—*v.t.* to incite, as a dog, by making a sibilant sound.

Histog'eny (-toj-) *n.* the formation and development of organic tissues.

Histol'ogy *n.* the science that treats of the minute structure of the tissues of plants, animals, etc.—**histol'ogist** *n.*

His'tory *n.* the study of past events; a record of these; past events; a train of events, public or private; course of life or existence; a systematic account of phenomena.—**histor'ian** *n.* a writer of history.—**histor'ic** *a.* noted in history.—**histor'-ical** *a.* of, or based on history; belonging to the past. — **histor'ically** *adv.*—**histori'city** *n.* being historical, not legendary.—**historiog'-rapher** *n.* a writer of history *esp.* as official historian.

Histrion'ic *a.* of acting, stagy. —*n.pl.* theatricals.

Hit *v.t.* to strike with a blow or missile; to affect injuriously; find; suit. — *v.i.* to strike; light (upon).—*n.* a blow; success.—**hitt'er** *n.*

Hitch *v.t.* to raise or move with a jerk; fasten with a loop, etc.—*v.i.* to be caught or fastened.—*n.* a jerk; a fastening, a loop or knot; a difficulty, obstruction.

Hith'er (-TH-) *adv.* to or towards this place.—*a.* situated on this side.—**hitherto'** *adv.* up to now.

Hit'lerite *n.* a supporter of the National Socialist Party in Germany; a follower of Hitler.

Hive *n.* a box in which bees are housed.—*v.t.* to gather or place (bees) in a hive.—*v.i.* to enter a hive.

Hoar (hor), **hoar'y** *a.* gray with age; grayish-white.—**hoar'-frost** *n.* white frost, frozen dew.

Hoard (hord) *n.* a stock, store, *esp.* hidden away. — *v.t.* to amass and hide away; store. *Syn.* accumulation, savings, cache. *Ant.* waste, loss.

Hoard'ing (hord-) *n.* a temporary board fence round a building or piece of ground, *esp.* when used for posting bills.

Hoarse (hors) *a.* rough and harsh sounding, husky; having a hoarse voice.—**hoarse'ly** *adv.*—**hoarse'ness** *n.*

Hoary *see* HOAR.

Hoax *v.t.* to deceive by an amusing or mischievous story.—*n.* such deception.

Hob *n.* flat-topped casing of fireplace; a peg used as a mark in some games.—**hob'nail** *n.* a large-headed nail for boot-soles.

Hob'ble *v.i.* to walk lamely.—*v.t.* to tie the legs together of (horse, etc.).—*n.* a limping gait; a rope for hobbling.

Hob'bledehoy *n.* a clumsy youth.

Hobb'y *n.* formerly a small horse; a favourite occupation as a pastime.—**hobb'yhorse** *n.* a wicker horse fastened round a dancer's waist; a stick with a horse's head as a toy; a rocking-horse; a roundabout horse.—**hobgob'-lin** *n.* a mischievous imp.

Hob'-nob *v.i.* to drink together; to be familiar (with).

Ho'bo *n.* in America, a shiftless, wandering workman.

Hock *n.* the joint of a quadruped's hind leg between knee and fetlock.—*v.t.* to disable by cutting the tendons of the hock.

Hock *n.* German white wine.

Hock'ey *n.* a game played with a ball and curved sticks.

Ho'cus-po'cus *n.* jugglery,

trickery; a conjuring formula.—*v.t.* to play tricks on.—**ho'cus** *v.t.* to play tricks on; to stupefy with drugs.

Hod *n.* a small trough on a staff for carrying mortar.

Hoe *n.* a tool for scraping up weeds, breaking ground, etc.—*v.t.* to break up or weed with a hoe.

Hog *n.* a pig, *esp.* a castrated male for fattening; a greedy or dirty person.—**hogs'head** *n.* a large cask; a liquid measure of 52½ gal.

Hogmanay' *n.* the last day of the year.

Hoist *v.t.* to raise aloft, raise with tackle, etc.—*n.* a hoisting; a lift, elevator.

Ho'key-po'key *n.* cheap ice-cream.

Hold (hō·) *v.t.* to keep fast, grasp; support in or with the hands, etc.; maintain in a position; have capacity for; own, occupy; carry on; detain; celebrate; keep back; believe.—*v.i.* to cling; not to give way; abide (by), keep (to); last, proceed, be in force; occur.—*n.* grasp; a fortress.—**hold'er** *n.*—**hold'-all** *n.* a portable wrapping as baggage.—**hold'fast** *n.* a clamp.

Hold (hō·) *n.* the space below deck of a ship for cargo.

Hole *n.* a hollow place, cavity; a perforation, opening.—*v.t.* to perforate, make a hole in.

Hol'iday *see* HOLY.

Holl'and *n.* a linen fabric.—**Holl'ands** *n.* a spirit, gin.

Holl'ow (-ō) *n.* a cavity, hole, valley.—*a.* having a cavity, not solid; empty; false; not full-toned.—*v.t.* to make a hollow in; bend hollow.

Holl'y *n.* an evergreen shrub with prickly leaves and red berries.

Holl'yhock *n.* a tall plant bearing many flowers along the stem.

Holm (hōm) *n.* an islet, *esp.* in a river; flat ground by a river.

Holm (hōm), **holm-oak** *n.* evergreen oak, ilex.

Hol'ocaust *n.* a sacrifice wholly burnt; a great slaughter or sacrifice.—**hol'ograph** *n.* a document wholly written by the signer.

Hol'ophote *n.* the apparatus used in lighthouses for reflecting all the light in the required direction. — **holopho'tal** *a.*

Hol'ster *n.* a leather case for a pistol fixed to a saddle or belt.

Holt *n.* a wood, or piece of woodland; *esp.* a woody hill.

Ho'ly *a.* belonging to, or devoted to, God; free from sin, divine.—**ho'lily** *adv.*—**ho'liness** *n.* the quality of being holy; a title of the Pope.—**hol'iday** *n.* a day or period of rest from work, or of recreation; a religious festival (now usually holy-day).—**Holy Week** *n.* that before Easter.

Ho'lystone *n.* soft sandstone for scouring a ship's deck.—*v.t.* to scour with this.

Hom'age n. formal acknowledgment of allegiance; tribute, respect paid.

Home n. dwelling-place; fixed residence; native place; institution for the infirm, etc. —a. of or connected with home; not foreign.—adv. to or at one's home; to the point aimed at.—**home'less** a.—**home'ly** a. plain.—**home'spun** a. spun or made at home.—n. cloth made of homespun yarn; anything plain or homely.—**home'stead** n. a house with out-buildings, a farm.—**home'ward** a. and adv.—**home'wards** adv.—**home'sick** a. depressed by absence from home.

Hom'icide n. the killing of a human being; the killer.—**hom'icidal** a.

Hom'ily n. a sermon.—**homilet'ic** a. of sermons.—n.pl. the art of preaching.

Hom'iny n. maize, hulled and ground, and boiled with water.

Homœop'athy (hō-mi-) n. the treatment of disease by small doses of what would produce the symptoms in a healthy person.—**homœopath'ic** a. — **homœopath'ically** adv.—**ho'mœopath** n.—**homœop'athist** n.

Homoge'neous a. of the same nature; formed of uniform parts.—**homogene'ity** n.—**homol'ogous** a. having the same relation, relative position, etc.—**hom'ologue** n. a homologous thing.—**hom'onym** n. a word of the same form as another but of different sense.

Homosexual'ity n. sexuality excited by an individual (usually male) of the same sex.

Hone n. a whetstone.—v.t. to sharpen on one.

Hon'est (on-) a. upright, dealing fairly; free from fraud; unadulterated.—**hon'estly** adv.—**hon'esty** n. uprightness; a plant with semi-transparent pods. Syn. faithful, veracious, honourable, pure. Ant. dishonest, disloyal, false.

Hon'ey (hun-i) n. the sweet fluid collected by bees.—**hon'eycomb** n. the structure of wax in hexagonal cells in which bees place honey, eggs, etc.—v.t. to fill with cells or perforations.—**hon'eydew** n. a sweet sticky substance found on plants.—**hon'eysuckle** n. a climbing plant, woodbine.—**hon'eymoon** n. the month after marriage; the holiday taken by a newly-wedded pair.

Hon'iton a. a superior kind of lace made at Honiton in Devonshire.

Honk n. the call of the wild goose; any sound resembling this, esp. the sound of a motor-horn.

Hon'our (on-ẹr) n. high respect; renown; reputation; sense of what is right or due; chastity; high rank or position; a source or cause of honour; a court-card.—pl. mark of respect; distinction in examination.—v.t. to respect highly; confer honour on; accept or pay (a bill, etc.) when due.—**hon'ourable** *a.*—**hon'ourably** *adv.*—**hon'orary** *a.* conferred for the sake of honour only; holding a position without pay or usual requirements; giving services without pay.—**honorif'ic** *a.* conferring honour.—**honora'rium** *n.* a fee.

Hooch (-tch) *n.* intoxicating liquor.

Hood (hood) *n.* a covering for the head and neck, often part of a cloak or gown.—*v.t.* to put a hood on.—**hood'wink** *v.t.* to deceive.

Hoof (hōōf) *n.* the horny casing of the foot of a horse, etc.

Hook (hōōk) *n.* a bent piece of metal, etc., for catching hold, hanging up, etc.; a curved cutting tool.—*v.t.* to catch or secure with a hook.

Hook'ah *n.* a pipe in which the smoke is drawn through water and a long tube.

Hook'er *n.* a small sailing ship.—**old hooker,** fondly or scornfully of any ship.

Hool'igan *n.* one of a band of young street roughs.—**hooliganism** *n.*

Hoop (hoop) *n.* a band of metal or other material for binding a cask, etc.; a circle of wood or metal for trundling as a toy; a circle of flexible material for expanding a woman's skirt.—*v.t.* to bind with a hoop.

Hoop'ing-cough *n.* a disease, *esp.* of children, in which a cough is followed by a long sonorous respiration.—**hoop** *v.i.* to make the sound *hoop,* or the sound heard with the cough.—*n.* the sound.

Hoop'oe (-ō) *n.* a crested bird with variegated plumage.

Hoot (hōōt) *n.* the cry of an owl; a cry of disapproval.—*v.t.* to assail with hoots.—*v.i.* to utter hoots.

Hop *n.* a climbing plant with bitter cones used to flavour beer, etc.—*pl.* the cones.—**hopping** *n.* gathering hops.—**hop'-garden** *n* a field of hops.

Hop *v.i.* to spring (of person, on one foot; of animals, on all feet at once; in aviation, to make a single flight).—*n.* an act or the action of hopping.—**hopp'er** *n.* one who hops; a device for feeding material into a mill or machine; a boat which takes away dredged matter.—**hop'scotch** *n.* a game in which a stone is pushed in hopping.

Hope *n.* expectation and desire of something desired; a thing that gives, or an object of, this feeling.—*v.i.* to feel hope.—*v.t.* expect and desire.—**hope'ful** *a.*—**hope'fully** *adv.*—**hope'less** *a. Syn.* optimism, sanguinity, confidence, trust. *Ant.* despair, distrust, suspicion.

Ho'ral, ho'rary *a.* pertaining to an hour; noting the hours; occurring once an hour, continuing an hour; hourly.

Horde *n.* a troop of nomads; a gang; a rabble.

Hore'hound *n.* a plant with

bitter juice used for coughs, etc.

Hori′zon n. the boundary of the part of the earth seen from any given point; the line where earth (or sea) and sky seem to meet; boundary of mental outlook.—**horizon′tal** a. parallel with the horizon, level.—**horizon′tally** adv.

Hor′mone n. a substance secreted by certain glands which stimulates the action of the organs of the body.

Horn n. the hard projection on the heads of certain animals, e.g. cows; the substance of it; various things made of it, or resembling a horn; a wind instrument originally made of a horn.—**horn′ed** (-nd) a. having horns.—**horn′y** a.—**horn′beam** n. a tree like a beech.—**horn′pipe** n. a lively dance, esp. with sailors.

Horn′blende n. a common mineral consisting of silica, with magnesia, lime, or iron.

Horn′et n. a large insect of the wasp family.

Horn′swoggle v.t. in North America, to hoodwink, deceive, swindle.

Hor′ologe n. a timepiece.—**horol′ogy** n. clock-making.—**hor′oscope** n. observation of, or a scheme showing the disposition of the planets, etc., at a given moment.

Horom′etry n. the art, practice, or method of measuring time by hours, etc.—**horometrical** a.

Horr′ent a. standing erect, as bristles; bristled.

Horr′or n. terror; intense dislike or fear of; something causing this.—**horr′ible** a. exciting horror, hideous, shocking.—**horr′ibly** adv.—**horr′id** a. horrible.—**horr′idly** adv.—**horr′ify** v.t. to move to horror.—**horrif′ic** a.

Horse n. a familiar four-footed animal used for riding and draught; cavalry; a vaulting-block; a frame for support.—v.t. to provide with a horse or horses; to carry or support on the back.—**horse′-chestnut** n. a tree with conical clusters of white or pink flowers and large nuts.—**horse′power** n. the unit of rate of work of an engine, etc.; 550 foot-pounds per second.—**horse′radish** n. a plant with a pungent root.—**horse′shoe** n. an iron shoe for a horse; a thing so shaped.—**horse′man** n.—**horse′-woman** fem. a rider on a horse.—**hors′y** a. having to do with horses; affecting the dress, etc., of a groom or jockey.

Hort′atory, hort′ative a. serving to exhort.

Horti′culture n. gardening.—**horticult′ural** a. — **horticul′turist** n.

Hor′tus, sicc′us (-sik-) n. a collection of specimens of plants dried and preserved.

Hose n. stockings; a flexible tube for conveying water.—v.t. to water with a hose.—**ho′sier** n. a dealer in stockings, etc.—**ho′siery** n. his goods.

Hos'pital n. an institution for the care of the sick; a charitable institution.—**hos'pice** (-is) n. a travellers' house of rest kept by a religious order.—**hospital'ity** n. friendly and liberal reception of strangers or guests.—**hos'pitable** a.—**hos'pitably** adv.—**hos'tel** n. a house of residence for students; an inn.—**hos'telry** n. an inn.—**host** (ho-) n. one who entertains another; the keeper of an inn.—**hostess** fem.

Host (hō') n. an army; a large crowd.—**hos'tile** a. of an enemy; opposed.—**hostil'ity** n.

Host (hō-) n. the bread consecrated in the Eucharist.

Hos'tage n. a person taken or given as a pledge.

Hos'tile a. warlike.

Hot a. of high temperature, very warm, giving or feeling heat; pungent; angry; severe.—**hot'ly** adv.—**hot'ness** n.—**hot'head** n. a hasty person.

Hotch'potch n. a dish of many ingredients; a medley.

Hotel (hō-) n. a large or superior inn.

Hough see HOCK.

Hound n. a hunting dog; a runner following scent in a paperchase; a despicable man.—v.t. to chase with, or as with, hounds.

Hour (owr) n. the twenty-fourth part of a day; the time of day; an appointed time.—pl. the fixed times or prayer; the prayers; a book of them.—**hour'ly** adv. every hour; frequently.—a. fre-

quent; happening every hour.—**hour'glass** n. a sand-glass running an hour.

Hou'ri (hōōr-i, howr-i) n. a nymph of the Mohammedan paradise; a beautiful woman.

House n. a building for human habitation; a building for other specified purpose; an inn; a legislative or other assembly; a family; a business firm.—v.t. to receive, store in a house; furnish with houses.—v.i. to dwell, take shelter.—**house'boat** n. a boat fitted for living in on a river, etc.—**house'breaker** n. a burglar; a man employed to demolish old houses.—**house'hold** n. the inmates of a house collectively.—**house'holder** n. one who occupies a house as his dwelling; the head of a household.—**house'keeper** n. a woman managing the affairs of a household.—**house'maid** n. a maidservant who cleans rooms, etc.—**house'-warming** n. a party to celebrate the entry into a new house.—**house'wife** n. the mistress of a household; (huss'if) a case for needles, thread, etc.

Hous'ing (-z-) n. a horse-cloth (usually pl.).

Hov'el n. a mean dwelling; an open shed.

Hov'er v.i. to hang in the air (of bird, etc.); loiter; be in a state of indecision.

How adv. in what way; by what means; in what condition; to what degree; (in direct or dependant question).—**howbe'it** adv. nevertheless.—**howev′er** *adv.* in whatever manner, to whatever extent; all the same.

How′dah *n.* a seat on an elephant's back.

Howe (how) *n.* a plain between hills.

How′itzer *n.* a short gun firing shells at high elevation.

Howl *v.i.* to utter a long, loud cry.—*n.* such cry.—**how′ler** *n.* one that howls; a S. American monkey remarkable for its strong voice; a stupid mistake.—**how′ling** *n.* in wireless, continuous oscillations of audible frequency occurring in a valve receiving circuit.

Hoy *n.* a small coasting vessel.

Hoy′den *n.* a boisterous girl.

Hub *n.* the middle part of a wheel, from which the spokes radiate; a central point of activity.

Hub′bub *n.* an uproar; confused din.

Huck′aback *n.* rough linen for towels.

Huck′leberry *n.* a N. Amer. shrub; its fruit.

Huck′ster *n.* a hawker; a mercenary person.—*v.i.* to haggle.—*v.t.* to deal in on a small scale.

Hud′dle *v.t.* and *i.* to heap, crowd together confusedly.—*n.* a confused heap.

Hue *n.* colour, complexion.

Hue *n.* hue and cry, an outcry after a criminal.

Huff *v.t.* to bully; offend; at draughts, to remove (opponent's man) as forfeit.—*v.i.* to take offence.—*n.* a fit of petulance.—**huff′y** *a.*—**huff′ily** *adv.*

Hug *v.t.* to clasp tightly in the arms; to cling; to keep close to.—*n.* a strong clasp.

Huge *a.* very big.—**huge′ly** *adv.* very much.

Hugg′er-mugg′er *n.* confusion; secrecy.—*a.* secret; confused. *adv.* in confusion or secrecy.

Hulk *n.* a dismantled ship; this used as a prison; a big person or mass.—**hulk′ing** *a.* big, unwieldy.

Hull *n.* a shell, husk; the frame or body of a ship.—*v.t.* to remove shell or husk; to send a shot into the hull of (a ship).

Hum *v.i.* to make a low continuous sound as a bee or top.—*v.t.* to sing with closed lips.—*n.* a humming sound.—**humm′ing-bird** *n.* a very small bird whose wings hum.—**humm′ing-top** *n.* one spinning with a hum.

Hu′man *a.* of man, relating to, or characteristic of the nature of man.—**hu′manly** *adv.*—**humane′** *a.* benevolent, kind; tending to refine.—**hu′manism** *n.* literary culture; devotion to human interests.—**hu′manist** *n.* a classical scholar.—**human′ity** *n.* human nature; the human race.—*pl.* humane studies or literature.—**humanitar′ian** *n.* a philanthropist.—*a.* of, or holding the views of a humanitarian.—**hu′manise** *v.t.* to make human; civilise.

Hum′ble *a.* not proud, lowly, modest.—*v.t.* to bring low, abase.—**hum′bly** *adv.*

Hum'ble-bee *n.* a large bee.

Hum bug *n.* sham, nonsense, deception; an impostor.—*v.t.* to delude.

Hum'drum *a.* commonplace.

Hu'mefy *v.t.* to make moist; to soften with water.

Hu'meral *a.* belonging to the shoulder.—**hu'merus** *n.* the long bone of the upper arm.

Hu'mid *a.* moist, damp.—**humid'ity** *n.*

Humil'iate *v.t.* to lower the dignity of, abase, mortify.—**humilia'tion** *n.*—**humil'ity** *n.* state of being humble, meekness.

Humm'ock *n.* a low knoll, a hillock.

Hu'mour *n.* state of mind, mood; temperament; the faculty of saying, of perceiving what excites amusement; a transparent fluid of an animal or plant.—*v.t.* to gratify, indulge.—**hu'morist** *n.*—**hu'morous** *a.*—**hu'morously** *adv.*—**hu'moursome** *a.* capricious, peevish.

Hump *n.* a normal or deforming lump, *esp.* on the back.—*v.t.* to make hump-shaped; in Australia, to carry on the back; to shoulder.—**hump'back** *n.* a person with a hump. —**hump'backed** *a.* having a hump.—**to hump bluey, to hump swag,** in Australia, to go on the tramp carrying one's pack on one's back.

Hu'mus (hū-) *n.* decayed vegetable matter; mould.

Hunch *v.t.* to thrust or bend into a hump.—*n.* a hump.—**hunch'back** *n.* a humpback.

Hun'dred *n.* and *a.* the cardinal number, ten times ten; a subdivision of a county.—**hun'dredth** *a.* the ordinal number. — **hun'dredfold** *a.* and *adv.*—**hun'dredweight** *n.* a weight of 112 lbs., the twentieth part of a ton.

Hun'ger (-ng-g-) *n.* discomfort or exhaustion caused by lack of food; strong desire.—*v.i.* to feel hunger.—**hung'ry** *a.* —**hung'rily** *adv.*

Hunk *n.* a thick piece.

Hunks *n.* a miser.

Hunt *v.i.* to go in pursuit of wild animals or game.—*v.t.* to pursue (game, etc.); to do this over (a district); to use (dogs, horses) in hunting; to search for.—*n.* hunting; a hunting district or society.—**hunts'man** *n.* a man in charge of a pack of hounds.—**hunt'er** *n.*—**hunt'ress** *fem.*

Hur'dle *n.* a portable frame of bars to make temporary fences or to be jumped over in a **hurdle-race** *n.*—**hurd'ler** *n.* one who makes, or races over, hurdles.

Hurl *v.t.* to throw with violence.—*n.* a violent throw. —**hur'ly-bur'ly** *n.* tumult.

Hurr'icane *n.* a violent storm, a tempest.—**hurr'icane-lamp** *n.* a lamp made to be carried in wind.—**hurr'icane-deck** *n.* the upper deck of steamboats.

Hurr'y *n.* undue haste; eagerness.—*v.i.* to move or act in great haste.—*v.t.* to cause to act with haste; urge to haste.—**hurr'iedly** *adv.*

Hurt *v.t.* to injure, damage,

give pain to, wound.—*n*. wound, injury, harm.— **hurt'ful** *a*.—**hur'tle** *v.i.* to move quickly with rushing sound.

Hus'band (-z-) *n*. a man married to a woman.—*v.t.* to economise.—**hus'bandman** *n*. a farmer.—**hus'bandry** *n*. farming.

Hush *v.t.* to silence.—*v.i.* to be silent.—*n*. silence.

Husk *n*. the dry covering of certain seeds and fruits; a worthless outside part.—*v.t.* to remove the husk from.— **husk'y** *a*. of, or full of, husks; dry as a husk, dry in the throat.

Hus'ky *n*. an Indian sledge-dog; an energetic man.

Hussar' (-z-) *n*. a light cavalry soldier.

Hus'sif *n*. a case for holding needles, thread, etc.

Huss'y *n*. a pert girl; a woman of bad behaviour.

Hust'ings *n.pl.* platform from which parliamentary candidates were nominated; a Guildhall court.

Hust'le (hus-l) *v.t* .to push about, jostle.—*v.i.* to push one's way, bustle.—*n*. bustle.

Hut *n*. a small mean dwelling; a temporary wooden house, *esp*. for troops.—**hut'ment** *n*. a camp of huts.

Hutch *n*. a pen for rabbits, etc.

Hy'acinth *n*. a bulbous plant with bell-shaped flowers, *esp*. of a purple-blue; this blue; an orange precious stone.

Hyæ'na (hī-ē-na) *n*. a wild animal related to the dog.

Hy'aline *a*. crystal-clear.

Hy'brid *n*. the offspring of two plants or animals of different species; a mongrel. —*a*. cross-bred.—**hy'bridise** *v.t.* and *i.*—**hy'bridism** *n*.

Hy'datid *n*. a tumour with aqueous contents, resulting from the development of the larva of the tape-worm.— **hy'datoid** *a*. watery.—*n*. the aqueous humour of the eye or its enveloping membrane.

Hy'dro- *prefix.* in:—**hy'drant** *n*. a water-pipe with a nozzle for a hose.—**hydraul'ic** *a*. relating to the conveyance of water; worked by water-power.—*n*. (in *pl*.) the science of water conveyance or water-power. — **hy'dro-a'eroplane** *n*. an aeroplane made to rise from or descend on water.—**hydrocar'bon** *n*. a compound of hydrogen and carbon.—**hydrodynam'ics** *n*. the science that treats of the motions of a system wholly or partly fluid.— **hydroelec'tric** *a*. effecting the development of electricity by the use of water or steam. —**hy'drogen** *n*. a colourless gas which combines with oxygen to form water.— **hydrog'raphy** *n*. the description of the waters of the earth.—**hydrog'rapher** *n*.— **hydrograph'ic** *a*. — **hydrop'-athy** *n*. the treatment of disease by water.—**hydro-path'ic** *a*.—**hy'drophone** *n*. an instrument for detecting sound through water.— **hy'droplane** *n*. a light skimming motor-boat —**hydro-pho′bia** n. aversion to water, *esp.* as symptom of rabies in man, and many other compounds.

Hye′na *see* HYENA

Hy′giene n. the principles of health; sanitary science.—**hygi′enic** (-gĕn-) a.—**hygi′enically** adv.—**hygi′enist** n.

Hygrom′eter n. an instrument for measuring the amount of moisture in the air.

Hymene′al a. of marriage.

Hymn (him) n. a song of praise, *esp.* to God.—v.t. to praise in song.—**hym′nal** a. of hymns.—n. a book of hymns.—**hym′nody** n. singing or composition of hymns. — **hymn′odist** n. — **hymnol′ogy** n. the study of hymns.

Hy′oscine n. a poisonous alkaloid, used as a sedative in cases of mania and delirium.

Hyper′bola n. a curve produced when a cone is cut by a plane making a larger angle with the base than the side makes.—**hyper′bole** (-li) n. rhetorical exaggeration.—**hyperbol′ical** a.

Hyperbor′ean a. of the extreme north.—n. a dweller in such region.

Hypercrit′ical a. too critical.

Hy′phen n. a short line (-) indicating that two words or syllables are to be connected.

Hypno′sis (hip-) n. a state like deep sleep in which the subject acts on external suggestion.—**hypnot′ic** a. of hyp-

nosis.—n. person under hypnosis; thing producing it.—**hyp′notism** n. the production of hypnosis.—**hyp′notist** n.—**hyp′notise** v.t.

Hypochon′dria (-kon) n. morbid depression.—**hypochon′driac** a. affected by this.—n. a sufferer from it.—**hypochondri′acal** a.

Hypoc′risy (hip-) n. the assuming of a false appearance of virtue; insincerity.—**hyp′ocrite** n.—**hypocrit′ical** a.—**hypocrit′ically** adv.

Hypoderm′ic a. introduced beneath the skin.

Hypogas′tric a. relating to, or situated in, the lower part of the abdomen.

Hypot′enuse n. the side of a right-angled triangle opposite the right angle.

Hypoth′ec n. a legal security over the effects of a debtor granted to his creditors.

Hypoth ecate (-th-) v.t. to pledge, mortgage.—**hypotheca′tion** n.—**hypoth′esis** n. a supposition as a basis for reasoning; an assumption.—**hypothet′ical** a.—**hypothet′ically** adv.

Hyss′op (his-) n. an aromatic herb.

Hys′teresis n. lag of magnetism behind the magnetising force.

Hyste′ria (his-) n. disturbance of (a woman's) nervous system with convulsions, disturbance of mental faculties, etc.; morbid excitement.—**hyster′ical** a.—**hyster′ically** adv.—**hyster′ics** n.pl. fits of hysteria.

I

I *pron.* the pronoun of the first person singular.

Iamb'us, i'amb *n.* a metrical foot of a short followed by a long syllable.—**iamb'ic** *a.*

Iat'ric, iat'rical *a.* pertaining to medicine or physicians.

Ibe'rian *a.* pertaining to Iberia, that is, Spain and Portugal.

I'bex *n.* wild goat with large horns.

I'bis *n.* a stork-like bird.

Ice *n.* frozen water; a frozen confection.—*v.t.* to cover with ice; cool with ice; cover with sugar.—**ice'berg** *n.* a large floating mass of ice.—**i'cicle** *n.* a tapering spike of ice hanging where water has dripped.—**i'cy** *a.*—**i'cily** *adv.*

I'chor *n.* in mythology, the blood of the gods; watery fluid from wound, etc.

Ichthyol'ogy (ikth-) *n.* the branch of zoology treating of fishes.—**ichthyosaur'us** *n.* a prehistoric marine animal.

I'cicle *see* ICE.

I'con *n.* an image.—**icon'oclast** *n.* a breaker of images.—**icon'oclasm** *n.*—**iconoclas'tic** *a.*

Id *n.* in psycho-analysis, the mind's reservoir of instinctive energies.

Ide'a *n.* a notion in the mind; way of thinking; vague belief; plan, aim.—**ide'al** *a.* existing only in idea; visionary; perfect.—*n.* perfect type.—**ide'ally** *adv.*—**ide'alism** *n.* imaginative treatment; philosophy that the object of external perception consists of ideas.—**ide'alist** *n.*—**ide'alise** *v.t.* to represent or look upon as ideal.—**idealisa'tion** *n.*

Ident'ity *n.* absolute sameness; individuality.—**ident'ical** *a.* the very same.—**ident'ically** *adv.*—**ident'ify** *v.t.* to establish the identity of; associate (oneself) with inseparably; treat as identical.—**identifica'tion** *n.*

Id'eograph *n.* a picture, symbol, figure, etc., suggesting an object without naming it. Also **id'eogram.**—**ideog'raphy** *n.* representation of things by pictures; phonetic art; shorthand writing.

Idiocy *see* IDIOT.

Id'iom *n.* one's language; the way of expression natural to a language; an expression peculiar to it.—**idiomat'ic** *a.* characteristic of a language; marked by the use of idioms, colloquial. — **idiomat'ically** *adv.*—**idiosyn'crasy** *n.* feeling or view peculiar to a person.

Id'iot *n.* a mentally deficient person.—**id'iocy** *n.* state of being an idiot.—**idiot'ic** *a.*—**idiot'ically** *adv.*

I'dle *a.* doing nothing; lazy; useless, vain, groundless.—*v.t.* to be idle.—*v.t.* to pass (time) in idleness.—**i'dleness** *n.*—**i'dly** *adv.*—**i'dler** *n. Syn.* indolent, unemployed, vacant, futile. *Ant.* hardworking, energetic, laborious, employed.

I'dol n. an image of a deity as an object of worship; false god; object of excessive devotion.—idol'ater n. a worshipper of idols.—idol'atress fem.—idol'atry n.—idol'atrous a.—i'dolise v.t. make an idol of; love or venerate to excess.

I'dyll n. a short description, usually in verse, of a picturesque scene or incident, esp. of rustic life.—idyll'ic a.

If conj. on the condition or supposition that; whether.

Ig'neous a. fiery; resulting from fire.—ignite' v.t. to set on fire.—v.i. to take fire.—igni'tion n.—ig'nis fat'uus n. phosphorescent light flitting over marshes, will-o'-the-wisp.

Igno'ble a. mean, base.—igno'bly adv.

Ig'nominy n. dishonour, disgrace; infamous conduct.—ignomin'ious a.—ignomin'iously adv. Syn. disgrace, humiliation, degradation. Ant. honour, elevation.

Ignore' v.t. to disregard, leave out of account.—ignora'mus n. an ignorant person.—ig'norance n. lack of knowledge.—ig'norant a.—ig'norantly adv.

Igua'na (igwä) n. a large tree lizard of tropical America.

I'lex n. holm-oak.

Ilk a. same, as in Mackintosh of that ilk meaning Mackintosh of Mackintosh.

Ill a. out of health; bad, evil; faulty.—n. evil, harm.—adv. not well; faultily; unfavourably.—ill'ness n.

Il- prefix, for in- before "l," negatives the idea of the simple word: e.g. ille'gal a. not legal.—illeg'ible a. not legible; etc., etc. Such words are not given where the meaning and derivation are clear from the simple word.

Illu'minate v.t. to light up; to decorate with lights; decorate with gold and colours.—illumina'tion n.—illu'minative a.—illu'minant n. an agent of lighting.—illu'mine, illume' v.t. to light up.

Illu'sion n. a deceptive appearance, belief, or statement.—illu'sionist n. a conjuror.—illu'sory a.—illu'sive a.

Ill'ustrate v.t. to make clear, esp. by examples or drawings; adorn with pictures.—illustra'tion n.—illus'trative a.—ill'ustrator n.—illus'trious a. famous.

Im'age n. a statue; semblance; type; simile, metaphor; counterpart; optical counterpart, as in a mirror.—v.t. to make an image of; reflect.—im'agery n. images; use of rhetorical figures.—imag'ine (-j-) v.t. to picture to oneself; conjecture; think.—imag'inable a.—imag'inary a. existing only in fancy.—imagina'tion n. the mental faculty of making images of things not present; fancy.—imag'inative a.—imag'inatively adv.

Ima'go n. an image; the last and perfected state of insect life, when the pupa case is dropped and the inclosed comes forth.

Imam′, imaum (-mawm) *n.* a minister or priest among the Mahommedans.

Im′becile *a.* mentally weak.—*n.* a person of weak mind.—**imbecil′ity** *n.*

Imbibe′ *v.t.* drink in.

Im′bricated *a.* bent and hollowed like a roof or gutter tile; lying over each other in regular order, like tiles or shingles on a roof.—**imbrica′tion** *n.*

Imbrogl′io (-brōl-yō) *n.* a complicated situation.

Imbue′ *v.t.* to saturate, dye, inspire.

Im′itate *v.t.* to take as model; mimic, copy.—**im′itable** *a.*—**imita′tion** *n.*—**im′itative** *a.*—**im′itator** *n.* *Syn.* ape, follow. *Ant.* originate, create.

Im- *prefix,* for *in-* before "*m*," negatives the idea of the simple word: e.g., **imm′ature** *a.* not mature.—**immo′bile** *a.* not mobile, etc., etc. Such words are not given where the meaning and derivation are clear from the simple word.

Immac′ulate *a.* spotless.

Immana′tion *n.* an entering or flowing in.

Imm′anent *a.* abiding in, inherent.—**imm′anence** *n.*

Imme′diate *a.* occurring at once; direct, not separated by others.—**imme′diately** *adv.*—**imme′diacy** *n.*

Immemor′ial *a.* beyond memory.—**immemor′ially** *adv.*

Immense′ *a.* huge, vast.—**immen′sity** *n.*—**immense′ly** *adv.*

Immerse′ *v.t.* to dip, plunge, into a liquid.—**immer′sion** *n.*

Imm′igrate *v.i.* to come into a country as a settler.—**immigra′tion** *n.*—**imm′igrant** *n.* and *a.*

Imm′inent *a.* close at hand.—**imm′inently** *adv.*—**imm′inence** *n.* *Syn.* threatening, hanging over. *Ant.* distant, remote.

Immit′ *v.t.* to send in; to inject; to infuse.

Imm′olate *v.t.* to sacrifice.—**immola′tion** *n.*

Immune′ *a.* secure, exempt; proof (against a disease, etc.).—**immu′nity** *n.*

Immure′ *v.t.* to imprison.

Imp *n.* a little devil; a mischievous child.

Im- *prefix,* for *in-* before "*p*," negatives the idea of the simple word: e.g. **impal′pable** *a.* not palpable, untouchable.—**impar′tial** *a.* not partial, fair; etc., etc. Such words are not given where the meaning and derivation are clear from the simple word.

Impact′ *n.* collision.

Impair′ *v.t.* weaken, damage.—**impair′ment** *n.*

Impale′ *v.t.* transfix, *esp.* on a stake, to put to death; combine (two coats of arms) by placing them side by side with a line between.—**impale′ment** *n.*

Impart′ *v.t.* to give a share of; communicate.

Impass′ible *a.* not liable to pain or suffering. — **impassability** *n.*—**impass′ive** *a.* without feeling or emotion; calm.—**impassiv′ity** *n.*

Impas'sioned *a.* deeply moved.

Impeach' *v.t.* call in question; accuse; accuse of treason.—**impeach'able** *a.*—**impeach'ment** *n.*

Impecc'able *a.* incapable of sin.

Impecu'nious *a.* having no money.—**impecunios'ity** *n.*

Impede' *v.t.* to hinder.—**imped'iment** *n.*—**impediment'a** *n.pl.* baggage, *esp.* of an army.—**imped'ance** *n.* in electricity, opposition offered to an alternating current by resistance, inductance, or capacity.

Impel' *v.t.* to drive, force.

Impend' *v.i.* be imminent.

Imper'ative *a.* expressing command; urgent, necessary.—*n.* the imperative mood.—**imper'atively** *adv.*

Impe'rial *a.* of an empire; of an emperor; majestic.—*n.* a small part of the beard left growing below the lower lip (after Napoleon III).—**impe'rialism** *n.* extension of empire; belief in colonial empire.—**impe'rialist** *n.*—**imperialis'tic** *a.*—**impe'rious** *a.* domineering.

Imper'il *v.t.* to bring into peril.

Imper'sonate *v.t.* play the part of.—**impersona'tion** *n.*—**imper'sonator** *n.*

Impert'inent *a.* insolent, saucy; irrelevant.—**impert'inence** *n.*—**impert'inently** *adv. Syn.* meddlesome, intrusive, impudent, rude. *Ant.* polite, courteous.

Impertur'bable *a.* incapable of being disturbed or agitated.—**impertur'bably** *adv.*

Imper'vious *a.* not admitting of passage through; impenetrable.—**imper'viously** *adv.*—**imper'viousness** *n.*

Im'petus *n.* force with which a body moves; impulse.—**impet'uous** *a.* ardent, vehement; acting or moving with a rush.—**impet'uously** *adv.*—**impetuos'ity** *n.*

Im'pi *n.* a brigade of Kaffir warriors.

Impinge' *v.i.* to dash, strike.

Implac'able *a.* inexorable; not to be assuaged.—**implacabil'ity** *n.*

Implant' *v.t.* to insert, fix.

Implead' *v.t.* to sue at law.—**implead'er** *n.*

Im'plement *n.* a tool, instrument, utensil.—*v.t.* carry (a contract, etc,) into effect.

Im'plicate *v.t.* to involve include; entangle; imply.—**implica'tion** *n.*—**implic'it** (-s-) *a.* implied but not expressed; involved in a general principle, exclusive of individual judgment.—**implic'itly** (-s-) *adv.*—**imply'** *v.t.* involve the truth of; to mean.

Implore' *v.t.* to entreat earnestly.

Impone' *v.t.* to lay down; to stake or wager.

Import' *v.t.* to bring in, introduce (*esp.* goods from a foreign country); imply, mean; express; be of consequence to.—**im'port** *n.* a thing imported; meaning; importance.—**importa'tion** *n.*—**import'er** *n.*—**import'able** *a.*—**import'ant** *a.* of consequence; momentous; pompous.—**import'antly** *adv.*—**import'ance** *n.*

Impor'tune *v.t.* to solicit pressingly.—**impor'tunate** *a.* persistent in soliciting.—**importu'nity** *n.*—**impor'tunately** *adv.*

Impose' *v.t.* to lay (a tax, duty, etc.) upon.—*v.i.* to be impressive; take advantage, practise deceit (on).—**imposi'tion** *n.*—**impos'tor** *n.* a deceiver, one who assumes a false character.—**impos'ture** *n.*—**im'post** *n.* duty, tax; upper course of a pillar.

Imposs'ible *a.* that cannot be done; not feasible.—**imposs'ibly** *adv.*—**impossibil'ity** *n.*

Im'potent *a.* powerless, ineffective.—**im'potence** *n.*—**im'potently** *adv.*

Impound' *v.t.* to shut up (cattle, etc.) in a pound; confiscate.

Impov'erish *v.t.* to make poor or weak.—**impov'erishment** *n.*

Impreca'tion *n.* an invoking of (evil).—**im'precate** *v.t.*

Impreg'nable *a.* proof against attack.—**impregnabil'ity** *n.*—**impreg'nably** *adv.*

Impreg'nate *v.t.* to make pregnant; saturate.—**impregna'tion** *n.*

Impresar'io *n.* an organiser of a public entertainment; operatic manager.

Impress' *v.t.* to imprint, stamp; fix; generate; affect deeply.—**im'press** *n.* act of impressing; mark impressed.—**impress'ible** *a.*—**impressibil'ity** *n.*—**impres'sion** *n.* impress; a printed copy; total of copies printed at once; effect produced, *esp.*

on mind or feelings; notion belief.—**impres'sionable** *a.*—**impressionabil'ity** *n.*—**impres'sionism** *n.* method of painting or writing to give general effect without detail.—**impres'sionist** *n.*—**impres'sionis'tic** *a.*—**impress'ive** *a.* making a deep impression.

Impress' *v.t.* to press into service.—**impress'ment** *n.*

Imprest' *v.t.* to advance on loan.—**im'prest** *n.* money advanced on loan.

Imprint' *v.t.* to impress; stamp.—**im'print** *n.* impression, stamp.

Impris'on (-z-) *v.t.* to put in prison.—**impris'onment** *n.*

Impromp'tu *adv.* and *a.* extempore.—*n.* something composed or said extempore.

Impro'priate *v.t.* to place (tithes, etc.) in hands of a layman.—**impropria'tion** *n.*

Improve' (-ōōv) *v.t.* to make better; make good use of.—*v.i.* to become better.—**improv'able** *a.*—**improve'ment** *n.*—**improv'er** *n.* *Syn.* amend, correct, ameliorate, rectify. *Ant.* spoil, deteriorate, mar, injure.

Improv'ident *a.* not provident; negligent; inconsiderate.—**improv'idence** *n.*

Im'provise *v.t.* to compose or utter extempore; get up, arrange, extempore.—**improvisa'tion** *n.*

Im'pudent *a.* pert, insolent, saucy.—**im'pudently** *adv.*—**im'pudence** *n.*

Impugn' (-ūn) *v.t.* to call in question, challenge.

Im'pulse *n.* sudden application of force; motion caused by it; sudden inclination to act; incitement.—impul'sion *n.* impulse, usually in the first sense.—impul'sive *a.* given to acting without reflection.—impul'sively *adv.*

Impu'nity *n.* freedom from injurious consequences.

Impure' *a.* not pure; mixed; defiled by sin; not grammatically correct.—impu'rity *n.*

Impute' *v.t.* to set to the account of; ascribe.—imputabil'ity *n.*—imputa'tion *n.*

In *prep.* expresses inclusion within limits of space, time, circumstance, etc.—*adv.* in or into some state, place, etc.

In- *prefix* negatives the idea of the simple word: e.g. inact'ive *a.* not active; inca'pable *a.* not capable, etc., etc. Such words are omitted where the meaning and derivation may easily be inferred from the simple word.

Inadvert'ent *a.* failing to pay attention; unintentional.—inadvert'ence, inadvert'ency *n.*—inadvert'ently *adv.*

Inane' *a.* empty, void; foolish, silly.—inan'ity *n.* a being empty; exhaustion.

In'asmuch *adv.* seeing that; (only in inasmuch as).

Inaug'urate *v.t.* admit to office; begin, initiate the use of, *esp.* with ceremony.—inaug'ural *a.*—inaug'urally *adv.*—inaugura'tion *n.*—inaug'urator *n.*

Inauspi'cious *a.* not auspicious;

ill-omened; unfortunate; evil; unfavourable.—inauspi'ciously *adv.*

In'board *a.* inside the hull or bulwarks.

In'born, inbred' *a.* born with, inherent.

Incal'culable *a.* not capable of being calculated; very great.

Incalesc'ent *a.* increasing in heat.—incalesc'ence *n.*

Incandes'cent *a.* glowing with heat, shining; of artificial light, produced by glowing filament.—incandes'cence *n.* —incandesce' *v.i.* and *t.*

Incanta'tion *n.* a magic spell, a charm.

Incar'cerate *v.t.* to imprison.—incarcera'tion *n.*—incar'cerator *n.*

Incarn'adine *v.t.* to dye crimson.—*a.* crimson.

Incarn'ate *v.t.* to embody in flesh, *esp.* in human form.—*a.* embodied in flesh.—incarna'tion *n.*

Incen'diary *a.* of the malicious setting on fire of property; guilty of this; inflammatory. —*n.* one guilty of arson, an incendiary person. — incen'diarism *n.*—incense' *v.t.* to enrage.—in'cense *n.* gum or spice giving a sweet smell when burned; its smoke; flattery.—*v.t.* to burn incense to; perfume with incense.

Incen'tive *a.* arousing.—*n.* something that arouses to feeling or action.

Incep'tion *n.* beginning.—incep'tive *a.* beginning, initial.

Incess'ant *a.* unceasing.

In'cest n. sexual intercourse of kindred within forbidden degrees.—incest'uous a.

Inch n. one-twelfth of a foot; a small island.

In'choate (in-kō-) a. just begun.

In'cident n. an event, occurrence.—a. naturally attaching to; striking, falling (upon).—in'cidence n. a falling on, or affecting.—incident'al a. casual, not essential.—incident'ally adv.

Incin'erate v.t. to consume by fire.—incin'erator n.—incinera'tion n.

Incip'ient a. beginning.

Incise' v.t. to cut into; engrave.—inci'sion (-siz-) n. —inci'sive (-sī-) a. sharp; pointed, trenchant.—inci'sor n. a cutting tooth.

Incite' v.t. to urge, stir up.—incite'ment n. Syn. rouse, stimulate, provoke, instigate. Ant. prevent, restrain, calm.

In'civism n. want of patriotism; neglect of one's duty as a citizen.

Inclem'ent a. of weather, stormy, severe, cold.—inclem'ency n.

Incline' v.t. to bend, turn from the vertical; dispose.—v.i. to slope; be disposed.—in'cline n. a slope.—inclina'tion n.

Include' v.t. to reckon in; comprise.—inclu'sion n.—inclu'sive a.—inclu'sively adv.

Incog'nito adv. with identity concealed or not avowed.—a. concealing or not avowing identity.—n. this condition.

Incoher'ent a. not coherent; loose; inconsistent. — incoher'ently adv.—incoher'ence n. want of cohesion.

In'come n. receipts, esp. annual, from work, investments, etc.

Incong'ruous (-ng-g-) a. not accordant, absurd.—incongru'ity n.—incong'ruously adv. Syn. inappropriate, unsuitable. Ant. fit, congruous, suitable, appropriate.

Incon'sequent a. not following from the premises; illogical.

Inconsid'erate a. not considerate.

Inconsis'tent a. incompatible; unsuitable; discordant.—inconsis'tence n.

Incorp'orate v.t. to unite into one body; form legally into a corporation; include.—incorpora'tion n.

Increase' v.i. to become greater in size, number, etc. —v.t. to make greater.—in'crease n. growth, enlargement, multiplication.—in'crement n. increase; profit. Syn. enlarge, expand, augment, amplify. Ant. decrease, diminish, contract.

Incrim'inate v.t. to charge with crime; involve in an accusation. — incrim'inatory a.

Incrust see ENCRUST.

In'cubate v.t. to hatch (eggs). —v.i. to sit on eggs; of disease germs, to pass through the stage between infection and appearance of symptoms.—incuba'tion n.—in'cubator n. an apparatus for artificially hatching eggs.

In'cubus *n.* a nightmare; an oppressive person or thing.

In'culcate *v.t.* to impress on the mind.—**inculca'tion** *n.*

Incumb'ent *a.* lying, resting (on).—*n.* the holder of a church benefice.—**incumb'ency** *n.* office or tenure of an incumbent.

Incur' *v.t.* to fall into, bring upon oneself.—**incur'sion** *n.* an invasion.

Incur'able *a.* incapable of being cured; hopelessly bad. —**incur'ably** *adv.*

Incuse' *v.t.* to impress by striking or stamping; —*a.* hammered.—*n.* an impression.

Indebt'ed (-det-) *a.* owing.—**indebt'edness** *n.*

Indeed' *adv.* in truth, really.

Indefat'igable *a.* untiring.—**indefat'igably** *adv.*

Indefeas'ible (-fēz-) *a.* that cannot be lost or annulled.

Indefen'sible *a.* untenable.—**indefen'sibly** *adv.*

Indel'ible *a.* that cannot be blotted out or effaced; permanent.—**indel'ibly** *adv.* —**indelibil'ity** *n.*

Indem'nity *n.* security against loss; compensation, *esp.* exacted by a victorious country after war.—**indem'nify** *v.t.* to give indemnity to; to compensate. —**indemnifica'tion** *n.*

Indent' *v.t.* to make notches or holes in; draw up a document in duplicate; make ar order (*upon* some one *for*); order by indent.—**in'dent** *n.* a notch; an order, requisition. —**indenta'tion** *n.* — **indent'-**
ure *n.* an indented document; a sealed agreement, *esp.* one binding apprentice to master.—*v.t.* to bind by indenture.

Indepen'dent *a.* not subject to others; self-directing; free; unconnected.— **indepen'dently** *adv.*—**indepen'dence, indepen'dency** *n.* state or quality of being independent; self-reliance; self-support.

Indescri'bable *a.* incapable of being described.—**indescri'bably** *adv.*

In'dex *n.* (in'dexes, in'dices (-sēz) *pl.*) forefinger; anything that points out, an indicator; an alphabetical list of references, usually at the end of a book.—*v.t.* to provide a book with an index; to insert in an index. —**in'dicate** *v.t.* to point out, state briefly.—**indica'tion** *n.* —**indic'ative** *a.* that indicates; *gram.* stating as a fact.—**in'dicator** *n.*

In'dia-rubber *n.* rubber, caoutchouc, *esp.* as used for rubbing out pencil marks.

In'dicate *see* INDEX.

Indict' (-dit) *v.t.* to accuse, *esp.* by legal process.—**indict'ment** *n.*—**indict'able** *a.*

Indiff'erent *a.* impartial; careless; unimportant; neither good nor bad; having no inclination for or against.—**indiff'erently** *adv.*—**indiff'erence** *n.*

Indi'genous (-dij-) *a.* born in or natural to a country.

In'digent (-j-) *a.* poor, needy. —**in'digence** *n.*—**in'digene** *n.*

Indig'nant *a.* moved by anger

and scorn; angered by injury.
—indig'nantly*adv.*—indigna'-
tion *n.*—indig'nity *n.* unworthy treatment; insult.

In'digo *n.* a blue dye obtained from a plant; the
plant.

Indite' *v.t.* to write, put into
words.

Individ'ual *a.* single; characteristic of a single person
or thing.—*n.* a single person.
—individ'ually *adv.*—individual'ity *n.* individual existence or character.—individ'-
ualism *n.* social theory of
free action of individuals.—
individ'ualist *n.*—individual-
is'tic *a.*

In'dolent *a.* lazy.—in'dolence
n.—in'dolently *adv.* *Syn.*
sluggish, slothful, listless,
inert. *Ant.* energetic, active, hard-working.

Indom'itable *a.* unyielding.—
indom'itably *adv.*

In'door *a.* within, used within,
etc., a house.—in'doors *adv.*

Indorse *see* ENDORSE.

Indu'bitable *a.* beyond doubt.

Induce' *v.t.* to persuade; bring
about, infer; produce (electricity) by induction.—induce'ment *n.* incentive, attraction.—induct' *v.t.* to
instal in office.—induc'tion
n. inducting; a general
inference from particular
instances; production of
electric or magnetic state in
a body by its being near
(not touching) an electrified
or magnetised body; in an
internal combustion engine,
that part of the piston's
action which draws the gas

from the carburettor.—
induc'tive *a.* — induc'tively
adv.—induc'tor *n.* *Syn.* incite, prevail on, influence.
Ant. dissuade, prevent,
check.

Indulge' *v.t.* to gratify; give
free course to; take pleasure
in freely.—indul'gent *a.*—
indul'gence *n.*—indul'gently
adv.

In'durate *v.t.* to harden.

In'dustry *n.* diligence; habitual
hard work; a branch of manufacture or trade.—indus'-
trious *a.* diligent.—indus'trial
a. of industries, trades.—
indus'trialism *n.* factory
system.

Ine'briate *v.t.* to make drunk.
—*a.* drunken.—*n.* a drunkard.—inebria'tion *n.*—ineb-
ri'ety *n.*

Ined'ible *a.* not eatable; unfit
for food.

Ineff'able *a.* unspeakable, too
great for words.—ineff'ably
adv.

Ineffi'cient *a.* not efficient.—
ineffi'ciency *n.*

Inel'igible (-ji-) *a.* incapable
of being elected to an office.
—ineligibil'ity *n.*

Inept' *a.* absurd, out of place.
—inept'itude *n.*

Inert' *a.* without power of
action or resistance; slow,
sluggish.—iner'tia (-shya) *n.*
the property by which
matter continues in its
existing state of rest or
motion in a straight line
unless that state is changed
by external force.—inert'ly
adv.—inert'ness *n.*

Inev'itable *a.* unavoidable,

not to be escaped.—inev'it-ably *adv.*—inevitabil'ity *n.*

Inex'orable *a.* relentless.—inex'orably *adv.*

Inexpug'nable *a.* impregnable; of argument, unanswerable.

Infall'ible *a.* not liable to fail.—infall'ibly *adv.*—infalli-bil'ity *n.*

In'famous *a.* of ill fame, shameless, bad.—in'famy *n.*—in'famously *adv. Syn.* disgraceful, disreputable, shameful, ignominious, base, scandalous. *Ant.*, of *a.* praiseworthy, commendable, honourable.

In'fant *n.* a child under seven; a person under twenty-one, a minor.—in'fancy *n.*—infant'icide *n.* murder of new-born child; person guilty of this.—in'fantile *a.* childish.

In'fantry *n.* foot soldiers.

Infat'uate *v.t.* affect to folly of foolish passion.—infatua'tion *n.*

Infect' *v.t.* to make noxious; affect (with disease).—infec'tion *n.*—infec'tious *a.* catching.

Infeft'ment *n.* in Scots Law, a deed or process of putting in possession of heritable property.

Infer' *v.t.* to deduce by reasoning, conclude.—in'ference *n.*—inferen'tial *a.*—infer'able *a.*

Infe'rior *a.* lower; of poor quality.—*n.* one lower (in rank, etc.).—inferior'ity *n.*

Inferior'ity complex *n.* in psycho-analysis, a deep-seated sense of inferiority.

Infern'al *a.* of the lower world; hellish.—infern'ally *adv.*

Infer'tile *a.* not productive; barren.—infertil'ity *n.*

Infest' *v.t.* haunt, swarm in.

In'fidel *n.* an unbeliever.—*a.* unbelieving.—infidel'ity *n.* disbelief (in religion); dis-loyalty.

Infilt'rate *v.i.* to percolate, trickle through.—*v.t.* to cause to pass through pores.—infiltra'tion *n.*

In'finite (-it) *a.* boundless.—infinites'imal *a.* extremely or infinitely small.—in'finitely *adv.*—infin'ity *n.*—infin'itive *a. gram.* in the mood expressing the notion of the verb without limitation by any particular subject.—*n.* a verb in this mood; the mood. *Syn.* immeasurable, illimitable, interminable, limitless, unbounded, im-mense, enormous, vast, stupendous. *Ant.* finite, limited, restricted, small, brief.

Infirm' *a.* physically weak; mentally weak, irresolute.—infirm'ity *n.*—infirm'ary *n.* a hospital.

Inflame' *v.t.* to set alight, to raise to heat or excitement.—*v.i.* to catch fire; become excited.—inflamm'able *a.* easily set on fire; excitable.—inflammabil'ity *n.*—inflamma'tion *n.* a morbid process affecting part of the body with heat, swelling and redness.—inflamm'atory *a.*

Inflate' *v.t.* to blow up with air or gas; raise (price)

artificially; increase (currency of a state) abnormally. —infla'tion n.

Inflect' v.t. to bend; to modify (words) to show grammatical relationships.—inflec'tion,inflex'ion n.

Inflex'ible a. incapable of being bent.—inflex'ibly adv. —inflexibil'ity n.

Inflict' v.t. to impose, deliver forcibly, cause to be borne.— inflic'tion n. inflicting; a boring experience.

Infloresc'ence n. the unfolding of blossoms.

In'fluence n. agent or action working invisibly (upon); moral power (over, with); thing or person exercising this.—v.t. to exert influence upon.—influen'tial a.—influen'tially adv.—influen'za n. a contagious feverish illness; severe catarrh.—in'flux n. a flowing in.

Inform' v.t. to tell; inspire.— v.i. to bring a charge against. —inform'ant n. one who tells.—informa'tion n. telling; what is told, knowledge.— inform'ative a.—inform'er n. one who brings a charge.

In'fra adv. below; under; after.—in'fra-red a. to denote the light rays below the red end of the visible spectrum.—in'fra-red photography n. photography with a special lens and plate giving a clearer photograph.

Infre'quent a. seldom happening.—infre'quently adv.—infre'quence.—infre'quency n.

Infringe' v.t. to transgress,

break.—infringe'ment n.— infrac'tion n.

Infu'riate v.t. to fill with fury.

Infuse' v.t. to pour in, instil; steep in order to extract soluble properties.—infu'sion n. infusing; liquid extracts obtained. Syn soak, macerate, implant, ingraft, inspire, introduce, inculcate.

Infuso'ria n.pl. microscopic animalcules found in water and other fluids.—infuso'rial a.

Inge'nious a. clever at contriving; cleverly contrived.— ingenu'ity n.—inge'niously adv.

Ingen'uous a. frank, artless, innocent.—ingen'uously adv. Syn. noble, generous, open, unreserved, plain, sincere, candid, fair. Ant. cunning, sly, artful, studied, insincere, artificial.

Ingestion n. act of throwing, or putting, into the stomach.

Ing'le (ing-gl) n. a fire on a hearth.—ing'le-nook n. a chimney-corner.

In'got (ing-g-) n. a brick of cast metal, esp. gold or silver.

Ingra'tiate v. refl. to get oneself into favour.

Ingre'dient n. a component part of a mixture.

Inhab'it v.t. to dwell in.— inhab'ilable a.—inhab'itant n.—inhabita'tion n.

Inhale' v.t. to breathe in.— v.i. to breathe in air.— inhala'tion n.

Inhere' v.i. of qualities, to exist (in); of rights, to be

vested (in person).—inhe′rent
a.—inhe′rently *adv.*—inhe′r-
ence *n.*

Inher′it *v.t.* to take as heir;
derive from parents.—*v.i.* to
succeed as heir.—inher′it-
ance *n.*—inher′itor *n.*—
inher′itress, inher′itrix *fem.*

Inhe′sion *n.* inherence.

Inhib′it *v.t.* to forbid; forbid
to exercise clerical functions;
hinder (action).—inhibi′tion
n.—inhib′itory *a.*

Inhume′ *v.t.* to bury —
inhuma′tion *n.*

Inim′ical *a.* hostile, hurtful.
Syn. adverse, ill-disposed,
antagonistic, repugnant, pernicious. *Ant.* friendly,
kindly-disposed, partial,
amicable.

Inim′itable *a.* defying imitation.—inim′itably *adv.*

Iniq′uity *n.* wickedness; gross
injustice.—iniq′uitous *a.*

Ini′tial (ish-) *a.* of the beginning, occurring at the beginning.—*n.* an initial letter.—
v.t. to mark, sign, with one's
initials.—ini′tiate *v.t.* to set
on foot, begin; admit, *esp.*
into a secret society.—*n.* an
initiated person.—initia′tion
n.—ini′tiative *n.* first step,
lead, power of acting in-
dependently.—*a.* originating.
—ini′tiatory *a.*

Inject′ *v.t.* to force in (fluid,
medicine, etc.), as with a
syringe; fill thus.—injec′tion
n.

Injunc′tion *n.* a judicial order
to restrain; an authoritative
order.

In′jury *n.* wrong, damage,
harm.—in′jure *v.t.* to do
wrong to, damage.—inju′ri-
ous *a.*—inju′riously *adv.*

Injus′tice *n.* want of equity;
wrong.—injust′ly *adv.*

Ink *n.* fluid used for writing;
paste used for printing.—
v.t. to mark with ink; cover
or smear with it.—ink′y *a.*—
ink′-pot *n.*—ink′bottle *n.*—
ink′well *n.* vessel for ink.—
ink′stand *n.*—ink′er *n.* an
instrument marking, or
recording with, ink.

Ink′ling *n.* a hint, slight
knowledge or suspicion.

In′land *n.* the interior of a
country.—*a.* in this; away
from the sea; within a
country.—*adv.* in or towards
the inland.

In′lay *v.t.* to embed; to
decorate thus.—*n.* inlaid
work.

In′let *n.* an entrance; a creek;
a piece inserted.

In′ly *adv.* in the heart, in-
wardly.

In′mate *n.* an occupant,
inhabitant.

In′most *a.* most inward.

Inn *n.* a public house for the
lodging or refreshment of
travellers.—inn′keeper *n.*—
Inns of Court *n.* the four
societies admitting to practice at the English Bar; their
buildings.

Innate′ *a.* inborn.

Inn′er *a.* lying within.—*n.*
the ring next the bull on a
target.

Inn′ings *n.pl.* in games, the
batsman's turn of play, a
side's turn of batting.

Inn′ocent *a.* free from guilt;
guileless; harmless.—*n.* an

innocent person, *esp.* a young child; an idiot.—**inn'ocence** *n.*—**inn'ocently** *adv.*—**inno-c'uous** *a.* harmless.

Inn'ovate *v.t.* to bring in changes, new things.—**inn'-ovator** *n.*—**innova'tion** *n.*

Innuen'do *n.* an allusive remark, hint (usually depreciatory).

Innu'merable *a.* not capable of being numbered; very numerous. — **innu'merably** *adv.*

Inoc'ulate *v.t.* to treat with disease germs, *esp.* as a protection; implant (disease germs).—**inocula'tion** *n.*

Ino'dorous *a.* wanting scent.

Inoffen'sive *a.* giving no offence.—**inoffen'sively** *adv.*—**inoffen'siveness** *n.*

Inop'erative *a.* not operative; producing no effect.

Inopp'ortune *a.* unseasonable in time.

Inord'inate *a.* excessive. *Syn.* irregular, disorderly, extravagant, immoderate. *Ant.* regular, systematic, reasonable, controlled, restricted, curbed.

Inorgan'ic *a.* devoid of organised structure; pertaining to substances without carbon.—**inorgan'ically** *adv.*

In'-patient *n.* a patient that stays in an infirmary or hospital.

In'put *n.* in electricity, power supplied to battery, condenser, etc.

In'quest *n.* a legal or judicial inquiry.

Inquire', enquire' *v.i.* to seek information.—*v.t.* to ask

to be told.—**inqui'rer, enqui'rer** *n.*—**inqui'ry, enqui'ry** *n.*—**inquisi'tion** *n.* an investigation, official inquiry. —**Inquis'ition** *n.* a tribunal for the suppression of heresy.—**inquis'itor** *n.*—**inquisitor'ial** *a.*—**inquis'itive** *a.* given to inquiring, curious; prying.—**inquis'itively** *adv.*

In'road *n.* an incursion.

Insane' *a.* unsound in mind: lunatic.—**insane'ly** *adv.*—**insan'ity** *n.*

Inscribe' *v.t.* to write (*in* or *on* something); mark; trace (figure) within another; dedicate.—**inscrip'tion** *n.* inscribing; words inscribed on a monument, coin, etc.

Inscru'table *a.* mysterious, impenetrable. — **inscru'tably** *adv.*—**inscrutabil'ity** *n.*

In'sect *n.* a small invertebrate animal with six legs, usually body divided into segments and two or four wings.—**insect'icide** *n.* a preparation for killing insects.—**insectiv'orous** *a.* insect-eating.

Insen'sate *a.* without sensibility; stupid, foolish.

Insert' *v.t.* to place or put (*in, into, between*); introduce (*into* written matter, etc.).—**inser'tion** *n.*

In'set *n.* something extra inserted.

In'shore *adv.* and *a.* near the shore.

In'side *n.* the inner side, surface, or part.—*a.* of, in, or on, the inside.—*adv.* in or into the inside.—*prep.* within, on the inner side.

Insid'ious *a.* stealthy, treacherous.—**insid'iously** *adv.* *Syn.* crafty, wily, artful, sly, designing, guileful, treacherous, deceitful, deceptive. *Ant.* open, frank, straightforward, straight, downright, truthful.

In'sight (-sīt) *n.* mental penetration.

Insig'nia *n. pl.* badges or emblems of an honour or office.

Insin'uate *v.t.* to bring or get (something *into* something) gradually or subtly to hint.—**insinua'tion** *n.*

Insip'id *a.* dull, tasteless.—**insipid'ity** *n.*

Insist' *v.i.* to dwell, maintain, demand persistently.—**insist'ent** *a.*—**insist'ently** *adv.*—**insist'ence** *n.*

In'solent *a.* insulting, offensively contemptuous.—**in'solently** *adv.*—**in'solence** *n.* *Syn.* domineering, arrogant, abusive, contemptuous, audacious, pert, impertinent, rude, saucy, impudent. *Ant.* humble, meek, respectful, polite, courteous.

Insom'nia *n.* sleeplessness.

In'span *v.t.* to yoke to a vehicle.

Inspect' *v.t.* to examine closely or officially.—**inspec'tion** *n.*—**inspec'tor** *n.*—**inspector'ial** *a.*

Inspire' *v.t.* to breathe in; infuse thought or feeling into; arouse, create a feeling or thought.—**inspira'tion** *n.*

Inspir'it *v.t.* to animate, put spirit into.

Install' *v.t.* to place (person in an office, etc.) with ceremony; establish, have put in.—**installa'tion** *n.*

Instal'ment (-awl-) *n.* a payment of part of a debt; any of parts of a whole delivered in succession.

In'stance *n.* an example; particular case; request; place in a series.—*v.t.* to cite.—**in'stant** *a.* urgent; belonging to the current month; immediate.—*n.* a moment, a point of time.—**in'stantly** *adv.*—**instanta'neous** *a.* happening in an instant.—**instanta'neously** *adv.*—**instant'er** *adv.* at once.

Instead' (-ed) *adv.* in place (of).

In'step *n.* the top of the foot between toes and ankle.

In'stigate *v.t.* to incite, bring about.—**instiga'tion** *n.*—**in'stigator** *n.*

Instil' *v.t.* to put in by drops.—**instilla'tion** *n.*—**instil'ment** *n.*

In'stinct *n.* inborn impulse or propensity; unconscious skill.—**instinct'** *a.* charged, full.—**instinct'ive** *a.*—**instinct'ively** *adv.*

Instito'rial *a.* in law, pertaining to an agent or factor.

In'stitute *v.t.* to establish, found; appoint; set going.—*n.* a society for promoting some public object, *esp.* scientific; its building.—**institu'tion** *n.* instituting; an established custom or law; an institute.—**institu'tional** *a.*—**in'stitutor** *n.*

Instruct' *v.t.* to teach, inform, give directions to.—**instruc'tion** *n.*—**instruc'tive** *a.*—**in-**

struc'tively *adv.*—instruc'tor *n.*—instruc'tress *fem.*

In'strument *n.* a tool or implement, *esp.* for scientific purposes; a person or thing made use of; a contrivance for producing music; a legal document.—instrument'al *a.*—instrument'ally *adv.*—instrumental'ity *n.*—instrumenta'tion *n.* arrangement of music for instruments.

Insubor'dinate *a.* not submissive; mutinous.—insubordina'tion *n.*

Insuffi'cient *a.* not sufficient.—insuffi'ciency *n.*

In'sular *a.* of an island; of islanders.—insular'ity *n.*—in'sulate *v.t.* to make into an island; to isolate, *esp.* by materials not conducting electricity.—insula'tion *n.*—in'sulator *n.*—in'sulin *n.* a cure for diabetes.—in'sulated tape *n.* adhesive tape of indiarubber for winding round conductors of electricity.

Insult' *v.t.* to assail with abuse in act or word.—in'sult *n.* scornful abuse, affront.

Insu'perable *a.* that can not be got over.—insu'perably *adv.*—insuperabil'ity *n.*

Insure' *v.t.* to secure the payment of a sum in event of loss, death, etc., by a contract and payment of sums called premiums; to make such contract about; make safe (*against*); make certain.—insu'rance *n.*—insur'able *a.*—insu'rer *n.*—insu'rance-policy *n.* a contract of insurance.

Insur'gent *a.* in revolt.—*n.* one in revolt.—insurrec'tion *n.* a revolt.

Insuscep'tible *a.* not capable of being moved or impressed.—insusceptibil'ity *n.*

Intact' *a.* untouched. *Syn.* undefiled, undamaged, unhurt, scathless, left complete. *Ant.* interfered with, damaged, incomplete, disturbed.

Inta'glio (-tal-) *n.* an incised design; a gem so cut.

In'take *n.* that which is taken in; a point where a tube narrows; in motoring, passage for air to enter carburettor.

Intan'gible *a.* not perceptible to the touch.—intangibil'ity *n.*

In'teger (-j-) *n.* a whole number.—in'tegral (-g-) *a.*—in'tegrate *v.t.* to combine into a whole.—integra'tion *n.*—integ'rity *n.* original perfect state; honesty, uprightness.

Integ'ument *n.* covering, skin, rind.

In'tellect *n.* the faculty of thinking and reasoning.—intellec'tual *a.* of, or appealing to, the intellect; having good intellect.—*n.* an intellectual person.—intellectual'ity *n.*—intell'igent *a.* having or showing good intellect; quick at understanding.—intell'igently *adv.*—intell'igence *n.* intellect; quickness of understanding; information, news.—intell'igencer *n.* an informant, spy.—intell'igible *a.* that can be understood. intell'igibly *adv.*—intelligibil'ity *n.*—intelligent'zia *n.* the part of a nation claiming power of independent thought.

Intem'erate *a.* inviolate; pure.

Intend' *v.t.* to design, purpose, mean.—**intense'** *a.* very strong or acute.—**intens'ify** *v.t.*—**intensifica'tion** *n.*—**intens'ity** *n.*—**intens'ive** *a.* giving emphasis; aiming at increased productiveness.—**intens'ively** *adv.*—**intent'** *n.* purpose.—*a.* eager; resolved, bent.—**intent'ly** *adv.*—**inten'tion** *n.* purpose, aim.—**inten'tional** *a.*—**intent'ness** *n.*

Inter' *v.t.* to bury.—**inter'ment** *n.*

In'ter-*prefix* meaning 'between, among, mutually; forms compounds, e.g. **inter-colo'nial** *a.* between colonies;—**in'terrela'tion** *n.* mutual relation; etc., etc. Such words are not given where the meaning and derivation may easily be inferred from the simple word.

In'teract *n.* a short performance to fill up the interval between the acts.—*v.i.* to act on each other.—**interac'tion** *n.*

Intercede' *v.t.* plead.—**interces'sion** *n.*—**intercess'or** *n.*

Intercept' *v.t.* cut off, seize in transit.—**intercep'tion** *n.*

In'tercourse *n.* mutual dealings; communication; connection.

In'terdict *n.* a prohibition.—**interdict** *v.t.* to prohibit; restrain.—**interdic'tion** *n.*—**interdict'ory** *a.*

In'terest *n.* concern, curiosity; the thing exciting this; money paid for use of borrowed money; legal concern; right; advantage; personal influence.—*v.t.* to excite interest; to cause to feel interest.—**in'teresting** *a.*—**in'terestingly** *adv.*

Interfere' *v.i.* to meddle; clash; of rays, etc., to strike together.—**interfe'rence** *n.*; in wireless, interruption of reception by atmospherics or by unwanted signals.

In'terim *n.* the meantime.—*a.* temporary, intervening.

Inte'rior *a.* situated within; inland.—*n.* inside; inland.

Interjec'tion *n.* a word thrown in, or uttered abruptly.—**interject'** *v.t.*

Interlace' *v.t.* to unite, as by lacing together.—**interlace'ment** *n.*

Interleave' *v.t.* to insert, as blank leaves in a book, between other leaves.—**in'terleaf** *n.*

Interloc'utor *n.* one who takes part in a conversation.—**interlocu'tion** *n.* dialogue.—**interloc'utory** *a.*

In'terloper *n.* one intruding in another's affairs.

In'terlude *n.* an interval in a play; something filling it; an interval.

Intermarr'y *v.i.* to connect families or races by a marriage between two of their members. — **inter-marr'iage** *n.*

Interme'diate *a.* coming between two; interposed.—**interme'diary** *n.*—**intermezz'o** (-dz-) *n.* a short performance between acts of a play or opera.

Interm'inable *a.* endless.—**interm'inably** *adv.*

Intermit' *v.t.* and *i.* to stop for a time.—**intermis'sion** *n.*—**intermitt'ent** *a.*

Intern' *v.t.* to oblige to live within prescribed limits.—**intern'ment** *n.*

Inter'nal *a.* inward; interior.—**inter'nally** *adv.*—**internal combustion** the process of exploding a mixture of air and fuel in a piston-fitted cylinder.

Interne'cine *a.* mutually destructive; formerly, deadly.

In'ternode *n.* the space between two nodes or points of the stem from which the leaves arise.—**interno'dal** *a.*

Interpell'ate *v.t.* in the French or other Chamber, to interrupt the business of the day to demand an explanation from a Minister.—**interpella'tion** *n.*

Inter'polate *v.t.* to put in new (*esp.* misleading) matter (in a book, etc.).—**interpola'tion** *n.*

Interpose' *v.t.* to insert; say as an interruption; put in the way.—*v.i.* to intervene; obstruct.—**interposi'tion** *n.* *Syn.* introduce, intervene, interfere, mediate, arbitrate, intercede.

Inter'pret *v.t.* to explain; explain to oneself; translate; in art, render, represent.—**inter'preter** *n.*—**interpreta'tion** *n.*

Interreg'num *n.* an interval between reigns.

Interr'ogate *v.t.* to question, *esp.* closely or officially.—

interroga'tion *n.*—**interrog'ative** *a.* questioning; used in asking a question.—**interr'ogator** *n.*—**interrog'atory** *a.* of enquiry.—*n.* question, set of questions.

Interrupt' *v.t.* to break in upon; stop the course of.—**interrup'tion** *n.*

Intersect' *v.t.* to cut into, or between; to divide.—*v.i.* to cut into one another; to meet and cross.—**intersec'tion** *n.*

Intersperse' *v.t.* to scatter; diversify.—**intersper'sion** *n.*

In'terstice *n.* chink, gap.—**intersti'tial** *a.*

In'terval *n.* a pause, break, intervening time or space; difference of pitch.

Intervene' *v.i.* to happen in the meantime; to be placed, come in, between others; interfere.—**interven'tion** *n.*

In'terview *n.* a meeting, *esp.* formally arranged; meeting of a journalist and person whose views he wishes to publish.—*v.t.* to have an interview with.—**in'terviewer** *n.*

Intest'ate *a.* not having made a will.—*n.* an intestate person.—**intes'tacy** *n.*

Intest'ine *a.* internal, civil.—*n.* (usually *pl.*) the lower part of the alimentary canal.—**intest'inal** *a.*

In'timate (-āt) *a.* familiar, closely acquainted; close.—*n.* an intimate friend.—**in'timacy** *n.*—**in'timate** (-āt) *v.t.* to make known; announce.—**intima'tion** *n.*

Intim'idate *v.t.* to force or

deter by threats.—intimida'-
tion n.—intim'idator n.

In'to prep. expresses motion
to a point within.

Intone' v.t. to recite in a
singing voice.—intona'tion
n. modulation of voice;
intoning.

Intox'icate v.t. to make
drunk; excite beyond self-
control.—intox'icant a. intoxicating.—n. intoxicating
liquor.—intoxica'tion n.

Intrep'id a. fearless.—intrepid'ity n. Syn. cour-
ageous, heroic, gallant, valorous. Ant. cowardly,
fearful, scared, afraid, timid,
cringing.

In'tricate a. involved, puzz-
lingly entangled. — in'tri-
cately adv.—in'tricacy n.

Intrigue' (-trēg) n. underhand
plotting or plot; a secret love
affair.—v.i. to carry on an
intrigue.—intri'guer n.

Intrin'sic a. inherent, essential.—intrin'sically adv.

Introduce' v.t. to bring in or
for ward; make known formally; bring to notice, insert.
introduc'tion n.—introduc'-
tory a.

Introspec'tion n. examination
of one's own thoughts.—
introspec'tive a.—introspec'-
tively adv.

Intrude' v.i. to thrust in
without invitation or right.—
v.t. to force in thus.—intru'-
sion n.—intru'sive a.

Intui'tion (-ish-) n. immediate
or direct apprehension by
the mind without reasoning;
immediate insight.—intu'i-
tive a.—intu'itively adv.

Intwine' v.t. to twine or twist
into or together.

In'undate v.t. to flood.—in-
unda'tion n.

Inure' v.t. to accustom.

Invade' v.t. to enter with
hostile intent; assail; encroach on.—inva'der n.—inva'sion n.

Inval'id a. not valid, of no
legal force.—inval'idate v.t.—
invalid'ity n.—invalid' (-ĕd)
a. ill, enfeebled by sickness
or injury.—n. a person so
disabled or enfeebled.

Inval'uable a. above price.

In'var n. a steel containing
36 per cent. of nickel, and
having a low coefficient of
expansion.

Inva'riable a. constant; always
uniform.—inva'riably adv.

Inva'sion see INVADE.

Inveigh' (-va) v.i. to speak
violently (against).—invec'-
tive n. abusive speech or
oratory.

Invei'gle (-vē-, -vā-) v.t. to
entice, seduce. — invei'gle-
ment n.

Invent' v.t. to devise, originate.
—inven'tion n.—invent'ive a
—invent'ively adv.—invent'-
or n. — in'ventory n. a detailed list of goods, etc.—v.t.
to enter in an inventory.
Syn. contrive, design, fabricate, forge.

Invert' v.t. to turn upside
down; reverse the position
or relations of.—in'verse a.
inverted.—in'versely adv.—
inver'sion n.

Inver'tebrate n. an animal
having no vertebral column.
—a. destitute of a backbone.

Māte, mēte, mīte, mōte, mūte, bōōt.

Invest' *v.t.* to lay out (money); to clothe; endue; cover as a garment; lay seige to.—**invest'iture** *n.* formal installation of person in office or rank.—**invest'ment** *n.* investing; money invested; stocks and shares bought.

Invest'igate *v.t.* inquire into.—**investiga'tion** *n.*—**invest'igator** *n.*

Invet'erate *a.* deep-rooted, long established.—**invet'eracy** *n.*

Invid'ious *a.* likely to arouse ill-will.—**invid'iously** *adv.*

Invig'orate *v.t.* to give vigour to.

Invin'cible *a.* unconquerable.—**invincibil'ity** *n.*

Invi'olate *a.* unhurt; unprofaned; unbroken.

Invis'ible *a.* incapable of being seen.—**invisibility** *n.*

Invite' *v.t.* to request courteously to come; to ask courteously; attract, tend to call forth.—**invita'tion** *n.* *Syn.* solicit, bid, call, summon, entice. *Ant.* forbid, prohibit, debar, interdict, repel, disgust.

In'voice *n.* a list of goods sent, with prices.—*v.t.* to make an invoice of.

Invoke' *v.t.* to call on; appeal to; ask earnestly for.—**invoca'tion** *n.*

Invol'untary *a.* not done willingly.—**involuntarily** *adv.*

Involve' *v.t.* wrap up, entangle, implicate; imply, entail.—**in'volute** *a.* intricate; rolled spirally.—**involu'tion** *n.*

I'odine *n.* a non-metallic element of the chlorine group, used in medicine.—**i'odise** *v.t.* to soak in iodine.—**io'doform** *n.* an antiseptic.

Ion *n.* an electrically charged atom or group of atoms.—**ionize** *v.t.* to divide into ions.—**ionization** *n.*

Io'ta (ī-ō-) *n.* the Greek letter *i*; an atom, jot.

I.O.U. *n.* a signed paper acknowledging a debt.

Ipecacuan'ha (ip-i-kak-u-an-a) *n.* the root of a S. Amer. plant used as an emetic; the plant.

Ire *n.* anger, wrath.—**irate'** (i-) *a.* angry.—**iras'cible** *a.* hot-tempered.—**irascibil'ity** *n.*—**iras'cibly** *adv.*

Iren'ic *a.* peaceful, desirous of peace.

I'ris *n.* a genus of plants with sword-shaped leaves and showy flowers; the circular membrane of the eye containing the pupil; formerly, rainbow.—**irides'cent** *a.* showing colours like a rainbow; changing colour with change of position.—**irides'cence** *n.*—**irid'ium** *n.* a white metal.

Irk *v.t.* to weary, trouble.—**irk'some** *a.*

I'ron (irn) *n.* a metal, much used for tools, utensils, etc., and the raw material of steel; a tool, etc., of this metal—*pl.* fetters.—*a.* of, or like, iron; inflexible, unyielding; robust.—*v.t.* to smooth, cover, bind, etc., with iron or an iron.—**i'ronclad** *a.* protected with iron.—*n.* a ship so protected.—**i'ronmaster** *n.* a manufacturer of iron.—**i'ronmonger**

n. a dealer in hardware. — i'ronmongery *n.* his wares.

I'rony *n.* speech in which the meaning is the opposite of that actually expressed; words used with an inner meaning. — iron'ical *a.* — iron'ically *adv.*

Ir- *prefix* for *in-* before "*r.*" Many words are omitted in which the prefix simply negatives the idea of the simple word, as in irreg'ular *a.* not regular, etc.

Irra'diate *v.t.* to shine upon, throw light upon. — irradia'tion *n.* impregnation by X-rays, light-rays.

Irref'ragable *a.* that cannot be refuted.

Irrespec'tive *a.* without taking account (of).

Irr'igate *v.t.* to water by channels or streams. — irriga'tion *n.* — irr'igator *n.*

Irr'itate *v.t.* to excite to anger; excite, inflame, stimulate. — irrita'tion *n.* — irr'itant *a.* causing irritation. — *n.* a thing doing this. — irr'itable *a.* easily annoyed. — irr'itably *adv. Syn.* to tease, exasperate, provoke, chafe. *Ant.* to allay, to soothe, to calm, to lessen the action of.

Irrup'tion *n.* invasion; bursting in.

I'singlass (iz-ing-glás) *n.* a gelatine obtained from fish, *esp.* sturgeon.

I'sland (īl-) *n.* a piece of land surrounded by water; anything resembling this, e.g. a street-refuge. — i'slander *n.* a dweller on an island.

Isle (īl) *n.* an island. — islet (īl-) *n.* a little island.

I'sobar *n.* a line on a map connecting places with the same mean barometric pressure. — isobar'ic *a.*

I'solate *v.t.* to place apart or alone. — isola'tion *n.*

Isos'celes *a.* of a triangle, having two of its sides equal.

I'sotherm *n.* a line passing through points of equal mean temperature.

I'sotopes *n.pl.* substances having different atomic weights, yet the same chemical qualities.

Iss'ue *n.* a going or passing out; an outlet; offspring, children; outcome, result; question, dispute; a sending or giving out officially or publicly; number or amount so given out. — *v.i.* to go out; result in; arise (from). — *v.t.* to emit, give out, send out.

Isth'mus (-th- *or* is-m-) *n.* a neck of land.

It *pron.*, the neuter pronoun of the third person.

Ital'ic *a.* of type, sloping. — italics *n.pl.* this type, now used for emphasis, foreign words, etc. — ital'icise *v.t.* to put in italics.

Itch *v.i.* to feel an irritation in the skin. — *n.* an irritation in the skin: an impatient desire. — itch'y *a.*

I'tem *n.* any of a list of things, a detail, an entry in an account or list. — *adv.* also.

It'erate *v.t.* to repeat. — itera'tion *n.* — it'erative *a.*

Itin'erant *a.* travelling from place to place; travelling on circuit; of Methodists, preaching in a circuit.—**itin'eracy** *n.*—**itin'erary** *n.* a record of travel; a route, line of travel; a guide-book.

I'vory *n.* the hard white substance of the tusks of elephants, etc.—**black ivory** *n.* Negro slaves.—**ivory black** *n.* black pigment from burnt ivory.

I'vy *n.* a climbing evergreen plant.—**i'vied** *a.* overgrown with ivy.

Iz'ard *n.* the wild goat of the Pyrenean mountains; the ibex.

J

Jab *v.t.* to poke roughly; thrust abruptly.—*n.* a poke.

Jabb'er *v.i.* to chatter rapidly.—*v.t.* utter thus.—*n.* gabble.

Jab'ot (zhab-ō) *n.* a frill on a bodice, etc.

Jac'inth (jas-) *n.* a reddish-orange precious stone.

Jack *n.* a knave at cards; various mechanical appliances; a flag; various small things; added to names of animals, indicates male, as in jack'ass, or small, as in jack-snipe.

Jack *n.* a leather coat; a leather bottle for liquor.

Jack'al (-awl) *n.* a wild animal like a dog.

Jack'anapes *n.* a pert child; an impertinent fellow.

Jackaroo' (-rōō) *n.* in Australia, an English newcomer gaining experience in the Australian backblocks.

Jack'ass *n.* the male of the ass; a blockhead.

Jack'boot *n.* a large boot coming above the knee.

Jack'et *n.* a sleeved outer garment, a short coat; an outer casing.

Jac'obean (-bē-an) *n.* of the reign of James I.—**Jac'obin** *n.* a Dominican friar; a member of a democratic club set up in 1789 in Paris in a Jacobin convent; an extreme radical.—**Jac'obite** *n.* an adherent of the Stuarts after the abdication of James II.—**ja'cob's-ladder** *n.* a plant; a rope-ladder with wooden rungs.

Jade *n.* a sorry nag, a worn-out horse; in contempt, a woman.—*v.t.* to tire out.

Jade *n.* an ornamental stone, usually green.

Jag *n.* a sharp projection, e.g. a point of rock.—**jagg'ed** *a.*

Jag'uar *n.* a large spotted wild animal of the cat tribe.

Jail *see* GAOL.

Jal'ap *n.* a purgative drug.

Jam *v.t.* to squeeze; cause to stick and become unworkable; pack together.—*v.i.* to stick and become unworkable.—*n.* fruit preserved by boiling with sugar.

Jamb (jam) *n.* the side post of a door, etc.

Jamboree' *n.* a spree, a celebration.

Jang'le (-ng-gl) *v.i.* to sound harshly, as a bell.—*v.t.* to make do this.—*n.* a harsh metallic sound; a wrangle.

Jan'issary, jan'izary *n.* formerly, a soldier of the bodyguard of the Turkish Sultan.

Jan'itor *n.* a doorkeeper, caretaker.

Jan'uary *n.* the first month.

Japan' *n.* a very hard varnish. —*v.t.* to cover with this.

Jape *n.* a joke.—*v.i.* to joke.

Jar *n.* a vessel of glass, earthenware, etc.

Jar *v.i.* to make a grating noise; vibrate gratingly; wrangle.—*v.t.* to cause to grate, vibrate.—*n.* a jarring sound; shock, etc.

Jar'gon *n.* barbarous or distorted language; gibberish; excessively technical language.

Jargonelle' *n.* an early pear.

Jarr'ah *n.* a gum-tree of Australia.

Jas'mine, jas'min, jess'amine, jess'amin *n.* a flowering shrub.

Jas'per *n.* a red, yellow, or brown stone.

Jaun'dice (-dis) *n.* a disease marked by yellowness of the skin.—**jaun'diced** *a.* jealous, of soured outlook.

Jaunt *n.* a short pleasure excursion.—*v.i.* to make one. —**jaunt'ing-car** *n.* a two-wheeled vehicle common in Ireland.

Jaunt'y *a.* sprightly; briskly pleased with life.—**jaunt'ily** *adv.*

Jav'elin *n.* a light spear for throwing.

Jaw *n.* one of the bones in which the teeth are set.— *pl.* mouth; gripping part of vice, etc.

Jay *n.* a noisy bird of brilliant plumage; a chatterer.—**jay-walker**, in America, a pedestrian who tries to cross a road at an unauthorised place, or who walks without care for traffic.

Jazz *n.* discordant syncopated music and dance.—*v.i.* to indulge in jazz.—*a.* discordant or bizarre in colour, etc.

Jeal'ous (jel-) *a.* suspiciously watchful; distrustful of the faithfulness (of); envious.— **jeal'ousy** *n.*—**jeal'ously** *adv.*

Jean (jān, jēn) *n.* a twilled cotton cloth.

Jeer *v.t.* and *i.* to scoff, deride.—*n.* a scoff.

Je'hu *n.* a driver.

Jejune' (-ōōn) *a.* poor, uninteresting, unsatisfying.

Jell'y *n.* a semi-transparent food made with gelatine, becoming stiff as it cools; anything of the consistency of this.—**jell'y-fish** *n.* a jelly-like small sea-animal.

Jemm'y *n.* a burglar's crowbar.

Jeop'ardy (jep-) *n.* danger.— **jeop'ardise** *v.t.* to endanger.

Jeremi'ad *n.* a doleful complaint.

Jerk *n.* a sharp, abruptly stopped movement, a twitch, start, sharp pull.—*v.t.* and *i.* to move, or throw with a jerk.—**jerk'y** *a.*—**jerk'ily** *adv.* —**jerk'iness** *n.*

Jerked *a.* cut into long strips and dried in the sun.

Jer'kin *n.* a close-fitting jacket, *esp.* of leather.

Jerr'an, jirrand *a.* in Australia, afraid.

Jer'ry-built *a.* of flimsy construction with bad materials. —**jer'ry-builder** *n.*

Jer'sey (-z-) *n.* a close-fitting knitted jacket.

Jest *n.* joke.—*v.i.* joke.— **jest'er** *n.* a joker, *esp.* a professional fool of a court.

Jes'uit (jez-) *n.* a member of the Society of Jesus, an Order founded by Ignatius Loyola in 1533. — **Jesuit'ical** *a.*

Jet *n.* a hard black mineral capable of a brilliant polish.

Jet *n.* a stream of liquid, gas, etc., *esp.* shot from a small hole; the small hole; spout, nozzle.—*v.t.* and *i.* spurt out in jets.

Jet'sam *n.* goods thrown out to lighten a ship and later washed ashore.—**jett'ison** *v.t.* to throw overboard thus.

Jett'y *n.* a small pier or landing-place.

Jew'el *n.* a precious stone; a personal ornament containing one; a precious thing.— **jew'eller** *n.* a dealer in jewels.—**jew'elry, jew'ellery** *n.*

Jib *n.* a ship's triangular staysail.—*v.t.* to pull over (a sail) to the other side; of a horse or person, to stop and refuse to go on, to object to proceed.—**jibboom'** *n.* a spar from the end of the bowsprit.—**jibb'er** *n.*

Jibe *see* GYBE.

Jig *n.* a lively dance; music for it; various mechanisms or fittings.—*v.i.* to dance a jig; to make jerky up-and-down movements.—**jig'saw**

n. a machine fretsaw.— **jigg'er** *n.*

Jigg'er *n.* in South Africa and America, a flea, the female of which burrows under human flesh to lay its eggs, particularly attacking the feet.

Jilt *v.t.* to cast off (a lover) after encouraging.—*n.* one who does this.

Jimm'y *n.* in South Africa, a newly-arrived immigrant.

Jing'le (-ng-gl) *n.* mixed metallic noise, as of shaken chain; repetition of same sounds in words.—*v.i.* to make the sound.—*v.t.* to cause to make it.

Jing'o (-ng-g-) *n.* a warmonger.—**by Jingo,** a form of asseveration.

Jiu-jitsu *n. see* JU-JUTSU.

Job *n.* a piece of work; an employment; an unscrupulous transaction.—*v.i.* to do odd jobs; to deal in stocks.— **jobb'er** *n.*—**jobb'ery** *n.*—**job'master** *n.* one who hires horses.

Job *v.t.* to prod.

Jock'ey *n.* a professional rider in horseraces.—*v.t.* to cheat; manœuvre.

Jocose' *a.* waggish, humorous. —**jocos'ity** *n.*—**joc'ular** *a.* joking, given to joking.— **jocular'ity** *n.*—**jocose'ly** *adv. Syn.* jocular, facetious, witty, merry, pleasant, sportive. *Ant.* dismal, ponderous, serious, heavy, dull, miserable, gloomy.

Joc'und *a.* merry.—**jocund'ity** *n.*

Jog *v.t.* to move or push with

a jerk.—*v.i.* to walk or ride with jolting pace; to go on one's way.—*n.* a jogging.—**jog'trot** *n.* a slow regular trot.—**jog'gle** *v.t.* and *i.* to move to and fro in jerks.—*n.* a slight jog.

John *n.* a proper name.—**John Collins** *n.* in N. America, a morning drink of gin, sugar, lemon, ice and soda-water.—**Johnny cake**, a cake made of the meal of Indian corn; in Australia, a cake of flour and water baked in hot ashes.

Join *v.t.* to put together, fasten, unite.—*v.i.* to become united or connected.—*n.* a joining; place of joining.—**join'er** *n.* one who joins; a maker of furniture and light woodwork.—**join'ery** *n.* his work.—**joint** *n.* an arrangement by which two things fit or are joined together, rigidly or loosely; a bone with meat on, as food.—*a.* common; shared of or by two or more.—*v.t.* to connect by joints; to divide at the joints.—**joint'ly** *adv.*—**joint'-stock** *n.* common stock, share, capital.—**join'ture** *n.* property settled on a wife for her use after the husband's death.

Joist *n.* a parallel beam stretched from wall to wall on which to fix floor or ceiling.

Joke *n.* a thing said or done to cause laughter, something not in earnest.—*v.i.* to make jokes.—*v.t.* to banter.—**jo'ker** *n.*

Joll'y *a.* festive, merry.—**joll'ity** *n.*—**jollifica'tion** *n.* merrymaking.

Joll'y-boat *n.* a small ship's boat.

Jolt (-ō-) *n.* a jerk throwing up, as from a seat.—*v.t.* and *i.* to move or shake with jolts.

Jon'quil *n.* a rush-leaved daffodil.

Jor'um *n.* a large drinking-bowl; its contents.

Jos'tle (-sl) *v.t.* and *i.* to knock or push against.—*n.* a jostling.—**joust** (jōō-), **just** *n.* an encounter with lances between two mounted knights.—*v.i.* to take part in a joust.

Jot *n.* a small amount.—*v.t.* to write (down) briefly.

Jour'nal (jer-nl) *n.* a daily record; a log-book; a daily newspaper or other periodical; the part of an axle or shaft resting on the bearings.—**jour'nalism** *n.* editing, or writing in periodicals.—**jour'nalist** *n.*—**journalis'tic** *a.*

Jour'ney (jer-) *n.* a going to a place; the distance travelled.—*v.i.* to travel.—**jour'neyman** *n.* one who has learned a trade and works as an artisan paid by the day; a hireling.

Joust *see* JOSTLE.

Jowl *n.* cheek, jaw; outside of the throat when prominent.

Joy *n.* gladness, pleasure, delight; a cause of this.—**joy'ful** *a.*—**joy'less** *a.*—**joy'fully** *adv.* *Syn.* happiness, felicity, transport, ecstasy, rapture, bliss, merriment, hilarity, gaiety, festivity. *Ant.* sorrow, sadness, gloom, bitterness, rue, woe, care, mourning, agony, regret, tribulation, lamentation.

Ju′bilate *v.i.* to rejoice.— **ju′bilant** *a.*—**ju′bilantly** *adv.* —**jubila′tion** *n.*

Ju′bilee *n.* a fiftieth anniversary; time of rejoicing.

Judge (juj) *n.* an officer appointed to try and decide cases in law courts; one who decides a dispute, question, contest; one fit to decide on the merits of a question or thing; an umpire; in Jewish history, a ruler.—*v.i.* to act as judge.—*v.t.* to act as a judge of; try, estimate; decide.—**judg′ment** *n.* sentence of a court; an opinion; faculty of judging; a misfortune regarded as a sign of divine displeasure.— **ju′dicature** *n.* administration of justice; the body of judges.—**judi′cial** (-ish-) *a.* of, or by, a court, or judge; proper to a judge; impartial; critical.—**judi′cially** *adv.*— **judi′cious** *a.* sensible, prudent. — **judi′ciously** *adv.* — **judi′ciary** *n.* courts of law, system of courts and judges.

Jug *n.* a deep vessel for liquids; the contents of one.— *v.t.* to stew (*esp.* a hare) on a jug or jar.

Jug′gle *v.i.* to play conjuring tricks, amuse by sleight of hand; practise deceit.—*v.t.* to trick or cheat (*out of*).— *n.* a juggling.—**jug′gler** *n.*— **jug′glery** *n.*

Jug′ular *a.* of or in the neck or throat.

Juice (jōōs) *n.* the liquid part of vegetable, fruit, or meat. —**juic′y** *a.*

Ju-ju *n.* a West African fetish, as an idol, to which sacrifices are sometimes made; hence, also, a talisman.

Ju′jube *n.* a lozenge of gelatine, sugar, etc.—a fruit; the shrub producing it.

Ju-jut′su, jiu-jitsu *n.* the Japanese art of wrestling and self-defence.

Ju′lep *n.* a sweet drink; a medicated drink.

Jul′ian *a.* belonging to or derived from Julius Cæsar.— **Julian calendar,** the calendar as adjusted by Julius Cæsar, in 46 B.C., in which the year was made to consist of 365 days, 6 hours, instead of 365 days.

Julienne′ *n.* a kind of clear soup.

July′ *n.* the seventh month.

Jum′ble *v.t.* to mingle, mix in confusion.—*v.i.* move about in disorder.—*n.* a confused heap, muddle.

Jump *v.i.* to spring from the ground.—*v.t.* to pass by jumping.—*n.* a leap, sudden upward movement.—**jump′er** *n.*—**jump′y** *a.* nervous.

Jum′per *n.* a sailor's loose jacket; a woman's loose outer garment slipped over the head and reaching to the hips.

Junc′tion *n.* a joining; a place of joining; a railway station where lines join.—**junc′ture** *n.* state of affairs. *Syn.*

union, combination, coalition, connection, linking, coupling, place of meeting. *Ant.* break, split, burst, parting, division, cleavage.

June (jōōn) *n.* the sixth month.

Jung′le (-ng-gl) *n.* tangled vegetation; land covered with it, *esp.* in India; a tangled mass.—**jung′ly** *a.*

Jun′ior (jōōn-) *a.* the younger; of lower standing.—*n.* a junior person.—**junior′ity** *n.*

Jun′iper (jōōn-) *n.* an evergreen shrub with berries yielding oil of juniper, used for medicine and gin.

Junk *n.* old rope; salt meat; old odds and ends.

Junk *n.* a sailing vessel of the Chinese seas.

Junk′et *n.* curdled milk flavoured and sweetened.—*v.i.* to feast, picnic.

Junt′a *n.* a council in Spain or Italy.

Ju′piter (jōō-) *n.* the Roman chief of gods; the largest of the planets.

Jupon′ (jōō-) *n.* a sleeveless jacket or coat; a petticoat.

Ju′ral (jōō-) *a.* pertaining to right.

Jurid′ical (joor-) *a.* relating to the administration of law, legal.—**jurisconsult′** *n.* one learned in law.—**jurisdic′tion** *n.* administration of justice; authority; territory covered by a court or authority. — **jurispru′dence** (-oo-) *n.* the science of, or skill in, law.—**jurist** *n.* one skilled in law.—**juris′tic** *a.*

Jur′y (joor-i) *n.* a body of persons sworn to render a verdict in a court of law; a body of judges in a competition.—**jur′or** *n.* one of a jury.

Jur′y-mast (joor-i-måst) *n.* a temporary mast rigged in place of a broken one.

Just *see* joust.

Just *a.* upright, fair; proper, right, equitable.—*adv.* exactly, barely.—**just′ly** *adv.*—**just′ice** (-is) *n.* quality of being just, fairness; judicial proceedings; a judge, magistrate.—**just′ify** *v.t.* to show to be right or true or innocent; to be sufficient grounds for.—**justifi′able** *a.*—**justifi′ably** *adv.*—**justifica′tion** *n.* *Syn.* legal, exact, accurate, regular, complete, due, suitable, deserved, merited, condign, righteous, good, virtuous, blameless, pure, conscientious, honourable, impartial. *Ant.* unjust, unfair, biassed, prejudiced, erroneous, misleading, uneven, unsatisfactory.

Jut *v.i.* to project.—*n.* a projection.

Jute (jōōt) *n.* fibre of certain plants, used for rope, canvas, etc.

Ju′venile (jōō-) *a.* young; of, or for, the youthful.—*n.* a young person, child.—**juven-il′ity** *n.*—**juves′cent** *a.* becoming young.—**juves′cence** *n.*

Juxtapose′ (-z) *v.t.* to put side by side.—**juxtaposi′tion** *n.*

Jyn′tee *n.* a plant from which harcoal, as used in gunpowder, is made.

Māte, mēte, mīte, mōte, mūte, bōōt.

K

Kaa'ins, ka'ins (kå-) *n.pl.* in South Africa, scraps from which the fat has been fried out; cracklings.

Kaff'ir, kaf'ir *n.* one of a woolly-haired race inhabiting the Eastern part of South Africa.

Kaik, kain'ga (kīk, kǐn-) *n.* in New Zealand, a Maori settlement or village.

Kale, kail *n.* cabbage, cole.—**kail'yard** *n.* kitchen garden.

Kaleid'oscope (-lid-) *n.* a tube in which patterns are produced by reflection of pieces of coloured glass, moved by rotating the tube. — **kaleidoscop'ic** *a.* swiftly changing.

Kanak'a *n.* a Sandwich Islander; a native labourer brought from the Pacific Islands to Australia.

Kangaroo' (-ng-ga-) *n.* an Australian animal with very strongly-developed hind legs for jumping.

Ka'olin (kå-, kā-) *n.* fine white China clay.

Ka'pok (kå-) *n.* fibre for cushions, etc.; a tree-cotton.

Ka'va (kå-) *n.* the beverage derived from a Polynesian plant of the pepper family.

Kedge *n.* a small anchor.—*v.t.* to move (a ship) by a cable attached to a kedge.

Kedg'eree *n.* a dish of rice, fish, eggs, etc.

Keel *n.* the lowest longitudinal timber, or steel substitute, on which a ship is built up.—*v.t.* to turn keel up, capsize —**keel'less** *a.*—**keel'son** *n.* line of timbers or plates bolted to the keel.

Keen *a.* sharp, vivid, acute, eager, strong.—**keenly** *adv.*

Keep *v.t.* to observe, carry out; retain possession of, not lose; maintain; detain; cause to continue; reserve, manage.—*v.i.* remain good; remain; continue.—*n.* maintenance, food; central tower of a castle, a stronghold.—**keep'er** *n.*—**keep'ing** *n.* act of keeping; charge, possession; harmony, agreement.—**keep'sake** *n.* a thing treasured for the sake of the giver.

Keg *n.* a small cask.

Kelp *n.* a large seaweed; ashes of it for extraction of iodine.

Ken *v.t.* to know.—*n.* range of knowledge.

Kenn'el *n.* a house or shelter for dogs; a mean dwelling.—*v.t.* to put into a kennel.

Kenn'el *n.* gutter.

Kerb *see* CURB.

Ker'chief (-if) *n.* a headcloth.

Kerm'es (-iz) *n.* an insect used for red dyestuff.

Kern'el *n.* the inner soft part of a nut or fruit-stone; central or essential part.

Ker'osene *n.* lamp-oil from petroleum or coal and shale.

Kers'ey (-zi) *n.* a coarse woollen cloth.

Kers'eymere (-zi-) *n.* twilled cloth of fine wool.

Kes'trel *n.* a small hawk.

Ketch *n.* a small two-masted or cutter-rigged coasting vessel.

Māte, mēte, mīte, mōte, mūte, bōōt.

Ketch'up *n.* sauce of mushrooms, tomatoes, etc.

Ket'tle *n.* a metal vessel with spout and handle for boiling.—**ket'tledrum** *n.* a drum of parchment stretched over a metal hemisphere.

Key *n.* an instrument for moving the bolt of a lock; *fig.* anything that "unlocks"; music, a set of related notes; a lever to play a note of piano, organ, etc.—**key'board** *n.* a set of keys on a piano, etc.—**key'note** *n.* the note on which a musical key is based; a dominant idea.—**key'stone** *n.* the central stone of an arch which locks all in position.

Kha'ki (ká-) *a.* dull yellowish-brown.—*n.* khaki cloth, military uniform.

Kham'sin *n.* a hot south-east wind that blows regularly in Egypt for about fifty days, beginning about the middle of March.

Kibb'le *v.t.* to bruise or grind closely; to clip roughly.

Kick *v.i.* to strike out with the foot; be recalcitrant; recoil.—*v.t.* to strike with the foot.—*n.* a blow with the foot; recoil.

Kid *n.* a young goat; leather of its skin.—*v.t.* (*sl.*) to hoax.

Kid'nap *v.t.* to steal (a child), abduct (a person).—**kid'napper** *n.*

Kid'ney *n.* either of the pair of organs which secretes the urine; nature, kind.

Kill *v.t.* to deprive of life, slay.

Kiln *n.* a furnace, oven.

Kil'ogramme *n.* a weight of 1,000 grammes.—**kil'ometre** *n.*—**kil'olitre** *n.*

Kilt *v.t.* to gather in vertical pleats; to tuck up.—*n.* a short skirt worn by Highlanders.

Kin *n.* family, relatives.—*a.* related by blood.—**kin'dred** *n.* relationship; relatives.—*a.* related.—**kin'ship** *n.*—**kins'man** *n.*; **kins'woman** *fem.*; **kins'folk** *n.*

Kind (kīnd) *n.* genus, sort, variety, class.—*a.* having a sympathetic nature, considerate, good, benevolent.—**kind'ly** *a.* kind, genial.—**kind'liness** *n.*—**kind'ly** *adv.* *Syn.* of *a.* bounteous, beneficent, congenial, obliging, humane. *An.* unkind, harsh, cruel, disagreeable, severe.

Kin'dergarten *n.* a school for teaching young children by games, object lessons, etc.

Kin'dle *v.t.* to set on fire.—*v.i.* to catch fire.—**kind'ling** *n.* act of lighting; small wood to kindle fires.

Kinemat'ic (kī-) *a.* relating to pure motion.—*n.* (in *pl.*) the science of this.—**kinemat'ograph** *see* CINEMATOGRAPH.—**kinet'ic** *a.* of motion in relation to force.—*n.* (in *pl.*) the science of this.

King *n.* a male sovereign ruler of an independent state; a piece in the game of chess; a card in each suit with a picture of a king.—**king'dom** *n.* state ruled by a king; realm, sphere.—**king'cup** *n.* marsh marigold.—**king'fisher** *n.* a small bird of bright plumage which dives for fish.—**king's evil** n. scrofula, which was thought to be curable by a king's touch.—**king'ly** a.—**king'ship** n.

Kink n. a short twist in a rope, wire, etc.—v.i. and t. to form a kink.

Kiosk' n. a small open pavilion.

Kip n. the skin of a young beast.—**kip-skin** leather prepared from the skin of young cattle, intermediate between calf-skin and cow-hide.

Kipp'er v.t. to cure (fish) by splitting open, rubbing with salt, and drying or smoking. —n. a kippered fish; a salmon in spawning time.

Kirk n. church. Northern form of *church*, q.v.

Kiss n. a caress with the lips. —v.t. to give a kiss to.—v.i. to exchange kisses.

Kit n. a wooden tub; an outfit; personal effects, *esp.* of traveller.—**kit'bag** n. a bag for soldier's or traveller's kit.

Kitch'en n. a room used for cooking.—**kitch'en-garden** n. a garden for vegetables and fruit.—**kitch'enmaid** n.— **kitch'ener** n. a cooking-range.

Kite n. a bird of prey; a light frame flown in wind.— **kite'-balloon** n. a military captive balloon.

Kith n. acquaintances (only in kith and kin).

Kitt'en n. a young cat.

Ki'wi-kiwi (kē-) n. any bird of the genus Apteryx (found in New Zealand).

Kleptoma'nia (-ā-) n. a morbid tendency to steal for the sake of theft.—**kleptoma'niac** n.

Klink'er n. in South Africa, a brick used for paving yards; a hard biscuit.

Kloof n. in S. Africa, a ravine, a gulley.

Knack (n-) n. acquired faculty for doing something adroitly; trick.

Knack'er (n-) n. a buyer of worn-out horses for killing.

Knap'sack (n-) n. a soldier's or traveller's bag to strap to the back.

Knave (nā-) n. a rogue; at cards, the lowest court card, the jack.—**kna'very** n.— **kna'vish** a.

Knead (nĕ-) v.t. to work up into dough; to work, massage.

Knee (n-) n. the joint between the thigh and lower leg; a corresponding joint in animals; a part of a garment covering the knee.—**knee'-breeches** n.pl. breeches reaching to or just below the knee.—**knee'cap** n. a protective covering for a knee; the bone in the front of the knee (also **kneepan** n.).

Kneel (n-) v.i. to fall or rest on the knees.

Knell (n-) n. the sound of a bell, *esp.* at a funeral or after a death.

Knick'erbocker (n-) n loose-fitting breeches gathered in at the knee (also **knick'ers** n.pl.).

Knick'-knack (n-, n-) n. a light dainty article, a tr nket.

Knife (n-) n. a cutting blade

in a handle.—*v.t* to cut or stab with a knife.—**knife'-board** *n.* one for cleaning knives on.

Knight (nīt) *n.* a person of a rank below the baronets, giving the right to prefix *Sir* to his name; a military follower, a champion· a piece in the game of chess.—*v.t.* to make (person) a knight.—**knight'hood** *n.*—**knight'age** *n.* the knights; a list of them.—**knight'ly** *a.*

Knit (n-) *v.t.* to form a fabric by putting together a series of loops in wool, or other yarn; to make close or compact.—*v.i.* to unite.

Knob (n-) *n.* a rounded lump, *esp.* at the end or on the surface of anything.—**knobb'y** *a.*—**knobb'ly** *a.*

Knock (n-) *v.t.* to strike, hit.—*n.* a blow, rap.—**knock'er** *n.* who or what knocks; a metal appliance for knocking on a door.—**knock'-kneed** *a.* having incurved legs.

Knoll (nōl) *n.* a small rounded hill.

Knot (n-) *n.* a twisting together of parts of two or more strings, ropes, etc., to fasten them together; a cockade, cluster; a hard lump, *esp.* of wood where a branch joins or has joined in, a measure of speed of ships, e.g. ten knots means ten nautical miles per hour; a difficulty.—*v.t* to tie with or in knots.—**knott'y** *a.* full of knots; puzzling, difficult.

Knout (n-) *n.* a whip formerly used in Russia.—*v.t.* to flog with this.

Know (nō) *v.t.* to be aware of, have information about, be acquainted with, recognise, have experience, understand. —*v.i.* to have information or understanding.—**know'-able** *a.*—**know'ing** *a.* that knows; cunning, shrewd.—**know'ingly** *adv.*—**knowl'edge** (nol-) *n.* knowing; what one knows; all that is or may be known. — **knowl'edgeable** (nolij-) *a.* intelligent, well-informed.

Knubs *n.pl.* waste silk formed in winding off the threads from a cocoon.

Knuc'kle (nuc-kl) *n.* a bone at a finger-joint.—*v.i.* knuckle down, to put the knuckles on the ground in playing marbles.—*v.t.* to strike with the knuckles. — **knuc'kle-dus'ter** *n.* a metal appliance worn on the knuckles to add force to a blow.

Knur (n-) *n.* a knot on a tree-trunk; a hard lump; a wooden ball.

Knurl (n-) *n.* a knob or ridge.—**knurled'** (-ld) *a.* knotty, gnarled.

Kohl (kōl) *n.* powdered antimony for darkening the eyelids.

Ko'la *n.* an African tree whose seeds or nuts, having stimulating properties, are used in preparations of chocolate, aerated waters, etc.; an aerated water.

Koo'doo (-ōō-) *n.* the striped antelope of Africa, with long, spiral-twisted horns.

Kop'je (-pi) *n.* in S. Africa, a hill.

Koran (kor-an, koran-) *n.* the sacred book of the Mohammedans.

Ko'sher *a.* of food, etc., fulfilling the Jewish law.—*n.* kosher food or shop.

Kotow' (kō), **kowtow'** *n.* in China, touching the ground with the head in respect or submission.—*v.t.* to do this; to act obsequiously.

Kraal (krâl) *n.* S. African village within a fence.

Kryp'ton *n.* one of the inert constituents of the atmosphere.

Ku'dos (kū-) *n. Colloq.* fame; glory; credit.

Kuk'ri (koo-) *n.* the heavy curved Gurkha knife.

Kum'mel *n.* a cumin-flavoured liqueur.

Kursaal' (kōōr-) *n.* a public room for the use of visitors at German health resorts.

L

Laa'ger (lâ-) *n.* in South Africa, an encampment.

La'bel *n.* a slip of paper, metal, etc., fixed to an object to give some information about it.—*v.t.* to affix a label to.

La'bial *a.* of the lips; pronounced with the lips.—*n.* a sound so pronounced.

La'bour (-bẹr) *n.* exertion of the body or mind; a task; pains of childbirth; workmen collectively.—*v.i.* to work hard; strive; to maintain normal motion with difficulty; *esp.* of a ship, to be tossed heavily.—*v.t.* to elaborate; stress to excess.—**la'bourer** *n.* one who labours, *esp.* a man doing manual work for wages.—**labor'ious** *a.* hard-working; toilsome.—**labor'iously** *adv.*—**lab'oratory** *n.* a place set apart for scientific investigations or for manufacture of chemicals. *Syn.* work, toil, effort, industry, task. *Ant.* idleness, play, inaction, rest.

Lab'yrinth *n.* a network of passages in which it is difficult to find the way, a maze. —**labyrin'thine** (-th-) *a.*

Labur'num *n.* a tree with yellow flowers.

Lac *n.* a dark resin.

Lac, lakh *n.* one hundred thousand (gen. of rupees).

Lace *n.* a cord to draw edges together, e.g. to tighten shoes, stays, etc.; ornamental braid; fine openwork fabric, often of elaborate pattern.—*v.t.* to fasten with laces; to flavour with spirit.

La'cerate (las-) *v.t.* to tear, mangle; distress.—**lacera'tion** *n.*

Lac'hrymal (-k-) *a.* of tears.—**lac'hrymatory** *n.* a tear bottle.—*a.* causing tears or inflammation of the eyes.—**lac'hrymose** *a.* tearful.

Lack *n.* deficiency, want.—*v.t.* to be without, or poorly supplied with.

Lackadai'sical (-dāz-) *a.* languid, avoiding enthusiasm.

Lack'ey *n.* a footman; an obsequious person.—*v.t.* to

be, or play the, lackey to.

Lacon'ic *a.* using, or expressed in, few words.—**lacon'ically** *adv.*—**lacon'icism** *n.* *Syn.* curt, terse, concise, short. *Ant.* verbose, wordy, diffuse.

Lac'quer (lak-ẽr) *n.* a hard varnish.—*v.t.* to coat with lacquer.

Lacrosse' (là-) *n.* a ball-game played with long-handled rackets.

Lac'tic *a.* of milk.—**lacta'tion** *n.* secreting of milk.—**lac'teal** *a.* of milk.

Lacu'na *n.* a gap, a missing portion in a document or series.

Lacus'tral, lacus'trine *a.* pertaining to lakes or swamps.

Lad *n.* a boy, young fellow.

Ladd'er *n.* an appliance consisting of two poles connected by cross-bars called rungs, used as a means of ascent.

Lade *v.t.* to load; ship; burden.

La'dle *n.* a spoon with a long handle and large bowl.—*v.t.* to lift out with a ladle.

La'dy *n.* a woman of good breeding or social position; title of women of rank; formerly mistress, wife, love.—our Lady, the Virgin Mary.—**la'dylike** *a.*—**la'dyship** *n.*—**la'dybird** *n.* a small beetle, usually red with black spots.—**La'dy-day** *n.* the Feast of the Annunciation, 25th March.

Lag *v.i.* to go too slow, fall behind.—**lagg'ard** *n.* one who lags.—*a.* loitering, slow.

La'ger-beer (là-gẽr-) *n.* a light German beer, so called from its being laid up or stored for some months before use.

Lagoon' *n.* a salt-water lake, often one enclosed by an atoll.

La'ic, la'icise see LAY.

Lair (lẽr) *n.* the resting-place of an animal.

Laird *n.* a Scottish landowner.

La'ity see LAY.

Lake *n.* a large body of water surrounded by land.—**lake'-let** *n.* a small lake.

Lake *n.* a red pigment.

Lam *v.t.* especially in North Amer., to beat or hit.—**lamming** *n.* a beating.

La'ma (là-) a Buddhist priest in Tibet.

Lamb (lam) *n.* the young of the sheep; its meat; an innocent or helpless creature.—*v.i.* of a sheep, to give birth to a lamb.—**lamb'like** *a.* meek.

Lam'bent *a.* playing on a surface; softly shining.

Lame *a.* crippled in a limb, *esp.* leg or foot; limping; of an excuse, etc., unconvincing.—*v.t.* to make lame.—**lame duck** *n.* a disabled person.

Lamell'a *n.*; *pl.* **lamellæ** a thin plate or scale.—**lamellar** *a.*

Lament' *n.* a passionate expression of grief; a song of grief.—*v.t.* and *i.* to feel or express sorrow (for).—**lamenta'tion** *n.*—**lam'entable** *a.* deplorable.

Lam'ina *n.* a thin plate, scale, flake.—**lam'inate** *v.t.* to beat into, cover with, plates or layers.—*v.i.* to split into layers.

Lamm'as *n.* the 1st August, formerly a harvest festival.

Lamp *n.* a vessel holding oil to be burnt at a wick for lighting; various other appliances as sources of light.—**lamp'black** *n.* a pigment made from soot.—**lamp'ion** *n.* a fairy-light glass.

Lampoon' *n.* a venomous satire on an individual.—*v.t.* to write lampoons against.

Lamp'rey *n.* a fish like an eel with a sucker mouth.

La'nary *n.* a store-place for wool.—**la'nate, la'nated** *a* woolly.

Lance (-à-) *n.* a horseman's spear.—*v.t.* to pierce with a lance or lancet.—**lan'cet** *n.* a pointed two-edged surgical knife.—**lan'cer** *n.* a cavalry soldier armed with a lance.—**lance-cor'poral** *n.*—**lance-ser'geant** *n.* non-commissioned officers in the army.—**lan'ceolate** *a.* lance-shaped

Land *n.* the solid part of the earth's surface; ground, soil; country; property consisting of land.—*pl.* estates.—*v.i.* to come to land, disembark.—*v.t.* to bring to land.—**land'fal** *n.* a ship's approach to land at the end of a voyage.—**land'ing** *n.* act of landing; a platform between flights of stairs.—**land'ing-stage** *n.* a platform for embarkation and disembarkation.—**land'lord** *n.*—**land'-lady** *fem.* a person who lets land or houses, etc.; master

or mistress of an inn, boarding-house, etc.—**land'-locked** *a.* enclosed by land.—**land'lubber** *n.* a person ignorant of the sea and ships.—**land'mark** *n.* a boundary-mark, a conspicuous object as a guide for direction, etc.—**land'rail** *n.* a corncrake —**land'slip** *n.*—**land'slide** *n.* a fall of earth from a cliff; a notable collapse of a politica party. —**lands'man** *n.* one who is not a sailor.—**land'ed** *a.* possessing, or consisting of. lands.—**land'ward** *a.* and *adv.*—**land'wards** *adv.*—**land'-scape** *n.* a piece of inland scenery; a picture of it.—**land'scape-paint'er** *n.*—**'and'-scape-gard'ening** *n.* the laying out of grounds.

Lan'dau (-aw) *n.* a four-wheeled carriage with a top which can be opened or closed.

Land'dros *n.* in South Africa, a sheriff.

Lande (land) *n.* a level sandy region unfit for cultivation and covered with heather or broom, as along the sea-coast in south-western France.

Lane *n.* a narrow road or street; a passage in a crowd of people.

Lang'uage (-ng-gw-) *n.* speech; the words used by a people; the words used in a branch of learning; style of speech.

Lang'uish (ng-gw-) *v.i.* to be or become weak or faint; to be in depressing or painful conditions; droop, pine.—

lang'uid *a.* weak, faint, spiritless, dull.—**lang'uidly** *adv.*—**lang'uor** (-ger) *n.* faintness; want of energy or interest; tender mood; softness of atmosphere.—**lang'uorous** *a.*

La'niary *a.* lacerating or tearing.—*n.* a slaughter-house.—**lania'tion** *n.*

Lank *a.* lean and tall; long and limp.—**lank'y** *a.* awkwardly tall and lean.

Lan'olin *n.* grease from wool.

Lan'tern *n.* a transparent case for a lamp or candle; an erection on a dome or roof to admit light.—**lan'thorn** *n.* a lantern.

Lan'yard *n.* a short cord, as for securing a knife or whistle.

Lap *n.* the front of a woman's skirt as used to hold anything; seat or receptacle made by a sitting person's thighs; a single turn of wound thread, etc.; a round of a racecourse.—*v.t.* to enfold, wrap round.—**lap'dog** *n.* a small pet dog.—**lapel'** *n.* the part of the front of a coat folded back towards the shoulders.—**lapp'et** *n.* a flap or fold.

Lap *v.t.* to drink by scooping up with the tongue; of waves, etc., to make a sound like an animal lapping.

Lap'idary *a.* of stones; engraved on stone.—*n.* a cutter or engraver of stones.—**lap'is laz'uli** *n.* a bright blue stone or pigment.

Lapse *n.* a slip; a mistake; fall from virtue; passing (of time, etc.)—*v.i.* to fall away; come to an end, *esp.* through some failure.

Lap'wing *n.* a plover.

Lar'board *n.* and *a.* formerly, port (side of ship).

Lar'ceny *n.* theft.

Larch *n.* a coniferous tree.

Lard *n.* prepared pig's fat.—*v.t.* to insert strips of bacon; to intersperse or decorate (speech with strange words, etc.).—**lard'er** *n.* a storeroom for meat and other food.—**lard'y** *a.*

Large *a.* broad in range or area; great in size, number, etc.; liberal; generous.—**large'ly** *adv.*—**lar'gesse** *n.* formerly, money or gifts scattered on an occasion of rejoicing.

Lar'iat *n.* a picketing-rope; a lasso.

Lark *n.* a familiar singing-bird.

Lark *n.* frolic, spree.—*v.i.* to indulge in one.—**lark'y** *a.*

Larr'igan *n.* in North America, a moccasin with a long leg made from deer-hide.

Larr'ikin, lar'akin *n.* in Australia, a rough; a disorderly person.—*a.* rowdy.

Lar'va *n.* (lar'væ *pl.*) an insect in the stage between grub and caterpillar.—**lar'val** *a.*

Lar'ynx *n.* the part of the throat containing the vocal chords.—**laryngi'tis** *n.* inflammation of this.

Las'car *n.* a native East Indian sailor employed in European vessels.

Lasciv'ious *a.* lustful. *Syn,*

lewd, sensual, libidinous, unchaste, licentious, prurient. *Ant.* pure, moral, chaste, clean, wholesome.

Lash *n.* a stroke with a whip; the flexible part of a whip.—*v.t.* to strike with a whip, thong, etc.—*v.i.* to aim a violent blow of a whip, etc.

Lash *v.t.* to fasten or bind with cord, etc.

Lass *n.* girl.

Lass'itude *n.* weariness. *Syn.* exhaustion, prostration, faintness, heaviness, ennui. *Ant.* vigour, strength, power, stamina, energy.

Lass'o (-ō, ōō) *n.* a rope with a noose for catching cattle, etc., by throwing the noose over the head.—*v.t.* to catch with a lasso.

Last (-à-) *n.* a model of a foot on which a shoemaker shapes boots, etc.

Last (-à-) *n.* a large measure of quantity.

Last (-à-) *a.* and *adv.* after all others, coming at the end.—*n.* a last person or thing.—**last'ly** *adv.*

Last (-à-) *v.i.* to continue, hold out, remain alive or unexhausted.

Lataki'a (-kē-) *n.* a superior quality of Turkish tobacco from *Latakia*, in Syria.

Latch *v.t.* to fasten with a latch.—*n.* a fastening for a door, consisting of a bar, a catch for it, and a lever to lift it; a small lock with spring action.

Lat'chet *n.* a shoe-lace.

Late *a.* after the proper time, backward; far on in a period

of time; that was recently but now is not; recently dead; recent in date; of a late stage of development.—*adv.* after the proper time; recently; at or till a late hour.—**late'ly** *adv.* not long since.

Lateen' *a.* **lateen sail,** a triangular sail on a long yard at an angle of 45° to the mast.

La'tent *a.* existing but not developed.

Lat'eral *a.* of or at the side.—**lat'erally** *adv.*

Lat'erite *n.* a brick-coloured rock found in India; a red ferruginous clay, often dried in the sun for use in building.—**lateri'ceous** *a.* like bricks; of the colour of bricks.

La'tex (la-) *n.* the vital sap or fluid of plants.—**laticif'erous** (-sif-) *a. Bot.* bearing or containing latex or sap.

Lath (làth) *n.* a strip of wood.—**lath'** *a.* like a lath; tall and thin.

Lathe (lāth) *n.* a machine for spinning an object while it is being cut or shaped.

Lath'er (-тн-) *n.* froth of soap and water; frothy sweat.—*v.t.* to cover (chin) with lather.—*v.i.* to form a lather.

Laticos'tate *a.* broad-ribbed.

Latiden'tate *a.* broad-toothed.

Latifo'lius *a.* broad-leaved.

Lat'in *a.* of the ancient Romans; of or in their language; speaking a language descended from theirs.—*n.* the language of the ancient Romans.—**latin'ity** *n.* manner of writing Latin;

Latin style.—lat′inism n. a word or idiom imitating Latin.

Lat′itude n. freedom from restriction; scope.—geog. angular distance on a meridian reckoned North or South from the equator.—pl. regions, climes.—latitudinar′ian (-ėr-) a. claiming or showing latitude of thought, esp. in religion.—n. a person with such views.—latitudinar′ianism n.

Latrine′ (-ēn) n. a camp substitute for a W.C.

Latt′en n. a kind of brass or bronze; sheet tin; iron-plate covered with tin.

Latt′er a. latter; recent; second or two.—latt′erly adv. lately.

Latt′ice n. a structure of laths crossing with spaces between; a window so made.—latt′iced a.

Laud n. praise, song of praise.—v.t. to praise.—laud′able a.—laud′ably adv.—lauda′tion n.—laudabil′ity n. Syn. extol, glorify, eulogise, applaud. Ant. disparage, reprove, censure, blame.

Laud′anum n. tincture of opium.

Laugh (lȧf) v.i. to make the sounds instinctively expressing amusement or merriment or scorn.—n. the sound or act of laughing.—laugh′able a. funny.—laugh′ably adv.—laugh′ing-stock n. an object of general derision.—laugh′ing-gas n. nitrous oxide as an anæsthetic.—laugh′ter n. laughing.—laughing-hyæna Hyæna striata, so called from its cry.

Launch v.t. to hurl; set going; set afloat.—v.i. to enter on a course.—n. the setting afloat of a vessel.

Launch n. a man-of-war's largest boat; a large power-driven boat.

Laun′dress n. a washerwoman.—laun′dry n. a place for washing clothes, esp. as a business.—laun′der v.t. to wash and iron, etc.

Lau′rel n. a glossy-leaved shrub, the bay tree.—pl. wreath of bay-leaves, emblem of victory or merit.—lau′reate a. (lawr′i-āt) crowned with laurels.—poet lau′reate, a poet with an appointment to the Royal Household, nominally to write court odes.—lau′reateship n.

Laur′in n. an acrid fatty substance found in the fruit of the laurel.

La′va (là-) n. matter thrown out by volcanoes in fluid form and solidifying as it cools.

Lave v.t. to wash, bathe.—lav′atory n. a room for washing; a place for water-closets, etc.

Lav′ender n. a shrub with fragrant flowers; the colour of the flowers, a pale blue tinged with red.

Laverock (-vr-) see LARK.

Lav′ish a. giving or spending profusely; very or too abundant.—v.t. to spend or give profusely.

Law *n.* a rule binding on a community; the system of these rules; a branch of this system; knowledge of it, administration of it; a general principle deduced from facts, an invariable sequence of events in nature.—**law′ful** *a.* allowed by the law.—**law′-giver** *n.* one who makes laws.—**law′less** *a.* regardless of the laws.—**law′fully** *adv.*—**law′lessly** *adv.*—**law′yer** *n.* a professional expert in law.—**law′-abiding** *a.* obedient to the laws.—**law′suit** *n.* the carrying on of a claim in a court.

Lawn *n.* a fine linen.

Lawn *n.* a stretch of carefully tended turf in a garden, etc.—**lawn′-mower** *n.* a machine for cutting grass.—**lawn′-tenn′is** *n.* a game played on a flat ground with a net across the middle.

Lawyer *see* LAW.

Lax *a.* loose, slack, negligent; not strict.—**lax′ative** *a.* loosening the bowels.—*n.* a laxative drug.—**lax′ity** *n.*—**lax′ly** *adv.*

Lay *v.t.* to deposit on a surface, cause to lie.—**lay′er** *n.* one who lays; a thickness of matter spread on a surface; one of several such; a shoot fastened down to take root.—*v.t.* to propagate plants by making layers.

Lay *n.* a minstrel's song, a ballad.

Lay *a.* not clerical; of or done by persons not clergymen; non-professional. — **lay′man** *n.*

Layette′ (-et) *n.* clothes needed for a new-born child.

Lay′-figure *n.* a jointed figure of the body used by artists.

Laz′ar *n.* a leper.—**lazarett′o** *n.* a leper-hospital.

La′zy *a.* averse to work, indolent.—**la′zily** *adv.*—**la′ziness** *n.*—**laze** *v.i.* to indulge in laziness. *Syn.* slothful, idle, inert, torpid. *Ant.* industrious, active, diligent, assiduous.

Lea (lē) *n.* a piece of meadow or open ground.

Lead (led) *n.* a soft, heavy gray metal; a plummet or lump of this used for sounding depths of water; the graphite in a pencil.—*pl.* a piece of roof covered with the metal; strips of it used to widen spaces in printing, etc.—*v.t.* to cover, weight or space with lead.—**leads′-man** *n.* the sailor who heaves the lead.—**lead′en** *a.* of or resembling lead.

Lead (lēd) *v.t.* to guide, conduct; persuade; serve as a way, conduct people.—*v.i.* to be or go or play the first.—*n.* leading; example; front place.—**lead′er** *n.* one who leads; an article in a newspaper expressing editorial views (also leading article).—**lead′ership** *n.*—**lead′ing case** *n.* a legal decision used as a precedent.—**lead′ing question** *n.* a question worded to prompt the answer desired.

Leaf *n.* (leaves *pl.*) a part of a plant's foliage consisting usually of a green blade on a stem; two pages of a book, etc.; a thin sheet; a flap or movable part of a table, etc. —leaf'let *n.* a small leaf; a single sheet, often folded, of printed matter for distribution, a handbill.—leaf'y *a.* —leaf'less *a.*

League (lēg) *n.* a measure of road distance, about three miles.

League (lēg) *n.* an agreement for mutual help; the parties to it; a federation of clubs, etc.—*v.t.* and *i.* to combine in a league.—leag'uer *n.* a member of a league.

Lea'guer (lē-) *n.* a camp; investment of a town or fort; siege.

Leak *n.* a hole or break through which a liquid undesirably passes in or out.— *v.i.* to let liquid in or out so; of a liquid, to find its way through a leak.—leak'age *n.* a leaking; gradual escape or loss.—leak'y *a.*

Leal *a.* loyal.

Lean *a.* lacking fat; thin.—*n.* the lean part of meat, mainly muscular tissue. *Syn.* slender, spare, meagre, lank, skinny, gaunt, emaciated, barren, jejune, scanty, not plentiful, poor. *Ant.* fat, stout, plump, burly, fleshy, brawny, corpulent, portly, plentiful, rich.

Lean *v.i.* to bend or incline; tend (towards).—*v.t.* to cause to lean, to prop (against).

Leap *v.i.* to spring from the ground.—*v.t.* to spring over. —*n.* a jump.—leap'-frog *n.* a game in which a player

vaults over another bending down.—leap'-year *n.* a year with February 29th as an extra day.

Learn (lẹrn) *v.t.* to gain skill or knowledge by study, practice or being taught.— *v.i.* to gain knowledge; to be taught; to find out.— learn'ed *a.* having much knowledge, deeply read; showing or requiring learning. —learn'edly *adv.*—learn'er *n.*—learn'ing *n.* knowledge got by study.

Lease *n.* a contract by which land or property is given for a stated time by an owner to a tenant, usually for a rent.—*v.t.* to take or give the use of by a lease.— lease'hold *n.*—less'or *n.*— less'ee *n.*

Leash *n.* a thong for holding dogs; a set of three animals.

Least *a.* smallest.—*n.* the smallest one.—*adv.* in smallest degree.

Leath'er (leᴛʜ-) *n.* skin of an animal prepared for use.— loath'ern *a.*—leath'ery *a.*— leather-jacket, in Australia, a tree; a fish; a kind of pancake.—leather-wood, a North American shrub of the genus *Dirca.*

Leave *v.t.* to go away from; deposit; allow to remain; depart without taking; bequeathe.—*v.i.* to go away, set out.

Leave *n.* permission; permission to be absent from duty.

Leav'en (lev-) *n.* yeast.—*v.t.* to treat with it.

Lecanor'a *n.* a genus of lichens,

species of which have been suggested for manna.

Lech'er *n.* a man given to lewdness.—*v.i.* to practise lewdness; to indulge in carnal desires.—**lech'erous** *a.* lewd; provoking lust; lascivious.—**lech'erously** *adv.*—**lech'erousness** *n.*—**lech'ery** *n.*

Lec'tern *n.* a reading desk in church.

Lec'tion *n.* a difference in copies of a manuscript or book; a reading.—**lec'tor** *n.* a reader.

Lec'tual *a.* that confines to bed.

Lect'ure *n.* a discourse for the instruction of an audience; a speech of reproof.—*v.t.* to reprove.—*v.i.* to deliver a discourse.—**lect'urer** *n.*—**lect'ureship** *n.* an appointment as lecturer.

Ledge *n.* a narrow flat surface sticking out from a wall, cliff, etc.; a ridge or rock below the surface of the sea.

Ledg'er *n.* a book of debit and credit accounts, the chief account book of a firm.—**ledger-line** *n.* in music, a short line, added above or below the stave.

Lee *n.* shelter; the side of anything, *esp.* a ship, away from the wind.—**lee'ward** *a.* on the lee side.—*adv.* towards this side.— **lee'way** *n.* the leeward drift of a ship.

Leech *n.* a blood-sacking worm; (formerly) a physician.

Leech *n.* the edge of a sail.

Leek *n.* a herb like an onion with long bulb and thick stem.

Leer *v.i.* to glance with malign, sly, or immodest expression. —*n.* such glance.

Lees *n.pl.* sediment of wine, etc.

Left *a.* denotes the side, limb, etc., opposite to the right; (*see* RIGHT).—*n.* the left hand or part.—*adv.* on or towards the left.

Leg *n.* one of the limbs on which a person or animal walks, runs, or stands; a support resembling this; part of a garment covering a leg.—**legg'ing** *n.* (usually in *pl.*) a covering of leather or other material for the leg.

Leg'acy *n.* anything left by a will; a thing handed down to a successor.

Le'gal *a.* of, appointed or permitted by, or based on, law.—**le'gally** *adv.*—**legal'ity** *n.*—**le'galise** *v.t.* to make legal.—**legalisa'tion** *n.* *Syn.* lawful, legitimate, authorised, allowable. *Ant.* illegal, illicit, contraband, unconstitutional, lawless.

Leg'ate *n.* an ambassador, *esp.* of the Pope.—**lega'tion** *n.* a diplomatic minister and his suite; their mission or residence.—**leg'ateship** *n.*

Legatee' *n.* one who receives a legacy.

Leg'end (lej-) *n.* a traditional story or myth; traditional literature; an inscription.—**leg'endary** *a.*

Leg'erdemain (lej-) *n.* juggling, conjuring.

Leg'horn (-gorn) *n.* a kind of straw; a breed of fowls.

Leg′ible (-j-) *a.* easily read.—**legibil′ity** *n.*—**leg′ibly** *adv.*

Le′gion (lē-jn) *n.* a body of infantry in the Roman army; various modern military bodies; an association of veterans; a large number.—**le′gionary** *a.* and *n.*

Leg′islator (-j-) *n.* a maker of laws.—**leg′islate** *v.i.* to make laws.—**legisla′tion** *n.*—**leg′islative** *a.*—**leg′islature** *n.* a body that makes laws.

Legit′imate (-j-) *a.* lawful, proper, regular.—**legit′imacy** *n.*—**legit′imate, legit′imatise, legit′imise** *v.t.* to make legitimate.—**legitimatisa′tion, legitima′tion** *n.*—**legit′imist** *n.* a supporter of an hereditary title to a monarchy.

Legu′minous (-g-) *a.* leguminous plants, those bearing fruit in valved pods, as peas and beans.

Leipo′a (lī-) *n.* a genus of Australian mound-birds, of the genus *megapodidæ.*

Lei′sure (lezh-er) *n.* freedom from occupation, spare time.—**leis′urely** *a.* deliberate.—**leis′urely** *adv.*—**leis′ured** *a.* having plenty of spare time.

Lek′ker *a.* in South Africa, delicious; tasty; slightly intoxicated.—*n.pl.* sweets.

Lemm′ing, lem′ing *n.* a burrowing animal of the rat family, of Northern Europe.

Lem′on *n.* a pale yellow fruit with acid juice; the tree bearing it; its colour.—**lemonade′** *n.* a drink made from lemon juice. — **lem′ony** *a.*

Le′mur (lē-) *n.* a nocturnal animal like a monkey.

Lend *v.t.* to give the temporary use of; let out for hire or interest; give, bestow.—**it lends itself to**, it is adapted to.—**lend′er** *n.*

Length (-th) *n.* the quality of being long; measurement from end to end; a long stretch; a piece of a certain length.—**length′en** *v.t.* and *i.* —**length′wise** *a.* and *adv.*—**length′y** *a.*—**length′ily** *adv.*

Le′nient *a.* mild, being without severity. — **le′nience, le′niency** *n.*—**le′niently** *adv.* —**len′ity** *n.*—**len′itive** *n.* a soothing or mildly laxative drug.

Len′inism *n.* politico-social theory and/or system of government; Russian bolshevism.

Lo′no *n.* a thin linen cloth made in imitation of muslin.

Lens (-z) *n.* a piece of glass with one or both sides curved, used for concentrating or dispersing light in cameras, spectacles, telescopes, etc.; a combination of such glasses in an instrument.

Lent *n.* a period of fasting from Ash Wednesday to Easter-Eve.—**lent′en** *a.* of, in, or suitable to, Lent.

Lent′il *n.* the eatable seed of a leguminous plant.

Lent′isk *n.* a tree yielding mastic.

Le′onine *a.* like a lion.

Leop′ard (lep-) *n.* a large carnivorous animal, with a

spotted fawn coat.—**leop'ard- ess** *fem.*

Lep'er *n.* one suffering from leprosy.—**lep'rosy** *n.* a disease forming silvery scales on the skin and eating away the parts affected.—**lep'rous** *a.*—**lepidop'terous** *a.* having wings covered with scales.

Lepidoden'dron *n.* a gigantic club-moss frequently found in coal.

Lepidop'tera *n.pl.* an order of insects having four wings covered with fine gossamer scales, as moths, butterflies, etc.

Lese-maj'esty (lēz-) *n.* treason.

Le'sion *n.* an injury, injurious change in the texture or action of an organ of the body.

Less *a.* (comparative of little), not so much.—*adv.* to a smaller extent or degree.—*pron.* a less amount or number.—*prep.* after deducting, minus.—**less'en** *v.t.* to diminish.—**less'er** *a. Syn.* of " lessen," reduce, abate, abridge, contract, narrow, curtail, retrench, weaken, impair, lower, degrade, be reduced, sink, shrink, dwindle. *Ant.* increase, grow, swell, spread, expand, dilate, extend, multiply, amplify, magnify, inflate, develop, strengthen.

Lessee *see* LEASE.

Less'on *n.* a portion of Scripture read in church; something to be learnt by a pupil; a part of a course of teaching; an experience that teaches.—*v.t.* to teach, discipline.

Lessor *see* LEASE.

Lest *conj.* in order that . . . not, for fear that.

Let *v.t.* to allow, enable, cause to; allow to escape; grant use of for rent, to lease.— *v.i.* to be leased.

Let *v.t.* to hinder.—*n.* a hindrance; in games, an obstruction of a ball or player cancelling the stroke.

Le'thal *a.* deadly.

Leth'argy *n.* drowsiness, apathy, want of energy or interest. — **lethar'gic** *a.* — **lethar'gically** *adv.*

Lett'er *n.* one of the symbols with which words are written; a written message. —*pl.* literature, knowledge of books.—*v.t.* to mark with letters.—**lett'ered** *a.* learned. —**lett'erpress** *n.* matter printed from type.

Lett'uce (-tis) *n.* a plant grown for use as salad.

Leu'cocyte (lū-ko-) *n.* one of the white corpuscles of the blood, which destroys bacteria and other organisms.

Levant' *v.i.* to run away; to decamp.—**levanter** *n.*

Lev'ee *n.* a sovereign's reception for men only; formerly, a great person's reception on rising; in U.S., a pier or embankment.

Lev'el *n.* an instrument for showing or testing a horizontal line or surface; such line or surface; a horizontal passage in a mine; a social or moral standard.—*a.* horizontal; even in surface; even in style, quality, etc. —*v.t.* to make level, bring to the same level; to lay low; to aim (a gun).—**level-head'ed** *a.* not apt to be carried away by emotion or excitement.—**lev'eller** *n.* one who would abolish social distinctions.

Le'ver *n.* a bar used to apply force at one end by pressure exerted at the other, a point in between resting against a fixed support.—**le'verage** *n.* the action or power of a lever.

Lev'eret *n.* a young hare.

Levi'athan *n.* a sea-monster; a huge ship; anything very large of its kind.

Lev'ity *n.* inclination to make a joke of serious matters, frivolity.—**levita'tion** *n.* the power of raising a solid body into the air by spiritualism. —**lev'itate** *v.t.* and *i.* *Syn.* buoyancy, inconstancy, fickleness, unsteadiness, volatility, flightiness. *Ant.* weight, gravity, oppressiveness, sadness, languor, sluggishness.

Lev'y *n.* the act of collecting taxes or enrolling troops; amount or number levied.— *v.t.* to raise or impose by compulsion.

Lewd *a.* indecent.—**lewd'ly** *adv.*— **lewd'ness** *n.*

Lew'isite (lōō-) *n.* an explosive compound with peculiarly destructive properties.

Lex'icon *n.* a dictionary.— **lexicog'raphy** *n.* the art of writing dictionaries. — **lexicog'rapher** *n.*

Li'able *a.* subject (to), exposed (to), answerable.—

liabil'ity *n.* state of being liable.—*pl.* debts.

Liai'son (li-ā-zong) *n.* union; connection; an intimacy, *esp.* secret; illicit intimacy between a man and a woman. —**liaison officer,** an officer employed to keep in touch with each other two or more bodies of troops under different commands.

Liar *see* LIE.

Liba'tion *n.* drink poured out as an offering to the gods.

Li'bel *n.* a published statement damaging to a person's reputation.—*v.t.* to publish a libel against.—**li'bellous** *a.*

Lib'eral *a.* generous; openminded; of a political party, favouring changes making towards democracy.—*n.* one of such a party.—**lib'eralism** *n.* the principles of a Liberal party.—**liberal'ity** *n.* munificence.—**lib'eralise** *v.t.*—**lib'erally** *adv.*—**lib'erate** *v.t.* to set free.—**libera'tion** *n.*—**lib'erator** *n.*—**lib'erty** *n.* freedom.—**lib'ertine** (-ēn) *n.* a dissolute man.—*a.* dissolute. —**lib'ertinism** *n.*

Libid'inous *a.* lustful.

Libi'do (-bē-) *n.* in psychology, the emotional craving which is said by psycho-analysis to lie behind all human impulse, and the repression of which may give rise to pathological conditions.

Li'brary *n.* a collection of books; a place where the books are kept; a reading or writing room in a house.— **librar'ian** (-ér-) *n.* a keeper of a library.—**librar'ianship**

n.—librett'o *n.* the book of words of an opera.—librett'ist *n.*

Li'cence *n.* leave, permission; formal permission; the document giving it; excessive liberty; dissoluteness; a writer's or artist's transgression of the rules of his art (often poetic licence).—li'cense, li'cence *v.t.* to grant a licence to.—licen'tiate *n.* one licensed to practise an art or profession.—licen'tious *a.* sexually immoral.—licen'tiously *adv.*—licensee' *n.* the holder of a licence.

Li'chen (-k-) *n.* a small flowerless plant forming a crust on rocks, trees, etc.—li'chened *a.*

Lich'-gate, lych'-gate *n.* the roofed gate of a churchyard, under which a corpse is placed to await the clergyman at a funeral.

Lick *v.t.* to pass the tongue over.—*n.* an act of licking.

Lid *n.* a movable cover; the cover of the eye.

Li'do (lē-) *n.* a pleasure resort, usually by the sea.

Lie *v.i.* to be horizontal or at rest; to be situated; to recline.—*n.* direction; state (of affairs, etc.). *Syn.* to remain, to lodge, to sleep, to consist in, to belong to. *Ant.* move, stir, stand.

Lie *v.i.* to make a false statement.—*n.* an untrue statement.—li'ar *n.*

Lief (lēf) *adv.* gladly.—*a.* dear.

Liege (lēj) *a.* bound to render feudal service.—*n.* a vassal; a lord; a loyal subject.

Lien (lē-en) *n.* a right to hold property until a claim is met.

Lieu (lū) *n.* in lieu of, instead of.—lieuten'ant (*Army* left-, *Navy and U.S.* lōōt-) *n.* a substitute; a junior army or navy officer.

Life *n.* lives *pl.* the active principle of the existence of animals and plants, animate existence; the time of its lasting; the history of such an existence; a manner of living; vigour, vivacity.—life'less *a.*

Lift *v.t.* to raise to a higher position.—*v.i.* to rise.—*n.* an apparatus to raise things, an elevator; an act of lifting.

Lig'ament *n.* a band of tissue joining bones.—lig'ature *n.* a thread for tying up an artery.

Light (līt) *a.* of, or bearing, little weight; gentle; easy, requiring little effort; trivial.—*adv.* in a light manner.—light'en *v.t.* to reduce or remove a load, etc.—light'ly *adv.*—light'ness *n.*—lights *n.pl.* lungs of animals.—light' *v.i.* to get down from a horse or vehicle; to come by chance (upon).—light'er *n.* a large boat used for unloading ships.

Light (līt) *n.* the natural agent by which things are visible; a source of this; a window; mental vision; the light part of anything.—*a.* bright; pale, not dark.—*v.t.* to set burning; to give light to.—*v.i.* to take fire; to brighten.—light'en *v.t.* to give light to.—light'ning *n.* a visible discharge of electricity in the atmosphere.—**light'house** *n.* a tower with a light to guide ships.—**light'some** *a.* radiant.

Lig'neous *a.* of, or of the nature of, wood.

Like *a.* similar, resembling.— *adv.* in the manner of.— *pron.* a similar thing.— **like'ly** *a.* probably true; hopeful, promising. — *adv.* probably.—**like'lihood** *n.*— **li'ken** *v.t.* to compare.— **like'ness** *n.* quality of being like; a portrait.—**like'wise** *adv.* in like manner.—**like** *v.t.* to find agreeable.—*v.i.* to be pleasing.—**like'able** *a. Syn.* correspondent, analogous, allied, parallel, likely, probable. *Ant.* different, distinct, dissimilar, varied, diverse, discordant.

Li'lac *n.* a shrub bearing pale violet flowers; their colour.— *a.* of this colour.

Lilt *v.t.* and *i.* to sing merrily.— *n.* a rhythmical effect in music.

Lil'y *n.* a bulbous flowering plant.

Limb (lim) *n.* an arm or leg, a branch of a tree.

Limb (lim) *n.* the edge of the sun or moon.

Lim'ber *n.* the detachable front part of a gun-carriage. —*v.t.* to attach the limber to (a gun).

Lim'ber *a.* pliant, lithe.

Lim'bo *n.* a supposed region on the borders of Hell for unbaptised persons, etc.; prison.

Lim'bo *n.* in South Africa, a coloured cotton fabric worn by the natives.

Lime *n.* a sticky substance used for catching birds; the alkaline earth from which mortar is made.— *v.t.* to smear, or catch, with lime, to treat (land) with lime.—**lime'stone** *n.* rock which yields lime when burnt.

Lime *n.* a small acid fruit like a lemon.

Lime *n.* an ornamental tree.

Lim'erick *n.* self-contained, nonsensical, humorous or wittily improper stanza, rhyming *aabba*; its essentials are lilt and point.

Lim'it *n.* a boundary; utmost extent or duration.—*v.t.* to restrict, bound.—**limita'tion** *n.*—**lim'itable** *a.*

Limn (lim) *v.t.* to paint, depict.

Lim'ousine (-zēn) *n.* a closed type of motor-car, with the top projecting over the driver's seat.

Limp *a.* without firmness or stiffness.—**Limp'ly** *adv.*

Limp *v.i.* to walk lamely.—*n.* a limping gait.

Limp'et *n.* a shellfish which sticks tightly to rocks.

Limp'id *a.* clear.—**limpid'ity** *n.*—**limp'idly** *adv.*

Lin'ament *n.* a tent for a wound; lint.

Linch'-pin *n.* a pin to hold a wheel on its axle.

Lincrus'ta *n.* a material, canvas-backed and designed in solid relief, used on walls and ceilings instead of paper, etc.

Lind'en *n.* the lime tree.

Line *n.* a linen thread; any cord or string; a wire; a

stroke made with a pen, etc.; a long narrow mark; continuous length without breadth; a row; a series; course; province of activity. —*v.t.* to cover inside; to mark with a line or lines; to bring into line.—li'ning *n.* a covering for the inside of a garment, etc.—lin'eage *n.* descent from, or the descendants of, an ancestor.—lin'eal *a.* of lines; in direct line of descent.—lin'eament *n.* feature.—lin'ear *a.* of or in lines.—lin'en *a.* made of flax.—*n.* cloth made of flax; linen articles collectively.

Ling *n.* a slender fish.

Ling *n.* a kind of heather.

Ling'er (-ng-g-) *v.i.* to tarry, loiter; remain long.

Ling'ual (-ng-gw-) *a.* of the tongue or language.—*n.* a lingual sound.—ling'uist *n.* one skilled in languages.—linguist'ic *a.* of languages.—*n.* in *pl.* the science of languages.

Lin'iment *n.* embrocation.

Link *n.* a ring of a chain.—*v.t.* to join with, or as with, a link.—*v.i.* to be so joined.

Link *n.* a torch.

Links *n.pl.* ground on which golf is played; grassed sandhills.

Linn'et *n.* a familiar songbird.

Lino'leum *n.* a kind of floorcloth in the manufacture of which linseed oil is largely used.

Li'notype *n.* a machine for producing lines of words cast in one piece.

Lin'seed *n.* the seed of flax.

Lint *n.* soft material for dressing wounds.

Lint'el *n.* the top piece of a door or window.

Li'on *n.* a large animal of the cat tribe; a person of importance.—li'oness *fem.*—li'onise *v.t.* to treat as a celebrity.

Lip *n.* either edge of the mouth; an edge or margin.

Liq'uid *a.* fluid, not solid or gaseous; bright, clear.—*n.* a liquid substance.—liq'uefy *v.t.* and *i.*—liquefac'tion *n.*—liques'cent *a.* tending to become liquid.—liques'cence *n.*—liq'uidate *v.t.* to pay (debt); to arrange the affairs of, and dissolve (a company).—liquida'tion *n.*—liq'uidator *n.*—liq'uor (lik-er) *n.* a liquid, *esp.* an alcoholic one for drinking.—liqueur' (li-kūr) *n.* an alcoholic liquor flavoured and sweetened.

Liq'uorice (-ker-is) *n.* a black substance used in medicine and as a sweetmeat; the plant or its root, from which the substance is obtained.

Lisle (līl) *n.* a fine handtwisted cotton thread used for making stockings.

Lisp *v.t.* and *i.* to speak with faulty pronunciation of the sibilants; speak falteringly. —*n.* a lisping.

Liss'om *a.* supple, agile.

List *n.* the border or edge of cloth; strips of cloth, *esp.* used as material for slippers; a roll or catalogue.—*pl.* a space for tilting.—*v.t.* to write down in a list.

List v.i. to desire; of a ship, to incline, lean to one side.— n. desire; inclination of a ship.—**list′less** a. indifferent, languid.—**list′lessly** adv.

List′ v.t. and i. to listen.—**list′en** (lis-en) v.i. to try to hear, give attention in order to hear.—**list′ener** n.

Lit′any n. a form of prayer.

Lit′eral a. of letters; exact as to words; according to the sense of actual words, not figurative.—**lit′erally** adv.—**lit′erary** a. of, or learned in, literature.—**li′terate** a. educated.—**lit′eracy** n.—**litera′tim** adv. letter for letter.—**lit′erature** n. books and writings of artistic value; the production of these; the profession of writers.

Lith′arge n. protoxide of lead, produced by exposing melted lead to a current of air.

Lithe a. supple.—**lithe′some** a.

Lithog′raphy n. the making of drawings on stone for printing.—**lith′ograph** n. a print so produced.—v.t. to print thus.—**lithog′rapher** n.—**lithograph′ic** a.

Lith′osphere n. the solid earth.

Lit′igate v.i. to go to law.—**lit′igant** a. and n.—**litiga′tion** n.—**liti′gious** (-j-) a. fond of going to law.

Lit′mus n. a blue colouring-matter turned red by acids.

Lit′otes (-o-tēz) n. a weaker expression meant to suggest a stronger.

Litre (lē-ter) n. the measure of capacity in the French decimal system.

Litt′er n. a portable couch; a kind of stretcher for the wounded; straw, etc., as bedding for animals; fragments lying about, untidy refuse of paper, etc.; the young of an animal produced at a birth.—v.t. to strew with litter; to bring forth.

Lit′tle a. small, not much.—n. a small quantity.—adv. slightly. Syn. minute, diminutive, tiny, pigmy, short, scanty, inconsiderable, petty, slender, feeble, weak, trivial, paltry, selfish, narrow, contemptible. Ant. large, big, huge, extensive, spacious, frequent, long.

Litt′oral a. of, or on, the seashore.—n. a littoral district.

Lit′urgy n. a form of public worship.—**litur′gical** a.

Live (liv) v.i. to have life; to pass one's life, continue in life; dwell; feed.—**liv′ing** n. the action of being in life; means of earning livelihood; a church benefice.

Live (liv) a. living; flaming.

Live′lihood n. means of living.

Live′long a. the livelong day, the whole day.

Live′ly a. brisk, active, vivid.—**live′liness** n. Syn. quick, nimble, smart, alert, sprightly, prompt, blithe, gleeful, jocund, vivacious, airy, expressive, forcible, energetic, spirited, glowing, effervescent. Ant. dull, slow, lethargic, vapid, inert, indifferent, spiritless, dead.

Liv′er n. the organ which secretes bile.

Liv′ery n. allowance of food

for horses; the distinctive dress of the members of a City Company, or of a person's servants.—**liv'ery-man** *n.* a member of a London guild.—**liv'ery-stable** *n.* a stable where horses are kept at a charge, or hired out.

Liv'id *a.* of a bluish pale colour.

Lixiv'iate *v.t.* to form into lye; to impregnate water with alkaline salt, by passing it through the ashes of wood.—**lixivia'tion** *n.*

Liz'ard *n.* a four-footed reptile.

Lla'ma, la'ma (lá-) *n.* a woolly animal used as a beast of burden in S. America.

Load *n.* a burden; the amount usually carried at once; in motoring, the actual load carried by vehicle; resistance against which engine has to work; in electricity, amount of electrical energy drawn from a source.—*v.t.* to put a load on or into; to charge (a gun); to weigh down.—**load'stone, lode'stone** *n.* magnetic iron ore; a magnet.—**load'star, lode'star** *n.* the Pole Star.—**lode** *n.* a vein of ore.

Loaf *n.* **loaves** *pl.* a mass of bread as baked; a cone of sugar.

Loaf *v.i.* to idle.

Loam *n.* a fertile soil.

Loan *n.* a thing lent; an act of lending.—*v.t.* to lend.

Loath, loth (-*th*) *a.* unwilling. —**loath'ly** *a.*—**loath'some** *a.* disgusting.—**loathe** (-TH) *v.t.* to hate, abhor.

Lobb'y *n.* a corridor into which rooms open.

Lobe *n.* the soft hanging part of the ear; any similar flap.

Lob'ster *n.* a shellfish with long tail and claws, which turns scarlet when boiled.

Lo'cal *a.* relating to place; of or existing in a particular place.—**local'ity** *n.* a place, situation; district.—**lo'cally** *adv.*—**lo'calise** *v.t.*—**locate'** *v.t.* to attribute to a place; to find the place of.—**loca'tion** *n.* a placing; situation.—**loc'ative** *a.* and *n.* a grammatical case denoting "place where."

Loch (guttural -ch) *n.* a lake; an arm of the sea.

Lock *n.* a tress of hair.

Lock *n.* an appliance for fastening a door, lid, etc.; the mechanism for discharging a firearm; an enclosure in a river or canal for moving boats from one level to another; a close crowd of vehicles.—*v.t.* to fasten with a lock; join firmly, embrace closely.—*v.i.* to become fixed or united.—**lock'er** *n.* a small cupboard with a lock.—**lock'jaw** *n.* tetanus.—**lock'out** *n.* the exclusion of workmen by employers as a means of coercion.—**lock'smith** *n.* one who makes and mends locks.—**lock'et** *n.* a small pendant of precious metal for a portrait, etc.

Locomo'tive (lō-) *a.* having the power of moving from place to place.—*n.* a steam engine moving from place to place by its own power.—

locomo'tion *n.* action or power of moving from place to place.

Lo'cus *n.*; *pl.* **lo'ci**, a geometrical line, all of whose points satisfy a certain geometrical condition to the exclusion of all other points.

Lo'cust *n.* a destructive winged insect; a tree: its fruit resembling a bean in shape.

Locu'tion *n.* a phrase

Lode *see* LOAD.

Lodge *n.* a house for a shooting or hunting party; a house at the gate of an estate; a meeting-place of a branch of freemasons, etc.; the branch. —*v.t.* to house; deposit.— *v.i.* to live in another's house at a fixed charge; to become fixed after being thrown —**lodg'er** *n.*—**lodge'ment** *n.* a lodging or being lodged.

Loft *n.* an attic; a room over a stable; a gallery in a church. —*v.t.* to send (a golf-ball) high. **loft'y** *a.* of great height; elevated.—**loft'ily** *adv.*

Log *n.* an unhewn portion of a felled tree; an apparatus for measuring the speed of a ship; a journal kept on board ship, etc.—a **log'-book** *n.*

Lo'ganberry *n.* a hybrid plant, being a cross between the blackberry and the raspberry; the fruit itself.

Log'arithm *n.* one of a series of arithmetical functions tabulated for use in calculation.—**logarith'mic** *a.*

Logg'erhead *n.* a blockhead. —at loggerheads, quarrelling.

Logg'ia (loj-a) *n.* a kind of open, elevated gallery in a building.

Log'ic (loj-) *n.* the art of reasoning.—**log'ical** *a.* relating to logic; according to reason; able to reason well. — **log'ically** *adv.* — **logi'cian** *n.*

Loin *n.* the part of the body on either side between ribs and hip.

Loi'ter *v.i.* to waste time on the way, hang about.— **loi'terer** *n.*

Loll *v.i.* to sit or lie lazily; of the tongue, to hang out.— *v.t.* to hang out (the tongue).

Loll'ipop *n.* a sweetmeat.

Lone *a.* solitary.—**lone'ly** *a.* alone; feeling sad because alone.—**lone'liness** *n.*—**lone'some** *a.*

Long *a* having length, *esp.* great length,—*adv.* for a long time. *Syn.* tedious, far-reaching, dilatory, extensive. *Ant.* short, brief, near, concise, laconic, prompt.

Long *v.i.* to have a keen desire.—**long'ing** *n.*

Longev'ity (-j-) *n.* long existence or life.—**longe'val** *a.*

Lon'gitude *n.* distance of a place east or west from a standard meridian.—**longitu'dinal** *a.* of length or longitude.

Loo'fah *n.* the pod of a plant used as a sponge; the plant.

Look *v.i.* to direct or use the eyes; to face; to take care; to seem; to hope.—*n.* a looking; expression; aspect. —**look'ing-glass** *n.* a mirror. —**look'-out** *n.* a watch; a place for watching; a watch-man.

Loom n. a machine for weaving.

Loom v.i. to appear dimly, esp. with vague or enlarged appearance.

Loop n. the figure made by a curved line crossing itself; a similar rounded shape in a cord or rope, etc., crossed on itself; in aviation, an aerial manœuvre in which the aeroplane describes a complete circle, the upper side of the aeroplane being always on the inside of the circle, and the lateral axis always parallel with the ground.—v.t. to form into a loop.—v.i. to form a loop.—**loop'line** n. a part of a railway line which leaves the main line and joins it again. —to loop the loop v.

Loop'hole n. a slit in a wall, esp. for shooting through; a means of escape, of evading a rule without infringing it.

Loose a. not tight or fastened or fixed, or exact or tense; slack; vague; dissolute.—v.t. to set free; unfasten; make slack.—v.i. to shoot, let fly.—**loose'ly** adv.—**loos'en** v.t. to make loose.—**loose'ness** n.

Loot n. and v.t. plunder.

Lop v.t. to cut away twigs and branches; chop off.

Lop v.i. to hang limply.—**lop'ear** n. a drooping ear; a rabbit with such ears.—**lopsi'ded** a. with one side lower than the other, badly balanced.

Loqua'cious a. talkative.—**loquac'ity** (-kwas-) n.

Lo'quat (lō-kwat) n. a low-growing Japanese plum tree, giving yellow, slightly acid fruit, used for preserving; also the fruit itself.

Lord n. a feudal superior; one ruling others; an owner; God; a title of peers.—v.i. to domineer.—**lord'ling** n. a petty lord.—**lord'ly** a.—**lord'liness** n.—**lord'ship** n. rule, ownership; domain; title of peers, e.g. your lordship, etc.

Lore n. learning; body of facts and traditions.

Lorgnette' (lorn-yet') n. eye-glasses with a handle.

Lor'iner n. a maker of bridles, bits, and stirrups;n ame of one of the livery companies of London.

Lorn a. abandoned.

Lorr'y n. a long wagon, without sides, set on four wheels.

Lose (lōōz) v.t. to be deprived of, fail to retain; let slip; fail to get; be late for; be defeated in.—v.i. to suffer loss.—**loss** n. a losing; what is lost; harm or damage resulting from losing. Syn. let fall, mislay, waste, miss, be bereaved of. Ant. gain, win, find, acquire, achieve.

Lot n. one of a set of objects used to decide something by chance (to cast lots); fate. destiny; an item at an auction; a collection; a large quantity.—**lott'ery** n. a gamble in which part of the money paid for tickets is distributed to some owners of tickets selected by chance.—**lott'o** n. a game of chance.

Lo'tion n. a liquid for washing wounds, improving the skin, etc.

Lo'tus n. a legendary plant supposed to yield a fruit causing forgetfulness when eaten: a water-lily.

Loud a. strongly audible; noisy; obtrusive.—**loud'ly** adv.

Lounge v.i. to loll; move lazily.—n. a place for, or a spell of, lounging; a deep chair or sofa.

Lour see LOWER.

Louse n. lice pl. a parasitic insect.—**lous'y** a.

Lout n. an awkward fellow lacking manners.

Lou'ver, lou'vre (lōō-ver) n. a set of boards or slats set parallel and slanting to admit air without rain; a ventilating structure of these.

Love (luv) n. warm affection; sexual passion; a sweetheart; a score of nothing.—v.t. to have love for.—v.i. to be in love.—**lov'able** a.—**love'less** a.—**love'lorn** a. forsaken by, or pining for, a lover.—**love'ly** a. beautiful, delightful.—**lov'er** n.—**love'-bird** n. a small green parrot.—**lov'ing-cup** n. a bowl passed round at a banquet.—**love'-in-a-mist** n. a blue-flowered garden plant.

Low (lō) a. not tall or high or elevated; humble; commonplace; vulgar; dejected; not loud.—**low'er** v.t. to cause or allow to descend; to diminish; degrade.—**low'-land** n. low-lying country.—**Low'lands** n. the less mountainous parts of Scotland.—**Low'lander** n.—**low'ly** a. modest, humble.—**lowli'ness** n.

Low (lō) v.i. of cattle, to utter their cry.—n. the cry.

Low'er, lour v.i. to scowl.—n. a scowl.

Loy'al a. faithful; true to allegiance.—**loy'ally** adv.—**loy'alty** n.—**loy'alist** n.

Loz'enge n. a diamond figure; a small sweetmeat or tablet of medicine.

Lubb'er n. a clumsy fellow.—**lubb'erly** a. awkward.

Lu'bra (-ōō-) n. in Australia, a black woman; a gin.

Lu'bricate v.t. to oil or grease; to make slippery.—**lu'bricant** n. a substance used for this.—**lubrica'tion** n.—**lu'bricator** n.—**lubri'city** n. slipperiness; lewdness.

Luce (-ōō-) n. a pike when full grown.

Lucerne' n. a fodder plant like clover.

Lu'cid (lōō-) a. clear; easily understood.—**lucid'ity** n.—**lu'cidly** adv.—**lu'cent** a. bright.—**Lu'cifer** n. the morning star; Satan.—**lu'cifer** a match.

Lu'cigen (lōō-si-jen) n. a modern light of very great power, produced by the mixture of compressed air and oil at a high temperature.

Lucim'eter (-sim-) n. a photometer, or instrument for measuring the intensity of light.

Luck *n.* fortune, good or ill; chance.—**luck′y** *a.* having good luck.—**luck′less** *a.* having bad luck.—**luck′ily** *adv.*

Lu′cre (lōō-kr) *n.* gain or profit as a motive.—**lu′crative** *a.* yielding profit.

Lu′dicrous (loo-) *a.* absurd, laughable.

Luff *n.* the part of a fore-and-aft sail nearest the mast.— *v.t.* and *i.* to bring (a ship) nearer the wind.

Lug *v.t.* to drag with effort.— *v.i.* to pull hard. — *n.* an act of lugging.—**lugg′age** *n.* traveller's baggage.

Luge (lōōj) *n.* a flat toboggan without runners, on which the rider lies face downwards.

Lug′sail *n.* an oblong sail fixed on a yard which hangs slanting on a mast.—**lugg′er** *n.* a vessel with such sails.

Lugu′brious *a.* mournful.

Luke′warm (look) *a.* moderately warm, tepid; lacking enthusiasm, indifferent.

Lull *v.t.* to soothe with sounds, sing to sleep; to make quiet.—*v.i.* to become quiet.—*n.* a brief time of quiet in storm or pain.—**lull′aby** (-bĭ) *n.* a lulling song or sounds.

Lum′bar *a.* relating to the loins.—**lumba′go** *n.* rheumatism in the loins.

Lum′ber *v.i.* to move heavily; obstruct.—*n.* disused articles, useless rubbish; timber, *esp.* sawn in planks.

Lu′minous (lōō-) *a.* bright, shedding light.—**lu′minary**

n. a heavenly body giving light; a person noted for learning.—**luminos′ity** *n.* *Syn.* radiant, brilliant, vivid, lucid, clear. *Ant.* black, dark, obscure, gloomy.

Lump *n.* a shapeless piece or mass; a swelling; a sum covering various items.— *v.t.* to throw together in one mass or sum.—*v.i.* to move heavily.—**lump′ish** *a.* clumsy; stupid.—**lumo′y** *a.*

Lu′nar (lōō-) *a.* relating to the moon.—**lunar caustic**, nitrate of silver.—**lu′natic** *a.* insane. —*n.* an insane person.— **lu′nacy** *n.*

Lunch *n.* a meal taken in the middle of the day.— **lunch′eon** (-shn) *n.* a lunch; a midday banquet.

Lung *n.* an air-breathing organ.

Lunge *v.i.* to thrust with a sword, etc.—*n.* such thrust, or thrusting movement of the body.

Lu′pus (-ōō-) *n.* a tuberculous inflammation of the skin.— **lu′pine** *a.* like a wolf.— **lu′pin**, **lu′pine** *n.* a leguminous plant having showy flowers.

Lurch *n.* **to leave in the lurch**, to leave in difficulties, abandon (a comrade).

Lurch *n.* a sudden roll to one side.—*v.i.* to make a lurch.

Lurch′er *n.* a poacher's mongrel dog.

Lure *n.* a falconer's apparatus for recalling a hawk; something which entices, a bait.— *v.t.* to recall (a hawk); to entice.

Lu'rid *a.* ghastly, pale, glaring. —lu'ridly *adv.*

Lurk *v.i.* to lie hidden; be latent.

Lus'cious (-shus) *a.* sweet; sickly sweet; over-rich. *Syn.* honeyed, delicious, savoury, palatable. *Ant.* sour, unpalatable, nauseous, disgusting.

Lush *a.* of grass, etc., luxuriant and juicy.

Lust *n.* sensuous desire; passionate desire.—*v.i.* to have passionate desire.—lust'ful *a.* —lust'y *a.* healthy, vigorous. —lust'ily *adv.*

Lus'tre *n.* gloss, shine; splendid reputation, glory; glossy material.—lus'trous *a.*

Lus'tre, lus'trum *n.* a period of five years.—lustra'tion *n.* purification by sacrifice.— lus'trate *v.t.*—lus'tral *a.*

Lute (lōōt) *n.* a stringed musical instrument played with the fingers.—lu'tanist *n.* a lute-player.

Lute, lu'ting (lōōt, lōō-ting) *n.* a composition of clay or other tenacious substance, used for making joints airtight.—*v.t.* to close or coat with lute.

Lux'ury *n.* possession and use of costly and choice things for enjoyment; an enjoyable but not necessary thing; comfortable surroundings.— luxu'rious *a.*—luxu'riously *adv.*—luxu'riate *v.i.* to indulge in luxury; to grow rank; to take delight (in).— luxu'riant *a.* growing profusely; abundant.—luxu'riantly *adv.*—luxu'riance *n.*

Lychgate *see* LICHGATE.

Lydd'ite *n.* a powerful explosive used in shells.

Lye *n.* water made alkali with wood ashes, etc., for washing.

Lymph *n.* colourless animal fluid; the matter from cowpox used in vaccination.— lymphat'ic *a.* of lymph; flabby, sluggish.—*n.* a vessel in the body conveying lymph.

Lynch *n.* lynch law, the procedure of a self-appointed court trying and executing an accused person.—*v.t.* to put to death without proper trial.

Lynx *n.* an animal of the cat tribe noted for keen sight.— lynx-eyed *a.* quick-sighted.

Lyre *n.* an instrument like a harp.—lyr'ic, lyr'ical (lir-) *a.* relating to the lyre; meant to be sung; of short poems, expressing the poet's own thoughts and feelings; describes a poet who writes such poems.—lyr'ic *n.* a lyric poem.—lyr'ist *n.* a lyric poet.

M

Maca'bre (-à-ber) *a.* gruesomely imaginative.

Macad'am *n.* road surface, layers of small broken stone. —macad'amise *v.t.* to pave a road with broken stones.

Macaro'ni *n.* Italian paste of wheat in long tubes.— macaroon' *n.* small cake containing ground almonds.

Macaw' *n.* a parrot.

Mace *n.* staff with a metal head; a staff of office carried before officials.

Mace *n.* spice made of the husk of the nutmeg.

Mac'erate *v.t.* to soften by steeping; to cause to waste away.—**macera'tion** *n.*

Machine' (-shēn) *n.* an apparatus combining the action of several parts, to apply mechanical force for some purpose; a person like a machine from regulation or sensibility; a controlling organisation; a bicycle, vehicle, motor car.—*v.t.* to sew, print with a machine. —**machin'ery** (-ĕ-) *n.* parts of a machine collectively; machines.—**machi'nist** *n.* one who makes or works machines.—**machine'-gun** *n.* gun firing repeatedly and continuously by a loading and firing mechanism.—**machina'tion** (-kin-) *n.* plotting, intrigue.—**mac'hinate** *v.i.* to lay plots.

Mack'erel *n.* a sea-fish with blue and silver barred skin.

Mack'inaw *n.* in N. America, a heavy woollen cloth; a thick blanket; a boat with sharp-pointed ends used by explorers, traders, etc.

Mack'intosh *n.* cloth waterproofed with a layer of rubber; a coat made of this.

Mac'rocosm *n.* the universe.

Mad *a.* suffering from mental disease, insane; wildly foolish; excited.—**mad'ly** *adv.*— **mad'man** *n.*—**mad'ness** *n.*—

mad'den *v.t.* to make mad.— **mad'cap** *n.* reckless person.

Mad'am *n.* polite form of address to women.

Madd'er *n.* a climbing plant; its root; a dye-stuff made from this.

Madeir'a (-dĕr-) *n.* a rich sherry wine, made in *Madeira*.

Madonn'a *n.* the Virgin Mary; a picture or statue of the Virgin Mary.

Mad'repore *n.* coral.

Mad'rigal *n.* short love poem or song; part-song for three or more voices.

Maff'ick *v.i.* to exult riotously.

Magazine' (-zēn) *n.* storehouse for explosives and the military stores; a periodical with stories and articles by different writers; an appliance for supplying cartridges automatically to a gun.

Magent'a (-j-) *n.* a crimson alkaline dye.—*a.* of this colour.

Magg'ot *n.* a grub, a lava; a crazy notion.—**magg'oty** *a.*

Mag'ic (-j-) *n.* the art of influencing events by controlling nature or spirits, any mysterious agency of power; witchcraft, conjuring. —**magic-lant'ern** *n.* an apparatus by which pictures are projected on a white screen in a darkened room. — **mag'ical** *a.* — **mag'ically** *adv.*—**magi'cian** *n.*—**ma'gi** *n.pl.* a priest of ancient Persia; the wise men from the East.

Mag'istrate (-j-) *n.* civil officer administering the

law.—**magiste'rial** *a.* at or referring to a magistrate or master; dictatorial.—**mag'istracy** *n.* the office of a magistrate; magistrates collectively.

Mag'ma *n.* a thick residuum; the glassy base of an igneous rock; any crude mixture in the form of a thin paste.

Magnan'imous *a.* great-souled, above resentment, etc.—**magnanim'ity** *n.*

Mag'nate *n.* a person of influence by wealth or position.

Magne'sium *n.* metallic chemical element.—**magne'sia** *n.* a white powder compound of this used in medicine.

Mag'net *n.* a piece of iron having the properties of attracting iron and pointing north and south when suspended; loadstone.—**magnet'ic** *a.*—**magnet'ically** *adv.*—**mag'netism** *n.* magnetic phenomena; the science of this; personal charm or power of attracting others.—**mag'netise** *v.t.* to make into a magnet.—**magnetisa'tion** *n.*—**magne'to** *n.* the apparatus for ignition in an internal combustion engine.—**magnetom'eter** *n.* an instrument used to measure magnetic intensity.—**magnetic equator**, a line round the earth where the magnetic needle has no dip.

Magnif'icent *a.* splendid, stately, imposing, excellent.—**magnif'icently** *a.*—**magnif'icence** *n.*—**mag'nify** (-fī) *v.t.* to exaggerate; to make greater; to increase the apparent size, as with a lens; to praise.

Magnil'oquent *a.* speaking loftily.—**magnil'oquence** *n.*

Mag'nitude *n.* size; importance.

Magno'lia *n.* flowering tree.

Mag'num *n.* a wine bottle holding two quarts.

Mag'pie *n.* a black-and-white chattering bird.

Mag'ra *n.* a contrivance used by aboriginal mothers in Australia to carry their infants on their backs.

Mahl'stick (mäl-) *n.* a shaft used by painters to support the right hand.

Mahog'any *n.* a reddish brown wood.

Ma'hout *n.* an elephant driver.

Maid'en *n.* a young unmarried woman.—*a.* unmarried; of, or suited to, a maiden; having a blank record.—**maid** *n.* a young unmarried woman; a woman servant.—**maid'enhair** *n.* a fern with delicate stalks and fronds.—**maid'enhead** *n.* virginity.—**maid'enhood** *n.*—**maid'only** *a.*

Mail *n.* armour made of interlaced rings or overlapping plates.—**mail'ed** *a.* covered with mail.

Mail *n.* bag of letters; the letters conveyed at one time; the official despatch of letters.—*v.t.* to send by mail.

Maim *v.t.* to cripple, mutilate.

Main *n.* an open ocean; the chief matter; strength, power.—*a.* chief, principal, leading.—**main'land** *n.* a stretch of land which forms the main part of the country.—main'ly **a**.—main'mast *n*. the chief mast in a ship.—main'sail *n*. the lowest sail of a mainmast.—main'-spring *n*. chief spring of a watch or clock.

Maintain' *v.t.* to carry on; to preserve; to support, sustain, keep up; to keep supplied; to affirm.—maintain'able *a.* —main'tenance *n.* *Syn.* to supply with, contend, uphold, assert. *Ant.* drop, neglect, abandon, discontinue, cease.

Maisonette' (mä-zon-et) *n.* a small house compactly built and internally arranged; part of house fitted as self-contained dwelling; a flat.

Maize *n.* Indian corn.

Majesty *n.* stateliness; kingship or queenship.—majes'tic *a.*—majes'tically *adv.*

Majol'ica *n.* fine glazed Italian pottery.

Ma'jor *a.* greater; out of minority.—*n.* one out of minority; an officer in the army, ranking next above a captain.—major'ity *n.* the state of being a major; the greater number; the larger party voting together; the excess of the vote on one side; the rank of a major.—major-do'mo *n.* head-servant of a large household.

Make *v.t.* to construct; produce; bring into being; establish; appoint; amount to; to cause to do something; to accomplish; to reach; to earn.—*v.i.* tend; contribute; of the tide, to rise.—*n.* style of construction, form, manufacture.—ma'ker *n.*—make'-shift *n.* a method, tool, etc., used for want of something better.—make'weight *n.* a trifle added to make something seem stronger or better. *Syn.* to fashion, create, effect, gain. *Ant.* break, destroy, lose, mar.

Malacc'a *n.* a brown cane used for walking-sticks, etc.

Mal'achite (-kīt) *n.* a green mineral.

Mal- *prefix* ill, badly, miss; not. — maladjust'ment *n.* faulty adjustment.—maladministra'tion *n.* faulty administration.—mal'content *a.* actively discontented.—*n.* a malcontent person.—malediction *n.* a curse.—mal'efactor *n.* a criminal.—malef'icent *a* hurtful.—malef'icence *n.*—malev'olent *a.* full of ill-will.—malev'olence *n.*—malforma'tion *n.* faulty formation.— malo'dorous *a.* evil-smelling.—malprac'tice *n.* wrong-doing.—mal'treat *v.t.* to treat ill, handle roughly.—maltreat'ment *a.*—malversa'tion *n.* corrupt handling of trust money.

Mal'ady *n.* a disease.

Mal'aga *n.* a wine from *Malaga*, Spain.

Malar'ia (-ēr-) *n.* a fever due to mosquito bites.—malar'ial *a.*—malar'ious *a.*

Male *a.* of the begetting sex; of men or male animals.—*n.* a male person or animal.

Mal'i (-ä-) *n.* in South Africa, money.

Ma'lic a. derived from the apple.

Mal'ice n. action of ill-will.—**malic'ious** a.—**malic'iously** adv. Syn. malevolence, maliciousness, rancour, malignity, vindictiveness, hate. Ant. benevolence, goodwill, sympathy, charity, kindness, love.

Malign' (-lin) a. hurtful.—v.t. to slander, misrepresent.—**malig'nant** a. feeling extreme ill-will; of a disease, very virulent.—**malig'nantly** adv.—**malig'nancy** n.—**malig'nity** n. malignant disposition.

Maling'erer (-ng-g-) n. one who pretends illness to escape duty.—**maling'er** v.i.

Mall (mel, mal) n. a level, shaded walk.

Mall'ard n. the male of the wild duck.

Mall'eable a. capable of being hammered into shape.—**malleabil'ity** n.—**mall'et** n. hammer, usually of wood.

Mall'ow n. a wild plant with purple flowers.

Malm'sey (màm-) n. a strong sweet wine.

Malt n. grain used for brewing.—v.t. to make into malt.—**malt'ster** n.

Malthu'sian (-ew-zi-) a. pertaining to or supporting the teaching of Malthus.—n. a follower of Malthus; one who holds that some check is necessary to prevent over-population.

Mam'ba n. a poisonous South African snake, usually black in colour.

Mamm'al a. an animal of the type feeding their young with their milk.—**mamma'lian** a.

Mamm'on n. wealth as an object of pursuit or of evil influence; the devil of covetousness.

Mamm'oth n. an extinct animal like an elephant.

Man n. men pl. a human being; person; the human race; an adult human male; a man-servant; a piece used in a game, e.g. chess.—v.t. to supply (a ship, etc.) with necessary men.—**man'ful** a. brave, resolute.—**man'fully** adv.—**man'hole** n. an opening through which a man may pass.—**man'hood** n.—**man'ikin** n. a little man; a model of the human body.—**mankind'** n. human beings in general.—**man'like** a.—**man'ly** a.—**man'liness** n.—**mann'ish** a. manlike.—**man'slaughter** n. killing of a human being unintentionally or in provocation.

Man'acle n. a fetter for the hand.—v.t. handcuff.

Man'age v.t. to carry on, conduct; to succeed in doing; to handle; to persuade.—v.i. to conduct affairs.—**man'ageable** a.—**man'agement** n.—**man'ager** n.—**man'ageress** fem.—**manage'rial** a. Syn. to govern, train, influence, husband. Ant. neglect, ignore, disregard.

Manda'mus n. a writ from a superior court to an inferior, to a corporation, or to a person, directing the performance of some duty.

Man'darin n. a Chinese provincial governor; figuratively, any high government official; a Chinese variety of orange.

Man'date a. command of, or commission to act for another; commission from the League of Nations to govern a people not qualified for independence; an instruction from an electorate to a representative. —**man'datary** n. a holder of a man'date.— **man'datory** a.

Man'dible n. a lower jaw bone; either part of a bird's beak. —**mandib'ular** a.

Man'dolin(e) n. a stringed musical instrument like a lute.

Man'drake, mandrag'ora n. a narcotic plant.

Man'drell n. an axis on which material revolves in a lathe; a rod round which metal is cast or forged.

Man'drill n. a large baboon.

Mane n. the long hair at the back of the neck of a horse, lion, etc.

Mang'anese (-ng-g-) n. a metallic element; a black oxide of this, used in glass-making, etc.

Mange (-ā-) n. a skin disease of dogs and other animals.— **ma'ngy** a.

Mang'el-wurz'el (-g-) **mang'-old-wurz'el** n. a variety of beet, used as cattle food.

Man'ger (mān-jer) n. an eating-trough in a stable.

Mang'le (mang-gl) n. a machine for rolling washed linen, etc.—v.t. to put through a mangle.

Mang'le (mang-gl) v.t. to hack, mutilate, spoil.

Mang'o (-ng-gō) n. an Indian fruit; the tree bearing it.

Mang'osteen n. fruit similar to an orange, but darker, with white, juicy pulp, found in the East Indies.

Manhatt'an n. a cocktail, orig. American, containing whisky, vermouth, gin, bitters.

Ma'nia n. madness; prevailing craze.—**ma'niac** a. affected by mania.—n. a mad person. —**ma'niacal** a.

Man'icure n. the treatment of the finger-nails and hands; person doing this professionally.—v.t. to apply such treatment to.—**man'icurist** n.

Man'ifest a. clearly revealed, visible, undoubted.—v.t. to make manifest.—n. a list of cargo for the Customs.— **manifesta'tion** n.—**manifes'to** n. a declaration of policy by a sovereign or commander or body of persons. *Syn.* clear, evident, obvious; —of v. to show, display, exhibit, evince. *Ant* of a. obscure, dim, shadowy.

Man'ifold a. numerous and varied.—v.t. to make copies of (a document).

Manikin see MAN.

Manil'a, manill'a n. fibre used for ropes; a cheroot.

Manip'ulate v.t. to handle; to deal with skilfully; to manage craftily.—**manip'ulator** n.— **manipula'tion** n.—**manip'ulative** a.

Mann'a n. the food of the Israelites in the wilderness;

a sweet tree-juice used in medicine.

Mann'equin (or -kin) n. live model employed by dress-makers, etc.

Mann'er n. the way a thing happens or is done; a sort or kind; custom; style.—pl. social behaviour.—mann'er-ism n. addiction to a literary or artistic manner; a habitual trick of style or behaviour.—mann'erly a. having good manners.

Manœuv're (-ōō-ver) n. a movement of troops or ships in war.—v.t. to cause to perform manœuvres.—v.i. to perform manœuvres; employ stratagems, to work adroitly.

Man'or n. a unit of land in the feudal period.—man'or-house n. the residence of the lord of the manor.—manor'ial a.

Man'sion n. a large dwelling-house.—manse n. a minister's house.

Man'suetude (-swit-) n. mild temper.

Man'tel n. the structure enclosing a fireplace.—man'tel-shelf n. a shelf at the top of the mantel.—man'telpiece n. a mantel or a mantel-shelf.

Man'ticore n. a fabulous monster with a human head, a lion's body and a scorpion's tail; an unidenti-fied monkey.

Mantill'a n. a scarf worn as a head-dress.

Man'tle n. a loose cloak; a covering; a hood fixed round a gas jet for incandescent light.—v.t. to cover; to con-ceal.—v.i. to become covered with scum; of the blood, to rush to the cheeks: of the face, to blush.—mant'let n. a short mantle; a movable bullet-proof screen. *Syn.* of *v.t.* and *v.i.* cloak, over-spread, disguise, expand, be suffused, flush, effervesce, foam, froth, cream. *Ant.* of *v.t.* uncover, expose, strip, lay bare, disclose.

Man'ual a. of, or done with, the hands.—n. a handbook, a text-book; an organ key-board.

Manufac'ture n. the making of articles or materials, *esp.* in large quantities, for sale.—v.t. to produce (articles), to work up (materials) into finished articles.—manufac'-tory n. factory or workshop.—manufac'turer n. the owner of a factory.

Manumit' v.t. to give freedom to (a slave).—manumis'sion n.

Manure' v.t. to enrich land.—n dung or other substances used for fertilising land.

Man'uscript a. written by hand.—n. a book, docu-ment, etc., written by hand; copy of matter to be printed.

Manx a. of the Isle of Man.—n. the Manx language.

Man'y (men-i) a. numerous.—n. a large number.

Mao'ri (mou-ri) n. an abor-igine of New Zealand.—a. pertaining to the aborigines of New Zealand.

Map n. flat representation of the earth or some part of it,

or of the heavens.—*v.t.* to make a map of.

Ma'ple *n.* a tree of the syca-more family, a variety which yields sugar.

Mar *v.t.* to spoil, impair.—**mar'plot** *n.* one who frus-trates plans.

Mar'abou *n.* a kind of stork; the soft white lower tail feathers of this bird, used to trim hats, etc.; also, a kind of silk; a Mohammedan sorcerer of North Africa.

Maraschi'no (-kĕ·) *n.* a li-queur distilled from cherries.

Maraud' *v.t.* and *i.* to make a raid for plunder.—**maraud'er** *n.*

Mar'ble *n.* a kind of lime stone capable of taking a polish; a slab of this; a small ball used in a game called marbles.—*v.t.* to colour so as to resemble veined marble.

March *n.* the third month.

March *n.* a border or frontier.—*v.i.* to border.

March *v.i.* to walk with a military step; to start on a march; to go.—*v.t.* to cause to march or go.—*n.* the action of marching; the distance marched in a day; a tune intended to accompany marching.

March'ioness (-shon-) *n.* the wife or widow of a mar-quis.

Marco'nigram *n.* a wireless telegram.

Mare (mĕr) *n.* the female of the horse or other equine animal.—**mare's' nest** *n.* fancied discovery.

Mar'garine (-g-) *n.* vegetable substance imitating butter.

Mar'gin (-j-) *n.* the border or edge; amount allowed be-yond what is absolutely necessary; the blank space round a printed page.—**marge** *n.* a margin.—**mar'ginal** *a.* *Syn.* rim, brink, brim, verge, skirt, limit, confine, room, space, latitude. *Ant.* centre, middle.

Mar'guerite (-ĕt) *n.* ox-eye daisy.

Mar'igold *n.* a plant with yellow flowers.

Marinade' *n.* a spiced liquor made of vinegar and wine in which fish are pickled to improve their flavour.

Marine' (-ĕn) *a.* of the sea or shipping; used at sea.—*n.* shipping collectively; a sol-dier serving on board a ship.—**mar'iner** *n.* a sailor.

Marionette' *n.* a puppet worked with strings.

Mar'ital *a.* relating to a hus-band or marriage.

Mar'itime *a.* bordering on the sea; connected with sea-faring or navigation.

Mar'joram *n.* an aromatic herb.

Mark *n.* something set up to be aimed at; a sign or token; an inscription; a line, dot, scar, or any visible trace or impression.—*v.t.* to make a mark on; to indicate, to be a distinguish-ing mark of; to watch.—*v.i.* to take notice.—**marks'man** *n.* one skilled in shooting.—**mark'er** *n.* *Syn.* symbol, stamp, brand, token, indication;—of *v.* to impress, note, notice, brand. *Ant.* deletion, erasure.

Mark *n.* a German coin; various old coins.

Mark'et *n.* an assembly for buying and selling; a place where goods are sold; demand for goods; a place or centre for trade.—*v.t.* to bring to or sell in a market. —**mark'etable** *a.*

Marl *n.* a clayey soil used as a fertiliser.—*v.t.* to fertilise with it.

Marl'ine (-in) *n.* two-strand cord. — **marl'inespike** *n.* a pointed hook for unravelling rope to be spliced.

Mar'malade *n.* orange jam.

Mar'moset *n.* small bushy-tailed monkey.

Mar'mot *n.* a rodent allied to the squirrel.

Mar'ocain (-kān) *n.* a dress material, usually silk.

Maroon' *n.* a brownish crimson colour; a kind of firework.— *a.* of the colour.

Maroon' *n.* a fugitive slave in the West Indies; a marooned person.—*v.t.* to leave on a desert island.

Marque (-k) *n.* **letters of marque,** a licence to act as a privateer.

Marquee' (-kē) *n.* a large tent.

Mar'quetry (-ket-) *n.* inlaid work.

Mar'quis, mar'quess *n.* nobleman of rank next below a duke.—**mar'quisate** *n.*

Ma'rrow (-rō) *n.* the fatty substance inside bones.— **vegetable marrow,** a gourd cooked as a table vegetable.

—**mar'rowfat** *n.* a large pea.

—**mar'rowy** *a.*

Ma'rry *v.t.* to join as husband and wife; to take as husband or wife.—*v.i.* to take a husband or wife.—**mar'riage** (-rij) *n.* the state of being married; an act of marrying. —**mar'riageable** *a.*

Mars *n.* the Roman god of war; the planet next to the earth.—**Martian** *n.* a supposed inhabitant of Mars.

Marseillaise (mar-se-lāz') *n.* the French National Anthem, sung first by *Marseilles* volunteers.

Marsh *n.* low-lying wet land. —**marshmall'ow** *n.* the herb growing near marshes.— **marsh-mar'igold** *n.* a plant with yellow flowers growing in wet places.—**marsh'y** *a.*

Marsh'al *n.* high officer of state.—**Field Marsh'al,** a military officer of the highest rank.—*v.t.* to arrange in due order; to conduct with ceremony.

Marsu'pial (-sōō-) *n.* an animal that carries its young in a pouch, e.g. the kangaroo.

Mart *n.* market place or market hall.

Mart'en *n.* an animal yielding a valuable fur.

Mar'tial (-shal) *a.* relating to war; warlike.

Mar'tin *n.* species of swallow.

Martinet' *n.* a strict disciplinarian.

Mar'tingale (-ng-g-) *n.* a strap to prevent a horse from throwing up its head; a system of doubling stakes at gambling.

Māte, mēte, mīte, mōte, mūte, bōōt.

Marti'ni (-tĕ-) *n.* a cocktail containing *esp.* vermouth, gin, bitters.

Mar'tinmas *n.* the feast of St. Martin, 11th November.

Mart'let *n.* a martin; in heraldry, a bird without feet.

Mar'tyr (-tẹr) *n.* one put to death for refusing to give up the Christian faith; one who suffers in some cause; one in constant suffering.— *v.t.* to make a martyr of.— **mar'tyrdom** *n.*—**martyrol'ogy** *n.* a list or history of martyrs.

Mar'vel *n.* a wonderful thing. —*v.i.* to wonder.—**mar'vellous** *a.*

Marx'ism (marks-ism) *n.* the doctrine of the materialist conception of history, taught by Carl Marx, German socialist.—**Marxian** *a.*

Mas'cot *n.* a thing supposed to bring good luck.

Mas'culine (-lin) *a.* relating to males; manly, vigorous; of the grammatical gender to which names of males belong.

Mash *n.* meal mixed with warm water; a warm food for horses, etc.—*v.t.* to make into a mash; to crush into a soft mass.

Mask (-à-) *n.* a covering for the face; a disguise or pretence.—*v.t.* to cover with a mask; to hide or disguise.— **masque** . a form of amateur theatrical performance; a masquerade. — **masquerade'** *n.* a masked ball.—*v.i.* to go about in disguise. *Syn.* subterfuge, revelry, pretence. *Ant.* frankness, naturalness.

Mas'ochism (kizm) *n.* in psycho-analysis, satisfaction of sexual impulses by endurance of pain.—**masochist** *n.* —**masochistic** *a.*

Ma'son *n.* a worker in stone; a freemason.—**mason'ic** *a.* of freemasonry.—**ma'sonry** *n.* stonework; freemasonry.

Mass *n.* the service of the Eucharist.

Mass *n.* a quantity of matter; a dense collection of this; a large quantity.—**the mass'es,** the populace.—*v.t.* and *i.* to form into a mass.—**mass'y** *a.* solid, weighty.—**mass'ive** *a.* having great size and weight.—**mass'age** (-àzh) *a.* rubbing and kneading the muscles, etc., as curative treatment.—*v.t.* to apply this treatment to.—**mass'eur** *n.;* **mass'euse** *fem.* one who practises massage.

Mass'acre (kẹr) *n.* a general slaughter; indiscriminate killing, *esp.* of unresisting people.—*v.t.* to make a massacre of.

Mast (-à-) *n.* a pole for supporting sails.

Mast (-à-) *n.* the fruit of beech, oak, etc., used as food for pigs.

Mast'er (mà-) *n.* one who employs another; the head of a household; an owner; one in control; the captain of a merchant ship; a teacher; an artist of great reputation. *v.t.* to overcome; to acquire knowledge of, or skill in.— **mast'erful** *a.* imperious, self-willed.—**mast'erly** *a.* skilfully done.—**mast'ery** *n.*

victory, authority. *Syn.* chief, ruler, proprietor, principal, director. *Ant.* servant, slave, mar. employee, pupil.

Mas'tic *n.* a gum got from certain trees.

Mas'ticate *v.t.* chew.—**mastica'tion** *n.*

Mas'tiff *n.* a large dog.

Mas'toids *n.* popular name for disease of the mastoid process, below the ear, including abscess on the brain and meningitis.

Mas'turbate *v.i.* to practise self-abuse.—**masturbation** *n.*

Mat *n.* a small carpet or strip of plaited rushes, straw, etc.; a thick tangled mass.—*v.t.* and *i.* to form into such a mass.

Mat *a.* dull, unpolished, slightly rough.

Mat'ador *n.* the man charged with slaying the bull in bull-fights.

Match *n.* a person or thing exactly corresponding to another; one able to contend equally with another; a trial of skill; a marriage; a person regarded as eligible for marriage.—*v.t.* to join in marriage; to meet equally in contest; to place in contest with; to get something corresponding to (a colour, pattern, etc.).—*v.i.* to correspond.—**match'less** *a.* unequalled.—**match'board** *n.* boards fitted into each other by tongue and groove along the edges.—**match'-maker** *n.* a woman fond of arranging marriages.

Match *a.* a small stick with a head which bursts into flame when rubbed; a fuse.—**match'lock** *n.* an old musket fired by a fuse.—**match'wood** *n.* small splinters.

Mate *n.* checkmate.—*v.t.* to checkmate.

Mate *n.* a comrade, a husband or wife; an officer in a merchant ship immediately below the captain.—*v.t.* to marry.—*v.i.* to keep company.

Mate'rial *a.* of matter or body; unspiritual; essential, important.—*n.* the stuff from which anything is made; a stuff or fabric.—**mate'rialism** *n.* an opinion that nothing exists except matter.—**mate'rialist** *a.* and *n.*—**materialis'tic** *a.*—**mate'rialise** *v.t.* to make material.—*v.i.* to come into existence.—**mate'rially** *adv.*

Mater'nal *a.* of, or related through, a mother.—**materu'ity** *n.* motherhood.

Mathemat'ics *n.pl.* the science of space and number.—**mathemat'ical** *a.*—**mathemat'ically** *adv.*—**mathemati'cian** *n.*

Mat'inee (-ā) *n.* a morning or afternoon performance.—**mat'ins** *n.pl.* morning prayers in the Church of England; one of the canonical hours, a midnight or daybreak office.

Mat'ricide *n.* one who kills his mother; the killer.

Matricu'late *v.t.* to enter on a college or university register.—*v.i.* to enter one's name on such register; to pass an examination entitling one to do this.— **matricula'tion** n.

Mat'rimony n. marriage.— **matrimo'nial** a. Syn. nuptials, wedding. Ant. divorce, single-blessedness, bachelordom, spinsterhood.

Ma'trix n. a mould for casting.

Ma'tron n. a married woman; a woman in charge of the domestic arrangements of a hospital, school, etc. — **ma'tronly** a.

Matt see MAT.

Matt'er n. the substance of which a thing is made up; physical or bodily substance in general; pus; the substance of a book, etc.; an affair; a reason, a cause of trouble.—v.i. to be of importance.

Matt'ock n. a tool for breaking up hard ground.

Matt'ress n. a stuffed flat case used as or under a bed; a frame with stretched wires for supporting a bed.

Mature' a. ripe, complete in development or growth.— v.t. to bring to maturity.— v.i. to come to maturity; of a bill, to become due.— **matu'rity** n. Syn. full-grown, mellow, developed, perfected, ready. Ant. immature, unripe, undeveloped, unprepared.

Maud'lin a. weakly sentimental.

Maul, mawl n. heavy wooden hammer.—**maul** v.t. to beat or bruise; to handle roughly.

Maund (mawnd) n. in the East Indies, a measure of weight, varying from about 24 lbs. to over 82 lbs., according to the article weighed and the district.

Maund'er v.i. to move or act dreamily; to wander in talking.

Maun'dy n. foot-washing ceremony on Thursday before Easter (cf. John xiii. 14); royal alms given on that day.

Mau'ser (mow-) n. a type of repeating magazine rifle, from the name of the German inventor.

Mausole'um n. stately building as a tomb.

Mauve (mōv) n. a bright purple aniline dye; the colour of this dye.—a. of this colour.

Mav'erick n. in North America, an unbranded steer; a strayed cow; something dishonestly obtained by appropriation, as land cattle, etc. —**maverick brand**, a brand used by dishonest cattle-raisers.

Maw n. the stomach.

Mawk'ish a. having a sickly flavour; weakly sentimental.

Max'im n. short saying expressing a general truth; a rule of conduct.

Max'im n. a machine-gun.

Max'imum n. the greatest possible size or number.—a. that is a maximum.

May n. the fifth month; the hawthorn, its flowers.—v.i. to take part in May-day festivities.

May v. aux. expresses possibility, permission, usually, opportunity, etc.

Mayonnaise′ n. a sauce.

May′or n. the head of a municipality.—**may′oral** a.—**may′oralty** n. the office, or time of office, of a mayor.—**may′oress** n. the mayor's wife; lady mayor.

Maze n. a labyrinth; a network of paths or lines.—v.t. stupefy.

Maz′er n. an old form of drinking bowl made of wood, often mounted in silver, and much valued by collectors.

Mazour′ka, mazur′ka n. a lively Polish dance; music for it.

Me pron. objective case singular of the 1st personal pronoun I.

Mead n. an alcoholic drink made from honey.

Mead n. a meadow.—**mead′ow** (med-) n. a piece of grassland.—**mead′ow-sweet** n. a sweet-smelling flowering plant.

Mea′gre (mē-gėr) a. lean, thin, scanty.

Meal n. grain ground to powder.—**meal′y** a.

Meal n. an occasion of taking food; the food taken.

Mean a. inferior; shabby; small-minded.—**mean′ly** a.—**mean′ness** n. Syn. despicable, niggardly, spiritless. Ant. splendid, high, praiseworthy, generous, liberal.

Mean a. intermediate in time, quality, etc.—n. anything which is intermediate.—pl. that by which something is done; money resources.—**mean′time** n.—**mean′while** n. the time between one happening and another.—adv. during this time.

Mean v.t. to intend, design; signify; import.—**mean′ing** n. sense, significance.—a. expressive.—**mean′ly** adv.

Meand′er (mē-and-) v.i. to flow windingly; to wander aimlessly.—n. (usually pl.) a winding; a roundabout way.

Meas′les (mez-ls) n.pl. an infectious disease with red spots.—**meas′ly** a. relating to measles; poor, wretched.

Meas′ure (mēzh-ėr) n. a size or quantity; a vessel, rod, line, etc.; for ascertaining size or quantity; a unit of size or quantity; poetical rhythm; an order or tune; musical time; a slow dance; a course or plan of action; a law.—v.t. to ascertain size or quantity of; to be (so much) in size or quantity; to estimate; bring into competition (with).—**meas′urable** a.—**meas′ured** a. carefully considered.—**meas′urement** n.

Meat n. food; the flesh of animals used as food.—**meat′y** a.

Mechan′ic (-k-) a. relating to a machine.—n. one employed in working with machinery; a skilled workman.—pl. the branch of science dealing with motion and tendency of motion.—**mechan′ical** a. concerned with machines or manual operation; worked or produced by, or as though by, a machine; like a machine; relating to mechanics. — **mechan'ically** *adv.* — **mechani'cian** *n.* — **mech'anism** *n.* the structure of a machine; a piece of machinery.

Mech'ani'sation (mek-) *n.* change from system of animal transport or power to mechanical.—**mech'anise** *v.t.* to render mechanical.—**mech'anised** *a.*

Med'al *n.* a piece of metal usually round or star-shaped with an inscription, etc., and used as a reward or memento.—**medall'ion** *n.* a large medal; various things like this in decorative work. —**med'allist** *n.* the winner of a medal; a maker of medals.

Med'dle *v.i.* to interfere, to busy oneself with unnecessarily.—**med'dlesome** *a.*

Mediæ'val *a.* relating to the Middle Ages.—**mediæ'valism** *n.*—**mediæ'valist** *n.* one who studies the Middle Ages.

Me'diate *v.i.* to go between in order to reconcile.—*v.t.* to bring about, a medium.—*a.* not immediate; depending on something intermediate. —**media'tion** *a.*—**me'diator** *a.*

Med'icine *n.* the art of healing by remedies and the regulation of diet; a remedy or mixture of drugs.—**med'ical** *a.*—**med'ically** *adv.*—**medic'-ament** *n.* a remedy.—**med'icate** *v.t.* to impregnate with medicinalsubstances.—**medica'tion** *n.*—**med'icative** *a.* healing.—**medic'inal** *a.* having healing properties.

Me'diocre *a.* neither bad nor good, ordinary.—**medioc'rity** *n.*

Med'itate *v.t.* to think about; to plan.—*v.i.* to be occupied in thought.—**medita'tion** *n.* —**med'itative** *a.*—**med'ita-tively** *adv.*

Me'dium *n.* **me'diums, me'dia** *pl.* a middle quality or degree; an intermediate substance conveying force; surroundings; environment; means, agency.—*a.* between two qualities, degrees, etc.— **medium waves**, in wireless, by the Hague definition, waves between 200 and 3000 metres.

Med'lar *n.* a tree with a fruit like a small apple, eaten when decayed; the fruit.

Med'ley *n.* a hand-to-hand fight; a miscellaneous mixture.

Médoc' *n.* a red wine from Médoc, Gironde, France.

Medu'sa *n.* in mythology, a Gorgon whose head turned beholders into stone; a kind of jelly-fish.

Meed *n.* a reward.

Meek *a.* submissive, humble. —**meek'ly** *adv.*—**meek'ness** *n. Syn.* mild, yielding, unassuming. *Ant.* assertive, pushful.

Meer'schaum (-shum) *n.* a white substance resembling clay used for bowls of tobacco pipes.

Meet *a.* fit, suitable.—**meet'ly** *adv.*

Meet *v.t.* to come face to face with; to encounter; to satisfy, pay.—*v.i.* to come face to face; to assemble; to come

---

into contact.—*n.* a meeting for a hunt.—**meet'ing** *n.* an assembly.

Megalith'ic *a.* consisting of great stones.—**megaloma'nia** *n.* a passion for great things. —**megaloma'niac** *a.* and *n.* —**meg'aphone** *n.* an instrument for carrying the sound of the voice to a distance.

Megger' *n.* in wireless, an instrument for measuring high resistances.

Mel'ancholy (-k-) *n.* sadness, dejection, gloom.—*a.*gloomy, dejected.—**melancho'lia** *n.* mental disease accompanied by depression.—**melanchol'ic** *a.*

Mêlé'e (melā) *n.* a mixed fight.

Mellif'luous *a.* sweet as honey. —**mellif'luence** *n.*

Mell'ow *a.* ripe; juicy; partly drunk.—*v.t.* and *i.* to make or become mellow.

Mel'odrama *n.* a play full of sensational happenings and ending happily.—**melodramat'ic** *a.*

Mel'ody *n.* sweet sound; series of musical notes arranged to make a tune.—**melo'dious** *a.*—**mel'odist** *n.* singer; composer of melodies.

Mel'on *n.* various gourds eaten as fruit.

Mel'rose *n.* honey of roses, a mixture of powdered redrose, honey, and diluted alcohol.

Melt *v.i.* to become liquid by heat; to be dissolved; to become softened; to waste away.—*v.t.* to cause to soften or dissolve or become liquid by heat.

Mem'ber *n.* a limb; any part of a complicated structure; any of the individuals making up a body or society. —**mem'bership** *n.*

Mem'brane *n.* a thin flexible tissue in a plant or animal body.

Mement'o *n.* a thing serving to remind.

Mem'oir (-war) *a.* record of events; an autobiography or biography.

Mem'ory *n.* the faculty of recollecting or recalling, to mind; a recollection; the length of time one can remember.—**memori'al** *a.* of or preserving memory.—*n.* something which serves to keep in memory; a statement in a petition.—**memor'ialise** *v.t.* to commemorate; to petition.—**memor'ialist** *n.*—**mem'orise** *v.t.* to commit to memory. — **mem'orable** *a.* worthy of being remembered. —**mem'orably** *adv.* **memoran'dum** *n.* a note to help the memory; a note of a contract; an informal letter. *Syn.* remembrance, reputation, fame. *Ant.* forgetfulness, oblivion.

Mem'sahib *n.* in India, a European married lady.

Men'ace *n.* a threat.—*v.t.* to threaten.

Menag'erie (-j-) *n.* a collection of wild animals kept for show.

Men'agogue *n.* a medicine that promotes the menstrual flow.

Mend *v.t.* to repair, correct,

put right.—*v.i.* to improve, *esp.* in health.—*n.* to repair breakage or hole.

Menda'cious *a.* untruthful.—**mendac'ity** *n.*

Mend'icant *a.* beggar.—*n.* a beggar.—**mend'icancy** *n.*

Men'hir *n.* a tall, massive, rude monumental stone.

Me'nial *a.* relating to a servant in a house: servile.—*n.* a household servant.

Meningi'tis (-jĭ-) *n.* inflammation of the membranes of the brain.

Mensura'tion *n.* measuring, *esp.* of areas.

Ment'al *a.* relating to or done by the mind.—**ment'ally** *adv.* —**mental'ity** *n.* quality of mind.

Men'thol *n.* a camphor obtained from oil of peppermint.

Men'tion (-shn) *n.* referring to or remark about (a person or thing).—*v.t.* to refer to, speak of.—**men'tionable** *a.*

Men'tor *n.* a wise and trusted adviser.

Men'u *n.* a list of dishes to be served.

Mephi'tis *n.* foul, pestilential exhalations. — **mephitic** *a.* *Syn.* of *a.* foul, fetid, poisonous, malarious. *Ant.* salubrious, wholesome, pure.

Mer'cantile (-k-) *a.* relating to trade; engaged in trade.

Mer'cenary (-s-) *a.* hired; working simply for reward.—*n.* hired soldier.

Mer'cer *n.* a dealer in fabrics, *esp.* silks.

Mer'cerise *v.* to give a lustre or gloss to cotton fabrics by treating with chemicals.—**mercer'ised** *a.*—**mercer'ising** *n.*

Mer'chant *n.* a wholesale trader.—**mer'chandise** *n.* the things in which he deals.—**mer'chantman** *n.* a trading ship.

Mer'cury *n.* a white metal, liquid at ordinary temperature; quicksilver.—**Mercury**, the Roman god of eloquence; the planet nearest to the sun.—**mercu'rial** *a.* lively, sprightly; relating to or containing mercury.

Mer'cy *n.* the quality of compassion; refraining from the infliction of suffering by one who has the right or power to inflict it.—**mer'ciful** *a.*—**mer'ciless** *a.* *Syn.* leniency, tenderness, charity, grace, favour, forgiveness. *Ant.* severity, cruelty, harshness.

Mere (mēr) *n.* a lake.

Mere (mēr) *a.* only; not of more value or size, etc., than name implies.—**mere'ly** *adv.*

Merge *v.i.* to lose identity, to mix in.—*v.t.* to cause to lose identity or to be absorbed.—**mer'ger** (-j-) *n.* a being absorbed into something greater; a combination of business firms into one.

Merid'ian *a.* relating to noon, or the position of the sun at noon. — *n.* noon; the highest point reached by a star, etc.; a period of greatest splendour; an imaginary circle in the sky passing through the celestial poles; a circle of the earth passing through the poles and a place stated.

Meringue' (me-rang) *n.* a mixture of white of eggs and sugar, slightly browned, used as icing; a cake made of this.

Merin'o (-ēn-) *n.* a variety of sheep; soft material made of merino wool.

Mer'it *n.* excellence, worth; a quality of deserving well.— *pl.* excellences or defects.— *v.t.* to deserve.—**meritor'ious** *a.* deserving well.

Mer'kin *n.* a wig; a mop for cleaning cannon.

Merle *n.* a blackbird.

Mer'lin *n.* a kind of hawk.

Mer'lon *n.* that part of a parapet which lies between two embrasures.

Mer'maid *n.* an imaginary sea creature having the upper part of a woman and the lower part like a fish.

Mer'ry *a.* joyous, cheerful.— **merr'ily** *adv.*—**merr'iment** *n.* —**merr'ythought** *n.* a forked bone between the head and breast of a bird.—**merr'y-go-round** *n.* a revolving machine with wooden horses, cars, etc.

Mer'saline *n.* a mercerised cotton for dress linings.

Mesh *n.* one of the open spaces of a net.—*v.t.* to catch in meshes.

Mes'merism *n.* a system of inducing a hypnotic state by influence on a patient.— **mesmer'ic** *a.*—**mes'merist** *n.* —**mes'merise** *v.t.*

Mess *n.* a portion of food; a state of untidy confusion; a company of people who regularly eat together; the place where they do this.— *v.i.* to take one's meals thus; to busy one's self untidily.— *v.t.* to make a mess of, to muddle.—**mess'mate** *n.* a companion at meals; a member of a mess.

Mess'age *n.* a communication from one person to another. —**mess'enger** *n.* one who carries a message.

Messi'ah *n.* the promised deliverer of the Jews; Christ.

Mess'uage (-swāj) *n.* a house with out-buildings and land.

Met'al *n.* any of a number of chemical elements usually bright and easy to melt, e.g. gold, iron, etc.; broken stone used for macadam roads.—**metall'ic** *a.*—**met'allurgy** *n.* the art of refining metals.—**met'allurgist** *n.*

Metamor'phosis *n.* change of shape, substance, character, etc.—**metamor'phose** *v.t.* to transform.

Met'aphor *n.* a figure of speech in which a term is transferred to something it does not literally apply to; an instance of this.—**metaphor'ical** *a.*

Metaphys'ics *n.pl.* theory of being and knowing.—**metaphys'ical** *a.* — **metaphysi'cian** *n.*

Metath'esis *n.* transposition, *esp.* of letters in a word, e.g. the movement of " r " in *bird*, OE. *bridd.*

Mete *v.t.* to measure.—**me'ter** *n.* an instrument for measuring.

Me'teor *n.* a shining body

Māte, mēte, mīte, mōte, mūte, bōōt.

appearing temporarily in the sky; a shooting star.—meteor'ic *a.*—me'teorite *n.* a fallen meteor.—meteorol'ogy *n.* the science of weather.—meteorolog'ical *a.*—meteorol'ogist *n.*

Methinks' *v. impers.* it seems to me.

Meth'od *n.* a way of doing something; orderliness, system.—method'ical *a.*—meth'odist *n.* a member of any of the churches originated by John Wesley and G. Whitefield. — meth'odism *n* — meth'odise *v.t.* to reduce to order. *Syn.* process, plan, order, arrangement. *Ant.* confusion. disorder.

Meth'yl *n.* a base of wood spirit.—meth'ylate *v.t.* to mix with methyl.

Metic'ulous *a.* over particular about details.

Mét'ier (mät-yā) *n.* one's happiest profession, vocation; one's forte.

Me'tre *n.* a verse, rhythm; the unit of length in the French decimal system, 39.37 inches.—met'rical *a.* of measurement or of poetic metre.—met'ric *a.* of that system of weights and measures in which the metre is a unit.

Metrop'olis *n.* the chief city of a state.—metropol'itan *a.* of a metropolis.—*n.* an archbishop or other bishop with authority over bishops of a province.

Metro'style *n.* the tone-modulating and time-changing part of a pianola.

Met'tle *n.* courage, spirit.—met'tlesome *a.*

Mew *v.i.* of a hawk, to molt.—*v.t.* to put (a hawk) into a cage for moving; to imprison, shut up.—*n.* a cage for molting hawks.—mews *n.pl.* (usually treated as *sing.*) a set of stables round an open space.

Mew *n.* the cry of a cat.—*v.i.* to utter this cry.

Mez'zanine *n.* a low story between two higher ones.

Mez'zo-sopra'no (met-so-) *n.* a voice between soprano and contralto; a singer with this voice.

Mez'zotint (met-sō-) *n.* the method of engraving in which lights and half lights are made for scraping a roughened surface; a print so produced.

Mi'a-mi'a *n.* in Australia, an aboriginal hut; a bed or rest.

Mias'ma *n.* harmful exhalations from marshes, etc.—miasmat'ic *a.*

Mi'ca *n.* a mineral found in glittering scales or plates.

Mich'aelmas (mik-al-) *n.* the feast of St. Michael the Archangel. 29th September.

Mi'crobe *n.* a minute plant or animal, *esp.* one causing disease or fermentation.—mi'crocosm *n.* the world of man; man as an epitome of the universe.—microcos'mic *a.*—mi'crophone *n.* an instrument for making sounds louder, e.g. as part of a telephone or of broadcasting apparatus.—mi'croscope *n.* an instrument by which a very small body is magnified and made visible.—micro-scop'ic *a.* relating to a microscope; so small as to be only visible through a microscope.—micros'copy *n.* the use of the microscope.

Mid *a.* intermediate, that is in the middle.—mid'day *n.* noon or about then.—mid'-land *n.* the middle part of a country.—*pl.* the middle counties of England.—mid'night *n.* twelve o'clock at night.—mid'shipmen *n.* a naval officer of the lowest commission rank. — mid'-summer *n.* the summer solstice; the middle part of the summer.—mid'way *a.* and *adv.* halfway.

Midd'en *n.* a dunghill.

Mid'dle *a.* equal distance or between two extremes; medium, intermediate.—*n.* the middle point or part.—mid'dleman *n.* the trader handling goods between the producer and the consumer.

Midge *n.* a gnat or similar insect.—mid'get *n.* a very small person or thing.

Midinette *n.* a Parisian shop-girl, who throngs the streets at midday.

Mid'riff *n.* the diaphragm.

Midst *n.* in the midst of, sur-rounded by, among.—*prep.* in the midst of.

Mid'wife *n.* a woman who assists others in childbirth.—mid'wifery (-wif-ri) *n.* the art or practice of doing this.

Mien (mēn) *n.* a person's bearing or look.

Might (mit) *n.* power, strength.—might'y *a.*—might'ily *adv.*

Mignonette' (min-yon-) *n.* a plant with sweet-smelling flowers.

Mi'grate *v.i.* to move from one place to another.—mi'grant *a.* and *n.*—migra'-tion *n.*—migra'tory *a.*

Mika'do *n.* the emperor of Japan.

Milch *a.* giving, or kept for, milk.

Mild (-ī-) *a.* gentle, merciful, indulgent; not strongly flavoured.—mild'ly *a.*—mild'-ness *n. Syn.* tender, soft, temperate. *Ant.* ungentle, rough, harsh, stormy.

Mil'dew *n.* a destructive fungus on plants or things exposed to damp.—*v.i.* to become tainted with mildew.—*v.t.* to affect with mildew.

Mile *n.* a measure of length, 1760 yards.—mi'leage *n.* dis-tance in miles.

Mileom'eter (-lom-) *n.* in motoring, an instrument for measuring and recording distance travelled.

Miles'ian *n.* an Irishman.—*a.* Irish.

Mil'itary *a.* of, or for, soldiers or armies of warfare.—*n.* soldiers.—mil'itant *a.* en-gaged in warfare; combative.—*n.* a militant person.—mil'itancy *n.*—mil'itarism *n.* enthusiasm for military force and methods.—mil'itarist *n.*—mil'itate *v.i.* to be an argument or influence (against).—mili'tia (-ish-a) *n.* a force of citizens, not pro-fessionally soldiers, which may be called on at need for military service.

Milk *n.* the white fluid with which animals feed their young.—*v.t.* to draw milk from.—**milk'sop** *n.* effeminate man or youth.—**milk'maid** *n.* a woman working with cows or in a dairy.—**milk'-teeth** *n.* the first set of animal teeth.—**milk'y** *a.* containing or like milk.

Mill *n.* machinery for grinding corn, etc.; building containing this; various manufacturing machines; a factory.—*v.t.* to put through a mill.—**mill'er** *n.*—**mill'-race** *n.* a stream of water driving a mill wheel.—**mill'stone** *n.* one of a pair of flat circular stones used for grinding.

Millenn'ium *n.* a period of a thousand years; a period of a thousand years during which some claim Christ is to reign on earth.—**millenn'ial** *a.*—**mill'iard** *n.* a thousand millions.—**mill'ion** *n.* a thousand thousands.—**millionaire** *n.* an owner of a million of money, an extremely rich person.—**mill'igram** *n.* the thousandth part of a gram.—**mill'imeter** *n.*—**mill'ilitre** *n.*

Mill'et *n.* the small grain of an Indian cereal plant; the plant.

Mill'iner *n.* one who makes up or deals in women's hats, ribbons, etc.—**mill'inery** *n.*

Milt *n.* the spawn of male fish.

Mim'bar *n.* a pulpit in a mosque.

Mime *n.* a jester; an old form of dramatic representation. —**mim'ic** *a.* imitated, feigned, *esp.* to amuse.—*n.* one skilled in amusing imitation.—*v.t.* to imitate, ludicrously or closely.—**mim'icry** *n.*

Mim'eograph *n.* an apparatus for producing stencils of written matter, from which copies may be obtained.

Mimo'sa *n.* a genus of leguminous plants which includes the sensitive plant.

Mim'otype *n.* a form of animal life which mimics another found in a different country.

Mim'ulus *n.* a genus of showy garden plants.

Minaret' *n.* tall slender tower by a mosque.

Mi'natory *a.* threatening.

Mince *v.t.* to cut or chop small; to utter with affected carefulness.—*v.i.* to walk in an affected manner.—*n.* minced-meat. — **mince'-meat** *n.* a mixture of chopped currants, spices, suet, etc.— **mince' pie** *n.* a pie containing mince-meat.

Mind (-i-) *n.* the thinking faculties as distinguished from the body, the intellectual faculties; memory; attention; intention; taste.— *v.t.* to attend to; care for; keep in memory.—**mind'ful** *a.* taking thought; keeping in memory. *Syn.* intellect, head, spirit, liking, disposition, intent;—of " mindful," obedient, observant. *Ant.* unmindful, forgetful, disobedient, inattentive.

Mine *pron.* that belonging to me.

Mine *n.* a deep hole for digging out coal, metals, etc.; an underground gallery with a charge of explosive; a large shell or canister of explosive placed in the sea to destroy ships.—*v.t.* to dig from a mine; to make a mine in or under.—*v.i.* to make or work in a mine.—**mi′ner** *n.*—**min′eral** *a.* got by mining; inorganic.—*n.* a mineral substance.—**mineral′ogy** *n.* the science of minerals.—**mineral′ist** *n.*—**mineralog′ical** (-j-) *a.*—**mine′layer** *n.* a ship used for laying mines. — **mine′-sweeper** *n.* a ship used to clear away mines.—**min′eral-water** *n.* water containing some mineral, *esp.* natural or artificial kinds used for drinking.

Min′gle (-ng-g-) *v.t.* and *i.* to mix; unite. *Syn.* combine, blend, merge. *Ant.* separate, clear, disentangle.

Min′iature *n.* a small painted portrait; a book or model on a small scale.—*a.* small-scale.—**min′iaturist** *n.* a painter of miniatures.

Min′ikin *n.* a pet; the smallest kind of pin; the second size of match-stick.—*a.* small, delicate.

Min′im *n.* in music, a note half the length of a semibreve; the smallest fluid measure, 1/60th of a fluid dram.—**min′imise** *v.t.* to bring to, or estimate at, the smallest possible amount.—**min′imum** *n.* the lowest size or quantity. —*a.* smallest in size or quantity.

Min′ion *n.* a favourite; a creature, servile dependent.

Min′ister *n.* a person in charge of a department of the State; a diplomatic representative; a clergyman.—*v.t.* to supply.—*v.i.* to serve; to contribute; to be serviceable or helpful.—**ministe′rial** *a.*—**min′istry** *n.* office of clergymen; the body of ministers forming a government; agency; action of ministering.—**ministe′rialist** *n.* a supporter of the government.—**min′istrant** *a.* ministering.—*n.* an officiating clergyman.—**ministra′tion** *n.* rendering a help, *esp.* to the sick or needy.

Mink *n.* a variety of the weasel tribe, valuable for its fur.

Minn′ow (-ō) *n.* a small freshwater fish.

Mi′nor *a.* lesser; under age.— *n.* a person under the age of twenty-one.—**minor′ity** *n.* the state of being a minor; the lesser number; the smaller party voting together.

Min′otaur *n.* a fabled monster, half bull, half man.

Min′ster *n.* a monastery church; a cathedral.

Min′strel *n.* a mediæval singer or musician.—*pl.* performers of Negro songs.—**min′strelsy** *n.* the art or poetry of minstrels.

Mint *n.* a place where money is coined.—*v.t.* coin.

Mint *n.* an aromatic plant used in cooking.

Minuet′ *n.* a stately dance; music for it.

Māte, mēte, mīte, mōte, mūte, bōōt.

Mi'nus *prep.* less, with the deduction of.—*a.* of quantities, negative.

Minute' (mĭ-nūt) *a.* very small; very precise.—**min'ute** (min-it) *n.* 60th part of an hour or of a degree or angle; a moment; a memorandum.—*pl.* record of the proceedings of a meeting, etc.—*v.t.* to make a minute of; to record in minutes.—**min'ute'ly** (mĭ-nū-) *adv.*—**minu'tiæ** (-shi-ē) *n.pl.* trifles, precise details.

Minx *n.* a pert girl, a hussy.

Mio'cene (mi-ō-sēn) *a.* a term denoting the geological period in which can be observed a minority of living species.

Mir'acle *n.* a supernatural event; a marvel.—**mirac'ulous** *a.*—**mirac'ulously** *adv.*—**mir'acle-play** *n.* a drama (*esp.* mediæval) based on the life of Christ or of some saint.

Mirage' (-àzh) *n.* a deceptive image in the atmosphere, e.g. of a lake in the desert.

Mire *n.* swampy ground, mud.—*v.t.* to stick in, or dirty with, mud.—**mi'ry** *a.*

Mirr'or *n.* a polished surface for reflecting images of objects.—*v.t.* to reflect an image of.

Mirth *n.* merriment.—**mirth'ful** *a.* *Syn.* jollity, laughter, hilarity, glee, cheerfulness. *Ant.* sadness, sorrow, melancholy, dejection.

Mir'za (mĕr-za) *n.* a Persian title placed before a name to denote a scholar and after one to denote a prince.

Mis- *prefix* meaning amiss, wrongly; makes compounds, e.g. **misapply'** *v.t.* to apply wrongly. — **misman'agement** *n.* bad management. Such words are not given where the meaning and derivation may easily be found from the simple word.

Misalli'ance *n.* an improper or degrading marriage.

Mis'anthrope *n.* a hater of mankind.—**misanthrop'ic** *a.* —**misan'thropy** *n.*—**misan'thropist** *n.*

Miscast' *v.t.* and *i.* to reckon erroneously; to distribute unsuitably, as the parts of a play for actors;—*a.* unsuitably distributed;—*n.* an erroneous reckoning.

Miscella'neous *a.* mixed, assorted.—**mis'cellany** *n.* a collection of assorted writings in one book, a literary medley.

Mis'chief (-chif) *n.* harmful, a source of harm or annoyance; annoying conduct. — **mis'chievous** *a.* having harmful effect; disposed to or full of mischief.

Mis'creant *n.* a wicked person.

Misdemea'nour *n.* offence less grave than a felony.—**misdemea'nant** *n.* one guilty of wrong conduct or petty crime.

Mi'ser (-z-) *n.* one who hoards instead of using money; a stingy fellow.—**mi'serly** *a.*—**mis'erable** *a.* very unhappy, wretched; mean; disappointing.—**mis'ery** *n.* great unhappiness; distress, poverty.

Mis'ericorde (-kord) *n.* mercy; a small dagger used by a knight to put a man out of misery.

Misno'mer *n.* a wrong name; the use of a wrong name.

Misog'amy *n.* hatred of marriage.—**misog'amist** *n.*

Misog'yny (-j-) *n.* hatred of women.—**misog'ynist** *n.*

Miss *n.* a title of an unmarried woman or girl; a girl.

Miss *v.t.* fail to hit, reach, find, catch, or notice; not to be in time for; to omit, to notice or regret absence of.—*n.* the fact of missing.

Miss'al *n.* a mass-book.

Miss'el-thrush *n.* a large thrush which feeds on mistletoe.

Miss'ile (-il) *n.* that which may be thrown or shot to do damage.

Mis'sion (mish-n) *n.* sending or being sent on some service; party of persons sent; a person's calling in life.—**mis'sionary** *a.* of religious missions.—*n.* one who goes on religious missions.—**miss'ive** *n.* a letter.

Mist *n.* water vapour in fine drops.—**mist'y** *a.*—**mist'ily** *adv.*

Mistake' *v.t.* not to understand; to form a wrong opinion about; to take (a person or thing) for another.—*v.i.* to be in error.—*n.* an error in thought or action.

Mis'tletoe (-sl-) *n.* a parasitic plant with white berries which grows on various trees.

Mis'tral *n.* a violent northwest wind that blows over the Gulf of Lyons.

Mis'tress *n.* a woman who employs other persons; a woman with mastery or control; a woman teacher; the object of a man's illicit love.

Mite *n.* a very small insect; a very small coin; a small but well-meant contribution; a very small child or person.

Mit'igate *v.t.* to make less severe.—**mitiga'tion** *n.* *Syn.* of *n.* relief, decrease. *Ant.* aggravation, increase.

Mi'tre (-ter) *n.* a bishop's headdress; joint between two pieces of wood, etc., meeting at right angles with the line of their joining, bisecting the right angle.—*v.t.* to put a mitre on; to join with or shape for a mitre-joint.

Mitt'en *n.* a glove with one compartment for the four fingers; a glove leaving the fingers and end of the thumb bare.

Mix *v.t.* to put together or to combine or blend, to mingle.—*v.i.* to be mixed; to associate.—**mix'ture** *n.*

Mizz'en, **miz'en** *n.* the lowest fore and aft sail on the aftermost mast of a ship.—**miz'(z)enmast** *n.* the aftermost mast on a full-rigged ship.

Mnemon'ic (n-) *a.* helping the memory.—*n.* something intended to help the memory.—*pl.* the art of improving the memory.

Moan *n.* a low murmur, usually indicating pain.—

v.t. to bewail.—*v.i.* to utter a moan.

Moat *n.* a deep wide ditch round a town or building.— *v.t.* to surround with a moat.

Mob *n.* a disorderly crowd of people; mixed assembly.— *v.t.* to attack in a mob, to hustle or ill-treat.

Mob'cap *n.* an indoor cap formerly worn by women.

Mo'bile (-bil) *a.* capable of movement; easily moved or changed. — **mobil'ity** *n.* — **mo'bilise** *v.t.* to prepare (forces) for active service.— *v.i.* of an army, to prepare for active service.—**mobilisa'tion** *n.*

Mocc'asin *n.* an Amer. Ind. soft shoe, usually of deerskin.

Mock *v.t.* to make fun of, to hold up to ridicule; to disappoint.—*v.t.* to scoff.—*n.* act of mocking; a laughing stock.—*a.* sham, imitation. —**mock'er** *n.*—**mock'ery** *n.* *Syn.* to deride, taunt, scoff at. *Ant.* respect, revere, take seriously.

Mode *n.* method, manner, fashion.—**mo'dish** *a.* in the fashion.

Mod'el *n.* a representation of an object made to scale; a pattern; a person or thing worthy of imitation; the person employed by an artist to pose, or by a dressmaker to show off clothes.— *v.t.* to work into shape; to make according to a model.

Mod'erate (-it) *a.* not going to extremes, not excessive, medium.—*n.* a person of moderate views.—(-āt) *v.t.* and *i.* to make or become less violent or excessive.— **modera'tion** *n.*—**mod'erator** *n.* go-between or mediator; president of a Presbyterian body.

Mod'ern *a.* of present or recent times; new fashioned.—*n.* a person living in modern times.—**mod'ernism** *n.* of modern character or views.— **mod'ernist** *n.*—**modern'ity** *n.* —**mod'ernise** *v.t.* to adapt to modern ways or views.— **modernisa'tion** *n.*

Mod'est *a.* unassuming, retiring, not over-rating one's qualities or achievements.— **mod'esty** *n.*

Mod'icum *n.* a small or moderate quantity.

Mod'ify (-fi) *v.t.* to make small changes in; to tone down.—**modifica'tion** *n.*

Modiste' (mō-dēst) *n.* a milliner or dressmaker.

Mod'ulate *v.t.* to regulate; vary in tone.—*v.i.* to change the key of music.—**modula'tion** *n.*

Mod'ule *n.* a model; in architecture, a measure to regulate the proportions of select parts of a building.

Mod'ulus *n.* a number, coefficient, or quantity, that measures a force, function, or effect.

Mo'dus *n.* a way or mode; a compensation in lieu of tithes.

Mo'hair *n.* a fine cloth of goat's hair.

Mohamm'edan *a.* of Mohammed or his religion.—*n.* a believer in Mohammed.— **Mohamm'edanism** *n.*

Moi′ety *n.* a half.

Moil *v.i.* to drudge.

Moir′é (-rā) *a.* watered.—*n.* a watered fabric, usually of silk.

Moist *a.* damp, slightly wet.—**moist′ened** *v.t.*—**moist′ure** *n.* liquid, especially diffused or in drops.

Mo′lar *a.* of teeth, serving to grind.—*n.* a molar tooth.

Molass′es (-ez) *n.* drainings of raw sugar, treacle.

Mole *n.* a small dark growth on the skin.

Mole *n.* a small burrowing animal.—**mole′skin** *n.* its fur; a kind of fustian like it.

Mole *n.* a pier or breakwater.

Mol′ecule *n.* one of the uniform small particles, composed of atoms, of which a homogeneous substance is made up.—**molec′ular** *a.*

Molest′ *v.t.* to interfere with, meddle with so as to annoy or injure.—**molesta′tion** *n.*

Moll′ify *v.t.* to calm down.—**mollifica′tion** *a. Syn.* soften, assuage, pacify, mitigate, temper. *Ant.* aggravate, irritate, provoke.

Moll′usc *n.* a soft-bodied and (usually)hard-shelled animal.

Mo′loch *n.* the deity of the Ammonites, to whom human sacrifices were offered, hence anything demanding unusual sacrifices.

Mo′ment *n.* a very short space of time.—**mo′mentary** *a.* lasting only a moment.—**mo′mentarily** *adv.*—**moment′ous** *a.* important.—**moment′um** *n.* force of moving body.

Mon′arch (-k) *n.* the sovereign ruler of a state.—**mon′archy** *n.* a state ruled by a sovereign; his rule.—**monarch′ic** *a.*—**mon′archist** *n.* a supporter of monarchy.

Mon′astery *n.* a house occupied by a religious order.—**monas′tic** *a.* relating to monks, nuns, or monasteries.—**monas′ticism** *n.*

Mon′day (mun-di) *n.* the second day of the week.

Mon′el met′al *n.* a nickel copper alloy.

Mon′ey (mun-) *n.* current coin; a medium of exchange.—**mon′etary** *a.*—**mon′etise** *v.t.* to make into or recognise as money.—**monetisa′tion** *n.*

Mon′eywort *n.* an evergreen trailing plant, named from its round leaves.

Mon′ger (mung-g-) *n.* a dealer or trader.

Mon′goose (-ng-g-) *n.* a small Indian animal noted for killing snakes.

Mon′grel (mung-g-) *n.* an animal, *esp.* a dog of mixed breed.—*a.* that is a mongrel.

Mon′itor *n.* one who gives a warning or advice; a senior pupil in a school charged with special duties and authority; a small warship with heavy guns.—**mon′itress** *fem.*—**mon′itory** *a.*—**moni′tion** *n.* a warning.

Monk (munk) *n.* one of a religious community of men living apart under vows.—**monk′ish** *a.*—**monk′s - hood** *n.* a herbaceous plant, extremely poisonous.

Monk′ey (munk-i) *n.* an

animal closely allied to man; an imitative or mischievous child.—*v.i.* to play tricks.—**monk'ey-nut** *n.* peanut.—**monkey-puzzle** *n.* a kind of prickly tree.

Mono- *prefix.*

Mon'obloc *n.* internal combustion engine, all the cylinders made in one casting.

Mon'ochrome *n.* representation in one colour.—*a.* of only one colour.—**monochromat'ic** *a.*—**mon'ochord** *n.* musical instrument with only one string.—**mon'ody** *n.* a lament.—**monog'amy** *n.* the custom of being married to only one person at a time. —**mon'ogram** *n.* two or more letters interwoven.— **mon'ograph** *n.* a short book on a single subject.— **mon'ologue** *n.* a dramatic composition with only one speaker.—**monoma'nia** *n.* madness on a single subject. —**monoma'niac** *n.*—**mon'o-mark** *n.* (trade name) a combination of letters and numbers used instead of the name of the owner to identify property.—**mon'o-plane** *n.* an aeroplane with single wings.—**monop'oly** *n.* exclusive possession of a trade, privilege, etc.—**monop'olise** *v.t.*—**monop'olist** *n.* —**mon'orail** *n.* a railway having cars running on or suspended from a single rail. —**mon'osyllable** *n.* a word of one syllable.—**monosyllab'ic** *a.*—**mon'otheism** *n.* belief that there is only one God.— **mon'otheist** *n.*—**mon'otone**

n. a continuing on one note.—**monot'onous** *a.* lacking in variety, wearisome.— **monot'ony** *n.*—**mon'otype** *n.* a machine for casting and setting printing type in individual letters.

Monsoon' *n.* the seasonal wind of the Indian Ocean.

Mon'ster *n.* misshapen animal or plant; a person of great wickedness; a huge animal or thing.—*a.* huge.—**mon'strous** *a.*—**mon'strously** *adv.* —**monstros'ity** *n.* a monstrous being; a monster.

Month (munth) *n.* one of the twelve periods into which a year is divided; the period of the revolution of the moon.—**month'ly** *a.* happening, payable, etc., once a month.—*adv.* once a month. —*n.* a monthly magazine.

Mon'ument *n.* anything that commemorates; a written record.—**monument'al** *a.* of or serving as a monument; vast, stupendous.

Mood *n.* state of mind and feelings.—**mood'y** *a.* changeable in mood; gloomy. *Syn.* of "moody," varying, morose, irritable, captious. *Ant.* phlegmatic, unruffled, consistent.

Mood *n.* in grammar, a group of forms indicating function of a verb.

Moo'i (mōō-i) *a.* in South Africa, fine; good-looking; handsome; pretty.

Moon *n.* the satellite revolving round the earth; a satellite of a planet.—*v.i.* to go about dreamily.—**moon'light** *n.*—

moon'shine *n.* nonsense.—
moon'stone *n.* a precious
stone.—moon'struck *a.* lunatic.

Moor *n.* a tract of waste land,
often hilly and covered with
heather; land preserved for
grouse shooting.—moor'cock
n. red grouse.—moor'hen *n*
water-hen.

Moor *v.t.* to fasten (a ship)
with chains or ropes.—*v.i.*
to secure a ship thus.—
mooring mast *n.* in aviation,
steel-girder structure fitted
at head with receiving arm
for holding air-ship while
allowing its free movement
in any direction.

Moot *n.* a meeting.—*v.t.* to
bring for discussion.—*a.* that
is open to argument.

Mop *n.* a bundle of yarn,
cloth, etc., fastened to the
end of a stick and used for
cleaning.—*v.t.* to clean or
wipe with a mop or with
any absorbent stuff.

Mope *v.i.* to be depressed.

Mor'al *a.* concerned with
right and wrong conduct;
of good conduct.—moral
victory, a failure or defeat
that inspirits instead of
crushing the loser.—moral
certainty, a thing that can
hardly fail.—*n.* a practical
lesson, e.g. of a fable.—*pl.*
habits with respect to right
and wrong, *esp.* in matters
of sex.—morale' (-àl) *n.*
discipline and spirit of an
army or other body of
persons.—mor'alist *n.* a
teacher of morals.—moral'ity
n. good moral conduct;

moral goodness or badness;
a kind of mediæval drama,
containing a moral lesson.—
mor'alise *v.t.* to interpret
morally.—*v.i.* to write or
think on the moral aspect of
things.—mor'ally *adv.* *Syn.*
ethical, virtuous, just, honourable, blameless. *Ant.*
wicked, sinful, vicious, dishonest, unjust, impure, dissolute, immoral.

Morass' *n.* a marsh.

Morato'rium (-tō-) *n.* literally,
a delay; an act authorising
the suspension of payments
by a bank or a debtor.

Mor'bid *a.* unwholesome,
sickly.

Mord'ant *a.* biting;—*n.* any
substance that fixes dyes.

More *a.* greater in quantity
or number.—*adv.* to a
greater extent, in addition.—
pron. greater or additional
amount or number.—more-
o'ver *adv.* besides.

Morganat'ic *a.* morganatic
marriage, a marriage of a
king or prince in which the
wife does not share her
husband's rank or posses-
sions and the children do
not inherit from their
father.

Mor'ibund *a.* dying.

Mor'mon *n.* one of a sect,
founded in the United States,
professing theocracy and
polygamy.—mor'monism *n.*

Morn *n.* the morning.—
morn'ing *n.* early part of the
day.

Morocc'o *n.* goatskin leather.

Morose' *a.* sullen, unsoci-
able.

Morph'ia *n.* **morph'ine** *n.* the narcotic part of opium.

Morphol'ogy *n.* the science of the structure of organisms.— **morpholog'ical** (-loj-) *a.*

Morr'is *n.* a dance by persons in fancy dress representing characters of the Robin Hood stories; a dance in imitation of a Moorish dance, a part of former May celebrations.

Morr'is tube *n.* a small-bore barrel for fixing in rifle or gun for practice at short range.

Morr'ow *n.* the following day.

Morse *a.* **morse-code**, a system of signalling in which the letters of the alphabet are represented by various combinations of dots and dashes, short and long flashes, etc.

Mor'sel *n.* mouthful; fragment.

Mort *n.* in hunting, a note sounded at the death of game.

Mort *n.* a salmon in the third year; a woman.

Mort'al *a.* subject to death; causing death.—*n.* a mortal creature.—**mortal'ity** *n.* being mortal; great loss of life; death rate.—**mort'ally** *adv. Syn.* human, deadly, fatal. *Ant.* immortal, eternal, superficial.

Mort'ar *n.* a vessel in which substances are pounded; short gun throwing at high angles; a mixture of lime, sand, and water for holding bricks and stones together.

Mort'gage (morg-ij) *n.* a conveyance of property as security for debt with provision that the property be reconveyed at payment within an agreed time.— *v.t.* to convey by mortgage. —**mort'gagor** (morg'a-jer) *n.* —**mortgagee'** *n.*

Mort'ify *v.t.* to subdue by self-denial; to humiliate.— *v.i.* of a part of the body, to be affected with gangrene. —**mortifica'tion** *n.*

Mort'ise (-is) *n.* a hole made in a piece of wood, etc., to receive the tongue at the end of another piece called a tenon.—*v.t.* to make a mortise in; to fasten by mortise and tenon.

Mort'uary *a.* of, or for, burial. —*n.* a building where dead bodies are kept for a time.

Mosa'ic *n.* a picture or pattern made by fixing side by side small bits of coloured stone, glass, etc.; this process of decoration.

Moselle' *n.* a light wine from the Moselle district.

Mos'lem *n.* a Mohammedan.— *a.* pertaining to the Mohammedans.

Mosque (mosk) *n.* Mohammedan place of worship.

Mosqui'to (-kē-tō) *n.* various kinds of gnat.

Moss *n.* a swamp; a small plant growing in masses on a surface.—*v.t.* to cover with moss.—**moss'y** *a.*

Most (mō-) *a.* greatest in size, number, or degree.—*n.* the greatest amount or degree.—*a.* in the greatest degree.—**most'ly** *adv.* for the most part.

Mot (mō) *n.* a pithy or witty saying.

Mote *n.* a particle of dust, a speck.

Moth'er (muth-) *n.* a female parent; the head of a religious community of women. —*a.* inborn.—*v.t.* to act as a mother to.—**moth'erhood** *n.* —**moth'erly** *a.*—**moth'er-in-law** *n.* the mother of one's wife or husband.—**moth'er of pearl'** *n.* an iridescent substance forming the lining of certain shells.

Mo'tif *n.* a subject; a dominating theme.

Mo'tion *n.* process or action or way of moving; proposal in a meeting; an application to a judge.—*v.t.* to direct by a sign.—**mo'tionless** *a.*—**mo'tive** *a.* causing motion.—*n.* that which makes a person act in a particular way; the chief idea in a work of art.—**mo'tor** *n.* that which imparts movement; a machine to supply motive power.—**mo'tor-car** *n.* a carriage moved by an engine carried inside it.—**mo'torist** *n.* the user of a motor-car.—**motorboat'ing** *n.* in wireless, very low-frequency oscillations produced in a receiver. *Syn.* movement, impulse, proposition. *Ant.* rest, inertness, idleness.

Mot'ley *a.* checkered.—*n.* a motley colour; a jester's dress.—**mot'tle** *n.* a blotch on a surface; an arrangement of blotches.—*v.t.* to mark with blotches.

Mott'o *n.* a saying adopted as a rule of conduct; a short inscribed sentence; a word or sentence accompanying an heraldic crest.

Moujik' (moo-zhik) *n.* a Russian peasant.

Mould (mold) *n.* loose or surface earth.—**mould'er** *v.i.* to decay into dust.

Mould (mold) *n.* a pattern for shaping; a hollow object in which metal is cast; character, object, form.—*v.t.* to shape or pattern.—**mould'ing** *n.* a moulded object; a decoration, *esp.* a long strip of ornamental section.

Mould (mold) *n.* a growth caused by dampness.—**mould'y** *a.*

Moult (molt) *v.i.* to change feathers.—*v.t.* to shed (feathers).—*n.* the action of moulting.

Mound *n.* a heap of earth or stones; a small hill.

Mount *n.* a hill; that on which anything is supported or fitted; a horse.—*v.i.* to go up; get on horseback; to rise.—*v.t.* to go up; get on the back of; to set on a mount; to furnish with a horse.—**mount'ain** *n.* a hill of great size.—**mountaineer'** *n.* one who lives among or climbs mountains.—**mount'ainous** *a.*

Moun'tebank *n.* a quack; a market-place entertainer.

Mourn (morn) *v.i.* to feel or show sorrow.—*v.t.* to grieve for.—**mourn'er** *n.*—**mourn'ful** *a.*—**mourn'fully** *adv.*—**mourn'ing** *n.* an act of mourning; the conventional signs of grief for a death;

the clothes of a mourner.
Syn. lament, bewail, deplore.
Ant rejoice, be glad.

Mouse *n.* mice *pl.* a small rodent animal.—*v.i.* to catch mice.—mous´er *n.* a cat good at catching mice.

Moustache´ (mus-tásh) *n.* hair on the upper lip.

Mouth (-th; *pl.* THZ) *n.* an opening in the head, used for eating, speaking, etc.; an opening into anything hollow; the outfall of a river, entrance to harbour, etc.—(-TH) *v.t.* to take into the mouth; to declaim.—*v.i.* to declaim.—mouth´piece *n.* an end of anything intended to be put between the lips; one who speaks for others.

Move (mōōv) *v.t.* to change the position of; to stir; to propose.—*v.i.* to change places; to take action.—*n.* a moving; a motion making towards some goal.—move´able *a.* and *n.*—move´ment *n.* the process or action of moving; the moving parts of a machine; a main division of a piece of music.

Mo´vies (mōō-) *n. collog.* the moving pictures, the cinematograph.

Mow (mō) *v.t.* to cut (grass, etc.).—*v.i.* to cut grass.—mow´ing-machine *n.*

Much *a.* existing in quantity. —*n.* a large amount; an important matter.—*adv.* in a great degree, nearly.

Mu´cilage *n.* gum.

Muck *n.* cattle dung; unclean refuse.—muck´y *a.*

Mud *n.* wet and soft earth.—

mud´dle *v.t.* to confuse; bewilder; mismanage.—*v.i.* to be busy in a fumbling way; confusion.—mudd´y *a.*

Mud´guard *n.* a guard over a wheel to prevent mud, water, etc., being splashed over vehicle and occupants.

Muez´zin (mōō-ed-zĕn) *n.* a crier who summons =he Mohammedans to prayer.

Muff *n.* covering to keep the hands warm.

Muff *n.* one with no practical skill or sense.

Muff´in *n.* a light round flat cake.

Muff´le *v.t.* wrap up, *esp.* to deaden sound.—muff´ler *n.* a scarf to cover the neck and throat; in motoring, a silencer.

Muf´ti *n.* a Mohammedan priest; plain clothes as distinguished from uniform.

Mug *n.* a drinking cup.

Mugg´y *a.* damp and stifling.

Mulatt´o (mū-) *n.* a person with one European and one Negro parent.

Mul´berry *n.* a tree of which the leaves are much used to feed silkworms; its fruit.

Mulch *n.* straw, leaves, etc., spread as a protection for the roots of plants.—*v.t.* to protect in this way.

Mulct *n.* a fine.—*v.t.* to fine.

Mule *n.* an animal which is a cross between a horse and an ass; a stupid, obstinate person.—muleteer´ *n.* a mule driver.—mu´lish *a.*

Mulieb´rity (-li-eb) *n.* womanhood; effiminacy.

Mull *v.t.* to heat (wine) with sugar and spices.

Mull'et *n.* a sea fish sought after as food.

Mulligataw'ny *n.* a soup made with curry powder.

Mull'ion *n.* an upright dividing bar in a window or screen.

Mul'tiple *a.* having many parts.—*n.* a quantity which contains another an exact number of times.—**multipli'city**, a variety, greatness in number.—**mul'tiply** *v.t.* to make many; to find the sum of a given number taken a stated number of times.—*v.i.* to increase in number or amount.—**multiplica'tion** *n.*—**mul'titude** *n.* great number; a great crowd. — **multitu'dinous** *a.* very numerous.

Mul'tiplex *a.* manifold; multiple; in telegraphy, equipped to carry numerous messages over the same wire.

Mul'tivalve *a.* having many valves; in wireless, consisting of several thermionic valves. —*n.* a mollusc with a shell of many valves or pieces.

Mum'ble *v.i.* and *t.* to speak indistinctly.

Mumm'er *n.* one who acts in a dumb-show.—**mumm'ery** *n.* dumb-show acting.

Mumm'y *n.* an embalmed body.—**mumm'ified** *v.t.*

Mumps *n.pl.* a contagious disease marked by swelling in the glands of the neck.

Munch *v.t.* to chew noisily.

Mun'dane *a.* belonging to this world.

Muni'cipal (-is'-) *a.* belonging to the affairs of a city or town.—**munieipal'ity** *n.* a city or town with local self-government; its governing body.

Munif'icent *a.* magnificently generous.—**munif'icence** *n.* *Syn.* beneficent, liberal, generous, bountiful. *Ant.* miserly, mean, niggardly.

Muni'tion (-ish-) *n.* (usually *pl.*) military stores.

Mu'ral *a.* of or on a wall.

Mur'der *n.* the unlawful and deliberate killing of a human being.—*v.t.* to kill thus.—**mur'derer** *n.* — **mur'deress** *fem.*—**mur'derous** *a.*

Murk *n.* thick darkness.—**murk'y** *a.*

Mur'mur *v.i.* making a low continuous sound; to complain.—*v.t.* to utter in a low voice.—*n.* a sound or act of murmuring.

Murr'ain *n.* cattle plague.

Mus'cat *n.* a musk-flavoured grape; a strong wine made from it.—**muscatel'** *n.* a muscat.

Mus'cle (mus-el) *n.* a part of the body which produces movement by contracting; the part of the body made up of muscles.—**mus'cular** *a.*

Muse (-z) *n.* one of the goddesses inspiring learning and the arts.—**muse'um** *n.* a place to show objects illustrating the arts, history, etc.

Muse (-z) *v.i.* to be lost in thought.—*n.* a state of musing.

Mush *n.* porridge of maize meal (*Amer.*); in wireless, interference from high-power

arc transmitting stations.—
mush-area n.

Mush'room n. an eatable fungus.

Mu'sic (-z-) n. the art of expressing or causing an emotion by melodious and harmonious combination of notes; the laws of this; composition in this art; such composition represented on paper.—**mu'sical** a.—**mu'sically** adv.—**musi'cian** (-zish-en) n.

Musk n. a scent obtained from a gland of the musk-deer; various plants with a similar scent.—**musk'y** a.

Mus'keg n. in North America, marshy land; a bog.

Musk'et n. an infantryman's gun. esp. unrifled.—**musketeer'** n.—**musk'etry** n. use of firearms.

Mus'lin (-z-) n. a fine cotton fabric.

Muss'el n. a bivalve shellfish.

Mussoli'ni n. a dictator; a dominating personality.

Must n. new or unfermented wine.

Must v. aux. to be obliged to, or certain to.

Mus'tang n. the wild horse of the prairies.

Must'ard n. powder made from the seeds of a plant used in paste as a condiment; the plant.

Must'er v.t. and i. to assemble. —n. an assembly, esp. for exercise, inspection.

Must'y a. mouldy.

Mu'table a. liable to change.—**muta'tion** n.

Mute a. dumb; silent.—n. a dumb person; a hired mourner.—**mute'ly** a.

Mu'tilate v.t. to deprive of a limb or other part; to damage.—**mutila'tion** n.

Mu'tiny n. rebellion against authority, esp. against the officers of a disciplined body. —v.i. to commit mutiny.—**mu'tinous** a.—**mutineer'** n. Syn. of a. rebellious, insubordinate. Ant. disciplined, obedient, loyal.

Mutt'er v.i. to speak with the mouth nearly closed, indistinctly.—v.t. to utter in such tones.—n. an act of muttering.

Mutt'on n. flesh of sheep used as food.

Mu'tual a. done, possessed, etc., by each of two with respect to the other; common to both.—**mu'tually** adv. Syn. reciprocal, interchangeable, common. Ant. separate, distinct, unrelated.

Muz'zle n. projecting mouth and nose of an animal; a thing put over these to prevent biting; the end of a firearm by which the projectile leaves.—v.t. to put a muzzle on.

Muz'zy a. bewildered; tipsy.

My pron. belonging to me.

Myal'gia n. cramp in a muscle.

My'all n. in Australia, an acacia tree; a wild native; wild cattle.

Myasthen'ia n. muscular debility.

Mynheer' (-hăr, hĕr) n. in South Africa a term of respect, used to a superior; a gentleman.

Myr'iad (mir-) *n.* ten thousand; an endless number.— *a.* innumerable.

Myrioph'yllous (-of-i-lus) *a.* (*bot.*) having many leaves.

Myriora'ma *n.* a device for combining in different ways sections of views.

Myr'midon (mer-) *n.* a servile follower.—*pl.* retinue following.

Myrrh(mer)*n.*anaromaticgum.

Myr'tle (mer-) *n.* an evergreen shrub.

Mysopho'bia *n.* a morbid fear of contamination.

Mys'tery (mis-) *n.* an obscure or secret thing; a state of being obscure; a religious rite; a miracle-play.—**myste'rious** *a.*—**myste'riously** *adv.*—**myst'ic** *a.* of hidden meaning, *esp.* in a religious sense.—*n.* one who seeks direct communication with God by self-surrender or contemplation.—**myst'ical** *a.*—**myst'icism** *n.*—**myst'ify** *v.t.* to bewilder.—**mystifica'tion** *n.*

Myth (mith) *n.* a tale with supernatural characters or events; an imaginary person or object.—**myth'ical** *a.*—**mythol'ogy** *n.* myths collectively; the study of them.—**mytholog'ical** (-j-) *a.*—**mythol'ogist** *n.*

Mythog'rapher *n.* a composer or writer of fables.

N

Nab *v.t.* to catch suddenly.

Na'bit *n.* pulverised sugar-candy.

Na'bob *n.* an Indian deputy governor; a rich retired Anglo-Indian.

Nac'arat *n.* a pale-red colour with a tinge of orange.

Nacelle' *n.* a small boat; in aviation, that part of aeroplane which houses engine, pilot, passengers and goods.

Nacht slang (nåht) *n.* in South Africa, a snake that moves about at night.

Na'cre (-ker) *n.* mother-of-pearl.

Na'dir *n.* the point opposite the zenith.

Nag *n.* a small horse for riding; a horse.

Nag *v.t.* and *i.* to worry, be worrying by constant fault-finding.

Nai'ad (nī-) *n.* a river nymph.

Nail (nāl) *n.* the horny shield of the ends of the fingers; a claw; a small metal spike for fixing wood, etc.—*v.t.* to fix with a nail.

Naïve (nå-ēv) *a.*, simple, unaffected. *Syn.* frank, candid, ingenuous. *Ant.* disingenuous, sophisticated, insincere.

Na'ked *a.* without clothes; exposed, bare.—**na'kedness** *n.*—**na'kedly** *adv.*

Nam'by-pam'by *a.* weakly, sentimental.

Name *n.* the word by which a person, thing, etc., is denoted; reputation.—*v.t.* to give a name to; to call by a name; appoint; mention.—**name'less** *a.*—**name'ly** *adv.* that is to say.—**name'sake** *n.* a person having the same name as another.

Namm'a hole n. in Australia, a native well.

Nan'du (-dōō) n. the South American ostrich.

Nankeen' n. yellow cotton cloth.

Na'os n. the chief chamber of a temple; an innermost sanctuary.

Nap n. roughish surface on cloth made by projecting fibres.

Nap v.i. to take a short sleep. —n. a short sleep.

Nap n. a card game.

Nape n. the back of the neck; the hollow there.

Na'pery n. the household linen, esp. for the table.

Naph'tha n. an inflammable oil distilled from coal, etc. **naph'thalene** n. a disinfectant.

Na'piform a. turnip-shaped.

Nap'kin n. a square piece of linen used for wiping fingers or lips at table.

Napoo' a. no more; finished.

Narciss'us n. a bulbous plant with a white scented flower.

Narco'sis n. the stupefying effect of a narcotic.

Narcot'ic n. a drug causing sleep or insensibility.—a. inducing sleep.

Nardoo' n. an Australian plant, whose spores are used as food.

Nar'ghile (-gi-lā) a hookah or tobacco-pipe in which the smoke is drawn through water.

Narrate' v.t. to relate, tell (story). — narra'tion n. — narr'ative n. an account or story.—a. relating.—narra'tor n.

Narr'ow (-ō) a. of little breadth —n. a narrow part of a strait.—v.t. to make narrow. —v.i. to become narrow.— narr'owly adv.—narr'owness n.

Nar'whal n. a sea animal with a tusk or tusks developed from teeth, the sea-unicorn.

Na'sal (-z-) a. relating to the nose.—n. a sound which is partly produced in the nose. —na'salise v.t. to make nasal in sound.

Nas'cent a. just coming into existence.

Na'sicorn a. having a horn on the nose.—n. an animal having a horn on the nose.

Nasi'tis n. nasal catarrh.

Nastur'tium (-shun) n. a genus of plants which includes the watercress and a garden plant with red or orange flowers.

Nas'ty (nà-) a. foul, disagreeable.—nast'ily adv.—nas'tiness n.

Na'tal a. relating to birth.

Na'tant a. floating.

Nata'tion n. swimming.

Natato'-res (-tō-rēz) n.pl. birds that swim.

Na'tion (-shn) n. a people or race organised as a state.— na'tional (nash-) a.—nat'ionally adv.—national'ity n. national quality or feeling; the fact of belonging to a particular nation.—nat'ionalist n. one who supports national rights.—nat'ionalise v.t. to convert into the property of a nation.—

na'tive *a.* inborn; born in a particular place; found in a pure state; that was the place of one's birth.—*n.* one born in a place; an oyster reared in an artificial bed.—nativ'ity *n.* *Syn.* natural, indigenous, inborn, innate. *Ant.* foreign, alien, strange, acquired.

Natt'erjack *n.* a kind of toad.

Natt'y *a.* neat and smart.—natt'ily *adv.*—natt'iness *n.*

Na'ture *n.* the innate or essential qualities of a thing; class, sort; life force; the power underlying all phenomena in the material world; the material world as a whole.—nat'ural *a.* of, according to, occurring in, provided by, nature.—*n.* a half-witted person.—nat'urally *adv.*—nat'uralist *n.* one who studies plants and animals.—nat'uralise *v.t.* to admit to citizenship; to accustom to a new climate.—naturalisa'tion *n.*

Naught (nawt) *n.* nothing, zero.—*a.* bad, useless.—naught'y *a.* wayward, not behaving well.—naught'ily *adv.*—naught'iness *n.*

Nau'sea (-si-a) *n.* sickness.—nau'seate *v.t.* to affect with sickness; to reject with loathing.—nau'seous *a.*

Nautch (nawch) *n.* in India, a ballet dance by women called nautch-girls.

Naut'ical *a.* of seamen or ships.—naut'ilus *n.* a shellfish with a membrane which acts as a sail.

Nau'tilus (naw-) *n.* a uni-

valvular shellfish; a form of diving-bell which requires no suspension.

Naval *see* NAVY.

Nave *n.* a hub of a wheel.

Nave *n.* the main body of a church building.

Na'vel *n.* the small pit on the belly.

Navic'ular *a.* relating to small ships or boats.—*n.* the scaphoid bone of the hand or the foot.

Nav'igate *v.i.* to sail.—*v.t.* to sail over; to direct the steering of a ship.—nav'igator *n.* one who navigates; a worker employed in digging a canal.—nav'igable *a.*—naviga'tion *n.*—navv'y *n.* a labourer (*navigator* in second sense).

Na'vy *n.* a fleet; the warships of a country with their crews and organisation.—na'val *a.*

Nawab (-wawb) *n.* a viceroy; a nabob (Hind.).

Nay *adv.* no.

Na'zi (nåt-) *n.* member of the Nationalist-Socialist party in Germany.

Nean'derthal *a.* to denote man of the earliest long-headed race in Europe, which became extinct at least 20,000 years ago.

Neap *a.* neap tide, the low tide at the first and third quarters of the moon.

Neaped *a.* (*nautical*) left aground.

Near *adv.* at or to a short distance.—*prep.* close to.—*a.* close at hand, close; closely related; stingy; of

horses, vehicles, etc., left.—
v.t. and *i.* to approach.—
—near'ly *adv.* closely; almost.—near'ness *n.*

Neat *n.* ox, cow; cattle.—
neat'herd *n.* a cowherd.

Neat *a.* pure, undiluted;
simple and elegant; cleverly
worded; deft.—neat'ly *adv.*
—neat'ness *n.*

Neb'ris *n.* a fawn's skin.

Neb'ula *n.* a cluster of stars.—
neb'ular *a.*—neb'ulous *a.*
cloudy; vague.

Nec'essary (nes-) *a.* needful,
requisite, that must be done.
—*n.* a needful thing.—
nec'essarily *adv.*—necess'ity
n. a constraining power or
state of affairs; a being
needful; a needful thing;
poverty.—necess'itate *v.t.* to
make necessary.—necess'itous *a.* poor, needy. *Syn.*
essential, needful, requisite.
Ant. unnecessary, inessen-
tial, needless.

Neck *n.* the part of the body
joining the head to the
shoulders; the narrower part
of a bottle, etc; a narrow
piece of anything between
wider parts.—neck'erchief
(-chif) *n.* a kerchief for the
neck.—neck'lace *n.* an ornament round the neck.—
neck'let *n.* an ornament,
piece of fur, etc., to go
round the neck.

Necrol'atry *n.* worship of the
dead, of ancestors.

Nec'romancy *n.* magic, *esp.* by
supposed communication
with the dead.—nec'roman-
cer *n.*—necrop'olis *n.* a
cemetery.

Necro'sis *n.* gangrene, *esp.* of
a bone.

Nec'tar *n.* the drink of the
gods; the honey of flowers.—
nect'arine *a.*—*n.* a variety of
peach.

Nec'tary *n.* the honey-gland
of a flower.

Need *n.* a want, requirement,
necessity; poverty.—*v.t.* to
want, require.—need'ful *a.*—
need'less *a.*—needs *adv.* of
necessity (only in needs
must or must needs).—need'y
a. poor.

Need'fire *n.* a fire produced
by friction; phosphorescent
light of rotten wood; a
beacon.

Need'le *n.* a pointed pin with
an eye and no head, for
passing thread through
cloth, etc.; a knitting pin;
the magnetised bar of a
compass; an obelisk.

Nefar'ious (-ēr-) *a.* wicked.

Neg'ative *a.* expressing denial
or refusal; wanting in
positive qualities; not positive.—*n.* a negative word
or statement; in photo-
graphy, a picture made by
the action of light on
chemicals in which the
lights and shades are
reversed.—*v.t.* to disprove,
reject.—negate' *v.t.* to deny.
—nega'tion *n.*

Neglect' *v.t.* to disregard,
take no care of; fail to do;
omit through carelessness.—
n. the fact of neglecting or
being neglected.—neglect'ful
a.—neg'ligence *n.*—neg'li-
gent *a.* — neg'ligently *adv.*
Syn. omit, overlook, slight.

Ant. care for, cherish, regard.

Neg′ligée (-zhā) *n.* an easy, unceremonious attire.

Nego′tiate *v.i.* to discuss with a view to finding terms of agreement.—*v.t.* to arrange by conference; transfer (a bill, cheque, etc.); get over (an obstacle).—**nego′tiable** *a.* —**negotia′tion** *n.*—**nego′tiator** *n.*

Ne′gro *n.* a member of the black African race.—**ne′gress** *fem.*—**ne′groid** *a.*

Ne′gus *n.* hot mixture of wine and water flavoured.

Neigh (nā) *v.i.* of a horse, to utter its cry. — *n.* the cry.

Neigh′bour (nāber) *n.* one who lives near another.—**neigh′bouring** *a.* situated near by. **neigh′bourhood** *n.* district; people of a district; region round about.—**neigh′bourly** *a.* as or fitting a good or friendly neighbour.

Nei′ther *a.* and *pron.* not the one or the other.— *adv.* not on the one hand; not either. —*conj.* nor yet.

Nek *n.* in South Africa, a narrow ridge of land joining together two mountains or hills.

Nelum′bo *n.* a genus of water-lilies (Ceylon).

Nem′esis *n.* retribution; the goddess of retribution.

Nemoph′ilous *a.* frequenting, or dwelling, in woods.

Neolith′ic *a.* of the later stone age.—**neol′ogism** *n.* a new coined word or phrase.—**ne′ophyte** *n.* a new convert; a beginner.

Ne′on *n.* one of the inert constituent gases of the atmosphere.

Neo-so′cialist *n.* a member of a political organisation (in France) which separated from the Socialist Party to combat fascism. — **neo-socialism** *n.*

Neoter′ic *a.* new; modern.

Neph′ew *n.* a brother's or sister's son.

Ne′potism *n.* favouritism.

Nep′tune *n.* the god of the sea; the planet farthest from the sun.

Nereid (nē′-rē-id) *n.* a sea-nymph.

Ner′oli *n.* the essential oil of the bitter-orange.

Nerve *n.* sinew, tendon; a fibre or bundle of fibres conveying feeling, impulses to motion, etc., to and from the brain and other parts of the body; assurance, coolness in danger.—*pl.* irritability, unusual sensitiveness to fear, annoyance, etc.—*v.t.* to give courage or strength to. —**nerve′less** *a.*—**nerv′ous** *a.* of the nerves; vigorous; excitable, timid.—**nerv′ously** *adv.* — **nerv′ousness** *n.* — **nerv′y** *a.*

Nes′cient (nesh-yent) *a.* ignorant.—**nes′cience** *n.*

Ness *n.* a headland.

Nest *n.* the place in which a bird lays and hatches its eggs; an animal's breeding place; any snug retreat.—*v.i.* to make or have a nest.—**nes′tle** (-sl) *v.i.* to settle comfortably, usually pressing in or close to something.—

nest'ling *n*. a bird too young to leave the nest.

Net *n*. an open-work fabric of meshes of cord, etc.; a piece of it used to catch fish, etc.—*v.t.* to cover with, or catch in, a net.—*v.i.* to make net.—netting *n*. string or wire net.

Net *a*. left after all deductions; free from deduction.—*v.t.* to gain as clear profit.

Ne'temere' (nĕ-tĕm-e-rē) *n*. Papal decree, that marriage between Roman Catholics and members of other faiths is not valid unless solemnised by a Roman Catholic bishop or his deputy.

Neth'er (-TH-) *a*. lower.

Net'suke (-sū-kā) *n*. carved wooden or ivory toggle or button worn by Japanese.

Nett'le *n*. a plant with stinging hairs on the leaves.—*v.t.* to irritate, provoke.—nett'le-rash *n*. a disorder of the skin like the effect of nettle stings.

Neural'gia (nū-) *n*. pain in the nerves, *esp*. in the face and head.—neural'gica.—neuras-the'nia *n*. nervous debility.—neurasthe'nic *a*.—neuri'tis *n*. inflammation of nerves.—neurot'ic *a*. suffering from nervous disorder; abnormally sensitive.—*n*. a neurotic person.

Neuro'sis *n*. nervous disease without lesion of parts.

Neut'er *a*. neither masculine nor feminine.—*n*. a neuter word; the neuter gender.—neut'ral *a*. taking neither side in a war, dispute, etc.; without marked qualities; belonging to neither of two classes.—*n*. a neutral state, or a subject of one.—neu-tral'ity *n*.—neut'ralise *v.t.* to make ineffective; to counterbalance.

Neu'trodyne *a*. in wireless, a form of valve control to prevent interference and gain clearness of sound.

Neve *n*. a mass of snow-ice, not yet converted into a glacier.

Nev'er *adv*. at no time.—nevertheless' *adv*. for all that.

Never-never *n*. the thinly-populated country far from settlement, *esp*. in Western Queensland and the Northern Territory.

New *a*. not existing before, fresh; that has lately come into some state or existence.—*adv*. (usually new-) recently, fresh.—newfang'led (-ng-gld) *a*. of new fashion.—new'ly *adv*.—new'ness *n*.—news'paper *n*. a periodical publication containing news.—news *n*. report of recent happenings. fresh information.—news'monger *n*. a gossip. *Syn*. novel, recent, modern. *Ant*. old, stale, worn, antiquated.

New'el *n*. the central pillar of a winding staircase; the post at the top or bottom of a staircase rail.

Newfound'land *n*. a kind of large dog.

Newt *n*. a small tailed amphibious creature.

Next *a*. nearest; immediately

following.—*adv.* on the first future occasion.

Nexus *n.* tie; connection.

Nib *n.* a split pen-point.—*pl.* crushed cocoa beans.

Nib'ble *v.t.* to take little bites of.—*v.i.* to take little bites.—*n.* a little bite.

Nib'lick *n.* a golf-club with a cup-shaped iron head.

Nice *a.* hard to please; careful, exact; difficult to decide; minute; subtle, fine; (*slang*) pleasant, friendly, kind, agreeable, etc., etc.—**nice'ly** *adv.*—**ni'cety** *n.* precision; minute distinction or detail.

Niche (-tsh) *n.* a recess in a wall.

Nick *v.t.* to make a notch in, indent; just catch in time.—*n.* a notch; the exact point of time.

Nick'el *n.* a silver-white metal much used in alloys and plating.

Nickname *n.* a name added to or replacing an ordinary name, e.g. William *the Silent, Boney* (for Napoleon), etc.—*v.t.* to give a nickname to.

Nic'otine (-ēn) *n.* a poisonous oily liquid in tobacco.—**nic'otinism** *n.* tobacco poisoning.

Nic'tate *v.i.* to wink.

Nidge *v.t.* to dress stones with a sharp-pointed hammer.

Niece *n.* a brother's or sister's daughter.

Nif'ty *a. colloq.* in North America, neat; smart; of the best quality.

Nigg'ard *n.* a stingy person.—**nigg'ardly** *a.* and *adv.*

Nigg'er *n.* a negro.

Nigh (nī) *a., adv.,* and *prep.* near.

Night (nīt) *n.* the time of darkness between day and day; end of daylight; dark.—**night'ly** *a.* happening or done every night; of the night.—**night'ly** *adv.* every night, by night.—**night'ingale** (-ng-g-) *n.* a small bird which sings usually at night.—**night'mare** *n.* a feeling of distress during sleep; a bad dream.—**night'shade** *n.* various plants of the potato family, some of them with very poisonous berries.

Ni'hilism *n.* rejection of all religious and moral principles; opposition to all constituted authority or government.—**ni'hilist** *n.*

Nil *n.* nothing, zero.

Nill *n.* the shining sparks of brass in melting the ore.

Nilom'eter *n.* an instrument for measuring the rise of the Nile.

Nimbif'erous *a.* bringing stormy weather.

Nim'ble *a.* active, quick.—**nim'bly** *adv.*

Nim'bus *n.* a cloud of glory, a halo; a rain-cloud or storm-cloud.

Nin'compoop *n.* a feeble character, a fool.

Nine *a.* and *n.* the cardinal number next above eight.—**ninth** (-ī-) *a.*—**ninth'ly** *adv.*—**nine'ty** *a.* and *n.* nine tens.—**nine'tieth** *a.*—**nine'pins** *n.pl.* a game in which nine wooden " pins " are set up to be knocked down by a ball rolled at them, skittles.

Ninn'y *n.* a fool; a simpleton; a doll.

Nio'bium *n.* a steel-gray metallic element.

Nip *v.t.* to pinch sharply; detach by pinching; check growth (of plants) thus.—*n.* a pinch; a check to growth; sharp coldness of weather.— **nipp'ers** *n.pl.* pincers.

Nipperkin *n.* a small cup.

Nipp'le *n.* the point of a breast, a teat.

Nirva'na (-vå-) *n.* in Buddhism, extinction of personality as the highest good.

Nit *n.* the egg of a louse or other parasite.

Nit'id *a.* shining, lustrous.

Ni'ton *n.* radium emanation.

Ni'tre *n.* potassium nitrate, saltpetre.—**ni'trate** *n.* a compound of nitric acid and an alkali.—**ni'trogen** *n.* one of the gases making up the air.—**nitrog'enous** (-j-) *a.* of or containing nitrogen.— **ni'tric** *a.*—**ni'trous** *a.*— **nitrogly'cerine** (-s-) *n.* an explosive liquid.

Nix *n.* in South Africa, nothing.—**nix'-nic** *n.* absolutely nothing.

No *a.* not any.—*adv.* expresses a negative reply to question or request.—**no'body** *n.* no person; a person of no importance.—**noth'ing** (nuth'-) *n.* not anything.

Nobb'ler *n.* in Australia, a drink of spirits.—**nob'lerise** *v.i.* to drink heavily.

No'ble *a.* distinguished by deeds, character, rank or birth; of lofty character; impressive; excellent.—*n.* a member of the nobility.— **nobil'ity** *n.* the class holding special rank, usually hereditary, in a state; a being noble.—**no'bly** *adv.*—**no'bleman** *n.* *Syn.* aristocratic, honourable, renowned, magnanimous. *Ant.* ignoble, dishonourable, ungenerous, humble.

No'cent *a.* injurious; hurtful; mischievous.

Noctur'nal *a.* of, in, or by, night; active by night.— **noc'turne** *n.* a dreamy piece of music; a night scene.

Noc'uous *a.* hurtful.

Nod *v.i.* to bow the head slightly and quickly in assent, command, etc.; to let the head droop with sleep.—*v.t.* to incline (the head) thus.—*n.* an act of nodding.

Nod'dle *n.* the head.

Node *n.* a knot or knob; a point at which a curve crosses itself.—**no'dal** *a.*

Nod'ule *n.* a little knot; a rounded irregular mineral mass.

Noet'ic *a.* relating to, or originating in the intellect; noetical.

Nog *n.* a tree-nail; a timber-brick.—**nogging** *n.* a wall of scantling filled with bricks.

Noggin *n.* a small mug; a gill.

Noil *n.* a short staple wool combed out from the long staple.

Noise *n.* clamour, din; any sound.—*v.t.* to rumour.—

noise'less *a.*—**nois'y** *a.*—**nois'ily** *adv.*

Nois'ome *a.* disgusting.

Nom'ad *a.* roaming from pasture to pasture.—*n.* a member of a nomad tribe; a wanderer.—**nomad'ic** *a.*

No-man's-land *n.* the ground between trenches occupied by hostile armies.

No'menclature *n.* a system of names or naming.

Nom'inal *a.* of a name or names; existing only in name.—**nom'inally** *adv.*—**nom'inate** *v.t.* to propose as a candidate; appoint to an office.—**nom'inator** *n.*—**nomina'tion** *n.* — **nominee'** *n.*

Non- *prefix* makes compounds which negative the idea of the simple word, e.g. **noncom'batant** *n.* one who does not fight; **noncommis'sioned** *a.* not commissioned. The meaning and derivation of those not given should be sought by reference to the simple word.

Non'age *n.* minority.

Nonagenar'ian (-ēr-) *a.* between ninety and a hundred years old.—*n.* a person of such age.

Non'agon *n.* a nine-sided figure.

Nonce *n.* **for the nonce,** for the occasion only.

Non'chalant (-sh-) *a.* unconcerned. — **non'chalantly** *adv.*—**non'chalance** *n.*

Nonconform'ist *n.* one who does not conform to the established church.—**nonconform'ity** *n.*

Non'descript *a.* not easily described, indeterminate.

None (nun) *pron.* no one.—*a.* no.—*adv.* in no way.

Nonen'tity *n.* non-existence; a non-existent thing; a person of no importance.

Nonpareil' (-rel) *a.* unequalled.—*n.* something unequalled.

Nonplus' *n.* a state of perplexity, a deadlock —*v.t.* to bring to a nonplus.

Non'sense *n.* lack of sense; language without meaning.

Noo'dle *n.* a simpleton, a foolish person.

Nook (-ōō-) *n.* a sheltered corner.

Noon (-ōō-) *n.* midday.—**noon'tide** *n.* the time about noon.

Noose (-ōō-) *n.* a running loop; snare.—*v.t.* to catch in a noose.

Nor *conj.* and not.

Norm *n.* a rule or authoritative standard; a model.

Nor'mal *a.* perpendicular; conforming to type, ordinary.—**nor'mally** *adv.*—**normal'ity** *n.* *Syn.* natural, regular, ordinary, customary. *Ant.* abnormal, unnatural, unusual, strange.

North (-th) *n.* the region or cardinal point opposite to the midday sun; the part of the world, of a country, etc., towards this point.—*adv.* towards or in the north.—*a.* to, from, or in, the north.—**nor'therly** (-TH-) *a.*—**nor'thern** *a.*—**nor'therner** *n.*—**north'wards** *adv.*

Nose *n.* the organ of smell, used also in breathing.—*v.t.*

to detect by smell.—*v.i.* to smell.—**nose'gay** *n.* a bunch of sweet-smelling flowers.

Nosol'ogy *n.* the branch of medicine treating generally of diseases; classification of the phases of disease.—**nosolog'ical.**

Nostal'gia *n.* home-sickness.

Nos'tril *n.* one of the openings of the nose.

Nos'trum *n.* a quack medicine; a pet scheme.

Not *adv.* expressing negation.

No'table *a.* worthy of note, remarkable.—**no'tably** *adv.* —**notabil'ity** *n.* an eminent person.—**no'tary** *n.* a person authorised to draw up deeds, etc.—**nota'tion** *n.* the representing of numbers, quantities, etc., by symbols; a set of such symbols.—**note** *n.* a symbol standing for a musical sound; a single tone; a mark, sign; a brief written message, memorandum, letter; fame, regard.—*v.t.* to observe; to set down.—**no'ted** *a.* well known.—**note'worthy** *a.* worth noting, remarkable. *Syn.* memorable, distinguished, prominent, important. *Ant.* unnoted, unknown, ordinary, commonplace.

Notal'gia *n.* pain in the back.

Notan'dum *n.* something to be noted.

Notch *n.* a V-shaped cut or indentation.—*v.t.* to make notches in; to score.

Note *n.* a mask; a brief comment; a short letter.—*v.t.* to observe, to record.

Noth'ing (nuth-) *n.* no thing; not anything, naught.—*adv.* not at all.

No'tice (-tis) *n.* warning, intimation, announcement. a bill, etc., with an announcement.—*v.t.* to mention; observe; give attention to.—**no'ticeable** *a.*—**no'tify** (-ī) *v.t.* to report, give notice of or to.—**notifica'tion** *n.*—**no'tion** *n.* an idea, opinion, belief; fancy.—**notor'ious** *a.* known for something bad; well known.—**notori'ety** *n.*

No'tochord *n.* the rudimentary backbone.

Notwithstand'ing *prep.* in spite of.—*adv.* all the same.—*conj.* although.

Nongat (nōōgà) *n.* a soft kind of toffee, usually containing nuts.

Nought (nawt) *n.* nothing; a cipher (O).

Noumenon *n.*; *pl.* **noumena,** a thing as discerned by the understanding.

Noun (nown) *n.* a word used as a name of person, or thing.

Nour'ish (nur-) *v.t.* to supply with food; keep up.—**nour'ishment** *n.*

Nous *n.* mind; sense.

Nova'tion *n.* the substitution of a new title for an old one.

Nov'el *a.* new, strange.—*n.* a fictitious tale published as a whole book.—**nov'elist** *n.* a writer of novels.—**nov'elty** *n.*—**novelette'** *n.* a short novel.

November *n.* the eleventh month.

Nov'ice *n.* a candidate for admission to a religious order; one new to anything.

—novi'tiate, novi'ciate(-vish-) *n.*

Now *adv.* at the present time.—now'adays *adv.* in these times.

Now'el (nou-, nō-) *n.* the inner part of a large mould used for castings.

Now'el, No'el *n.* Christmas.

Nox'ious (-kshus) *a.* hurtful. *Syn.* harmful, dangerous, insalubrious. *Ant.* innocuous, harmless, safe, wholesome.

Noz'zle *n.* a pointed spout, *esp.* at the end of a hose.

Nu'ance (nū-ãns) *n.* a shade of difference.

Nu'bile *a.* marriageable.—nubility *n.*

Nu'cleus *n.* a centre, kernel; a beginning meant to receive additions.

Nude *a.* naked.—nu'dity *n.*

Nudge *v.t.* to touch slightly with the elbow.—*n.* such touch.

Nu'gatory *a.* trifling.

Nugg'et *n.* a rough lump of native gold.

Nui'sance (nū-) *n.* something harmful, offensive, or annoying.

Null *a.* of no effect, void.—null'ity *n.*—null'ify *v.t.*

Null'a-null'a (nŏŏl-) *n.* in Australia, a club used in battle by the Aborigines.

Null'ah *n.* a water-course.

Numb (num) *a.* deprived of feeling, *esp.* by cold.—*v.t.* to make numb.

Num'ber *n.* sum or aggregate; word or symbol saying how many; a single issue of a paper, etc., issued in regular series; classification as to singular or plural; rhythm; metrical feet or verses; a company or collection.—*v.t.* to count; to class, reckon; give a number to; amount to.—num'berless *a.* that cannot be counted.—nu'meral *a.* of or expressing number.—*n.* a sign or word denoting a number.—nu'merate *v.t.* to count.—numera'tion *n.*—nu'merator *n.* the top part of a fraction, the figure showing how many of the fractional units are taken.—numer'ical *a.* of, or in respect of, number, or numbers.—nu'merous *a.* many.

Num'bles *n.pl.* the entrails of a deer.

Numismat'ic *a.* of coins.—*n.* in *pl.* the study of coins.—numis'matist *n.*

Num'nah *n.* a thick cloth placed under a saddle.

Num'skull *n.* a dolt.

Nun *n.* a woman living in a convent under religious vows.—nunn'ery *n.* a convent of nuns.

Nun'cio (-shi-) *n.* a representative of the Pope at a foreign court.

Nuncu'pate *v.t.* to vow publicly; to dedicate.

Nup'tial *a.* of or relating to marriage or a marriage.—*n.* in *pl.* a marriage.

Nur *n.* a knot in wood; a knob.—nur and spell, a game played with a trap and ball.

Nurse *n.* a person trained for the care of the sick or

injured; a woman tending another's child.—*v.t.* to act as a nurse to.—**nurs′ery** *n.* a room for children; a rearing place for plants.—**nurs′eryman** *n.* an owner of a nursery garden.—**nurs′ling** *n.* an infant.

Nur′ture *n.* bringing-up.—*v.t.* to bring up.

Nut *n.* a fruit consisting of a hard shell and a kernel; a small block with a hole to be screwed on a bolt.—*v.i.* to gather nuts.—**nut′meg** *n.* the aromatic seed of an Indian tree.

Nu′tant *a.* nodding; bent downwards, of flowers; **nuta′tion** *n.* a slight declination of the earth's axis.

Nu′tria *n.* the fur of a South American rodent about the size and shape of a beaver.

Nu′trient *a.* nourishing.—*n.* something nutritious.

Nu′triment *n.* food.—**nutri′tion** (-trishn) *n.* the receiving or supply of food; food.—**nutri′tious** *a.* good in effects as food.—**nu′tritive** *a.*

Nux vom′ica *n.* the seed of an Eastern tree which yields strychnine.

Nuz′zle *v.i.* to burrow or press with the nose; nestle.

Nyctalo′pia (nik-ta-lō-) *n.* night blindness.—**nyc′talops** *n.* one afflicted with nyctalopia.

Nyl′ghau (-gaw) *n.* a large Indian antelope.

Nymph *n.* a legendary semi-divine maiden living in the sea, woods, mountains, etc.

Nym′pha *n.* a pupa or chrysalis.

O

Oaf *n.* a changeling; a dolt.

Oak *n.* a familiar forest tree.—**oak′en** *a.*

Oak′um *n.* loose fibre got by picking old rope.

Oar *n.* a wooden lever with a broad blade worked by the hands to propel a boat.—**oars′man** *n.*—**oars′manship** *n.*

Oa′sis (ō-ā-) *n.* a fertile spot in the desert.

Oast *n.* a kiln for drying hops.

Oat *n.* a grain of a common cereal plant (usually *pl.*), the plant.—**oat′en** *a.*—**oat′meal** *n.*

Oath *n.* the confirmation of the truth of a statement by the naming of something sacred; an act of swearing.

O′cor′date *a.* heart-shaped, but having the broader notched end at the base.

Obduce′ *v.t.* to draw over as a covering.

Ob′durate *a.* stubborn.—**ob′duracy** *n.* *Syn.* hard, callous, impenitent, inflexible. *Ant.* yielding, flexible, obedient, docile.

Obedient *see* OBEY.

Obeis′ance (-bās-, or -bēs-) *n.* a bow; a curtsey.

Ob′elisk *n.* a tapering stone shaft of rectangular section.

Obese′ *a.* very fat.—**obe′sity** *n.*

Obey (-bā) *v.t.* to do the bidding of; to be moved by.—**obe′dience** *n.*—**obe′dient** *a.*—**obe′diently** *adv.*

Ob′fuscate *v.t.* to stupefy.

Māte, mēte, mīte, mōte, mūte, bōōt.

Ob'iter *adv.* incidentally.— **obiter dictum,** an incidental opinion.

Obit'uary *n.* a notice or record of a death or deaths.

Ob'ject *n.* a material thing; that to which feeling or action is directed; an end or aim; a word dependant on a verb or preposition.— **object'** *v.t.* to state in opposition.—*v.i.* to feel dislike or reluctance to something.— **objec'tion** *n.*—**objec'tionable** *a.*—**objec'tive** *a.* external to the mind.—*n.* a thing or place aimed at.—**objectiv'ity** *n.*—**objec'tor** *n.*

Ob'jurgate *v.t.* to scold.— **objurga'tion** *n.*

Oblate' *a.* of a sphere, flattened at the poles.

Obla'tion *n.* an offering.— **ob'late** *n.* a person dedicated to religious work.

Obliga'to *a.* an accompaniment necessary to the effect.

Oblige' *v.t.* to bind morally or legally to do a service to; to compel.—**obliga'tion** *n.* a binding promise; a debt of gratitude; a favour; duty.— **oblig'atory** *a.* required; binding.—**ob'ligate** *v.t.*—**obli'ging** *a.* ready to serve others. *Syn.* to gratify, accommodate, compel, necessitate. *Ant.* incommode, embarrass, hinder, thwart.

Oblique' (-lĕk) *a.* slanting; indirect.—**obliq'uity** *n.*—**oblique'ly** (-lĕk-li) *adv.*

Oblit'erate *v.t.* to blot out.— **oblitera'tion** *n.*

Obliv'ion *n.* forgetting or being forgotten.—**obliv'ious** *a.*

Ob'long *a.* rectangular with adjacent sides unequal.—*n.* an oblong figure.

Ob'loquy *n.* abuse; disgrace. *Syn.* disgrace, odium, infamy. *Ant.* favour, respect, esteem.

Obnox'ious (-okshus) *a.* offensive, disliked.

O'boe (-boi) *n.* a wood wind instrument.

Ob'ole *n.* (*pharmacy*) a weight of 10 grains.

Obo'vate *a.* (*botany*) inversely ovate.

Obrep'tion *n.* act of creeping in by secrecy and surprise.

Obscene' *a.* indecent.—**obscen'ity** *n.*

Obscure' *a.* dark, dim; indistinct; unexplained; humble. —*v.t.* to dim; conceal; make unintelligible.—**obscu'rant** *n.* one who opposes enlightenment or reform.—**obscu'rantism** *n.*—**obscu'rity** *n.*

Ob'secrate *v.t.* to beseech; to entreat.—**obsecra'tion** *n.* act of imploring.

Ob'sequies (-iz) *n.pl.* funeral rites.

Obse'quious *a.* servile, fawning.

Observe' (-z-) *v.t.* to keep, follow; watch; note systematically; notice; remark.—*v.i.* make a remark.—**observ'able** *a.* — **observ'ably** *adv.* — **observ'ant** *a.* quick to notice.— **observ'ance** *n.* paying attention; keeping.—**observa'tion** *n.* action or habit of observing; noticing; a remark.— **observ'atory** *n.* a place for watching stars, etc.—**observ'er** *n.*

Obsess' *v.t.* to haunt, fill the mind.—**obses'sion** *n.*

Obsid'ian *n.* a fused volcanic rock.

Obsig'nate *v.t.* to seal; to ratify.

Ob'solete *a.* no longer in use, out of date.—obsoles'cent *a.* going out of use. *Syn.* old, ancient, archaic, effete. *Ant.* current, used, modern, recent.

Ob'stacle *n.* a thing in the way.

Obstet'ric *a.* of midwifery.— *n.* in *pl.* midwifery.—obstetric'ian *n.* one skilled in obstetrics.

Ob'stinate *a.* stubborn.— ob'stinacy *n.*—ob'stinately *adv.*

Obstipa'tion *n.* a stopping; costiveness.

Obstrep'erous *a.* unruly.

Obstruct' *v.t.* to hinder; block up. — obstruc'tion *n.* — obstruc'tionist *n.*—obstruc'tive *a.*

Ob'struent *a.* blocking up; hindering.—*n.* anything that obstructs.

Obtain' *v.t.* to get.—*v.i.* to be customary.—obtain'able *a.*

Obtec'ted *a.* covered; protected.

Obtem'per *v.t.* Scots law, to obey; to comply with.

Obtest' *v.t.* to beseech.— obtesta'tion *n.* supplication.

Obtrude' *v.t.* to thrust forward unduly.—obtru'sion *n.*—obtru'sive *a.*—obtru'sively *adv.*

Obtuse' *a.* not sharp or pointed; greater than a right angle; stupid.—obtuse'ly *adv.*

Ob'verse *n.* the side of a coin or medal opposite the side with the chief design.

Ob'viate *v.t.* to prevent.

Ob'vious *a.* clear, evident. *Syn.* plain, manifest, open. *Ant.* hidden, obscure, doubtful.

Ocari'na (-rē-) *n.* a small wind instrument of music made of terra-cotta.

Occa'sion *n.* opportunity; reason, need; immediate but subsidiary cause; time when a thing happens.— *v.t.* to cause. — occa'sional *a.* happening or found now and then.—occa'sionally *adv.* sometimes, now and then.

Occa'sive (o-ka'-siv) *a.* pertaining to the setting sun.

Oc'cident (-ks-) *n.* the West.— occident'al *a.*

Oc'ciput (ok'-si-) *n.* the hind part of the head.—occip'ital *a.* pertaining to the occiput.

Occlu'sion *n.* act of shutting up; absorption.—oc'clude *v.t.* to shut up.

Occult' *a.* secret, mysterious. —*v.t.* to hide from view.— occulta'tion *n.*

Occ'upy *v.t.* to take possession of; inhabit; fill; employ.— occ'upancy *n.* fact of occupying; residing.—occ'upant *n.* —occupa'tion *n.* seizure; possession; employment.— occ'upier *n.*

Occur' *v.i.* to happen; come to mind.—occurr'ence *n.*

O'cean (ō-shn) *n.* the great body of water surrounding the land of the globe; a large division of this; the sea.—ocean'ic (ō-shi-, or ō-si-) *a.*

Oceanol'ogy (ō-shē-a-nol-o-ji) *n.* that branch of science which relates to the ocean.

O'celot n. the leopard cat of America.

O'chre (ō-ker) n. various earths used as yellow or brown pigments.

Oct-, oc'ta-, oc'to- prefix eight.—oc'tagon n. a figure with eight angles.—octag-onal a.—oc'tave n. a group of eight days; eight lines of verse; a note eight degrees above or below a given note; this space.—octa'vo n. a size of book in which each sheet is folded into eight leaves.—Octo'ber n. the tenth month (Roman eighth).—octogen-a'rian a. of an age between eighty and ninety.—n. a person of such age.—oc'topus n. a mollusc with eight arms covered with suckers.—octosyll'able n. a word of eight syllables.—octet' n. a group of eight.

Oc'tad n. a system or series of eight.

Octan'dria n. a class of plants which have hermaphrodite flowers, with 8 stamens.

Oc'tant n. the eighth part of a circle; an instrument for measuring angles; having an arc of 45°.

Octenn'ial a. happening every eighth year; lasting eight years.

Oc'topod a. having 8 feet.—n. an animal with 8 feet.

Oc'troi(-trwa) n. a duty paid on goods entering French cities.

Oc'ular a. of the eye or sight.—oc'ularly adv.—oc'ulist n. an eye surgeon.

Oc'ulomotor a. connected with movement of the eye.

Od n. a natural power supposed to produce the phenomena of mesmerism.

Odd a. that is one in addition when the rest have been divided into two equal groups; not even; not part of a set; strange, queer.—odd'ity n. quality of being odd; an odd person or thing.—odd'ments n.pl. odd things.—odds n.pl. difference, balance; advantage to one of two competitors; advantage conceded in betting; likelihood.—odds and ends, odd fragments or left-over things.

Ode n. a lyric poem of lofty style.

O'dium n. hatred, widespread dislike.—o'dious a. hateful.

O'dograph n. a device for recording the rapidity, length, and number of strides in walking.

O'dour n. smell.—o'dorise v.t. to fill with scent.—o'dorous a.—o'dourless a.—odorif'erous a. spreading an odour.

Of prep. denotes removal, separation, ownership, attribute, material, quality, etc.

Off adv. away.—prep. away from.—a. distant; of horses, vehicles, etc., right.—off-hand' a. and adv. without previous thought or preparation.—off'scourings n.pl. worst part, dregs.—off'set n. side branch.—off'spring n. children, issue.—off'ing n. the more distant part of the sea visible to an observer.

Off'al n. parts cut out in preparing a carcase for food; refuse.

Offend' *v.t.* to displease.—*v.i.* to do wrong.—**offence'** *n.*—**offend'er** *n.*—**offen'sive** *a.* causing displeasure.—*n.* position or movement of attack. *Syn.* to annoy, shock, insult. *Ant.* please, humour, delight.

Off'er *v.t.* to present for acceptance or refusal; propose; attempt.—*v.i.* present itself.—*n.* an offering, bid.—**off'erer** *n.*—**off'ertory** *n.* collection in a church service.

Off'ice *n.* a service; a duty; official position; form of worship; a place for doing business; a corporation carrying on business.—*pl.* the parts of a house in which the domestic work is done.—**off'icer** *n.* one in command in an army, navy, ship, etc.—*v.t.* to supply with officers.—**offi'cial** (-fish'-) *a.* having or by authority.—*n.* one holding an office, *esp.* in a public body.—**offi'cialism** *n.* undue official authority or routine.—**offi'cialdom** *n.* officials collectively; their work, usually in a contemptuous sense.—**officiate** *v.i.* to perform the duties of an office; perform a service.—**offi'cious** (-ishus) *a.* meddlesome, importunate in offering service.

Off'ing, off'shoot, etc., *see* OFF.

Off'ward *adv.* (*naut.*), away from the land.

Oft, of'ten (of-n) *adv.* many times. frequently.

Og'doad (-do-ad) *n.* anything consisting of eight parts.

O'gee *n.* a moulding of two members, the one concave the other convex, somewhat like an S.

Ogive' (-i-) *n.* a pointed arch.

O'gle *v.i.* to make eyes.—*v.t.* to make eyes at.—*n.* an amorous glance.

O'gre (-ger) *n.* a man-eating giant.—**o'gress** *fem.*

Oh *interj.* an exclamation of surprise, pain, anxiety.

Ohm *n.* the unit of electrical resistance.

Oil *n.* a light inflammable viscous liquid, obtained from various plants, animal substances, and minerals.—*v.t.* to apply oil to.—**oil'y** *n.*

Oil'et, oillett, oillette (oil'-et) *n.* a loophole.

Oint'ment *n.* a greasy preparation for healing or beautifying the skin.

O.K. *abbrev.* an expression signifying approval.

Old (old) *a.* advanced in age, having lived or existed long; belonging to an earlier period.—**old'en** *a.* old.—**old-fash'ioned** *a.* in the style of an earlier period, out of date; fond of old ways. *Syn.* venerable, antiquated, ancient. *Ant.* young, new, modern.

Oleag'inous (ō-lē-aj-) *a.* oily, producing oil; unctuous.—**oleag'inousness** *n.* — **o'leograph** *n.* a picture printed in oils.—**oleom'eter** *n.* an instrument for ascertaining the weight and purity of oils.

Olean'der (ō-lē-an-) *n.* an evergreen flowering shrub.

O'leograph *n.* a lithograph in oil-colours.

Olfac'tory *a.* of smell.

Ol'igarchy (-ki) *n.* government by a few.—ol'igarch *n.*—oligarch'ic *a.*

Ol'ive (-iv) *n.* an evergreen tree; its oil-yielding fruit.—*a.* gray-green in colour.

Oma'sum *n.* the third stomach of ruminants.

Om'elet, om'elette *n.* a dish of fried eggs with seasoning, etc.

O'men *n.* a prophetic object or happening.—om'inous *a.* portending evil.

Omit' *v.t.* to leave out, neglect.—omis'sion *n.*

Om'nibus *n.* a road vehicle travelling on a fixed route and taking passengers at any stage; a vehicle taking hotel guests to or from a railway station.—*a.* serving or containing several objects.

Om'ni-direc'tional *a.* in wireless, denotes transmission in which the waves are radiated in all directions.

Omnip'otent *a.* all-powerful.—omnip'otence *n.*—omnipres'-ent *a.* everywhere at the same time.—omnipres'cence *n.*—omnis'cient (shi-ent) *a.* knowing everything.—omnis'cience *n.*—omniv'orous *a.* devouring all foods.

On *prep.* above and touching, at, near, towards, etc.—*adv.* so as to be on, forwards, continuously, etc.—on'ward *a.* and *adv.*—on'wards *adv.*

Once (wuns) *adv.* one time; ever; formerly.

On dit' (ŏn dē') *n.* a rumour; a common report.

One (wun) *a.* the lowest cardinal number; a single; a united; only, without others; identical.—*n.* the number or figure 1; unity; a single specimen.—*pron.* a particular but not stated person; any person.—oneself *pron.*—one'ness *n.*

On'erous *a.* burdensome.

On'ion (un'yun) *n.* a plant with a bulb of pungent flavour.

On'ly (ō-) *a.* that is the one specimen.—*adv.* solely, merely, exclusively.—*conj.* but then, excepting that.

Onol'ogy *n.* foolish talk.

Onomatol'ogy *n.* the science of, or a treatise on, names.

Onomatopœ'ia (-pē-ya) *n.* formation of a word by using sounds that resemble or suggest the object or action to be named.—onomatopoe'-ic, onomatopoet'ic (-po-et-) *a.*

On'set *n.* a violent attack; an assault.

On'to *prep.* on top of.

On'slaught(-slawt)*n.*an attack.

O'nus *n.* the burden.

On'ward *a.* advanced or advancing.—*adv.* in advance.

On'yx *n.* a variety of quartz.

O'olite (ō-o-līt) *n.* a limestone grained loosely like fish roe.

Ool'ogy (ō-ol-) *n.* study of eggs, and of birds during the nesting season.

Oo'long *n.* a variety of black tea possessing the flavour of green tea.

Oom *n.* in South Africa, uncle; a term of affection and respect.

Ooze *n.* wet mud, slime; sluggish flow.—*v.i.* to pass slowly through, exude.

O'pal *n.* a white or bluish stone with iridescent reflections.—opales'cent *a.* showing changing colours.

Opaque' (ŏ-pāk) *a.* not allowing the passage of light.—opa'city (ŏ-pas-) *n.*

Ope *a.* and *v.* open (used poetically).

O'pen *a.* not shut or blocked up; without lid or door; bare; undisguised; not enclosed or covered or limited or exclusive.—*v.t.* to set open, uncover, give access to; disclose, lay bare; begin; make a hole in.—*v.i.* to become open.—*n.* clear space, unenclosed country.—o'penly *adv.* without concealment.—o'pening *n.* a hole, gap; beginning.

Op'era *n.* musical drama.—operat'ic *a.*

Operam'eter *n.* an instrument for recording the number of movements made by a part of a machine.

Opera'tion *n.* working, way a thing works; scope; an act of surgery.—op'erate *v.i.*—op'erative *a.* working.—*n.* a mechanic.—op'erator *n.*

Oper'culum (ŏ-per-) *n.* a lid or cover.

Ophthal'mia *n.* inflammation of the eye.—ophthal'mic *a.*

Opiate *see* OPIUM.

Opin'ion *n.* what one thinks about something; belief, judgment.—opine' *v.t.* to think; utter an opinion.—opin'ionated *a.* stubborn in holding an opinion.

O'pium *n.* a sedative and narcotic drug made from the poppy.—o'piate *v.t.* to mix with opium.—*n.* an opiated drug.

Opop'anax (ŏ-pop-) *n.* a gum resin used in perfumes and formerly in medicines.

Oposs'um *n.* a small American marsupial animal.

Oppo'nent *n.* an adversary. *Syn.* foe, enemy, adversary. *Ant.* friend, ally, supporter.

Opp'ortune *a.* seasonable, well timed.—opportu'nity *n.* a favourable time or condition.—opp'ortunism *n.* the policy of doing what is expedient at the time regardless of principle. *Syn.* timely, welcome, seasonable. *Ant.* inopportune, unseasonable, untimely.

Oppose' (-z) *v.t.* to set against; contrast; resist, withstand.—*past p.* adverse.—oppo'ser *n.*—opp'osite (-zit) *a.* contrary, facing, diametrically different.—opposi'tion (-ish) *n.* a being opposite; resistance; a party opposed to that in power.

Oppress' *v.t.* to govern with tyranny; weigh down.—oppress'ive *a.*—oppress'ively *adv.*—oppres'sion *n.*—oppress'or *n.*

Oppro'brium *n.* disgrace.—oppro'brious *a.* *Syn.* abase, insult, disgrace. *Ant.* praise, fame, honour.

Oppugn' (o-pūn) *v.t.* to fight against; to oppose.—oppug'nant *a.* opposing.—*n.* an opponent.

Opsoma'nia *n.* a morbid liking for some particular kind of food.

Op'tative *n.* a mood of the verb expressing desire.

Op'tic *a.* of the eye or sight.— *n.* the eye; in *pl.* the science of sight or light.—op'tical *a.* —opti'cian (-ish-) *n.* a maker or dealer in optical instruments.

Op'timism *n.* belief that the world is the best possible world; doctrine that good must prevail in the end; disposition to look on the bright side.—op'timist *n.*— optimis'tic *a.*—optimis'tically *adv.*

Op'tion *n.* choice.—op'tional *a.*

Op'ulent *a.* rich.—op'ulence *n.*

O'pus *n.* a work; a musical composition.

Opus'cule (ō-pus-) *n.* a little work or treatise.

Or *conj.* introduces alternatives; if not.

Or'ach *n.* one of various plants used as spinach.

Or'acle *n.* a place where divine utterances were supposed to be given; an answer there given, often ambiguous; a wise or mysterious adviser.— orac'ular *a.* of an oracle; of dogmatic or doubtful meaning.

Or'al *a.* by mouth.—or'ally *adv.*

Or'ange (-inj) *n.* a familiar bright reddish-yellow round fruit; the tree bearing it; the colour of the fruit.—*a.* of the colour of an orange.

Orang'-outang', orang'-utan' *n.* a large ape.

Or'ator *n.* a maker of a speech, a skilful speaker.—ora'tion *n.* a formal speech.—ora-

tor'ical *a.* of an orator or oration.—or'atory *n.* speeches; eloquent language; a small chapel.—orator'io *n.* a semi-dramatic composition of sacred music.

Orb *n.* a globe, sphere.— orb'it *n.* the cavity holding the eye; the track of a heavenly body.

Orch'ard *n.* an enclosure containing fruit-trees.

Or'chestra (-k-) *n.* a band of musicians; the place occupied by such band in a theatre, etc.—orches'tral *a.* —or'chestrate *v.t.* to compose or arrange music for an orchestra.—orchestra'tion *n.*

Or'chid, or'chis (-k-) *n.* various flowering plants.

Ordain' *v.t.* to admit to the Christian ministry; confer holy orders upon; decree, destine. — ordina'tion *n.*— ord'inance *n.* a decree.

Or'deal *n.* a method of trial by requiring the accused to undergo a dangerous physical test; a trying experience.

Or'der *n.* rank, class, group; monastic society; sequence, succession, arrangement; command, pass, instruction. —*v.t.* to arrange; command; require.—or'derly *a.* methodical.—*n.* a soldier following an officer to carry orders; a soldier in a military hospital acting as attendant.—or'derliness *n.*—or'dinal *a.* showing position in a series.—or'dinary *a.* usual, commonplace. —*n.* a bishop in his province; a public meal supplied at a fixed time and price. *Syn* regularity, rule, system, injunction. *Ant.* chaos, confusion, rebellion, disorganisation.

Ordin'ance *n.* an established rule, rite, or ceremony.

Ord'nance *n.* guns, cannon; military stores.

Or'dure *n.* dung; filth.

Ore *n.* native mineral from which metal is extracted.

O'read (ō're-ad) *n.* a mountain nymph.

Or'gan *n.* a musical instrument of pipes worked by bellows and played by keys; a member of an animal or plant carrying out a particular function; a means of action; a newspaper.—**organ'ic** *a.* of the bodily organs; affecting bodily organs; having vital organs; organised, systematic.—**organ'ically** *adv.*—**or'ganism** *n.* an organised body or system.—**or'ganist** *n.* one who plays an organ.—**or'ganise** *v.t.* to furnish with news; to give a definite structure; to get up, arrange, put into working order.—**organisa'tion** *n.* — **or'ganiser** *n.*

Or'gandie *n.* a muslin of great transparency and lightness.

Or'gasm *n.* immoderate action or excitement.

Or'geat (or'-zhat) *n.* a flavouring liquor extracted from barley and sweet almonds.

Or'geis (-jē-is) *n.* a large kind of ling.

Or'gy (-ji) *n.* a drunken or licentious revel.

Or'iel *n.* a projecting part of an upper room with a window.

Or'ient *n.* the East; the lustre of the best pearls.—*a.* rising; Eastern; of pearls, from the Indian seas.—*v.t.* to place so as to face the east; to find one's bearings.—**orien'tal** *a.* and *n.*—**orienta'tion** *n.* —**orien'talist** *n.* an expert in Eastern languages and history.

Or'ifice *n.* opening, mouth of a cavity.

Or'igin *n.* beginning, source, parentage.—**ori'ginal** (-ij-) *a.* primitive, earliest; new, not copied or derived; thinking or acting for oneself; eccentric.—*n.* a pattern, thing from which another is copied; an eccentric person. —**ori'ginally** *adv.*—**original'ity** *n.*—**ori'ginate** *v.t.* to bring into existence.—**origina'tion** *n.*—**ori'ginator** *n.* *Syn.* commencement, foundation, derivation. *Ant.* end, finish, culmination.

O'riole (ō'-ri-ōl) *n.* a tropical thrush-like bird.

O'rion *n.* a bright constellation.

Or'ison *n.* a prayer.

Orle *n.* (*heraldry*) a bearing consisting of a band half the width of the border, extending round the shield near the edge.

Or'lop *n.* the lowest deck in a ship that has three decks.

Or'mer *n.* an ear-shell or sea-ear.

Or'molu (-lōō) *n.* gilded bronze; a gold-coloured alloy.

Or'nament *n.* decoration.—

v.t. to adorn.—ornament'al *a.*—ornamenta'tion *n.*—ornate' *a.* highly decorated.

Ornithol'ogy *n.* the science of birds.—ornitholo'gical *a.*—ornithol'ogist *n.*

Orog'raphy *n.* the geography of mountains. — orograph'ical *a.*

O'roide (ō-rō-id) *n.* a gold coloured alloy of copper, zinc, etc., used for cheap jewellery.

O'rotund *a.* full, clear, and musical; pompous.

Or'phan *n.* a child bereaved of one or both of its parents. —or'phanage *n.* an institution for the care of orphans. —or'phanhood *n.*

Or'piment *n.* a yellow mineral of the arsenic group, used as colouring.

Or'pington *n.* a breed of poultry, white, black or buff, of general utility.

Orr'ery *n.* an instrument constructed to show the revolutions of the planets, their relative sizes, distances, etc.

Orr'is *n.* the plant iris.

Ort *n.* a scrap of food; a fragment.

Ortho- *prefix.*—or'thodox *a.* holding accepted views; conventional.—or'thodoxy *n.* —orthog'raphy *n.* correct spelling.—orthopæd'ic *a.* for curing deformity.

Ort'olan *n.* a small bird, a bunting, *esp.* as a table delicacy.

Or'yx *n.* a genus of African antelope.

Os'cillate *v.i.* to swing to and fro; vary between extremes; set up wave motion in wireless apparatus.—oscilla'tion *n.*—os'cillator *n.* one that oscillates, *esp.* a person setting up unauthorised wireless waves from a radio receiving set.

Os'culate *v.t.* and *i.* to kiss.—oscula'tion *n.*

O'sier (-z-) *n.* a species of willow.

Os'prey *n.* the fishing eagle; egret plume.

Oss'eous *n.* of or like bone.—oss'ify *v.t.* and *i.* to turn into bone.—ossifica'tion *n.*

Osten'sible *a.* professed, used as a blind.—osten'sibly *adv.* —ostenta'tion *n.* show, display.—ostenta'tious *a.*—ostenta'tiously *adv.*

Osteop'athy *n.* art of treating diseases by removing structural derangement by manipulation, *esp.* of spine. — os'teopath *n.* one skilled in this art.

Os'tler (-sl-) *n.* a man who attends to horses.

Os'tracise *v.t.* to exclude from society, exile.—os'tracism *n.*

Os'trich *n.* a large swift-running bird.

Oth'er (UTH-) *a.* not this, not the same; alternative, different.—*pron.* other person or thing.—oth'erwise (-īz) *adv.* differently.

Otiose' (ō-shi-ōz) *a.* lazy, futile; at leisure.

Ott'er *n.* a furry aquatic fish-eating animal.

Ott'oman *n.* a cushioned seat without back or arms.

---

thère, fàther, hẹr; *awl, oil, owl.*

Ouch, nouch n. the setting of a jewel.

Ou'denarde n. a decorative tapestry, representing foliage.

Ought (awt) v. aux. expressing duty or obligation or advisability.

Ounce n. a weight, the twelfth of the troy pound, sixteenth of the avoirdupois pound.

Ounce n. a lynx; a snow-leopard.

Our pron. belonging to us.

Ou'sel (ōō-gl) n. the blackbird; applied to others of the thrush family.

Oust v.t to put out.

Ous'titi (wis-) n. a marmoset.

Out adv. from within, from among, away, not in the usual or right state.—out'ing n. a pleasure, excursion.—out'ward a. and adv.—out'wards adv.—out'wardly adv.

Out- as prefix makes many compounds with the sense of beyond, in excess, etc., e.g. outflank' v.t. to get beyond the flank.—out'put n. quantity put out, etc. These are not given where the meaning and derivation may easily be found from the simple word.

Out'back n. in Australia, remote, sparsely populated country.—a.

Out'balance v.t. to outweigh; to exceed.

Out'cast n. a vagabond; a pariah.—a. cast-out.

Outclass' v.t. to excel.

Out'crop n. (geol.) the coming out of a stratum to the surface.—v.i. to come out to the surface.

Out'door a. out of doors.

Out'fit n. a fitting-out; equipment.

Outflank' v.t. to go round the flank of.

Outgrow' v.t. to surpass in growth; to become too large or too old-for.

Out'house n. a building connected with and beside a main house.

Out'land n. foreign country.—outland'ish a. queer, extravagantly strange.

Out'law n. one placed beyond the protection of the law, an exile.—out'lawry n.

Out'rage n. violation of others' rights; gross or violent offence or indignity.—v.t. to injure, violate, ravish, insult.

Ou'tre (ōōtrā) a. extravagantly odd; bizarre.

Out'rigger n. a frame outside a ship's gunwale; a frame on the side of a rowing boat with a rowlock at the outer edge; a boat with one.

Outspan' n. in South Africa a reserved space, where animals may be unyoked and allowed to graze.

O'val a. egg-shaped, ellipitcal. —n. an oval figure or thing. —o'vary n. an egg-producing organ.

Ova'tion n. an enthusiastic burst of applause.

Ov'en (uv-) n. a heated iron box or other receptacle for baking in.

O'ver adv. above, above and beyond, going beyond, in excess, too much, past, finished, in repetition, across, etc.—*prep.* above, on, upon, more than, in excess of, along, etc.—*a.* upper, outer.

O'ver- as *prefix* makes compounds with meaning of too, too much, in excess, above, e.g. o'verdo *v.t.* to do too much.—overdraw' *v.t.* to draw in excess of what is in credit; etc. These words are not given where the meaning and derivation may easily be found from the simple word.

Overhaul' *v.t.* to come up with in pursuit; to examine and set in order.—*n.* a thorough examination, *esp.* for repairs.

Overlay' *v.t.* to spread over; to smother.

O'vert *a.* open, unconcealed.—o'vertly *adv.*

Overtake' *v.t.* to come up with in pursuit; to catch up.

Overthrow' *v.t.* to upset or overturn; to defeat.—*n.* ruin; defeat.

O'verture *n.* an opening of negotiations; a proposal; an introduction of an opera, etc.

Overween'ing *a.* thinking too much of oneself.

Overwhelm' (-whelm) *v.t.* to crush; to submerge and bear down.—overwhelm'ingly *adv.*

Ovic'ular *a.* pertaining to an egg.

O'vine (-ī-) *a.* of, or like, sheep.

Owe (ō) *v.t.* to be bound to repay, be indebted for.—ow'ing *a.* owed, due.—owing to, caused by.

Owl *n.* a night bird of prey.—owl'et *n.* a young owl.—owl'ish *a.* solemn and dull.

Own (ōn) *a.* emphasises possession.—*v.t.* to possess; acknowledge.—*v.i.* to confess. — own'er *n.* — own'ership *n.*

Ox *n.* ox'en *pl.* a large cloven-footed and usually horned animal used for draft, milk, and meat, a bull or cow.—ox'-eye *n.* a large daisy.—ox'-lip *n.* a hybrid between cowslip and primrose.

Oxal'ic *a.* of wood-sorrel.

Ox'ygen *n.* the gas in the atmosphere which is essential to life, burning, etc.——ox'ide *n.* a compound of oxygen.—ox'idise *v.t.* to cause to combine with oxygen; to cover with oxide, make rusty.—*v.i.* to combine with oxygen, to rust.

Oyez' (ū-yes) *n.* a call, usually uttered three times, by a public crier or court official to attract attention.

Oy'ster *n.* a bivalve mollusc or shellfish, usually eaten alive.

O'zone *n.* a condensed form of oxygen with a pungent odour; a refreshing influence.

P

Pace *n.* a step; the length of a step; walk or speed of stepping; speed.—*v.i.* to step.—*v.t.* to cross or measure with steps; to set the speed for.—pa'cer *n.*

Pach'yderm (-k-) *n.* thick-skinned animal, e.g. an

elephant. — **pachyderm'atous** *a.*

Pac'ify *v.t.* to calm; establish peace.—**pacifica'tiob** *n.*—**pacif'icatory** *a*—**pacif'icist, pa'cifist** *n.* an advocate on the abolition of war; one who refuses to help in war.—**paci'ficism** *n. Syn.* to quiet, still, allay. *Ant.* to rouse, incite, disturb.

Pack *n.* a bundle; company of animals; large set of people or things; a set of playing cards; a mass of floating ice. —*v.t.* to make into a bundle; to put together in a box, etc.; to fill with things; to order off.—**pack'age** *n.* a parcel.—**pack'er** *n.*—**pack'et** *n.* a small parcel.—**pack'horse** *n.* a horse for carrying bundles of goods.—**pack'-saddle** *n.* a saddle to carry goods.

Pact *n.* a covenant or agreement.

Pad *v.i.* to travel on foot.—*n.* an easy-paced horse.

Pad *n.* a piece of soft stuff used as a cushion; a shin-guard; sheets of paper fastened together in a block; foot or sole of various animals.—*v.t.* to make soft, fill in, protect, etc., with a pad or padding.—**padd'ing** *n.* material used for stuffing; literary matter put in simply to increase quantity.

Pad'dle *n.* a short oar with a broad blade at one or each end; a blade of a paddle-wheel.—*v.i.* to move by paddles; to roll gently.—*v.t.* to propel by paddles.—**pad'dle-wheel** *n.* a wheel with

crosswise blades which strike the water successively to propel ship.—**pad'dle-box** *n.* the upper casing of a paddle-wheel.

Pad'dle *v.i.* to walk with bare feet in shallow water.

Padd'ock *n.* a small grass field or enclosure.

Padd'y *n.* an Irishman.

Padd'y *n.* rice in the husk.—**paddyfield** *n* the field where rice is grown.

Padd'ymelon *n.* in Australia, a species of kangaroo.

Padell'a *n.* a shallow vessel in which fat is burned by means of a wick.

Pad'kost *n.* in South Africa, food for a journey.

Pad'lock *n.* a detachable lock with a hinged hoop to go through a staple or ring.—*v.t.* to fasten with padlock.

Pa'dre (pà-drā) *n.* a chaplain with H.M. Forces.

Pæan *n.* a shout or song of triumph.

Pædiat'rics *n.* care of children in sickness and in health.

Pædobap'tism *n.* the baptism of infants.

Pa'gan *a.* heathen.—*n.* a heathen.—**pa'ganism** *n.*

Page *n.* a boy servant or attendant.

Page *n.* one side of a leaf of a book.—*v.t.* to number the pages of. — **pa'ginate** *v.t.* to number the pages of.—**pagina'tion** *n.*

Pa'geant (paj-ent) *n.* a show of persons in costume in procession, dramatic scenes, etc., usually illustrating history; a brilliant show.—pa′geantry n.

Pago′da n. a temple or sacred tower of Chinese or Indian type.

Pag′ter n. in South Africa, a tenant farmer; a retailer licensed to sell spirits.

Pah interj. an exclamation of disgust or contempt.

Pai′gle (pa-gl) n. the cowslip; buttercup, etc.

Pail n. a bucket.—pail′ful n.

Paill′asse, pall′iasse (palyas) n. a straw mattress.

Paillette′ n. a piece of metal or coloured foil used in enamel painting; a sponge.

Pain n. bodily or mental suffering; penalty or punishment.—v.t. to inflict pain upon.—pain′ful a.—pain′fully adv.—pain′less a.—pain′lessly adv.—pains′taking a. diligent, careful. Syn. anguish, agony, distress, torment. Ant. ease, comfort. solace.

Paint n. colouring matter prepared for putting on a surface with brushes.—v.t. to portray, colour, coat, or make a picture of, with paint; to describe.—paint′er n.—paint′ing n. a picture in paint.

Paint′er n. a rope for fastening the bow of a boat to a ship, etc.

Pair (pàr) n. a set of two, esp. existing or generally used together.—v.t. to arrange in a pair or pairs.—v.i. to come together in a pair or pairs.

Pais (pā) n. the people from whom a jury is drawn.

Paja′mas, pyjamas (pa-já-maz, pi-) n.pl. loose drawers or trousers, worn by both sexes in India; a chamber garment.

Pal n. (colloquial) a mate or partner.

Pal′ace n. the official residence of a king, bishop, etc.; a stately mansion.—pala′tial a.—pal′atine a. having royal privileges.

Pal′adin n. a chivalrous person (originally one of the twelve peers of Charlemagne).

Pal′ama n. the webbing of the toes of a bird.

Pal′ate n. roof of the mouth; the sense of taste.—pal′atable a. agreeable to eat.—pal′atal a. of the palate; made by placing the tongue against the palate.—n a palatal sound.

Palatial, palatine see PALACE.

Pala′ver (-à-) n. a conference; empty talk.—v.i. to use many words.

Pale a. faint in colour, dim, whitish.—v.i. to grow white.

Pale n. a stake, boundary.—paling n. (usually in pl.) a fence.

Pal′ette n. an artist's flat board for mixing colours on.

Pal′frey n. a small saddle-horse.

Palisade′ n. a fence of stakes.—v.t. to enclose with one.

Pall (pawl) n. a cloth spread over a coffin.

Pall (pawl) v.i. to become tasteless or tiresome.

Pall′et n. a straw bed; a mean bed.

Pall′iate v.t. to relieve without

curing; to excuse. — **pallia'tion** n.—**pall'iative** a. giving temporary or partial relief.— n. a thing doing this. *Syn.* to lessen, extenuate, gloss. *Ant.* to aggravate, irritate, provoke.

Pall'id a. pale.—**pall'or** n. paleness.

Pall-mall' n. an old game which was played in St. James's Park, London, and gave name to the adjacent street.

Palm (päm) n. the flat of the hand; a tropical tree; a leaf of the tree as a symbol of victory.—v.t. to conceal in the palm of the hand; to pass off by trickery.—**palm'istry** n. fortune-telling from the lines on the palm of the hand.—**palm'ist** n.—**palm'ary** a. worthy of a palm of victory, distinguished.—**palm'er** n. a pilgrim returned from the Holy Land.—**Palm Sunday** n. the Sunday before Easter.—**palm'y** a. flourishing.

Pal'miped a. web-footed.—n. a swimming bird.

Pal'pable a. that may be touched or felt; certain, obvious.—**pal'pably** adv.—**pal'pitate** v.i. to throb.—**palpita'tion** n. *Syn.* visible, evident, manifest, plain. *Ant.* invisible, obscure, intangible.

Pal'staff (pawl-) n. an ancient weapon or implement resembling a chisel.

Pal'sy (pawl-) n. paralysis.—**pal'sied** a. affected with palsy.

Pal'ter (pawl-) v.t. to shuffle, deal evasively.—**pal'try** a worthless, contemptible.

Pam'pas n.pl. vast grassy, treeless plains in South America.

Pam'per v.t. to over indulge

Pamph'let n. a thin paper cover book, stitched but not bound.—**pamphleteer'** n. a writer of pamphlets.

Pan n. broad, shallow vessel.—**pan'cake** n. a thin cake of fried batter.—**pan'tile** n. a curved roofing tile.

Pan *prefix*, all.

Panace'a n. a universal remedy.

Panache' (-ash) n. a plume of feathers used as a headdress.

Pana'da n. bread boiled in water and sweetened.

Pan'ama (-mä) n. a hat made of fine strawlike material.

Pan'cake n. a thin cake of batter fried in a pan.—v.i. in aviation, to land clumsily.

Pan'da n. a small raccoon-like animal of India.

Pandemo'nium n. a scene of din and commotion.

Pan'der n. a go-between in illicit love affairs; procurer.—v.t. to minister basely.

Pane n. a piece of glass in a window.

Panegyr'ic (-i-jir-) n. a speech of praise.—**panegyr'ical** a.—**panegyr'ist** n.

Pan'el n. a compartment of a surface, usually raised or sunk, e.g. in a door; a strip of different material in a dress; a thin board with a picture on it; a list of jurors.

doctors, etc.—*v.t.* decorate with panels.—**pan'elling** *n.* panelled work.

Pang *n.* a sudden pain.

Pan'ic *n.* a sudden and infectious fear.—*a.* of fear, etc.; due to uncontrollable general impulse.

Pann'ier *n.* a basket of the type carried by a beast of burden or on a person's shoulders; part of a skirt looped up round the hips.

Pann'ikin *n.* a small metal drinking-cup.

Pan'oply *n.* a full suit of armour.

Panoram'a (-ăm-a) *n.* a picture arranged round a spectator or unrolled before him; a wide or complete view.—**panoram'ic** *a.*

Pan'sy (-zi) *n.* a flowering plant; a species of violet.

Pant *v.i.* to gasp for breath.—*n.* a gasp.

Pantaloon' *n.* in pantomime, a foolish old man who is the butt of the clown.—*pl.* wide trousers.

Pantech'nicon (-k-) *n.* storehouse or van for furniture.

Pan'theism *n.* identification of God with the universe.—**pan'theist** *n.*—**pan'theon** *n.* a temple of all the gods; a building for memorials of a nation's great dead.

Pan'ther *n.* a variety of leopard.

Pan'til *n.* a tile with a cross-section like the letter S.

Pan'tograph *n.* an instrument for copying diagrams, maps, etc., to any scale.

Pantol'ogy *n.* universal knowledge; a work of universal information.

Pantom'eter *n.* an instrument for measuring angles or determining perpendiculars.

Pan'tomime *n.* a dramatic entertainment in dumb show; Christmas-time dramatic entertainment.—**pantomim'ic** *a.*

Pan'try *n.* a room for storing food or utensils.

Pants *n.pl.* trousers; long tight drawers.

Pap *n.* soft food for infants, etc.

Pa'pacy *n.* the office of the Pope; the papal system.—**pa'pal** *a.* of, or relating to, the Pope.—**pa'pist** *n.*—**papist'ic** *a.*

Pa'per *n.* a material made by pressing pulp of rags, straw, wood, etc., into thin flat sheets; a sheet of paper written or printed on; a newspaper; an article or essay.—*pl.* documents, etc.—*v.t.* to cover with paper.—

Pap'ier-mâché (pap-ya-ma-sha) *n.* pulp from rags or paper mixed with size, shaped by moulding and dried hard.

Papy'rus *n.* a species of reed; a manuscript written on papyrus.

Par *n.* equality of value or standing; equality between market and nominal value.—**par'ity** *n.* equality.

Par'a- *prefix,* beside.

Par'able *n.* an allegory, story told to point out a moral.

Parab'ola *n.* a section of a cone made by a plane

parallel to the surface of the cone.

Parachute' (-sh-) *n.* an apparatus extending like an umbrella to enable a person to come safely to earth from a great height.

Parade' *n.* display; a muster of troops; a parade ground.—*v.t.* to muster; display.—*v.i.* to march with display.

Par'adigm *n.* an example; a model.

Par'adise *n.* the Garden of Eden; Heaven; state of bliss.

Pa'rados *n.* the back wall of a firing trench in warfare.

Par'adox *n.* statement that seems absurd but may be true.—**paradox'ical** *a.* *Syn.* enigma, riddle. *Ant.* platitude, commonplace, truism.

Par'affin *n.* a wax or oil distilled from shale, wood, etc.

Par'agon *n.* a pattern of excellence.

Parago'ne *n.* a touchstone; black marble admitting of an excellent polish.

Par'agraph *n.* a play upon words; a pun.

Par'agraph *n.* a section of a chapter or book; a short record.—*v.t.* to arrange in paragraphs.

Par'akeet, par'oquet *n.* a small parrot.

Paral'dehyde *n.* a narcotic particularly useful against insomnia.

Paraleipsis (-lip-sis) *n.* a pretended omission for rhetorical effect.

Par'allel *a.* continuously at equal distances; precisely corresponding.—*n.* a line of latitude; a thing exactly like another; a comparison.—*v.t.* to represent as similar, compare.—**par'allelism** *n.*

aral'ysis *n.* an incapacity to move or eel, due to damage to the nerve system.

Paramatt'a *n.* a fabric of wool and cotton.

Par'amount *a.* supreme. *Syn.* eminent, pre-eminent, supreme. *Ant.* unimportant, insignificant, small.

Par'amour (-ōōr) *n.* one for whom a married person has illicit love.

Par'ang *n.* a large, heavy knife used in felling trees, etc. (Malay).

Par'apet *n.* a low wall; a breast-high defence; a mound along the front of a trench.

Parapherna'lia *n.pl.* personal belongings, odds and ends of equipment.

Par'aphrase *n.* an expression of a meaning of a passage in other words.—*v.t.* to put the meaning of in other words.

Paraple'gia *n.* paralysis of the lower part of the body.

Par'asite *n.* a self-interested hanger-on; an animal or plant living in or on another.—**parasit'ic** *a* —**parasit'ically** *adv.*—**par'asitism** *n.*

Parasol' *n.* a light umbrella for protection against the sun.

Par'ataxis *n.* an arrangement of sentences which omits connecting words.

Par'avane *n.* a contrivance for cutting the moorings of submerged mines.

Par'boil v.t. to scald the surface in boiling water, to boil partly; to scorch.

Par'buckle n. a rope for raising or lowering round objects, the middle being secured at the higher level and the ends passed under and round the object.—v.t. to raise or lower in this way.

Par'cel n. a packet of goods, specially one enclosed in paper; a quantity dealt with at one time; a piece of land. —v.t. to divide into parts; to make up in a parcel.

Parch v.t. and i. dry by exposure to heat, to roast slightly, to make or become hot and dry.

Parch'ment n. skin prepared for writing; a manuscript of this.

Pard n. leopard.

Pard n. in North America, partner, friend, chum.

Par'don v.t. to forgive.—n. forgiveness.—par'donable a. — par'donably adv. — par'doner n. Syn. to absolve, remit, condone. Ant. to grudge, resent, to be implacable.

Pare (pér) v.t. to trim by cutting away the edge or surface of.—par'ing n. a piece pared off.

Paregor'ic a. soothing.—n. a soothing medicine; a tincture of opium.

Par'ent (pēr-) n. a father or mother.—parent'al a.—par'enthood n.—par'entage n. descent.

Paren'thesis n. paren'theses pl. n. a word or sentence inserted in a passage independently of the grammatical sequence and usually marked off by brackets, dashes, or commas.—pl. round brackets, (), used for this.—parenthet'ic a.

Par'esis n. an incomplete form of paralysis, affecting the movements but not sensation.

Parget v.t. to cover with plaster.—n. gypsum; rough plaster; pargeting.

Par'iah n. an Indian of no caste; a social outcast.— pariah dog, a yellow roaming dog in India.

Par'ish n. a district under a priest; a sub-division of a county.—parish'ioner n. an inhabitant of a parish.

Parity see PAR.

Park n. a large enclosed piece of ground, usually with grass or woodland, attached to a country house or set aside for public use; a recreation ground in a town; the artillery of a military force; its space in a camp; a place set aside for storing motorcars, aeroplanes, etc.—v.t. to arrange or leave in a park.

Par'kin n. a kind of gingerbread or cake made of oatmeal.

Parka n. an Eskimo outer garment of undressed skin.

Parky a. (colloq.) cold; chilly.

Parl'ance n. a way of speaking.—parl'ey n. a meeting between leaders or representatives of opposing forces to discuss terms.—v.i. to hold a discussion about terms.—**parl'iament** n. the legislature of the United Kingdom; any legislative assembly. — **parliament'ary** a. — **parliamenta'rian** — a. **parl'our** n.—a sitting-room or room for receiving company in a small house; a private room in an inn.

Parl'ous a. hard to escape from, unsatisfactory.

Parman'tig a. in South Africa overbearing; impertinent; haughty; fashionable.

Paro'chial (-k-) a. of a parish; narrow, provincial. — **paro'chialism** n. concentration on the local interests.

Par'o ly n. a composition in which the author's characteristics are made fun of by imitation; a burlesque; a feeble imitation.—v.t. to write a parody of.—**par'odist** n.

Parol' n. oral declaration; pleadings in a suit.—a. oral.

Parole' n. a promise given by a prisoner of war not to attempt to escape or to abstain from taking up arms again.

Par'onym n. a word resembling another in sound.

Parot'id n. the salivary gland situated near the ear.

Paroquet see parokeet.

Par oxysm n. a sudden violent attack of pain, rage, laughter, etc.

Par'quet (-ket) n. flooring of wooden blocks.—v.t. to lay a parquet.—**par'quetry** n. parquet work.

Parr n. a young salmon.

Parr'icide n. murder or murderer of a parent.

Parr'ot n. a bird with short hooked beak, some varieties of which can be taught to imitate speaking; an unintelligent imitator.

Parr'y v.t. to ward off.—n. an act of parrying, esp. in fencing.

Parse (-z) v.t. to describe (a word) or analyse (a sentence) in terms of grammar.

Par'sec n. a unit of length used in expressing the distance of the stars.

Par'simony n. stingyness; undue economy. — **parsimo'nious** a.

Par'sley n. a herb used for seasoning, etc.

Par'snip n. a plant with a yellow root cooked as a vegetable.

Par'son n. a clergyman of a parish or church; a clergyman.—**par'sonage** n. the parson's house.

Part n. a portion, section, share; duty; character given to an actor to play; interest.—v.t. to divide; separate; distribute.—v.i. to divide; separate from.—**parta'ker** n. one taking a share.—**partake'** v.t. to have a share in—v.i. to take or have a share.—**part'ly** adv.—**par'tial** a. prejudiced; fond of; being only in part.—**partial'ity** n.—**par'tially** adv.

Par'terre n. an ornamental arrangement of beds in a flower garden; the pit of a theatre.

Partic'ipate (-is-) v.t. and i. to

share in.—partic'ipant n.—partic'ipator n.—participa'tion n.—part'iciple n. an adjective made by inflection from a verb and keeping the verb's relation to dependent words.—particip'ial a.

Part'icle n. a minute portion of matter; least possible amount; a minor part of speech.

Par'ticoloured a. differently coloured in different parts, variegated.

Partic'ular a. relating to one, not general; considered apart from others; minute; very exact, fastidious.—n. a detail or item.—pl. a detailed account.—particular'ity n.—partic'ularly adv.—partic'ularise v.t. to mention in detail. Syn. special, fastidious, exact. Ant. indiscriminate, careless, commonplace.

Partisan' (-z-) n. an adherent of a party.—a. adherent to a faction.

Parti'tion n. division; dividing wall.—v.t. to divide.

Part'ner n. a member of a partnership; one that dances with another; a husband or wife.—part'nership n. association of persons for business, etc.

Part'ridge n. a small game bird of the grouse family.

Parturi'tion n. act of bringing forth young.

Part'y n. a number of persons united in opinion; side; a social assembly.—a. of or belonging to, a faction.

Par'venu n. an upstart; one newly risen into notice or power.

Par'vis n. the area round a church; a room over the church; a church porch.

Pas'chal (-sk-) a. of the Passover or Easter.

Pas'ma n. a powder for sprinkling.

Pas op' interj. in South Africa, a cry of warning, with meaning "take care!"

Pass (-à-) v.t. to go by; beyond, through, etc.; to exceed; to be accepted by.—v.i. to go; to be transferred from one state to another; to elapse; to undergo examination successfully.—n. a way, esp. a narrow and difficult way; a passport; condition; successful result from a test.—pass'able a. — pass'age n. journey; voyage; fare; part of a book, etc.; an encounter pass'port n. a document granting permission to pass.—past a. ended.—n. bygone times.—adv. by; along.—prep. beyond; after.

Passade n. a thrust; a turn or course of a horse backward or forward.

Pass'enger (-jer) n. a traveller, esp. by some conveyance.

Passe-partout n. a master-key; a mount or light frame for a picture.

Pass'ible a. capable of feeling or suffering.

Pas'sion n. suffering; strong feeling; wrath; object of ardent desire.—pas'sionate a. easily moved to anger; moved by strong emotions.

Pass'ive a. suffering; submissive; denoting the grammatical mood of a verb in which the action is suffered by the subject. *Syn.* inactive, unresisting, quiescent. *Ant.* active, energetic, vigorous.

Pass'over (-à-) *n.* a feast of the Jews to commemorate the time when God, smiting the first-born of the Egyptians, *passed over* the houses of the Israelites.

Paste *n.* a soft composition, as of flour and water; a fine glass to imitate gems.—*v.t.* to fasten with paste.—**past'y** *n.* a pie enclosed in paste.—*a.* like paste.—**pa'stry** *n.* articles of food made chiefly of paste.—**paste'board** *n.* a stiff, thick paper.

Pas'tel *n.* a coloured crayon; woad.

Pasteur'ism (-ter-) *n.* cure of diseases by inoculation.

Pas'til, -ille' (pastĕl) *n.* a lozenge; an aromatic substance burnt as a fumigator.

Pas'time (-à-) *n.* that which serves to make time pass agreeably.

Pas'tor (-à-) *n.* a minister of the gospel.—**pas'toral** *a.* relating to shepherds or rural life; relating to the office of pastor.—*n.* a poem describing rural life.—**past'orate** *n.* office or jurisdiction of a spiritual pastor.

Pas'toralist *n.* in Australia, a sheep or cattle farmer.

Past'ure (-à-) *n.* grass for food of cattle; ground on which cattle graze.—*v.t.* to feed on grass.—*v.i.* to graze.—**past'urage** *n.* the business of grazing cattle; pasture.

Pat *n.* a small mass, as of butter, beaten into shape.

Pat *n.* a light, quick blow.—*v.t.* to tap.

Pat'amar *n.* a coasting-vessel of Bombay and Ceylon.

Patch *n.* a piece of cloth sewed on a garment; a spot or plot; a plot of ground.—*v.t.* to mend; to repair clumsily.—**patch'y** *a.* full of patches.

Patchou'li *n.* a herb furnishing perfume; the perfume itself.

Pate *n.* the head; the top of the head.

Pate (pà-tā) *n.* a kind of platform.

Patell'a *n.* a small vase; the knee-cap; a limpet.

Pa'tent *a.* open; evident; manifest; open to public perusal, as letters *patent.*—*n.* a deed securing to a person the exclusive right to an invention.—*v.t.* to secure a patent.—**patentee'** (pā-ten-tĕ, pat-en-tŏ) *n.* one that has a patent.

Paterfamil'ias *n.* the father of a family.

Pater'nal *a.* of a father; fatherly.—**patern'ity** *n.* relation of a father to his offspring.

Path (-à-) *n.* a way or track; a course of action.

Pathol'ogy *n.* the science of diseases.

Pa'thos *n.* power of exciting tender emotions.—**pathet'ic, pathet'ical** *a.* affecting or moving the tender emotions.

—pathol'ogy n. the science of diseases.

Pa'tient (-shent) a. bearing trials without murmuring.—n. a person under medical treatment.—pa'tience n. the quality of enduring. Syn. passive, submissive, enduring. Ant. impatient, rebellious, restive.

Pati'na n. a bowl; rust on antique bronze.

Pat'io n. an uncovered enclosure connected with a house.

Pat'ois (-waw) n. a rustic or provincial form of speech.

Pa'triarch (-k) n. the father and ruler of a family, esp. in Biblical history; a venerable old man.

Patri'cian (-shn) n. a noble of ancient Rome; a person of noble birth.—a. of noble birth (cf. PLEBEIAN).

Pat'rimony n. right or estate inherited from ancestors.

Pat'riot n. one that loves his country, and maintains its interests.—a. patriotic.—patriot'ic a. inspired by love of one's country.—pat'riotism n. love of, desire to serve, one's country.

Patrol' (-ōl) n. a marching round of a guard; a small body patrolling; a unit of Boy Scouts.—v.i. to go round on guard, or reconnoitring.

Pa'tron n. a man under whose protection another has placed himself; a guardian saint; one that has the disposition of a church-living, etc.—pat'ronage n. special countenance or support; right of presentation to a church-living, etc.—pat'ronise v.t. to assume the air of a superior towards; to frequent as a customer.

Patronym'ic n. a name derived from that of a parent or an ancestor.

Patt'en n. a raised wooden shoe or sole; the base of a column.

Patt'er v.i. to tap in quick succession; to make a noise, as the sound of quick, short steps; to pray or talk rapidly.—n. a quick succession of small sounds.

Patt'ern n. model for imitation; a specimen.

Patty' n. a little pie.

Pau'city n. scarcity; smallness of quantity.

Paunch n. the belly.

Pau'per n. a poor person, esp. one supported by the public.—pau'perism n. state of being destitute of the means of support.—pau'perise v.t. to reduce to pauperism.

Pause n. a stop or rest.—v.i. to cease for a time.

Pav'an, paven n. a Spanish dance or its music.

Pave v.t. to form a surface with stone or brick.—pave'ment n. a paved floor or footpath; material for paving n.

Pavil'ion n. a tent raised on posts; a club-house on a playing-field, etc.

Pav'on n. a small triangular flag attached to a lance.

Paw n. the foot of an animal having claws.—v.i. to scrape with the fore foot.

Pawn *n.* goods deposited as security for money borrowed.—*v.t.* to pledge.—**pawn'broker** *n.* one that lends money on goods pledged.

Pawn *n.* a piece in a game, *esp.* chess.

Pawky' *a.* cunning; sly; arch.

Pax *interj.* (*colloq.*) peace! leave me alone.

Pay *v.t.* to give money, etc., for goods received or services rendered; to compensate.—*v.i.* to be remunerative.—*n.* wages.—**pay'able** *a.* justly due.—**pay'ment** *n.* discharge of a debt.

Pay *v.t.* to pitch the seams of a ship.

Paynim *n.* a pagan; a heathen.

Pea *n.* fruit, growing in pods, of a leguminous plant; the plant.

Peace *n.* calm; repose; freedom from war; quietness of mind.—**peace'able** *a.* disposed to peace.—**peace'ful** *a.*—**peace'fully** *adv.* *Syn.* quiet, tranquillity, concord. *Ant.* war, strife, uproar.

Peach *n.* a stone fruit of delicate flavour.

Peach *v.i.* to inform against.

Pea'cock *n.* a bird, remarkable for the beauty of its plumage and fan-like spotted tail.

Pea'-jacket *n.* a thick woollen jacket worn by seamen.

Peak *n.* the pointed end of anything, *esp.* the sharp top of a hill; maximum point in a cure or record.

Peal *n.* a loud sound, or succession of loud sounds; chime.—*v.i.* to sound loudly.

Pear (pér) *n.* a tree yielding delicious fruit; the fruit.

Pearl (purl) *n.* a hard, smooth, lustrous substance, found in several molluscs, particularly the pearl oyster; a jewel.—**pear'ly** *a.* clear; pure.

Pearl'-barley *n.* barley with the skin ground off.

Peas'ant (pez'-) *n.* a rural labourer; a rustic.—*a.* rural.—**peas'antry** *n.* peasants collectively.

Peat *n.* a decomposed vegetable substance, used for fuel.

Pe'ba *n.* a kind of armadillo.

Peb'ble *n.* a small, roundish stone; transparent and colourless rock-crystal.

Pecc'able *a.* liable to sin.

Peccadill'o *n.* a slight offence; a petty crime.

Pecc'ary *n.* a vicious animal allied to the hog.

Peck *n.* the fourth part of a bushel; a great deal.

Peck *v.t.* and *i.* to pick or strike with a beak.

Pec'tin *n.* a jelly obtained from ripe fruits.—**pectic** *a.* congealing; denoting pectin.

Pec'toral *a.* pertaining to the breast.—*n.* a lung medicine.

Pec'ulate (pek-ū-) *v.t.* and *i.* to embezzle.—**pecula'tion** *n.*—**pec'ulator** *n.*

Pecu'liar *a.* one's own; particular; strange.—**peculiar'ity** *n.* something that belongs to, or is found in, one person or thing; only. *Syn.* special, exceptional, unique. *Ant.* normal, ordinary, usual.

Pecu'niary *a.* relating to, or consisting of, money.

Ped'agogue (-gog) *n.* a schoolmaster; a pedantic teacher.

Ped'al *a.* of a foot.—*n.* something to transmit motion from the foot.—*v.i.* to use a pedal.

Ped'ant *n.* one who overvalues, or insists out of season on, petty details of book-learning, grammatical rules, etc.—**pedant'ic** *a.*

Pedd'le *v.t.* to retail, as a lawyer.

Pedere'ro *n.* a kind of gun.

Ped'estal *n.* the base of a column, pillar, etc.

Pedes'trian *a.* going on foot.—*n.* one that walks on foot.—**pedes'trianism** *n.* the practice of walking.

Pediat'rics *n.* that part of medicine dealing with children and children's diseases.

Ped'igree *n.* register of ancestors; genealogy.

Ped'iment *n.* the triangular space over a Greek portico, etc.

Ped'lar, -ler *n.* one who travels about hawking small commodities.

Pedom'eter *n.* an instrument resembling a watch, which measures the distance walked in a given time.

Peel *n.* an old, square fortified tower.

Peel *n.* a wooden shovel used by bakers; the blade of an oar.

Peel *v.t.* to strip off the skin or rind.—*v.i.* to come off, as the skin or rind.—*n.* rind, skin.

Peen *n.* the point or rounded end of a hammer-head.

Peep *v.i.* to cry, as a chick; to chirp.—*n.* the cry of a young chicken.

Peep *v.i.* to look slyly or momentarily.—*n.* such look.

Peer *n.* one of the same rank; a nobleman.—**peer'less** *a.*—**peer'age** *n.* the rank of a peer; the body of peers.

Peer *v.i.* to peep; to look narrowly, as with short-sighted eyes.

Peev'ish *a.* fretful; querulous. —**peev'ishly** *adv.*—**peev'ishness** *n.*

Pee'wit *n.* the lapwing.

Peg *n.* a wooden nail or pin.— *v.t.* to fasten with pegs.— *v.i.* to persevere.

Peg *n.* a drink of soda-water and whisky.

Pelf *n.* money (in contempt).

Pel'ican *n.* a large water-fowl, remarkable for its enormous pouch beneath its bill.

Pell'et *n.* a little ball.

Pell'-mell *adv.* in utter confusion.

Pellu'cid *a.* translucent; clear.

Pel'met *n.* a canopy, or valance, for a window frame, to hide the curtain rods.

Pelt *v.t.* to strike with missiles. —*v.i.* to throw missiles; to fall persistently, as rain.

Pelt *n.* a hide or skin.

Pel'vis *n.* the bony cavity at the base of the human trunk.

Pen *n.* an instrument for writing.—*v.t.* to compose and commit to paper; write.

Pen *n.* a small enclosure, as for sheep.—**pent** *a.* shut up.

Pen *n.* in South Africa a threepenny-bit.

Pe'nal *a.* relating to, incurring, or inflicting, punishment.—**pen′alty** n. punishment for a crime or offence.

Pen′ance n. suffering submitted to as an expression of penitence.

Pena′tes n.pl. the household gods of the ancient Romans.

Penchant (páng′-sháng) n. inclination, decided taste.

Pen′cil n. a small brush used by painters; an instrument, as of graphite, for writing, etc.—v.t. to paint or draw; to mark with a pencil.

Pend′ant n. a hanging ornament.—a. suspended; hanging; projecting.—**pend′ing** prep. during.—**pend′ulous** a. hanging loosely; swinging.—**pend′ulum** n. a suspended weight swinging to and fro, esp. as a regulator for a clock.

Pen′etrate v.t. to enter into; to pierce; to arrive at the meaning of.—**pen′etrable** a. capable of being pierced.—**penetrabil′ity** n. quality of being penetrable.—**penetra′tion** n. insight; acuteness.—**pen′etrative** a. piercing; discerning.

Pen′guin n. a swimming bird, unable to fly.

Pen′icil n. a brush of hairs; a tent or pledge for wounds.

Penin′sula n. a portion of land nearly surrounded by water.

Pe′nis n. the male organ of generation.

Pen′itent a. affected by a sense of guilt; one that repents of sin.—**pen′itence** n. sorrow for sin; repentance.—**peniten′tial** a. of, or expressing, penitence.—**peniten′tiary** a. relating to penance, or to the rules of penance.—n. a prison. Syn. repentant, contrite, remorseful. Ant. unrepentant, impenitent, obdurate.

Penn′ant n. a narrow piece of bunting, esp. a long narrow flag on a lance, etc. (also pennon).

Penn′y n. **penn′ies** pl. (denoting the number of coins).—**pence** pl. (amount of pennies in value), a copper coin; the twelfth part of a shilling.—**penn′iless** a. having no money.—**penn′yweight** n. a troy weight of 24 grains.

Pennyroy′al n. an aromatic herb.

Pen′sile a. hanging; suspended; pendulous.

Pen′sion n. an allowance for past services; an annuity paid to retired public officers, soldiers, etc.—v.t. to grant a pension to.—**pen′sioner** n.

Pen′sive a. thoughtful with sadness.

Pent′agon n. a plane figure having five angles.—**pentag′onal** a.—**pent′ateuch** (-k) n. the first five books of the Old Testament.

Pentam′eter n. a verse of five feet.

Pent′ecost n. a Jewish festival on the fiftieth day after the Passover; Whitsuntide.

Pent′house n. a shed standing with its roof sloping against a higher wall.

Pen′tode n. in wireless, a five-electrode thermionic valve

thére, fáther, her; awl, oil, owl.

which contains filament, plate and three grids.

Pe'nult n. the last syllable but one of a word.—**penul'timate** a. next before the last.

Pen'ury n. want; extreme poverty.—**penu'rious** a. miserly; niggardly.

Peon n. in India, a native constable or soldier; in Mexico, a labourer or serf.

Pe'ony n. a plant with showy flowers.

Peo'ple (pē-pl) n. the body of persons that compose a community, nation; persons generally.—v.t. to stock with inhabitants.

Pepp'er n. the fruit of a climbing plant, which yields a pungent aromatic spice.—v.t. to sprinkle with pepper; to pelt with shot.—**pepp'ery** a. having the qualities of pepper; irritable.—**pepp'ermint** n. a plant noted for the aromatic pungent liquor distilled from it.

Pep'sin, pep'sine n. a ferment in gastric juice (used as a drug).

Peradven'ture adv. perhaps.

Peram'bulator v.t. to walk through or over.—v.i. to walk about.—**peram'bulator** n. a small carriage for a child.

Perceive' v.t. to obtain knowledge of through the senses; to observe; to understand.—**perceiv'able** a.—**percep'tible** a. discernible.—**perceptibil'ity** n.—**percep'tion** n. the faculty of perceiving.

Percent'age n. proportion or rate per hundred.—**per cent**, in each hundred.

Perch n. a fresh-water fish.

Perch n. a pole or rod; a measure of five yards and a half; a roost.—v.t. to place, as on a perch.—v.i. to light or settle on a fixed body; to roost.

Perchance' adv. perhaps.

Percip'ient a. having the faculty of perception; perceiving.

Per'colate v.t. and i. to pass through small interstices, as a liquor; to filter.—**percola'tion** n.

Percus'sion n. collision; vibratory shock.

Perdi'tion (-ish-) n. ruin; future misery.

Per'egrinate v.i. to travel from place to place.—**peregrina'tion** n.

Perempt'ory a. authoritative; forbidding debate. Syn. express, final, compulsory. Ant. mild, persuasive, conciliatory.

Perenn'ial a. lasting through the years; perpetual; (bot.) continuing more than two years.

Per'fect a. complete; finished. —n. a tense denoting a complete act.—v.t. to finish; to make skilful.—**perfect'able** a. capable of becoming perfect.—**perfec'tion** n. state of being perfect.

Per'fidy n. treachery.—**perfid'ious** a.

Per'forate v.t. to pierce.—**perfora'tion** n. a hole bored through anything.

Perforce' adv. of necessity.

Perform' *v.t.* to bring to completion; to fulfil; to represent on the stage.—*v.i.* to act a part; to play, as on a musical instrument.—**perform'ance** *n.*

Per'fume *n.* an agreeable scent; fragrance.—*v.t.* to scent.—**perfu'mer** *n.*—**perfu'mery** *n.* perfumes in general.

Perfunct'ory *a.* done indifferently, careless.

Perfuse' (-fūz) *v.t.* to sprinkle, pour, or spread over.

Per'gola *n.* an arbour, or covered walk formed of growing plants.

Perhaps' *adv.* it may be; possibly.

Pe'ri *n.* a fairy [in Eastern mythology.

Perihe'lion *n.* that point in the orbit of a planet or comet nearest to the sun.

Per'il *n.* danger; exposure to injury.—**per'ilous** *a.* full of peril.

Perim'eter *n.* the outer boundary of a plane figure.

Pe'riod *n.* the time in which a heavenly body makes a revolution; a particular portion of time; a complete sentence; a full stop (.).—**period'ic** *a.* recurring at regular intervals.—**period'ical** *a.* relating to a period; periodic.—*n.* a publication issued at regular intervals.

Peri'pety *n.* sudden change, *esp.* of fortune.

Periph'ery *n.* circumference; surface.

Per'iscope *n.* an instrument used *esp.* in submarines, for giving a view of objects that are on a different level.

Per'ish *v.i.* to die, to waste away.—**per'ishable** *a.*

Peritone'um *n.* the membrane investing the internal surface of the abdomen.—**peritoni'tis** *n.* inflammation of the peritoneum.

Per'iwig *n.* a peruke; a wig.

Per'iwinkle *n.* a flowering plant; a common mollusc.

Per'jure (-jer) *v.t.* to forswear.—*v.i.* to bear false witness.—**per'jury** *n.* false swearing; crime of false testimony on oath.

Per'manent *a.* continuing in the same state; lasting.—**per'manence, per'manency** *n.* fixedness. *Syn.* enduring, abiding, perpetual. *Ant.* temporary, ephemeral, fugitive.

Per'meate *v.t.* to pass through the pores of; to saturate.—**per'meable** *a.* admitting of the passage of fluids.

Permit' *v.t.* to allow; to give leave to; to give leave.—(per-) *n.* a written permission.—**permis'sion** *n.* leave, liberty. — **permiss'ible** *a.* allowable. — **permiss'ive** *a.* allowing. *Syn.* to suffer, let, consent. *Ant.* to veto, prohibit, forbid.

Permute' *v.t.* to interchange.—**permuta'tion** *n.* mutual transference; (*Alg.*) change in the arrangement of a number of quantities.

Pern *n.* a honey buzzard.

Perni'cious (-nish-) *a.* having the quality of destroying or injuring; hurtful. *Syn.* injurious, noxious, deadly. *Ant.* salutary, wholesome, beneficial.

Pernick'ety *a.* (*colloq.*) fussy; fastidious about trifles.

Pernocta'tion *n.* a passing the whole night in watch or prayer.

Per'one (per-u-nē) *n.* the fibula.

Perora'tion *n.* the concluding part of an oration.

Perox'ide (-ok-sid *n.* that oxide of a given base which contains the greatest quantity of oxygen.

Perpend' *v.i.* to weigh in the mind.

Perpendic'ular *a.* exactly upright; at right angles to the plane of the horizon; at right angles to a given line or surface.—*n.* a line at right angles to the plane of the horizon; a line falling at right angles on another line or plane.

Per'petrate *v.t.* to commit (something bad).—**perpetra'tion** *n.*—**per'petrator** *n.*

Perpet'ual *a.* continuous, lasting for ever.—**perpet'ually** *adv.*—**perpet'uate** *v.t.* to make perpetual; not to allow to be forgotten.—**perpetua'tion** *n.*—**perpetu'ity** *n.*

Perplex' *v.t.* to puzzle; complicate.—**perplex'ity** *n.* a puzzled or tangled state.

Per'quisite (-it) *n.* a casual payment in addition to salary belonging to an employment; a thing that after serving its purpose is customarily taken possession of by servant, etc.

Perr'on (per-un) *n.* an external flight of steps leading up to the principal floor.

Perr'y *n.* a fermented drink made from pears.

Per'secute *v.t.* to oppress for the holding of an opinion; to subject to persistent ill-treatment.—**persecu'tion** *n.* —**per'secutor** *n.*

Persevere' *v.i.* to persist, maintain an effort.—**perseve'rance** *n.*

Per'siflage (-flàzh) *n.* idle talk; frivolous style of treating a subject.

Persist' *v.i.* to continue in a state or action in spite of obstacles or objections.—**persist'ent** *n.*—**persist'ence** *n.*

Per'son *n.* an individual human being; an individual divine being; a character in a play, etc.; in grammar a classification, or one of the classes, of pronouns and verb-forms according to the person speaking, spoken to, or spoken of.—**per'sonable** *a.* good-looking.—**per'sonage** *n.* a notable person.—**per'sonal** *a.* individual, private, of one's own; of or relating to grammatical person.—**personal property or estate**, all property except land and interests in land that pass to an heir.—**personal'ity** *n.* distinctive character.—**per'sonally** *adv.* in person.—**per'sonalty** *n.* personal property.—**per'sonate** *v.t.* to pass oneself off as.—**persona'tion** *n.*—**person'ify** *v.t.* to represent as a person; to typify.—**personifica'tion** *n.*—

personnel' *n.* staff employed in a service or institution.

Perspect'ive (-iv) *n.* the art of drawing on a flat surface to give the effect of solidity and relative distances and sizes; drawing in perspective; mental view.—**perspic'uous** *a.* clearly expressed.—**perspic'uity** *n.*—**perspica'cious** *a.* having quick mental insight.—**perspica'city** (-kas'-) *n.*

Perspec'tograph *n.* a contrivance for drawing objects in perspective.

Perspire' *v.i.* to sweat.—**perspira'tion** *n.*

Persuade' (-sw-) *v.t.* to convince; to bring (any one to do something) by argument, etc. — **persua'sion** *n.* — **persua'sive** *a.* *Syn.* to influence, urge, entreat. *Ant.* to dissuade, discourage, deter.

Pert *a.* forward, saucy.

Pertain' *v.i.* to belong, to relate.—**pert'inent** *a.* to the point.—**pert'inence** *n.*—**pertina'cious** *a.* obstinate, persistent.—**pertina'city** (-as-) *n.*

Perturb' *v.t.* to disturb gradually; to alarm.—**perturb'able** *a.*—**perturba'tion** *n.*

Pertu'sion *n.* act of punching; perforation.

Pertuss'is *n.* whooping-cough.

Peruke' (-ōōk) *n.* a wig.

Peruse' (-ōōz) *v.t.* to read, *esp.* in a slow or careful manner.—**peru'sal** *n.*

Pervade' *v.t.* to spread through. — **perva'sion** *n.* — **perva'sive** *a.*

Pervert' *v.t.* to turn to a wrong use; to lead astray.—**per'vert** *a.* one who has turned to error, *esp.* in religion.—**perver'sion** *n.*—**per'ver'sive** *a.*—**perverse'** *a.* obstinately or unreasonably wrong, wayward, etc.—**perver'sity** *n.*

Per'vious *a.* permeable; penetrable.

Pesade' *n.* rearing of a saddle horse.

Pes'ky *a.* in North Amer., annoying; vexatious, troublesome.

Pess'imism *n.* a theory that everything turns to evil; tendency to see the worst side of things.—**pess'imist** *n.*—**pessimist'ic** *a.*

Pest *n.* troublesome or harmful thing or person; a plague.—**pestif'erous** *a.* bringing plague; harmful, deadly—**pest'ilent** *a.* troublesome; deadly.

Pest'er *v.t.* to trouble or vex persistently.

Pes'tilence *n.* the disease known as the plague; any epidemic disease.—**pestilen'tial** *a.*

Pes'tle (-tl) *n.* an instrument with which things are pounded in a mortar.

Pet *n.* an animal or person kept or regarded with affection.—*v.t.* to make a pet of.

Pet *n.* a fit of ill-temper or sulking.

Pet'al *n.* coloured flower leaf.

Petard *n.* a small bomb for bursting things open.

Pe'ter *v.i.* (usually with out) in North American mining, to become exhausted; to thin out.

Pe'tersham *n.* a heavy overcoat; also breeches; a heavy woollen cloth; a corded silk ribbon.

Pet'it *a.* small; petty.

Peti'tion (-ish'-) *n.* a request, *esp.* one presented to a sovereign or parliament.—*v.t.* to present a petition to.—**peti'tionary** *a.*—**peti'tioner** *n.*

Petong' *n.* a white alloy of nickel and copper.

Pet'rel *n.* a small sea-bird.

Pet'rify *v.t.* to turn into stone.—**petrifac'tion** *n.*

Petrog'eny (-roj'-) *n.* science of origin of rocks.

Petrog'lyphy (-li-fi) *n.* carving on stone or rock.

Petro'leum *n.* a mineral oil.—**pet'rol** *n.* a refined petroleum.

Pet'ronel (-ru-nel) *n.* a horseman's pistol.

Pe'trous *a.* like stone; stony.

Pett'icoat *n.* a woman's underskirt.

Pett'ifogger *n.* a low-class lawyer; one given to mean dealing in small matters.—**pett'ifog** *v.i.* to be or act like a pettifogger.

Pett'y *a.* unimportant, trivial; on a small scale.

Pet'ulant *a.* given to small fits of temper.—**pet'ulance** *n.* *Syn.* hasty, cross, fretful. *Ant.* contented, placid, serene.

Pew *n.* a fixed seat in a church.

Pe'wit *see* PEEWIT.

Pew'ter *n.* an alloy of tin and lead; ware made of this.

Phae'ton (fā-) *n.* a light four-wheeled open carriage.

Pha'lanx (fa-langks) *n.* a body of men formed in close array.

Phan'tasm *n.* an illusion; a vision of an absent person.—**phantas'mal** *a.*—**phantasmagor'ia** *n.* an exhibition of illusions, a crowd of dim or unreal figures.—**phan'tasy** *n.* *see* FANTASY.—**phan'tom** *n.* an apparition or ghost.

Phan'tom *n.* an apparition; a spectre; a fancied vision.

Pharisa'ic, pharisa'ical *a.* hypocritical.

Pharmaceut'ic *a.* relating to pharmacy.—*n.* in *pl.* the science of pharmacy.—**pharmaceut'ical** *a.*—**pharmacopœ'ia** *n.* official book with a list and directions for the use of drugs.—**phar'macy** *n.* the preparation and dispensing of drugs; drugstore.

Pha'ros *n.* a lighthouse; a beacon.

Phar'ynx (-lngks) *n.* the cavity forming the back part of the mouth and terminating in the gullet.

Phase (-z) *n.* an aspect of the moon or a planet; a stage of development.

Pheas'ant (fez-) *n.* a game-bird.

Phe'nol *n.* carbolic acid.

Phenom'enon *n.* **phenom'ena** *pl.* anything appearing or observed; a remarkable person or thing.—**phenom'enal** *a.* recognisable or evidenced by the senses; relating to the phenomena; remarkable.

Phe'on *n.* the barbed head of a dart; in *heraldry* a broad arrow.

Phi'al *see* VIAL.

Phil- *prefix* loving.—philan'der *v.i.* to amuse oneself with love-making.—philan'thropy *n.* love of mankind; practice of doing good to one's fellow-men. — philanthrop'ic *a.*—philan'thropist *n.*—philat'ely *n.* stamp collecting.—philat'elist *n.*—philatel'ic *a.*—phil'harmon'ic *a.* musical (only for titles of societies). — philol'ogy *n.* science of the structure and the development of languages.—philolo'gical *a.*—philol'ogist *n.*—philos'ophy *n.* the pursuit of widsom; the study of realities and the general principles; a system of theories on the nature of things or on conduct; a calmness of mind expected of a philosopher.—philos'opher *n.* one who studies, or possesses, or originates, philosophy.—philosoph'ic, philosoph'ical *a.*—philos'ophise *v.i.*—phil'tre (-tẹr) *n.* a love-potion.

Phil'omath *n.* a lover of learning.

Phil'omel *n.* the nightingale.

Phlebi'tis (-bī-) *n.* inflammation of a vein.

Phlegm (flem) *n.* a viscid substance formed by the mucous membrane and ejected by coughing, etc.; calmness, sluggishness. — phlegmat'ic (-eg-) *a.* not easily agitated.

Phlox *n.* a flowering plant.

Pho'bia *n.* morbid fear or aversion.

Phœ'nix *n.* a fabulous bird, the only one of its kind, which dies by burning and rises renewed from the ashes; a unique thing.

Phonau'tograph (fŏn-aw-tu-) *n.* a device for recording sound vibrations in a vi¯ible form.

Phone *n., a.,* and *v.i.* an abbreviated form of telephone.

Phono- *prefix.*—phonet'ic *a.* of, or relating to, vocal sounds.—*n.* in *pl.* the science of vocal sounds.—phoneti'cian *n.*—pho'nofilm *n.* a combination of phonograph and cinematograph. — pho'nograph *n.* an instrument recording and reproducing sounds.—phonograph'ic *a.*

Pho'noscope *n.* an instrument for recording music as played, or testing musical strings.

Phos'phorus *n.* a non-metallic element which appears luminous in the dark.—phos'phate *n.*—phos'phide *n.*—phos'phite *n.* compounds of phosphorus. — phosphores'cence *n.* a faint glow in the dark.

Pho'to- *prefix* light.—pho'to-electri'city *n.* electricity produced or affected by the action of light.—pho'tograph *n.* a picture made by the chemical action of light on a sensitive film.—*v.t.* to take a photograph of.—photog'rapher *n.* — photograph'ic *a.*—photog'raphy *a.*—photogravure' *n.* process of etching a product of photography.—*n.* a picture so reproduced.—photom'eter *n.* an instrument for measuring the intensity of light.— **photom'etry** *n.*—**pho'toplay** *n.* a film drama.

Phrase (-z) *n.* a mode of expression; a small group of words; a pithy expression. —*v.t.* to express in words.— **phraseol'ogy** (-i-ol-) *n.* manner of expression, choice of words.

Phren'ic *a.* pert. to the diaphragm.—**phrenet'ic** *a.* having the mind disordered.

Phrenol'ogy *n.* the study of the shape of the skull; the theory that mental powers are indicated by the shape of the skull.—**phrenol'ogist** *n.*

Phthi'sis (th-) *n.* consumption of the lungs.—**phthi'sical** *a.*

Phut *n.* the sound of a bullet passing, of a bladder collapsing, etc.—*adv.* to go phut, to collapse.

Phylac'tery *n.* an amulet.

Phys'ic (-iz'-) *n.* medicine.— *pl.* the science of the properties of matter and energy.— *v.t.* dose with medicine.— **phys'ical** *a.* relating to physic, or physics, or the body.— **phys'ically** *adv.*—**physi'cian** a qualified medical practitioner.—**phys'icist** *n.* a student of physics.—**physiog'nomy** *n.* judging character by face; the face.—**physiog'raphy** *n.* science of the earth's surface.—**physiog'rapher** *n.*—**physiol'ogy** *n.* the science of the normal function of living things.— **physiol'ogist** *n.*—**physique'** (-ēk) *n.* bodily structure and development.

Piac'ular *a.* having power to atone; expiatory; atrociously bad.

Piaffe' *v.i.* to move as in trotting, but more slowly.

Pian'o *a.* and *adv.* in a low tone or voice.—*n.* a pianoforte.—**pian'oforte** (-ti) *n.* a musical instrument with strings which are struck by hammers worked by a keyboard.—**pi'anist** (pē-) *n.* performer on the pianoforte.— **piano'la** *n.* a mechanical device for playing on the piano.

Piazz'a *n.* a square, open space surrounded by buildings.

Picaresque' (-esk) *a.* of fiction, dealing with the adventures of rogues.

Picc'olo *n.* a small flute.

Pick *n.* a tool consisting of a curved iron crossbar and a wooden shaft for breaking up hard ground or masonry. —**pick'axe** *n.* a pick.

Pick *v.t.* to break the surface of; to skin with something pointed; to gather; to choose, select carefully; to find an occasion for.—*n.* an act of picking; the choicest part.— **pick'ings** *n.pl.* odds and ends of profit. *Syn.* to pluck, choose, cull. *Ant.* to leave, neglect, ignore.

Pick'-a-back *n.* a ride on the back of a man or animal, given to a child.

Pick'et *n.* a prong or pointed stake; a small body of soldiers on police duty; a party of trade unionists posted to deter would-be

workers during a strike.—
v.t. to tether to a peg; to
post as a picket; to beset
with pickets.

Pic′kle (pik′l) *n.* a brine or
other liquid for preserving
food; a sorry plight; a troublesome child.—*pl.* pickled
vegetables.—*v.t.* to preserve
in pickle.

Pick-up *n.* in printing, standing matter which is used
more than once; in wireless,
a device for direct conversion of the mechanical
vibration imparted by a
gramophone record to the
need'e into electric currents
which may be amplified to
work a loud-speaker.

Pic′nic *n.* a pleasure excursion
including a meal out of
doors.—*v.i.* to take part in
a picnic.

Pic′ric *a.* a powerful acid used
in dyeing, medicine, and as
an ingredient in certain
explosives.

Pic′ture *n.* a drawing or
painting.—*v.t.* to represent
in, or as in, a picture.—
pictor′ial *a.* of, in, with,
painting or pictures; graphic.
—*n.* a newspaper with many
pictures.—**pictor′ially** *adv.*—
picturesque′ (-csk) *a.* such
as would be effective in a
picture; striking, vivid.

Pi′cus *n.* the spotted wood-
pecker.

Pidd′ock *n.* a mollusc used for
bait.

Pie *n.* a magpie, wood-pecker;
a dish of meat, fruit, etc.,
covered with paste; a mass
of printer's type in confusion,

etc.—**pie′bald** *a.* irregularly
marked with black and
white; motley.—*n.* a piebald
horse or other animal.—**pied**
a. piebald.

Piece (pēs) *n.* a separate part
or fragment; a single object;
a literary or musical composition, etc.—*v.t.* to mend,
put together. — **piece′meal**
adv. by, in, or into pieces.

Pier (pēr) *n.* a piece of solid
upright masonry, *esp.* supporting a bridge or between
two windows; a structure
running into the sea as a
landing-stage, etc.

Pierce (pērs) *v.t.* to make a
hole in; to make a way
through.

Pier′rot (pēr′-ō) *n.* a French
pantomime character; a
member of a troupe of enter-
tainers, usually in white
costume trimmed with black
pom-pons.

Pi′ety *n.* godliness, devout-
ness; dutifulness. *Syn.* holiness, sanctity, devotion.
Ant. impiety, ungodliness,
wickedness.

Piff′le *n.* (*colloq.*) rubbish,
twaddle.—*v.i.* to trifle, behave foolishly.

Pig *n.* a swine; an oblong
mass of smelted metal.—*v.i.*
of a sow, to produce a litter;
herded together in a dirty
untidy way.—**pigg′ery** *n.* a
place for keeping pigs.—
pigg′ish *a.*—**pig′tail** *n.* a plait
of hair hanging from the
back of the head.

Pi′geon (pij′en) *n.* a bird of
many wild and domesticated
varieties, often trained to

carry messages, etc.—**pi'geon'hole** n. a compartment for papers.

Pigg'in n. a small wooden vessel with erect handle, used as a dipper.

Pig'ment n. colouring matter, paint or dye.

Pigmy see PYGMY.

Pike n. a spear formerly used by infantry; a peaked hill; a large freshwater fish.

Pike'let, pike'lin n. a light cake.

Pike'staff n. plain as a pikestaff, easy to see or understand.

Pilas'ter n. a square column, usually set in a wall.

Pilau (pi-lō') n. meat or fowl boiled with rice, raisins and spice.

Pil'chard n. a small sea fish.

Pile n. a beam driven into the ground, esp. as a foundation for building in water or wet ground.

Pile n. a heap; a great mass of building; an electric battery.—v.t. heaped up.

Pile n. a nap of cloth, esp. of velvet, carpet.

Piles n. (in pl.) tumours of veins of rectum.

Pil'fer v.t. to steal in small quantities.—**pil'ferage** n.

Pil'garlick n. a forsaken wretch.

Pil'grim n. one who walks to a sacred place; a wanderer.—**pil'grimage** n.

Pill n. a small ball of medicine.

Pill'age n. seizure of goods by force; esp. in war; plunder.—v.t. and i. to plunder.

Pill'ar n. a slender upright structure, a column.

Pill'ion (-yun) n. a cushion or seat for a person to ride behind a man on a horse or motor-cycle.

Pill'ory n. a frame with holes for head and hands in which an offender was confined and exposed to pelting and ridicule.—v.t. to set in pillory; to expose to ridicule and abuse.

Pill'ow n. a cushion for the head, specially in bed.—v.t. to lay on a pillow.

Pi'lot n. a person qualified to take charge of a ship entering or leaving a harbour, or where knowledge of local waters is needed; a steersman; navigator of an aeroplane; a guide.—v.t. to act as pilot to.—**pi'lotage** n. work or payment of a pilot.

Pil'ule n. a small pill.

Pimen'to n. allspice, or the tree producing it.

Pimp n. a pander.—v.i. to pander.

Pim'pernel n. a plant with small scarlet or blue or white flowers closing in dull weather.

Pim'ple n. a small tumour of the skin.—**pim'ply** a.

Pin n. a short thin piece of stiff wire with a point and head for fastening soft materials together; a wooden or metal peg or rivet.—v.t. to fasten with a pin or pins; to seize and hold fast.—**pin-money** n. an allowance made to a woman for her private expenditure.

Pin'afore n. a child's washing apron or overall.

Pinang' n. the betel-nut palm, or its fruit (Malay).

Pince'-nez (pangs'-nā) n. eye-glasses kept on the nose by a spring.

Pin'cers n.pl. a tool for gripping, composed of two limbs crossed and pivoted.—**pinch** v.t. to nip or squeeze.—n. a nip; stress; as much as can be taken up between finger and thumb.

Pinch'beck n. a zinc and copper alloy; cheap jewellery.—a. counterfeit, flashy.

Pind v.t. to inclose in a pound.

Pine n. an evergreen coniferous tree.—**pine'apple** n. the fruit of a tropical tree.

Pine v.i. to waste away with grief, want, etc.

Pin'fold n. a place in which cattle are confined; a pound.

Ping'-pong n. a table game similar to lawn-tennis.

Pin'guid (ping-gwid) a. fat; unctuous.

Pin'ion n. a wing.—v.t. to disable by binding wings, arms, etc.

Pin'ion n. a small cog-wheel.

Pink n. a garden plant; height of excellence.—a. pale red in colour.—v.t. to pierce; to ornament with perforations.

Pink n. a boat with a very narrow stern.

Pink'ing n. an engine noise similar to knocking.

Pinn'ace n. a man o' war's eight-oared boat; formerly, a small ship attending on a larger one.

Pinn'acle n. a pointed turret on a buttress or roof; a mounted peak; highest pitch or point.

Pinnock n. a hedge-sparrow; a tit-mouse.

Pint (pint) n. liquid measure, half a quart.

Pintle n. a pivot-pin; the bolt on which a rudder turns.

Pioneer (pī-on-) n. one of an advanced body preparing a road for troops; an explorer; one who first originates.—v.i. to act as pioneer or leader.

Pi'ous n. devout. Syn. godly, devout, religious. Ant. impious, irreverent, ungodly.

Pip n. a disease of fowls.

Pip n. a spot on playing cards, dice, or dominoes.

Pip n. a seed in a fruit.

Pipe n. a tube of metal or other material; a musical instrument, a whistle; a shrill voice, or bird's note; a tube with a small bowl at the end for smoking tobacco; a wine cask.—v.i. and t. to play on a pipe.—**pipe'clay** n. clay used for tobacco pipes and for whitening military equipment, etc.—v.t. to whiten with pipeclay.—**pi'per** n. a player on a pipe or bagpipes.

Pipette' n. a small tube to transfer fluids from one vessel to another.

Pip'it n. a bird of many becies.

Pip'kin n. a small earthenware jar or pan.

Pipp'in n. various sorts of apple.

Pi'quant (pēk'ant) a. pungent; stimulating.—**pi'quancy** n.—

pique (pēk) v.t. to irritate; hurt the pride of; stimulate. —n. feeling of injury or baffled curiosity. — **pi′qué** (pē′kā) n. stiff ribbed cotton fabric.

Piquet′ (-ket) n. a card game for two.

Pi′rate n. a sea-robber; publisher, etc., who infringes copyright.—v.t. to publish or reproduce regardless of copyright.—**pi′racy** n.—**pirat′ical** a.—**pirat′ically** adv.

Pirn n. a bobbin; the reel of a fishing-rod.

Pirouette′ n. a spinning round on the toe.—v.i. to do this.

Pisces (pis-ēz) n.pl. the Fishes, the twelfth sign of the Zodiac.

Pis′mire n. the ant or emmet.

Pista′chio n. the nut of a turpentine tree, containing a kernel of a pleasant taste.

Pist′il n. the female organ of a flower.

Pist′ol n. a small firearm used with one hand.—v.t. to shoot with a pistol.

Pist′on n. a plug fitting a cylinder and working up and down, e.g. as in a steam engine, etc.

Pit n. a deep hole in the ground; a coal mine or its shaft; a depression in any surface; the part of a theatre behind the stalls; an enclosure in which animals were set to fight.—v.t. to set to fight; to mark with small scars.—**pit′fall** n. a covered pit for catching animals or men.

Pit n. in South Africa, the name for a fruit kernel as a plum stone.

Pit′a-pat adv. in a flutter; with palpitation.

Pitch n. a dark sticky substance obtained from tar or turpentine.—v.t. to coat with this.—**pitch′-pine** n. resinous kind of pine.—**pitch′y** a. covered with pitch; black as pitch.

Pitch v.t. to set up; to cast or throw.—v.i. to fix upon; to fall headlong; of a ship to plunge lengthwise.—n. an act of pitching; degree, height, station; a slope.—**pitch fork** n. a fork for lifting and pitching hay, etc.—v.t. to throw with, or as with, a pitchfork.

Pitch′er n. large jug.

Pith n. the tissue in the stems and branches of certain plants; essential substance, most important part.—**pith′less** a.—**pith′y** a. consisting of pith; terse, concise.—**pith′ily** adv.

Pitt′acal n. a blue dye-stuff obtained from wood-tar.

Pitt′ance n. a small allowance; inadequate wages.

Pitu′itary a. secreting phlegm or mucous.—**pituitary gland** n. a ductless gland at the base of the brain.

Pit′y n. sympathy or sorrow for others′ suffering; a regrettable fact.—v.t. to feel pity for.—**pit′eous** a. deserving pity.—**pit′iable** a.—**pit′iably** adv.—**pit′iful** a. full of pity; contemptible.—**pit′iless** a.

Piv′ot n. a shaft or pin on which something turns.—

v.t. to furnish with a pivot.—*v.i.* to turn on one.

Pix'y, pix'ie *n.* a fairy.

Plac'ard *n.* a paper with a notice on one side for posting up.—*v.t.* to post placards on; to advertise or display on placards.

Placate' *v.t.* to conciliate, pacify.—plac'able *a.*

Place *n.* a particular part of space, spot; position; town, village, residence, buildings; office or employment.—*v.t.* to put in a particular place.

Placen'ta (-sen-) *n.* the soft disk which connects the fetus with the mother; the after-birth.

Pla'cid (as-) *a.* calm.—placid'ity *n.* *Syn.* unruffled, serene, tranquil. *Ant.* ruffled, troubled, tempestuous.

Pla'giary *n.* one who publishes borrowed or copied literary work as original.—pla'giarism *n.*—pla'giarist *n.*—pla'giarise *v.t.* and *i.*

Pla'gium *n.* the crime of kidnapping.

Plague (plāg) *n.* pestilence; affliction.—*v.t.* to trouble or annoy.—pla'guy *a.*—pla'guily *adv.*

Plaice *n.* a flat fish.

Plaid (plad) *n.* a long Highland shawl.

Plain *a.* flat, level; unobstructed, not intricate; easily understood; simple, ordinary; without decoration; not beautiful.—*n.* a tract of level country. — *adv.* clearly. — plain'ly *adv.* *Syn.* homely, artless. even. *Ant.* intricate, uneven, beautiful, attractive.

Plaint *n.* a statement of complaint in a law court; a lament.—plaint'iff *n.* one who sues in a law court.—plaint'ive *a.* sad.

Plait (plat) *n.* a fold; a braid of hair, straw, etc.—*v.t.* to form into plaits.

Plak'at *n.* the fighting fish (*Siamese*).

Plan *n.* a drawing representing a thing's horizontal section; diagram, map; a project, design; way of proceeding.—*v.t.* to make a plan of; make a design to arrange beforehand.

Plan'chet *n.* a disc of metal for a coin.

Plane *n.* a tree with broad leaves.

Plane *n.* a carpenter's tool for smoothing wood.—*v.t.* to make smooth with one.

Plane *a.* perfect, flat, or level; a smooth surface.

Plane *v.t.* to glide' in an aeroplane.

Plan'et *n.* a heavenly body revolving round the sun.—plan'etary *a.*

Plank *n.* a long flat piece of sawn timber.

Plant (-à-) *n.* a member of the vegetable kingdom, a living organism feeding on inorganic substances and without power of locomotion; equipment for machinery needed for a manufacture; in Australia, something hidden away.—*v.t.* set in the ground, to grow; to fix firmly; to support or establish; to stock with plants; in Australia, to hide.—planta'tion *n.* a wood of planted trees; an estate for cultivation of tea, tobacco, etc.; formerly, a colony.—**plant'er** *n.* one who plants; a grower of tropical produce; in Australia, a cattle-thief.

Plant'ain *n.* a low-growing herb with broad leaves.

Plant'ain *n.* a tropical tree like a banana; its fruit.

Plap *v.i.* to plash; to fall with a plashing sound.

Plaque (plak) *n.* the plate of a clasp or brooch; a plate of metal on which enamels are painted.

Plash *n.* a puddle; a splash.

Plas'ma *n.* formless matter; protoplasm.

Plast'er *n.* a piece of fabric spread with a medicinal or adhesive substance for application to the body; a mixture of lime, sand, etc., to spread on walls, etc.—*v.t.* to apply plaster to.—**plast'erer** *n.*—**plast'ic** *a.* produced by moulding, easily moulded; moulding shapeless matter. — **plast'icene** (-á-) (trade name) *n.* a kind of modelling clay.—**plasti'city** *n.* aptness to be moulded.

Plas'tron *n.* a breast-plate worn by fencers.

Plat *n.* a plot of ground.

Plat *v.t.* to plait.—*n.* strawplait.

Plate *n.* a flat thin sheet of metal, glass, etc.; utensils of gold or silver; shallow round dish from which food is eaten.—*v.t.* to cover with a thin coating of gold, silver, or other metal.—**plat'eau** (-ō)

n. a tract of level high land. —**plate'ful** *n.*—**plat'form** *n.* raised level surface or floor. —**plat'itude** *n.* commonplace remark.—**platitu'dinous** *a.*—**platt'er** *n.* a flat dish.

Plat'en *n.* in a printing-press, a plate by which paper is pressed against type; the roller in a type-writer.

Plat'inum *n.* a white heavy malleable metal.—**plat'inotype** *n.* a photographic process or print in which platinum is used.

Platoon' *n.* a small body of soldiers employed as a unit; sub-division of an infantry company.

Plau'sible *a.* something fair or reasonable; fair-spoken.— **plau'sibility** *n.*—**plau'dit** *n.* an act of applause. *Syn.* specious, superficial, ostensible. *Ant.* real, authentic, positive.

Play (plā) *v.i.* to move with light or irregular motion, to flicker, etc.; amuse oneself; to take part in a game; to perform on a musical instrument.—*v.t.* to use or work (an instrument); to take part in (a game); to contend with in a game; to perform (music), perform on (an instrument); to act; to act the part of.— *n.* brisk or free movement; activity; sport; amusement; gambling; a dramatic piece or performance.—**play'er** *n.* —**play'ful** *a.*—**play'thing** *n.* a toy.—**play'wright** *n.* an author of plays.

Plea (plē) *n.* that is pleaded; excuse; statement of a

prisoner or defendant.—
plead v.i. to address a court of law; to make an earnest appeal.—v.t. to bring forward as an excuse or plea.

Pleach v.t. to intertwine the branches of.

Please v.t. to be agreeable to. —v.i. to like; to be willing.— **pleas'ance** (plez-) n. delight; a pleasure-ground. — **pleas'ure** n. enjoyment; satisfaction, will, choice.—**pleas'urable** a. giving pleasure.—**pleas'ant** a. pleasing, agreeable.— **pleas'antly** adv.—**pleas'antry** n. a joke.

Pleat n. a three-fold band on a garment, etc., made by folding the material on itself.—v.t. to make a pleat in.

Plebe'ian a. belonging to the common people; low or rough.—n. one of the common people.—**pleb'-iscite** n. a decision by direct voting of a whole people.

Plebic'olist n. one that courts the common people.

Pleo'trum n. a small rod for plucking the strings of a lyre.

Pledge n. a thing given over as security; a toast; promise. —v.t. to give over as security; to engage; to drink the health of.

Pledg'et n. a small plug; a flat mass of lint laid over a wound.

Ple'nary a. complete, without limitations.—**plenipoten'tiary** a. having full powers.—n. an envoy or ambassador with full powers.—**plen'itude** n. completeness.—**plent'y** n.

quite enough; abundance.— **plent'eous** a.—**plent'iful** a. abundant.

Ple'num n. space as considered to be full of matter, opposed to vacuum.

Ple'onasm n. the use of more words than are needed for the sense.—**pleonast'ic** a.

Ple'onexia n. morbid selfishness.

Plet n. a whip for chastising prisoners.

Pleth'ora n. an excess of red corpuscles in the blood; oversupply.—**plethor'ic** a.

Pleur'isy (plōō-) n. inflammation of membrane round the lungs.

Plex'us n. network of nerves, or fibres; collection of related parts.

Pli'able a. easily bent or influenced. — **pliabil'ity** n. — **pli'ant** a. pliable.—**pli'ancy** n.

Pli'ers n.pl. small pincers.

Plight (plīt) n. promise.—v.t. to promise, engage oneself to.

Plight (plīt) n. state (usually of a distressing kind).

Plim'solls n.pl. rubber-soled shoes with fabric uppers for physical drill, etc.

Plinth n. a square slab as the base of a column, etc.

Pli'ocene n. the most recent tertiary deposits.

Plod v.i. to walk or work doggedly.

Plot n. a small piece of land; the plan or essential facts of a story, play, etc.; a secret design, a conspiracy. —v.t. to make a map of; to devise secretly.—v.i. to take part in conspiracy.

Plough (plow) *n.* an implement for turning up the soil. —*v.t.* to turn up with a plough, to furrow.

Plough *v.t.* to reject, as a candidate in an examination.

Plo'ver (pluv-) *n.* various birds, including the lapwing.

Pluck *v.i.* to pull or pick off; to strip the feathers from; to reject in an examination. —*n.* a plucking; a beast's heart, lungs, etc.; courage.— **pluck'y** *a.*—**pluck'ily** *adv.*

Plug *n.* something fitting into and filling a hole; tobacco pressed hard; a piece of this for chewing.—*v.t.* to stop with a plug; (*colloq.*) in North America, to hit or strike with the fist; to shoot.

Plum *n.* a stone fruit; the tree bearing it.

Plumb (-m) *n.* a ball of lead attached to a string and used for sounding, finding the perpendicular, etc.—*a.* perpendicular.—*adv.* perpendicularly; exactly.—*v.t.* to find the depth of; to set exactly upright.—**plumb'er** (-mer) *n.* one who works in lead, etc.—**plumm et** *n.* plumb.—**plumb'line** *n.* a cord with a plumb attached. **plumba'go** (-m-bā-) *n* black lead, graphite.

Plume (-ōōm) *n.* feather; ornament consisting of feathers or horse-hair.—*v.t.* to furnish with plumes; to strip of feathers; to boast.— **plu'mage** *n.* the feathers of a bird.

Plump *a.* of rounded form, moderately fat.

Plump *v.i.* to sit or fall abruptly; vote only for.— *v.t.* to drop or throw abruptly. —*adv.* abruptly, bluntly.

Plum'per *n.* a voter that plumps; the vote given; an unqualified lie.

Plu'mule *n.* a down-feather.

Plun'der *v.t.* to rob systematically; to take by open force. —*v.i.* to rob.—*n.* a violent robbery; property so obtained, spoils.

Plunderage *n.* embezzlement of goods on board ship.

Plunge *v.t.* to put forcibly (into).—*v.i.* to throw oneself (into); to enter or move forward with violence.—*n.* a plunge, dive.—**plun'ger** *n.*

Plu'per'fect (plōō-) *a.* of a tense, expressing action completed before a past point of time.

Plus *prep.* with addition of (usually indicated by the sign +); to be added; positive.—**plu'ral** *a.* more than one; denoting more than one person or thing.— *n.* a word in its plural form. —**plu'ralism** *n.* holding more than one appointment, vote, etc.—**plu'ralist** *n.*—**plural'ity** *n*

Plush *n* a fabric with a long soft nap.

Plutoc'racy *n.* government by the rich, the wealthy class.— **plu'tocrat** *n.* a wealthy person.—**plutocrat'ic** *a.*

Plu'tonian *a.* pertaining to the god Pluto, or his home; dark; subterranean.

Plu'vial *a.* very rainy.

Ply *n.* a fold or thickness.

Ply *v.t.* to wield, work at; supply pressingly.—*v.i.* to go to and fro.

Pne'ograph (nē-) *n.* an instrument for indicating expiratory movement.

Pneumat'ic (nū-) *a.* of, or coated by, or inflated with, wind or air.—**pneumo'nia** *n.* inflammation of the lungs.

Poach *v.i.* to cook (an egg) by dropping without the shell into boiling water.

Poach *v.t.* to pierce; to spear, as fish.—*v.i.* to be swampy or soft.

Poach *v.t.* to take (game) illegally.—*v.i.* to trespass for this purpose.—**poach'er** *n.*

Pochette' *n.* a pocket wallet.

Pock *n.* a pustule, as in small-pox.

Pock'et *n.* a small bag inserted in a garment; a cavity filled with ore, etc.; a mass of water or air differing in some way from that surrounding it.—*v.t.* to put into one's pocket; appropriate.

Pod *n.* a long seed-vessel, as of peas, beans, etc.—*v.i.* form pods.—*v.t.* to shell.

Podge *n.* a puddle; a plash.—**pod'gy** *a.* short and fat; thick.

Poe'-bird *n.* a bird valued for its plumage, song, and powers of mimicry (N. Zealand).

Po'em *n.* an imaginative composition in verse.—**po'et** *n.* a writer of poems.—**po'etess** *fem.*—**po'etry** *n.* the art or work of a poet.—**po'esy** *n.* poetry.—**poet'ic**, **poet'ical** *a.*—**poet'ically** *adv.*

—**po'etaster** *n.* an inferior or paltry verse-writer.

Pog'rom *n.* organised plunder and massacre of political opponents.

Poign'ant (poin-) *a.* pungent, stinging, moving, vivid.—**poign'ancy** *n.*

Poilu (pwā-lōō) *n.* a French private soldier.

Poin'ding *n.* enforcement of a claim by seizing a debtor's property.

Point *n.* a dot or mark; a punctuation mark; an item, detail; a unit of value; position, degree, stage; moment; the essential object or thing; a sharp end; the headland; a movable rail changing a train to other rails; one of the direction marks of a compass; striking or effective part or quality; an act of pointing.—*v.t.* to sharpen; to give value to (words, etc.); to fill up joints with mortar; to aim or direct.—*v.i.* to show direction or position by extending a finger, stick, etc.; to direct attention; of a dog, to indicate the position of game by standing facing it.—**point'ed** *a.*—**point'edly** *adv.*—**point'er** *n.* an index, indicating rod, etc., used for pointing; a dog trained to point.—**point'less** *a.*—**point'-blank'** *a.* aimed horizontally.—*adv.* with level aim (there being no necessity to elevate for distances), at short range.

Poise *v.t.* to place or hold in a balanced or steady position.—*v.i.* to be so held;

to hover.—*n.* balance, equilibrium, carriage (of body, etc.).

Poi son (-z-) *n.* substance which kills or injures when introduced into living organism.—*v.t.* to give poison to; to infect; to pervert, spoil.—poi′soner *n.*—poi′sonous *a.*

Poi′trine *n.* the breast-plate of a knight.

Poke *v.t.* to push or thrust with a finger, stick, etc.; a thrust forward.—*v.i.* to make thrusts; to pry.—*n.* an act of poking.—po′ker *n.* a metal rod for poking a fire.—po′ky *a.* small, confined.

Poke *n.* a bag.

Pol′der *n.* a bog; a morass; marshy land reclaimed and cultivated.

Pole *n.* a long rounded piece of wood; a measure of length, 5½ yards; a measure of area, 30¼ square yards.—*v.t.* to propel with a pole.

Pole *n.* each of the two points about which the stars appear to revolve; each of the ends of the axis of the earth; each of the opposite ends of a magnet, electric cell, etc.—po′lar *a.*—polar′ity *n.*—po′larise *v.t.* to give magnetic polarity to; to affect light so that its vibrations are kept to one plane. —polarisa′tion *n.*

Pole′-axe *n.* a battle-axe, a butcher's axe.

Pole′cat *n.* a small animal of the weasel family.

Polem′ic *a.* controversial.—*n.* a war of words.—polem′ical *a.*

Polem′oscope *n.* a glass with mirror to view obliquely.

Polen′ta *n.* a porridge made of maize.

Police′ (-ēs) *n.* public order; the civil force which maintains public order.—*v.t.* to keep in order.—police′man. *n.* a member of the police.—pol′icy *n.* political wisdom; a course of action adopted *esp.* in state affairs; prudent procedure.—polit′ic *a.* wise, shrewd, expedient, cunning. —*n.* in *pl.* the art of government; political affairs of life. —polit′ical *a.* of the state or its affairs.—politi′cian *n.* one engaged in politics.— pol′ity *n.* civil government; form of government; a state.

Pol′icy *n.* a contract of insurance.

Pol′icy *n.* in Scotland, the grounds about a gentleman's country house.

Pol′ish *v.t.* to make smooth and glossy; to refine.—*n.* the act of polishing; smoothness; a substance used in polishing.—polite′ *a.* refined; having refined manners, courteous.—polite′ly *adv.*—polite′-ness *n.* *Syn.* to burnish, brighten, furbish. *Ant.* to tarnish, sully, stain.

Polit′ical econ′omy *n.* the science dealing with the nature and distribution of wealth.

Pol′ka *n.* a dance; music for it.

Poll (pōl) *n.* the head or top of the head; a counting of voters; voting; the number of votes recorded.—*v.t.* to cut off the top of; to take the votes of; to receive (votes).—*v.i.* to vote.—

poll'ard *n.* a tree on which a close head of young branches has been made by polling; a hornless animal of a normally horned variety. —*v.t.* to make a pollard of (a tree).

Poll'en *n.* fertilising dust of a flower.

Poll'iwig, poll'iwog *n.* a tadpole.

Pollute' (-ōōt) *v.t.* to make foul; to desecrate.—**pollu'tion** *n.* *Syn.* to defile, stain, contaminate. *Ant.* to purify, cleanse, clear.

Po'lo *n.* a game like hockey played by men on ponies.

Polonaise' *n.* a Polish dance; the music for it.

Polo'ny *n.* a sausage of partly cooked pork.

Poltroon' *n.* a coward.— **poltroon ery** *n.*

Pol'verin *n.* the calcined ashes of a plant used in the manufacture of glass.

Poly- *prefix* many.—**polyan'dry** *n.* polygamy in which one woman has more than one husband.—**polyan'thus** *n.* a cultivated primrose.—**pol'ychrome** *a.* many colours.—*n.* a work of art in many colours.—**polychromat'ic** *a.*—**polyg'amy** *n.* the custom of being married to several persons at a time.— **polyg'amist** *n.*—**pol'yglot** *a.* speaking, writing, or written in several languages.—**pol'ygon** *n.* a figure with many angles or sides.—**polyg'onal** *a.*—**polyg'yny** *n.* polygamy in which one man has more than one wife.—**polyhe'dron** *n.* a solid figure contained by many faces.—**pol'yp** *n.* a coral insect or other creature of low organisation.—**polysyll'able** *n.* a word of many syllables.—**polysyllab'ic** *a.*— **polytech'nic** *a.* dealing with various arts and crafts.—*n.* a school doing this.—**pol'ytheism** *n.* the belief that there are many gods.—**pol'ytheist** *n.*—**polytheist'ic** *a.*

Pol'yp *n.* the sea anemone, or some allied animal.

Pol'ypus *n.*—*pl.* **pol'ypi** (-pī) a polyp; a kind of tumour.

Pom'ace *n.* the substance of apples, etc., crushed by grinding.

Pomade' *n.* a scented ointment for the head or hair.— **poma'tum** *n.* pomade.

Pome *n.* a fleshy fruit with one or more cells, as the apple.

Pom'egranate *n.* a large fruit with thick rind containing many seeds in a red pulp.

Pomera'nian *n.* a breed of small dogs.

Pomm'el *n.* the knob of a sword hilt; the front of a saddle.—*v.t.* to strike repeatedly; to strike with a sword-pommel.

Pomol'ogy *n.* the art or science of raising fruits.

Pomp *n.* splendid display or ceremony.—**pomp'ous** *a.* self-important; puffed up; of language, inflated. — **pompos'ity** *n.*

Pom-pom n. an automatic quick-firing gun.

Pom'-pon n. a tuft of ribbon, wool, etc., decorating a hat, shoe, etc.

Pon'cho n. a loose garment or cloak worn in South America.

Pond n. a small body of still water, esp. for watering cattle, etc.

Pon'der v.t. and i. to meditate, think over.—**pond'erable** a. capable of being weighed.—**pond'erous** a. heavy, unwieldy.

Pone n. bread made of maize, or with milk and eggs.

Pon'iard n. a dagger.—v.t. to stab with one.

Pont n. in South Africa, a large ferry-boat worked by a cable.

Pon'tac n. in South Africa, a dark 'grape; wine resembling port.

Pon'tiff n. the Pope; a high priest.—**pontif'ical** a.—**pontif'icate** n.

Pontoon' n. a flat-bottomed boat or metal drum for use in supporting a temporary bridge.

Po'ny n. a horse of a small breed.

Poo'dle n. a variety of pet dog with long curly hair often clipped fancifully.

Pooh interj. an exclamation of scorn or contempt.

Pooh-bah n. a person holding many offices.

Pool (-ōō-) n. a small body of still water (esp. of natural formation; a deep place in a river).

Pool (-ōō-) n. the collective stakes in various games; a variety of billiards; a combination of capitalists to fix prices and divide business; the common fund.—v.t. to throw into a common fund.

Poop (-ōō-) n. a stern of a ship.—v.t. to break over the poop of.

Poop n. in South Africa, porridge made from mealie flour.

Poor a. having little money; unproductive, inadequate, insignificant, unfortunate.—**poor'ly** adv.—**poor'ly** a. not in good health.—**poor'ness** n.

Poort n. in South Africa a mountain-pass.

Pop n. an abrupt small explosive sound.—v.i. to make such sound; to go or come unexpectedly or suddenly.—v.t. to put or place suddenly.

Pope n. the bishop of Rome as head of the Roman Catholic Church.—**po'pery** a. the papal system.—**po'pish** a.

Pop'injay n. a fop.

Pop'lar n. a tree noted for slender tallness and tremulous leaves.

Pop'lin n. a corded fabric of silk and worsted.

Popp'et n. timber to support a vessel while being launched; one of the heads of a lathe.

Popp'y n. a bright flowered plant which yields opium.

Pop'ulace n. the common people.—**pop'ular** a. of or by the people; finding general favour.—**popular'ity** n. being generally liked.—**pop'ularise** v.t. to make popular.—**popularisa'tion** n. — **pop'ularly** adv.—**pop'ulate** v.t. to fill with inhabitants.—**popula'tion** n. inhabitants; the number of them.—**pop'ulous** a. thickly populated.

Poran'gi n. in Australia, foolishness; silliness.—a. silly, crazy.

Por'celain n. fine earthenware, china.

Porch n. a covered approach to the entrance of a building.

Por'cine (-sīn) a. of or like a pig or pigs.

Porc'upine n. a rodent animal covered with long pointed quills.

Pore n. a minute opening, *esp.* in the skin.—**por'ous** a. full of pores; allowing a liquid to soak through.—**poros'ity** n.

Pore v.i. to fix the eyes or mind upon.

Pork n. pig's flesh as food.—**pork'er** n. a pig raised for food.—**pork'y** a. fleshy; fat.

Porph'yry n. a reddish stone with embedded crystals.

Por'poise (-pus) n. a blunt-nosed sea-animal about five feet long.

Porr'idge n. a soft food of oatmeal or other meal boiled in water.—**porr'inger** n. a small basin.

Port n. a harbour or haven; a town with a harbour.

Port n. a city gate; an opening in the side of a ship.—**port'hole** n. a small opening in the side of a ship for light and air.

Port n. the larboard or left side of a ship; — v.t. to turn to the left or larboard side of a ship.

Port n. a strong red wine.

Port n. bearing.—v.t. to carry (a rifle) slanting upwards in front of the body.—**port'able** a. easily carried.—**port'age** n. carrying or transporting; in North America, the interval of land between two navigable bodies of water over which boats have to be carried.—**portfo'lio** n. a case for papers, etc.—**port'ly** a. large and dignified in appearance.

Portend' v.t. to foretell; to be an omen of.—**port'ent** n. an omen, a marvel.—**portent'ous** a.

Port'er n. a door-keeper.—**por'tal** n. a large door or gate.—**portcull'is** n. a grating to raise or lower in front of a gateway.

Port'er n. a person employed to carry burdens; a dark beer.

Portfo'lio n. a portable case for loose papers; the office of a minister of state.

Port'ico n. colonnade; covered walk.

Portiere' (tyār) n. a door curtain.

Por'tion n. a part or share; destiny, lot; dowry.—v.t. to divide into shares; to give a dowry to.—**por'tionless** a.

Port'ly a. having a dignified mien; bulky. *Syn.* stately, grand, corpulent. *Ant.* undignified, puny, slim.

Portman'teau n. a bag for carrying apparel.

Portray' v.t. to make a picture of, describe.—**port'rait** n. a likeness.—**port'raiture** n.—**portray'al** n.

Port'reeve n. the chief magistrate of a port.

Pose v.t. to lay down; place in an attitude.—v.i. to assume an attitude, to give oneself out as.—n. an attitude, esp. one assumed for effect.

Pose v.t. to puzzle.—po'ser n. a puzzling question.

Pos'it (poz'-) v.t. to place; to lay down as a principle.

Posi'tion n. the way a thing is placed; situation, attitude; state of affairs; an office for employment; a strategic point.—pos'itive a. firmly laid down; definite, absolute, unquestionable; confident; overconfident; not negative; greater than zero.—n. positive degree; in photography, a print in which the lights and shadows are not reversed. —pos'itively adv.—pos'itivism n. a philosophy recognising only matters of fact and experience.—pos'itivist n.

Poss'e n. a body of men.

Possess' (zes) v.t. to own; of an evil spirit, to have the mastery of.—posses'sion n.— possess'ive a. of or indicating possession.—n. the possessive case in grammar.—possess'or n. Syn. to have, occupy, hold. Ant. disown, renounce.

Poss'et n. milk curdled as by wine.

Poss'ible a. that can or may be, exist, happen, be done.— possibil'ity n.—poss'ibly adv. Syn. potential, practicable, feasible. Ant. impossible, impracticable, unfeasible.

Post (pōst) n. an upright pole of timber or metal fixed firmly, usually as a support for something.—v.t. to display; stick up (on a post, notice board, etc.).—post'er n. a placard.

Post (pōst) n. official carrying of letters or parcels; a collection or delivery of these; a point, station, or place of duty; a place where a soldier is stationed, a place held by a body of troops, a fort; an office or situation.— v.t. to put into the official box for carriage by post; to transfer (entries) to a ledger; to supply with latest information; to station (soldiers, etc.) in a particular spot.—v.i. to travel with posthorses. — adv. in haste. —post'age n. the charge for carrying a letter.—post'al a. —post'master n. an official in charge of a post office.— post'horse n. a horse (formerly) kept for hire at intervals on main roads for use in relays.—post'-chaise n. travelling carriage hired and drawn from stage to stage by posthorses.—post'-man n. man who collects or delivers the post.—post'-mark n. an official mark with the name of the office, etc., stamped on letters.

Postdate' (pōst-) v.t. to give a date later than the actual date.—post-grad'uate a. carried on after graduation.— post-prand'ial a. after-dinner. —poste'rior (post-) a. later; hinder.—poster'ity n. descendants; later generations.

—post'ern n. a back or private door.—post-mortem (pōst-) a. taking place after death.—n. a medical examination of a dead body.—postpone' v.t. to put off to a later time.—postpone'ment n.—post'script n. an addition to a letter or book.

Poster'ity n. offspring; descendants.

Pos'tern n. a private entrance; a small door or gate.

Pos'thumous (-tū-) a. born after the death of the father; published after the death of the author.

Postil'lion n. a man who rides one of a pair of horses drawing a carriage.

Postmerid'ian a. belonging to the afternoon.—n. the afternoon.—contr. p.m.

Posto'ral a. being behind the mouth.

Postor'bital a. being on the hinder part of the orbit of the eye.—n. a postorbital bone.

Pos'tulate v.t. to claim, demand, take for granted.—n. something taken for granted.

Pos'ture n. attitude, position.

Po'sy n. a bunch of flowers.

Pot n. a round vessel; a cooking vessel.—v.t. to put into or preserve in a pot.—pott'er n. a maker of earthenware.—pott'ery n. a place where earthenware is made; earthenware; the art of making it.

Po'table a. drinkable.—pota'tion n. a drink or drinking.

Pot'ash n. an alkali used in soap, etc.; crude potassium carbonate.—potass'ium n. a white metal.

Pota'to n. a plant with tubers grown for food.

Poteen', potheen' n. Irish whiskey, esp. illicitly distilled.

Po'tent a. powerful.—po'tency n.—po'tentate a. a ruler.—poten'tial a. latent, that may or might but does not now exist or act.—n. amount of potential energy or work.—potential'ity n.—po'tently adv. Syn. strong, cogent, efficacious. Ant. weak, infirm, impotent.

Poth'er (-TH-) n. disturbance, fuss.

Po'tion n. a dose of medicine or poison.

Pot-pourri' (pō-pōō-rē') n. a mixture of rose petals, spices, etc.; a musical or literary medley.

Pott'age n. soup or stew.

Pott'er v.i. to work or act in a feeble, unsystematic way.

Pott'le'(-l) n. a liquid measure of 4 pints; a little pot; a small fruit basket.

Pott'o n. a small African lemuroid; the kinkajou.

Pouch n. a small bag.—v.t. to put into one.

Poult (pōlt) n. chicken.—poult'erer n. a dealer in poultry.—poult'ry n. domestic fowls.

Poult'ice (pōlt-is) n. a mass of bread, linseed, or other substance mixed with hot water, spread on a cloth, and applied to the skin.—v.t. to put a poultice on.

Pounce *v.i.* to spring upon suddenly, swoop.—*n.* a swoop or sudden descent upon something.

Pounce *n.* a fine powder used to prevent ink from spreading on unsized paper, etc.

Pound *n.* a weight, 12 ozs. troy, 16 ozs. avoirdupois; a unit of money, 20 shillings. —**pound'age** *n.* payment or commission of so much per pound (money); charge of so much per pound (weight).

Pound *n.* an enclosure for stray cattle.—*v.t.* to shut up in one.

Pound *v.t.* to crush to pieces or powder; to thump; cannonade.

Poun'son *n.* a dense, soft clay under the coal seam.

Pour (pawr) *v.i.* to come out in a stream, crowd, etc.— *v.t.* to give out thus; cause to run out.

Pourpar'ler (pōōr-pàr-lā) *n.* a preliminary consultation or conference.

Pout *v.i.* to thrust out the lips.—*v.t.* to thrust out (the lips).—*n.* an act of pouting. —**pout'er** *n.* a pigeon with the power of inflating its crop.

Pov'erty *n.* the condition of being poor; poorness, lack. *Syn.* penury, need, want. *Ant.* affluence, opulence, wealth.

Pow'der *n.* a solid matter in fine dry particles; a medicine in this form; gun-powder.— *v.t.* to apply powder to, to reduce to powder.—**pow'dery** *a.*

Pow'er *n.* ability to do or act; authority; person or thing having authority.—**pow'erful** *a.*—**pow'erless** *a.*

Pow'-wow (pou-wou) *n.* in North America, a conjurer; a medicine man; (*colloq.*) conference *esp.* a noisy or futile one.

Prac'tise *v.t.* to do habitually; to put into action; to work at; to exercise oneself in.— *v.i.* to exercise oneself; to exercise a profession.—**prac'tice** *n.* habitual doing; action as distinguished from theory; a habit; exercise in an art or profession.—**prac'tical** *a.* relating to action or real existence; given to action rather than theory; that is (something) in effect though not in name.—**prac'tically** *adv.*—**prac'ticable** *a.* that can be done or used or passed over. — **practicabil'ity** *n.* — **practi'tioner** *n.* one engaged in a profession.

Præmuni're *n.* the offence of disobeying the sovereign's mandate, incurring forfeiture; the writ grounded on that offence; the penalty incurred.

Pragmat'ic *a.* of the affairs of a state; concerned with practical consequence; dogmatic. — **pragmat'ical** *a.* — **prag'matism** *n.*—**prag'matist** *n.*

Prair'ie *n.* a large tract of grass-land without trees.

Praise *v.t.* to express approval or admiration of; to glorify. —*a.* commendation; the fact or state of being praised.— **praise'worthy** *a.*

Pram *n.* a flat-bottomed lighter used in the Baltic.

Pram *n.* in South Africa, a woman's breast.

Prance (-à-) *v.i.* to walk with bounds; a prancing.

Pran'dial *a. pert.* to dinner.

Prank *n.* a trick or escapade.

Prank *v.t.* to adorn or rig out showily.

Prase *n.* a leek-green quartz.

Prate *v.i.* to talk idly, chatter. —*n.* chatter.—**prat'tle** *v.i.* and *t.* to utter childishly.— *n.* childish chatter.

Prat'incol (-ing-kŏl) *n.* any one of a species of plover-like birds having long pointed wings and [deeply forked tail.

Pra'tique (-tēk) *n.* licence to trade with a place after quarantine.

Prawn *n.* an eatable sea crustacean like a shrimp.

Pray *v.t.* to ask earnestly.— *v.i.* to offer prayers, especially to God.—**pray'er** (prèr) *n.* an earnest entreaty; an action or practice of praying to God.—**pray'erful** *a.*

Pre- *prefix* makes compounds with the meaning of before, or beforehand; e.g. **pre-deter'mine** *v.t.* to determine beforehand.—**pre-war** *a.* before the war. These are not given where the meaning and derivation can easily be found from the simple word.

Preach *v.i.* to deliver a sermon.—*v.t.* to set forth in religious discourse.— **preach'er** *n.*

Pream'ble *n.* the introductory part.

Prearrange' (-ranj) *v.t.* to arrange beforehand.

Preb'end *n.* the stipend of a canon or member of a cathedral chapter.—**preb'endary** *n.* holder of a prebend.

Precar'ious (-kèr-) *a.* unsecure, unstable, perilous. *Syn* dubious, perilous, unsteady. *Ant.* certain, sure, safe.

Precau'tion *n.* previous caution; previous care to prevent evil or secure good.

Precede' *v.t.* to go or come before in rank, order, time, etc.—*v.i.* to go or come before.—**prece'dence** *n.* a higher or more honourable place; the right to this.— **prec'edent** (pres-) *n.* a previous case or occurrence taken as a rule.

Precent'or *n.* a leader of singing.

Pre'cept *n.* a rule for conduct; a maxim.—**precept'or** *n.* a teacher.—**precept'ress** *fem.*— **preceptor'ial** *a.*

Precess'ion (-sesh-) *n.* the act of going before or forward.

Pre'cinct *n.* ground attached to a sacred or official building.

Prec'ious (presh-us) *a.* of great value, highly valued; affected, over-refined. — **prec'iously** *adv.*—**prec'iousness** *n.* —**precios'ity** *n.* over-refinement in art or literature. *Syn.* valuable, rare, beloved. *Ant.* cheap, common, valueless.

Pre'cipe (-sipe) *n.* a writ requiring something to be

done, or the reason for non-fulfilment.

Pre'cipice (pres-) *n.* a very steep cliff or rockface.—**precip'itance, precip'itancy** *n.* rashness, speed, hastiness.—**precip'itate** *v.t.* to throw headlong; hasten the happening of; in chemistry, to cause to be deposited in solid form from a solution.—*a.* over-sudden, rash.—*n.* a substance chemically precipitated. — **precip'itately** *adv.*—**precipita'tion** *n.* — **precip'itous** *a.*

Pre'cis (prā-sē) *n.* an abstract or summary.

Precise' *a.* exact, strictly worded; particular; careful in observance. — **precise'ly** *adv.*—**preci'sian** *n.* punctilious or formal person.—**preci'sion** *n.*

Preclude' *v.t.* prevent.

Preco'cious (-ō-) *a.* developed too soon.—**precoc'ity** (-os-) *n.*

Preconceive' *v.t.* to form a notion or idea of beforehand.

Precon'sign (-kon-sin) *v.t.* to make over in advance; in psycho-analysis, relating to all.

Precur'sor *n.* a forerunner.

Predate' *v.t.* to antedate.

Pred'atory *a.* relating to plunder; given to plundering.—**preda'cious** *a.* of animals, living by capturing prey.

Predecease' (-sēs) *v.t.* and *v.i.* to die before.—*n.* death before another.

Pre'decessor *n.* one who precedes another in an office, etc.

Predes'tine (-tin) *v.t.* to decree beforehand; to foreordain.—**predes'tinate** *v.t.* to ordain beforehand by an unchangeable purpose.

Pred'icate *v.t.* to affirm or assert.—*n.* that which is predicated; in grammar, a statement made about a subject. — **pred'icable** *a.* — **predica'tion** *n.*—**predic'ative** *a.*—**predic'ament** *n.* a state or situation, usually an unpleasant one.

Predict' *v.t.* to foretell.—**predic'tion** *n.*

Predilec'tion *n.* a preference or liking.

Predispose' *v.t.* to incline beforehand.

Predom'inate *v.i.* to be the main or controlling element. — **predom'inance** *n.* — **predom'inant** *a.*

Predor'sal *a.* in front of the back.

Pre-em'inent *a.* excelling all others.—**pre-em'inently** *adv.*—**pre-em'inence** *n.*

Pre-emp'tion *n.* buying, or the right to buy, before opportunity is given to others.—**pre-emp'tive** *a.*

Preen *n.* a forked instrument used in dressing cloth.

Preen *v.t.* to trim (feathers) with a beak; smarten oneself.

Pre-estab'lish *v.t.* to establish beforehand.

Pre-exist' (-eg-zist) *v.i.* to exist beforehand, or before something else.

Pref'ace *n.* an introduction to a book, etc.—*v.t.* to introduce.—**pref'atory** *a.* *Syn.* prelude, preliminary, foreword. *Ant.* postscript, epilogue, conclusion.

Pre′fect *n.* a person put in authority; Roman official; a head of a French department; a schoolboy with responsibility for maintaining discipline. — **pre′fecture** *n.* office, residence, district of a prefect.

Prefer′ *v.t.* to like better; to promote.—**pref′erable** *a.* **pre-f′erably** *adv.*—**pref′erence** *n.* — **preferen′tial** *a.* giving or receiving a preference.—**prefer′ment** *n.* promotion.

Prefig′ure *v.t.* to exhibit, or suggest, by previous types; to foreshadow.

Pre′fix *n.* a proposition or particle put at the beginning of a word or title.—**prefix′** *v.t.* to put as introduction; put before a word to make a compound.

Pregla′cial (-glā-shal) *a.* before the glacial or drift period.

Preg′nant *a.* full of meaning; with child.—**preg′nancy** *n.*

Pregusta′tion *n.* act of tasting before.

Prehen′sile *a.* capable of grasping.

Prehistor′ic *a.* prior to the period in which history begins.

Prejudge′ (-juj) *v.t.* to judge before hearing; to condemn beforehand.

Prej′udice (-is) *n.* judgment or bias decided beforehand; harm likely to happen to a person or his rights as a result of others′ action or judgment; prepossession (usually unfavourable).—*v.t.* to injure.—**prejudi′cial** *a.* *Syn.* harm, prejudgment, bigotry. *Ant.* fairness, impartiality, equity.

Prel′ate *n.* bishop or other church dignitary of equal or higher rank.—**prel′acy** *n.*—**prelat′ical** *a.*

Prelim′inary *a.* preparatory, introductory.—*n.* an introductory or preparatory statement or action.

Prel′ude *n.* a performance, event, etc., serving as an introduction; in music, an introductory movement.—*v.i.* and *t.* to serve as prelude.

Prem′ature *a.* happening or done before the proper time.

Prem′ier *a.* chief, foremost.—*n.* a prime minister.

Prem′ise (prem′is) *n.* in logic, a proposition from which an inference is drawn.—*pl.* in law, beginning of a deed; house or buildings with its belongings.—**premise′** (-īz) *v.t.* to state by way of introduction.—**prem′iss** *n.* a (logical) premise.

Pre′mium *n.* a reward; sum paid for insurance; bonus; excess over nominal value.

Pren′tice *n.* an apprentice.

Preocc′upy (-pī) *v.t.* to occupy to the exclusion of other things.—**preoccupa′tion** *n.* mental concentration with the appearance of absent-mindedness.

Preopin′ion *n.* prepossession.

Preop′tion *n.* right of first choice.

Preordain′ *v.t.* to ordain beforehand; to foreordain.

Prepare' *v.t.* to make ready; to make.—*v.i.* to get ready.—**prepara'tion** *n.*—**prepar'atory** *a.*

Prepay' *v.t.* to pay in advance.

Prepense' (-pens) *a.* deliberate; premeditated.

Prepond'erate *v.i.* to be of greater weight or power.—**prepond'erance** *n.*

Preposi'tion *n.* a part of speech, a word marking the relation between two other words.—**preposi'tional** *a.*

Prepos'itor (-poz-) *n.* a scholar appointed to superintend others; a monitor.

Prepossess' (prē-) *v.t.* to impress, *esp.* favourably beforehand.—**prepossess'ion** *n.*

Prepos'terous *a.* utterly absurd. *Syn.* irrational, ridiculous, perverted. *Ant.* sound, reasonable, just.

Prerog'ative *n.* a peculiar power or right, *esp.* as vested in a sovereign.

Pres'age *n.* an omen, an indication of something to come.—**presage'** *v.t.* to foretell.

Presbyo'pia *n.* indistinct vision of near objects.

Pres'byter (-z-) *n.* an elder in a church; a priest.—**pres'bytery** *n.* a priest's house (in the Roman Catholic Church); the eastern part of the chancel; in certain churches, a court composed of ministers and elders.—**presbyte'rian** *a.* — **presbyte'rianism** *n.*

Pres'cience (preshyens) *n.* foreknowledge. — **pres'cient** (preshyent) *a.*

Prescind' *v.t.* to consider apart from other things.—*v.i.* to abstract the attention.

Prescribe' *v.t.* and *i.* to order, point; to order the use of (a medicine).—**prescrip'tion** *n.* prescribing; the thing prescribed; a written statement of it; in law, uninterrupted use as the basis of a right or title; such title.—**prescrip'tive** *a.*

Pres'ent *a.* that is here, now existing or happening.—*n.* the present time.—**pres'ently** *adv.* soon.—**pres'ence** *n.* a being present.

Present' *v.t.* to introduce formally; to show; to point or aim; to give, offer.—**pres'ent** *n.* a gift.—**present'able** *a.* fit to be seen.—**presenta'tion** *n.*—**present'ment** *n.*

Present'iment (-z-) *n.* a foreboding.

Presentoir' (-twor) *n.* a tray; a salver; a cup-holder.

Preserve' (-z-) *v.t.* to keep from harm or injury or decay.—*n.* jam; a place where game is kept for shooting.—**preserva'tion** *n.*—**preserv'ative** *a.* and *n.* *Syn.* to hold, secure, shield. *Ant.* endanger, expose, imperil.

Preside' (-z-) *v.i.* to be chairman; to superintend.—**pres'ident** *n.* the head of a society, company, republic.—**pres'idency** *n.*—**presiden'tial** *a.*

Presid'ial *a.* pertaining to or having a garrison.

Press *v.t.* to subject to push or squeeze; to urge steadily or earnestly.—*v.i.* to bring weight to bear.—*n.* a crowd; a machine for pressing, *esp.* a printing machine; the printing house; its work or art; newspapers collectively; a large cupboard.—**pres'sure** *n.*

Press *v.t.* to force to serve in the navy or army; to take for royal or public use.—**press'gang** *n.* a body of men employed in pressing men for the navy.

Prestidig'itator (-j-) *n.* a conjurer —**prestidigita'tion** *n.*

Prestige (ēzh) *n.* reputation, or influence depending on it.

Pres'timony *n.* a fund for the support of a priest.

Pres'to *adv.* (*mus.*) quick.

Presume' (-z-) *v.t.* to take for granted.—*v.i.* to take liberties.—**presu'mable** *a.*—**presu'mably** *adv.*—**presump'tion** *n.*—**presump'tive** *a.* that may be assumed as true or valid until the contrary is proved. —**presump'tuous** *a.* forward, taking liberties.—**presump'tuously** *adv.*

Presuppose' (-su-pōz) *v.t.* to take for granted.—**presupposi'tion** *n.* previous supposition.

Pretend' *v.t.* to feign, make believe.—*v.i.* to lay claim, to feign.—**pretence'** *n.*— **pretend'er** *n.*—**preten'tion** *n.* —**preten'tious** *a.* making claim to special merit or importance.

Pret'erite (-it) *a.* past expressing; past state or action.

Pretermit' *v.t.* to pass by; to omit; to disregard.

Preternat'ural (prē-) *a.* out of the ordinary way of nature.

Pre'text *n.* an excuse.

Pre'tor *n.* among the ancient Romans, a civil magistrate or judge.

Prett'y (prit'-i) *a.* having beauty that is attractive rather than imposing; charming, etc.—*adv.* fairly, moderately.—**prett'ily** *adv.*

Pret'zel *n.* a biscuit of wheaten flour baked crisp.

Prevail' *v.i.* to gain the mastery; to be in fashion or generally established.— **prev'alence** *n.*—**prev'alent** *a.*

Prevar'icate *v.i.* to make evasive or misleading statements.—**prevarica'tion** *n.*— **prevar'icator** *n.*

Preven'ient *a.* going before; preceding.

Prevent' *v.t.* to stop from happening.—**preven'tion** *n.*— **prevent'ive** *a.* and *n.*—**prevent'able** *a.*

Pre'vious *a.* preceding; happening before.—**pre'viously** *adv.* *Syn.* antecedent, foregoing, former. *Ant.* subsequent, succeeding, later.

Previse' *v.t.* to foresee; to forewarn.—**previ'sion** *n.* foresight, foreknowledge.

Pre-war *a.* prior to 28th July 1914; old-fashioned.

Prey *n.* that is hunted and killed by carnivorous animals; victim.—*v.i.* to prey upon; to treat as prey, to afflict.

Price *n.* that for which a thing is bought or sold.—*v.t.* to fix or ask a price of.— **price'less** *a.* invaluable.

---

thére. fàther, her; *awl, oil, owl*

Prick *n.* a slight hole made by pricking; a pricking or being pricked.—*v.t.* to pierce slightly with a sharp point; to mark by a prick; to erect (the ears).—**prick'le** *n.* a thorn or spike.—*v.i.* to feel a tingling or pricking sensation.—**prick'ly** *a.*

Prick'et *n.* a candlestick; a wax-taper; a buck in his second year; the wall-pepper.

Pride *n.* too high an opinion of oneself; feeling of elation or great satisfaction; something causing this.—**London pride**, the flower.—*v.refl.* to take pride. *Syn.* vanity, conceit, arrogance. *Ant.* modesty, diffidence, humility.

Prid'ian *a.* of or pert. to the previous day.

Prie-dieu' (prē-dye) *n.* a praying desk.

Priest *n.* an official minister of a religion; a clergyman.—**priest'ess** *fem.*—**priest'hood** *n.*—**priest'ly** *a.*

Prig *n.* a self-righteous person who professes superior ul ture, morality, etc.—**prig'gish** *a.*

Prill *n.* the superior parts of ore; a metal globule from an assay.

Prim *a.* very restrained, formally prudish.

Pri'ma (prē-) *n.* first.—**pri'ma-donna**, the first female singer in an opera.

Pri'mage (-mij) *n.* a small payment, originally paid to the master of a ship for his case of goods, now retained by the shipowner.

Pri'mal *a.* of the earliest age.—**pri'mary** *a.* chief; of the first stage, decision, etc.—**pri'marily** *adv.*—**prim'er** *n.* an elementary school book.—**pri'mate** *n.* an archbishop.—**pri'macy** *n.* pre-eminence; the office of archbishop.—**prime** *a.* first in time, quality, etc.—**Prime minister**, the leader of the government.—*n.* an office for the first hour of the day; first or best part of anything.—**prime'val** *a.* of the earliest age of the world.—**prim'itive** *a.* of an early, undeveloped kind.—**primogen'iture** *n.* the rule by which real estate passes to the firstborn.—**primor'dial** *a.* existing at or from the beginning.

Prime *v.t.* to fill up, e.g. with information.

Prime *v.t.* to prepare (a gun, explosive charge, etc.), for being let off by laying a train of powder.

Prime *v.t.* to prepare for paint w.th preliminary coating of oil, etc.

Pri'mo (prē-) *n.* first part in music.

Primp *v.t.* to prink.—*v.i.* to b formal or affected.

Prim'rose *n.* a plant bearing pale yellow flowers in spring; the colour of the flowers.—*a.* of this colour.

Prim'ula *n.* a genus of plants, including primrose.

Pri'mus *n.* in the Scottish Episcopal Church, the head bishop.

Pri'mus *n.* an oil stove in which the fuel is supplied

by air pressure created by a force pump.

Prince *n.* a ruler or a chief; the son of a king or queen.—**prin'cess** *fem.*—**prince'ly** *a.*—**prince'ling** *n.* a young prince; a petty ruler.—**prin'cipal** *a.* chief in importance.—*n.* the head of certain institutes, *esp.* schools or colleges; person for whom another is agent or second; a sum of money lent and yielding interest. — **principal'ity** *n.* territory or dignity of a prince.—**prin'ciple** *n.* a fundamental truth or element; a moral rule or settled reason of action; uprightness.

Princip'ia *n.pl.* first principles; elements.

Prink *v.t.* to dress to ostentation.—*v.i.* to strut.

Print *v.t.* to impress; to reproduce (words, pictures, etc.), by pressing inked types on blocks to paper, etc.; to produce in this way; to stamp (a fabric) with a coloured design.—*n.* an impression, mark left on a surface by something that has pressed against it; printed cotton fabric; printed lettering; a photograph; written imitation of printed type.—**print'er** *n.* one engaged in printing.

Pri'or *a.* earlier.—*adv.* prior to, before.—*n.* chief of a religious house or order.—**pri'oress** *fem.*—**prior'ity** *n.*—**pri'ory** *n.* a monastery or nunnery under a prior or prioress.

Prise *n.* a lever.— *v.t.* to raise as by means of a lever.

Prism (-zm) *n.* a solid whose two ends are similar, equal, of parallel rectilineal figures and whose sides are parallelograms; a transparent body of this form usually with triangular ends by which light can be reflected.—**prismat'ic** *a.* of prism shape; of colour, such as is produced by refraction through a prism, rainbow-like.

Pris'on (-z-) *n.* a jail.—**pris'oner** *n.* one kept in prison; one captured in war.

Prist'ine *a.* original, primitive, unspoiled.

Prith'ee (pRITH-) a corruption of *I pray thee.*

Pri'vate *a.* not public, reserved for or belonging to or concerning an individual only; of a soldier, not holding any rank.—*n.* a private soldier.—**pri'vacy** *n.* — **pri'vately** *adv.*—**privateer'** *n.* a privately owned armed vessel authorised by a government to take part in a war; the captain of such a ship.—**privateer'ing** *n.* the use of privateers.—**priva'tion** *n.* an act of depriving; want of comforts or necessaries; hardship.—**priv'ative** *a.* denoting privation or negation. *Syn.* retired, isolated, secret. *Ant.* public, general, unconcealed.

Priv'et *n.* a bushy evergreen shrub used for hedges.

Priv'ilege *n.* a right or advantage belonging to a person or class; an advantage or favour that only a few obtain.—*v.t.* to give an advantage to. *Syn.* prerogative, right, exemption. *Ant.* disqualification, liability, disadvantage.

Priv'y *a.* private, confidential. —**Privy Council**, a body of persons appointed by the sovereign, *esp.* in recognition of great public services.—**priv'ily** *adv.*

Prize *n.* a reward given for success in competition; a thing striven for; a thing that is won, e.g. in a lottery, etc.—*v.t.* to value highly.

Prize *n.* a ship or property captured in naval warfare.—**prize'-money** *n.* money from the sale of prizes.

Pro. *prefix* before; in front, etc.

Pro'a *n.* a long narrow sail canoe, noted for its speed.

Prob'able *a.* likely.—**probabil'ity** *n.*—**prob'ably** *adv.*—**pro'bate** *n.* a proving of a will; a certificate of this.—**proba'tion** *n.* testing of a candidate before admission to full membership of some body; a system of releasing offenders, *esp.* juvenile ones, so that their punishment may be cancelled by a period of good behaviour.—**proba'tioner** *n.* a candidate on trial.—**probe** *n.* a blunt rod for examining a wound.—*v.t.* to explore with a probe; to examine into.

Probe *n.* an instrument for examining a wound.—*v.t.* to examine thoroughly into.

Pro'bity *n.* honesty, uprightness.

Prob'lem *n.* a question or difficulty set for or needing a solution. —**problemat'ic, problemat'ical** *a.*

Probos'cis (-sis) *n.* a trunk or long snout, e.g. of an elephant.

Proca'cious (-shus) *a.* pert; saucy.—**procacity** *n.* petulance.

Procar'dium *n.* the pit of the stomach.

Proceed' *v.i.* to go forward; to be carried on; to go to law.—**proce'dure** *n.* act or manner of proceeding; conduct.—**pro'ceeds** *n. pl.* price or profit.—**pro'cess** *n.* a state of going on, a series of actions or changes; method of operation; an action of law; an outgrowth. —**proces'sion** *n.* a body of persons going along in a fixed or formal order.—**proces'sional** *a.* *Syn.* to advance, emanate, progress. *Ant.* to stop, retreat, recede.

Proc'erite (pros-) *n.* a filament of many joints terminating the feeler, as of a lobster.

Pro'chronism *n.* an error consisting in antedating.

Proclaim' *v.t.* to announce, make public.—**proclama'tion** *n.*

Procliv'ity *n.* inclination.

Procon'sul *n.* a Roman officer that discharged the duties of a consul; the governor of a province.

Procras'tinate *v.i.* to put off, delay.—**procrastina'tion** *n.*—**procrast'inator** *n.*

Pro'create *v.t.* to beget.—**procrea'tion** *n.*

Proc'tor *n.* a university official with disciplinary powers; an attorney in an ecclesiastical court.

Procure' *v.t.* to obtain; bring about.—**procu'rable** *a.*—**procura'tor** *n.* a Roman official in a province; one who manages another's affairs.—**procura'tion** *n.* the appointment or authority of a procurator.—**procure'ment** *n.* —**procu'rer** *n.*—**procu'ress** *fem.*

Prod *n.* a pointed instrument; goad; awl.

Prod *v.t.* to poke with something pointed.—*n.* a prodding.

Prod'igal *a.* wasteful.—*n.* a spendthrift.—**prodigal'ity** *n.* *Syn.* extravagant, profuse, free. *Ant.* thrifty, careful, prudent.

Prod'igy (-ji) *n.* a marvel; a person with some marvellous gift.—**prodi'gious** *a.* —prodi'giously *adv.*

Produce' *v.t.* bring forward; to bring into existence, make; to extend in length.—**prod'uce** *n.* that which is yielded or made.—**produ'cer** *n.*—**prod'uct** *n.* the result of a process of manufacture; a number resulting from a multiplication. — **produc'tion** *n.* producing; things produced.—**produc'tive** *a.*—**productiv'ity** *n.*

Pro'em *n.* preface; introduction.

Proempto'sis *n.* the addition of a day, necessary to prevent the new moon's happening a day too soon.

Profane' *a.* not sacred; blasphemous, irreverent.— *v.t.* to pollute, desecrate.— **profana'tion** *n.*—**profan'ity** *n.* profane talk or behaviour. *Syn.* impious, wicked, irreligious. *Ant.* pious, devout, holy.

Profess' *v.t.* to assert; to lay claim to; to have as one's profession or business; to teach as a professor.— **profess'edly** *adv.* avowedly.— **profes'sion** *n.* a professing, a vow of religious faith; entering a religious order; calling or occupation, *esp.* learned or scientific or artistic.—**profes'sional** *a.* of a profession.—*n.* a paid player.—**profess'or** *n.* a teacher of the highest rank in a university.—**professo'rial** *adj.*—**profess'orship** *n.*—**profess'orate** *n.* a professorship. —**professor'iate** *n.* a body of professors of a university.

Proff'er *v.t.* to offer.—*n.*

Profi'cient (-ish-) *a.* skilled.— *n.* one who is skilled.— **profi'ciency** *n.*

Pro'file (-fēl) *n.* an outline of anything as seen from the side.

Prof'it *n.* benefit obtained; money gains.—*v.t.* and *i.* to benefit.—**prof'itable** *a.* yielding profit.—**prof'itless** *a.*

Prof'ligate *a.* dissolute; reckless.—*n.* a dissolute man.— **prof'ligacy** *n.*

Profound' *a.* deep; very learned.—**profun'dity** *n.*

Profuse' *a.* abundant, prodigal.—**profu'sion** *n.*

Prog *v.i.* to wander about and

beg; to filch.—*n.* victuals sought by begging; one that seeks his victuals by begging.

Pro'geny (-oj-) *n.* descendants. —pro'gen'itor (prō-) *n.* an ancestor.

Prognath'ic *a.* having projecting jaws.

Progno'sis *a.* forecast.—prognost'ic *n.*—a prediction.—prognost'icate *v.t.* to foretell. —prognostica'tion *n.*

Pro'gramme *n.* a plan or detailed notes of intended proceedings.

Pro'gress *n.* onward movement; development; a state journey.—progress' *v.i.* to go forward. — progres'sion *n.* progress'ive *a.*

Prohib'it *v.t.* to forbid.—prohibi'tion *n.*—prohib'itive *a.*—prohib'itory *a.*

Proj'ect *n.* a plan.—project' *v.t.* to throw; to plan; to cause to appear on a distant background.—*v.i.* to stick out.—project'ile *a.* capable of being thrown.—*n.* a heavy missile, *esp.* a shell or cannon ball.—projec'tion *n.*—project'or *n.*

Projet' (-zhā) *n.* a draft of a proposed treaty in international law.

Prolap'sus *n.* the falling down of a part of the body from its normal position.

Prolegom'ena *n.pl.* preliminary observations; introductory remarks prefixed to a book.

Prolep'sis *n.* a figure by which objections are anticipated and answered; an error in chronology when an event is antedated.—prolep'tic *a.* anticipating the usual time.

Proletar'iat, proletar'iate (-tér-) *n.* the lowest class of a community, the common people. —proletar'ian *a.*

Pro'licide *n.* crime of killing one's offspring.

Prolif'ic *a.* fruitful; producing much.

Pro'lix *a.* wordy, long-winded. —prolix'ity *n.* *Syn.* long, protracted, discursive. *Ant.* concise, succinct, terse.

Proloc'utor *n.* the speaker or chairman of a convocation.

Pro'logue *n.* a preface, *esp.* a speech before a play.

Prolong' *v.t.* to lengthen out.—prolonga'tion *n.*

Prolu'sion *n.* a prelude or introduction; a preparatory essay.

Promenade' (-ăd) *n.* a leisurely walk; a place made or used for this.—*v.i.* to take a leisurely walk; to go up and down.

Prom'inent *a.* sticking out; distinguished. — prom'inence *n.*

Promis'cuous *a.* mixed without distinction, indiscriminate.—promiscu'ity *n.*

Prom'ise (-is) *n.* an undertaking to do or not to do something.—*v.t.* to make a promise of.—*v.i.* to make a promise.—prom'issory *a.* containing a promise.

Prom'ontory *n.* a point of high land jutting out into the sea.

Promote' *v.t.* to move up to a higher rank or position; to help forward; to begin the process of forming or making.—promo'ter *n.*—promo'tion *n.*

Prompt *a.* do or done at once; ready.—*v.t.* and *i.* to suggest, help out (an actor or speaker) by reading his next words or suggesting words.—prompt'er *n.*—prompt'itude *n.*—prompt'ly *adv.*

Prom'ulgate *v.t.* to proclaim or publish.—promulga'tion *n. Syn.* to disclose, declare, reveal. *Ant.* conceal, withhold.

Prona'os *n.* an open space in front of a temple.

Pro'nate *v.t.* to turn the palm of the hand downwards

Prone *a.* lying face or front downward.

Prong *n.* one spike of a fork or similar instrument.

Prong'buck *n.* the American antelope; also prong'horn.

Pro'noun *n.* a word used to represent a noun.—pronom'inal *a.*

Pronounce' *v.t.* to utter formally; to form with the organs of speech.—*v.i.* to give an opinion or decision. —pronounce'able *a.* - pronounced' *a* strongly marked, decided.—pronounce'ment *n.* a declaration.—pronuncia'tion *n.* the way a word, etc., is pronounced.

Proof *n.* something which proves; test or demonstration; a standard of strength of spirits; a trial impression from type or an engraved plate.—*a.* of proved strength; giving impenetrable defence against.

Proof-plane *n.* a small insulated metal disc for carrying electricity.—proof-sheet a printer's proof.

Prop *n.* a pole, beam, etc., used as a support.—*v.t.* to support, hold up.

Prop *v.i.* in Australia, to halt suddenly, *esp.* of a horse.—*n.*in aviation, abbrev. for propeller; in Australia, a sudden stop, *esp.* of a horse.

Propagand'a *n.* an association or scheme for propagating a doctrine; an attempt, or material used, to propagate a doctrine.—propagand'ist *n.*

Prop'agate *v.t.* to reproduce or breed; to spread by sowing, breeding, example, instruction, persuasion, etc. —*v.i* to breed or multiply.—propaga'tion *n.*

Propel' *v.t.* to cause to move forward.—propell'er *n.* a revolving shaft with blades for driving a ship or aeroplane.—propul'sion *n.*

Propense' *a.* inclined; disposed either to good or evil; prone.

Propen'sity *n.* inclination or bent.

Prop'er *a.* own, peculiar, individual; of a noun, denoting an individual person' or place; fit, suitable; strict; conforming to etiquette, decorous.—prop'erly *adv.*—prop'erty *n.* owning; being owned; that is owned; a quality or attribute belonging to something; article used on the stage in a play, etc.

Proph'et *n.* an inspired

teacher or revealer of the Divine Will; one who foretells future events.—proph'etess *fem.* — proph'ecy (-si) *n.* a prediction or prophetic utterance.—proph'esy (-sī) *v.i.* to utter predictions.—*v.t.* to foretell.—prophet'ic *a.* —prophet'ically *adv.*

Prophylact'ic (prō-) *a.* done or used to ward off disease.— *n.* a prophylactic medicine or measure.

Propina'tion *n.* act of drinking to one's health.

Propin'quity *n.* nearness.

Propi'tiate (-ish-) *v.t.* to appease, gain the favour of. —propitia'tion *n.*—propi'tiatory *a.*—propi'tious *a.* favourable. *Syn.* to appease, conciliate, reconcile. *Ant.* to antagonise, incite, to render unfavourable.

Pro'plasm *n.* a mould; matrix. —proplas'tic *a.* forming a proplasm.

Prop'olis *n.* a resinous substance collected by bees to stop the holes in hives.

Propo'nent *n.* one that makes a proposal.

Propor'tion *n.* a share; relation; comparison; relative size or number; due relation between connected things or parts.—*v.t.* to arrange proportions of.—propor'tional *a.*—propor'tionable *a.* in due proportion.—propor'tionally *adv.*

Propose' *v.t.* to put forward for consideration.—*v.i.* to offer marriage.—propo'sal *n.* —propo'ser *n.*—proposi'tion *n.* a statement or assertion;

a suggestion of terms.— propound' *v.t.* to put forward for consideration or solution.

Propri'etor *n.* an owner.— propri'etress *fem.*—propri'etary *a.* holding or held as property.—propri'ety *n.* properness, correct conduct.

Props *n.pl.* a gambling game played with four shells.

Prore *n.* the prow or beak of a ship.

Prorogue' (-rōg) *v.t.* to dismiss at the end of a session without dissolution.

Prosce'nium *n.* the part of the stage in front of the dropscene.

Proscribe' *v.t.* outlaw, condemn.—proscrip'tion *n.*

Prose *n.* speech or writing not verse.—*v.t.* to talk or write prosily.—prosa'ic *a.* commonplace.—prosa'ical *a.* —pro'sy *a.* tedious, dull.— pro'sily *adv.*—pro'siness *n.*— pro'sing *n.* dull and tedious speech or writing.

Prosect' *v.t.* to dissect beforehand for anatomical illustration.—prosect'or *n.*—prosect'ion *n.*

Pros'ecute *v.t.* to carry on, to bring legal proceedings against.—prosecu'tion *n.*— pros'ecutor *n.*—pros'ecutrix *fem.*

Pros'elyte *n.* a convert.— proselytise' *v.t.*

Prosen'chyna (pros-eng-ki-na) *n.* the cells composing the tissues of plants.

Proseu'cha (-ū-ka) *n.* a place of devotion, *esp.* Jewish chapel that was not a synagogue.

Pros'ody *n.* a science of versification.—**pros'odist** *n.*

Prosopope'ia *n.* a figure of speech by which inanimate things, dead or absent persons, are introduced as speaking.

Pros'pect *n.* a view; mental view; that is to be expected. —*v.t.* and *i.* to explore, *esp.* for gold.—**prospect'ive** *a.* future.—**prospect'ively** *adv.* —**prospect'or** *n.*—**prospect'us** *n.* a circular describing a company, school, etc.

Pres'per *v.i.* to do well.—*v.t.* to cause to do well.— **prosper'ity** *n.* good fortune, well-being.—**pros'perous** *a.*— **pros'perously** *adv.*

Pros'titute *n.* a woman who hires herself for sexual intercourse.—*v.t.* to make a prostitute of; to sell basely, put to an infamous use.—**prostitu'tion** *n.*

Pro'tean (-ti-an) *a.* variable.

Protect' *v.i.* to defend or guard.—**protec'tion** *n.*—**protect'ive** *a.*—**protec'tionist** *n.* one who advocates protecting industries by taxing competing imports.—**protect'or** *n.* one who protects; a regent.—**protect'orate** *n.* an office or period of a protector of a state; relation of a state to a territory that it protects and controls; such territory.

Prot'égé (-ezhā) *n.*—**pro'tégée** *fem.* a person who is under the care and protection of another.

Pro'tein (-tēn) *n.* kinds of organic compound which

form the most essential part of the food of living creatures.

Protest' *v.i.* to assert formally; to make a declaration against.—**pro'test** *n.* a declaration of objection.— **prot'estant** *a.* belonging to any branch of the Western Church outside the Roman communion.—*n.* a member of such church.—**prot'estantism** *n.*—**protesta'tion** *n.*

Pro'tocol *n.* a draft of terms signed by the parties as the basis of a formal treaty.

Pro'ton *n.* the positively charged nucleus of the hydrogen atom.

Pro'toplasm *n.* a soft, inelastic substance, from which the primitive tissue of animal and vegetable life is formed.

Protract' *v.t.* to lengthen; to draw to scale.—**protrac'tion** *n.*—**protract'or** *n.* an instrument for setting out angles on paper.

Protrude' *v.i.* and *t.* to stick out.—**protru'sion** *n.*—**protru'sive** *a.* thrusting forward. —**protru'sively** *adv.*—**protru'siveness** *n.*—**protru'sile** *a.* protrude and withdrawn.

Protu'berant *a.* bulging out.— **protu'berance** *n.* a bulge or swelling.—**protu'berate** *v.i.* to bulge out.—**protubera'tion** *n.* act of swelling beyond the surrounding surface.

Pro'tyle *n.* a supposed primitive matter.

Proud *a.* feeling or displaying pride; that is the cause of pride; stately.—**proud'ly** *adv.*

—**proud flesh** n. an excessive granulation in wounds or ulcers.

Prous'tite n. a light red mineral of arsenic and silver.

Prove (prōōv) v.t. to demonstrate, test; to establish the validity of (a will, etc.).— v.i. to turn out (to be, etc.). —**prov'en** a. proved. Syn. to verify, justify, test, confirm, establish. Ant. disprove, confute, refute.

Prov'edor n. a purveyor.

Prov'ender n. fodder.

Prov'erb n. short pithy saying in common use. —**proverb'ial** a.

Provide' v.i. to make preparation.—v.t. to supply or equip, get in what will be required.—**prov'ident** a. thrifty; showing foresight.— **prov'idence** n. foresight, economy; kindly care of God or nature.—**providen'tial** a. strikingly fortunate.— **providen'tially** adv.—**provi'sion** n. a providing; a thing provided.—pl. food.—v.t. to supply with food.—**provi'sional** a. temporary.—**provi'so** n. a condition.—**provi'sor** n. one appointed, esp. by the Pope, to a benefice before the death of the incumbent, the steward of a religious house; a vicar-general.

Prov'ince n. division of a country; a sphere of action. —pl. any part of the country outside the capital.—**provin'cial** a. and n.—**provin'cialism** n.

Provine' v.t. to lay a stock or branch of a vine in the ground for generation.

Provoke' v.t. to bring about, to irritate.—**provoca'tion** n. —**provoc'ative** a. Syn. exasperate, arouse, rouse, incense, aggravate, enrage, inflame, anger. Ant. pacify, allay, soothe, quiet.

Prov'ost n. the head of certain colleges; in Scotland, an official corresponding to a mayor.—**prov'ost-mar'shal** (prov-ō) n. the head of a body of military police.

Prow n. the prow of a ship.

Prow'ess n. bravery, fighting capacity.

Prowl v.i. to roam stealthily, esp. in search of prey, etc.

Prox'imate a. nearest, next, immediate.—**proxim'ity** n.— **prox'imo** adv. in the next month.

Prox'y n. an authorised agent or substitute; a writing authorising a substitute.

Prude n. a woman who affects excessive propriety with regard to relations of the sexes. — **pru'dish** a. — **pru'dery** n.

Pru'dent a. careful, discreet.— **pru'dence** n.—**pruden'tial** a.

Prune n. a dried plum.

Prune v.t. to cut out dead parts, excessive branches, etc.—**prun'ing-hook** n. a knife with curved blade for pruning trees.

Pru'rient a. given to or springing from lewd thoughts. —**pru'rience** n.

Prus'sian a. of Prussia.— **Prus'sian blue**, a blue pigment.—**pruss'ic acid** n. a poison, orig. got from Prussian blue.

Pry v.i. to look curiously; make furtive enquiries.

Prytane'um (prit-a-nē-um) n. a public hall in Greek cities, esp. in Athens, where strangers and honoured citizens were entertained.

Psalm (sâm) n. a sacred song.—**psalm'ist** n. a writer of psalms.—**psalm'ody** n. the art or practice of singing sacred music.—**psal'ter** n. the book of psalms; a copy of the psalms as a separate book.—**psal'tery** n. obsolete stringed instrument.

Psammit'ic a. like sandstone in structure.

Psell'ism (sel-) n. indistinct pronunciation.

Pseu'donym (sū-) n. a false name.—**pseudon'ymous** a.—**pseudo-** prefix, sham.

Pshaw (shaw) int. an exclamation expressing contempt or dislike.

Psittacid (sit-) n. a parrot.—**psittacine** a. pertaining to or resembling parrots.—**psittacosis** n. a dangerous infectious disease the germ of which is carried by parrots.

Psy'chic (sī'kik) a. of the soul or mind; that appears to be outside the region of physical law.—**psy'chical** a. psychic. — **psy'cho-anal'ysis** n. theory that the mind can be divided into conscious and unconscious or subconscious elements; medical practice based on this.—**psy'cho-an'alyst** n.—**psychol'**-

ogy n. the study of the mind.—**psycholo'gical** a.—**psychol'ogist** n.—**psy'chother'apy** n. the treatment of disease by mental influence.

Ptar'migan (t-) n. a bird of the grouse family, which turns white in winter.

Pto'maine (t-) n. poisonous alkaloid found in putrefying animal or vegetable matter.

Pu'berty n. sexual maturity.

Pub'lic a. of or concerning the public as a whole; not private; open to general observation or knowledge.—n. the community or its members.—**pub'lic-house** n. a house licensed to sell alcoholic liquors to be drunk on the premises.—**pub'lican** n. one who keeps a public-house.—**pub'lish** v.t. to make generally known; to prepare and issue for sale (books, music, etc.).—**pub'lisher** n.—**publica'tion** n.—**pub'licist** n. a writer on public concerns.—**publi'city** n. a being generally known; notoriety.—**pub'licly** adv. Syn. announced, divulged, advertised, proclaimed, declared, disclosed.

Puce n. flea colour, purplish brown.—a. of this colour.

Puck'a, pukk'a a. of full weight; substantial; real; superior.

Puc'ker v.t. and i. to gather into wrinkles.—n. wrinkle.

Pudd'er n. a tumult; a confused noise.

Pudd'ing (pood-) n. a form of cooked food usually in a soft mass.

Pu′dding-ball n. in Australia, a fish resembling a mullet.

Pud′dle n. a small muddy pool; a rough cement for lining ponds, etc.—v.t. to line with puddle.

Pudic′ity n. modesty; chastity.

Pu′erile a. childish.

Puer′peral a. pertaining to childbirth.

Puff n. a short blast of breath of wind, etc.; its sound; a piece of pastry; a laudatory notice, a piece of advertisement.—v.i. to blow abruptly; to breathe hard.—v.t. to send out in a puff; to blow up; to advertise; to smoke hard.—**puff′y** a.

Puff′in n. a sea bird with a large parrot-like beak.

Pug n. a small snub-nosed dog.—**pug′nose** n. a snub nose.

Pu′gilist n. a boxer.—**pu′gilism** n.—**pugilist′ic** a.

Pugna′cious a. given to fighting.—**pugna′city** n.

Pug′ree (-rē) n. a scarf round the hat to keep off the sun's rays.

Puis′ne (pū-nē) a. younger or inferior in rank.—**puis′ne judge** n.

Pu′issant a. powerful and mighty.—**pu′issantly** adv.—**pui′ssance** n. power, strength, might.

Puke v.i. to vomit.—n. vomiting.—**pu′ker** n.

Pul′chritude n. comeliness, beauty.

Pull (pool) v.t. to pluck or tug at; to draw or haul; to propel by rowing.—n. an act of pulling; force exerted by it; draught of liquor.

Pull′et (pool-) n. a young hen.

Pull′ey (poo-) n. a wheel with a groove in the rim for a cord, used to raise weights by a downward pull.

Pull′-over n. a form of jersey or sweater without fastening, to be pulled over the head.

Pul′monary a. of the lungs.

Pulp n. soft moist vegetable or animal matter.—v.t. to reduce to pulp.

Pul′pit (poo-) n. an erection or platform for a preacher.

Pulse n. throbbing of the arteries, esp. in the wrist; vibration.—**pulsate′** v.i. throb, quiver.—**pulsa′tion** n.

Pulse n. eatable seeds of such plants as beans, lentils, etc.

Pul′verise v.t. to reduce to powder.—**pulverisa′tion** n. Syn. to grind, crush. Ant. to build up, amalgamate.

Pu′ma n. a large American carnivorous animal.

Pum′ice (-is) n. a light porous variety of lava.

Pumm′el v.t. to pommel, q.v.

Pump n. an appliance in which the piston and handle are used for raising water, or putting in or taking out air or liquid, etc.—v.t. to raise, put in, take out, etc., with a pump.—v.i. to work a pump.

Pump n. a light shoe.

Pump′kin n. a large gourd used as food.

Pun n. a play on words.—v.i. to make one.—**pun′ster** n.

Punch n. a tool for perforating or stamping; a blow with the fist.—v.t. to stamp or perforate with a punch; to strike with the fist.

Punch *n.* a drink made of spirit or wine with water or milk, lemon, spice, etc., usually taken hot.

Punchay'et *n.* a court of arbitration in Hindustan consisting of five persons.

Punctil'io *n.* a minute detail of conduct; a mere form.—**punctil'ious** *a.* making much of punctilios.—**punc'tual** *a.* in good time, not late.—**punctual'ity** *n.*—**punc'tually** *adv.*—**punc'tuate** *v.t.* to put in punctuation marks.—**punctua'tion** *n.* putting in marks, e.g. commas, colons, etc., in writing or printing to assist in making the sense clear.—**punc'ture** *n.* an act of pricking; a hole made by pricking.—*v.t.* to prick a hole in.—**pun'gent** *a.* biting; irritant.—**pun'gency** *n.*

Punc'to *n.* the point of a foil in fencing.

Pun'dit *n.* a learned Brahmin; an expounder of the Sanskrit language, literature and laws.

Pu'nic *a.* pertaining to the Carthaginians; faithless; treacherous, deceitful.

Pun'ish *v.t.* to cause to suffer for an offence, to inflict a penalty on.—**pun'ishable** *a.*—**pun'ishment** *n.*—**pu'nitive** *a.* inflicting or intending to inflict punishment. *Syn.* to castigate, chastise, correct, discipline, scourge, whip, lash, chasten. *Ant.* reward, commend, indulge, spoil, pamper.

Punk *n.* fungus or some decayed wood used as tinder; in North America, idle, empty talk; any worthless object.—*a.* worthless, bad, poor in quality, stale, insipid.—**punk'y** *a.*

Punt *n.* a flat-bottomed, square-ended boat, propelled by pushing with a pole.—*v.t.* to propel with a pole.

Pun'to *n.* a dot or point in music; a thrust or pass in fencing.

Pu'ny *a.* small and feeble.

Pup *see* PUPPY.

Pu'pil *n.* a person being taught; the opening in the middle of the eye.

Pupp'et *n.* a figure of a human being often with jointed limbs controlled by wires.—**pupp'et-show** *n.* a show with puppets, worked by a hidden showman.

Pupp'y *n.* a young dog; conceited, young man.—**pup** *n.* puppy.

Pur'blind *n.* dim-sighted.

Pur'chase *v.t.* to buy.—*n.* buying; what is bought; leverage, grip, good position for applying force.

Purdah' *n.* a curtain; a curtain serving to screen women of high rank from the sight of men; a mark of caste.

Pure *a.* unmixed, untainted; simple; spotless; faultless; innocent. — **pure'ly** *adv.*—**pu'rify** *v.t.* and *i.*—**puri'fica'tion** *n.*—**purifica'tory** *a.*—**pu'rism** *n.* excessive insistence on correctness of language.—**pu'rist** *n.*—**pu'rity** *n.* a state of being pure.—

---

pu'ritan *n.* a member of the extreme Protestant party, who desired further *purification* of the church after the Elizabethan reformation; a person of extreme strictness in morals or religion.—pu'ritanism *n.*—puritan'ical *a.*

Purge *v.t.* to make clean, clear out.—*n.* an aperient.—purga'tion *n.*—purg'ative *a.* and *n.*—purg'atory *n.* a place for spiritual purging; a state of pain or distress.—purgator'ial *a.*

Pu'riform *a.* like pus.

Purl *n.* an edging of gold or silver wire or of small loops; a stitch that forms a rib in knitting.—*v.t.* to ornament with purls.—*v.i.* to knit in purl.

Purl *v.i.* to flow with a burbling sound.

Pur'lieu (lyōō) *n.* formerly tract of land on the edge of a royal forest; ground bordering on something, outskirts (usually *pl.*).

Pur'lin *n.* a timber lying across the rafters to support them underneath.

Purloin' *v.t.* to steal.

Pur'ple *n.* a colour between crimson and violet.—*a.* of this colour.—*v.t.* to make purple.

Purport' *v.t.* to mean; be intended to seem.—pur'port *n.* meaning, apparent meaning.

Pur'pose (-pus) *n.* intention, design, aim.—*v.t.* to intend.—pur'posely *adv.*

Purpres'ture *n.* an encroachment on public property.

Purprise' *n.* a close or enclosure; precincts of a manor.

Purr *n.* a noise which a cat makes when pleased.—*v.i.* to make this sound.

Purse *n.* small bag for money.—*v.t.* to contract in wrinkles.—*v.i.* to become wrinkled and drawn in.—pur'ser *n.* an officer who keeps accounts, etc., on a ship.

Pursue' (-sū) *v.t.* to run after; aim at; engage in.—*v.i.* to go in pursuit; to continue.—pursu'ance *n.* carrying out.—pursu'ant *adv.* accordingly.—pursu'er *n.*—pursuit' (-sūt) *n.* a running after, attempt to catch; occupation.—pur'suivant *n.* an officer of the College of Arms ranking below a herald. *Syn.* to follow, go after, trail. *Ant.* to precede, go before.

Pur'sy *a.* short-winded, fat.

Purtenance *n.* that which pertains or belongs to, *esp.* the heart, liver and lungs of an animal.

Purvey' *v.t.* to supply.—purvey'or *n.*

Pur'view *n.* scope or range.

Pus *n.* matter formed or discharged in a sore or inflammation.—pu'rulent *a.* forming pus.—pu'rulence *n.*

Push (poosh) *v.t.* to move or try to move away by pressure. —*v.i.* to make one's way.—*n.* an act of pushing; persevering self assertion; in Australia, a band of toughs; a military unit; a political party.—pusher *n.* in aviation, an aeroplane engine designed to work an air screw at the rear of the aero-plane.—push'ful *a.* given to pushing oneself.

Pusillan'imous (pū-) *a.* cow-ardly.—pusillanim'ity *n.*

Puss (poos) *n.* a cat; a hare.—puss'y *n.*

Puss'yfoot *n.* (*slang*) an ad-vocate of total prohibition.

Put (poot) *v.t.* to place or set; to express.

Pu'trid *a.* rotten.—pu'trefy *v.t.* and *i.* to make or become rotten.—putrefac'tion *n.*—putres'cent *a.* becoming rotten.— putres'cence *n.*—putrid'ity *n.*

Putt (put) *v.t.* to throw (a weight or shot) from the shoulder; to strike (a golf ball) along the ground in the direction of the hole.—putt'er *n.* a golf club for putting.

Putt-ee' *n.* a strip of cloth wound round the leg like a bandage, serving as a gaiter.

Putt'ock *n.* a species of kite; the buzzard.

Putt'y *n.* a paste of whiting and oil used by glaziers; polishing powder of calcined tin used by jewellers.—*v.t.* to fix or fill with putty.

Puy (puĕ) *n.* one of the small volcanic cones of Auvergne, hence a conical hill of volcanical origin.

Puz'zle *n.* a bewildering or perplexing question, problem or toy.—*v.t.* to perplex.—*v.i.* to think in perplexity. *Syn.* a riddle, enigma, be-wilderment.

Pyc'nite *n.* a variety of topaz from Saxony and Bohemia.

Pycnom'eter *n.* a instrument to ascertain the specific gravity of a body.

Pye'mia *n.* a disease caused by the absorption of pus or fetid matter; blood poison-ing.—pyem'ic *a.* pertaining to, or affected with, pyemia.

Pyg'my, pig'my *n.* a dwarf.—*a.* dwarf.

Pyja'mas (-ä-) *n.pl.* sleeping suit of loose trousers and jacket. *See* PAJAMAS.

Py'lon *n.* a tower for sus-pension of electric cables; a mark set up to guide aeroplanes during a flight over a stated course; a V-shaped mechanism on an aeroplane from which wires are taken.

Pyor'rhœa (-rĕ-a) *n.* an affec-tion of the gums.

Pyr'amid *n.* solid figure with sloping sides meeting at an apex; a solid structure of this shape, *esp.* the ancient Egyptian monuments; a group of persons or things highest in the middle.—pyram'idal *a.*

Pyre *n.* a pile of wood for burning a dead body.—pyrotech'nics (-k-) *n.* art of making or using fireworks; a firework display.

Py'rene *n.* a hydrocarbon obtained from coal-tar.

Py'roscope *n.* an instrument for ascertaining the intensity of radiant heat.

Pyrr'hic *n.* in verse, a foot con-sisting of two short syllables.

Py'thon (-th-) *n.* a large non-poisonous snake that crushes its prey.

Pyx (piks) *n.* a vessel in which the Host is reserved; a box in which specimen coins are placed to be tested at the Mint.

Q

Quab *n.* a flat soft fish; the eel-ponds.

Quack *n.* the harsh cry of the duck; a pretender to medical or other skill.—*v.i.* of a duck, to utter its cry.

Quadrages'ima *n.* the forty days of fast preceding Easter; Lent.—**quadrages'-imal** *a.* belonging to, or used in, Lent.

Quad'rangle (-ng-gl) *n.* a four-sided figure; a four-sided court in a building.—**quad-rang'ular** *a.*—**quad'rant** *n.* a quarter of a circle; an instrument for taking angular measurements.—**quadrate'v.t.** to make square.—**quadrate'** *a.* square. — **quadrat'ic** *a.* of an equation, involving the square of an unknown quantity.—**quadri'ga** *n.* a four-horsed chariot.—**quadri-lat'eral** *a.* four-sided.—*n.* a four-sided figure.—**quadrille'** *n.* a square dance.—**quad'-ruped** *n.* a four-footed animal.—**quad'ruple** *a.* fourfold. *v.t.* and *i.* to make or become four times as much.

Quad'ricorn *a.* having four horns or antennæ.—*n.* an animal with four horns, or antennæ.

Quaff *v.i.* to drink deeply.— *v.t.* to drink, drain.

Quag, quag'mire *n.* a marshy tract with quaking surface.

Quagg'a *n.* a S. African animal related to the zebra.

Quaich, quaigh (kwāн) *n.* a small drinking vessel, with two ears as handles.

Quail *n.* a small bird of the partridge family.

Quail *v.i.* to flinch.

Quaint *a.* interestingly old-fashioned or odd.—**quaint'ly** *adv.*

Quake *v.i.* to shake or tremble. —**Qua'ker** *n.* a member of the Society of Friends.— **Qua'keress** *fem.*—**qua'ky** *a.*

Qual'ify (kwol-) *v.t.* to ascribe a quality to, describe; to make competent; to moderate.—*v.i.* to make oneself competent, *esp.* by passing an examination.—**qualifica'-tion** *n.* qualifying, thing that qualifies.—**qual'ity** *n.* attribute, characteristic, property; degree of excellence; rank.—**qual'itatives** *a.* relating to quality. *Syn.* to fit, adapt, capacitate, equip, prepare, enable, dilute, assuage, restrict.—*Ant.* unfit, incapacitate, disable.

Qualm (kwâm) *n.* sudden feeling of sickness; misgiving; scruple.

Quandary (kwon-, or kwon-der-) *n.* a state of perplexity, a puzzling situation.

Quan'tity (kwon-) *n.* size, number, amount; specified or considerable amount.— **quan'titative** *a.*—**quan'tum** *n.* a desired or required amount.

Quar'antine (kwor-ĕn-) *n.*

isolation to prevent infection.—*v.t.* to put in quarantine.

Quarr'el (kwor-) *n.* an angry dispute; break-up of friendship.—*v.i.* to fall out with; find fault with.—**quarr'elsome** *a.*

Quarr'y (kwor-i) *n.* the object of a hunt.

Quarr'y (kwor-i) *n.* a place where stone is got from the ground for building, etc.—*v.t.* and *i.* to get from a quarry.

Quart (kwort) *n.* a quarter of a gallon.—**quart'er** *n.* a fourth part; region, district; mercy.—*pl.* lodgings.—*v.t.* to divide into quarters.—**quart'erdeck** *n.* part of the upper deck used by officers.—**quart'erday** *n.* day on which payments are due for the preceding quarter of the year.—**quart'ermaster** *n.* a naval or military rank.—**quart'erstaff** *n.* a long staff for fighting.—**quart'erly** *a.* happening, due, etc., each quarter of the year.—*n.* a quarterlyperiodical.—**quart'ern-loaf** *n.* a four-pound loaf.—**quartet'** *n.* music for four performers; a group of four musicians.—**quart'o** *n.* a size of book in which each sheet is folded into four leaves.—*a.* of this size.

Quartz (kworts) *n.* a stone of silica, often containing gold.

Quash (kwosh) *v.t.* to annul, *esp* by legal procedure.

Qua'ver *v.i.* to tremble, shake.—*v.t.* to say or sing in quavering tones.—*n.* a trill; a musical note half the length of a crotchet.

Quay (kē) *n.* a solid, fixed landing-stage.

Quea'chy (kwē-chi) *a.* yielding or trembling under the feet, as moist or boggy ground.

Queas'y *a.* inclined to, or causing, sickness.

Queen *n.* the wife of a king; a female sovereign; a piece in the game of chess; a perfect female bee, wasp, etc.; a court card. — **queen'ly** *adv.*

Queer *a.* odd, strange.—**queer'ly** *adv.*

Quell *v.t.* to crush, put down.

Quench *v.t.* to extinguish, put out; slake.

Quer'cus *n.* a genus of trees, obtaining the oaks.—**quer'cine** *a.* pertaining to oak.—*a.* the dyer's oak, a dye-stuff.

Quern *n.* a rude hand-mill for grinding grain.

Quer'ulous (-roo-) *a.* full of complaints. *Syn.* petulant, fault-finding, cross. *Ant.* placid, uncomplaining, content.

Que'ry *n.* a question; a mark of interrogation.—*v.t.* to question, ask.—**que'rent** *n.*

Quest *n.* a search.—*v.i.* to search.—**ques'tion** (-chn) *n.* a sentence seeking for an answer; a problem; debate, strife.—*v.t.* to ask questions of, to interrogate; to dispute.—**ques'tionable** *a.* doubtful, *esp.* not clearly true or honest.

Questionnaire' (kes-ti-on-năr) *n.* a list of questions drawn up for formal answer, and submitted in general to a series of individuals or bodies.

Queue (kū) n. a plait of hair; a line of waiting persons.

Quib'ble n. a play on words; an evasion, a merely verbal point in argument.—v.i. to evade a point by a quibble.

Quick a. rapid, swift, keen, brisk; living.—n. sensitive flesh.—adv. rapidly.—quick'-ly adv.—quick'en v.t. to give life to; make speedier, stir up.—v.i. to become living; to become faster.—quick'lime n. unslaked lime. —quick'sand n. loose wet sand which swallows up animals, ships, etc.—quick'-set a. of a hedge, made of living plants.—quick'-silver n. mercury. Syn. speedy, active, nimble, hasty, pregnant. Ant. slow, tardy, dilatory, inactive, stupid.

Quid n. a lump of tobacco for chewing.

Quid'nunc n. one that is curious, or that pretends to know everything that passes.

Qui'et a. undisturbed; with little or no motion or noise, —n. a state of peacefulness, absence of noise or disturbance.—v.t. and i. to make or become quiet.—qui'etly adv.—quies'cent a. at rest.— quies'cent aerial n. in wireless, a method of wireless telephony in which the carrier wave is suppressed unless speech is actually taking place. — quies'cence n. — qui'etude n.—qui'etism n. a passive attitude to life, esp. as a matter of religion.—

qui'etist n.—quie'tus (kwī ē-) n. death; being got rid of; formerly, a receipt for a bill.

Quill n. the hollow stem of a large feather; the spine of a porcupine; a pen, fishing-float, etc., made of a feather-quill. — quill'-driver n. a writer.

Quilt n. a padded coverlet.— v.t. to stitch (two pieces of cloth) with padding between.

Qui'nate n. in botany, having five leaflets on a petiole.

Quince n. an acid pear-shaped fruit; the tree bearing it.

Quinine' (-ēn) n. a bitter drug made from the bark of a tree and used to cure fever, etc.

Quin'querene n. a galley having five tiers of rowers.

Quin'sy (-zi) n. inflammation of the throat or tonsils.

Quintes'sence n. the purest form or essential feature.— quintessen'tial a.

Quintet' n. composition for five voices, or instruments; a company of five singers or players.

Quip n. a smart saying, an epigram.

Quire n. twenty-four sheets of writing paper.

Quit a. free, rid.—v.t. to leave, go away from.—v.refl. to bear oneself.—quits a. on equal or even terms by repayment, etc.—quitt'ance n. receipt, discharge.—quite a. wholly, completely. — quit'rent n. a rent reserved in grants of land, by the payment of which the tenant is quit from all other service.

Quiv'er *n.* a carrying-case for arrows.

Quiv'er *v.i.* to shake or tremble.—*n.* an act of quivering.

Qui vive (kē vēv) *int.* Who goes there? the challenge of a French sentinel.

Quizot'ic *a.* showing enthusiasm for visionary ideals, neglecting own interests for honour or generosity.

Quiz *v.t.* to make fun of; look at curiously or critically.—*n.* a person given to quizzing.— quizz'ical *a.*

Quod'libet *n.* a nice point; a subtlety; a musical medley improvised by several performers.

Quoit (k-) *n.* a ring for throwing at a mark as a game.

Quon'dam *a.* former, that was once.

Quor'um *n.* the number that must be present in a meeting to make its transactions valid.

Quo'ta *n.* a share to be contributed or received.

Quote *v.t.* to copy or repeat passages from; refer to, *esp.* to confirm a view; state a price for.—quota'tion *n.*— quo'table *a.*

Quoth (-ō-) *v.t.* said.

Quotid'ian *a.* daily; everyday, commonplace.

Quo'tient (-shent) *n.* the number resulting from dividing one number by another.

R

Rab'bi *n.* a Jewish title of respect for a teacher or doctor of the law.

Rabb'it *n.* a small rodent animal which resembles the hare.—*v.i.* to hunt rabbits.

Rab'ble *n.* a crowd of vulgar, noisy people; a mob.

Rab'id *a.* raging; mad.— rab'idly *adv.* — rab'idness *n.* —ra'bies *n.* canine madness.

Race *n.* the descendants of a common ancestor; one of the distinct varieties of the human species; a peculiar breed, as of horses, etc.— ra'cy *a.* having a strong flavour; spicy; spirited; piquant.—ra'cily *adv.*—ra'ciness *n.*—ra'cial *a.* of race or lineage.

Race *n.* running; act of running in competition for a prize; a strong current of water, *esp.* leading to a water-wheel.—*pl.* meeting for the sport of horse-racing. —*v.t.* to cause to run rapidly. —*v.i.* to run swiftly.—ra'cer *n.*

Ra'ceme *n.* a flower-cluster with short and equal flowered pedicels as in the currant.— racema'tion *n.* the trimming or harvesting of clusters of grapes.

Rach *n.* a dog that hunts by scent.

Ra'chis *n.* the vertebral column in animals; the stem of a plant or a feather.

Rack v.t. to stretch or strain; to stretch on the rack or wheel; to torture.—n. an instrument for stretching anything—hence, torture; a wooden frame in which hay is laid; a framework on which earthenware, bottles, or other articles are arranged; in mechanics, a straight bar with teeth on its edge, to work with a pinion.—rack'-rent n. the highest rent that can be exacted.

Rack n. thin, flying clouds.

Rack'et n. the bat used in tennis.—pl. a ball game played in a paved court surrounded by four walls.—rack'et-court n.—racketeer' (-e-tēr) n. in America, slang for gangster; one who blackmails business men.

Rack'et n. loud noise, uproar. —v.i. to make a noise.

Ra'diate v.i. to emit rays.—v.t. to emit in rays.—radia'tion n.—ra'diance n. brightness.—ra'diant a.—ra'diator n. that which radiates, esp. a heating apparatus for a room, or a part of an engine for cooling it. Syn. of a. shining, beaming, lustrous, brilliant, resplendent. Ant. dull, dim, murky, sombre.

Rad'ical a. of a root; fundamental; thorough.—n. a politician desiring thorough reforms.—rad'icalism n.

Radio- prefix, of rays of radiation, of radium.—ra'dioact'ive a. emitting invisible rays that penetrate matter. —ra'dio-activ'ity n.—radiol'-

ogy n. science of use of rays in medicine.

Ra'dio n. a wireless telegraphy or telephony.—ra'dio-drama n. a drama for broadcast production.—ra'diogram n. telegram sent by radio.

Rad'ish n. a pungent root.

Ra'dium n. a rare metal named from its radio-active power.

Ra'dius n. a straight line from the centre to the circumference of a circle or sphere. —ra'dial a. of a ray or rays; of a radius; of radium.

Ra'don n. a gaseous, radio-active element, formed by the disintegration of radium.

Rafale' n. a short intensive bombardment.

Raff n. a promiscuous heap; the rabble; the mob; a worthless fellow.

Raff'ia n. a prepared palm fibre used for making mats, etc.

Raff'ish a. disreputable.

Raff'le n. a lottery in which an article is assigned by lot to one of those buying tickets.—v.t. to dispose of by raffle.

Raft (-à-) n. a number of logs or planks, etc., of wood tied together and floating.—rafts'man n. a man that manages a raft.

Raft'er (-à-) n. one of the main beams of a roof.

Rag n. a fragment of cloth; a torn piece.—ragg'ed a. shaggy; torn; clothed in frayed or torn clothes; wanting smoothness.—rag'man n. a man that deals in rags;

a coward; the devil.—**rag'-stone** *n.* a rough sandy lime-stone, so named from its rag-like fracture.—**rag'time** *n.* music with much syncopation.

Rag'amuffin *n.* a ragged person or boy.

Rage *n.* violent anger or passion; fury.—*v.i.* to speak or act with fury; to be widely and violently prevalent. *Syn.* anger, choler, frenzy. *Ant.* calm, equity, sang-froid, phlegm, self-control.

Raid *n.* a rush, attack; a foray. —*v.t.* to make a raid on.— **raid'er** *n.* in aviation, a fighting aeroplane for bombing.

Rail *n.* a horizontal bar, *esp.* as part of a fence, railway line, etc.—*v.t.* to enclose with rails.—**rail'ing** *n.* fence of rails.—**rail'way** *n.* a road with lines of iron rails on which trains run.—**rail'road** *n.* railway.—**rail-car** *n.* a railway motor-car.—**railway-chairs**, grooved pieces of cast-iron bolted on to the sleeper.

Rail *v.i.* to utter abuse.— **raill'ery** *n.* banter.

Rai'ment *n.* clothing.

Rain *n.* moisture falling in drops from the clouds; the fall of such drops.—*v.i.* to fall as rain.—*v.t.* to pour down like rain.—**rain'y** *a.*— **rain'bow** *n.* an arch of prismatic colours formed in the sky by the sun's rays.— **rain'coat** *n.* a light rainproof overcoat.—**rain-gauge** *n.* an instrument for measuring the quantity of rain that falls at any given place in a given time.

Raise (-z) *v.t.* to set up, rear; lift up; breed, bring into existence; levy, collect; end (a siege).

Rai'sin (-z-) *n.* a dried grape.

Raj (räj) *n.* sovereignty; rule. —**ra'jah** *n.* an Indian king or ruler.

Rake *n.* a tool consisting of a long handle with a cross-piece armed with teeth for drawing together hay, etc., or breaking the ground.— *v.t.* to draw or break with a rake; to sweep or search over; sweep with shot.

Rake *n.* a dissolute man.— **ra'kish** *a.*

Rale *n.* a rattling noise in the lungs.

Rallentan'do *a.* in music, becoming slower.

Rall'y *v.t.* to bring together, *esp.* what has been scattered, as a routed army or dispersed troops.—*v.i.* to come together; regain health or strength.—*n.* an act of rallying.

Rall'y *v.t.* to tease.

Ram *n.* a male sheep; a swinging beam with a metal head for battering; a hydraulic machine; a beak projecting from the bow of a warship.—*v.t.* to beat down; stuff; strike with a ram.— **ram'rod** *n.* a rod for pressing down the charge of a muzzle-loading gun.

Ramazan', **Ra'madan** *n.* the ninth Mohammedan month;

the great annual fast or Lent of the Mohammedans.

Ram'ble *v.i.* to walk without definite route; wander; talk incoherently.—*n.* a rambling walk.—ram'bler *n.* one who rambles; a climbing rose.

Ram'ekin *n.* toasted bread covered with cheese and eggs.

Ram'iiy (-fī) *v.t.* and *i.* to spread in branches.—ramifica'tion *n.*

Ramm'ish *a.* rank; strong-scented; lustful.—ramm'ishness *n.*

Ramollisse'ment *n.* a morbid softening of some organ or tissue, *esp.* of the brain.

Ramp *v.i.* to stand on the hind legs.—*n.* a slope.—ramp'ant *a.* rearing; violent.

Ramp'art *n.* a mound for defence.

Ram'shackle *a.* tumbledown, rickety.

Ranch *n.* a cattle farm in America.—*v.i.* to conduct one.—ranch'er *n.*

Ran'cid *a.* smelling or tasting like stale fat.—rancid'ity *n.*

Ran'cour (-ker) *n.* bitter and inveterate ill-feeling.—ran'corous *a.* *Syn.* malice, malevolence, ill-will, grudge, venom. *Ant.* benevolence, friendliness, sweetness, goodwill.

Rand *n.* a border; a high land above a river valley.

Ran'dom *n.* at ran'dom, haphazard.—*a.* made or done at random.

Rangati'ra *n.* in Australia, a chief, male or female; a person of rank, an employer.

Rank *n.* a row or line; order; social position; high social position; relative place or position.—*v.t.* to draw up in a rank, classify.—*v.i.* to have rank or place.—rank'er *n.* a commissioned officer in the army promoted from the ranks.—range *n.* a rank; area, scope, sphere; the distance a gun can reach; distance of a mark shot at; place for practising shooting; a kitchen stove.—*v.t.* to set in a row; to roam.—*v.i.* to extend; roam.—rang'er *n.*

Rank *a.* growing too thickly or coarsely; offensively strong; vile; flagrant.—rank'ly *adv.*

Rank'le (rang-kl) *v.i.* to fester, continue to cause anger.

Ran'sack *v.t.* to search thoroughly.

Ran'som *n.* release from captivity by payment; the amount paid.—*v.t.* pay ransom for.

Rant *v.i.* to rave in violent, high-sounding language.—*n.* boisterous speech; wild gaiety.—*a.* boisterous.—ranter *n.*

Ranti'pole *n.* a wild romping child.—*v.i.* to run about wildly.—*a.* wild; romping; rakish.

Rap *n.* a smart slight blow.—*v.t.* to give a rap to.—*v.i.*

Rapa'cious *a.* greedy, grasping.—rapa'city (-pas-) *n.*

Rape *n.* a plant with oil-yielding seeds; a plant used to feed sheep.

Rape *v.t.* to violate.—*n.* an act of raping.

Rap'id *a.* quick, swift.—rapid'ity *n.*—rap'idly *adv.*

Ra'pier *n.* a light sword for thrusting only.

Rap'ine *n.* plunder.—**rapt** *a.* snatched away; lost in thought; intent.—**rap'ture** *n.* ecstasy.—**rap'turous** *a.*

Rare (rêr) *a.* uncommon; of uncommon quality.—**rare-bit** *n.* Welsh rabbit.—**rar'efy** *v.t.* to lessen the density of.—**rarefac'tion** *n.*—**rare'ly** *adv.*—**rar'ity** *n.* anything rare.

Rare *a.* imperfectly cooked.

Rare'ripe *n.* an early fruit, *esp.* a kind of peach that ripens early.

Ras *n.* a governor or visier in Abyssinia; a cape or headland.

Ras'cal *n.* a rogue, knave.—**ras'cally** *a.*—**rascal'ity** *n.*

Rase *see* RAZE.

Rash *n.* a skin eruption.

Rash *a.* hasty, reckless.—**rash'ly** *adv.* *Syn.* headstrong, foolhardy, incautious, venturesome, daring, indiscreet. *Ant.* cautious, careful, discreet, timid, guarded, wary.

Rash'er *n.* a thin slice of bacon or ham.

Rasp (-à-) *n.* a coarse file.—*v.t.* to scrape with one.—*v.i.* to scrape; make a scraping noise.

Rasp'berry (râzb-) *n.* a familiar soft fruit: the plant.

Rat *n.* a small rodent animal; one who deserts his party.—*v.i.* to hunt rats; to desert one's party.—**rats'bane** *n.* poison for rats.—**ratt'y** *a.* (*slang*) ill-tempered, either habitually or on a special occasion.

Ratafi'a *n.* a spirituous liquor flavoured with fruit kernels and sweetened with sugar.

Rat'chet *n.* a set of teeth on a bar or wheel allowing motion in one direction only.

Rate *n.* proportion between two things; charge; local taxation; degree of speed, etc.—*v.t.* to estimate the value of; value or assess for local taxation.—**rate'able** *a.* that can be rated; liable to pay rates.—**rate'payer** *n.*—**rated horse-power**, in motoring, horse-power according to R.A.C. formula.

Rate *v.t.* to scold.

Rath *n.* a prehistoric hill-fort.

Ra'ther (râther) *adv.* to some extent; in preference.

Rat'ify *v.t.* to confirm.—**ratifica'tion** *n.*

Ra'tio (-shi-ō) *n.* proportion.—**ratio'cinate** *v.i.* to reason.—**ratiocina'tion** *n.*—**ra'tion** (rashun) *n.* a fixed daily allowance.—*v.t.* to supply with, or limit to, rations.—**ra'tional** *a.* reasonable.—**ra'tionalism** *n.* the philosophy which regards reason as the only guide or authority.—**ra'tionalist** *n.*—**ra'tionalise** *v.t.* to explain away by reasoning.—**rational'ity** *n.*—**ra'tionally** *adv.*

Rat'lines (-inz) *n.pl.* cords fixed across a ship's shrouds.

Ratoon' *n.* a new shoot from the root of a sugar-cane.

Rattan' *n.* a palm with long

thin jointed stems; a cane of this.

Ratteen' n. a kind of thick woollen stuff, quilted or twilled.

Rat'tle v.i. to give out a succession of short sharp sounds, as of shaking small stones in a box.—v.t. to cause to sound thus.—n. the sound; an instrument for making it; the set of horny rings in a rattlesnake's tail.—rat'tlesnake n. a poisonous snake.

Rauc'ous a. hoarse.

Rav'age v.t. to lay waste.—n. destruction.

Rave v.i. to talk in delirium or with great enthusiasm.

Rav'el v.t. to entangle or disentangle; fray out.

Rave'lin n. a detached work with two faces meeting in a salient angle at the front and open at the rear.

Ra'ven n. a black bird of the crow family.

Rav'en v.i. and t. to seek prey or plunder.—rav'enous a. very hungry.—ravine' (ēn) n. a narrow gorge.—rav'ish v.t. to carry off, sweep away; commit rape upon (a woman); to enrapture.—rav'ishment n.

Raw a. uncooked; not manufactured; crude; stripped of skin; sensitive; chilly.—raw deal n. in North America, unfair or dishonest treatment.

Ray n. a single line or narrow beam of light, heat, etc.; any of a set of radiating lines.—v.i. to come out in rays.

Ray n. a flat-fish.

Ray n. a disease of sheep.

Ray'ah n. a Turkish subject who is not a Mohammedan.

Rayon n. a radius.—n. artificial silk (trade name).

Raze v.t. to destroy completely; wipe out, delete.—ra'zor n. an instrument for shaving.

Razee' n. an armed ship having her upper deck cut down and thus reduced to the next inferior rate or class.

Ra'zzia (rat-zi-a) n. a raid; a foray.

Re, in re prep. in the matter of.

Re- prefix, makes compounds with meaning of again, e.g. readdress' v.t. to address afresh.—recap'ture v.t. to capture again. These are not given where the meaning and derivation may easily be found from the simple word.

Reach v.t. succeed in touching; arrive at.—v.i. to stretch out the hand; extend.—n. act of reaching; power of touching, grasp, scope; a stretch of river between two bends.

React' v.i. to act in return or opposition or towards a former state.—reac'tion n.—reac'tionary n. one advocating backward movement, in politics, etc.—a. of or inclined to such reaction.—reac'tion coil n. in wireless, coil by which energy is fed back in reaction.—reac'tion for'mation n. in psychoanalysis, a habit contracted

---

Māte, mēte, mīte, mōte, mūte, bōōt.

as protection against repressed impulse. — **rea'gent** n. a chemical substance that reacts with another and is used to detect the presence of the other.

Read v.t. to look at and understand written or printed matter; to interpret mentally; learn by reading; read and utter.—v.i. to be occupied in reading; to find mentioned in reading.—**read'able** a. that can be read, or read with pleasure.—**readabil'ity** n.—**read'er** n.

Read'y (red'i) a. prepared, prompt. — **read'iness** n. — **read'ily** adv.

Re'al a. existing in fact; happening; actual; of property, consisting of land and houses.—**re'alism** n. regarding things as they are; artistic treatment with this outlook.—**re'alist** n.—**realist'ic** a.—**real'ity** n. real existence.—**re'alise** v.t. to make real; to convert into money. — **realisa'tion** n. — **re'ally** adv.—**re'alty** n. real estate *Syn.* substantial, absolute, positive, veritable, genuine, authentic, intrinsic, essential, internal. *Ant.* unreal, negative, spurious, counterfeit, adventitious.

Realm (relm) n. kingdom, province, sphere.

Ream n. twenty quires of paper.

Reap v.i. to cut grain.—v.t. to cut (grain).—**reap'er** n.

Rear n. the back part.—**rear'guard** n. troops protecting the rear of an army.

Rear v.t. to set on end; build up; breed, bring up.—v.i. to rise on the hind feet.

Rear'mouse, rere'mouse n. the leather-winged bat.

Reas'on (-z-) n. ground or motive; faculty of thinking; sensible or logical thought or view.—v.i. to think logically in forming conclusions.—v.t. to persuade by logical argument (*into* doing, etc.).—**roas'onable** a. sensible, not excessive; suitable; marked by logic. *Syn.* judgment, intellect, sense, principle, consideration, account, object, design, purpose, aim, wisdom, propriety, moderat on, argument, exposition, ratiocination. *Ant.* stupidity, senselessness, dullness, foolishness, absurdity, excess.

Reave v t. and i. to plunder.— **reav'er** n.

Re'bate n. a discount.—v.t. to diminish.

Re'bec, re'beck n. a musical instrument akin to the violin, with three strings and p ayed with a bow.

Rebel' v.i. to revolt. take arms against the ruling power.—**reb'el** n. one who rebels; one resisting authority.—a. in rebellion.—**rebell'ion** n. organised open resistance to authority. — **rebell'ious** a.—**rebell'iously** adv.

Rebor ing n. in the internal combustion engine, boring of cyl nder to regain true shape.

Rebound' v.i. to drive back; to reverberate.—v.i. to spring back; to re-echo.—*n.* act of flying back upon collision with another object.

Rebuff' *n.* a blunt refusal; check. — *v.t.* to repulse, snub.

Rebuke' *v.t.* to reprove, reprimand, find fault with.—*n.* an act of rebuking.

Re'bus *n.* a riddle in which the names of things, etc., are represented by pictures standing for the syllables, etc.

Rebut' *v.t.* to force back, refute.—rebutt'al *n.*

Recal'citrant *a.* refractory.

Recant' *v.t.* to withdraw a statement, opinion, etc.—recanta'tion *n.*

Recapit'ulate (rē-) *v.t.* to state again briefly.—recapitula'tion *n.*

Recede' *v.i.* to go back.

Receipt' (-sēt) *n.* written acknowledgment of money received; fact of receiving or being received; a recipe.—receive' (-sēv) *v.t.* to take, accept, get; experience.—receiv'er *n.*—receiv'able *a.*

Re'cent *a.* that has lately happened.—re'cently *adv.*

Recep'tacle *n.* a containing vessel, place or space.—recep'tion *n.* receiving; manner of receiving.—recep'tive *a.* able or quick to receive, *esp.* impressions.—receptiv'ity *n.*

Recess' *n.* a vacation or holiday; niche or alcove; secret hidden place.—recess'ional *n.* a hymn sung while the clergy are retiring.—recess'ive *a.* receding.

Rechauffe' (rā-shō-fā) *n.* a warmed-up dish; a literary rehash.

Recherche (re-sher-shā) *a.* of studied elegance; exquisite.

Recid'ivist *n.* one who relapses into crime.

Recif' *n.* in South Africa, a reef or bar on the sea floor, running parallel to the shore.

Re'cipe (resi-pe) *n.* directions for cooking a dish, a prescription.—recip'ient *a.* that can or does receive.—*n.* that which receives.

Recip'rocal *a.* in return, mutual.—recip'rocally *adv.* —recip'rocate *v.i.* to move backwards and forwards.—*v.t.* to give in return, give and receive mutually.—reciproca'tion *n.* - recipro'city *n.* *Syn.* alternate, correlative, convertible, interchangeable. *Ant.* individual, personal, peculiar, uninterchangeable.

Recis'ion *n.* the act of cutting off.

Recite' *v.t.* to repeat aloud, *esp.* to an audience.—reci'tal *n.* —recita'tion *n.*—recitative' (-ĕv) *n.* musical declamation. —reci'ter *n.*

Reck *v.i.* to care, heed.—reck'less *a.*

Reck'on *v.t.* to count; include; consider.—*v.i.* to make calculations, cast accounts.—reck'oner *n.*

Reclaim' *v.t.* to bring back (from wrong); to make fit for cultivation.—reclaim'able *a.*—reclama'tion *n.*

Recline' *v.i.* to sit or lie with back supported on a slope; repose.

Recluse' *a.* living in complete retirement.—*n.* a hermit.

Recoc'tion *n.* a second coction or preparation; something dressed up a second time.

Rec'ognise *v.t.* to know again; treat as valid; notice.— **recogni'tion** *n.*—**recogni'sable** *a.*—**recog'nisance** (or -kon-) *n.* a bond by which a person undertakes before a court to observe some condition.

Recoil' *v.i.* rebound, *esp.* of a gun when fired.—*n.* draw or spring back; an act of recoiling.

Recollect' *v.t.* to call back to mind.—**recollec'tion** *n.*

Recommend' *v.t.* to entrust; present as worthy of favour or trial; make acceptable.— **recommenda'tion** *n.*

Rec'ompense *v.t.* reward or punish; make up for.—*n.* reward.

Rec'oncile *v.t.* to bring back into friendship; adjust, settle, harmonise. **reconcilia'tion** *n.* —**reconcile'ment** *n.*—**reconci'lable** *a.*

Rec'ondite *a.* obscure, abstruse. *Syn.* deep, occult, unfathomable. *Ant.* plain, clear, obvious, evident.

Reconnoi'tre (-ter) *v.i.* to survey the position of an enemy, a strange district, etc.—*v.i.* to make a reconnaissance. — **reconn'aissance** *n.* such survey.

Record' *v.t.* to put down in writing.—**rec'ord** *n.* a being recorded; document or other thing that records; of a gramophone, a disc on which are cut impressions which a gramophone transforms into sound; the best recorded achievement.—**record'er** *n.* one who records; a city or borough chief magistrate; formerly, a large flute.

Recount' *v.t.* to tell in detail.

Recoup' *v.t.* to recompense; recover what has been expended or lost.

Recourse' *n.* a resorting to.

Recov'er (-kuv) *v.t.* to get back.—*v.i.* to get back health.—**recov'erable** *a.*—**recov'ery** *n.*

Rec'reant *a.* craven, cowardly; apostate.—*n.* a recreant person. *Syn.* false, mean, unfaithful. *Ant.* honest, trusty, sincere, faithful.

Rec'reate *v.t.* to restore.—*v.i.* to take recreation.—**recrea'tion** *n.* agreeable or refreshing occupation. — **rec'reative** *a.*

Recrim'inate *v.i.* to make a counter charge or mutual accusation. — **recrimina'tion** *n.*—**recrim'inatory** *a.*

Recrudesce' (-es) *v.i.* to break out again.—**recrudes'cence** *n.*

Recruit' (-ōōt) *n.* a newly-enlisted soldier; one newly joining a society.—*v.i.* to enlist.—*v.t.* to enlist fresh soldiers, etc.; to recover health.—**recruit'ment** *n.*—**recruit'ing-sergeant** *n.*

Rect'angle *n.* a four-sided figure with four right-angles. —**rectang'ular** *a.*—**rect'ify** (-fī) *v.t.* to put right, purify. —**rectifica'tion** *n.* act of setting right; process of refining by repeated distillation; in wireless, conversion of an alternating current into unidirectional pulsating current.—rec'tifying detector *n.* in wireless, a detector which performs rectification. —rectilin'eal, rectilin'ear *a.* in a straight line, of or characterised by straight lines.— rect'itude *n.* moral uprightness.—rect'o *n.* right-hand page, front of a leaf.—rect'um *n.* the final section of the large intestine.

Recum'bent *a.* lying down.

Recu'perate *v.t.* and *i.* to restore, be restored from illness, losses, etc.—recupera'tion *n.*

Recur' *v i.* to go or come back in mind; happen again.— recurr'ent *a.* — recurr'ence *n.*

Rec'usant *a.* obstinate in refusal, specifically, refusing to conform to the rites of the Established Church.

Red *a.* of a colour varying from crimson to orange and seen in blood, rubies, glowing fire, etc.—*n.* the colour.— red'breast *n.* the robin.— redd'en *v.t.* and *i.*—redd'ish *a.* —red'start *n.* a song-bird.— red'skin *n.* an Amer. Indian.

Redeem' *v.t.* to buy back; set free; free from sin; make up for.—redemp'tion *n.*—redeem'able *a.*—redeem'er *n.*

Red'ingote *n.* a double-breasted outside coat.

Red'olent *a.* smelling strongly (of).—red'olence *n.*

Redoub'le (-dub-) *v.t.* and *i.* to increase, multiply.

Redoubt' (-dowt) *n.* a detached outwork in fortifications.

Redoubt'able (-dowt-) *a.*

dreaded, formidable.—redoubt'ed *a.*

Redound' *v.i.* to contribute or turn to.—redund'ant *a.* superfluous.—redund'ancy *n.*

Redress' *v.t.* to set right.—*n.* compensation.—redress'er *n.* —redressible *a.* capable of being remedied or restored to a right state.—redress'ive *a.* affording relief.

Red'sear *v.i.* to break or crack when red hot, as iron under the hammer.

Red'start *see* RED.

Reduce *v.t.* to bring down, lower, lessen; bring by force or necessity to some state or action; in chemistry, to separate a substance from other substances with which it is combined; in Scots law, to set aside, as a deed, etc.— redu'cible *a.*—reduc'tion *n.*— reducing agent, a substance used to remove oxygen from other substances.—redu'cing-box, in motoring, a gear-box to reduce speed and increase turning power. *Syn.* to humble, degrade, diminish, curtail, shorten, depreciate. *Ant.* enlarge, increase, lengthen, enhance, exalt, elevate.

Redu'plicate *v.t.* to double.— reduplica'tion *n.*—redup'licative *a.*

Reed *n.* various marsh or water plants; the tall straight stem of one; the vibrating part of certain musical instruments.—reed'y *a.* full of reeds; like a reed instrument in tone.

Reef *n.* a part of a sail which

can be rolled up to reduce the area; a ridge of rock near the surface of the sea; a lode of auriferous quartz.—*v.t.* to take in a reef of.

Reek *n.* strong smell or smoke.—*v.i.* to smoke, emit fumes.

Reel *n.* a winding apparatus; a cylinder for winding cotton, etc., on; a lively Scottish dance; music for it; an act of staggering; in cinematography, a spool on which a film is wound; a portion of film, usually 1000 ft.—*v.t.* to wind on a reel.—*v.i.* to stagger, sway.

Reeve *v.t.* to pass (a rope) through a hole, in a block, etc.

Refash'ion *v.t.* to fashion anew.

Refec'tory *n.* a room for meals.—**refec'tion** *n.* a meal.

Refer' *v.i.* to trace or ascribe to; to submit for decision; to send to for information.—*v.i.* to have relation, allude.—**ref'erable** *a.*—**referee'** *n.* an umpire.—**ref'erence** *n.*—**referen'dum** *n.* the submitting of a question to a whole body of voters.

Refine' *v.t.* to purify.—**refine'ment** *n.*—**refi'ner** *n.*—**refi'nery** *n.* a place where sugar, etc., is refined.

Reflect' *v.t.* to throw back, *esp.* rays of light; to cast (discredit, etc.), upon.—*v.i.* to meditate.—**reflec'tion**, **reflex'ion** *n.*—**reflect'ive** *a.*—**reflect'or** *n.* a polished surface for reflecting light, etc.—**re'flex** *a.* reflected, bent

back; of muscular action, involuntary.—**reflex'ive** *a.* in grammar, describes a verb denoting the agent's action on himself.—**condi'tional re'flex**, reflex action due to associative attachment as shrinking from something because of some previous unpleasant association.—**re'flex cir'cuit**, in wireless, thermionic valve circuit giving dual amplification, high frequency and low frequency.

Re'flux *n.* a flowing back.

Reform' *v.t.* and *i.* to amend, improve.—*n.* amendment, improvement.—**reforma'tion** *n.*—**reform'atory** *n.* an institution for reforming juvenile offenders.—*a.* reforming.—**reform'er** *n.*

Refract' *v.t.* to break the course of (light, etc.).—**refrac'tion** *n.*—**refract'ive** *a.* **refract'ory** *a.* unmanageable, difficult to treat or work.—**refran'gible** *a.*

Refrain' *n.* chorus.

Refrain' *v.i.* abstain from.—*v.t.* to check. *Syn.* curb, govern, forbear, withhold. *Ant.* indulge, gratify, yield to, proceed, advance.

Refresh' *v.t.* to give freshness to.—**refresh'er** *n.* one that, or that which, refreshes; an extra fee to counsel in addition to the retaining fee.—**refresh'ment** *n.* that which refreshes, *esp.* food or drink.

Refrig'erate (-j-) *v.t.* to freeze, cool.—**refrigera'tion** *n.*—**refrig'erator** *n.* an apparatus for cooling or freezing.

Ref'uge n. shelter, protection. —**refugee'** n. one who seeks refuge, esp. in a foreign country.

Reful'gent (-j-) a. shining.—**reful'gence** n.—**reful'gency** n.

Refund' v.t. to pay back.

Refur'bish v.t. to furbish or polish anew.

Refuse' (-z) v.t. and i. to decline.—**ref'use** (-s) a. discarded.—n. rubbish, useless matter.—**refu'sal** n. Syn. to reject, repel, rebuff, repudiate. Ant. accept, receive, welcome, embrace.

Refute' v.t. to disprove.—**refu'table** a.—**refuta'tion** n.

Re'gal a. of, or like, a king.—**rega'lia** n.pl. the insignia of royalty, as used at a coronation, etc.—**re'gally** adv.—**regal'ity** n.

Re'gal n. a small portable organ in use in the 16th and 17th centuries.

Regale' v.t. to feast.—**regale'ment** n. refreshment.

Regard' v.t. to look at; consider (as); heed; relate to.—n. a look; particular respect; esteem.—pl. an expression of goodwill.—**regard'ful** a.—**regard'less** a. Syn. mark, watch, remark, contemplate, heed, mind, value, respect, admire, consider, reckon, deem, think, hold.

Regatt'a n. a meeting for yacht or boat races.

Re'gelate v.t. to become congealed again.—**regela'tion** n. the freezing together of two pieces of melting ice.

Re'gent a. ruling.—n. one who rules a kingdom during the absence, minority, etc., of its king.—**re'gency** n.—**régime'** n. system of government.—**reg'imen** (-j-) n. a prescribed system of diet.—**reg'iment** n. an organised body of troops as a unit of an army.—**regiment'al** a. of a regiment.—n. in pl. uniform.—**re'gius** a. appointed by the crown.

Re'gicide n. one who kills a king; his crime.

Regiment see REGENT.

Re'gion (-jn) n. an area, district.

Reg'ister (-j-) n. a written record; compass of a voice; a device for registering.—v.t. to set down in writing; to enter in a register.—**registrar'** n. the keeper of a register.—**registra'tion** n.—**reg'istry** n. registering; a place where registers are kept.

Re'gium do'num (rē-gi-um dō-num) n. an annual grant of money, orig. made by Charles II. to the Irish Presbyterian ministers (commuted in 1871), and in later reigns to the nonconforming clergy of England and Scotland.

Reg'let n. a kind of flat, narrow moulding; a fillet; a thin strip of wood used instead of a printer's lead.

Reg'nal a. pertaining to the reign of a sovereign.—**reg'nal years**, the number of years a sovereign has reigned.

Reg'nant a. reigning.—**reg'nancy** (reg-nan-si) n. rule; predominance.

Regorge' (rĕ-gorj) *v.t.* to vomit up; to swallow again; to swallow eagerly.

Regraft' *v.t.* to graft again.

Regrant' *v.t.* to grant back.

Regrate' (re-grāt) *v.t.* to remove the outer surface of, as of an old hewn stone, so as to give it a fresh appearance; to buy, as provisions, in order to sell again in or near the same market or fair; to engross; to forestall, as the market.—**regrat'er** (re-grā-tẹr) *n.* one that regrates.

Regreet' (rĕ-grēt) *v.t.* to greet or salute again.

Re'gress *n.* passage back; the power of passing back.—**regres'sive** *a.* passing back.—**regres'sively** *adv.*—**regres'sion** *n.* act of returning; retrogression.

Regret' *v.t.* to grieve for the loss of, or on account of.—*n.* grief for something done or left undone or lost.—**regret'ful** *a.*—**regrett'able** *a.*

Reguer'don (rĕ-ger-don) *n.* a reward, recompense.—*v.t.* to reward.

Reg'ula (reg-ŭ-la) *n.* a rule; a book of rules or directions in monastic institutions; (*arch.*) a fillet or listel.

Reg'ular *a.* done according to rule; habitual; living under rule; belonging to the standing army.—*n.* a regular soldier.—**regular'ity** *n.*—**reg'ulate** *v.t.* to adjust; put under rule.—**regula'tion** *n.*—**reg'ulator** *n. Syn.* normal, methodical, punctual, precise, exact, usual, systematic, uniform. *Ant.* unusual, strange, eccentric, inconsistent, variable, chaotic, muddled, exceptional.

Reg'ulus *n.* any metal that still retains to some extent the impurities of the ore; a star of the first magnitude in the constellation Leo.

Regur'gitate *v.t.* to throw or pour back in great quantity.—*v.i.* to be thrown or poured back.—**regurgita'tion** *n.* act of throwing or pouring back by the orifice of entrance; the act of swallowing again.

Rehabil'itate (rē-) *v.t.* to restore to reputation or former position.—**rehabilita'tion** *n.*

Rehearse' (-hẹrs) *v.t.* to repeat aloud; say over again; to practise (a play, etc.).—**rehears'al** *n.*

Rehibi'tion, redhibi'tion (rē-hibish-un, red-hi-bish-un) *n.* the returning of a thing purchased to the seller, on the ground of some defect or fraud; the annulling of a sale.

Reif (rēf) *n.* robbery; forcible theft; plunder.

Reign (rān) *n.* royal power; period of a sovereign's rule.—*v.i.* to be sovereign.

Reimburse' (rē-im-) *v.t.* to pay back.—**reimburse'ment** *n.*

Rein (rān) *n.* a narrow strap attached to the bit to check or guide a horse.—*v.t.* to check or manage with reins.

Reincarna'tion *n.* a rebirth of the soul in successive bodies; one of the series in the transmigration of souls.

—reincar'nate v.t.—reincarna'tionist n. one who believes in reincarnation.

Rein'deer (rān-) n. a deer of cold regions.

Reinforce' (rē-in-) v.t. to strengthen, esp. by sending fresh men.—reinforce'ment n.

Reins (rānz) n.pl. the kidneys; the lower part of the back over the kidneys; the affections and passions (formerly supposed to have their seat in that part of the body).

Reinstate' (rē-in-) v.t. to replace, restore.—reinstate'ment n.

Reiter (rī'tẹr) n. a mounted trooper; one of the hired bands, chiefly German, in the religious wars of the 14th and 15th centuries.

Reit'erate v.t. to repeat again and again.—reit'erative n. a word, or part of a word, repeated so as to form a reduplicated word.—reitera'tion n. repetition.

Reject' v.t. to refuse to have, put aside, cast up.—rejec'tion n.

Rejoice' v.t. and i. to make or be joyful.

Rejoin' v.t. to say in answer.—rejoin'der n. an answer.

Reju'venate v.t. to restore to youth.—rejuvena'tion n.—rejuvenes'cence n.—rejuvenes'cent a.

Relais' (re-lā') n. in fortification, a narrow walk just outside the rampart.

Relapse' v.i. to fall back, into evil, illness, etc.—n.

Relate' v.t. to narrate, recount; establish relation between; to have reference or relation to.—rela'tion n. narration; a narrative; correspondence, connection; connection by blood or marriage.—rel'ative a. dependent on relation to something else, not absolute; having reference or relation to.—n. a relative word or thing; one connected by blood or marriage.—rel'atively adv. — rela'tionship n.

Relax' v.t. to make loose or slack.—v.i. to become loosened or slack; become more friendly.—relaxa'tion n. relaxing recreation.

Re'lay n. a fresh set of horses to replace tired ones; a gang of men, supply of material, etc., used similarly; in electricity, a device for making or breaking a local circuit; in wireless, a broadcasting station receiving its programmes from another station.—re'lay-race n. a race between teams of which each runner does part of the distance.

Release' v.t. to give up, surrender, set free.—n. a releasing; a written discharge.

Rel'egate v.t. to banish, consign.—relega'tion n.

Relent' v.i. to give up harsh intention, become less severe.—relent'less a.

Rel'evant a. having to do with the matter in hand.—rel'evance n.

Rel'ic n. something remaining as a memorial of a saint, etc.; a thing kept as a memento.—pl. dead body; remains, surviving traces.—rel'ict *n.* a widow. :

Relief *n.* alleviation or end of pain, distress, etc.; money or food given to victims of a disaster, poverty, etc.; release from duty; one who relieves another; projection of a carved design from a surface; distinctness, prominence.— **relieve** *v.t.* to bring or give relief to.

Reli'gion (-ijn) *n.* a system of faith and worship.—reli'gious *a.*—reli'giously *adv.*—reli'giousness *n.*

Relin'quish (inkw-) *v.t.* to give up. — relin'quishment *n.*

Rel'iquary *n.* a case or shrine for relics.

Rel'ish *n.* taste or flavour; a savoury taste; a liking.—*v.t.* to enjoy, like.

Reluct'ant *a.* unwilling.—reluct'ance *n.*

Rely' *v.i.* to depend (on).—reli'able *a.* trustworthy.—reliabil'ity *n.*—reli'ance *n.*—reli'ant *a.* confident.—reliabil'ity trial *n.* a public test of strength and speed of aeroplanes, motor-cars or motorcycles.

Remain' *v.i.* to stay or be left behind; continue.—remains *n. pl.* a dead body.—remain'der *n.* rest, what is left after subtraction.—rem'anence *n.* magnetic flux remaining in iron parts of electro-magnet after the current is switched off.—rem'anet *n.* a parliamentary bill postponed to another session. *Syn.* to tarry, sojourn, wait, dwell, endure. *Ant.* to go, depart, leave, quit, retire, withdraw, disappear.

Remand' (-à-) *v.t.* to send back, *esp.* into custody.

Remark' *v.t.* to take notice of; to say.—*v.i.* to make a remark (on).—*n.* an observation, comment.—remark'able *a.* noteworthy, unusual.—remark'ably *adv.*

Rem'blai (ron'-blā) *n.* a portion of an earthwork formed by the excavated materials.

Rem'edy *n.* a means of curing, counteracting or relieving a disease, trouble, etc.—*v.t.* to put right.—reme'dial *a.*—reme'diable *a.*

Remem'ber *v.t.* to retain in or recall to the memory.—*v.i.* to have in mind.—remem'brance *n.*—remem'brancer *n.* one who or that which reminds, *esp.* as a title of an official.

Re'mex *n.* (*pl.* re'miges) one of the quill feathers of a bird's wing.

Remind' (-mind) *v.t.* to put in mind (of).—remind'er *n.*

Reminis'cence *n.* remembering; thing recollected.—reminis'cent *a.* reminding.

Rem'iped *n.* having oar-shaped feet.—*n.* a remiped animal.

Remise' (rĕ-mīz) *n.* a granting back; a surrender; a coach-house; a carriage hired from a livery stable; in fencing, a thrust following up one that has missed, before the opponent can recover.—*v.i.* to make a remise.—*v.t.* to grant back; to surrender.

Remiss' *a.* negligent.—re-miss'ly *adv.*—remit'. *v.t.* to forgive, not to exact, give up; slacken.—*v.i.* to slacken, give up.—remiss'ibl'e *a.*—remis'sion *n.*—remitt'ance *n.* a sending of money; money sent.—remittance man, in the colonies, a man who does no work but lives on money sent from his family. *Syn.* careless, heedless, neglectful, slack, inattentive, dilatory. *Ant.* careful, mindful, attentive, painstaking.

Rem'nant *n.* a fragment or small piece remaining.

Remon'etise (re-mun-e-tīz) *v.t.* to make legal tender again; to make basis of credit again, e.g. remonetise silver, to make a silver standard alongside, or instead of, the gold standard.

Remon'strate *v.i.* to protest, expostulate, argue.—remon'strance *n.*

Remorse' *n.* regret and repentance.—remorse'ful *a.*—remorse'fully *adv.*—remorse'less *a.* pitiless.

Remote' *a.* far away.—remote'ly *adv.* — remove' (-mōōv) *v.t.* to take away or off.—*v.i.* to go away; change residence.—remo'val (-ōō-) *n.*—remo'vable *a.*

Remu'nerate *v.t.* to reward, pay.—remunera'tion *n.*—remu'nerative *a.*

Re'nal *a.* pertaining to the kidneys.

Renas'cent *a.* springing up again.—renas'cence *n.* revival, *esp.* the revival of learning in the fourteenth to sixteenth centuries.—renais'-sance *n.* renascence.

Rencoun'ter, rencon'tre (ren-koun'-tẹr, rang-on'-tr) *n.* a meeting of two persons or bodies—hence, a meeting in opposition; action or engagement; a sudden contest; conflict; collision; clash.—*v.t.* to attack hand to hand.—*v.i.* to meet an enemy unexpectedly; to fight hand to hand.

Rend *v.t.* and *i.* to tear.

Rend'er *v.t.* to give in return, deliver up; submit, present; portray, represent; melt down.—rend'ezvous (rondi-vōō) *n.* a meeting-place.—*v.i.* to meet, come together.—rendi'tion *n.* surrender; translation.

Ren'egade *n.* a deserter, apostate.

Renew' *v.t.* to make new; to revive; to restore to a former state; to re-establish; to grant, or to accept, a new bill or note for the amount of a former one; to begin again; to implant holy affections in the heart.—*v.i.* to be made new; to grow again. —renew'al *n.* revival; restoration; regeneration; a re-loan on a new vote given in place of a former note.—renew'able *a.*—renewabil'ity *n.* the quality of being renewable.—renew'ing *a.* regenerating; quickening; reviving, as grace.—*n.* act of regenerating; act of quickening or imparting new impulse to the regenerated soul.

Reni'tent *a.* resisting pressure

or the effect of it, as an elastic body.—reni'tency *n.* the resistance of a body to pressure; moral resistance; reluctance.

Renn'et *n.* a preparation for curdling milk.

Renn'et *n.* a species of French apple; queen-apple.

Renounce' *v.t.* to give up, cast off.—*v.i.* at cards, to fail to follow suit.—renuncia'tion *n.*

Ren'ovate *v.t.* to restore, repair.—renova'tion *n.*

Renown' *n.* fame.

Rent *n.* payment for the use of land or buildings.—*v.t.* to hold as a tenant; to let.—rent'al *n.* sum payable as rent.—renter *n.* in the cinema, a person that rents films to theatre proprietors.

Rent *n.* a tear.

Rente (rŏnt) *n.* interest; *esp.* in *pl.*, that paid by a government on public loans.—rentier (rŏn-tyā) *n.* a person whose income is derived from invested capital.

Ren'ter *v.t.* to sew together so that the seam is scarcely visible; to fine-draw; to darn neatly.

Renu'ent *a.* throwing back the head, applied to muscles that do this.

Renuncia'tion *see* RENOUNCE.

Rep *n.* a fabric with corded surface.

Repair' *v.i.* to resort, betake oneself (to).

Repair' *v.t.* to mend.—*n.* a mend.—repair'able *a.*—repara'tion *n.* a repairing; amends, compensation.

Repartee' *n.* a witty retort; gift of making them.

Repast' *n.* a meal.

Repat'riate *v.t.* to restore to his own country.

Repay' *v.t.* to pay back; make return for.—repay'ment *n.*—repay'able *a.*

Repeal' *v.t.* to annul, cancel.—*n.* act of repealing.

Repeat' *v.t.* to say or do again, reproduce.—repeat'edly *adv.*—repeat'er *n.*—repeti'tion *n.*

Repel' *v.t.* to drive back, ward off, refuse.—repell'ent *a.* *Syn.* resist, withstand, check, confront, parry, rebuff, reject, decline. *Ant.* invite, welcome, accept, attract, entice.

Repent' *v.i.* to wish one had not done something, feel regret for a deed or omission.—*v.t.* to feel regret for.—repent'ant *a.*—repent'ance *n.*

Repercus'sion (rĕ-) *n.* recoil; echo; indirect effect.

Rep'ertory *n.* a store; a repertoire.—rep'ertoire (-twar) *n.* a stock of plays, songs, etc., that a player or company is prepared to give.

Repetend' *n.* that part of a repeating decimal which recurs continually.

Repine' *v.i.* to fret.

Replace' *v.t.* to put back; fill up with a substitute for.—replace'ment *n.*

Replen'ish *v.t.* to fill up again.

Replete' *a.* filled.—reple'tion *n.*

Replev'y *v.t.* to take or get back goods wrongfully taken or detained, upon giving security to try the right to them in a suit at law —

replev'in n. a personal action to recover possession of goods.—**replev'iable, replev'-isable** a. that may be replevied.

Rep'lica n. a copy of a work of art made by the artist.

Reply' v.i. and t. to answer.—n. an answer.

Repone (re-pōn) v.t. to restore; to replace in an office or rank.

Report' v.t. to relate; take down in writing; make or give an account of; name as an offender.—v.i. to make a report.—n. a rumour; account or statement; repute; a bang.—**report'er** n. one who reports, esp. for a newspaper.

Repose' v.i. to take rest.—v.t. to give rest to; put (trust, etc.).—n. rest.—**repos'itory** n. a store or shop.

Repouss'é (rē-pōōs-ā) a. embossed; hammered into relief from the reverse side.—n. metal work so produced.—**repoussage** (re-pōō-sazh, re-pōōs-ij) n. the process of producing repoussé work, or the work itself.

Reprehend' v.t. to find fault with.—**reprehen'sible** a.—**reprehen'sion** n.

Represent' v.t. to call up by description or portrait; make out to be; act, play, symbolise; act as deputy for; stand for.—**representa'tion** n.—**represent'ative** n. and a.

Repress v.t. to keep down or under.—**repress'ive** a.—**repres'sion** n.

Reprieve' v.t. to suspend the execution of (condemned person); a reprieving or warrant for it.

Rep'rimand n. a sharp rebuke.—v.t. to rebuke sharply.

Repri'sal n. retaliation.

Reproach' v.t. to scold, rebuke.—n. a scolding or upbraiding; expression of this; a thing bringing discredit.—**reproach'ful** a.

Rep'robate v.t. to disapprove of, reject.—a. depraved, cast off by God.—n. a reprobate person.—**reproba'tion** n.

Reproduce' (rē-) v.t. to produce anew; produce a copy of; bring new individuals into existence.—**reprodu'cible** a.—**reproduc'tion** n.—**reproduc'tive** a.—**reprodu'cer** n. in the cinema, a projector.

Reprove' (-ōōv) v.t. to blame, rebuke.—**reproof'** n.

Rep'tile n. a crawling animal such as a snake, lizard, tortoise, etc.—**reptil'ian** a.

Repub'lic n. a state in which the supremacy of the people or its elected representatives is formally acknowledged.—**repub'lican** a. and n.—**repub'licanism** n.

Repu'diate v.t. to cast off, disown.—**repudia'tion** n.

Repug'nant a. contrary; distasteful.—**repug'nance** n.

Repulse' v.t. to drive back; rebuff.—n. a driving back, rejection, rebuff.—**repul'sion** n. repulsing; distaste, aversion.—**repul'sive** a. loathsome, disgusting. Syn. to repel, disagree, revolt. Ant. to attract, entice, charm, invite, allure.

Repute' *v.t.* to reckon, consider.—*n.* reputation, credit. —**reputa'tion** *n.* what is generally thought or believed about a character; good fame. —**rep'utable** *a.* of good repute.

Request' *n.* asking; thing asked for.—*v.t.* to ask.

Req'uiem (-kwi-em) *n.* a mass for the dead.

Requies'cence (rek-wi-es-ens) *n.* a state of quiescence.

Require' *v.t.* to demand; want, need.—**require'ment** *n.*—**req'uisite** (-zit) *a.* needed.—*n.* something necessary.—**requisi'tion** *n.* a formal demand, usually for military supplies, etc.—*v.t.* to demand by an order of requisition; press into service.

Requite' *v.t.* to repay; retaliate on.—**requi'tal** *n.*

Rere'dos (rēr-dos) *n.* an ornamental screen on a wall behind an altar.

Rescind' (-s-) *v.t.* to cancel, annul.—**rescis'sion** *n.*

Re'script (rē-skript) *n.* among the Romans, the answer of an emperor consulted on some question—hence, an edict or decree.—**rescribe'** *v.t.* to write back; to answer; to write over again.—**rescrip'tion** *n.* a writing back; the answering of a letter. —**rescrip'tive** *a.* pertaining to a rescript.—**rescriptively** *adv.*

Res'cue *v.t.* to save, deliver.— **res'cuing** *n.*—**res'cuer** *n.*

Research' *n.* investigation, *esp.* scientific study to try and discover facts.—**research'er** *n.*

Resect' *v.t.* to cut or pare off.—**resec'tion** *n.* the act of cutting or paring off.

Resem'ble (-z-) *v.t.* to be like. —**resem'blance** *n.*

Resent' (-z-) *v.t.* to show or feel indignation at, retain bitterness about. — **resent'-ment** *n.*—**resent'ful** *a.*

Reserve' (-z-) *v.t.* hold back, set apart, keep for future use.—*n.* something reserved; part of an army only called out in emergency; reticence, concealment of feelings or friendliness.—*pl.* troops in support.—**reserva'tion** *n.* a reserving or thing reserved; an exception or limitation.— **reserved'** *a.*— not showing feelings, lacking cordiality.— **reserv'ist** *n.* one serving in the reserve.—**res'ervoir** *n.* a receptacle for liquid, *esp.* a large one built for storing water.

Reset' *v.t.* and *i.* to receive stolen goods.—*n.* the receiving of stolen goods.—**resett'er** *n.*

Reside' (-z-) *v.i.* dwell.— **res'idence** *n.* dwelling; house. —**res'idency** *n.* official residence of a British agent at an Indian court.—**res'ident** *a.* and *n.*—**residen'tial** *a.*

Res'idue (-z-) *n.* what is left.— **resid'ual** *a.*—**resid'uary** *a.*

Resign' (-zīn) *v.t.* to give up.— *v.i.* to give up an office, employment, etc.—**resigned'** *a.* content to endure.— **resigna'tion** (-zig-nā-) *n.* resigning; being resigned. *Syn.* to yield, renounce, relinquish, abandon, forgo, quit, leave. *Ant.* remain, retain, stay.

Resil'ient (-z-) *a.* rebounding. —resil'ience *n.*—resil'iency *n.*

Res'in (-z-) *n.* a sticky substance formed in and oozing from plants, *esp.* firs and pines.—res'inous *a.*—ros'in *n.* resin.

Resipisc'ence *n.* wisdom after the event; repentance.

Resist' (-z-) *v.t.* to withstand. —*v.i.* to oppose.—resist'ance *n.* in electricity, the opposition offered by a circuit to the passage of a current through it.—resist'ances *n.pl.* in psycho-analysis, mental forces opposed to self-knowledge. — resist'ant *a.* — resist'ible *a.*—resist'less *a.*

Res'onant (-z-) *a.* echoing, resounding.—res'onance *n.*

Resort' (-z-) *v.i.* to have recourse; frequent.—*n.* recourse; a frequented place.

Resound' (-z-) *v.i.* to echo, ring, go on sounding.

Resource' (-sors) *n.* skill in devising means.—*pl.* means of supplying a want; stock that can be drawn on, means of support.—resource'ful *a.* —resource'fully *adv.*

Respect' *v.t.* to refer to, to treat with esteem.—*n.* reference, relation; deference, esteem; point or aspect.— respect'able *a.* worthy of respect.—respectabil'ity *n.*— respect'ful *a.*—respect'ive *a.* several, separate.—respect'- ively *adv.*

Respire' *v.i. and t.* to breathe. —respi'rable *a.*—respira'tion *n.*—res'pirator *n.* an appar-

atus worn over the mouth and breathed through as a protection against dust, poison-gas, etc. — res'piratory *a.*

Res'pite *n.* a delay; suspension of the execution of a capital sentence; reprieve; suspension of labour.—*v.t.* to grant a respite to; to reprieve; to relieve by an interval of rest.

Resplend'ent *a.* brilliant, shining.—resplend'ence *n.* *Syn.* radiant, lustrous, effulgent, beaming, glorious. *Ant.* dull, gray, dismal, gloomy, drab, plain, ordinary, dowdy.

Respond' *v.i.* to answer; act in answer.—respond'ent *a.* replying.—*n.* one who answers; a defendant.—response' *n.* an answer.—respon'sions (re-spon-shuns) *n.* at Oxford, the first examination undergone by candidates for the B.A. degree.— respon'sible *a.* liable to answer for something; of good credit or position.—responsibil'ity *n.*—respon'sive *a.*— responden'tia *n.* a loan on a ship and cargo, payment depending on the safe arrival of the vessel.

Ressaldar' *n.* a native captain in an Indian cavalry regiment.

Rest *n.* repose; freedom from exertion or activity; a pause; a supporting appliance.— *v.i.* to take rest; be supported.—*v.t.* to give rest to; to place on a support.— rest'ful *a.*—rest'less *a.*

Rest *n.* remainder.—*v.i.* to be left over.

Rest *n.* an appliance holding the butt of a lance when charging.

Restaur' *n.* a claim against a guarantor.

Rest'aurant (-ān) *n.* an eating-house. — **restaurateur'** *n.* keeper of one.

Restitu'tion *n.* giving back or making up.

Resti've *a.* stubborn, resisting control.

Restore' *v.t.* to build up again, repair, renew; re-establish; give back. — **restora'tion** *n.* — **restor'ative** *a.* restoring. — *n.* a medicine to strengthen, etc.

Restrain' *v.t.* to check, hold back. — **restraint'** *n.* restraining, or means of restraining. — **restrict'** *v.t.* to limit, bound. — **restric'tion** *n.* — **restric'tive** *a.*

Restri'all *a.* in heraldry, divided barwise, palewise and pilewise.

Result' (-z-) *v.i.* to follow as a consequence; end. — *n.* effect, outcome. — **result'ant** *a.*

Resume' (-z-) *v.t.* to begin again; to summarise. — **rés'umé** *n.* a summary. — **resump'tion** *n.* a resuming. — **resump'tive** *a.*

Resurge' *v.i.* to rise again. — **resur'gent** *a.* — **resurrec'tion** *n.* rising again; revival. — **resurrect'** *v.t.* to restore to life.

resus'citate *v.t.* to revive, bring back from being nearly dead. — **resuscita'tion** *n.*

Ret *v.t.* to expose to moisture. — **rett'ing** *n.* the process of soaking flax. — **rett'ory, rett'-ery** *n.* a place where retting is carried on.

Re'tail *n.* sale in small quantities. — *v.t.* to sell in small quantities; to recount. — *adv.* by retail. — **re'tailer** *n.*

Retaille' (re-tā-lyā) *a.* in heraldry, divided twice, as an escutcheon.

Retain' *v.t.* to keep; engage services of. — **retain'er** *n.* fee to retain a barrister; a follower of a nobleman, etc. — **reten'tion** *n.* — **retent'ive** *a.*

Retal'iate *v.t.* and *i.* to repay in kind. — **retalia'tion** *n.* — **retal'iatory** *a.*

Retard' *v.t.* to make slow or late. — **retarda'tion** *n.*

Retch *v.i.* to make effort to vomit.

Ret'icent *a.* reserved in speech, not communicative. — **ret'i-cence** *n.*

Retic'ulate, retic'ulated *a.* made or arranged like a net. — **retic'ulate** *v.t.* and *i.* to make or be like a net. — **reticula'tion** *n.* — **ret'icule** *n.* lady's handbag.

Ret'ina *n.* the sensitive layer at the back of the eye.

Ret'inue *n.* a band of followers.

Ret'irade *n.* in fortification, a central retrenchment to which a garrison may retreat to prolong a defence.

Retire' *v.i.* to withdraw, give up office or work; go away; go to bed. — *v.t.* to cause to retire. — **retired'** *a.* that has retired from office, etc. — **retire'ment** *n.* — **reti'ring** *a.* unobtrusive, shy.

Retort' *v.t.* to repay in kind; reply; hurl back (a charge, etc.).—*n.* a thing done or said as vigorous reply or repartee; a vessel with a bent neck used for distilling.

Retract' *v.t.* to draw back, recant.—*v.t.* to recant.—retracta'tion *n.*

Retrax'it (trak-sit) *n.* in law, the withdrawing of a suit in court, by which the plaintiff loses his action.

Retreat' *n.* an act of, or military signal for, retiring; a sunset call on a bugle, etc.; a place of seclusion.—*v.i.* to retire.

Retrench' *v.t.* to cut down, reduce amount of (expense, etc.).—retrench'ment *n.*

Retribu'tion *n.* recompense, *esp.* for evil deeds; vengeance. —retrib'utive *a.*

Retrieve' *v.t.* to bring in; regain; restore; rescue from a bad state.—retriev'al *n.*—retriev'er *n.* a dog trained to find and bring in shot game.—retriev'able *a.*

Ret'rograde *a.* going backwards, reverting;reactionary. —retrogres'sion *n.*—retrogress'ive *a.*—ret'rospect *n.* a looking back, survey of the past. — retrospect'ive *a.* — retrospec'tion *n.*—retroces'sion *n.* ceding back again.

Retrousse (re-troo-sä) *a.* turned up, as the end of a nose; pug.

Retund' *v.t.* to blunt or dull.

Return' *v.i.* to go or come back.—*v.t.* to give or send back; to report officially; report as being elected;

elect.—*n.* returning; being returned; profit; official report.

Retuse' *a.* terminating in a round end, the centre of which is indented.

Re'us *n.* in law, a defendant.

Reveal' *v.t.* to make known; disclose.—revela'tion *n.* *Syn.* divulge, unveil, uncover, open, discover, impart, communicate, publish. *Ant.* conceal, hide, secrete.

Reveill'e, revell'y (-vali) *n.* a morning bugle-call, etc., to waken soldiers.

Rev'el *v.i.* to make merry.— *n.* a merrymaking.—rev'eller *n.*—rev'elry *n.*

Rev'enant *n.* one that returns from a long absence; a ghost.

Revenge' *v. refl.* to avenge oneself.—*v.t.* to make retaliation for; avenge.—*n.* a revenging, desire for vengeance; act that satisfies this.—revenge'ful *a.*

Rev'enue *n.* income, *esp.* of a state or institution.—inland revenue *n.* public money derived from income tax, excise, etc.

Reverb'erate *v.t.* and *i.* to echo or throw back.—reverbera'tion *n.*

Revere' *v.t.* to hold in great regard or religious aspect.—rev'erence *n.* revering; capacity for revering.—rev'erend *a.* worthy of reverence, *esp.* as a prefix to a clergyman's name.—rev'erent *a.* showing reverence.—reveren'tial *a.* marked by reverence.

Rev'erie *n.* a daydream, fit of musing.

Revers' (rĕ-vär-, rĕ-vĕr) *n.* that part of a garment which is turned back.

Reverse' *v.t.* to turn upside down or the other way round; change completely.—*n.* the opposite or contrary; the side opposite the obverse; a defeat.—*a.* opposite, contrary.—**revers'al** *n.*—**revers'ible** *a.*—**rever'sion** *n.* the return of an estate at the expiry of a grant to the person granting it; the right to succeed to an estate, etc., on a death or other condition; a returning to a state or condition.—**rever'sionary** *a.*—**rever'sioner** *n.* one holding a reversionary right.—**revert'** *v.i.* to return to a former state; come back to a subject.—**reverse' gear** *n.* mechanism to enable a vehicle to move backwards.—**reverse'light** *n.* in motoring, a light fitted at the rear of a car.—**rever'si** *n.* a game played by two persons on a draught-board with sixty-two counters.

Revet' *v.t.* to face a wall with masonry, sand-bags, etc.—**revet'ment** *n.*

Review (-vū) *n.* revision; survey, inspection, *esp.* of massed military forces; a critical notice of a book, etc.; a periodical with critical articles, discussion of current events, etc.—*v.t.* to hold, make, or write, a review of.—**review'er** *n.* a writer of reviews.

Revile' *v.t.* to call by ill names, abuse. *Syn.* to asperse, defame, malign, slander, upbraid.

Revise' *v.t.* to look over and correct.—**revi'ser** *n.*—**revi'sion** (-vizh-) *n.*

Revive' *v.i.* to come back to life, vigour, etc.—*v.t.* to bring back to life, vigour, use, etc.—**revi'val** *n.* a reviving, *esp.* of religious fervour.—**revi'valist** *n.* an organiser of religious revival.

Revoke' *v.t.* to annul.—*v.i.* at cards, to fail to follow suit though able to.—*n.* at cards, an act of revoking.—**rev'ocable** *a.*—**revoca'tion** *n.*

Revolt' (-ō-) *v.i.* to rise in rebellion; to feel disgust.—*v.t.* to affect with disgust.—*n.* a rebellion.—**revolt'ing** *a.* disgusting, horrible.

Revolve' *v.i.* to turn round, rotate.—*v.t.* to rotate; meditate upon.—**revolu'tion** *n.* a rotation or turning round; turning or spinning round; a great change; the violent overthrow of a system of government.—**revolu'tionary** *a.* and *n.*—**revolu'tionise** *v.t.*—**revol'ver** *n.* a repeating pistol with a revolving cartridge-magazine.

Revue' *n.* a theatrical entertainment, partly burlesque and partly musical comedy.

Revul'sion *n.* sudden violent change of feeling.

Reward' (-word) *v.t.* to pay, or make return, for service, conduct, etc.—*n.* a recompense or return.

Rex (reks) *n.* a king.

Rhab'domancy (rab-do-man-si) n. divination by means of rods.—**rhab'doid** (rab-doid) n. a small rod-like body found in certain vegetable cells.—**rhabdoid'al** (rab-doi-dal) a. rod-like.—**rhab'dosphere** (rab-do-sfēr) n. microscopic spherical body found in abysmal muds and believed to be an alga.

Rhadaman'thine, rhadaman'-tine (rad-a-man-thin, -tin) a. judicially strict; severe.

Rhap'sody n. an enthusiastic or high-flown composition.—**rhapsod'ic** a.—**rhap'sodist** n.

Rhe'toric n. the art of effective speaking or writing; artificial or exaggerated language.—**rhetor'ical** a.—**rhetori'cian** n.

Rheum (rōōm) . n. watery discharge.—**rheum'atism** n. painful inflammation of joints.—**rheumat'ic** a.

Rhino'ceros (-os-) n. a large thick-skinned animal with one or two horns on its nose.

Rhododen'dron n. a flowering shrub.

Rhom'bus, rhomb n. an equilateral but not right-angled parallelogram, a diamond or lozenge.

Rhon'chus n. a rattling or wheezing sound, as of disordered respiration, heard in auscultation.

Rho'tacism n. the change of s into r; excessive or peculiar pronunciation of r.

Rhu'barb n. a plant of which the fleshy stalks are cooked and used as fruit; a purgative from the root of a Chinese plant.

Rhyme see RIME.

Rhyparog'raphy n. genre and still-life painting, esp. of low subjects.

Rhysim'eter n. an instrument for measuring the velocity of fluids and the speed of ships.

Rhythm (riꞘHm) n. measured beat or flow, esp. of words, music, etc.—**rhyth'mic** a.—**rhyth'mical** a.—**rhyth'mically** adv.

Rhy'ton n. a drinking-horn without a foot, generally ending in a beast's head.

Rib n. one of the curved bones springing from the spine and making the framework of the upper part of the body; a curved timber of the framework of a boat; a strengthening ridge on cloth, etc.—v.t. to furnish or mark with ribs.

Rib'ald a. irreverent, scurrilous; indecent.—n. a ribald person.—**rib'aldry** n. ribald talk.

Ribb'on, rib'and n. a narrow band of fine fabric.

Rice n. the white seeds of an Eastern plant, used as food; the plant.—**rice'-paper** n. fine Chinese paper.

Rich a. wealthy; fertile; abounding in some product or material; valuable; of food, containing much fat or sugar; mellow; amusing.—**rich'es** n. pl. wealth.—**rich'ly** adv. Syn. opulent, plentiful, splendid, affluent, abundant, golden. Ant. poor, needy, unfertile, barren, skimpy, mean.

Rick *n.* a stack of hay, etc. —rick-stand, a basement on which a rick may be built.

Rick'ets *n.* a disease of children marked by softening of bones, bow-legs, etc.— **rick'ety** *a.* suffering from rickets; shaky, insecure.

Ric'ochet (-shā) *n.* a skipping on water or ground of a bullet or other projectile; a hit made after it.—*v.i.* to skip thus.—*v.t.* to hit or aim with a ricochet.

Rid *v.t.* to clear, relieve of.— **ridd'ance** *n.*

Rid'dle *n.* a question made puzzling to test the ingenuity of the hearer, an enigma; a puzzling fact, thing, or person.—*v.i.* to speak in or make riddles.

Rid'dle *n.* a coarse sieve.—*v.t.* to pass through a sieve; to pierce with many holes like those of a sieve.—**rid'dlings** *n.pl.* siftings.

Ride *v.i.* to go on horseback or in a vehicle; lie at anchor; float lightly.—*n.* a journey on a horse or other animal or in any vehicle; a road for riding on horseback.—**ri'der** *n.* one who rides; a supplementary clause; a mathematical problem on a given proposition.—**ri'derless** *n.*

Ridge *n.* the line of meeting of two sloping surfaces; a long narrow hill; a long and narrow elevation on a surface.—*v.t.* to form into ridges.

Ridic'ulous *a.* deserving to be laughed at, absurd, foolish. —**rid'icule** *v.t.* to laugh at,

hold up as ridiculous.—*n.* treatment of a person or thing as ridiculous.

Ri'ding *n.* an administrative division of Yorkshire or New Zealand.

Ridott'o *n.* a favourite Italian public entertainment, consisting of music and dancing; a public assembly or merry-making.

Riem (rēm) *n.* a raw-hide thong.

Riet'bok (rēt-bok) *n.* an African species of antelope.

Rife *a.* prevalent.

Riff'-raff *n.* rabble, disreputable people.

Ri'fle *v.t.* to search and rob; to make spiral grooves in (gun-barrel, etc.).—*n.* a rifled musket.—**ri'fling** *n.* the arrangement of grooves in a gun barrel.

Rift *n.* a crack, split.

Rig *v.t.* to provide (a ship) with spars, ropes, etc.; to equip; to set up, *esp.* as a makeshift.—*n.* the way a ship's masts and sails are arranged; costume; style of dress.—**rigg'ing** *n.* the spars and ropes of a ship.

Rigadoon' *n.* a lively dance for one couple; the music for such a dance.

Right (rīt) *a.* straight; just; proper; true; correct; genuine.—**right side**, the side of a person which is to the east when he faces north, the opposite of left.—*v.t.* to bring back to a vertical position; to do justice to.— *v.i.* to come back to a vertical position.—*n.* what is right, just, or due.—right-of-way *n*. in law, the right to pass through a field, etc.; in Australia, a lane.—*adv.* straight; properly; very; on or to the right side.—right'eous (richus) *a*. just, upright.—right'eousness *n*.—right'ful *a*.—right'ly *adv*.

Ri'gid (rij-) *a*. stiff; harsh.—rigid'ity *n*. *Syn*. severe, inflexible, unyielding, rigorous. *Ant*. pliable, adaptable, elastic, relaxed.

Rig'marole *n*. a meaningless string of words.

Ri'gor *n*. a sudden coldness attended by shivering.—ri'gor mor'tis, *n*. the stiffening of the body, caused by the contraction of the muscles after death.

Rig'our *n*. harshness, severity, strictness.—rig'orous *a*.

Rill *n*. small stream.

Rim *n*. the outer ring of a wheel; edge, border.—rim'-less *a*.

Rime, rhyme *n*. identity of sound of the ends of verse lines from the last accented syllable; verse marked by rime.—*v.t.* to make rimes.—ri'mer, rhy'mer, rhym'ster *n*. a maker of rimes.

Rime *n*. hoar-frost.

Rime *n*. a fissure; a chink; a long aperture.—ri'mer *n*. a carpenter's tool for boring holes or rimes.

Rim'ose *a*. full of rimes or chinks, like those in the bark of trees. Also rim'ous.

Rind (-I-) *n*. the outer coating of trees, fruits, etc.

Ring *n*. a small circle of gold, etc., *esp.* as worn on the finger; any circular appliance, band, coil, rim, etc.; a circle of persons.—*v.t.* to put a ring round.—ring'er *n*. in Australia, the man who shears most sheep in a day.—ring'let *n*. a curly lock of hair.—ring'-leader *n*. the instigator of a mutiny, riot, etc.—ring'dove *n*. a wood-pigeon.—ring-neck *n*. in Australia, a newly arrived immigrant, *esp.* from England.—ring'worm *n*. a skin disease in circular patches.

Ring *v.i.* to give out a clear resonant sound, as a bell; to resound.—*v.t.* to cause (a bell) to sound.—*n*. a ringing.

Rink *n*. a sheet of ice for skating; a floor for roller-skating.

Rinse (-s) *v.t.* to clean by putting in and emptying out water; to wash lightly.—*n*. a rinsing.

Ri'ot *n*. tumult, disorder; loud revelry; unrestrained indulgence or display.—*v.i.* to make or engage in a riot.

Rip *v.t.* to cut or tear away, slash, rend.—*n*. a rent or tear.

Rip *n*. a wicker basket in which to carry fish.

Ripa'rian *a*. of or on the banks of a river.

Ripe *a*. matured, ready to be reaped, eaten, etc.—ri'pen *v.i. and t. Syn.* mature, full, mellow, complete, finished, perfect. *Ant*. unripe, immature, sour, imperfect, callow.

Rip'ple *v.i.* to flow or form

into little waves.—*v.t.* to form ripples on.—*n.* a slight wave or ruffling of surface.

Rip'ple *n.* a kind of comb through which flax plants are passed to remove the seed-vessels.—*v.t.* to separate the seed from flax.

Rip'rap *n.* a foundation of stones thrown irregularly together, as in deep water or on a soft bottom; a firework giving a succession of loud reports.

Rip'saw *n.* a hand-saw with coarse but narrow-set teeth (used for cutting wood in the direction of the fibre).

Rise *v.i.* to get up; to move upwards; to reach a higher level; appear above the horizon; adjourn.—*n.* rising; upslope; increase; beginning.

Ris'ible (-z-) *a.* laughable; inclined to laugh.—**risibil'ity** *n.*

Risk *n.* danger.—*v.t.* to venture.—**risk'y** *a.*—**risk'ily** *adv.*

Ris'per, rus'per *n.* in South Africa, a species of small, very destructive caterpillar.

Riss'ole *n.* a cake of chopped meat, etc., fried.

Rite *n.* a formal practice or custom, *esp.* religious.—**rit'ual** *a.* concerning rites.—*n.* a prescribed order or book of rites.—**rit'ualism** *n.* practice of ritual.—**rit'ualist** *n.*

Ri'val *n.* one that competes with another for favour, success, etc.—*v.t.* to vie with.—*a.* in the position of a rival.—**ri'valry** *n.*

Rive *v.t.* and *i.* to split.

Riv'er *n.* a large stream of water.

Riv'et *n.* a bolt for fastening plates of metal together, the end being put through the holes and then beaten flat.—*v.t.* to fasten with rivets; clinch.

Riv'ulet *n.* a small stream.

Roach *n.* a freshwater fish.

Road *n.* a track or way prepared for passengers, vehicles, etc.; direction, way; a roadstead.—**road'-hog** *n.* in North America, anyone driving to the danger of the public.—**road'stead** *n.* a piece of water near the shore where ships may lie at anchor.—**road'ster** *n.* a horse, bicycle, etc., suited for the road; a type of open touring motor-car.

Roam *v.t.* and *i.* to wander about, rove.

Roan *a.* having a coat in which the main colour is thickly interspersed with another, *esp.* bay or sorrel or chestnut mixed with white or gray.—*n.* an animal with such a coat.

Roan *n.* a soft sheepskin leather.

Roan'-tree *n.* native British tree; the mountain ash; wild service-tree producing clusters of berries of a bright red colour and acid taste; also **row'an-tree, rod'dan**, etc.

Roar (rawr) *n.* a loud deep hoarse sound as of a lion, thunder, voice in anger, etc.—*v.i.* to make such sound.—

v.t. to utter in roaring voice, shout out.

Roast *v.t.* to cook by exposure to an open fire.—*v.i.* to be roasted.—*n.* a roasted joint.—*a.* roasted.

Rob *v.t.* to plunder, steal from. —**robb'er** *n.*—**robb'ery** *n.* *Syn.* to thieve, despoil, pillage. *Ant.* to restore, benefit.

Rob'be *n.* in South Africa, a fur seal.

Robe *n.* a long outer garment. —*v.t.* to dress.—*v.i.* to put on robes or vestments.

Rob'in *n.* a bird with breast red in winter.—**robin-red'-breast** *n.*

Ro'bot *n.* a mechanical slave.

Robust' *a*, sturdy.

Roc (rok) *n.* the monstrous bird well known in the mythology of the Arabians. —**roc's-egg**, something marvellous, but untrue.

Roch'et *n.* a garment like a surplice, with tight sleeves, worn by bishops.

Rock *n.* stone; a large rugged mass of stone; a hard toffee. —**rock'ery** *n.* a mound or grotto of stones or rocks for plants in a garden.—**rock'y** *a.*

Rock *v.i.* to sway to and fro.— *v.t.* to cause to do this.— **rock'er** *n.* a curved piece of wood, etc., on which a thing may rock.

Rock'et *n.* a firework on a stick that can be shot up in the air by igniting its contents (used for display, signalling, carrying a line to a wrecked ship, etc.).

Roco'co *a.* of furniture, architecture, etc., having much conventional decoration, tastelessly florid; antiquated —*n.* the rococo style.

Rod *n.* a slender straight round bar, wand, stick or switch; a birch or cane; a measure (=a pole).

Ro'dent *a.* gnawing.—*n.* a gnawing animal.

Ro'deo *n.* a gathering of cattle to be branded or marked.

Rodomontade' *n.* boastful language.

Roe *n.* a small species of deer.

Roe *n.* a mass of eggs in a fish.

Ro'ger de Cov'erley *n.* an English country-dance.

Rogg'enstein (-stīn) *n.* an oolite in which the cementing matter is argillaceous.

Rogue (rōg) *n.* a rascal, knave; mischief-loving person or child; a wild beast of savage temper living apart from its herd.—**ro'guish** (-gĭsh) *a.*— **ro'guery** *n.* *Syn.* scamp, villain, caitiff, scoundrel, sharper, swindler.

Rois'ter *v.i.* to bluster, to swagger.—**rois'terer** *n.*

Rôle *n.* an actor's part.

Roll (rōl) *n.* a piece of paper, etc., rolled up; a list or catalogue; a small loaf.—*v.t.* to move by turning over and over; to wind round; to smooth out with a roller. —*v.i.* to move by turning over and over; to move or sweep along; of a ship, to swing from side to side.— **roll'er** *n.* a cylinder used for pressing or smoothing, supporting something to be moved, winding something on, etc.—**roll'ing plant** *n.* locomotives, carriages, etc., of a railway.

Roll'icking *a.* boisterously jovial.

Ro'ly-po'ly *n.* a pudding of paste covered with jam and rolled up.

Romal' *n.* a species of silk fabric brought from the East; a braided thong of leather, or horsehair, serving as a horseman's whip.

Ro'man *a.* of Rome or the Church of Rome.—**Ro'man type,** plain upright letters, the ordinary script of printing. **Ro'man fig'ures,** the letters I, V, X, L, C, D, M, used to represent numbers in the manner of the Romans. —**Romance'** *n.* the vernacular language of certain countries, developed from Latin and developing into French, Spanish, etc.—**romance'** *n.* a tale of chivalry; a tale with scenes remote from ordinary life; literature like this; an event or love-affair or atmosphere suggesting it; sympathetic imagination; exaggeration; picturesque falsehood.—**romanc'er** *n.*—**Roman'ic** *a.* evolved from Latin.—**roman'tic** *a.* characterised by romance; of literature, etc., preferring passion and imagination to proportion and finish.— **Ro'manise** *v.t.* to make Roman or Roman Catholic. —**romant'icism** *n.*

Rom'any *n.* a gipsy; the gipsy language.—*a.* gipsy.

Romp *v.i.* to frolic.—*n.* a spell of romping; a child given to romping.

Ron'deau (-dō) *n.* a poem, usually of thirteen iambic lines of eight or ten syllables, with two rhymes, the opening words recurring additionally, as a burden, after the eighth and thirteenth lines; a rondo.—**ron'del** *n.* a poem of thirteen or fourteen iambic lines of eight or ten syllables, with two rhymes, the first line recurring as a closing refrain, and the first two as the seventh and eighth; a small round tower erected at the foot of a bastion.—**ron'delet** *n.* a poem of seven lines, of which two are refrains.

Rood (-ōō-) *n.* the Cross; a crucifix; a quarter of an acre.

Roof (-ōō-) *n.* the outside upper covering of a building.—*v.t.* to put a roof on, be a roof over.

Rook (-ōō-) *n.* a bird of the crow family.—**rook'ery** *n.* a colony of rooks; a cluster of mean houses.

Rook (-ōō-) *n.* a piece at chess, also called a castle.

Room (-ōō-) *n.* space; space enough; a division of a house.—**room'y** *a.* having plenty of space.

Roor'back *n.* in North America, an untrue story or rumour spread in political intrigue.

Roost (-ōō-) *n.* a perch for fowls; a henhouse.—*v.i.* to perch.

Root (-ōō-) *n.* the part of a plant that grows down into the earth and conveys nourishment to the plant; source, origin; original or vital part.—*v.t.* to cause to take root; to pull by the roots.—*v.i.* to take root.

Rope *n.* a thick cord.—*v.i.* to secure or mark off with a rope; in Australia, to lasso.—**ropable** *a.* in Australia, of cattle, wild and intractable.—**ro'py** *a.* sticky and stringy.

Roque'fort (rōk-fōr) *n.* a cheese of ewes' milk.

Ro'quelaure (rō-ke-lōr) *n.* a kind of short cloak.

Roquet' (rō-kā') *v.t.* in croquet, to strike one ball with another.—*n.* the stroke so made.

Rose *n.* a beautiful flower of many varieties; a rose-bush; a perforated flat nozzle for a hose, etc.; a pink colour.—*a.* of this colour.—**ro'sary** *n.* a string of beads for keeping count of prayers; a form of prayer, a rose-garden.—**ros'eate** *a.* rose-coloured, rosy.—**rosette'** *n.* a rose-shaped bunch of ribbon; a rose-shaped architectural ornament.—**rose'wood** *n.* a fragrant wood.—**ro'sy** *a.* rose-coloured; flushed; hopeful.

Rose'mary *n.* an evergreen fragrant shrub.

Ros in *see* RESIN.

Ros'land *n.* moorland.

Roso'lio (-li-ō) *n.* a red wine of Malta; a sweet cordial.

Ross'ignol (-nyol) *n.* the nightingale.

Ros'ter *n.* a list or plan showing turns of duty.

Ros'trum *n.* a platform for public speaking.

Rot *v.t.* and *i.* to decompose naturally.—*n.* decay, putrefaction; a disease of sheep; nonsense.—**rott'en** *a.* decomposed; corrupt.

Ro'ta *n.* a wheel; a course; a roster; an ecclesiastical tribunal in the R.C. church.—**rotam'eter** *n.* an opisometer, i.e. an instrument that, with a small wheel, measures the curved lines of a map.

Ro'tang, ro'ttang *n.* in South Africa, the name of several species of East Indian climbing plants; a walking-stick cut from the strong, tough stem of the plant.

Ro'tary *a.* of movement, circular.—**rotate'** *v.i.* to move round a centre or on a pivot.—*v.t.* to cause to do this.—**rota'tion** *n.*—**rota'tory** *a.*—**rotund'** *a.* round.—**rotund'ity** *n.*—**rotary pump** *n.* pump in which fluid is pumped by rotary action.

Rote *n.* **by rote**, by memory without understanding.

Rotund' *see* ROTARY.

Rouge (rōōzh) *n.* a red powder used to colour the cheeks or lips.—*v.t.* and *i.* to colour with rouge.

Rough (ruf) *a.* not smooth, of irregular surface; violent, boisterous; lacking refinement; approximate; in a preliminary form.—*v.t.* to make rough; to plan out approximately.—*n.* a disorderly ruffian; a rough state.—rough'en *v.t.*—rough'-cast *a.* coated with a mixture of lime and gravel.—*n.* such mixture.—*v.t.* to coat with it.—rough'-hew' *v.t.* to shape roughly.—rough'ly *adv. Syn.* unpolished, harsh, discordant, stormy, brutal, terrible. *Ant.* polished, level, smooth, gentle, courteous, polite, calm.

Roulade' *n.* in music, an embellishment; a flourish.

Roul'eau (rōō-lŏ) *n.* a cylindrical packet of coins.

Roulette' (rōō-) *n.* a game of chance played on a table with a revolving centre; a small toothed wheel used by engravers to roll over the surface of a plate to produce dots; a hair-curling roller; (*geom.*) a kind of curve.

Round (rownd) *a.* spherical or cylindrical or circular, or nearly so; roughly correct; large; plain.—*adv.* with a circular or circuitous course. —*n.* something round in shape; a rung; movement in a circle; recurrent duties; customary course, as of a postman or military patrol; a cartridge for a firearm.—*prep.* about; on all sides of. —*v.t.* to make round; to get round.—*v.i.* to become round.—round'about *n.* a merry-go-round.—*a.* to denote extension of one-way traffic round a central point. —Round'head *n.* a supporter of the Parliament in the Civil War.—round'ly *adv.*—round'ers *n.pl.* a ball game.

—round'-rob'in *n.* a petition signed with names in a circle so that it may not be known who signed first.

Roup *v.t.* in Scotland, to expose for sale by auction.—*n.* a sale of goods by auction.

Rouse (rowz) *v.t.* to wake up, stir up, cause to rise.—*v.i.* to waken.

Rout (rowt) *n.* a troop; a disorderly crowd; a large evening party; a disorderly retreat.—*v.t.* to put to rout.

Route (rōōt) *n.* a road, way. —routine' (-ēn) *n.* regular course; regularity of procedure.

Rove *v.i.* to wander without fixed destination.—*v.t.* to wander over.—ro'ver *n.* one who roves; an elder Boy Scout; a pirate.

Row (rō) *n.* a number of things in a straight line.

Row (rō) *v.i.* to propel a boat by oars.—*v.t.* to propel by oars.—*n.* a spell of rowing.

Row *n.* a disturbance or dispute.

Row'an *n.* the mountain ash.

Rowd'y *n.* a rough.—*a.* disorderly.

Row'el *n.* a small wheel with points on a spur.

Row'lock (rol'ok) *n.* an appliance serving as point of leverage for an oar.

Roy'al *a.* of, worthy of, befitting, patronised by, a king or queen; splendid.—roy'alist. *n.* a supporter of monarchy.—roy'alty *n.* royal dignity or power; royal persons; payment to an owner of land for the right to work minerals, or to an inventor for use of his invention; payment to an author depending on sales. *Syn.* regal, noble, illustrious, august, majestic. *Ant.* plebeian, ignoble, vulgar, low-born.

Rub *v.t.* to subject to friction; pass the hand over; abrade, chafe; remove by friction.— *v.i.* to come into contact accompanied by friction; become frayed or worn with friction.—*n.* a rubbing; an impediment.—**rubb'er** *n.* one who rubs; a thing for rubbing; indiarubber.

Rubb'er *n.* a series of three games at various card games; a series of an odd number of games or contests at various games; two out of three games won.

Rubb'ish *n.* refuse, waste material; trash, nonsense.— **rubb'ishy** *a.*—**rub'ble** *n.* fragments of stone.

Rube *n.* in North America, a farmer; a rustic.

Rubesc'ent *a.* growing or becoming red; tending to a red colour.—**rubes'cence** *n.* a reddening; a flush.

Ru'bicund (rōō-) *a.* ruddy.— **ru'bric** *n.* a chapter-heading; a direction in a liturgy (properly one printed in red).—**ru'bric** *v.t.* to mark, write, or print in red; supply with rubrics.—**rubrica'tion** *n.* —**ru'by** *n.* a red precious stone; its colour.—*a.* of this colour.

Ruche *n.* a kind of plaited or goffered quilling; rouche.

Ruck *n.* crowd; band.

Ruck *n.* a crease.—*v.t.* and *i.* to make or become wrinkled.

Ruck'sack *n.* a pack carried on the back.

Rudd'er *n.* a flat piece hinged to the stern of a ship or boat to steer by.—**rudd'er-wheel** *n.* a small wheel on a plough, to help in guiding it.

Rudd'y *a.* of a fresh or healthy red; ruddy-faced.

Rude *a.* primitive; roughly made; uneducated; uncivil. —**rude'ly** *adv.*—**ru'diment** *n.* beginning, germ.—*pl.* elements, first principles.— **rudimen'tary** *a. Syn.* violent, boisterous, tumultuous; ignorant, untaught, barbarous, shapeless, unformed, inelegant, clumsy. *Ant.* calm, gentle, serene, refined, smooth, shapely, dainty.

Rue (rōō) *n.* a plant with strong-smelling bitter leaves.

Rue (rōō) *v.t.* and *i.* to repent. —*n.* repentance.—**rue'ful** *a.* —**rue'fully** *adv.*

Ruff *n.* a starched and frilled collar.; a bird allied to the woodcock and sandpiper; a species of pigeon.—**ruf'fle** *n.* a frilled cuff. — *v.t.* to crumple, disorder; frill or pleat; annoy, put out.

Ruff *n.* at cards, an act of trumping.—*v.t.* and *i.* to trump.

Ruff'ian *n.* a rough lawless fellow, a desperado.—**ruff'ianly** *a.*

Rug *n.* a thick woollen wrap; a mat for the floor, of shaggy or thick-piled surface.— **rugg'ed** *a.* rough, broken; furrowed; unpolished; harsh.

Rug'by n. a form of football in which the ball may be seized and run with.

Rugg'ens n.pl. in South Africa, undulating hills or slopes.

Ru'in n. downfall; fallen or broken state; decay, destruction.—pl. ruined buildings, etc.—v.t. to reduce to ruins; bring to decay or destruction, spoil; cause loss of fortune to.— **ruina'tion** n. — **ru'inous** a. — **ru'inously** adv.

Rule n. a principle or precept; what is usual; government; a strip of wood, etc., for measuring length.—v.t. to govern; decide.—**ru'ler** n. one who governs; a strip of wood, etc., for measuring or drawing straight lines.

Rum n. a spirit distilled from sugar-cane.

Rum'ble v.i. to make a noise as of distant thunder, a heavy cart moving along, etc.—n. such noise.

Rumbooze' n. any alcoholic drink. Also **rum'bo**, **rumbull'ion**.

Ru'minate v.i. to chew the cud; meditate.—**ru'minant** a. cud-chewing.—n. a cud-chewing animal.—**rumina'tion** n.—**ru'minative** a.

Rumm'age v.t. and i. to search thoroughly.—n. a ransacking; odds and ends.

Rumm'er n. a large drinking-glass.

Rumm'y n. a simple card game.

Ru'mour n. hearsay, common talk; current but unproved statement.—v.t. to put round as a rumour.

Rump n. tail-end; buttocks.

Rum'ple v.t. to crease or wrinkle.—n. a crease.

Rum'pus n. a disturbance; noise and confusion.

Rum'py n. a tailless cat.

Rum'swizzle (-swiz-l) n. an undyed Irish wool fabric.

Run v.i. to move rapidly on the legs; to go quickly; flow; flee; compete in a race; revolve; continue; have a certain meaning.—v.t. to cross by running; expose oneself, be exposed; cause to run; land and dispose of (smuggled goods).—n. an act or spell of running; a rush; tendency, course.—**runn'er** n.

Run'agate n. a deserter, fugitive.

Rune n. a character of the earliest Teutonic alphabet.—**ru'nic** a.

Rung n. a cross-bar or spoke, esp. in a ladder.

Runn'el n. a gutter.

Run'rig n. the ownership of alternate ridges in a field.

Runt n. any animal small below the usual size of the species; a variety of pigeon; stem of a cabbage.

Rupee' n. the Indian unit of money; a silver coin worth about 1s. 4d.

Rup'ture n. a breaking or breach; a hernia.—v.t. and i. to break or burst. Syn. fracture, disruption, quarrel, contention. Ant. union, coalition, junction, harmony, peace.

Ru'ral a. of the country.

Ruse (-z-) *n.* a stratagem, trick.

Rush *n.* a plant with a slender pithy stem growing in marshes, etc.; the stems as a material for baskets.—**rush'y** *a.* full of rushes.

Rush *v.t.* to impel or carry along violently and rapidly; to take by sudden assault.—*v.i.* to move violently or rapidly.—*n.* a rushing.

Rusk *n.* a piece of bread re-baked; various biscuits.

Russ'et *a.* of reddish-brown colour.—*n.* the colour; a variety of apple.

Rust *n.* the reddish-brown coating formed on iron by oxidation and corroding it; a disease of plants.—*v.i.* and *t.* to contract or affect with rust.—**rust'y** *a.*

Rust'bank *n.* in South Africa, a wooden couch or bed.

Rust'ic *a.* of, or as of, country people; rural; of rude manufacture; made of untrimmed branches.—*n.* a countryman, peasant.—**rusti'city** *n.*—**rust'-icate** *v.t.* to banish from a university.—*v.i.* to live a country life.—**rustica'tion** *n.* *Syn.* rude, unpolished, coarse, plain, simple, artless. *Ant.* polished, refined, accomplished, cultured.

Rus'tle (-sl) *v.i.* to make a sound as of blown dead leaves, etc.—*n.* the sound.

Rut *n.* the periodical sexual excitement of the male of deer and certain other animals.—*v.i.* to be under the influence of this.

Rut *n.* a furrow made by a wheel; a settled habit or way of living.—**rutt'y** *a.*

Rutt'er *n.* a trooper; a marine chart.

Ruth (rōōth) *n.* pity.—**ruth'-less** *a.* pitiless.—**ruth'lessly** *adv.*

Rye *n.* a grain used for fodder and in some places for bread; the plant bearing it.

Rye-grass *n.* kinds of grass cultivated for fodder.

Ry'ot *n.* an Indian peasant.

S

Saam *prep.* in South Africa, too; as well.

Sabb'ath *n.* the Jewish Sunday or seventh day.—**Sabbata'-rian** *n.* a strict observer of Sunday.—**Sabbatar'ianism** *n.* **Sabbat'ical** *a.*

Sa'ble *n.* a small Arctic animal; its fur; black.—*a.* black.

Sab'ot (-ō) *n.* a wooden shoe worn by lower classes in some European countries.—**sab'otage** *n.* intentional damage done by workmen to their materials, etc.

Sa'bre (-ber) *n.* a cavalry sword.—*v.t.* to strike with one.

Sab'ulous *a.* sandy; gritty.—**sabulos'ity** *n.* the quality of being sabulous; sandiness; grittiness.

Sac *n.* a cavity in an animal or vegetable body.

Sacc'harin(e) *a.* pertaining to sugar.—*n.* an extremely sweet substance from coal-tar.

Sacerdo'tal (sas'-) *a.* of priests.
—**sacerdo'talism** *n.*

Sa'chem *n.* a chief of a tribe of the American Indians; a sagamore.

Sach'et (sash-ā) *n.* a scent-bag.

Sack *n.* a large bag, usually of some coarse textile material.—*v.t.* to pillage (a captured town, etc.).—**sack'cloth** *n.* a coarse fabric used for sacks.—**sack'ing** *n.* material used for sacks.

Sack *n.* a dry wine; a warmed and spiced drink.

Sack'but *n.* a wind instrument of music; a trombone.

Sac'rament *n.* one of certain ceremonies of the Christian Church, *esp.* the Eucharist.—**sacrament'al** *a.*—**sa'cred** *a.* dedicated, regarded as holy.—**sa'credly** *adv.*—**sac'rifice** *n.* making of an offering to a god; the thing offered; giving something up for the sake of something else; the act of giving up; the thing so given up as a sacrifice.—*v.t.* to offer as sacrifice.—**sacrifi'cial** *a.*—**sac'ristan** *n.* an official in charge of the vestments and vessels of a church.—**sac'rosanct** *a.* secure by religious fear against desecration or violence.—**sac'rilege** *n.* violation of something sacred.—**sacrili'gious** *a.*

Sa'crum (-krum) *n.* five vertebræ forming a compound bone at the base of the spinal column.

Sad *a.* sorrowful; deplorably bad: of colour, dull, sober.—**sad'ly** *adv.*—**sadd'en** *v.t. Syn.*

dejected, downcast, distressing, dark-coloured, sombre, heavy. *Ant.* happy, joyous, gay, bright, light.

Sad'dle *n.* rider's seat to fasten on a horse, or form part of a bicycle, etc.; a part of a shaft; a joint of mutton or venison; a ridge of a hill.—*v.t.* to put a saddle on.—**sadd'ler** *n.* a maker of saddles, etc.—**sadd'lery** *n.*

Sadd'ucee *n.* one of a sect among the ancient Jews who denied the resurrection, a future state, and the existence of angels.—**Sadduce'-an** *a.* pertaining to the Sadducees; sceptical; irreligious.

Sa'dism *n.* a form of sexual perversion marked by love of cruelty.—**sa'dist** *n.*

Safe *a.* uninjured, out of danger; not involving risk; cautious; trustworthy.—*n.* a strong box; a ventilated cupboard for meat, etc.—**safe'ly** *adv.*—**safe'ty** *n.*—**safe-con'duct** *n.* a passport or permit to pass somewhere.—**safe'guard** *n.* a protection.—*v.t.* to protect.

Saff'ian *n.* leather of goatskin or sheepskin, tanned with sumach and dyed in bright colours.

Saff'ron *n.* the orange-red colouring matter obtained from the crocus.—*a.* of this colour.

Sag *v.t.* to sink in the middle, to hang sideways or curve downwards under pressure.

Sa'ga (sā-ga) *n.* a mediæval tale of Norse heroes.

Saga'cious *a.* shrewd, mentally

acute.—**saga'ciously** *adv.*—
saga'city *n.*

Sag'amore *n.* the head of a
tribe among North American
Indians.

Sage *n.* an aromatic herb.

Sage *a.* wise, discreet.—*n.* a
very wise man.—**sage'ly** *adv.*

Sagitta'rius *n.* the Archer,
one of the twelve signs of
the zodiac, which the sun
enters about 22nd November.

Sa'go *n.* a starch, a foodstuff
made from it, obtained
from palms.

Sa'hib (sa-ib) *n.* a term of
respect used by natives of
India and Persia in addressing Europeans.

Sail *n.* a piece of canvas
stretched to catch the wind
for propelling a ship; a wind-
catching appliance form-
ing the arm of a windmill;
ships collectively; the act of
sailing.—*v.i.* to travel by
water; to begin a voyage.—
v.t. to navigate.—**sail'or** *n.*

Saint *adj.* holy; title of a
canonised person.—*n.* one
who has been canonised.—
saint'ly *adj.*—**saint'ed** *a.*
canonised; sacred.—**saint'liness** *n.*

Sake *n.* for the sake of, on
behalf of, to please or
benefit, or get, or keep.

Sa'ker *n.* a bird of the falcon
genus; a hawk; a small piece
of artillery.

Salaam', **salam'** (-lâm) *n.* a
salutation or mark of
respect in the East.—*v.t.* to
salute.

Sala'cious *a.* lustful.—**sala'city**
n.

Sal'ad *n.* vegetable as food
without cooking; a lettuce
or other plant suitable for
this use.

Sal'amander *n.* a fabulous
animal like a lizard, supposed to live in fire; a
variety of lizard.

Salam'ba *n.* a fishing contrivance used in the East.

Sal'angane *n.* a Chinese swift
whose nest is edible.

Sal'ary *n.* fixed payment of
persons employed in non-
manual or non-mechanical
work.—**sal'aried** *a.*

Sale *n.* a selling; a special
disposal of stock at low
prices. — **sales'man** *n.* a
shop assistant or traveller.
—**sales'manship** *n.*

Sal'ic *a.* designating a law
by which only males can
inherit the throne.

Sal'icin *n.* a bitter substance
obtained from the bark and
leaves of willows and pop-
lars.—**salicyl'ic** *a.* derived
from the willow.—**salicyl'ic
acid**, an antiseptic acid.—
salic'ylate *n.* a salt, *esp.* the
sodium salt, of salicylic
acid, used as a specific in
acute rheumatism.

Sa'lient *a.* jutting out.—*n.* a
salient angle, *esp.* in fortification.—**sa'lience** *n.*

Sa'line *n.* a fruit salt.—*a.*
salty.

Sali'va *n.* a liquid which
forms in the mouth.—
sali'vary *a.*

Sall'ow *a.* of a sickly yellow
or pale in colour.

Sall'y *v.i.* to rush; to set out.
—*n.* a rushing out, *esp.* from

a fort; an outburst; witty remark.

Salm'on (sam-) *n.* a large silvery - scaled fish with orange-pink flesh valued as food; the colour of its flesh. —*a.* of this colour.

Saloon' *n.* a large reception room; a public dining-room; the principal cabin or sitting-room in a passenger ship; a drawing-room car on a railway; a public room for specified use, such as billiards; in motoring, a limousine with all seats enclosed.

Sal'picon *n.* stuffing; chopped meat or bread used to stuff legs of veal.

Salse *n.* a mud volcano.

Salt (solt) *n.* sodium chloride, a substance which gives sea-water its taste; a chemical compound of an acid and a metal.—*a.* preserved with, or full of, or tasting like, salt.—*v.i.* preserved with salt; to put salt on.—**salt'y** *a.* —**salt'ness** *n.*—**salt'-cellar** *n.* a small vessel for salt on the table.—**salt'petre** *n.* potassium nitrate used in gunpowder.

Sal'tant *a.* leaping; dancing.— **sal'tatory** *a.*—**salta'tion** *n.*

Saltarell'o *n.* a very animated Italian and Spanish dance for a single couple; music for such a dance.

Sal'tire, sal'tier *n.* in heraldry, an ordinary in the form of a St. Andrew's cross, formed by two bends crossing each other.

Salu'brious *a.* favourable to health.—**salu'brity** *n.* *Syn.* healthful, beneficial, good. *Ant.* unhealthy, bad.

Sal'utary *a.* wholesome, resulting in good.—**salute'** *v.t.* to greet with words or sign; to kiss.—*v.i.* to perform a military salute.—*n.* a word or sign by which one greets another; a kiss; a prescribed motion of the arm as a mark of respect to a superior, etc., in military usage.—**saluta'-tion** *n.*

Sal'vage *n.* a payment for saving a ship from danger; the act of saving a ship or other property from danger; property so saved.—**salva'-tion** *n.* fact or state of being saved.—**salve** *v.i.* to save from peril.

Salve (salv *or* såv) *n.* healing ointment. — *v.i.* to anoint with such.

Sal'ver *n.* a tray for refreshments, visiting cards, etc.

Sal'vo *n.* simultaneous discharge of guns as a salute, or in battle.

Sal'-volat'ile (-ili) *n.* a preparation of ammonia used to restore persons who faint, etc.

Samar'itan *a.* pertaining to *Samaria*, in Palestine.—*n.* native or inhabitant of Samaria; a benevolent person.

Sama'rium *n.* a rare-earths metal discovered in *Samarskite*; the latter is notable as containing uranium.

Sam'bo *n.* the offspring of a black person and a mulatto—hence, humorously, a negro.

thére, fáther, her; awl, oil, owl.

Sam Browne *n.* leather belt, part of British officer's service uniform.

Same *a.* identical, not different, unchanged, unvarying. —**same'ness** *n.* monotony.

Sa'miel (sā'-mi-el) *n.* a hot wind that blows in Arabia from the desert.

Sam'isen *n.* a guitar or banjo of three strings used in Japan.

Sam'phire *n.* a herb that grows on rocks by the seashore; St. Peter's wort; sea-fennel.

Sam'ple *n.* a specimen.—*v.i.* to take or give a sample of. —**sam'pler** *a.* beginner's exercise in embroidery.

Sanator'ium *n.* an establishment for the treatment of invalids; a health resort.

Sanc'tify *v.t.* to set apart as holy; to free from sin.— **sanctifica'tion** *n.* —**sanctimo'nious** *a.* making a show of piety.—**sanct'imony, sanctimo'niousness** *n.* assumed outward holiness.—**sanc'tity** *n.* saintliness, sacredness; inviolability.—**sanc'tuary** *n.* a holy place; a place where a fugitive was safe from arrest or violence.—**sanc'tum** *n.* a sacred place or shrine; a person's private room.— **sanc'tion** *n.* a penalty or reward following the breaking or observing of the law; permission with authority; countenance given by custom.—*v.t.* to allow or authorise. *Syn.* to venerate, reverence, dedicate, purify, enshrine. *Ant.* to desecrate, profane, pollute, pervert.

Sand *n.* a powdery substance made by the wearing down of rock.—*pl.* stretches or banks of this, usually forming a seashore.—*v.t.* to cover or mix with sand.—**sand'stone** *n.* a rock composed of sand. —**sand'bag** *n.* a bag filled with sand or earth and used in fortification.—**sand'paper** *n.* paper with sand stuck on it for scraping or polishing wood, etc.—**sand'shoe** *n.* a canvas shoe for beach wear, etc.—**sand'y** *a.*

San'dal *n.* a shoe consisting of a sole attached by straps.

San'dalwood *n.* a scented wood.

Sand'wich *n.* two slices of bread with meat or other substance between.—*v.t.* to insert between two other different things.

Sandy-blight *n.* in Australia, a form of ophthalmia which makes the eyes feel full of sand.

Sane *a.* of sound mind, sensible.—**san'ity** *n.*—**san'itary** *a.* helping or not hindering the protection of health against dirt, etc.—**sanita'tion** *n.* the improving of sanitary conditions.

Sang-froid' (-frwaw) *n.* freedom from agitation; coolness; indifference.

San'guine (ng-gwin) *a.* hopeful or confident; florid.—**san'guinary** *a.* bloodthirsty; accompanied by bloodshed. *Syn.* plethoric, full-blooded, cheerful, ardent, confident. *Ant.* hopeless, diffident, dejected, cold.

Sa'orstat Eireann (sā-or-stat e-rĭn) *n.* Irish Free State.

Sap *n.* juice of plants.—**sap'less** *a.*—**sap'ling** *n.* a young tree.

Sap *n.* the covered trench approaching a besieged place or enemy trench.—*v.t.* to construct such trenches.—*v.i.* to undermine; to destroy insidiously.—**sapp'er** *n.*

Sa'pient *a.* wise (usually ironical).—**sa'pience** *n.*

Sapona'ceous *a.* of or containing soap.

Sapph'ic *a.* pertaining to Sappho, a Grecian poetess; noting a kind of verse in which three lines of five feet each are followed by a line of two feet.—*n.* a Sapphic verse.

Sapph'ire (saf-) *n.* a blue precious stone.

Sar'aband, sar'abande *n.* a stately Spanish dance; the music for such a dance.

Sar'acen *n.* an Arabian; a Mussulman; an adherent of Mohammedanism in countries farther west than Arabia.

Sar'casm *n.* a bitter or wounding ironic remark; such remarks; the power of using them.—**sarcast'ic** *a.*—**sarcast'ically** *adv.*

Sarcoph'agus *n.* a stone coffin.

Sard *n.* a precious stone; a variety of chalcedony.

Sardine' (-dĕn) *n.* a small fish of herring family, usually packed in oil.

Sardon'ic *a.* of a smile or laughter, bitter, scornful.

Sargass'um *n.* a genus of sea-weeds.—**sargass'o** *n.* the gulf-weed.—**Sargasso Sea**, the part of the Atlantic covered by the gulf-weed.

Sark *n.* a shirt; a chemise; the body garment.—**sar'king** *n.* thin boards for lining, to be used under slates; linen for shirts.

Sarong' *n.* a garment worn in the East Indies.

Sartor'ial *a.* pertaining to a tailor.

Sash *n.* a frame forming a window, usually sliding up or down.

Sash *n.* a scarf wound around the body.

Sa'tan *n.* the devil.—**satan'ic** *a.* devilish.—**satan'ically** *adv.*

Sat'chel *n.* a small bag, or bag for school books.

Sate *v.t.* to gratify to the full.

Sateen' *see* SATIN.

Sat'ellite *n.* a hanger-on; in astronomy, a planet revolving round another; a moon.

Sa'tiate (sāsh-i-āt) *v.t.* to satisfy to the full; surfeit.—**sa'tiable** *a.*—**satia'tion** *n.*—**sati'ety** *n.* the feeling of having had too much.

Sat'in *n.* a silk fabric with a glossy surface on one side.—**sateen'** *n.* a glossy cotton or woollen fabric.—**sat'inwood** *n.* an ornamental wood of a tropical tree.—**sat'iny** *a.*

Sat'ire (-ir) *n.* a composition in which vice or folly, or a foolish person, is held up to ridicule; use of ridicule or sarcasm to expose vice and folly.—**satir'ic, satir'ical** *a.*—**sat'irist** *n.*—**sati'rise** *v.t. Syn.*

irony, sarcasm, wit, burlesque.

Sat'isfy *v.t.* content, to meet the wishes of; to pay, fulfil, supply adequately; convince; to have sufficient.—**satisfac'tion** *n.*—**satisfac'tory** *a.*

Sat'urate *v.t.* to soak thoroughly; to cause to dissolve a maximum amount.—**satura'tion** *n.*

Sat'urday *n.* the seventh day of the week.—**Sat'urn** *n.* a Latin god; one of the planets.—**sat'urnine** *a.* gloomy; sluggish in temperament.

Sat'yr (-ẹr) *n.* a woodland god, part man and part beast.—**satyr'ic** *a.*

Sauce *n.* liquid added to food to give relish.—*v.t.* to add sauce to.—**sauce'pan** *n.* a cooking-pot.—**sau'cer** *n.* a curved plate put under a cup. etc., to catch spilt liquid.—**sau'cy** *a.* impudent, cheeky.—**sau'cily** *adv.*

Sauer'-kraut (sour-krout) *n.* a German dish of chopped cabbage pressed with salt till it ferments.

Saugh *n.* the willow.

Saun'ter *v.i.* to walk in leisurely manner, to stroll.—*n.* a leisurely walk or stroll. *Syn.* ramble, dawdle, linger, loiter. *Ant.* speed, hasten, hurry, run.

Saus'age (sos-) *n.* minced meat enclosed in a tube of thin membrane.

Sauter (sō-tā) *v.i.* to fry quickly with little grease.

Sauterelle' *n.* an instrument used by stone cutters for tracing and forming angles.

Sauterne (sō-tẹrn) *n.* a kind of French wine, from *Sauterne*, in the Gironde.

Sav'age *a.* uncivilised, primitive; wild.—*n.* a member of a savage tribe, a barbarian.—*v.t.* to attack with trampling and biting.—**sav'agery** *n.*—**sav'agely** *adv.*

Savann'a *n.* an extensive open plain covered with grass.

Save *v.t.* to rescue, preserve; keep for the future, lay by; to prevent the need of.—*v.i.* to lay by money.—*prep.* except.—*conj.* but.—**sa'viour** *n.* a deliverer or redeemer.

Sav'eloy *n.* a highly-seasoned dried sausage.

Sa'vour (-ver) *n.* characteristic taste.—*v.i.* to smack of.—**sa'voury** *a.* having an appetising taste or smell.—*n.* a savoury dish at the beginning or end of a dinner.

Savoy' *n.* a variety of cabbage.

Saw *n.* old saying, maxim.

Saw *n.* a tool for cutting wood, etc., by tearing it with a toothed edge.—*v.t.* to cut with a saw.—*v.i.* to make the movements of sawing.—**saw'dust** *n.* fine wood fragments made in sawing.—**saw'fish** *n.* a fish armed with a toothed snout.—**saw'yer** *n.* a workman who saws timber.

Saw'der *n.* flattery.

Saxe *n.* a shade of blue.

Sax'horn *n.* an instrument of the trumpet class.—**sax'ophone** *n.* a large instrument like a clarinet.

Sax'ifrage *n.* an Alpine or rock plant.

Say *v.t.* to utter or deliver with the speaking voice; state; express; take as an example or as near enough; form and deliver an opinion; to try; to assay.—*n.* what one has to say; chance of saying it; share in a decision.—**say'ing** *n.* a maxim, proverb.

Scab' *n.* a crust formed over a wound; a skin disease; a disease of plants; a blackleg.—**scabb'y** *a.*

Scabb'ard *n.* a sheath for sword or dagger.

Scabb'le *v.t.* to dress stones with a broad chisel.

Scaff'old *n.* a temporary platform for workmen; a gallows. **scaff'olding** *n.* a framework of poles and platforms for workmen.

Scal'awag *n.* an undersized animal; a worthless fellow.

Scald (skawld) *v.t.* to injure with boiling liquid or steam; to clean with boiling water.—*n.* injury by scalding.

Scale *n.* a pan of a balance; a weighing instrument.—*v.t.* to weigh in scales; to have the weight of.

Scale *n.* one of the plates forming the outer covering of fishes and reptiles; a thin flake.—*v.t.* to remove the scales from.—*v.i.* to come off in scales.

Scale *n.* a series of musical notes, degrees, or graduations; the steps of graduating measuring instrument; relative size, ration of enlarging or reduction (e.g. in a map, etc.).—*v.t.* to climb or attack with ladders.

Sca'lene *a.* of a triangle, having its three sides unequal.

Scall'op *n.* an eatable shellfish; edging in small curves imitating the edge of a scallop shell.—*v.t.* to shape in this way; to cook in a scallop shell or a dish resembling one.

Scalp *n.* the skin and hair of the top of the head.—*v.t.* to cut off the scalp of.

Scal'pel *n.* a small surgical knife.

Scamp *n.* a rascal.

Scamp *v.t.* to do hastily or negligently.

Scamp'er *v.i.* to run about; to run hastily from place to place.—*n.* a scampering.

Scan *v.t.* to look at carefully; to measure or read (verse) by its metrical feet.—**scan'sion** *n.*

Scan'dal *n.* malicious gossip; a feeling that something is an outrage or cause of discussion, the thing causing such feeling.—**scan'dalize** *v.t.* to shock.—**scan'dalous** *a.* outrageous; disgraceful. *Syn.* opprobrium, defamation, gossip, rumour. *Ant.* praise, commendation, reticence.

Scanso'res *n.pl.* birds having the toes arranged to facilitate climbing, as the woodpeckers, parrots, etc.—**scanso'rial** *a.* climbing, or adapted for climbing.

Scant *a.* barely sufficient; not sufficient.—*v.t.* to put on short allowance; to supply grudgingly. — **scant'y** *a.*—**scant'ily** *adv.*

Scant'ling n. a size to which stone or wood is to be cut; a small beam, *esp.* one under five inches square.—**scantle** v.t. to cut into small pieces.

Scape n. and v.t. to escape.—**scape'goat** n. a person bearing blame due to others.—**scape'grace** n. an incorrigible fellow.

Scaphan'der n. a diver's watertight suit.

Scap'ula n. the shoulder-blade.—**scap'ular** a. pertaining to the scapula.—n. a part of the habit of certain religious orders in the R.C. church, consisting of two bands of woollen stuff, of which one crosses the back and the other the stomach.

Scar n. the mark left by a healed wound, burn or sore.—v.t. to mark with a scar.—v.i. to heal with a scar.

Scar'ab n. the sacred beetle of ancient Egypt; a gem cut in the shape of this beetle.

Scar'amouch n. a buffoon in motley dress; a personage in the old Italian comedy characterised by boastfulness and poltroonery.

Scarce (skers) a. hard to find; existing or available in insufficient quantity.—**scarce'ly** adv. only just; not quite.—**scarce'ness** n.—**scar'city** n.

Scare (skėr) v.t. to frighten.—n. fright or panic.

Scarf n. scarfs, scarves pl. a long narrow strip of material to put round the neck, over the shoulders, etc.

Scar'ify v.t. to scratch or cut slightly all over; to criticise mercilessly.—**scarifica'tion** n.

Scar'let n. a brilliant red colour; cloth or clothing of this colour, *esp.* military uniform.—a. of this colour.—**scar'let fe'ver** n. an infectious fever with a scarlet rash.—**scar'let runn'er** n. a trailing bean with scarlet flowers.—**scarlati'na** (-tē-) n. scarlet fever.

Scarp n. the inside slope of a ditch in fortifications.—v.t. to make steep.

Scathe (-TH) n. injury.—v.t. to injure, especially by withering up.—**scathe'less** a. unharmed.

Scatt'er v.t. to throw or put here and there; to sprinkle.—v.i. to disperse.

Scaup n. a bed of shell-fish.

Scav'enger n. one employed in cleaning streets, removing refuse, etc.—**scav'enge** v.t. to clean (streets).—v.i. to work as a scavenger.

Scene (sēn) n. the place of the action of a novel, play, etc.; the place of any action; a subdivision of a play; a view; an episode; a stormy conversation, *esp.* with display of temper.—**sce'nery** n. stage scenes; the natural features of a district.—**sce'nic** a. picturesque; of, or on, the stage.—**scenar'io** n. the written version of a play to be produced by cinematograph.

Scent (s-) v.t. to track by smell; to detect; to give a perfume to.—n. a smell; liquid perfume.

Scep'tic (sk-) n. one who

maintains doubt.—scep'tical *a.*—scep'ticism *n.* *Syn.* unbeliever, infidel, atheist, heretic, deist. *Ant.* believer, Christian, theist.

Scep'tre (s-) *n.* an ornamental staff as a symbol of royal power; royal or imperial dignity.

Schaap'sticker *n.* in South Africa, the night - adder, erroneously believed to kill sheep.

Schanz *n.* in South Africa, a defensive protection made of earth, stones, etc.

Schappe *n.* a silken fabric.

Sched'ule (sh-; in U.S. sk-) *n.* an appendix to an Act of Parliament; a tabulated statement.—*v.t.* to enter in a schedule.

Schelm, shell'um, skell'um *n.* in Scotland and in South Africa, a thief; pest; scoundrel; ne'er-do-well; a bad-tempered animal.

Scheme (sk-) *n.* a plan or design; a project; a list or table; an outline or syllabus. —*v.i.* to make plans, especially as a secret intrigue.— *v.t.* to plan, to bring about.— sche'mer *n.*

Schimm'el *n.* in South Africa, a gray horse.

Schis'm (sizm) *n.* a division in a church or party.— schismat'ic *n.* and *a.*— schismat'ical *a.*

Schlen'ter *a.* in South Africa, colloquial for false, unreliable.

Schnapps, schnaps *n.* Holland gin.

Scho'lium *n.* a marginal annotation; note; comment; usually a grammatical or philological note; (*math.*) a remark or observation subjoined to a demonstration.— scho'liast *n.* a commentator or annotator.—scholias'tic *a.* pertaining to a scholiast or his pursuits.

School (skōōl) *n.* an institution for teaching boys or girls or both, or for giving instruction in any subject; the buildings of such institution; time of lessons; a group of thinkers, writers, artists, etc., with principles or methods in common.—*v.t.* to educate; to bring under control, to train. — school'man *n.* a medieval philosopher. — schol'ar *n.* one taught in a school; one quick to learn; a learned person; a person holding a scholarship.— schol'arly *a* —schol'arship *n.* learning; a prize or grant to a student for payment of school or college fees.— scholast'ic *a.* relating to schools or schoolmen; pedantic.

School (sk-) *n.* a shoal (of fish, whales, etc.).

Schoon'er (sk-) *n.* a ship with fore and aft sails on two or more masts.

Schottische' (shot-ēsh) *n.* a variety of polka; music for this.

Schrik *n.* in South Africa, a fright; a start.

Sciat'ica (sī-) *n.* pain in the sciatic nerve.—sciat'ic *a.* of the hip.

Sci'euce (sī-) *n.* systematic

knowledge; the investigation of this; any branch of study concerned with a body of observed material facts.— scientif'ic *a.*—scientif'ically *adv.*—sci'entist *n.*

Scim'itar (s-) *n.* a short curved sword.

Scintill'a (s-) *n.* a spark.— scin'tillate *v.i.* to sparkle.— scintilla'tion *n.*

Sci'on (s-) *n.* a slip for grafting; a descendant or heir.

Sciss'ors (siz-) *n.pl.* a cutting instrument of two blades pivoted together so that the edges slip over each other.

Sciss'ure *n.* a longitudinal opening made by cutting; a cleft; a fissure.

Sclero'sis *n.* a hardening.

Scobs *n. sing.* and *pl.* raspings of ivory, hartshorn, metals, etc.; the dross of metals.

Scoff (sk-) *n.* taunt; mocking words.—*v.t.* to jeer or mock. —scoff'er *n. Syn.* mockery, taunt, ridicule. *Ant.* admiration, respect.

Scold (sk-) *n.* a nagging woman.—*v.i.* to find fault noisily.—*v.t.* to rebuke.

Sconce (sk-) *n.* a bracket candlestick on a wall.

Soonce *n.* the top of the head.

Scone (skon) *n.* a round cake baked on a griddle.

Scoop *n.* an article for ladling; a kind of shovel; a tool for hollowing out.—*v.t.* to ladle out; to hollow out or rake in with a scoop.

Scoot *v.i.* (*slang*) to move off quickly.—scoot'er *n.* a small vehicle with four wheels and a guiding handle, to carry one person.

Scope *n.* range of activity or application; room, play.

Scorbu'tic *a.* affected with, or concerning, scurvy.

Scorch *v.t.* to burn the surface of.—*v.i.* to be burnt on the surface.

Score *n.* a group or set of twenty; a cut, notch, stroke, or mark; a written or printed piece of orchestral music; a tally; reason; sake; number of points made in a game.— *v.t.* to notch or mark; to cross out; to record; to make (points) in a game.—*v.i.* to achieve a success.—scor'er *n.*

Scorn *n.* contempt, derision.— *v.i.* to despise.—scorn'er *n.*— scorn'fully *adv.*—scorn'ful *a.*

Scorp'ion *n.* a small lobster-shaped animal with a sting at the end of its jointed tail.

Scorse *n.* a course or manner of dealing; barter.—*v.t.* to exchange.

Scor'tatory *a.* pertaining to fornication or lewdness.

Scot *n.* a payment or a person's share of it.—scot-free' *a.* free from payment, punishment, etc.

Scot *n.* a native of Scotland.— Scott'ish *a.* (also Scotch, Scots).—Scots'man *n.*—scot'icism *n.* a Scottish turn of speech.

Scotch *v.t.* to disable or wound.

Scoto'graph *n.* an instrument by which one may write in the dark, or for aiding the blind to write.

Scoto'ma, scot'omy *n.* dimness

of sight, accompanied by giddiness.

Scoun'drel n. a villain.—**scound'relly** a.

Scour v.t. to clear or polish by rubbing; to clear out.

Scour v.i. to run or move hastily.—v.t. to move rapidly along or over in search of something.

Scourge (skurj) n. a whip or lash.—v.t. to flog. Syn. evil, calamity, plague, pestilence.

Scout n. a man sent out to reconnoitre; a ship used for reconnoitering; a small fast aeroplane; a boy scout.—v.i. to go out or act as a scout.

Scout v.t. to reject scornfully; to dismiss as absurd.

Scow n. a large, flat-bottomed boat.—v.t. to transport in a scow.

Scowl v.t. to frown gloomily or sullenly.—n. gloomy frown.

Scrag n. a lean person or animal; the lean end of a neck of mutton.—**scragg'y** a.

Scram'ble v.i. to move along or up by crawling, climbing, etc.; to struggle with others for; to cook (eggs) by stirring them, when broken, in the pan.—n. a scrambling; a disorderly proceeding.

Scran n. scraps; broken victuals.

Scrap n. a small detached piece or fragment.—**scrapp'y** a.

Scrape v.t. to rub with something sharp; to clean or smooth in this way; to rub with harsh noise.—v.i. to make an awkward bow.—n. an act or sound of scraping; an awkward situation, esp. one resulting from an escapade.—**scra'per** n.

Scratch v.t. to score or mark a narrow surface wound with claws, nails, or anything pointed; to make marks on with pointed instruments; to remove from a list.—v.i. to use claws or nails.—n. a wound or mark or sound made by scratching; a line or starting point.—a. got together at short notice; impromptu.—**scratch'ily** a.

Scrawl v.t. to write or draw untidily. —n. something scrawled; careless writing.

Scream v.i. to utter a piercing cry; to whistle or hoot shrilly.—n. a shrill, piercing cry.

Screech v.i. and n. scream.

Screed n. a long letter or passage; list of grievances, etc.

Screen n. a piece of furniture to shelter from heat, light, draught or observation; anything used for such purpose; a sheet or board to display lantern pictures, etc.; in the cinema, the sheet on which films are exhibited and from which sound is reflected; in motoring, the wind-screen; a wooden or stone partition in a church.—v.t. to shelter or hide; to protect from detection.

Screw (-ōō) n. a cylinder with a spiral ridge running round it, outside or inside; a ship's propeller; a turn of a screw;

a twist; a miser; a worn-out horse.—*v.t.* to fasten with a screw; to press or stretch with a screw; to obtain by pressure, to extort; to work by turning, to twist round.—**screw'-driv'er** *n.* *Syn.* to force, squeeze, press, distort, twist. *Ant.* to unscrew, to loosen, to straighten.

Scrib'ble *v.t.* to write or draw carelessly.—*v.i.* to write or draw carelessly; to make meaningless marks with a pen or pencil.—*n.* something scribbled.—**scribe** *n.* a writer; a copyist; an author.

Scrim *n.* thin, strong cotton or woollen cloth, used in upholstery for linings, etc.

Scrimm'age *n.* a scuffle.

Scrimp *v.t.* to make too small or short; to stint.—*a.* scanty; *n.* niggard.—**scrimp'ly** *adv.*—**scrimp'ness** *n.*

Scrip *n.* a small wallet.

Scrip *n.* a certificate of holding stocks or shares.

Script *n.* handwriting; written characters. — **scrip'ture** *n.* sacred writings; the Bible.—**script'ural** *adv.*—**scriv'ener** *n.* a copyist or clerk.

Scrof'ula *n.* a constitutional disease which affects the lymphatic glands, oftenest those of the neck; king's-evil.—**scrof'ulous** *a.* diseased with scrofula.—**scrof'ulously** *adv.*—**scrof'ulousness** *n.*

Scrog *n.* a thick, stunted bush or shrub.—**scrogg'ya.**stunted.

Scroll (-ōl) *n.* a roll or parchment or paper; a list; an ornament shaped like a scroll of paper.

Scrounge *v.t.* and *i.* (*slang*) to pilfer.

Scrub *n.* a stunted tree; brushwood.—**scrubb'y** *a.* covered with scrub; insignificant.—**scrubb'er** *n.* in Australia, a bullock which has escaped into the scrub.—**scrub dan'ger** *n.* in Australia, a wild bullock.

Scrub *v.t.* to clean with a hard brush and water.—*n.* a scrubbing.—**scrubb'ing-brush** *n.*

Scruff *n.* nape (of neck).

Scru'ple *n.* a small weight; a feeling of doubt about a proposed action; a conscientious objection.—*v.i.* to hesitate.—**scru'pulous** *a.* extremely conscientious, thorough; attentive to small points of conscience.—**scrupulos'ity** *n.* *Syn.* of " scrupulous," precise, exact, conscientious,cautious, captious. *Ant.* unscrupulous, careless, incautious.

Scru'tiny *n.* an investigation, an official examination of votes; a searching look.—**scrutineer** an examiner of votes.—**scru'tinise** *v.t.* to examine closely.

Scru'to *n.* a kind of trap door in theatres.

Scry'ing *n.* foretelling the future by gazing steadily into a crystal ball; crystal gazing.

Scud *v.i.* to run quickly; to run before the wind.—*n.* the act of scudding.

Scuf'fle *v.i.* to struggle at close quarters.—*n.* a confused struggle.

Scull *n.* an oar used for the

stern of a boat; a short oar used in pairs.—*v.t.* and *i.* to propel or move by means of a scull or sculls.

Scull'ery *n.* a place for washing dishes, etc.

Scull'ion *n.* a kitchen under-servant.

Sculp'ture *n.* the art of forming figures in relief or solid; the product of this art.—*v.t.* to represent, by sculpture.—**sculp'tural** *a.*—**sculp'tor** *n.*

Scum *n.* froth or other floating matter on a liquid; the waste part of anything.

Scunn'er *v.i.* to feel disgust at; to loathe.—*v.t.* to disgust.—*n.* loathing; disgust.

Scupp'er *n.* a hole in the side of a ship level with the deck.

Scurf *n.* dried flakes detached from the skin.—**scurf'y** *a.*

Scurr'ilous *a.* coarse or indecent language.—**scurril'ity** *n.*

Scurr'y *v.i.* to run hastily.—*n.* bustling haste.

Scur'vy *n.* a disease characterised by spots, debility, etc.—*a.* afflicted with the disease; mean, low, contemptible.

Scut *n.* the tail of a hare, or other animal whose tail is short.

Scu'tage *n.* in feudal law, a tax on a knight's fee; a commutation for personal service.

Scutch'eon *see* ESCUTCHEON.

Scut'tle *n.* a vessel for coal; a large open basket.

Scut'tle *v.i.* to rush away.

Scut'tle *n.* a hole with a lid in the side or deck of a ship.

—*v.i.* to make a hole in a ship, *esp.* to sink it.

Scy'phus (sī-fus) *n.* a footless bowl - shaped drinking - cup with two handles not carried above the rim; in botany, a cup-shaped organ, as the crown of the corolla in the narcissus.

Scythe (sīth) *n.* a mowing implement consisting of a long curved blade swung by a bent handle held in both hands.—*v.t.* to cut with a scythe.

Sea *n.* the mass of solid water covering most of the earth; a broad tract of this; waves; swell.—**sea'board** *n.* coast.—**sea'faring** *a.* occupied in sea voyages.—**sea'man** *n.* a sailor.—**sea'weed** *n.* a plant growing in the sea.—**sea'worthy** *a.* in a fit condition to put to sea.

Seal *n.* an amphibious marine animal with flippers as limbs, of which some varieties have valuable fur.—*v.i.* to hunt seals.—**seal'skin** *n.* the skin or fur of seals.—**seal'er** *n.* a man or ship engaged in sealing.

Seal *n.* a piece of metal or stone engraved with a device for impression on wax, etc.; the impression made by this (on letters, documents, etc.).—*v.t.* to affix a seal to; to ratify; to mark with a stamp as evidence of some quality; to keep close, or secret; to settle, as doom.—**Great Seal** *n.* official seal of the United Kingdom.—**seal'ing wax** *n.*

Seal'yham *n.* a breed of Welsh terrier.

Seam *n.* a line of junction of two edges, e.g. of, two pieces of cloth, or two planks; a thin layer of stratum.— *v.t.* to mark with furrows or wrinkles. — **seam'less** *a.* — **seam'stress, semp'stress** *n.* a sewing woman.—**seam'y** *a.* marked with seams; worst side.

Sean'ad Eireann' (sen-ad-e-rin) *n.* senate of the Irish Free State.

Se'ance (sā-ōñs) *n.* a session of a public body; a meeting of Spiritualists.

Seaplane *n.* in aviation, an aeroplane designed to rise from, and land on, water.

Sear *v.t.* to scorch or brand with a hot iron; to deaden.

Search *v.t.* to look over or through in order to find something; to probe into.— —*v.i.* to explore, to look for something.—*n.* the act of searching; a quest.— **search'light** *n.* an electric arc-light which sends a concentrated beam in any desired direction. *Syn.* to examine, scrutinise, investigate. *Ant.* overlook, neglect, disregard, find, discover.

Seas'on (sēz-) *n.* one of the four divisions of the year associated with a type of weather and a stage of agriculture; a proper time; a period during which something happens, grows, is active, etc.—*v.t.* to bring into sound condition; to flavour with salt or condi-ments, etc.—**seas'onable** *a.* suitable for the season.— **seas'onal** *a.* depending on, or varying with, seasons.— **seas'oning** *n.* flavouring materials.

Seat *n.* a thing made or used for sitting on; manner of sitting (of riding, etc.); a right to sit (e.g. in a council, etc.); the sitting part of the body; the locality of a disease, trouble, etc.; a country house.—*v.t.* to make to sit; to provide sitting accommodation for.

Seba'ceous *a.* made of, or pertaining to, tallow or fat.

Sebun'dy *n.* in East Indies, a native soldier or policeman.

Sec *a.* dry (said of wines).

Secede' *v.i.* to withdraw from a federation, alliance, etc.— **seces'sion** *n.* — **seces'sionist** *n.*

Seck'el *n.* a small, delicious variety of pear.

Seclude' *v.t.* to guard from, remove from sight or resort. —**seclu'sion** *n.*

Sec'ond *a.* next after the first. —*n.* a person or thing coming second; one giving aid, *esp.* assisting a principal in a duel; the sixtieth part of a minute.—*v.t.* to support; further; to support (a motion in a meeting) so that discussion may be in order.— **sec'ondly** *adv.*—**sec'ondary** *a.* subsidiary, or of less importance; of education, coming between primary and university stages.—**sec'ondarily** *adv.*—**sec'onder** *n.*— **sec'ondhand'** *a.* to buy after use by a previous owner, not original.

Se'cret *a.* kept or meant to be kept from general knowledge; hidden.—*n.* something kept secret.—**se'cretly** *adv.*—**se'crecy** *n.* a keeping or being kept secret; an ability to keep secrets.—**sec'retary** *n.* one employed by another or appointed by a society to deal with papers and correspondence, keep records, prepare business, etc.—**secreta'rial** *a.*—**secretar'iat** *n.* a body of secretaries.—**sec'retaryship** *n.*—**secrete'** *v.t.* to hide; of a gland, etc., to collect and supply a particular substance in the body.—**secre'tion** *n.*—**secre'tory**—*a.*—**secre'tive** *a.* given to making secrets, uncommunicative.—**secre'tiveness** *n. Syn.* hidden, occult, private, secluded, privy, clandestine, mysterious. *Ant.* public, open, unconcealed.

Sect *n.* a party within a church; a religious denomination.—**sect'ary** *n.*—**secta'rian** *a.*

Sec'tile *a.* capable of being cut; capable of being cut smoothly without fracture (said of minerals).

Sec'tion *n.* a cutting; a part cut off; a drawing of anything as if cut through.—**sec'tional** *a.*—**sec'tor** *n.* a part of a circle enclosed by two radii and the arc which they cut off; a sub-division of the front occupied by an army.

Sec'ular *a.* worldly; lay; not monastic; lasting for, or occurring once in, an age.—**sec'ularist** *n.* one who would exclude religion from schools.—**sec'ularism** *n.*—**sec'ularise** *v.t.* to transfer from religious to lay possession or use.—**secularisa'tion** *n.*

Secure' *a.* safe; free from care; firmly fixed.—*v.t.* to make safe; to free (a creditor) from risk of loss; to make firm; to gain possession of.—**secure'ly** *adv.* — **secu'rity** *n.*

Secu'rifer *n.* one of a family of hymenopterous insects, having a saw-shaped or hatchet-shaped appendage to the posterior part of the abdomen.

Sedan' *n.* a small covered vehicle for one, carried on poles by two men.—(also **sedan'-chair**).

Sedate' *a.* calm, collected, serious. — **sedate'ly** *adv.* — **sed'ative** *a.* soothing.—*n.* soothing drug.—**sed'entary** *a.* sitting much; done in a chair.—**sed'iment** *n.* a matter which settles to the bottom of liquid. *Syn.* quiet, tranquil, serene, undisturbed, sober, serious. *Ant.* restless, disturbed, indiscreet, rash.

Sede'runt *n.* a single sitting or meeting of a court.

Sedge *n.* a plant resembling coarse grass which grows in swampy ground.—**sedge-flat**, sedgy land below high-watermark.—**sedge'-war'bler**, a British summer bird.

Sedil'ia *n.pl.* stone seats on the south side of the altar in churches for the priest, deacon, and sub-deacon.

Sedi'tion *n.* talk or speech urging to rebellion.—**sedi'tious** *a.*

Seduce' *v.t.* to lead astray, to persuade to commit some sin or folly; to induce (a woman) to surrender her chastity. — **seduc'tion** *n.*— **seduct'ive** *a.* alluring, winning.

Sed'ulous *a.* persevering.—**sedu'lity** *n.*

See *v.t.* to perceive with the eyes or mentally; to find out. to reflect; to come to know; to interview.—*v.i.* to perceive; understand.—**seer** *n.* a prophet.—**see'ing** *conj.* since.

See *n.* the diocese and work of a bishop.

See'catchie *n.* the male furseal, or the sea-bear of Alaska.

See'cawk *n.* the skunk.

Seed *n.* the reproductive germs of flowering plants; one grain of this; such grains saved or used for sowing; offspring.—*v.i.* to produce seed.—*v.t.* to sow with seed.—**seed'ling** *n.* a young plant raised from seed. —**seed'y** *a.* run to seed; shabby; feeling ill.

Seek *v.t.* to make search or enquiry for.—*v.i.* to search.

Seem *v.i.* to appear (to be or to do).—**seem'ingly** *adv.*— **seem'ly** *a.* becoming and proper.—**seem'liness** *n.*

See'-saw *n.* a game in which children sit at opposite ends of a plank supported in the middle and swing up and down; the plank used for this.—*v.i.* to move up and down.

Seethe *v.t.* to boil, cook or soak in hot liquid.—*v.i.* to be agitated or in confused movement.

Seg'ment *n.* a piece cut off; a section.

Seg'regate *v.t.* to set apart from the rest. — **segrega'tion** *n.*

Seid'litz-powders (sĕd-, sĭd-, sed-litz-) *n.pl.* aperient powders, containing bicarbonate and potasso-tartrate of soda, and tartaric acid.

Seine (sēn, sān) *n.* a large net for catching fish.—*v.t.* to catch fish with a seine.

Seis'mic (sīz-) *a.* pertaining to earthquakes. — **seis'mograph** *n.* an instrument to record earthquakes.—**seis'mogram** *n.* the record made by a seismometer.—**seismol'ogy** *n.* doctrine of earthquakes.—**seismolog'ic, seismolog'ical** *a.* pertaining to seismology.—**seismol'ogist** *n.* one versed in seismology.— **seismom'eter** *n.* an instrument for measuring the time of occurrence, duration, direction, and intensity of earthquakes. — **seis'moscope** *n.* an instrument for showing visibly the movements or undulations of the ground in an earthquake.

Seize (sēz) *v.t.* to grasp; lay hold of; perceive.—**seiz'able** *a.*—**seiz'ure** *n.*

Sel'dom *adv.* rarely.

Select' *v.t.* to pick out, choose. —*a.* choice, picked; exclusive.—**selec'tion** *n.*—**select'or** *n.*—**selectiv'ity** *n.* in wireless, the degree to which a receiver is capable of selecting one wave-length or frequency to the exclusion of all others.

Sele'nium *n.* an elementary substance, allied to sulphur and tellurium.—**sel'enite** *n.* a transparent variety of gypsum. — **selen'ium cell**, primary cell used for the transmission of pictures, the resistance of which varies according to the amount of light falling on it.

Selenog'raphy *n.* a description of the surface of the moon.

Self *pron.*, **selves** *pl.* is used to express emphasis or a reflexive usage.—*a.* of a colour, uniform, the same throughout.—*n.* one's own person or individuality.—**self'ish** *a.* concerned unduly over personal profit or pleasure, lacking consideration for others.—**self'ishly** *adv.*—**self'less** *a.*—**self-possessed'** *a.* calm, composed.—**self-posses'sion** *n.*—**self'-same** *a.* very same.—**self-star'ter**, an automatic contrivance for starting a motor-car; a car so fitted.

Sell *v.t.* to hand over for a price; to betray or cheat.—*v.i.* to find purchasers.—*n.* a disappointment.—**sell'er** *n.*

Sel'vedge, sel'vage *n.* an edge of cloth finished to prevent ravelling out.

Sem'aphore *n.* a post with movable arm or arms used for signalling; a system of signalling by human or mechanical arms.

Sema'tics *n.* the science of the origin and evolution of language.

Sem'blance *n.* appearance; image.

Semen *n.* seed, *esp.* the male generative product of animals; sperm.

Semi- *prefix,* half as in **sem'ibreve** *n.* a musical note half the length of a breve.—**sem'icircle** *n.* the half of a circle.—**semicir'cular** *a.*—**semico'lon** *n.* a punctuation mark (;).—**sem'iquaver** *n.* a musical note half the length of a quaver.—**sem'itone** *n.* a musical half tone.—**sem'i-detached'** *a.* of a house, joined to another on one side only.

Sem'inary *n.* a school or college.

Semolin'a (-ĕn-a) *n.* hard grains left after the sifting of flour, used for puddings, etc.

Semp'stress *see* SEAMSTRESS.

Sen'ate *n.* the upper council of a state, university, etc.—**sen'ator** *n.*—**senator'ial** *a.*

Send *v.t.* to cause to go or be conveyed; to despatch; to discharge.

Se'nile *a.* showing the weakness of old age.—**senil'ity** *n.*—**se'nior** *a.* older; superior in rank or standing.—*n.* an elder person; a superior.—**senior'ity** *n.*

Sen'night *n.* a week.

Sense *n.* any of the bodily faculties of perception or

feeling; sensitiveness of any or all of these faculties; ability to perceive, mental alertness; consciousness; meaning; coherence, intelligible meaning.—**sensa'tion** *n.* an operation of a sense, feeling; excited feeling or state of excitement; an exciting event.—**sensa'tional** *a.* —**sensa'tionalism** *n.*—**sense'less** *a.*—**sense'lessly** *adv.*— **sen'sible** *a.* that can be perceived by the senses; aware, mindful; considerable; appreciable; reasonable, wise.— **sensibly** *adv.*—**sensibil'ity** *n.* —**sen'sitive** *a.* open to or acutely affected by external impressions; easily affected or altered; responsive to slight changes.—**sen'sitively** *adv.*—**sen'sitiveness** *n.*—**sensitise'** *v.t.* to make sensitive, *esp.* to make (photographic film, etc.), sensitive to light. —**sen'sual** *a.* depending on the senses only and not on the mind; given to the pursuit of pleasures of sense, self-indulgent; licentious.— **sensual'ity** *n.*—**sen'sualist** *n.* —**sen'sualism** *n.*—**sen'suous** *a.* stimulating, or apprehended by, the senses. *Syn.* of " sensational," startling, exciting. *Ant.* unexciting, commonplace, ordinary, everyday, humdrum.

Sen'tient *a.* feeling or capable of feeling.—**sent'iment** *n.* a mental feeling; an emotion; a tendency to be moved by feeling rather than reason; a verbal expression of feeling.—**sentiment'al** *a.*—**senti**ment'alist *n.*—**sentimental'ity** *n.*

Sent'inel *n.* sentry.

Sent'ry *n.* a soldier on watch.

Sep'arate *v.t.* to put apart; to occupy a place between.— *v.i.* to withdraw, to become parted from.—*a.* disconnected, apart.—**sep'arately** *adv.*—**sep'arable** *a.*—**separa'tion** *n.*—**sep'arator** *n.* that which separates, *esp.* an apparatus for separating cream from milk.

Se'pia *n.* a brown pigment made from a fluid secreted by the cuttle fish.—*a.* of this colour.

Se'poy *n.* an Indian soldier in the British Indian army.

Septem'ber *n.* the ninth month (seventh in the Roman reckoning).—**septenn'ial** *a.* occurring every seven years. —**septet'(te)** *n.* music for seven instruments or voices.

Sep'tic *a.* causing or caused by blood poisoning or putrefaction.—**sep'sis** *n.* a septic state.—**septice'mia** *n.* bloodpoisoning.

Septuages'ima (sep-tū-a-jesi-må) *n.* the third Sunday before Lent (so called because it is seventy days before Easter).

Sep'tuagint *n.* a Greek version of the Old Testament (so called because it was said to be the work of seventy, or rather of seventy-two, translators, at Alexandria, about 270 years B.C.). Also written LXX.

Sep'tum *n.; pl.* **sep'ta**, a partition; in botany, a partition that separates the cells of the fruit; in anatomy, a partition that separates two cavities, as of the nostrils.

Sep'tuple *a.* seven times as much; sevenfold.—*v.t.* to multiply by seven.—*v.i.* to become septuple.

Sep'ulchre (-kẹr) *n.* a tomb.—**sepul'chral** *a.*—**sep'ulture** *n.* burial.

Se'quel *n.* a consequence or continuation.—**se'quent** *a.* following.—**se'quence** *n.* a connected series, a succession.

Sequest'er *v.t.* to seclude.—**sequest'rate** *v.t.* to confiscate; to divert to satisfy claims against its owner.—**sequestra'tion** *n.*

Se'quin *n.* an ornamental metal disk on dresses, etc.; formerly, a Venetian gold coin.

Seragl'io (se-rál-yō) *n.* the palace of the Grand Seignior or Turkish sultan, in which are confined the females of the harem; a harem; a house of debauchery.

Serai' (-rā) *n.* a place for the accommodation of travellers in India.

Serang' *n.* the boatswain of a Lascar crew.

Ser'aph *n.* one of the highest of the order of angels.—**seraph'ic** *a.*—**seraphim** *n.*

Sere *a.* dried up, withered.

Serenade' *n.* music sung or played at night below a person's window, *esp.* by a lover.—*v.t.* to entertain with a serenade.

Serene' *a.* calm, tranquil.—

serene'ly *a.*—**seren'ity** *n.* *Syn.* peaceful, undisturbed, unruffled, placid. *Ant.* agitated, troubled, unsettled, deranged.

Serf *n.* one of a class of labourers bound to, and transferred with, land.—**serf'dom** *n.*

Serge *n.* a strong twilled worsted fabric.

Serg'eant, serj'eant (sarj-ant) *n.* a non-commissioned officer a police officer; formerly, a member of the highest rank of English barristers.—**sergeant-ma'jor** *n.* highest non-commissioned officer in regiment.

Ser'ies (sĕr-ēz) *a.* a sequence, succession, set.—**se'rial** *a.* of and forming a series; published in instalments.—*n.* a serial story or publication.—**seria'tim** *adv.* one after another.

Ser'ious (sĕr-) *a.* earnest, sedate, thoughtful; not jesting; of importance.—**se'riously** *adv.* *Syn.* solemn, sober, thoughtful, momentous, weighty. *Ant.* jocular, joyful, trivial, mirthful, careless, unimportant.

Ser'mon *n.* a discourse of religious instruction or exhortation spoken or read from a pulpit; any similar discourse.—**ser'monise** *v.i.* to talk like a preacher; to compose sermons.

Serp'ent *n.* a snake; a kind of firework; an obsolete wind instrument.—**serp'entine** *a.* like or shaped like a serpent or snake; tortuous.

Serra'ted *a.* notched like a saw.—**serra'tion** *n.*

Ser'ried *a.* in close order, pressed shoulder to shoulder.

Ser'um (sĕr-) *n.* a watery animal fluid, *esp.* a thin part of blood as used for inoculation. — **ser'ous** *a.* — **serum therapy** *n.* cure of disease by inoculation with serum.

Serve *v.i.* to work under another; to carry out duties; to be a member of a military unit; to be useful or suitable or enough; in tennis, to start play by striking the ball.—*v.t.* to work for, attend on, help to food; supply something; be useful to; contribute to; to deliver formally; to treat in a specified way.—**ser'vant** *n.* a personal or domestic attendant.—**ser'vice** *n.* the state of being a servant; work done for and benefit conferred on another; a department of State employ; employment of persons engaged in this; a set of dishes, etc.—**ser'viceable** *a.* useful or profitable.—**ser'vile** *a.* slavish, without independence.—**servil'ity** *n.*—**ser'vitor** *n.* a servant; a student assisted out of college funds in certain colleges.—**ser'vitude** *n.* bondage or slavery.

Ser'vice *n.* a tree like a mountain ash with a pear-shaped fruit.

Ses'ame *n.* an annual herbaceous plant, from the seeds of which an oil is expressed.—**open sesame**, a charm, mentioned in the *Arabian Nights*, by which the door of the robber's dungeon flew open; a specific for gaining entrance to a place; a key to a difficulty.

Ses'sion *n.* a meeting of a court, etc.; a continuous series of such meetings.—**ses'sional** *a.*

Set *v.t.* to cause to sit, to put in place; to fix, point, to put up; to make ready; to put to music; to put in position, etc.—*v.i.* of the sun, to go down, to become firm or fixed; to have a direction.—*a.* deliberate; formal, arranged beforehand; unvarying.—*n.* a setting; a tendency; a habit.

Set *n.* a number of things or persons associated as being similar or complementary or used together, etc.

Seta'ceous *a.* consisting of bristles.

Sett *n.* a match; a number of mines taken on lease.

Settee' *n.* a couch.

Set'tle *n.* a bench with a back and arms.—*v.t.* to put in order; to establish, make firm or secure or quiet; to decide upon; to bring (a dispute, etc.) to an end; to pay.—*v.i.* to come to rest; subside; to become clear; to take up an abode; to come to an agreement.—**set'tlement** *n.*—**sett'ler** *n.* *Syn.* arrange, decide, compose, regulate. *Ant.* unsettle, disarrange, postpone.

Sev'en *a.* and *n.* a cardinal number, next after six.—

sev'enth *a.* the ordinal number.

Sev'er *v.t.* separate, divide; cut off.—*v.i.* to divide.—**sev'erance** *n.*—**sev'eral** *a.* separate; individual; some, a few.—*pron.* a few.—**sev'erally** *adv.*

Severe' (-ēr) *a.* strict; rigorous; hard to do or undo.—**severe'ly** *adv.* — **sever'ity** *n.*

Sew (sō) *v.t.* to join with thread.—*v.i.* to be occupied in sewing.

Sew'er (sū-) *n.* an underground drain to remove waste water and refuse.—**sew'age** *n.* refuse so carried off.

Sex *n.* the state of being male or female; males or females collectively.—**sex'ual** *a.*—**sex'ually** *adv.*

Sexag'enary *a.* pertaining to the number sixty; proceeding by sixties.—**sexagena'rian** *n.* a person of the age of sixty years.—*a.* sixty years old.

Sexages'ima *n.* the second Sunday before Lent, the next to Shrove-Tuesday (so called as being about the sixtieth day before Easter).

Sexenn'ial *a.* lasting si. years, or happening once in six years.

Sex'tain *n.* a stanza of six lines.

Sext'ant *n.* an instrument with a graduated arc of a sixth of a circle to measure angles, altitudes of a heavenly body, etc.

Sext'on *n.* an official in charge of a church, often acting as gravedigger.

Sfumato (sfōō-) *a.* having hazy outline, as a drawing or painting.

Shabb'y *a.* poorly dressed; faded, worn; dishonourable. — **shabb'ily** *adv.* — **shabb'iness** *n.*

Shack *n.* a shanty.

Shac'kle *n.* a fetter; a link to join two pieces of chain, etc.; anything that hampers.—*v.t.* to fetter or hamper.

Shad *n.* a fish of the herring tribe.

Shadd'ock *n.* tree of orange genus; a fruit of this tree.

Shade *n.* partial darkness; the darker part of anything; depth of colour; a tinge; shelter or a place sheltered from light, heat, etc.; a ghost.—*v.t.* to screen from light, to darken; to represent shades in a drawing.—**shad'ow** *n.* a patch of shade; a dark figure projected by anything that intercepts rays of light.—*v.t.* to cast a shadow over; to follow and watch closely.—**shad'owy** *a.* —**sha'dy** *a.*

Shadoof, shaduf (-dōōf) *n.* a contrivance, used in Egypt and the East generally, for raising water, *esp.* for the irrigation of small areas of land.

Shaft (-à-) *n.* a straight rod, stem, or handle; one of the bars between which a horse is harnessed; the entrance boring of a mine; a revolving rod for transmitting power.

Shag *n.* matted wool or hair; cloth with a long nap; a fine cut tobacco.—**shagg'y** *a.*

Shagreen' *n.* a rough untanned leather.

Shah (shà) *n.* the king of Persia; the ruler of a land.

Shake *v.i.* to tremble, totter, vibrate; — *v.t.* to cause to shake; in Australia, to steal. —*n.* the act of shaking; vibration; jolt.—**sha'ky** *a.*—**sha'kily** *adv.*

Shako' *n.* a military cap with a peak.

Shale *n.* a clay rock like slate but softer.

Shall *v.aux.* makes compound tenses or moods to express obligation, command, condition or intention.

Shall'op *n.* a sort of large boat with two masts; a small boat with lug-sails.

Shallot' *n.* a small onion.

Shall'ow (-ō) *a.* not deep.—*n.* a shallow place.

Sham *n.* an imitation, a counterfeit.—*a.* imitation.—*v.t.* and *i.* to pretend.

Sham'ble *v.i.* to walk with shuffling gait.

Shamb'les *n.pl.* a slaughter-house; butcher's stall.

Shame *n.* the emotion caused by consciousness of something wrong or dishonouring in one's conduct or state; a cause of disgrace.—*v.t.* to cause to feel shame; to disgrace.—**shame'faced** *a.* (earlier *shamefast*) shy.—**shame'ful** *a.*—**shame'fully** *adv.*—**shame'less** *a.* *Syn.* of *a.* infamous, disgraceful, scandalous, indecent, degrading. *Ant.* proper, becoming, decent, honourable.

Shampoo' *v.t.* to wash (the scalp) with something forming a lather in rubbing.—*n.* a shampooing.

Sham'rock *n.* a trefoil plant taken as the emblem of Ireland.

Shan'dry *n.* a light, two-wheeled cart or gig; any old, rickety conveyance. Also **shandrydan.**

Shan'dygaff *n.* a mixture of bitter ale or beer with ginger-beer.

Shanghai' *n.* a long-legged hen; in Australia, a catapult. —*v.t.* to drug and ship a sailor.—**Shanghai-shot** *n.* in Australia, a short distance.

Shank *n.* the lower leg; the shinbone; a stem of a thing.

Shant'y *n.* a hut; in Australia, a public-house, *esp.* an unlicensed one.

Shant'y *n.* a sailor's song with chorus.

Shape *n.* external form or appearance; a mould or pattern. -*v.t.* to give shape to, mould, fashion, make.—**shape'less** *a.*—**shape'ly** *a.* well-proportioned.

Shard *n.* a broken fragment, *esp.* of earthenware.

Share (shèr) *n.* the blade of a plough.

Share (shèr) *n.* a portion.—*v.t.* to give or allot a share.—*v.i.* to take a share.

Shark *n.* a large fish, of which some varieties are man-eaters; a grasping person; a sharper.

Sharp *a.* having a keen edge or fine point; apt, keen; brisk; harsh; dealing cleverly but unfairly; shrill; strongly marked, *esp.* in outline.—*n.* in music, a note half a tone above the natural pitch.— **sharp'ly** *adv.*—**sharp'en** *v.t.* —**sharp'er** *n.* a swindler.— **sharp'ness** *n.*—**sharp'shooter** *n.* a marksman. *Syn.* penetrating, pointed, cutting, keen, acute, bitter, acrid. *Ant.* blunt, dull, stupid.

Shatt'er *v.t.* to break in pieces.—*v.i.* to fly in pieces.

Shave *v.t.* to pare away; to cut close, *esp.* the hair of the face or head; to graze.— *v.i.* to shave oneself.—*n.* a shaving; a narrow escape.— **shave'ling** *n.* a tonsured monk.

Sha'vian *a.* in the manner of George Bernard Shaw.

Shawl *n.* a square of fabric mainly used to cover the shoulders.

Shawm *n.* a musical instrument like an oboe, used in Middle Ages.

She *pron.* the third person singular feminine pronoun.

Sheaf *n.* bundle, *esp.* corn.

Shea'ling *n.* a hut used by shepherds or fishermen.

Shear *v.t.* to cut through; to clip or cut; to clip the hair or wool from.—*n.* in *pl.* a cutting implement like a large pair of scissors; a scissor-shaped erection of beams used as a crane.— **shear'er** *n.*

Sheath *n.* a close-fitting cover, *esp.* for a knife or sword; a scabbard.—**sheathe** *v.t.* to put into a sheath.

Shed *n.* a roofed shelter used as a store or workshop.

Shed *v.t.* to cast off, scatter, throw off.—*n.* a dividing ridge.

Sheen *n.* gloss.—**sheen'y** *a.*

Sheep *n.* a ruminant animal with a heavy coat of wool.— **sheep'ish** *a.* shy.—**sheep'cot**, **sheep'cote** *n.* a shelter for sheep.

Sheer *a.* pure; perpendicular.

Sheer *v.i.* to deviate from a course.

Sheet *n.* a large piece of linen, etc., to cover a bed; a broad piece of any thin material; a large expanse.—*v.t.* to cover with a sheet.

Sheet *n.* a rope fastened in the corner of a sail.—**sheet'-anchor** *n.* a large anchor used only in an emergency.

Sheikh (-āk, -ēk) *n.* an Arab chief.

Shek'el *n.* a Jewish weight and coin.

Shelf *n.* a board fixed horizontally (on a wall, etc.), on which to put things.—**shelve** *v.t.* to put on a shelf; to put off.

Shell *n.* a hard outer case of an animal, fruit, etc.; an explosive projectile; an inner coffin; the outer part of a structure left when the interior is removed.—**shell-back** *n.* an old sailor; a barnacle. — **shell - proof** *a.* proof against bombshells.— **shell-shock** *n.* a nervous disorder caused by bursting of shells or bombs near' the patient.—*v.t.* to take a shell from, or out of a shell; to fire at with shells.

Shellac' *n.* lac in scales.

Shelt'er *n.* a place or structure giving protection; protection.—*v.t.* to give protection to, to screen.—*v.i.* to take shelter.

Shelve *v.i.* to slope gradually.

She'ol *n.* the place, or state, of the dead; the Hebrew Hades.

Shep'herd (shep-ęrd) *n.* a man who tends sheep.—shep'-herdess *fem.*

Sher'bet *n.* a cooling drink of water and fruit juices.

Sher'iff *n.* a county or city officer.

Sherr'y *n.* a Spanish wine.

Shibb'oleth *n.* a test word.

Shield *n.* a plate of armour carried on the left arm; a protective covering.—*v.t.* to cover, screen.

Shift *v.t.* to move, remove.—*v.i.* to remove; change position.—*n.* an evasion; an expedient; a relay of workmen; the time of their working; a removal; formerly, a woman's undergarment.—shift'less *a.* lacking in resource or character.—shift'y *a.* shuffling, full of evasions.—shift'iness *n.*

Shille'lagh (-āla) *n.* a cudgel.

Shill'ing *n.* a silver coin= twelve pence.

Shill'y-shally *v.i.* to waver.—*n.* wavering, indecision.

Shimm'er *v.i.* to shine with faint quivering light.—*n.* such light.

Shin *n.* the front of the lower leg.—*v.i.* to climb with arms and legs.

Shin'dy *n.* a row.

Shine *v.i.* to give out or reflect light.—*n.* brightness.—shi'ny *a.*

Shin'gle (-ng-gl) *n.* a flat piece of wood used as a tile.—*v.t.* to cover with shingles; to cut (a woman's hair) close.

Shin'gle (ng-gl) *n.* pebbles on the shore.

Shin'gles (-ng-gl) *n.* a disease with eruptions often forming a belt round the body.

Shin'to *n.* the system of nature-worship formerly prevailing in Japan.

Shin'ty *n.* a Scottish game similar to hockey.

Ship *n.* a large sea-going vessel.—*v.t.* to put on or send in a ship.—*v.i.* to embark; to take service in a ship.—ship'ment *n.* act of shipping; goods shipped.—shipp'ing *n.* ships collectively.—ship'shape *a.* orderly trim.

Shir'allee *n.* in Australia, *sl.* a bundle of blankets; clothes, provisions, etc., tied up in a blanket, ready to be carried on the back.

Shire *n.* a county.

Shirk *v.t.* to evade, try to avoid (a duty, etc.).—shirk'er *n.*

Shirt *n.* an undergarment for the upper part of the body.

Shiv'er *n.* a splinter.—*v.t.* to splinter, break in pieces.—*v.i.* to split into pieces.

Shiv'er *v.i.* to tremble, usually with cold or fear.—*n.* an act or state of shivering.

Shoal *n.* a sandbank or bar, a shallow; a school of fish.—*v.i.* to become shallow; to collect in a shoal.

Shock *v.t.* to horrify, scandalise.—*n.* a violent or damaging blow; a collision.

Shock *n.* a mass of hair.—*a.* shaggy.

Shoddy *n.* a cloth made of mixed old and new wool.—*a.* worthless, second-rate, of poor material.

Shoe (shōō) *n.* a covering for the foot, like a boot, but not enclosing the ankle; a metal rim or curved bar put on a horse's hoof; various protective plates or under-coverings.

Shooldarr'y *n.* in India, a small tent.

Shoot *v.i.* to move swiftly and suddenly; to let off a gun, bow, etc.; to go after game with a gun; to sprout. —*v.t.* to pass quickly under or along; to dump; to discharge; to kill or wound with a missile; in cinematography, to photograph a film.—*n.* an act of shooting; an expedition to shoot; a young branch or stem.

Shop *n.* a place where goods are made, or bought and sold.—*v.i.* to visit shops.— **shop'lifter** *n.* one who steals from a shop.

Shore *n.* the edge of the sea, or large lake.

Shore *n.* a prop.—*v.t.* to prop.

Short *a.* having little length; brief; hasty; friable.—*n.* in *pl.* breeches coming to, and open at, the knee.—*adv.* abruptly.—**short'age** *n.* deficiency.—**short'-cir'cuit** *n.* in electricity, a connection, often accidental, of very low resistance between two parts of a circuit.—**short'en** *v.t.* and *i.*—**short'hand** *n.* a method of rapid writing by signs or contractions.— **short'ly** *adv.* soon; briefly.— **short waves** *n.* in wireless, waves between 10 and 50 metres. *Syn.* of " shorten," abridge, diminish, reduce, curtail. *Ant.* expand, lengthen, increase, magnify.

Shot *n.* an act of shooting; a shooter; a missile; lead in small pellets; a bill at a tavern.—*a.* woven so that the colour is different according to the angle of the light.

Shoul'der (-ōl-) *n.* the part of a body to which an arm or foreleg is attached; a support or bracket.—*v.t.* to put on one's shoulder.—*v.i.* to make a way by pushing.—**shoulder'-blade** *n.* shoulder bone.

Shout *n.* a loud cry.—*v.i.* to utter one.—*v.t.* to utter with a very loud voice; in Australia, to stand someone a drink.

Shove (-uv) *v.t.* and *n.* push.

Shov'el (-uv-) *n.* a broad spade with a long or short handle.—*v.t.* to lift or move with a shovel.

Show (-ō) *v.t.* to expose to view, point out; guide; accord (favour, etc.).—*v.i.* to appear, be visible.—*n.* something shown; a display, spectacle.—**show'y** *a.*—**show'-ily** *adv.*—**show'man** *n.*

Show'er *n.* a short fall of rain; anything coming down like rain.—*v.t.* and *i.* to rain. —**show'ery** *a.*

Shrap'nel *n.* a shell filled with bullets which are discharged by the explosion of the shell.

Shred *n.* a fragment, torn strip.—*v.t.* to break or tear to shreds.

Shrew *n.* an animal like a mouse; a malicious person; a scold.—**shrew'mouse** *n.* shrew.—**shrew'ish** *a.*—**shrewd** *a.* intelligent; crafty; coming near the truth.—**shrewd'ly** *adv.*—**shrewd'ness** *n.*

Shriek *v.t.* and *i.* and *n.* screech.

Shriev'alty *n.* the office of sheriff.

Shrike *n.* butcher-bird.

Shrill *a.* piercing, sharp in tone.—**shril'ly** *adv.*

Shrimp *n.* a small crustacean of lobster shape.—*v.i.* to go catching shrimps.—**shrimp'er** *n.*

Shrine *n.* a case with relics of a saint; a chapel for this; a temple.

Shrink *v.i.* to become smaller; to retire, flinch.—*v.t.* to make shrink.—**shrink'age** *n.*

Shrive *v.t.* to give absolution to.—**shrift** *n.*

Shriv'el *v.i.* to shrink and wrinkle.

Shroff *n.* in India, a banker or money-changer.—*v.t.* to ascertain the quality of coins. — **shroff'age** *n.* the examination of coins by an expert, and the separation of the good from the debased or defaced.

Shroud *n.* a sheet for a corpse; a covering.—*pl.* a set of ropes to a masthead.—*v.t.* to put a shroud on; to screen; wrap up.

Shrove'tide *n.* the days just before Lent.—**Shrove Tues'-day.**

Shrub *n.* a woody or bushy plant.—**shrubb'y** *a.*—**shrub-b'ery** *n.* a plantation of shrubs, a part of a garden filled with them.

Shrug *v.i.* to raise and narrow the shoulders, as a sign of disdain, etc.—*v.t.* to move (the shoulders) thus.—*n.* a shrugging.

Shudd'er *v.i.* to tremble violently, *esp.* with horror.—*n.* a shuddering.

Shuf'fle *v.i.* to move the feet without lifting them; to act evasively.—*v.t.* to mix (cards); (with *off*) to evade, pass to another.—*n.* a shuffling.—**shuff'ler** *n.*

Shun *v.t.* to avoid, abstain from.

Shunt *v.t.* to move (a train) from one line to another; to push aside.

Shut *v.t.* and *i.* to close.—**shutt'er** *n.* a movable screen for a window, usually hinged to the frame.

Shut'tle *n.* an instrument which threads the woof between the threads of the warp in weaving; a similar appliance in a sewing machine.—**shut'tlecock** *n.* a cork with a cup-shaped fan of feathers stuck in it for use with a battledore.

Shy *a.* timid, bashful, awkward in company: reluctant.—*v.i.* to start back in sudden fear; to show sudden reluctance.—*n.* a sudden start of fear by a horse.—shy'ly *adv.*—shy'ness *n.*

Shy *v.t.* and *n.* throw.

Sib'ilant *a.* having a hissing sound.—*n.* a speech sound with a hissing effect.

Sib'yl *n.* a woman supposed to be endowed with a spirit of prophecy.—sib'ylline *a.*

Sick *a.* ill; inclined to vomit, vomiting.—sick'en *v.t.* and *i.*—sick'ly *a.*—sick'ness *n.*—sick'-bay *n.* a place set aside for treating the sick.

Sic'kle *n.* a reaping hook.

Side *n.* one of the surfaces of an object, *esp.* an upright inner or outer surface; either surface of a thing having only two; part of the body that is to the right or left; the region nearer or farther than, or right or left of, a dividing line, etc.; one of two parties or sets of opponents.—*v.i.* to take up the cause of.—side'arms *n.pl.* weapons worn at the side.—side'board *n.* a piece of furniture for holding dishes, etc., in a dining-room.—side-car *n.* in motoring, a small canoe-shaped body attached to a motor-cycle.—side'long *adv.* obliquely.—sides'man *n.* assistant to churchwardens.—side'ways *adv.*—si'ding *n.* a track added at the side of a railway.—si'dle *v.i.* to edge along.—side'slip *n.* a skid.

Sider'eal (-dĕr-) *a.* relating to the stars.

Sid'erite *n.* the lodestone; a meteorite wholly composed of iron.—sid'erolite *n.* a meteorite composed partly of iron and partly of stone.—siderog'raphy *n.* art of steel-engraving.

Siege *n.* a besieging of a town or fortified place.

Sienn'a *n.* an earthy pigment of a brownish-yellow colour, a silicate of iron and alumina.

Sierr'a *n.* a chain of mountains with saw-like ridges.

Siest'a (sĕ-est-a) *n.* a rest or sleep in the afternoon.

Sieve (siv) *n.* a utensil with network or a perforated bottom for sifting.—sift *v.t.* to separate coarser portion from finer; solid from liquid.

Sigh (sī) *v.i.* to utter a long audible breath.—*n.* such a breath.

Sight (sīt) *n.* faculty of seeing; a seeing something seen; a device for guiding the eye.—*v.t.* catch sight of.—sight'less *a.*—sight'ly *a.* good to look at.

Sign (sīn) *n.* a movement, mark, or indication to convey some meaning.—*v.t.* to put one's signature to.—*v.i.* to make a sign or gesture; to affix a signature.—sig'nature *n.* a person's name written by himself; the act of writing it.—sig'natory *n.* one of those who sign a document.—sign'manual (sīn-) *n.* an autograph signature, *esp.* of a sovereign.—sign'post (sīn-) *n.* a post supporting a signboard, *esp.* to show the way at cross roads.—sign'board (sīn-) *n.* a board with some device or inscription.—

sig'nal n. a sign to convey an order, etc.; a semaphore, *esp.* on a railway.—*v.t.* to make signals to.—*v.i.* to give orders, etc., by signals.—*a.* remarkable, striking.—**sig'nally** adv.—**sig'nalise** v.t. to make notable.—**sig'net** n. a small seal.—**sig'nify** v.t. to mean; to imitate.—*v.i.* to be of importance.—**signif'icant** a. expressing the importance.—**signif'icantly** adv. —**signif'icance** n.—**significa'tion** n. the meaning.

Si'lence n. stillness, absence of noise; a refraining from speech.—*v.t.* to make silent. —**si'lent** a.

Silhouette' n. a portrait or picture cut from black paper or done in solid black on white; an outline of an object seen against the light.

Sil'ica n. silicic acid in a state of purity.—**sil'icate** n. a salt formed by the union of silica and a base, as alumina, lime, soda, magnesia, potassa, etc.—**sil'icon, silic'ium** n. a dark, nut-brown, elementary substance, destitute of metallic lustre, which communicates valuable properties when incorporated in steel. —**silic'eous, silic'ious** a. containing silica, or partaking of its qualities.—**silic'ic** a. pert. to flint or quartz.

Silk n. a fibre made by the larvæ of certain moths; thread or fabric made from this. — **silk'en** a. — **silk'y** a. —**silk'iness** adv.—**silk'ily** a.

Silk'-worm n. the caterpillar that produces silk.

Sill n. slab of wood or stone at bottom of a door or window.

Sill'y a. foolish; weak in intellect.—**sill'iness** n.

Si'lo n. a pit or tower for storing fodder or grain.

Silt n. mud deposited by water.—*v.t.* and *i.* to fill with silt.

Sil'van a. wooded; rural.

Sil'ver n. a white precious metal; things made of it; silver coins.—*v.t.* to coat with silver.—**sil'very** a.

Sil'verside n. a silver-fish, sand-smelt, or atherine; the lower and choicer part of the round of beef.

Sim'ian a. of apes; ape-like.

Sim'ilar a. resembling, like.— **sim'ilarly** adv.—**similar'ity** n. likeness.—**sim'ile** (sim-i-li) n. a comparison of one thing with another, *esp.* in poetry. —**simil'itude** n. outward appearance; guise.

Simm'er v.t. and i. to keep or be just bubbling or just below boiling-point; to be in a state of suppressed anger or laughter.

Si'mony n. the buying or selling of church preferment.

Si'moom n. a hot, dry wind that blows from the Arabian desert.

Sim'per v.i. to smile in a silly or affected way.

Sim'ple a. plain; straightforward; ordinary, mere.— **sim'ply** adv.—**sim'pleton** n. a foolish person.—**simpli'city** n.—**sim'plify** (-fī) v.t.—**simplifica'tion** n. *Syn.* uncomplicated, elementary, artless, easy. *Ant.* intricate, artful, involved, difficult.

Sim'ulate *v.t.* to pretend to be.—**simulac'rum** *n.*—**simulac'ra** *pl.* a shadowy likeness; an unreal thing.—**simula'tion** *n.*

Simulta'neous *a.* occurring at the same time.—**simulta'neously** *adv.* — **simul'taneity** *n.* — **simulta'neous broadcasting** *n.* broadcasting of programme transmitted by one station by others connected by telephone.

Sin *n.* a transgression against divine or moral law, *esp.* one committed consciously; conduct or state of mind of a habitual or unrepentant sinner.—*v.i.* to commit sin.—**sin'ful** *a.* of the nature of sin; guilty of sin. — **sin'fully** *a.*—**sinn'er** *n.*

Since *adv.* from then till now; subsequently; ago.—*prep.* at some time subsequent to.—*conj.* from the time that; seeing that.

Sincere' *a.* not assumed or merely professed; actually moved by or feeling the apparent motives; straightforward.—**sincere'ly** *adv.*—**sincer'ity** *n.* *Syn.* unfeigned, true, genuine, unaffected. *Ant.* hypocritical, affected, false, dishonest.

Si'necure *n.* an office with pay but no duties.

Sin'ew *n.* a tendon.—*pl.* muscles, strength; mainstay or motive power.—**sin'ewy** *a.*

Sing *v.i.* to utter musical sounds.—*v.t.* to utter (words) with musical modulation; to celebrate in song or poetry.—**sing'er** *n.*

Singe (-nj) *v.t.* to burn the surface of.—*n.* an act or effect of singeing.

Sin'gle (-ng-gl) *a.* one only; alone, separate; unmarried; formed of only one part, fold, etc.—*v.t.* to pick (out).—**sing'let** (-ng-gl-) *n.* an unlined woollen undergarment.—**sin'gleton** *n.* a single thing; the only card of a suit in a hand.—**sin'gly** *adv.*—**sin'gle-stick** *n.* fencing with a basket-hilted stick; the stick.—**sin'gular** *a.* unique; remarkable; odd; denoting one person or thing.—*n.* a word in singular.—**sin'gularly** *adv.* — **singular'ity** *n.*

Sin'ister *a.* evil-looking; wicked; in heraldry, on the left-hand side. *Syn.* unlucky, inauspicious, unfortunate, evil. *Ant.* lucky, auspicious, fortunate, good.

Sink *v.i.* to become submerged in water; to drop, give way, decline.—*v.t.* to cause to sink; to make by digging out; to invest.—*n.* a receptacle with a pipe for carrying away waste water.—**sink'er** *n.*

Sinn Fein' (shin fān') *n.* Irish policy and movement aiming at independent self-government and cultural and economic development for Ireland on national lines.

Sin'uous *a.* curving, winding.—**sin'uously** *adv.*—**sinuos'ity** *n.*

Si'nus *n.* an opening; a hollow;

a recess in the shore; a bay; *Surg.* a cavity in a bone or other part; an abscess with a small orifice.

Sip *v.t.* and *i.* to drink in very small draughts.—*n.* a portion of liquid sipped.

Si'phon *n.* a bent tube for drawing off liquids; a bottle with a tap at the top through which liquid is forced by pressure of gas inside.

Sir *n.* the title of a knight or baronet; a public or respectful form of address.

Sir'dar *n.* a military commander in India; the commander-in-chief of the Egyptian army.

Sire *n.* a term of address to a king, a father.

Si'ren *n.* a legendary female monster supposed to lure sailors to destruction; a fog signal.

Sirene' (-rēn) *n.* an instrument for ascertaining the number of vibrations corresponding to any given pitch.

Sir'loin *n.* upper part of a loin of beef.

Sirocc'o *n.* a hot Mediterranean wind.

Sis'al, si'sal *n.* fibre of the S. American aloe.

Sis'ter *n.* daughter of the same parents or having a common parent.—*a.* closely related, exactly similar.—**sis'terly** *a.* —**sis'terhood** *n.* the relation of sister; an order or band of women.—**sis'ter-in-law** *n.* a sister of a husband or wife; the wife of a brother.

Sit *v.i.* to rest on the lower part of the body as on a chair, to seat oneself; to hold a session; to incubate.—*v.t.* to sit upon (horse).

Site *n.* a place, situation, a plot of ground for, or with, a building.—**sit'uate**, **sit'uated** *a.* placed.—**situa'tion** *n.* place or position; an employment or post; state of affairs.

Six *a.* and *n.* a cardinal number, one more than five. —**sixth** *a.* the ordinal number. —*n.* a sixth part.—**six'pence** *n.* the sum of six pence; the silver coin of this value.— **six'penny** *a.* costing sixpence.

Si'zar *n.* a student at Cambridge or Dublin admitted at lower fees.—**sizarship** *n.* the station of a sizar at Cambridge or Dublin.

Size *n.* bigness, dimensions.— *v.t.* to sort or estimate by size.

Size *n.* a substance resembling glue.—*v.t.* to coat or treat with size.

Sizz'le *v.i.* to make a hissing or sputtering sound; to dry and shrivel up with hissing by the action of the fire.—*n.* a hissing sound; extreme heat.

Sjam'bok (syäm-) *n.* a short whip.—*v.t.* to beat with such a whip.

Skate *n.* a flat fish.

Skate *n.* a steel blade with a framework to attach it to a boot, used for gliding over ice.—*v.i.* to glide on skates.

Skein (-ā-) *n.* a quantity of yarn, wool, etc., in a loose knot.

Skel'eton *n.* bones of an animal.

Sketch *n.* a rough drawing; a brief account; essay, etc.—*v.t.* to make a sketch of.—*v.i.* to practise sketching.—**sketch'y** *a.*

Skew *v.i.* to move obliquely.—*a.* slanting.

Skew'bald *a.* bay and white in patches.

Skew'er *n.* a pin to fasten meat together.—*v.i.* to pierce or fasten with a skewer.

Ski (shē) *n.* a long wooden runner fastened to the foot for sliding over snow.—*v.i.* to slide on skis.

Skid *n.* a drag for a wheel.—*v.t.* to apply a skid to.—*v.i.* of a wheel, to slip without revolving or to slip sideways.

Skiff *n.* small boat.

Skill *n.* practical ability, cleverness.—**skil'ful** *a.*—**skil'-fully** *adv.* *Syn.* dexterity, aptitude. *Ant.* awkwardness, clumsiness, inaptitude.

Skill'et *n.* a small vessel with a handle, used for heating water, etc.

Skill'y *n.* watery broth or soup.

Skim *v.t.* to rid of floating matter; to remove from the surface of a liquid; to cover over lightly and rapidly; to read in this way.—*v.i.* to move thus.

Skimp *v.t.* to give short measure; to do a thing imperfectly.

Skin *n.* an outer covering, *esp.* of an animal or fruit.—*v.t.* to remove the skin of.—**skinn'y** *a.* thin.—**skinless** *a.*—**skin-deep**, superficial; slight.—**skin-grafting**, the operation of transplanting a piece of healthy skin to a wound to form a new skin.—**skin-effect**, in electricity, tendency of alternating current to spread over surface of conductor rather than distribute equally over whole area.—**skin-tight**, fitting close to the skin.

Skip *v.i.* to leap lightly; to jump a rope as it is swung under one.—*v.t.* to pass over.—*n.* an act of skipping.

Skipp'er *n.* the captain of a ship.

Skirm'ish *n.* a fight between small parties, a small battle.—*v.i.* to fight slightly or irregularly.

Skirt *n.* the lower part of a woman's dress, a coat, etc., an outlying part.—*v.t.* to border; to go round.

Skit *n.* a satire or caricature.—**skitt'ish** *a.* frisky, frivolous.

Skit'tles *n.pl.* the game of nine-pins.

Skulk *v.i.* to sneak out of the way, to lurk.

Skull *n.* the bony case that encloses the brain.—**skullcap** *n.* a close-fitting cap.

Skunk *n.* a small North American animal like a weasel, which defends itself by emitting an evil-smelling fluid; a mean fellow.

Sky *n.* the apparent canopy of the heavens; the heavenly regions. — **sky'-writing** *n.* smoke writing executed in the sky by an aeroplane.

Slab *n.* thick broad piece.

Slack *a.* loose; sluggish; not busy.—*n.* a loose part.—*v.t.* to mix (lime) with water.—

v.i. to be idle or azy.—
slack'ly *adv.*—**slack'en** *v.t.*
and *i.*

Slack *n.* small coal.—**slag** *n.*
refuse of smelted metal.

Slake *v.i.* to moderate.—*v.t.*
to quench; to slack (lime).

Slam *v.t.* to shut noisily; to
dash down.—*v.i.* to shut with
a bang.—*n.* a noisy shutting
or other bang.—slam (grand
or little) thirteen or twelve
tricks taken in one deal in
cards.

Slan'der (-å-) *n.* a false or
malicious statement about a
person.—*v.t.* to utter such
statement.—**slan'derer** *n.*—
slan'derous *a.*

Slang *n.* a colloquial language.
—*v.t.* to scold violently.

Slant (-å-) *v.t.* and *i.* and *n.*
slope.—*adv.* in a slanting
manner.—*a.* sloping, oblique.

Slap *n.* a blow with the open
hand or a flat instrument.—
v.t. to strike thus.

Slash *v.t.* to gash; to lash.—
n. a gash; a cutting stroke.

Slat *n.* a narrow strip of wood
or metal; a thin, flat stone.

Slate *n.* a kind of stone which
splits easily in flat sheets; a
piece of this for covering a
roof or for writing on.— *v.t.*
to cover with slates.

Slatt'ern *n.* a slut.—**slatt'ernly**
a.

Slaught'er (slawt'-) *n.* killing.
—*v.t.* to kill.—**slaught'erous**
a.—**slaught'er-house** *n.* a
place for killing animals for
food.

Slave *n.* a captive, a person
without freedom or personal
rights.—*v.i.* to work like a

slave.—**sla'very** *n.*—**sla'vish**
a.—**sla'ver** *n.* a person or ship
engaged in slave traffic.

Slav'er *v.i.* to let saliva run
from the mouth.—*n.* saliva
running from mouth; gross
flattery.

Slay *v.t.* to kill.—**Slay'er** *n.*

Sledge, sledge'-hammer *n.* a
heavy blacksmith's hammer.

Sledge *n.* a carriage on runners
for sliding on snow; a toboggan. (also SLED.)

Sleek *a.* glossy and smooth.

Sleep *n.* an unconscious state
regularly occurring in man
and animals.—*v.i.* to take
rest in sleep, to slumber.—
sleep'er *n.* one who sleeps; a
beam supporting a rail of a
railway; a sleeping-car.—
sleep'less *a.*—**sleep'iness** *n.*—
sleep'y *a.*—**sleep'ily** *adv.*

Sleet *n.* partly-thawed snow.

Sleeve *n.* the part of a garment
which covers the arm; in
motoring, case surrounding
shaft; in aviation, wind indicator at aerodrome.—*v.t.* to
furnish with sleeves; to put
sleeves into.—**sleeved** *a.*—
sleeveless *a.*— **sleeve-band**, the
wrist-band or cuff.— **sleeve-
link**, two buttons linked together, and securing the edges
of a cuff or wristband.—
sleeve valve, sliding-valve.—
leg of mutton sleeve, a sleeve
full in the middle and narrow
at each end.—**to hang upon
one's sleeve**, to be dependent
upon one.—**to have up one's
sleeve**, to have something in
readiness for an emergency,
without letting others know
of it.

Sleigh (slā) *n.* a sledge.

Sleight (slīt) *n.* dexterity.—**sleight'-of-hand'** *n.* conjuring.

Slen'der *a.* slim, slight, small. *Syn.* moderate, trivial, meagre, spare, abstemious, simple. *Ant.* considerable, large, plentiful, ample, stout.

Sleuth *n.* a track; a bloodhound; a relentless tracker; a detective.—**sleuth'hound** *n.*

Slew *v.t.* and *i.* to swing round.

Slice *n.* a thin flat piece cut off.—*v.t.* to cut into slices.

Slick *a.* smooth; smooth-tongued; smart.—*adv.* deftly.—*v.t.* to make glossy.

Slide *v.i.* to slip smoothly along.—*v.t.* to cause to slide.—*n.* a sliding; a track on ice made for or by sliding; the sliding part of mechanism.—**sliding-roof**, roof of saloon motor-car designed to open by sliding.

Slight (-īt) *a.* slim, slender; not substantial; trifling.—*v.t.* to disregard; to neglect.—*n.* indifference; an act of discourtesy.—**slight'ly** *adv.* *Syn.* weak, fragile, thin, faint, transient, silly, soft, gentle, cursory, superficial. *Ant.* important, serious, strong, weighty, sturdy.

Slim *a.* thin, slight; crafty.

Slime *n.* sticky mud.—**sli'my** *a.*

Sling *n.* a pocket with a string attached at each end for hurling a stone; a hanging bandage for a wounded limb; any rope, belt, etc., for hoisting or carrying weights.—*v.t.* to throw; to hoist or swing by means of a rope.

Slink *v.i.* to move stealthily.

Slip *n.* a twig cut for grafting or planting; a long narrow slip; a landing place; a slope on which ships are built; a leash; a mistake; an act of slipping; in cricket, a position on the offside, a few yards behind the wicket; the fieldsman in this position; in motoring, revolution of wheels without movement along the surface of the road; in aviation, pitch of an airscrew, less distance it actually travels in one revolution.—*v.i.* to lose one's foothold.—*v.t.* to cause to slip; to put on or off easily or gently; to release (a dog).—**slipp'er** *n.* a light shoe for indoor use.—**slipp'ery** *a.* so smooth as to cause slipping or to be difficult to hold or catch.—**slip'shod** *a.* slovenly, careless.

Slips *n.pl.* the upper side-boxes in a theatre; wings.

Slit *v.t.* to cut open, to sever.—*a.* cut, torn.—*n.* a straight narrow cut.

Slith'er (-TH-) *v.i.* to slide and bump (down a slope, etc.).

Sliv'er *n.* a slip or splinter of wood; a long strip.—*v.t.* to divide into long, thin or very small pieces.—*v.i.* to split; to become split off.

Sloam *n.* layers of clay between those of coal.

Sloat *n.* a narrow piece of timber which holds together large pieces; a slat.

Slobb'er *v.i.* to slaver.—*v.t.* to wet with saliva.—*n.* running saliva.—**slobb'ery** *a.*

Sloe *n.* the blackthorn; its

blue-black fruit.—**sloe-gin** n. the liqueur made from sloes.

Slo'gan n. a Highland war-cry; catchword, motto.

Sloop n. a one-masted cutter-rigged vessel; a gun-boat.

Slop n. an overall.—pl. ready-made clothing.

Slop n. dirty liquid; semi-liquid food.—v.t. to spill or splash.—v.i. to spill.—**slopp'y** a.

Slope n. a slant, an upward or downward inclination.—v.i. to move obliquely.—v.t. to place slanting.

Slot n. a narrow hole or depression.

Slot n. the trail of an animal.

Sloth (-ō-) n. sluggishness; a sluggish S. Amer. animal.—**sloth'fully** adv.

Slouch n. a stooping, awkward, or shambling walk.—v.i. to walk in this way.—v.t. to pull down (a hat).

Slough (-ow) n. a bog.

Slough (-uf) n. the skin shed by a snake.—v.i. of such tissue, to be shed.—v.t. to shed (skin).

Slov'en (-uv-) n. a dirty, untidy person.—**slov'enly** a.

Slow (-ō) a. moving at a low rate of speed; behindhand; dull.—v.i. to slacken speed.—**slow'ly** adv.—**slow'ness** n.

Slow'-worm (slō-) n. a small lizard; a blind worm.

Slug n. a land snail with no shell; a lazy fellow; an oval or cylindrical bullet.—**slug'ard** n.—**slugg'ish** a. slow moving; lazy.—**slugg'ishness** n.

Sluice (-ōōs) n. a gate or door to control a flow of water.—v.t. to pour water over.

Slum n. squalid street or neighbourhood.—v.i. to visit slums.   [sleep.

Slum'ber v.i. to sleep.—n.

Slump v.i. of prices, etc., to fall suddenly or heavily.—n. such fall.

Slur v.t. to pass over lightly; to depreciate.—n. a slight.

Slush n. liquid mud; half-melted snow.—**slush'y** a.

Slut n. a dirty untidy woman.—**slutt'ish** a.

Sly a. cunning, wily; done with artful dexterity.—**sly'ly** adv.—**sly'ness** n.

Smack n. a taste, flavour.—v.i. to taste (of).

Smack v.t. to open (the lips) with a loud sound; to slap.—n. a smacking or slap; the sound of a slap.

Smack n. a small sailing vessel, usually for fishing. (See p. 517.)

Small (-awl) a. little.—**small'ness** n.—**small'clothes** n.pl. breeches.—**small'pox** n. a contagious disease.—**small-arms**, muskets, rifles, pistols, etc.—**small debts**, debts that are in England under £20; in Scotland, £12.—**small end**, in internal-combustion engine, bearing of a connecting rod connecting it to piston.—**small holding**, an allotment. *Syn.* diminutive, tiny, insufficient, inadequate. *Ant.* large, considerable, big, important.

Smalt n. common glass tinged of a fine deep blue by the protoxide of cobalt, ground fine, and used as a pigment in various arts.

Smart a. brisk; clever; trim, well dressed; fashionable.— v.i. to be very painful; to suffer acutely.—n. a sharp pain.—smart′en v.t.—smart′ly adv.—smart′ness n.

Smash v.t. to shatter; to dash. —v.i. to break.—n. a heavy blow; wrecked state; an accident wrecking vehicles.

Smatt′ering n. a superficial knowledge.—smatt′er v.i. to have a smattering.—smatt′erer n.

Smear v.t. to rub with grease, etc.—n. a mark made thus.

Smell v.t. to perceive by the nose.—v.i. to use the nose; to give out an odour.—n. an odour; the faculty of perceiving odours by the nose.

Smelt n. a small fish.

Smelt v.t. to extract metal from ore.

Smew n. a diving bird, visiting Britain in the winter.

Smi′lax n. a climbing shrub.

Smile v.i. to assume a pleased or amused expression.—n. an act of smiling.

Smirch v.t. to dirty; to disgrace.

Smirk v.i. to smile affectedly. —n. such smile.

Smite v.t. to strike; attack; affect, esp. with love.

Smith n. a worker in iron, etc. —smith′y (-TH-) n. his workshop.

Smock n. a loose garment with the upper part gathered.—v.t. to gather by diagonal lines of sewing.—smock′-frock n. a labourer's smock.

Smoke n. the cloudy mass of suspended particles that rises from fire or anything burning; a spell of tobacco smoking.—v.i. to give off smoke; to inhale and expel the smoke of burning tobacco.—v.t. to expose to smoke (esp. in curing fish, etc.); to consume (tobacco) by smoking.— smo′ker n.—smo′ky a.— smo′kily adv.

Smolt n. a salmon in its second year, when it has acquired its silvery scales.

Smooth (-TH) a. not rough, even of surface; plausible.— v.t. to make smooth; to quieten.—smooth′ly adv.— smoothing circuit, Elec. a device used for eliminating a pulsating component from a unidirectional current, such as that obtained from a rectifier. Syn. level, flat, polished, sleek, bland, fluent, deceptive. Ant. rough, uneven, unpolished, rude, uncivil, blunt, tempestuous.

Smoth′er (-UTH-) n. dense smoke, spray, foam, etc.— v.t. to suffocate, choke; suppress.—v.i. to be suffocated.

Smoul′der v.i. to burn slowly without flame.

Smudge n. a smear, stain, dirty mark.—v.t. to make a dirty mark on.

Smug a. self-satisfied, complacent.—smug′ly adv.

Smug′gle v.t. to bring into a country without payment of customs duties payable.— smugg′ler n.

Smut n. a piece of soot, a black particle of dirt; a disease of

grain; lewd or obscene talk.
—*v.t.* to blacken, smudge.—
smutt'y *a.*

Snack *n.* a light meal.

Snaf'fle *n.* a light bit for a
horse.—*v.t.* to put one on.

Snag *n.* a stump, *esp.* a tree-
trunk in a river.

Snail *n.* a slow-moving mollusc
with a shell, common in
gardens.

Snake *n.* a long scaly limbless
reptile.—sna'ky *a.*

Snake'stone *n.* a fossil ammon-
ite; any substance applied as
a specific for snake-bites.

Sna'king *n.* the act or process
of hauling a log; a snake-like
curl or spiral.

Snap *v.i.* to make a quick bite
or snatch.—*v.t.* to snatch or
bite; break abruptly.—*n.* a
quick sharp sound; a bite;
a break.—snapp'y *a.*—snapp'-
ish *a.*—snap'-dragon *n.* a
plant with flowers resembling
a mouth; a game of snatching
raisins from burning brandy.

Snare *n.* a noose used as a trap.
—*v.t.* to catch with one.

Snarl *n.* the growling sound
made by an angry dog.—*v.i.*
to make this sound; to
grumble.

Snar'ling *n.* process of forming
raised work or convex lines,
figures, etc., in vessels or
vases of sheet-metal, where
the direct action of the hammer is precluded by the
narrowness of the vase or
vessel.—snarling-iron, snar-
ling-tool, a curved tool for
embossing or fluting hollow
metal-ware.

Snatch *v.i.* to make a quick

grab or bite (at).—*v.t.* to
seize, catch.—*n.* a grab; a
short spell.

Sneak *v.i.* to slink.—*n.* a mean
or treacherous person.

Sneer *v.i.* to smile, speak or
write scornfully.—*n.* a sneering.

Sneeze *v.i.* to emit breath with
a sudden convulsive spasm
and noise.—*n.* a sneezing.

Snell *a.* keen; active; cold;
bitter.

Snib *v.t.* to fasten; to bolt.—
n. a fastening of a door;
latch.

Snick *n.* a small cut or mark;
notch; nick.—*v.t.* to cut; to
clip; to nick.—snick'ersnee *n.*
a kind of knife.

Snick'er *v.i.* to laugh slyly; to
laugh with small, audible
catches of voice.—*n.* a half
suppressed, broken laugh.

Sniff *v.i.* to draw in breath
through the nose with a sharp
hiss; to express disapproval,
etc., by sniffing.—*v.t.* to take
up through the nose, to smell.
—*n.* a sniffing.

Snip *v.t.* to cut, cut bits off.—
n. a bit cut off; a small cut.
—snipp'et *n.* a shred, a
fragment.

Snipe *n.* a bird.—*v.i.* to shoot
at enemy individuals from
cover.—*v.t.* to hit by so shooting.—sni'per *n.*

Sniv'el *v.i.* to make a sniffing
to show real or sham emotion,
esp. sorrow.

Snob *n.* judges by social rank
or wealth rather than merit.
—snobb'ery *n.*—snobb'ish *a.*
—snobb'ishly *adv.*

Snoo'ker *n.* a game resembling

pool or pyramids played on a billiard table.

Snooze *v.i.* to take a short sleep, to be half-asleep.—*n.* a nap.

Snore *v.i.* to make noises with the breath when asleep.—*n.* an act of snoring.

Snort *v.i.* to make a noise by driving breath through the nostrils.—*n.* such noise.

Snout *n.* nose of an animal.

Snow *n.* frozen vapour which falls in flakes.—*v.i.* it snows, snow is falling.—*v.t.* to let fall or throw down like snow; to cover with snow.—**snow'y** *a.*—**snow'drop** *n.* a bulbous plant with white flowers in early spring.

Snub *v.t.* to mortify or repress intentionally; to rebuke.—*n.* a snubbing.—**snub'nose** *n.* a turned-up stumpy nose.

Snuff *n.* charred candle-wick; powdered tobacco for inhaling through the nose; an act of snuffing.—*v.t.* to free (a candle) from snuff; to put out; to draw up or through the nostrils.—*v.i.* to draw air or snuff into the nose.

Snug *a.* cosy; trim.—**snug'ly** *adv.*—**snugg'ery** *n.* a cosy room.

So *adv.* in such manner; very; the case being such.—*conj.* therefore; in case that.

Soak *v.i.* to lie in a liquid.—*v.t.* to steep, make thoroughly wet.—*n.* a soaking.

Soap *n.* a compound of alkali and oil used in washing.—*v.t.* to apply soap to.

Soar *v.i.* to fly high.

Soar'ing *n.* act of mounting on the wings, as a bird; lofty flight; also, act of rising high in thought; intellectual flight; in aviation, flight in motorless aeroplanes.

Sob *v.i.* to catch the breath, *esp.* in weeping.—*n.* a sobbing.

So'ber *a.* temperate; subdued; not drunk.—*v.t.* and *i.* to make or become sober.—**so'berly** *adv.*—**sobri'ety** *n.* *Syn.* abstemious, moderate, dispassionate, serious. *Ant.* intemperate, extreme, passionate, careless.

So'briquet (-kā) *n.* a nickname.

So'cial *a.* living in communities; relating to society; sociable.—**so'cially** *adv.*—**so'ciable** *a.* inclined to be friendly, of ready companionship.—**sociabil'ity** *n.* — **so'ciably** *adv.*—**soci'ety** *n.* companionship; living associated with others; those so living; fashionable people collectively; an association or club.—**sociol'ogy** *n.* social science.—**so'cialism** *n.* a policy aiming at ownership of means of production and transport, etc., by the community.—**so'cialist** *n.*—**socialist'ic** *a.*

Sock *n.* a short stocking; an inner sole.

Sock'et *n.* a hole for something to fit into.

Sod *n.* a flat piece of earth with grass.

So'da *n.* an alkali.—**so'dawater** *n.* water charged with gas.—**so'dium** *n.* a metallic element.

Sodal'ity n. a fellowship or fraternity.

Sodd'en a. soaked; like dough.

Sod'omy n. unnatural sexual intercourse.

So'fa n. a long padded seat with a back and one or two ends.

Soft a. yielding easily to pressure, not hard; mild; easy; subdued; over-sentimental.—soft'ly adv.—soft'en (sof'n) v.t. and i.

Sogg'y a. soaked with water; damp and heavy.

Soil n. earth, ground.

Soil v.t. and i. to make or become dirty.—n. dirt; sewage.

Soiree' (swå-rā) n. an evening party; a public meeting of a society, congregation, etc., where refreshments are served, with speeches and business reports.

Soj'ourn (suj'ern) v.i. to stay for a time.—soj'ourner n.

So'lace n. and v.t. comfort.—sola'tium n. money compensation.

So'lan n. a large sea-bird like a goose; a gannet.

So'lar a. of the sun.

Sol'der (sōl-, sol-, sod-) n. an easily-melted alloy used for joining metal.—v.t. to join with it. — sol'dering-iron n.

Sol'dier (sō-) n. one serving in an army.—v.i. to serve in the army. — sol'dierly a. — sol'diery n. troops.

Sole n. the flat of the foot; the under part of a boot or shoe, etc.; a flat-fish.—v.t. to supply with a sole.

Sole a. only, unique.—sole'ly adv.

Sol'ecism n. a breach of grammar or etiquette.

Sol'emn (-em) a. serious; formal; impressive.—sol'emnly adv.—solem'nity n.—sol'emnise v.t. to celebrate, perform; make solemn.—solemnisa'tion n. Syn. grave, melancholy, ceremonious, stately. Ant. cheerful, gay, jovial, informal, unceremonious.

So'lenoid n. cylindrical coil of wire (without fixed iron core) forming an electro-magnet.

Soli'cit (-lis'-) v.t. to urge; request; entice.—solicita'tion n.—soli'citor n. one who solicits; a lawyer.—soli'citous a. anxious.—soli'citude n.

Sol'id a. not hollow; compact. —n. a body of three dimensions.—sol'idly adv.—solid'ity n.—solid'ify v.t. and i.—solidifica'tion n.—solidar'ity n. united state.

Solil'oquy n. a talking with oneself.—solil'oquise v.i.

Sol'iped n. an animal whose foot is not cloven; a solidungulate.

Sol'itary a. alone, single.—n. a hermit.—sol'itude n.—solitaire' n. a single precious stone set by itself; a game for one.—so'lo n. music for one performer; in motoring, abbr. for solo-machine, i.e. motor-cycle without sidecar attached.—a. not concerted; driving car, or piloting aeroplane alone.—so'loist n.

Solive' n. a joist or rafter, or other subordinate beam.

Sol'stice n. a period of the year when the sun is overhead at one of the tropics.—**solsti'tial** a.

Solve v.t. to work out, clear up, find the answer of.—**sol'uble** a. capable of solution.—**solubil'ity** n.—**solu'tion** n. the answer to a problem; a dissolving; a liquid with something dissolved in it.—**sol'vable** a.—**sol'vent** a. able to pay debts, having more assets than liabilities.—n. a liquid with a power of dissolving.—**sol'vency** n.

Som'bre a. dark or gloomy. Syn. cloudy, dismal, mournful. Ant. bright, clear, glad.

Sombre'ro n. wide-brimmed hat.

Some (sum) pron. a portion, a quantity.—a. one or other; an amount of; certain; approximately.—**some'body** n.—**some'how** adv. — **some'thing** n.—**some'time** a. former —adv. formerly; at some (past or future) time.—**some'times** adv. on occasion.—**some'what** n. something.—adv. to some extent, rather.—**some'where** adv.

Som'ersault (sum-) n. a tumbling head over heels.

Somnam'bulist n. a sleepwalker.—**somnam'bulism** n.

Som'nolent a. sleepy.—**som'nolence** n.

Son n. a male child.—**son'-in-law** n. a daughter's husband.

Sona'ta (-ä-) n. a piece of music in several movements.—**sonati'na** (-tē-) n. a short and simple sonata.

Song n. singing; a poem for singing.—**song'ster** n.—**song'stress** fem.

Son'ifer n. an acoustic instrument for collecting sound, and conveying it to the ear of a particularly deaf person.

Sonn'et n. a fourteen-line poem with a rhyme system.—**sonneteer'** n.

Sonor'ous a. giving out deep sound, resonant. — **son'orously** adv.—**sonor'ity** n.

Son'sy, son'cy a. plump; well-conditioned; good-humoured; hearty.

Soon (-ōō-) adv. before long; early.

Soot (-ōō-) n. a black substance formed by the burning of coal, etc.—**soot'y** a.

Sooth (-ōō-) n. truth.—**sooth'sayer** n. a person professing to foretell the future.

Soothe (-ōōTH) v.t. to calm, soften; please with soft words. Syn. quiet, pacify, appease, assuage, mollify. Ant. excite, irritate, inflame, enrage.

Sop n. a piece of bread, etc., soaked in liquid; a bribe.—v.t. to steep in water, etc.

Soph'ist n. a captious reasoner. —**soph'ism** n. a specious argument.—**sophist'ical** a.—**soph'istry** n.—**sophist'icate** v.t. to make artificial, spoil, falsify.—**sophistica'tion** n.

Soporif'ic (sop- or sō-) a. causing sleep.

Sopra'no (-rä-) n. the highest voice in women and boys; a singer with this voice; musical part for it.

Sor'cerer n. a wizard.—**sor'cer-**

ess *fem.*—sor'cery *n.* witchcraft, magic.

Sor'did *a.* mean, squalid.—sor'didly *adv.* — sor'didness *n.*

Sore *a.* painful; distressed.—*adv.* grievously.—*n.* a sore place, an ulcer or boil, etc.—sore'ness *n.*—sore'ly *adv.*

Sorr'el *n.* a plant.

Sorr'el *n.* a reddish-brown colour; a horse of this colour.—*a.* of this colour.

Sorr'ow (-ō) *n.* pain of mind, grief.—*v.i.* to grieve.—sorr'owful *a.*—sorr'owfully *adv.*

Sorr'y *a.* distressed; mean, poor.—sorr'ily *adv.*

Sort *n.* a kind of class.—*v.t.* to classify.—sort'er *n.*

Sort'ie (-ē) *n.* a sally by besieged forces.

Sot *n.* drunkard.—sott'ish *a.*

Sott'o *adv.* under.—sott'o vo'ce (vō-chā) under one's breath; in an aside.

Soul (sōl) *n.* the spiritual part of a human being; a person.—soul'ful *a.* expressing elevated feeling.—soul'less *a.* mean, prosaic.

Sound *n.* that which is heard.—*v.i.* to make a sound.—*v.t.* to cause to sound.—sounder *n.* telegraphic device, for transmission of messages by clicking sounds. — soundscreen, screen for reproduction of noises including talk, synchronised with showing of film.

Sound *a.* in good condition; solid; of good judgment.—sound'ly *adv.* thoroughly. *Syn.* healthy, perfect, strong, correct, well-founded, trustworthy. *Ant.* unsound, unhealthy, imperfect, fallacious.

Sound *n.* a channel or strait.

Sound *v.t.* to find the depth of—*v.i.* to find the depth of water.

Soup (sōōp) *n.* a liquid food made by boiling meat or vegetables.

Sour *a.* acid; peevish.—*v.t.* and *i.* to make or become sour.—sour'ly *adv.*—sour'ness *n.*

Source (sors) *n.* a spring; origin.

Souse *v.t.* to pickle; soak.—*v.i.* to soak; to fall into water, etc.—*n.* an act of sousing.

Soutane' (sōō-) *n.* a cassock; the outer garment worn by R.C. ecclesiastics.

South *n.* the cardinal point opposite the north; the region, or part of a country etc., lying to that side.—*a.* that is towards the south.—*adv.* towards the south.—south'erly (suTH-) *a.*—south'ern (suTH) *a.*—south'wards *a.* and *adv.*—south'wester, sou'wester *n.* a waterproof hat.—south'down *a.* of, or pert. to the Hampshire or Sussex Downs.—*n.* a sheep bred on the Hampshire or Sussex Downs.

Sou'venir (sōō'ven-ēr) *n.* keepsake.

Sov'ereign (sov'ran) *n.* a king; a gold coin = 20 shillings.—*a.* supreme; efficacious.—sov'ereignty *n.*

Soviet' *n.* council, *esp.* of soldiers and workmen, in Russia.

Sow *n.* female of the swine.

Sow (sō) *v.i.* to scatter seed.— *v.t.* to scatter or deposit (seed); to spread abroad.— **sow'er** *n.*

Soy *n.* a kind of sauce for fish or meat, prepared from a bean; the plant from which this sauce is obtained.

Spa (spä) *n.* a medicinal spring; a place with one.

Space *n.* extent; period; area; expanse; the expanse of the universe; an empty place.— *v.t.* to place at intervals.— **spa'cious** *a.* roomy.—**space charge**, in wireless, an electric field set up by the stream of electrons from the filament of a thermionic valve, and tending to impede the flow of electrons.

Spade *n.* a tool for digging.

Spade *n.pl.* one of the suits at cards.—*sing.* a card of this suit.

Spaghett'i *n.* a kind of macaroni.

Span *n.* the space from thumb to little finger as a measure; an extent or space; the stretch of an arch, etc.; a team of oxen.—*v.t.* to stretch over; to measure with the hand; to harness or yoke.— **spann'er** *n.* a tool for gripping the nut of a screw.

Span'gle (-ng-gl) *n.* a small piece of glittering metal as an ornament.

Span'iel *n.* a dog with long ears and hair.

Spank *v.i.* to move with vigour or spirit.—**spank'ing** *a.* brisk; fine, big.—**spank'er** *n.* a fast-going horse, ship, etc.

Spank *v.t.* to slap with the flat of the hand, *esp.* in chastising children.

Spar *n.* a pole, *esp.* as part of a ship's rigging.

Spar *n.* a crystalline mineral.

Spar *v.i.* to box; dispute, *esp.* in fun.

Spare (-èr) *a.* additional, in reserve; not in use.—*v.t.* to leave unhurt; abstain from using; do without, give away.

Spark *n.* a small glowing or burning particle; a trace; in internal-combustion engines, electric spark which ignites explosive mixture in cylinder. —*v.i.* to emit sparks.— **spar'kle** *v.i.* to glitter.— **sparkler** *n.*—**sparkless** *a.*— **sparklessly** *adv.*—**sparklet** *n.* a small spark.—**spark-arrester**, in electricity, a contrivance to prevent sparking where undesirable.—**spark-ing-plug**, in internal-combustion engines, plug screwed into cylinder head to carry electric current from outside to inside of cylinder.

Spark *n.* a gay, lively, showy man; a lover.—*v.i.* to play the spark; to court.

Sparr'ing *n.* boxing for exercise or amusement; also prelusive contention preparatory to close hitting—hence, a slight debate; contest in argument and repartee.

Sparr'ow (-ō) *n.* a small brownish bird, common in towns.

Sparse *a.* thinly scattered.

Spar'tan *a.* hardy; frugal.

Spasm (-zm) *n.* a convulsive muscular contraction.—**spas-**

mod'ic *a.* of the nature of a spasm; jerky; intermittent; disjointed.

Spat *n.* a short gaiter.

Spatch'cock *n.* a cock killed and cooked hastily on some sudden demand. — *v.t.* to thrust hastily into the middle of, as some additional matter in a written or telegraphed communication.

Spate *n.* a sudden flood in a river.

Spatt'er *v.t.* to splash, cast drops over.—*n.* a slight splash.—spatt'erdash *n.* a protection against splashes.

Spat'ula *n.* a broad blade, used for mixing paint, etc.

Spav'in *n.* a tumour on a horse's leg.

Spawn *n.* eggs of fish.—*v.i.* of fish, to cast eggs.

Spay *v.t.* to castrate a female by taking out the ovaries.

Speak *v.i.* to utter words; to converse; to deliver a discourse.—*v.t.* to utter; communicate with (a passing ship).—speak'able *a.*—speak'er *n.*

Spear *n.* a long pointed weapon, a pike.—*v.t.* to pierce with a spear.

Spe'cial (spesh'l) *a.* beyond the usual; particular, individual; distinct; limited.—spe'cially *adv.*—spe'cialist *n.* one who devotes himself to a special subject or branch of a subject.—spe'cialism *n.*—spe'cialise *v.i.* to be a specialist. —*v.t.* to make special.—special'ity *n.* a special product, characteristic, etc.—spe'cie (spē'shi) *n.* coined

money.—spe'cies *n.* a class; a subdivision; a sort or kind. —specif'ic *a.* characteristic of a thing or kind; definite; specially efficacious for something.—specif'ically *adv.*—spe'cify (-fī) *v.t.* to state definitely or in detail.—specifica'tion *n.* detailed description.—spe'cimen *n.* an individual example; a part used to typify a whole.—spe'cious (spē-) *a.* having a fair appearance; plausible.—spe'ciously *adv. Syn.* peculiar, exceptional, unique, specific. *Ant.* general, usual, common.

Speck *n.* a small spot, particle. —*v.t.* to spot.—spec'kle *n.* and *v.* speck.

Spec'tacle *n.* a show; a thing exhibited.—*pl.* an arrangement of lenses to help defective sight.—spectac'ular *a.* —specta'tor *n.* one who looks on.—spec'tre *n.* a ghost.—spec'trum *n.*—spec'tra *pl.* the coloured band into which a beam of light can be decomposed.—spec'troscope *n.* an instrument for decomposing light and examining spectra. —spec'ulate *v.i.* to make theories or guesses; to engage in risky commercial transactions.—spec'ulator *n.*—spec'ulative *a.*—specula'tion *n.*

Spec'ulum *n.* a mirror; a reflector of polished metal, *esp.* such as is used in reflecting-telescopes.—spec'ular *a.* having the qualities of a speculum; having a smooth, reflecting surface; affording a view.

Speech *n.* act or faculty of

speaking; words; language; conversation; a discourse.—
speech'ify *v.i.* to make a speech.—**speech'less** *a.*

Speed *n.* swiftness; rate of progress. — *v.i.* to move quickly; to succeed.—*v.t.* to further; expedite; bid farewell to.—**speedom'eter** *n.* an instrument to show the speed of a moving vehicle.—**speed'y** *a.*—**speed'ily** *adv.*—**speed'well** *n.* a plant with blue flowers.

Spell *n.* a magic formula; an enchantment.

Spell *n.* a turn of work, etc.; a bout.

Spell *v.t.* to read letter by letter; to give the letters of in order.

Spelt'er *n.* an alloy of zinc.

Spend *v.t.* to lay out; disburse; employ.—**spend'thrift** *n.* a wasteful person, a prodigal.—**spend'er** *n.* *Syn.* dispense, consume, squander, devote, bestow. *Ant.* save, hoard retain, reserve.

Spermace'ti *n.* a fatty substance obtained from the head of the sperm-whale and used for making candles, ointment, etc. — **sperm'-whale** *n.* the cachalot.

Spew *v.t.* to vomit.

Sphere *n.* a globe; range, province. — **spher'ical** *a.*—**sphe'roid** *n.* a body nearly a sphere in shape.

Sphinx *n.* a monster, half woman, half lion; a statue of this; an enigmatic person.

Spice *n.* an aromatic or pungent vegetable substance; spices collectively; a trace.—

v.t. to season with spices.—**spi'cy** *a.*—**spi'cily** *adv.*

Spick and span *a.* new and neat.

Spi'der *n.* an animal which spins a web to catch its prey.

Spig'ot *n.* a peg for a hole in a cask.

Spike *n.* an ear (of corn, etc.), a sharp-pointed piece of metal or wood, a nail.—*v.t.* to drive a spike into, supply with spikes, fasten with spikes.

Spike'nard *n.* an aromatic substance got from an Eastern plant; the plant.

Spill *n.* a splinter or twist of paper for use as a taper.

Spill *v.t.* to shed; pour out; throw off.—*v.i.* to flow over.—*n.* a fall.

Spin *v.t.* to twist into thread; to revolve rapidly.—*v.i.* to make thread; to revolve rapidly.—*n.* a rapid run or ride; a spinning.—**spin'dle** *n.* a rod or axis for spinning.—**spinn'er** *n.*—**spin'ster** *n.* an unmarried woman; a woman who spins.

Spin'ach (ij) *n.* a vegetable.

Spine *n.* a thorn; various things like this; a backbone.—**spi'nal** *a.*

Spin'et *n.* an instrument like a harpsichord.

Spinn'aker *n.* a large yacht sail spread by a boom.

Spinn'ey *n.* a small wood.

Spinn'ing *n.* the act or process of drawing out and twisting into threads, as wool, cotton, flax, etc.—**spinn'ing-jenn'y**, a machine for spinning wool or cotton.—**spinn'ing-wheel**, a machine for spinning wool, cotton, or flax into threads, in which a wheel drives a single spindle.

Spin'ster *see* SPIN.

Spire *n.* the pointed part of a steeple; a pointed stem.

Spire *n.* a coil.—**spi'ral** *n.* a continuous curve round a cylinder, like the thread of a screw.—*a.* of this form.—**spi'rally** *adv.*

Spir'it *n.* soul; a ghost; essential character or meaning; courage, liveliness; a frame of mind; a liquid got by distillation, *esp.* an alcoholic one.—*v.t.* to carry away mysteriously. — **spir'itual** *a.*—**spir'itually** *adv.*—**spir'itless** *a.*—**spir'ituality** *n.*—**spir'itualism, spir'itism** *n.* belief that the spirits of the dead can communicate with living people.—**spir'itualist, spir'itist** *n.*—**spir'ituous** *a.* alcoholic.

Spirt *v.t.* and *i.* to send or come out in a jet. — *n.* a jet.

Spit *n.* a sharp rod to put through meat for roasting; a sandy point projecting into the sea.—*v.t.* to thrust through.

Spit *v.i.* to eject saliva.—*v.t.* to eject from the mouth.—*n.* a spitting; saliva.—**spit'tle** *n.* saliva.—**spittoon'** *n.* a vessel to spit into.

Spite *n.* malice.—*v.t.* to thwart spitefully. — **spite'ful** *a.*—**spite'fully** *adv.*

Splash *v.t.* to spatter liquid over.—*v.i.* to dash, scatter (of liquids).—*n.* the sound or result of splashing.—**splash'board** *n.* a mudguard.—

splash lubrica'tion, internal-combustion engine, lubrication depending on splash of cranks rotating in oil.

Splay *v.t.* to spread out; make slanting.—*n.* slanting surface; spread.—*a.* slanting.

Spleen *n.* an organ in the abdomen; irritable or morose temper.—**splenet'ic** *a.*

Splen'did *a.* magnificent, gorgeous; excellent.—**splen'didly** *adv.*—**splen'dour** *n.* *Syn.* shining, bright, effulgent, glorious. *Ant.* dull, insignificant, inglorious.

Splice *v.t.* to join by interweaving strands; to join (wood) by overlapping.—*n.* a spliced joint.

Splint *n.* a rigid strip of material for holding a broken limb in position.—**splin'ter** *n.* split-off fragment, a chip.—*v.i.* to break into fragments.

Split *v.t.* and *i.* to break asunder.—*n.* a crack or fissure.

Splutt'er *v.t.* to utter incoherently with spitting sounds.—*v.i.* to emit such sounds.—*n.* such sounds or speech.

Spoil *v.t.* to damage or injure; to pillage; to damage the manners or behaviour of by indulgence.—*v.i.* to go bad.—*n.* booty.—**spolia'tion** *n.*

Spoke *n.* a radial bar of a wheel.—**spoke'shave** *n.* a tool for shaping wood.

Spokes'man *n.* one deputed to speak for others.

Sponge (-unj) *n.* a marine growth used to absorb

liquids.—*v.t.* to wipe with a sponge.—*v.i.* to live craftily at the expense of others.—spon'gy *a.*

Spon'sor *n.* one who answers for an infant at baptism; a surety.

Sponta'neous *a.* voluntary (said of persons); acting from its own energy, or by the law of its being; produced without external force (said of physical effects, as growth, combustion, etc.). — spon-ta'neously *adv.*—sponta'neousness *n.*—spontane'ity *n.* voluntariness. *Syn.* free, unconstrained, natural, automatic. *Ant.* involuntary, compulsory, artificial, mechanical.

Spook *n.* a ghost.

Spool *n.* a reel.

Spoon *n.* an implement with a shallow bowl at the end of a handle for carrying food to the mouth, etc.—*v.t.* to transfer with a spoon.

Spoon'erism *n.* an amusing transposition of initial consonants of a phrase such as, "half-warmed fish" for "half-formed wish."

Spoor *n.* the trail of wild animals; scent.—*v.i.* to follow a spoor.—spoorer, one that tracks game by the spoor.

Sporad'ic *a.* occurring at intervals or in small numbers.

Sporr'an *n.* a pouch worn in front of the kilt by Highlanders.

Sport *n.* pastime; merriment. *v.i.* to amuse oneself, take part in a game, etc.—sport'-ive *a.* playful. — sports'man *n.* one who hunts, shoots, etc.

Sports *a.* suitable for, designed for, or connected with outdoor occupations of a recreational, athletic, or informal nature, *e.g.* sports clothes.—sports mod'el, a fast open car.

Spot *n.* a small mark or stain; a place.—*v.t.* to mark with spots; detect.—spot'less *a.*—spot'lessly *adv.*

Spouse *n.* a husband or wife.

Spout *v.t.* and *i.* to pour out.—*n.* a projecting tube for pouring a liquid; a copious discharge.

Sprag *n.* a billet of wood used to lock the wheel of a vehicle; ratchet and pawl device to prevent vehicle running backwards on a hill.—*v.t.* to stop by a sprag.

Sprain *n.* and *v.t.* wrench or twist (of a muscle, etc.).

Sprat *n.* a small sea fish.

Sprawl *v.i.* to lie or toss about awkwardly.

Spray *n.* twigs; a graceful branch or twig.

Spray *n.* flung drops of water. —*v.t.* to sprinkle with spray.

Spread (-ed) *v.t.* to stretch out; scatter.—*v.i.* to become spread.—*n.* extent.—spread'er *n.* a bar to stretch.

Sprig *n.* a small twig; a small nail.

Spright'ly (-rīt-) *a.* lively, brisk. —spright'liness *n.*

Spring *v.i.* to leap; appear; crack.—*v.t.* to produce unexpectedly.—*n.* a flow of water from the earth; the first season of the year; a leap; recoil; a piece of coiled or bent metal with much resilience.—**spring'-tide** *n.* a high tide at new or full moon.—**springe** *n.* a snare.—**spring'y** (-g-) *a.* having elasticity.

Sprin'kle (-ng-kl) *v.t.* to scatter small drops on. — **sprink'ler** *n.*

Sprint *v.i.* to run a short distance at great speed.—*n.* such run or race.—**sprint'er** *n.*

Sprit *n.* a small spar crossing the sail of a boat, which it is used to extend and elevate.

Sprite *n.* a fairy.

Sprit'sail *n.* a sail extended by a sprit.

Sprock'et *n.* a projection on the periphery of a wheel or capstan for engaging a chain.

Sprout *v.i.* to put forth shoots, spring up.—*n.* a shoot.

Spruce *n.* a variety of fir.—*a.* neat in dress.

Sprue *n.* a projection from a casting, being the metal that has solidified in a passage, or sprue-hole, to the mould.

Spru'it (sprōō) *n.* a small stream, feeder of a large one; *esp.* one dry in the hot weather.

Spud *n.* a small spade-like implement for cutting roots of weeds, etc.; *slang*, a potato.

Spume *n.* and *v.i.* foam.

Spur *n.* a pricking instrument attached to a horseman's heel; a projection on the leg of a cock; a projecting mountain range; a stimulus.—*v.t.* to apply spurs to; urge.—*v.i.* to ride hard.

Spu'rious *a.* sham. *Syn.* illegitimate, false, fictitious,

counterfeit. *Ant.* genuine, true, authentic.

Spurn *v.t.* to reject with scorn.

Spurt *n.* a short sudden effort, *esp.* in a race.—*v.i.*

Sputt'er *v.t.* and *i.* and *n.* splutter.

Spu'tum *n.* spittle.

Spy *n.* one who enters hostile territory to observe and report.—*v.i.* to act as a spy.—*v.t.* to catch sight of.

Squab (-ob) *n.* an unfledged bird; a sofa cushion.

Squab'ble (-ob-) *n.* a petty noisy quarrel.—*v.i.* to engage in one.

Squad (-od) *n.* a small party, *esp.* of soldiers.—**squad'ron** *n.* a division of a cavalry regiment or of a fleet, or of an air force.

Squal'id (-ol-) *a.* mean, and dirty.—**squal'or** *n.*

Squall (-awl) *n.* a scream; a sudden gust of wind.—*v.i.* to scream.

Squan'der (-on-) *v.t.* to spend wastefully.

Squan'derma'nia *n.* passion for reckless spending, particularly of public money, without promise of profitable return.—**squan'dermaniac** *n.*

Square (-er) *n.* an equilateral rectangle; an area of this shape; the product of a number multiplied by itself; an instrument for drawing right angles.—*a.* square in form; honest.—*v.t.* to make square; to find the square of; to pay; bribe.—*v.i.* to fit, suit.—**square'ly** *adv.*

Squash (-osh) *v.t.* to crush flat or to pulp.—*n.* a crowd.

Squat (-ot) *v.i.* to sit on the heels.—*a.* short and thick.—**squatt'er** *n.* one who settles on land without title.

Squaw *n.* a Red Indian wife or woman.

Squeak *v.i.* to make a short shrill sound.—*n.* such sound.

Squeal *n.* a long squeak.—*v.i.* to make one.

Squeam'ish *a.* easily made sick; over-scrupulous.

Squee'gee (-je) *n.* a piece of gutta-percha or rubber, fixed to a handle, for cleaning windows, pavements, etc.; a rubber roller used in photography, printing, etc.—*v.i.* to use as a squeegee on.

Squeeze *v.t.* to press; subject to extortion.—*n.* an act of squeezing.

Squib *n.* a small firework; a short satire.

Squid *n.* a cuttle-fish.

Squint *v.i.* to have the eyes turned in different directions. —*n.* this affection of the eyes; a glance.

Squire *n.* a country gentleman; a lady's escort.—*v.t.* to escort (a lady).

Squirm *v.i.* and *n.* wriggle.

Squirr'el *n.* a small graceful animal living in trees and having a large bushy tail.

Squirt *v.t.* and *i.* to eject, be ejected, in a jet.—*n.* an instrument for squirting.

Stab *v.t.* to pierce with a pointed weapon.—*v.i.* to strike with such weapon.—*n.* a blow or wound so inflicted.

Stab'ilise *v.t.* to make steady, restore to equilibrium, *esp.* of money values, prices and wages.—**stabilisation** *n.*

Sta'ble *n.* a building for horses.—*v.t.* to put into one.

Sta'ble *a.* firmly fixed; resolute.—**sta'bly** *adv.*—**stabil'ity** *n.* *Syn.* firm, enduring, steady, durable. *Ant.* unstable, shaky, vacillating, transitory.

Stack *n.* a pile or heap, *esp.* of hay or straw; a tall chimney. —*v.t.* to pile in a stack.

Staff *n.* staffs, staves *pl.* a pole; a body of officers or workers; the five lines on which music is written.

Stag *n.* a male deer.

Stage *n.* a raised floor or platform; the platform of a theatre; dramatic art or literature, scene of action; point of development; a stopping-place on a road, the distance between two of them. —*v.t.* to put (a play) on the stage.—**sta'gy** *a.* theatrical.

Stagg'er *v.i.* to walk or stand unsteadily.—*v.t.* to shock.— *n.* an act of staggering.

Stag'nate *v.i.* to cease to flow, be motionless.—**stag'nant** *a.* —**stagna'tion** *n.*

Staid *a.* of sober and quiet character. — **staid'ness** *n.*— **staid'ly** *adv.*

Stain *v.t.* and *i.* to discolour, soil.—*n.* a spot or mark.— **stain'less** *a.*

Stair *n.* a set of steps, *esp.* as part of a house.—**stair'case** *n.*

Stake *n.* a sharpened stick or post; money wagered or contended for.—*v.t.* to secure or mark out with stakes; to wager.

Stal'actite *n.* a deposit of lime

---

like an icicle on the roof of a cave.—**stal'agmite** n. a similar deposit on the floor.

Stale a. old, lacking freshness. —n. urine of horses.—v.i. of horses, to make water.— **stale'mate** n. in chess, a draw through one player being unable to move. *Syn.* insipid, musty, commonplace, hackneyed. *Ant* sparkling, fresh, new, unusual.

Stalk (-awk) n. a plant's stem.

Stalk (-awk) v.i to steal up to game; to walk in a stiff and stately manner.—v.t. to steal up to (game, etc.).—n. a stalking.

Stall (-awl) n. a compartment in a stable; an erection for the display and sale of goods; a seat in the chancel of a church; a front seat in a theatre, etc.—v.t. to put in a stall.— v.i. to stick fast; of an aeroplane, to lose flying speed.—**stalling speed**, that speed of an aeroplane below which steady flight becomes impossible.

Stall n. an ambush; a stale; a stalking-horse; pretext; a thief's assistant.

Stall'ion n. a horse not castrated, so called because kept in a stall and not allowed to work.

Stal'loy n. a silicon steel; used in wireless for cores of low-frequency transformers.

Stal'wart a. strong, sturdy, brave.—n. a stalwart person.

Sta'men n. the male organ of a flowering plant.—**stam'ina** n. power of endurance.

Stamm'er v.i. to speak with

repetitions of syllables.—v.t. to utter thus.—n. the habit of so speaking.—**stamm'erer** n.

Stamp v.i. to put down a foot with force.—v.t to impress a mark on; to affix a postage stamp.—n. a stamping with the foot; an imprinted mark; an appliance for marking; a piece of gummed paper printed with a device as evidence of postage, etc.; character.—**stampede'** n. a sudden frightened rush, *esp.* of a herd of cattle, a crowd, etc.—v.t. and i. to put into, take part in, a stampede.

Stance n. a site; an area for building; a stand or stall in a market; position of the feet in certain games.

Stanch see STAUNCH.

Stanch'ion (-un) n. a post or prop.

Stand v.i. to have an upright position; to be situated; to become or remain firm or stationary; to be a symbol of, etc.—v.t. to set upright; to endure—n. a stoppage; a holding firm; something on which a thing may be placed; a structure for spectators to stand on for better view.

Stand'ard n. a flag; a weight or measure to which others must conform; degree, quality; a post.—**stan'dardise** v.t. to regulate by a standard.

Stan'za n. a group of lines of verse.

Sta'ple n. a U-shaped piece of metal with pointed ends to drive into wood for use as a ring; a main commodity;

the thread or pile of wool, cotton or flax.—*a.* pertaining to commodities; regularly produced or made for market. —*v.t.* to sort or classify according to the length of fibre.—**stapler** *n.* a dealer in staple commodities.

Star *n.* a shining celestial body, seen as a twinkling point of light; an asterisk (*) a celebrated player; a medal or jewel, etc., of the apparent shape of a star (*).—*v.t.* to adorn with stars; to mark with an asterisk.

Star'board *n.* the right-hand side of a ship, looking forward.—*a.* of, or on, this side. —*v.t.* to put (the helm) to starboard.

Starch *n.* a substance forming the main food element in bread, potatoes, etc., and used, mixed with water, for stiffening linen, etc.—*v.t.* to stiffen with it.—**stark** *a.* stiff; downright.—*adv.* quite (e.g. in *stark-mad*).

Stare *v.t.* to look fixedly at; to be prominent or obvious — *v.t.* to abash by staring at.— *n.* a staring.

Stark-na'ked *a.* quite naked.

Star'ling *n.* a speckled bird.

Start *v.i.* to make a sudden movement; to begin, *esp.* a journey.—*v.t.* to begin; set going.—*n.* an abrupt movement; an advantage of less distance to run in a race.

Star'tle *v.t.* to give a fright to.

Starve *v.i.* to suffer from cold or hunger; to die of hunger. —*v.t.* to kill or distress with lack of food, warmth, or other necessary thing.— **starve'ling** *n.* a starving person.—**starva'tion** *n.*

State *n.* condition; a politically organised people; rank; pomp.—*v.t.* to express in words; fix.—**state'ly** *a.* dignified.—**state'ment** *n.* an expression in words; an account.—**states'man** *n.* one who is able in managing the affairs of a state. — **states'manship** *n.* his art. — **state'room** *n.* a separate cabin on ship. *Syn.* of "stately, lofty, formal, ceremonious. *Ant.* undignified, informal, unceremonious.

Stat'ic, stat'ical *a.* pert. to bodies at rest, or in equilibrium. — **statically** *adv.*— **static characteristic**, in wireless, graph showing relation between steady voltage and current of a thermionic valve.

Stat'ic *a.* dealing with forces in equilibrium.—*n.* in *pl.* the branch of physics studying such forces.

Station *n.* a place where a thing stops or is placed; position in life; a stopping place for railway trains.—*v.t.* to put in a position.—**sta'tionary** *a.* not moving or not intended to be moved.

Sta'tioner *n.* one who deals in writing materials, etc.—**sta'tionery** *n.* his wares.

Statist'ics *n.pl.* numerical facts collected systematically and arranged; the study of them. —**statisti'cian, stat'ist** *n.* one who deals with statistics.— **statist'ic** *a.*—**statist'ically** *adv.*

---

there, father, her; awl, oil, owl.

Stat'ue n. a solid carved or cast image of a person, etc.—stat'uary n. statues collectively.—statuesque' a. like a statue.—statuette' n. a small statue.

Stat'ure n. height (of a person).

Sta'tus n. position, rank, "standing"; position of affairs.

Stat'ute n. a written law.—stat'utory a.

Staunch, stanch v.t. to stop a flow (of blood) from.—a. trustworthy loyal.

Stave n. one of the pieces forming a cask; a verse or stanza. — v.t. to break a hole in; to ward (off).

Stay v.t. to stop.—v.i. to remain; sojourn; pause.—n. a remaining or sojourning.

Stay n. a support, prop; a rope supporting a mast, etc. —pl. corsets.—v.t. to prop or support.

Stead (-ed) n. in stead, in place; in good stead, of service.—stead'y a. firm; regular; temperate.—stead'ily adv.—stead'fast a. firm, unyielding.—stead'fastly adv. —stead'iness n. Syn. of "steadfast," fixed, established, resolute. Ant. unsteady, vacillating, irresolute.

Steak (stāk) n. a slice of meat for broiling.

Steal v.i. to rob; to move silently.—v.t. to take without right or leave.—stealth (stelth) n. secrecy, slinking way.—stealth'y a.—stealth'ily adv.

Steam n. vapour of boiling water.—v.t. to cook or treat with steam.—v.i. to give off steam; to rise in vapour; to move by steam power.—steam'er n. a vessel for cooking or treating with steam; a steam-propelled ship.

Steed n. a horse.

Steel n. a hard and malleable metal made by mixing carbon in iron; a tool or weapon of steel.—v.t. to harden.

Steel'yard n. balance with unequal arms.

Steep a. having an abrupt or decided slope.—n. a steep place.—steep'ly adv.—stee'ple n. a church tower with a spire.—stee'plechase n. cross-country horse-race.

Steep v.t. to soak.

Steer v.t. to guide, direct the course of.—v.i. to direct one's course.—steer'age n. the effect of a helm; the part of a ship allotted to the passengers paying lowest fare.—steers'man n. one who steers a ship.—steering column, in motoring, hollow column carrying steering-wheel at top.—steering connecting-rod, in motor, rod connecting lever arms on road-wheels with lever.—steering-lock, maximum angular amount wheels can swivel from side to side.—steering stagger, violent wobbling of steering road-wheels of vehicle.

Steer n. a young male ox.

Stell'ar a. of stars.

Stem n. a stalk or trunk; the part of a word to which inflectional endings are added; the foremost part of a ship.

Māte, mēte, mīte, mōte, mūte, bōōt.

Stem *v.t.* to check.

Stench *n.* an evil smell.

Sten'cil *v.t.* to paint with figures, etc., by passing a brush over a pierced plate. —*n.* the plate; the pattern made.

Stenog'raphy *n.* shorthand writing.—**stenog'rapher** *n.*— **stenograph'ic** *a.*

Stentor'ian *a.* very loud.

Step *v.i.* to move and set down a foot.—*v.t.* to measure in paces; to set up (a mast).— *n.* an act of stepping; the mark made by the foot; a measure, an act, a stage in a proceeding; a board, rung, etc., to put the foot on; a degree in a scale; a mast socket. — **step-down trans-for'mer**, electricity, a transformer having secondary voltage lower than primary voltage, and secondary current higher than primary.— **step-up transfor'mer**, transformer having secondary voltage higher than primary, and secondary current lower than primary.

Step'child *n.* the child of a husband or wife by a former marriage.—so **step'father** *n.* —**step'mother** *n.* — **step'-brother** *n.*—**step'sister** *n.*

Steppe *n.* an extensive treeless plain in European and Asiatic Russia.

Ster'eoscope *n.* an instrument in which two pictures taken at different view-points are combined into one image with an effect of solidity.— **stereoscop'ic** *a.*—**ster'eotype** *n.* a plate for printing cast from set-up type.—*v.t.* to make a stereotype from; to make into an empty formula.

Ster'ile *a.* barren; free from disease germs.

Sterilisa'tion *n.* the act of making sterile; the process of freeing from living germs; rendering mental defectives, or persons having hereditable disease, incapable of procreating children.—**ster-ilise** *v.t.* to render sterile; to free from living germs.— **steriliser** *n.*

Ster'ling *a.* of standard value or purity; of solid worth; in English coin.

Stern *a.* severe, strict.— **stern'ly** *adv.*—**stern'ness** *n. Syn.* harsh, unrelenting, hard, afflictive, cruel, immovable, dark, gloomy, threatening. *Ant.* lax, gentle, mild, yielding, irresolute.

Stern *n.* the after part of a ship.

Ster'ol *n.* a solid alcohol, such as ergosterol.

Ster'torous *a.* characterised by a deep snoring; hoarsely breathing.—**stertorously** *adv.* —**stertorousness** *n.*

Stet "let it stand" (a proof-reader's direction to cancel an alteration previously made).

Steth'oscope *n.* an instrument for listening to the action of the heart or lungs.

Ste'vedore *n.* one who loads or unloads ships.

Stew *v.t.* and *i.* to cook slowly in a closed vessel.—*n.* food so cooked.

Stew'ard *n.* one who manages

another's property; an attendant on a ship's passengers; an official managing a race-meeting, an assembly, etc.—stew'ardess *fem*.

Stick *v.t.* to jab, stab, fix, fasten.—*v.i.* to adhere, project, come to a stop, etc.—*n*. a rod. — stick'y *a*. adhesive, viscous.

Stic'kleback (-klb-) *n*. a small fish with spines on its back.

Stick'ler *n*. one who insists on trifles of procedure, authority, etc.

Stiff *a*. rigid; awkward.—stiff'ly *adv*.—stiff'en *v.t.* and *i*.—stiff'ness *n*. *Syn*. inflexible, formal, constrained. *Ant*. pliant, flexible, informal, unconstrained.

Sti'fle *v.t.* to smother.

Stig'ma *n*. a brand, a mark.—stig'matise *v.t.* to mark out, describe (as something bad).

Stile *n*. an arrangement of steps for climbing a fence.

Stile *n*. a pin set on the face of a dial to form a shadow; a style.—stilar *a*. pertaining to a stile. Also STYLE.

Stilett'o *n*. a small dagger.

Still *a*. motionless, noiseless.—*v.t.* to quiet.—*adv*. to this time; yet; even.—still'ness *n*.—still'y *a*. quiet.—still'-born *a*. born dead.—still life *n*. painting of inanimate objects.

Still *n*. an apparatus for distilling. — still'-room *n*. a housekeeper's store-room.

Still *n*. in the cinema, a photograph taken by an ordinary camera during the production of a film; an enlargement of one unit of a film.

Stilt *n*. one of a pair of poles with footrests for walking raised from the ground.—stilt'ed *a*. stiff in manner, pompous.

Stil'ton *n*. a fine cheese, originally made at *Stilton*, in Huntingdonshire.

Stim'ulus *n*. something that rouses to activity.—stim'ulate *v.t.* to rouse up, spur.—stim'ulant *a*. producing a temporary increase of energy.—*n*. a drug, etc., doing this.—stim'ulative *a*. — stimula'tion *n*.

Sting *v.t.* to thrust a sting into; to cause sharp pain to.—*v.i.* to be affected with sharp pain.—*n*. a pointed weapon, often poisoned, of certain insects and animals; the thrust, wound, or pain of one.

Stin'gy (-ji) *a*. meanly; avaricious; niggardly.—stingily *adv*.—stinginess *n*.

Stink *v.i.* to give out a strongly offensive smell.—*n*. such smell.

Stint *v.t.* to keep on short allowance.—*n*. limitation of supply or effort.

Sti'pend *n*. salary.—stipend'iary *a*. receiving a stipend.—*n*. a stipendiary magistrate

Stip'ple *v.t.* to engrave in dots.—*n*. this process.

Stip'ulate *v.i.* to insist on, mention in making a bargain.—stipula'tion *n*.

Stir *v.t.* to set or keep in motion.—*v.i.* to begin to move; to be out of bed.—*n*. commotion.

Stirr'up n. a metal loop hung from a strap for supporting the foot of a rider on a horse. —**stirr'up-cup** n. a drink given to a departing rider.

Stitch n. a movement of the needle in sewing; its result in the work; a sharp pain in the side.—v.t. and i. to sew.

Sti'ver n. a Dutch coin and money of account, of the value of about a halfpenny.

Stoat n. the ermine.

Stock n. a stump or post; a stem; a handle or piece to hold by; lineage; animals, materials, etc., requisite for farming, trade; a supply; the liquor used as a foundation of soup; various sweet-smelling flowers; money invested in a concern.—pl. a frame of timber supporting a ship while building; a frame with holes to confine the feet of offenders.—v.t. to supply with, or keep, a stock. —**stock'broker** n. an agent for buying and selling shares in companies.—**stock'-jobber** n. a dealer in stocks and shares.—**stock'-still'** a. motionless.

Stockade' n. an enclosure of stakes.

Stock'ing n. a close-fitting covering for the leg and foot.

Stod'gy a. heavy, dull, indigestible.—**stodge** n. heavy food.

Sto'ic n. a philosopher holding virtue to be the highest good and teaching indifference to pleasure and pain; a person of great self-control.

—**sto'ic, sto'ical** a.—**sto'ically** adv.—**sto'icism** n.

Sto'ker n. one who tends a fire.—**stoke** v.t. and i. to tend (a fire).

Stole n. a long, loose garment, reaching to the feet; a narrow band of silk or stuff, worn by deacons, and by bishops, and priests.—**stoled** a.

Stol'id a. hard to excite.—**stol'idly** adv.—**stolid'ity** n. Syn. heavy, obtuse, slow, insensible. Ant. acute, active, susceptible.

Stom'ach (-umak) n. the bag forming the chief digestive organ; appetite; inclination. —v.t. to put up with.—**stomach'ic** a.

Stone n. a piece of rock; a gem; the hard seed of a fruit; a weight = 14 lbs.— v.t. to throw stones at; to free (fruit) from stones.— **stone'-blind'** a. quite blind. —**stone'-deaf'** a. — **stone'ware** n. heavy common pottery.—**sto'ny** a.—**sto'nily** adv.

Stook n. a collection of sheaves, usually twelve, set up in the field.—v.t. to set-up, as sheaves of grain, in stooks.

Stool n. a chair with no back; a place for evacuating the bowels; what is evacuated.

Stoop v.i. to lean forward or down.—n. a stooping carriage of the body.

Stop v.t. to fill up; to check, bring to a halt.—v.i. to cease, stay.—n. a stopping or being stopped; a punctuation mark; a set of organ pipes; the lever for putting it in

action.—**stopp'age** n.—**stopp'-
er** n. a plug for closing a
bottle.—**stop-light,** red light
at rear of motor-car automatically switched on by
application of brakes.—**stop-
press news,** news put into
newspaper at latest possible
moment.

Store n. abundance; stock; a
place for keeping goods.—pl.
stocks of goods, provisions,
etc.—v.t. to stock, furnish,
keep.—**stor'age** n.—**stor'age
battery,** an accumulator.

Stor'ey n. a horizontal division
of a house.

Stork n. a wading bird.

Storm n. a violent wind or
disturbance of the atmo-
sphere; an assault on a fortress.—v.t. to take by storm.
—v.i. to rage.—**storm'y** a.

Stor'y n. a tale; an account; a
storey.—**stor'ied** a. celebrated
in tales.

Stout a. sturdy; fat.—n. a
kind of beer.—**stout'ly** adv.
—**stout'ness** n.

Stove n. an apparatus for
cooking, warming a room,
etc.

Sto'ver n. fodder for cattle.

Stow v.t. to pack away.—
Stow'age n. — **stow'away** n.
one who hides himself on a
ship to obtain passage.

Strad'dle v.i. to spread the
legs wide.—v.t. to bestride
something in this way.

Straffe v.t. punish; shell,
bomb, attack.—n. bombard-
ment, attack.

Strag'gle v.i. to stray, get dispersed.—**strag'gler** n.

Straight (strāt) a. without
bend; honest; level; in
order.—n. straight state or
part.—adv. direct.—**straight'-
en** v.t. and i. — **straightfor'-
ward** a. open, frank, simple.
—**straightfor'wardly** adv. —
straight'way adv. at once.

Strain v.t. to stretch tightly;
stretch to the full or to excess; filter.—v.i. to make
great effort.—n. stretching
force; violent effort; injury
from being strained; a burst
of music or poetry; tone of
speaking or writing.—**strain'-
er** n. a filter.

Strain n. a breed or race.

Strait a. narrow, strict.—n. a
channel of water connecting
two larger areas.—pl. a position of difficulty or distress.—
strait'laced a. puritanical.—
strait'-waistcoat n. a jacket
to confine the arms of mani-
acs, etc.

Strake n. a continuous range
of planks on the bottom or
sides of a vessel, reaching
from the stem to the stern.

Strand n. shore.—v.t. and i. to
run aground.

Strand n. one of the strings or
wires making up a rope.

Strange (-ānj) a. unaccus-
tomed, singular.—**strange'ly**
adv. — **strange'ness** n.—
stra'nger n. an unknown
person; a foreigner; one un-
accustomed (to). Syn. un-
usual, peculiar, foreign, alien.
Ant. usual, familiar, customary, native.

Stran'gle (-ng-gl) v.t. to kill by
squeezing the windpipe.—
strangula'tion n.

Strap n. a strip of leather or

metal.—*v.t.* to fasten with a strap; to beat with one.—**strapp'ing** *a.* tall and well-made.

Strat'agem *n.* an artifice in war; a trick, device.—**strat'egy** *n.* the art of handling troops, ships, etc., to the best advantage.—**strat'egist** *n.*—**strate'gic** *a.*

Stra'tosphere *n.* upper part of the atmosphere, in which temperature does not decrease with height.

Stra'tum (strā-) *n.* a layer.—**stra'tify** *v.t.* to arrange thus.—**stratifica'tion** *n.*

Straw *n.* dry cut stalks of corn.—**straw'berry** *n.* a creeping plant producing a red fruit; the fruit.

Straw'board *n.* cardboard made of straw.

Stray *v.i.* to wander, get lost.—*a* strayed; occasional.—*n.* a stray animal.

Strays *n. pl.* in wireless, atmospherics.

Streak *n.* a long line or band.—*v.t.* to mark with streaks.—**streak'y** *a.*

Stream *n.* a flowing body of water, or other liquid.—*v.i.* to flow; to run with liquid; to float or wave in the air.—**stream'er** *n.* a ribbon to stream in the air.—**stream'let** *n.* a small stream.

Stream'line *n.* that shape of a body (e.g. motor-car, aeroplane) calculated to present the smallest amount of resistance to the air when passing through it.—*v.t.* to design a body streamline.—**streamlined** *a.* built, shaped so as to present least resistance to the air.—**stream'lining.** *n.*

Street *n.* a road in a town or village with houses at the side.

Strength *n.* power.—**strength'en** *v.t.* and *i.*

Stren'uous *a.* energetic, earnest.—**stren'uously** *adv.*

Stress *n.* strain; impelling force; effort; emphasis.—*v.t.* to emphasise; to put mechanical stress on.

Stretch *v.t.* to tighten, pull out; to reach out; to exert to the utmost.—*v.i.* to reach; to have elasticity. — *n.* a stretching or being stretched; an expanse; a spell.—**stretch'er** *n.* a person or thing that stretches; a bar in a boat for a rower's feet; an appliance on which a disabled person can be carried.

Strew (-rōō) *v.t.* to scatter over a surface.

Stri'a *n.*; *pl.* **stri'æ**, a small channel or threadlike line in the surface of a shell or other object.—**stri'ate** *a.* streaked.—**striate'** *v.t.* to mark with streaks.—**stria'tion** *n.*

Strict *a.* defined; without exception; stern, not lax or indulgent.—**strict'ly** *adv.*—**strict'ness** *n.*—**stric'ture** *n.* a critical remark; a morbid contraction.

Stride *v.i.* to walk with long steps.—*v.t.* to pass over with one step.—*n.* a step, or its length.

Stri'dent *a.* harsh in tone.

Strife *n.* conflict.

Strike v.t. to hit.—v.i. to hit; to cease work in order to enforce a demand.—n. such stoppage of work.—stri'ker n. one that, or that which, strikes; in motoring (i) selector arm, (ii) rocking lever actuating valve from cam, (iii) in low-tension magnets ignition arm of rocking lever which breaks control inside cylinder.—stri'king a. noteworthy.

String n. fine cord; a row or series.—v.t. to tie with or thread on string.—string'y a. fibrous.

Strin'gent a. strict.—strin'-gency n.—strin'gently adv.

Strip v.t. to lay bare, take the covering off.—v.i. to take off one's clothes.—n. a long narrow piece.—strip'ling n. a youth. Syn. uncover, divest, plunder, undress. Ant. cover, dress, to put on.

Stripe n. a narrow mark or band; a blow with a scourge.

Strive v.i. to try hard, struggle.

Stroke n. a blow; an attack of paralysis; a mark of a pen; a completed movement in a series; the rower sitting nearest the stern; an act of stroking.—v.t. to set the time in rowing; to pass the hand lightly over.

Stroll (-ō-) v.i. to walk in a leisurely or idle manner.—n. a leisurely walk.

Strong a. powerful.—strong'-hold n. a fortress.—strong'ly adv.

Stron'tium n. a metallic element.—stron'tia n. oxide of strontium.

Strop n. a piece of leather for sharpening a razor.—v.t. to sharpen on one.

Structure n. make, construction.—n. a building, something made of various pieces.—struc'tural a. — struc'turally adv.

Strug'gle v.i. to contend, fight; proceed or work with difficulty and effort.—n. a contest, effort.

Strum v.i. to strike the notes of a stringed instrument unskilfully.—n. a careless performance on a stringed instrument.

Strut v.i. to walk affectedly or pompously.—n. such gait; a brace; in aviation, a member in compression to hold, or steady, two constructional parts relatively to each other; more generally, any short spar on an aeroplane.

Strut n. a rigid support, usually set obliquely.—v.t. to stay with struts.

Strych'nine (-ik'nēn) n. a poison got from nux vomica seeds.

Stub n. the stump of a tree; a remnant of anything;—v.t. to strike, as the toes against a fixed object.—stub-axle, in motoring, a short swivelling axle on which the steering road wheels run. [grain.

Stub'ble n. stumps of cut

Stubb'orn a. unyielding, obstinate.—stubb'ornly adv.—stubb ornness n. Syn. refractory, unbending, intractable, obdurate. Ant. yielding, manageable, docile, tractable.

Stucc'o n. plaster.

Stud n. a movable double-button; a nail with large head sticking out; a boss.—v.t. to set with studs.

Stud n. a set of horses kept for breeding.—stud'-farm n.

Stud'y n. effort to acquire knowledge; a subject of this; a room to study in; a sketch.—v.t. to make a study of; to try constantly to do.—v.i. to be engaged in learning.—stu'dent n. one who studies.—stu'dio n. the workroom of an artist, etc.—stu'dious a.—stu'diously adv.

Stuff n. material, fabric.—v.t. to stop or fill up.—v.i. to eat greedily.—stuff'y a. lacking fresh air.

Stult'ify v.t. to make look ridiculous, make of no effect.—stultifica'tion n.

Stum'ble v.i. to trip and nearly fall. — n. a stumbling.—stum'bling-block n. an obstacle.

Stump n. the remnant of a tree, etc., when the main part has been cut away; one of the uprights of the wicket at cricket.—v.i. to walk noisily.—v.t. to tour making speeches; to break the wicket of (a batsman out of his ground in playing the ball).—stump'y a.—stump'-orator n. a travelling speaker (as using tree stumps for platforms).

Stun v.t. to knock senseless.

Stunt n. (U.S. slang) a spectacular effort or feat.

Stunt v.t. to check the growth of.

Stu'pefy v.t. to make stupid, deprive of full consciousness. — stupefac'tion n.—stupen'dous c. amazing.—stu'pid a. slow-witted, dull.—stupid'ity n.—stu'pidly adv.—stu'por n. dazed state.

Stur'dy a. robust, strongly built.—stur'dily adv.—stur'diness n.

Stur'geon n. a large fish valued as food.

Stutt'er v.i. and t. to speak with difficulty, esp. with repetition of initial consonants; to stammer.—n. an act or habit of stuttering.

Sty n. a place to keep pigs in.

Sty, stye n. an inflammation on the eyelid.

Style n. manner of writing, doing, etc.; designation; sort; superior manner or quality; a pointed instrument for writing on waxed tablets.—v.t. to designate.—sty'lish a. fashionable.—sty'lishly adv.—sty'list n. one cultivating style in literary or other execution.

Sty'mie n. in golf-playing, a position in which a player has to putt for the hole with his opponent's ball directly in the line of approach, the balls being more than six inches apart.

Styp'tic a. stopping bleeding.

Suave a. smoothly polite.—sua'vity n. Syn. affable, gentle, mild, soft. Ant. rude surly, rough, haughty.

Sub- prefix meaning under, in lower position, etc. Often used separated as abbreviation for the whole compound,

---

e.g. "sub"=a subscription.

Subac'id *a.* moderately acid.

Suba'gent *n.* a deputy-agent.

Sub'altern *a.* of inferior rank. —*n.* an officer below the rank of captain.

Sub'committ'ee *n.* a section of a committee functioning separately.

Subcon'scious *a.* partially or feebly conscious.—*n.* in psycho-analysis, the unapprehended; that part of the human mind which is absolutely unknown to the possessor.

Subdivide' *v.t.* to divide again. —**subdivis'ion** *n.*

Subdue' *v.t.* overcome.

Subhu'man *a.* under, or beneath, the human.

Sub'inspector *n.* an under or assistant inspector; a school inspector of the third class.

Sub'ject *a.* liable to, owning allegiance; — **subject to**, conditional upon.—*n.* one owing allegiance; that about which something is predicated; conscious self; topic, theme.— **subject'** *v.t.* to make liable, or cause to undergo. —**subjec'tion** *n.*—**subject'ive** *a.* relating to the self; displaying an artist's individuality.—**subjectiv'ity** *n.*

Subjoin' *v.t.* to add at the end.

Sub'jugate *v.t.* conquer.—**subjuga'tion** *n.*

Subjunc'tive *n.* a mood used mainly in subordinate clauses. —*a.* in or of that mood.

Sublet' *v.t.* of a tenant, to let the whole or part of what he has rented to another.

Sublime *a.* inspiring awe.—

sub'limate *v.t.* to purify; to heat into vapour and allow to solidify again.—*n.* a sublimated substance. — **sublima'tion** *n.*—**sublime'ly** *adv.* —**sublim'ity** *n.* *Syn.* lofty, stately, dignified, glorious, grand. *Ant.* lowly, abject, ignominious.

Sublu'nary (-ōō-) *a.* earthly.

Sub'marine *a.* below the surface of the sea.—*n.* a vessel that can be submerged.

Submerge' *v.t.* to place under water.—*v.i.* to go under.— **submer'sion** *n.*

Sub-microscop'ic *a.* beyond the range of, i.e. too small to be seen through, a high-power microscope, e.g. filter-passing viruses; the atom.

Submit' *v.t.* to put forward for consideration; surrender.— *v.i.* surrender; urge. — **submiss'ive** *a.*—**submis'sion** *n.*

Submul'tiple *n.* number that divides another without a remainder; an aliquot part.

Subord'inate *a.* of lower rank or importance.—*n.* one under the orders of another.—*v.t.* to make or treat as subordinate.—**subord'inately** *adv.* —**subordina'tion** *n.*

Suborn' *v.t.* to bribe to do evil.—**suborna'tion** *n.*

Subox'ide *n.* an oxide containing one equivalent of oxygen and two of another element.

Subpoen'a (-pēn'a) *n.* a writ requiring attendance at a court of law.—*v.t.* to summon by one.

Subrep'tion *n.* the act of obtaining a favour by surprise or unfair representation, as by concealing the trúth.

Subroga'tion *n.* the substitution or succession of one person in place of another, with succession to his rights; succession of any kind.

Subscribe' *v.t.* to write one's name at the end of a document; to pay or promise to pay (a contribution).—**subscri'ber** *n.*—**subscrip'tion** *n.*

Subsec'tion *n.* a division of a section.

Sub'sequent *a.* later.—**sub'sequence** *n.*—**sub'sequently** *adv.*

Subserve' *v.t.* to be useful to.—**subserv'ient** *a.* servile.—**subserv'iently** *adv.*—**subserv'ience** *n.*

Subside' *v.i.* to sink, settle; come to an end.—**Sub'sidence** *n.*—**sub'sidy** *n.* money granted.—**sub'sidise** *v.t.* to pay a grant to.—**subsid'iary** *a.* supplementing.

Subsist' *v.i.* to exist.—**subsist'ence** *n.*

Sub'soil *n.* the soil beneath the surface soil.

Sub'stance *n.* matter; a particular kind of matter; chief part, essence; wealth.—**substan'tial** *a.* solid, big, important.—**substan'tially** *adv.*—**substantial'ity** *n.* — **substan'tiate** *v.t.* to bring evidence for.—**substantia'tion** *n.*—**sub'stantive** *a.* having independent existence.—*n.* a noun.

Substa'tion *n.* a subordinate station.

Sub'stitute *n.* a thing or person put in place of another.

—*v.t.* to put in exchange for.—**substitu'tion** *n.*

Substra'tum *n.* ; *pl.* **substra'ta**, that which is laid or spread under; a layer of earth lying under another; the subsoil; in metaphysics, the ultimate matter or substance forming the subject of perception, cognition and cause of phenomena.

Subtend' *v.t.* to be opposite to.

Sub'terfuge *n.* an evasion, lying excuse.

Subterra'nean *a.* underground.

Subtle (sut'l) *a.* ingenious, clever; acute; crafty; tenuous.—**subt'ly** *adv.*—**subt'lety** *n.*

Subtract' *v.t.* to take away.—**subtrac'tion** *n.*

Sub'urb *n.* an outlying part of a city.—**suburb'an** *a.*

Subven'tion *n.* a subsidy.

Subvert' *v.t.* to overthrow.—**subver'sive** *a.*—**subver'sion** *n.*

Sub'way *n.* an underground passage.

Succeed' (-ks-) *v.t.* to follow, take the place of.—*v.i.* to follow; to accomplish a purpose.—**success'** *n.* accomplishment, attainment; issue, outcome.—**success'ful** *a.*—**success'fully** *adv.*—**succes'sion** *n.* a following; a series; a succeeding.—**success'ive** *a.*—**success'ively** *adv.* — **success'or** *n.*

Succinct' (-ks-) *a.* terse.—**succinct'ly** *adv.*—**succinct'ness** *n.* *Syn.* brief, short, compendious. *Ant.* rambling, loose, discursive.

Succ'our *v.t.* and *n.* help.

Succ'ulent *a.* juicy.—**suco'ulence** *n.*

Succumb' (-kum) *v.i.* to yield; to die.

Such *a.* of the kind or degree mentioned; so made, etc.; of the same kind.

Suck *v.t.* to draw into the mouth; to roll in the mouth. *n.* a sucking.—**suck'er** *n.* a person or thing that sucks; an organ or appliance which adheres by suction. —**suc'kle** *v.t.* to feed from the breast. —**suck'ling** *n.* an unweaned child.—**suc'tion** *n.* drawing in or sucking, *esp.* of air.

Sudd *n.* a mass of floating water-plants, interlaced with trunks of trees, etc., forming floating islands on the White Nile.

Sudd'en *a.* done or occurring unexpectedly; abrupt. —**sudd'enly** *adv.*—**sudd'enness** *n.*

Suds *n.pl.* froth of soap and water.

Sue *v.t.* to seek justice from. — *v.i.* to make application or entreaty.

Suède (swād) *n.* soft kid leather.

Suet (sōō'it) *n.* hard animal fat.

Suff'er *v.t.* to undergo; permit. —*v.i.* to undergo pain, hurt, etc. — **suff'erable** *a.* — **suff'erance** *n.* toleration.—**suff'erer** *n.*

Suffice' *v.i.* to be enough.— *v.t.* to meet the needs of.— **suffi'cient** *a.* enough.—**suffi'ciency** *n.*

Suff'ix *n.* a letter or word added to the end of a word.

—(-fiks'). — *v.t.* to add or annex to the end.

Suff'ocate *v.t.* to kill by stopping breathing.—*v.i.* to feel suffocated.—**suffoca'tion** *n.*

Suff'ragan *n.* an assistant bishop.—*a.* assisting (a bishop).

Suff'rage *n.* a vote or right of voting.—**suff'ragist** *n.* one claiming a right of voting.— **suffragette'** *n.* a woman suffragist.

Suffuse' *v.t.* to well up and spread over.—**suffu'sion** *n.*

Su'gar (shoog-) *n.* a sweet crystalline vegetable substance.—*v.t.* to sweeten with it.—**su'gary** *a.*

Suggest' (suj-) *v.t.* to propose; call up the idea of.—**suggest'ive** *a.*—**suggest'ively** *adv.* —**sugges'tion** *n.*

Su'icide *n.* one who kills himself intentionally. —**suici'dal** *a.*—**suici'dally** *adv.*

Su'int *n.* the natural grease of wool.

Suit (sūt) *n.* an action at law; a set, *esp.* of man's outer clothes; one of the four sets in a pack of cards.— *v.t.* to go with, be adapted to; meet the desires of; make fitting, etc.—*v.i.* to be convenient. —**suit'able** *a.* fitting, convenient.—**suit'ably** *adv.*—**suitabil'ity** *n.*—**suite** (swēt) *n.* a set of things going, or used, together, *esp.* furniture; a retinue.—**suit'or** (sūt-) *n.* one who sues; a wooer.

Sul'ky *a.* sullen.—**sulk** *n.* sulky mood.—*v.i.* to be sulky.—**sulk'ily** *adv.*

Sull'en *a.* resentful, ill-hum-

oured; dismal.—**sull'enny** adv.
Sull'y v.t. to stain, tarnish.
Sul'phonal n. a heavy crystalline compound used as a sedative, hypnotic, drug.
Sul'phur n. a pale-yellow non-metallic element. — **sul'phurous** a. — **sulphu'ric** a. —**sulphu'reous** a.—**sul'phate** n. a salt formed by sulphuric acid in combination with any base.—**sulphat'ing** n. a deposit of white lead sulphate on the plates of an electric accumulator left uncharged.
Sul'try a. hot and close.
Sum n. amount, total.—v.t. to add up.—**summ'ary** a. done quickly.—n. an abridgement or statement of the chief points of a longer document, speech, etc.—**summ'arily** adv. — **summ'arise** v.t.—**summa'tion** n. an adding up.
Summ'er n. the second season. —v.i. to pass the summer.— **summ'ery** a.
Summ'it n. top.
Summ'on v.t. to demand the attendance of; to call on; gather up (energies, etc.).— **summ'ons** n. a call, authoritative demand.
Sump n. the bottom of a shaft in which water collects; in motoring, a well in the crankcase containing lubricating oil; in warfare, a hole dug to take off water from a trench.
Sump'tuary a. regulating expenditure. — **sump'tuous** a. lavish, magnificent.—**sump'tuously** adv. — **sump'tuousness** n.

Sun n. the luminous body round which the earth revolves; its rays.—v.t. to expose to the sun's rays.—
Sun'day n. the first day of the week.—**sun'flower** n. a plant with large golden flowers like pictures of the sun. — **sunn'y** a. — **sun'less** a.
Sun'dæ (-dă) n. an ice-cream decked with fragments of fruit and nuts.
Sund'er v.t. to separate.— **sund'ry** a. several, divers.— n.pl. odd items not mentioned in detail.
Sup v.t. to take by sips.—v.i. to take supper.—n. a mouthful of liquid.
Su'per- prefix. makes compounds with meaning of above, in excess, e.g. **superhu'man** a. more than human. —**superabund'ant** a. excessively abundant, etc. These are not given where the meaning and derivation may easily be found from the simple word.
Su'perable a. that can be overcome.
Superann'uate v.t. to pension off, or discharge as too old. —**superannua'tion** n.
Superb' a. splendid, grand, impressive.—**superb'ly** adv.
Su'percargo n. one in charge of the commercial affairs of a ship.
Supercharge' v.t. to charge or fill to excess.—**superchar'ger** n. in the internal-combustion engine, a device to ensure complete filling of the cylinder with explosive mixture

when running at high speed.
—supercharged a.

Supercil'ious a. indifferent
and haughty. — supercil'-
iously adv.—supercil'iousness
n.

Supereroga'tion n. a doing
more than duty requires.—
supererog'atory a.

Superfi'cies (-fish'i-ēz) n. surface, area.—superfi'cial a.
of or on a surface; without
depth.—superficial'ity n.

Super'fluous a. extra, unnecessary.—superflu'ity n.—super'-
fluously adv. Syn. redundant,
excessive, needless. Ant.
necessary, essential, requisite,
indispensable.

Superintend' v.t. to have charge
of, overlook.—superintend'-
ent n.—superintend'ence n.

Supe'rior a. upper, higher in
position or rank or quality;
showing a consciousness of
being so.—superior'ity n.

Super'lative a. of or in the
highest degree.—n. the superlative degree of an adjective
or adverb.

Supernat'ural a. being beyond the powers or laws of
nature; miraculous.—supernat'urally adv.

Supernu'merary a. in excess
of the normal number.—n.
a supernumerary person or
thing.

Superphos'phate n. manure
made of bones treated with
sulphuric acid.

Supersede' v.t. to set aside;
supplant; take the place of.
—superses'sion n.

Supersti'tion n. a religion or
opinion or practice based on

a belief in luck or magic.—
supersti'tious a.—supersti'-
tiously adv.

Su'per-tax n. a tax on large
incomes in addition to income tax. Also known as
surtax'.

Super-tuned' (tūnd) a. in
motoring, tuned to racing
pitch.

Supervene' v.i. to happen as
an interruption or change.—
superven'tion n.

Su'pervise v.t. to superintend.
—supervi'sion n.

Su'pine a. indolent. Syn.
sluggish, torpid, careless.
Ant. alert, brisk, quick, industrious, careful.

Supp'er n. the last meal of the
day when dinner is not the
last.—supp'erless a.

Supplant v.t. to take the place
of, esp. unfairly.—supplant'er
n.

Sup'ple a. pliable.—sup'ply
adv.

Supple'ment n. something
added to fill up, supply a
deficiency.—v.t. to add to.
—supplement'ary a.

Supp'licate v.t. and i. to beg
humbly. — supplica'tion n.
—supp'licatory a. — supp'-
liant a. petitioning.—n. a
petitioner.

Supply' v.t. to furnish; substitute for.—n. a supplying,
a substitute; stock, store.

Support' v.t. to hold up; assist; sustain.—n. a supporting or being supported, or
means of support.—support'-
able a.—support'er n.

Suppose' v.t. to assume as a
theory; take for granted;

accept as likely.—**suppo'sable** *a*. — **supposition** *n*. — **suppositi'tious** *a*. sham.

Suppress' *v.t*. to put down, restrain, keep or withdraw from publication.—**suppres'sion** *n*. *Syn*. overthrow, overwhelm, stifle, smother, repress, check, stop. *Ant*. advertise, reveal, sustain, preserve.

Supp'urate *v.i*. to fester.—**suppura'tion** *n*.

Supracos'tal *a*. above, or upon, the ribs.

Supralat'eral *a*. situated on the upper part of the side.

Supralu'nar (-lōō-) *a*. being beyond the moon; very lofty.

Supreme' *a*. highest.—**supreme'ly** *adv*.—**suprem'acy** *n*.

Surcease' *v.t*. to cause to cease.—*v.i*. to cease.—*n*. cessation.

Sur'charge *n*. an additional charge; a charge against a responsible official.—*v.t*. to exact such charge.

Surd *a*. not capable of being expressed in rational numbers, as the square root of 2; radical; not sonant.—*n*. a quantity that cannot be expressed by rational numbers.

Sure (shōōr) *a*. certain; trustworthy.—*adv*. certainly.—**sure'ly** *adv*.—**sure'ty** *n*. one who makes himself responsible for the obligations of another.

Surf *n*. foam of breaking waves.

Sur'face (-fis) *n*. outside face of a body; a plane; the top visible side.

Sur'feit (-fit) *n*. excess.—*v.t*. and *i*. to feed to excess.

Surge *v.i*. to move in large waves.—*n*. wave; in electricity, a sudden rush of current in a circuit.

Sur'geon (-jn) *n*. a medical expert who performs operations.—**sur'gery** *n*. treatment by operation; a doctor's consulting room.—**surg'ical** *a*.—**sur'gically** *adv*.

Sur'ly *a*. gloomily morose; ill-natured; cross and rude. —surlily *adv*.—surliness *n*.

Surmise' *v.t*. and *i*. and *n*. guess.

Surmount' *v.t*. to get over, overcome.—**surmount'able** *a*.

Sur'name *n*. family name.

Surpass' *v.t*. to outdo.

Surp'lice (-plis) *n*. a loose white vestment worn by clergy and choristers.

Sur'plus *n*. what remains over or in excess.

Surprise' *n*. what takes unawares; the emotion roused by being taken unawares; a taking unawares.—*v.t*. to cause surprise to.

Surren'der *v.t*. to hand over. —*v.i*. to yield.—*n*. an act of surrendering.

Surrepti'tious *a*. done secretly or stealthily. — **surrepti'tiously** *adv*.

Surr'ogate *n*. a deputy, *esp*. of a bishop.

Surround *v.t*. to be or come all round.

Surroy'al *n*. the crown-antler of a stag.

Sursol'id *a*. pert. to the fifth

power.—*n.* the fifth power of a number.

Sur'tax *n.* an additional tax. —*v.t.* to impose one on.

Surveill'ance (ser-vāl'-) *n.* close watching.

Survey *v.t.* to view; to measure or map (land).—**sur'vey** *n.* a surveying.—**survey'or** *n.*

Survive' *v.t.* to outlive; to come alive through.—*v.i.* to continue to live or exist.—**survi'val** *n.*—**survi'vor** *n.*

Suscep'tible *a.* sensitive; impressionable. — **susceptibil'ity** *n.*

Suscep'tion *n.* the act of taking upon one's self or undertaking.—**suscep'tor** *n.*

Sus'citate *v.t.* to rouse; to excite.—**suscita'tion** *n.*

Suspect' *v.t.* to have an impression of the existence or presence of; to be inclined to believe, to doubt the innocence of.—*a.* of suspected character.—*n.* a suspected person.—**suspi'cion** *n.* a suspecting or being suspected. —**suspi'cious** *a.*—**suspi'ciously** *adv.*

Suspend' *v.t.* to hang up; to sustain in fluid; to cause to cease for a time, keep inoperative.—**suspend'er** *n.*—**suspense'** *n.* a state of uncertainty.—**suspen'sion** *n.* a state of being hung up, or debarred; in motoring, the duty of supporting the frame and body of a motor-vehicle on the axles, performed by springs.—**suspen'sory** *a.*

Sustain' *v.t.* to keep or hold up; endure; confirm.—**sustain'able** *a.*—**sus'tenance** *n.* food.

—**sustenta'tion** *n.* maintenance. *Syn.* nourish, aid, support, approve, justify. *Ant.* let down, abandon, lose, deny.

Sut'ler *n.* a camp follower selling provisions.

Su'zerain *n.* a feudal lord; a sovereign with rights over an autonomous state.—**su'zerainty** *n.*

Svelte *a.* lightly built; supple (of the human figure); in art, free, easy, bold.

Swab (-ob) *n.* a mop; a pad of surgical wool.—*v.t.* to clean with a swab.—**swabb'er** *n.*

Swad'dle (-od-) *v.t.* to swathe. —**swaddling-bands** (-clothes) *n.pl.* clothes in which an infant is swathed.

Swagg'er *v.i.* to strut; to talk boastfully. — *n.* a strutting gait; a boastful or overconfident manner.

Swain *n.* a rustic; a lover.

Swall'ow (-ol'ō) *n.* a migratory bird with a skimming manner of flight.

Swall'ow (-ol-ō) *v.t.* to cause to allow to pass down the gullet. —*n.* an act of swallowing.

Swamp (-omp) *n.* a bog.—*v.t.* to entangle in a swamp; to overwhelm, flood.—**swamp'y** *a.*

Swan (-on) *n.* a large water bird with graceful curved neck.

Swank *a.* pliant, agile; active. —*v.i.* (*colloq.*) to swagger; to boast; to show off.—*n.* (*colloq.*) bluster; swagger.— **swanky** *a.* (*colloq.*) smart; showy; swaggering; pretentiously grand.

Swap, swop, *v.t.* to exchange;

to barter.—*v.t.* to barter.— *n.* an exchange; barter.

Swara'ji *n.* a political party in India formed from the Indian Congress party, and advocating home rule, and relying largely on the use of obstructionist methods.— Swara'jist *n.* and *a.*

Sward (-ord) *n.* turf.

Swarm (-orm) *n.* a large cluster of insects; a vast crowd.— *v.i.* of bees, to emigrate in a swarm; to gather in large numbers.

Swarm (-orm) *v.i.* to climb grasping with hands and knees.

Swart (-ort) *a.* dark in colour. —swar'thy *a.* dark-complexioned.

Swasti'ka (-tēk'a) *n.* a form of cross (卐).

Swat (swot) *v.t.* to hit smartly; to kill, *esp.* insects.

Swath *n.* a line of grass or grain cut and thrown together by the scythe; the whole sweep of a scythe.

Swathe *v.t.* to cover with wraps or bandages.

Sway *v.i.* to swing unsteadily. —*v.t.* to make to do this; to govern; wield.—*n.* swaying motion; government.

Swear *v.t.* to promise on oath; to cause to take an oath.— *v.i.* to use profane oaths.

Sweat (swet) *n.* moisture oozing from the skin.—*v.i.* to exude sweat; to toil.—*v.t.* to cause to sweat; to employ at wrongfully low wages.— sweat'er *n.* an athlete's woollen jersey.

Swede *n.* a variety of turnip.

Sweep *v.i.* to pass quickly or magnificently; to extend in a continuous curve.—*v.t.* to clean with a broom; to carry impetuously.—*n.* a sweeping motion; a wide curve; range; an act of cleaning with a broom; a long oar; one who cleans chimneys. — sweep'-stake *n.* a gamble in which the winner takes the stakes contributed by all.

Sweet *a.* tasting like sugar; agreeable; tuneful; in good condition.—*n.* the sweet part; a sweetmeat.—*pl.* sweet dishes at table; delights.— sweet'bread *n.* an animal's pancreas as food.—sweet'-brier *n.* a wild rose.—sweet'-meat *n.* a piece of confectionery.—sweet'heart *n.* a lover.—sweetpea' *n.* a plant of the pea family with bright flowers.—sweet'en *v.t.* and *i.* —sweet'ly *adv.*—sweet'ish *a.* *Syn.* luscious, redolent, soft, harmonious, dulcet, lovely, delightful, charming, mild, tender. *Ant.* bitter, acid, sour, grating, harsh, disagreeable, offensive.

Swell *v.i.* to expand.—*v.t.* to cause to expand.—*n.* an act of swelling or being swollen; the heave of the sea after a storm; a mechanism in an organ to vary the volume of sound.

Swelt'er *v.i.* to be oppressive, or oppressed with heat.

Swerve *v.i.* to swing round, change direction during motion; a swerving.

Swift *a.* rapid, quick, ready.— *n.* a bird like a swallow.—

swift'ly *adv.* *Syn.* speedy, expeditious, eager, sudden. *Ant.* slow, dilatory, tardy, gradual.

Swill *v.t.* to pour water over or through; to drink greedily. —*v.i.* to drink greedily. —*n.* a rinsing; liquid food for pigs.

Swim *v.i.* to support and move oneself in water; to float; to be flooded. —*v.t.* to cross by swimming. — *n.* a spell of swimming. —swimm'er *n.*

Swim *v.i.* to have a feeling of dizziness.

Swind'ler *n.* a cheat. —swin'dle *v.t.* and *i.* and *n.* cheat.

Swine *n.* pig. —swine'herd *n.*

Swing *v.i.* to move to and fro, *esp.* as a suspended body; to revolve. —*v.t.* to cause to swing; to suspend. —*n.* an act of swinging; a seat hung to swing on.

Swirl *v.i.* to move with an eddying motion. —*v.t.* to cause to do this. —*n.* such motion.

Swish *v.i.* to swing a rod, etc., with an audible hissing sound; to move with a similar sound. —*v.t.* to swing thus; to cane. —*n.* the sound; a stroke with a cane, etc.

Switch *n.* a flexible stick or twig; a mechanism to complete or interrupt an electric circuit, etc. —*v.t* to strike with a switch; to affect (current, etc.) with a switch; to swing round abruptly. —switchboard *n.* a device by means of which connections can be established readily between the many circuits

employed in systems of telegraphy, telephony, electric lighting, etc.

Swiv'el *n.* a mechanism of two parts which can revolve the one on the other. —*v.t.* and *i.* to turn on a swivel.

Swoon *v.i.* and *n.* faint.

Swoop *v.i.* to come down like a hawk. —*n.* an act of swooping.

Sword (sord) *n.* a weapon, a long blade for cutting or thrusting. —sword'-fish *n.* a fish with a long sharp upper jaw.

Swot *v.t.* and *i.* (*colloquial*) to study hard.

Syb'arite *n.* a luxurious person.

Sy'bo *n.* a young onion.

Syc'amore *n.* a tree.

Syc'ophant *n.* a flatterer. —sycophant'ic *n.* —syc'ophancy *n.*

Syll'able *n.* a division of a word as a unit for pronunciation. —syllab'ic *a.*

Syll'abus *n.* a programme.

Syllep'sis *n.* the agreement of a verb or adjective with one, rather than another, of two nouns, with either of which it might agree. —syllep'tic *a.*

Syll'ogism (-j-) *n.* a form of logical reasoning consisting of two premisses and a conclusion. —syllogist'ic *a.*

Sylph *n.* a sprite.

Syl'van *see* SILVAN.

Symbio'sis *n.* the community of mutually-dependent dissimilar organisms. —symbiot'ic *a.* —symbiot'ically *adv.*

Sym'bol *n.* a sign; a thing representing or typifying something. —symbol'ic *a.* —symbol'ically *adv.* — sym'bolise *v.t.*

Symm'etry *n.* proportion between parts, balance of arrangement between two sides. —symmet'rical *a.*—symmet'rically *adv. Syn.* shapeliness, harmony. regularity, order. *Ant.* disparity, incongruity, discord, disorder, irregularity, confusion.

Sym'pathy *n.* feeling for another in pain, etc.; sharing of emotion, interest, desire, etc.—sympathet'ic *a.*—sympathet'ically *adv.*—sym'pathise *v.i.*

Sym'phony *n.* a harmony of sounds; a composition for a full orchestra.—symphon'ic *a.*—sympho'nious *a.* harmonious.

Sympo'sium *n.* a drinking party; a friendly discussion; a set of magazine articles by various writers on the same subject.

Symp'tom *n.* a sign or token; a change in the body indicating its state of health or disease.—symptomat'ic *a.*

Syn'agogue *n.* a Jewish congregation or its meeting-place.

Syn'chronise *v.t.* to make agree in time.—*v.i.* to happen at the same time.—syn'chronism *n.*—synchronisa'tion *n.* —syn'chronous *a.*

Syncli'nal *a.* sloping downward in opposite directions so as to meet in a common point or line; dipping.

Syn'cope (-pi) *n.* fainting; a syncopated spelling, etc.—syn'copate *v.t.* to shorten by the omission of an interior element (in words, music, etc.).

Syn'dicalism *n.* an economic movement aiming at the combination of workers in all trades to enforce the demands of labour by sympathetic strikes.

Syn'dicate *n.* a body of persons associated for some enterprise.

Synec'doche (-nek'-do-kē) *n.* a figure or trope by which the whole of a thing is put for a part, or a part for the whole.

Synecphone'sis *n.* a contraction of two syllables into one.

Syn'esis *n.* construction according to the sense rather than the syntax.

Syn'od *n.* a church council.

Syn'onym *n.* a word with the same meaning as another.—synon'ymous *a.*—synonym'ity *n.*

Synop'sis *n.* a summary.—synop'tic *a.* having the same viewpoint.

Syn'tax *n.* the part of grammar treating of the arrangement of words.—syntact'ic *a.*—syntact'ically *adv.*

Syn'thesis *n.* a putting together, combination.—synthet'ic *a.*—synthet'ically *adv.*

Syph'ilis *n.* an infectious venereal disease.

Syr'inge *n.* an instrument for drawing in liquid by a piston and forcing it out in a fine stream or spray; a squirt.—*v.t.* to spray with a syringe.

Syr'up *n.* a thick solution of sugar; treacle.—syr'upy *a.*

Sys'tem *n.* a complex whole;

an organisation; method; classification.—systemat'ic *a.* methodical. — systemat'ically *adv.*—sys'tematise *v.t.*

Sys'tole (-to-lē) *n.* the shortening of a long syllable; the contraction of the heart and arteries for expelling the blood and carrying on the circulation.—systol'ic *a.* contracting.

Syz'ygy (siz-i-ji) *n.* the conjunction or opposition of two celestial bodies.

T

Tab *n.* a tag, label, short strap.

Tab'ard *n.* a herald's coat.

Tabb'y *n.* a brindled cat; a she-cat.

Tab'ernacle *n.* a tent or booth; a nonconformist meeting-house.

Ta'ble *n.* a piece of furniture consisting mainly of a flat board supported by legs, brackets, etc., about three feet from the ground; a tablet; food; a set of facts or figures arranged in lines or columns.—*v.t* to lay on a table.—ta'ble-land *n.* a plateau.—tab'leau (-lō) *n.*—tab'leaux (-lō) *pl.* a dramatic situation. — tableau - vivant (tab'lō vē'vān) *n.* a group of persons, silent and motionless, arranged to represent some scene. — tab'let *n.* a small flat slab.—tab'ular *a.* shaped or arranged like a table.—tab'ulate *v.t.* to arrange (figures, facts, etc.) in tables.—tabula'tion *n.*

Taboo' *n.* a setting apart of a thing as sacred or accursed; a ban or prohibition.—*a.* put under a taboo.—*v.t.* to put under a taboo.

Ta'bor *n.* a small drum.—tab'ouret *n.* a low stool.

Tac'it (tas'-) *a.* implied but not spoken.—tac'itly *adv.*—tac'iturn *a.* talking little, habitually silent.—taciturn'ity *n.* *Syn.* inferred, understood, secret, quiet, still, taciturn. *Ant.* overt, manifest, spoken, express, explicit.

Tack *n.* a small nail; a long loose stitch; a rope at the corner of a sail; the course of a ship obliquely to windward.—*v.t.* to nail with tacks; to stitch lightly; to beat to windward with tacks; to change from one tack to another.

Tac'kle *n.* equipment, apparatus, *esp.* lifting appliances with ropes.—*v.t.* to take in hand; grip.

Tact *n.* skill in dealing with people or situations.—tact'ful *a.*— tact'less *a.*—tact'fully *adv.*—tact'lessly *adv.*—tact'ile *a.* of or relating to the sense of touch.

Tact'ics *n.pl.* the art of handling troops or ships in battle.—tact'ical *a.*—tacti'cian *n.*

Tad'pole *n.* a young frog in the tailed stage.

Taff'erel, taff'rail *n.* the rail at the stern of a ship, the flat ornamental part of the stern.

Taff'eta *n.* a smooth, lustrous, silk fabric.

Tag *n.* a ragged end; pointed end of lace, etc.; a trite quotation; an address label; any appendage.—*v.t.* to append.—**tag'rag** *n.* rabble.

Tail *n.* the projecting continuation of the backbone at the hinder end of an animal; in aviation, a group of stabilising planes or fins at rear of aeroplane to which are attached elevating rudder controls.—**tailed** *a.*—**tail'less** *a.*—**tailplane** *n.* in aviation, a stabilising surface at rear of aeroplane, the function of which is to secure steady motion in a vertical plane.—**tailskid** *n.* in aviation, a metal rod, situated below the fin, with foot along which an aeroplane slides in taxying. —**tail-spin** *n.* in aviation, a vertical dive by an aeroplane, nose foremost and describing a spiral, tail descending in a straight line.—**tail-light** *n.* in motoring, a light carried at the rear of a vehicle, showing a red warning light to the rear, and illuminating the rear number plate.

Tail'or *n.* a maker of outer clothing.

Taint *n.* a stain; an infection. —*v.t.* to stain slightly; corrupt.—*v.i.* to become corrupted.

Take *v.t.* to grasp, get hold of; get; receive, assume, adopt; accept; understand; consider; carry or conduct.—*v.i.* to be effective.

Talc *n.* a white or green powder of soapy feel.

Tale *n.* a story; number, count.

Tal'ent *n.* a natural ability or power; an ancient weight or money.

Tal'isman *n.* an object supposed to have magic powers.

Talk (tawk) *v.i.* to speak or converse.—*v.t.* to express in speech; to use (a language); to discuss.—*n.* speech; conversation; rumour. — **talk'ative** *a.*—**talk'er** *n.*—**talk'y** *n.* (slang) a combination of phonograph and cinematograph, a " talking film."

Tall *a.* high; of great stature.

Tall'ow (tal'ō) *n.* melted and clarified animal fat.—*v.t.* to smear with tallow.—*a.* made of tallow.

Tall'y *n.* a notched rod for keeping accounts; an account so kept; a reckoning.—*v.t.* to record by a tally.—*v.i.* to agree, correspond.

Tal'on *n.* a claw.

Tam'bour (-ōōr) *n.* a large drum; a round frame for embroidery.—**tambourine'** *n.* a flat half-drum with jingling discs of metal attached.

Tame *a.* not wild; domesticated; without excitement, uninteresting.—*v.t.* to make tame.—**tame'ly** *adv.*—**ta'mer** *n.* *Syn.* tractable, mild, gentle. *Ant.* wild, untamed, fierce, savage.

Tamp'er *v.i.* to interfere (with) improperly; meddle.

Tan *n.* crushed oak-bark; the colour of this.—*v.t.* to make into leather; to make brown.

Tan'dem *adv.* one behind the other.—*n.* a vehicle with two horses one behind the other;

a bicycle for two riders one behind the other.

Tan'gent (-j-) *a.* touching, meeting without cutting.— *n.* a line tangent to a curve. —**tangen'tial** *a.*—**tangen'tially** *adv.*—**tan'gible** *a.* that can be touched; definite.— **tangibil'ity** *n.*

Tan'gle (-ng-gl) *v.t.* to twist together in a muddle.—*n.* a tangled mass.

Tan'gram *n.* a puzzle or game of mosaic pieces.

Tank *n.* a storage vessel for liquids, *esp.* a large one; an armoured motor-vehicle used in trench warfare.— **tanker** *n.* a steamer fitted with oil-tanks; a motor-vehicle or railway container-wagon for carrying liquid fuel.

Tank'ard *n.* a large drinking-cup of metal.

Tan'talise *v.t.* to torment by presenting and then taking away something desired.— **tan'talus** *n.* an appliance for keeping decanters locked up.

Tan'tamount *a.* equivalent in value or signification; equal.

Tan'trum *n.* an outburst of temper.

Tap *n.* a hollow plug for drawing off liquid; a valve with a handle to regulate or stop the flow of a fluid in a pipe, etc.—*v.t.* to put a tap in; to draw off.—**tap'root** *n.* a long tapering root growing directly downwards.—**tap'ster** *n.* one who draws beer in an inn.

Tap *v.t.* to strike lightly but with some noise.—*n.* a slight blow or rap.

Tape *n.* a narrow long strip of fabric, paper, etc.—**tape'-worm** *n.* a flat worm parasitic on animals.

Ta'per *n.* a long wick covered with wax: a thin candle.— *v.i.* to become gradually thinner towards one end.

Tap'estry *n.* a fabric decorated with woven designs in colours.

Tapio'ca *n.* a granular food made from the cassava-root.

Ta'pir (-er) *n.* an American animal, with flexible proboscis, allied to the pig.

Tapp'et *n.* in an internal-combustion engine, a short steel rod conveying to the valve stem movement imparted by the lift of a cam.

Tar *n.* a thick black liquid distilled from coal, etc.—*v.t.* to coat with tar.

Taran'tula *n.* a large, poisonous spider found in Southern Europe.

Tard'y *a.* slow, behind-hand. —**tard'ily** *adv.* *Syn.* sluggish, slack, late, procrastinating. *Ant.* quick, prompt, lively, early, timely, premature.

Tare (tēr) *n.* a weed, the vetch.

Tare (tēr) *n.* allowance made for the weight of box, cart, etc., when goods are weighed in such container.

Tar'get (-g-) *n.* a mark to aim at in shooting; a small shield. —**targe** *n.* a shield.

Tar'iff *n.* a list of charges.

Tar'mac *n.* mixture of tar and road metal or macadam used for giving a smooth, non-friable road surface for motor traffic.

Tarn *n.* a small mountain lake.

Tar′nish *v.t.* to discolour (*esp.* metal). — *v.i.* to become stained, lose shine.—*n.* discoloration.

Tarpaul′in *n.* canvas treated with tar or oil.

Tar′pon, tarpum *n.* a large edible fish.

Tarr′y *v.i.* to linger, delay.

Tart *n.* an open pie of fruit, etc.; a small covered fruit pie.

Tart *a.* sour. *Syn.* bitter, pungent, biting, harsh, testy, snappish. *Ant.* agreeable, mild, sweet, gentle.

Tart′an *n.* a woollen cloth woven in a pattern of stripes crossing at right angles; a pattern used in this cloth.

Tar′tar *n.* a crust deposited on the teeth; deposit on wine-casks, etc.

Tar′tar *n.* a native of Tartary; a person of an irritable temper.—**to catch a Tartar,** to encounter a person that proves too strong for the assailant.

Taseom′eter *n.* an instrument for measuring strains in a structure.

Tasim′eter *n.* an electrical instrument for detecting minute changes in pressure, temperature, moisture, etc.

Task (-à-) *n.* a piece of work set or undertaken.—*v.t.* to put a task on, to take to task, to reprove.—**task′-master** *n.*

Tass′el *n.* an ornament consisting of a bunch of threads on a knob.

Taste *v.t.* to perceive or try the flavour of; to eat or drink; to experience.—*v.i.* to have a flavour.—*n.* a small quantity; flavour; sense of tasting; appreciation and judgment in matters of beauty, style, etc.; style or manner. —**taste′ful** *a.*—**taste′fully** *adv.* —**taste′less** *a.*

Tat *v.t.* to make trimming by tatting.—*v.i.* to make tatting. —**tatting** *n.* lace-edging, woven or knit from common sewing thread, with a peculiar stitch.—**tatter** *n.*

Tatt′er *n.* a rag.—**tatterdema′lion** *n.* a ragged fellow.

Tat′tle *v.i.* to gossip.

Tattoo′ *n.* a beat of drum and bugle-call; a military spectacle.

Tattoo′ *v.t.* to mark the skin in patterns, etc., by pricking and filling the punctures with colouring matter.—*n.* a mark so made.

Tau (taw) *n.* the toad-fish.

Taube (toub) *n.* a German monoplane.

Taunt *n.* a reproach, insulting words.—*v.t.* to insult, reproach bitterly.

Taut *a.* drawn tight.

Tautol′ogy *n.* repetition of the same thing in other words.—**tautolo′gical** *a.*

Tav′ern *n.* an inn or ale-house.

Taw′dry *a.* showy but cheap and without taste.—**taw′drily** *adv.*

Tawn′y *a.* yellowish-brown.— *n.* this colour.

Tawse *n.pl.* a leather strap fringed at the end for whipping children.

Tax *v.t.* to exact a contribution to the cost of government; to examine accounts; to put a burden or strain on.—*n.* the charge imposed; a burden.—taxa'tion *n.*—tax'able *a.*—taxim'eter *n.* an instrument for measuring the time and distance to reckon the charge for a cab fitted with it.—tax'-payer *n.*

Tax'i- (cab) *n.* a motor-cab for hire with driver.—tax'i *v.i.* to go in a taxi; (of an aeroplane) to run along the ground under its own power.—*pres. part.* tax'ying.

Tax'idermy *n.* the art of stuffing animals.—tax'idermist *n.*

Tea *n.* the dried leaves of a plant cultivated in China, India, etc.; an infusion of it as a beverage; various herbal infusions; an afternoon meal at which tea is served.

Teach *v.t.* to instruct; to impart knowledge of.—*v.i.* to act as teacher.—teach'er *n. Syn.* train, school, preach, discipline, direct, advise. *Ant.* misdirect, mislead, deceive, misguide.

Teak *n.* an East Indian tree; the very hard wood obtained from it.

Teal *n.* a small water-fowl allied to the duck.

Team *n.* a set of animals, players of a game, etc., associated in an activity.—team'ster *n.* one who drives a team of draught animals.

Tear *n.* a drop of fluid in, or falling from, the eye.—tear'ful *a.*—tear'less *a.*—tear'drop *n.*—tear'-stained *a.*

Tear (tér) *v.t.* to pull apart, rend.—*v.i.* to become torn; to rush.—*n.* a rent.

Tease *v.t.* to pull apart the fibres of; to torment, irritate.—*n.* one who torments.—teas'ing *a.*

Tea'sel *n.* a plant of which one species bears a large burr, used for raising a nap in woollen cloth; the burr of the plant.

Teat *n.* the nipple of a female breast; an artificial substitute for this.

Tech'nical (tek-) *a.* of or used in an art or arts; belonging to a particular art.—technical'ity *n.* state of being technical; that which is technical.—tech'nically *adv.*—technique' (tek-nēk') *n.* method of performance in an art.—techni'cian *n.*—technol'ogy *n.* systematic knowledge of industrial arts.—technol'ogist *n.*

Technoc'racy (-nok'-) *n.* a movement founded in America in 1920 for scientific and technical study of factors, *esp.* economic, affecting modern life.

Te'dium *n.* boredom or quality of boring.—te'dious *a.* wearisome.—te'diously *adv.*

Tee *n.* a mark at which missiles are aimed; in golf, the sand, or earth, on which the ball is slightly raised at the beginning of play for each hole.—*v.t.* to place a ball on the tee.

Teem *v.i.* to abound with, swarm, be prolific.

Teethe (-TH) *v.i.* to cut teeth.

Teeto'tal *a.* abstaining or pledged to abstain from intoxicating drink; relating to

such abstinence or pledge.—
teeto'taller *n.*—**teeto'talism** *n.*

Teeto'tum *n.* a top, *esp.* one with marked sides for gambling, etc.

Teg, tegg *n.* a female fallow deer; a doe in the second year.

Teg'ument *n.* a covering; the covering of the living body.—**tegumen'tal** *a.*—**tegumen'tary** *a.* consisting of teguments.

Telau'tograph *n.* a form of telegraph that transmits messages as set out by hand, whether writing or drawing.

Teleg'ony (-leg-) *n.* theory of the supposed influence exercised by a male on the children begotten on his mate by a later cohabitor.

Tel'egraph *n.* an apparatus for sending messages mechanically to a distance, as by semaphore, electricity, etc.—*v.t.* and *i.* to communicate by telegraph.—**teleg'raphist** *n.* one who works a telegraph.—**telegraph'ic** *a.*—**telegraph'ically** *adv.*—**teleg'raphy** *n.*—**tel'egram** *n.* a message sent by telegraph.—**telep'athy** *n.* the action of one mind on another at a distance.—**telepath'ic** *a.*—**telepath'ically** *adv.*—**tel'ephone** *n.* an apparatus for communicating sound to a distance.—*v.t.* and *i.* to communicate or speak by telephone.—**telephon'ic** *a.*—**teleph'ony** *n.*—**teleph'onist** *n.*—**tel'eprinter** *n.* an apparatus resembling a typewriter, by means of which a subscriber can call up on the telephone another subscriber and send and receive typed messages.—**tel'escope** *n.* an instrument of lenses to see things more clearly at a distance.—**telescop'ic** *a.*—**tel'evision** *n.* seeing at a distance by the use of wireless transmission.

Tell *v.t.* to narrate, make known; count.—*v.i.* to give an account; to be of weight or importance.—**tell'er** *n.*—**tell'ing** *a.* effective. *Syn.* relate, report, communicate, repeat, inform. *Ant.* conceal, withhold.

Tellu'rian *a.* of the earth.

Tellu'rium *n.* a substance of a silver-white colour, sometimes reckoned among the metals.

Tel'otype *n.* an electric telegraph which prints the messages; an automatically-printed telegram.

Temer'ity *n.* rashness.—**temera'rious** *a.* foolhardy.

Temp'er *v.t.* to harden; to bring to proper condition; to restrain, moderate.—*n.* degree of hardness of steel, etc.; mental constitution; frame of mind; anger, *esp.* in noisy outburst.—**temp'erament** *n.* mental constitution.—**temperament'al** *a.* — **temperament'ally** *adv.*—**temp'erate** *a.* showing or practising moderation.—**temp'erance** *n.* moderation, self-restraint.—**temp'erately** *adv.* — **temp'erature** *n.* degree of heat or coldness.

Temp'est *n.* a violent storm.—**tempest'uous** *a.*—**tempest'uously** *adv.*

Tem'ple n. a building for worship.

Tem'ple n. the flat part on either side of the head above the cheekbone.

Tem'plet, tem'plate n. a mould used by bricklayers and masons, machinists, millwrights, etc.

Temp'oral a. relating to time, or this life or world; secular.—**temporal'ity** n.—**temp'orary** a. lasting or used only for a time.—**temp'orarily** adv.—**temp'orise** v.t. to gain time by negotiation, etc.; to conform to circumstances.—**temp'oriser** n. Syn. temporary, transitory, fleeting, impermanent, worldly, earthy. Ant. permanent, lasting, spiritual, ecclesiastical, unworldly.

Tempt v.t. to try; to try to persuade, esp. to evil.—**tempt'er** n.—**tempta'tion** n.

Ten n. and a. the cardinal number next after nine.—**tenth** a. the ordinal number.

Ten'able a. that may be held or defended.—**tena'cious** a. holding fast.—**tenac'ity** n.—**ten'ant** n. one who holds lands or house, etc., on a rent, or lease.—**ten'ancy** n.—**ten'antry** n. a body of tenants.—**ten'antable** a. fit for habitation.

Tench n. a fresh-water fish.

Tend v.t. to take care of.—**tend'ance** n.—**tend'er** n. a vessel attending a larger one; a carriage for fuel and water attached to a locomotive.

Tend v.i. to incline; make in direction of.—**tend'ency** n.—

tend'er v.t. to offer.—n. an offer; what may legally be offered in payment.

Tend'er a. delicate, soft; easily injured; gentle, loving, affectionate.—**tend'erly** adv.—**tend'erness** n.

Tend'on n. a sinew attaching a muscle to a bone, etc.

Tend'ril n. a slender curling stem by which a climbing plant attaches itself to anything.

Ten'ebrous, tenebrose a. dark; obscure.—**tenebrousness** n.—**tenebros'ity** n. darkness; gloom.

Ten'ement n. a piece of land or a house; a part of a house forming a separate dwelling.—**ten'ement-house** n.

Tenen'dum n. the clause in a deed defining the tenure of the land.

Ten'et n. a doctrine.

Ten'nis n. a game in which a ball is struck between players on opposite sides of a net in a covered court; a variation of this played on a grass or other court (also called lawn-tennis).

Ten'on n. a tongue cut on the end of a piece of wood, etc., to fit into a mortise.

Ten'or n. meaning; general course; a male voice between alto and bass; music for this; a singer with this voice.

Tense n. a modification of a verb to show time of action, etc.

Tense a. stretched tight.—**ten'sile** a. capable of being stretched. — **ten'sion** n. stretching or strain when stretched.—tent n. a portable shelter of canvas.—tent'-pole n.—tent'-peg n.

Tent'acle n. a feeler.—tent'ative a. done as a trial.—n. an attempt.—tent'atively adv.

Tent'er n. a frame for stretching cloth.—tent'er-hook n. a hook for holding the cloth.—on tent'er-hooks, in painful suspense.

Ten'uous a. thin.—tenu'ity n.

Ten'ure n. conditions or period of holding land, an office, etc.

Tep'id a. moderately warm.

Tercente'nary n. a three-hundredth anniversary.—a. pertaining to one.

Ter'ebine n. a disinfectant derived from oil of turpentine.—ter'ebinth n. a tree or shrub yielding a limpid, balsamic resin; the turpentine tree.

Tere'do n. a genus of worm-like molluscs (a species, the ship-worm, perforates submerged wood).

Tergiversa'tion (-j-) n. shuffling; desertion of party.

Term n. a limit or end; a fixed day for regular payment, e.g. rent; a period during which courts sit, schools are open, etc.—pl. conditions, mutual relationship; a word or expression.—v.t. to name.—term'inal a. at or forming an end.—n. a terminal part or structure.—term'inate v.t. to bring to an end.—v.i. to come to an end.—termina'tion n.—term'inable a.—terminol'ogy n. the study of terms; a set of technical terms or vocabulary.—terminolo'gical (-j-) a.

—term'inus n. a finishing point; a station at the end of a railway.

Term'agant n. a brawling woman.

Ter'mite n. the so-called white ant.—termita'rium, ter'mitary n. a nest or mound made by termites.

Terr'ace n. a raised level place, a level cut out of a hill; a row or street of uniform houses.—v.t. to form into a terrace.

Terra-cott'a n. a hard unglazed pottery; its colour, a brownish-red.

Terr'ain (-ān) n. in geology, any rock, or series of rocks; in military affairs, an extent of ground or country.

Terrapin n. a fresh-water or tide-water tortoise.

Terrest'rial a. of the earth; of land.

Terr'ible a. causing fear; excessive.—terr'ibly adv.—terrif'ic a. terrible, awe-inspiring.—terrif'ically adv.—terr'ify v.t. to frighten. — terr'or n. a state of great fear.—terr'orise v.t. to force or oppress by fear.—terr'orism n. Syn. of "terror," fright, dismay, consternation, horror. Ant. boldness, courage, assurance, confidence.

Terr'ier n. a small dog of various breeds, orig. for following a quarry into a burrow.

Terr'itory n. a region; the land subject to a ruler. — territor'ial a. relating to a territory.—Territorial Force n. an army primarily for home de-

---

fence, of volunteer part-time soldiers.

Terr'y *n.* a textile fabric of wool or silk, woven like velvet, but with the loops uncut.

Terse *a.* expressed in few words, pithy.

Ter'tiary *a.* third.

Tess'ellate *v.t.* to form into squares or checkers; to lay with checkered work.—tessellated, tessellar *a.*—tessella'tion *n.*

Test *n.* means of trial.—*v.t.* to try, put to the proof.—testing *n.* the act of trying for proof; in motoring, proving of correctness of every adjustment in a car, with examination for faults.—testcase *n.* in law, a lawsuit viewed as a means of establishing a precedent the one way or the other.

Test'ament *n.* a will; one of the two divisions of the Bible.—testament'ary *a.*—test'ate *a.* that has left a will.—test'acy *n.* state of being testate.—testa'tor *n.*—testa'trix *fem.*

Test'icle *n.* a male genital organ.

Test'ify *v.i.* to bear witness.—*v.t.* to bear witness to.—test'imony *n.* evidence.—testimo'nial *n.* a certificate of character, ability, etc.; a gift by a number of persons to express their regard for the recipient.

Test'y *a.* irritable, short-tempered. *Syn.* fretful, peevish, querulous, captious, hasty. *Ant.* placid, genial,

jovial, serene, gentle, tranquil.

Tet'anus *n.* lockjaw, rigidity of some or all muscles.

Teth'er (-TH-) *v.t.* to tie up (a horse, etc.) with a rope.—*n.* a rope or chain for fastening a grazing animal; limit of endurance (*at the end of his tether*).

Tet'ragon *n.* a figure with four angles and four sides.—tetrag'onal *a.*—tetrahe'dron *n.* a solid contained by four plane faces.

Tet'rode *n.* in wireless, a four-electrode thermionic valve.

Text *n.* the actual words of a book, passage, etc.; the main body of a literary work; letterpress; a passage from the Scriptures, etc., *esp.* as the subject of a discourse.—text'-book *n.* a manual of instruction.—text'ual *a.* of or in a text.—text'ile *a.* woven; capable of being woven; relating to weaving.—text'ure *n.* the character or structure of a textile fabric.

Than (TH-) *conj.* and *prep.* introduces second part of a comparison.

Thank *v.t.* to give thanks to, express gratitude to.—thanks *n.pl.* words of gratitude.—thank'ful *a.* feeling grateful.—thank'less *a.* having or bringing no thanks.

That (TH-) *a.* demonstrates or particularises.—*dem. pron.* the particular thing meant.—*adv.* as.—*rel. pron.* which, who.—*conj.* introduces noun clauses.

Thatch *v.t.* to roof (a house)

with straw or similar material.—*n.* straw used in thatching.

Thaum'aturge *n.* a wonder-worker. — **thaum'aturgy** *n.* magic, miracle-working.

Thaw *v.t.* and *i.* to melt.—*n.* a melting (of frost, etc.).

The (TH-) is the definite article.

The'atre (-ter) *n.* a place where plays are performed; the drama or dramatic works generally; a surgical operating room.—**theat'rical** *a.* of or for the theatre; showy, spectacular.—**theat'rically** *adv.*—**theat'ricals** *n.pl.* amateur dramatic performances.

Theft *n.* stealing.

Their (THêr) *a.* theirs.—*pron.* belonging to them.

The'ism *see* THEOLOGY.

Them *pron.* objective case of *they*; those persons or things.

Theme *n.* subject of a composition; an essay.

Then (TH-) *adv.* at that time; next; that being so.

Thence (TH-) *adv.* from that place, point of reasoning, etc.

Theod'olite *n.* a surveying instrument for measuring angles, etc.

Theol'ogy *n.* the science treating of God.—**theolo'gical** *a.*—**theolo'gically** *adv.*—**theolo'gian** (-lŏj-) *n.*—**theoc'racy** *n.* government by God.—**theocrat'ic** *a.*—**the'ism** *n.* belief in divine creation of the universe without denial of revelation.—**the'ist** *n.*—**theos'opy** *n.* a system of philosophy basing knowledge of nature on intuitional knowledge of God. — **theos'ophist** *n.*

The'orem *n.* a proposition which can be demonstrated by argument.—**the'ory** *n.* a supposition to account for something; a system of rules and principles; rules and reasoning, etc., as distinguished from practice.—**theoret'ical** *a.* — **theoret'ically** *adv.*—**the'orist** *n.*—**the'orise** *v.i.* *Syn.* of "theory," hypothesis, speculation, conjecture, philosophy, explanation. *Ant.* truth, fact, reality.

Therapeut'ic *a.* relating to healing.—*n.* in *pl.* the art of healing.

Ther'apy *n.* in medicine, curative treatment; usually in compound words as RADIOTHERAPY.

There (TH-) *adv.* in that place, to that point.—**there'fore** *adv.* in consequence, that being so.

Ther'mal *a.* of or pertaining to heat.—**ther'mic** *a.* thermal.—**thermom'eter** *n.* an instrument to measure temperature. — **thermomet'ric** *a.*—**thermion'ic valve** *n.* an apparatus for changing wireless waves into vibrations audible in telephony, and for amplifying and generating such waves.—**ther'mos flask** *n.* a flask keeping its contents hot or cold by a double wall with a vacuum between.

Ther'mion *n.* a positively or negatively charged particle or ion, emitted by an incandescent body.—**thermionic** *a.* pertaining to a thermion.—**thermionic valve**, a vacuum tube with incandescent filament and auxiliary electrodes, used as generator, detector or amplifier of wireless signals.

Ther'mit, ther'mite (-mīt) *n.* aluminium powder mixed with a metal oxide, which when ignited, emits tremendous heat, used *esp.* for welding.

Thermodynam'ics *n.* the science that deals with the conversion of heat into mechanical energy.

Thermo-electric'ity *n.* electricity developed by the action of heat.

Ther'mograph *n.* a self-registering thermometer.

The'sis *n.* proposition; dissertation.

Thes'pian *a.* theatrical; belonging to the stage.

Thews *n.pl.* a person's muscular strength.

They (THā) *pron.* the third person plural pronoun.

Thick *a.* having great thickness, not thin; dense, crowded; viscous; foggy.— **thick'ly** *adv.*—**thick'en** *v.t.* and *i.*—**thick'ness** *n.* the dimension of anything measured through it, at right angles to the length and breadth.—**thick'et** *n.* a thick growth of small trees.— **thick'set** *a.* set closely together; sturdy and solid in limbs and frame.

Thief *n.* thieves *pl.* one who steals.—**thieve** *v.t.* and *i.* to steal.—**thiev'ish** *a.*

Thigh (thī) *n.* the upper part of the leg.

Thim'ble *n.* a metal cover for the end of the finger in sewing.

Thin *a.* of little thickness; of little density; loose, not closely packed.—*v.t.* and *i.* to make or become thin.— **thin'ness** *n.* *Syn.* spare, slender, scanty, lean, dilute, slight, flimsy, insufficient. *Ant.* thick, bulky, dense, close, compact, numerous, fat.

Thine (THīn) *pron.* and *a.* belonging to thee.

Thing *n.* a material object; any possible object of thought.

Think *v.i.* to have one's mind at work; to reflect; hold an opinion.—*v.t.* to conceive or consider in the mind.— **think'er** *n.*

Third *a.* the ordinal number corresponding to *three.*—*n.* a third part.

Thirst *n.* the feeling caused by lack of drink.—*v.i.* to feel the lack of drink.—**thirst'y** *a.* —**thirst'ily** *adv.*

Thirteen' *a.* and *n.* a number, three and ten.—**thirt'y** *n.* and *a.* a number, three times ten.

This (TH-) *dem. a.* and *pron.* denotes a thing or person near, or just mentioned, etc.

This'tle (-sl) *n.* a prickly plant with a purple flower.

Thith'er (THITH'-) *adv.* to or toward that place.

Thole *v.t.* to bear; to undergo; to stand; to suffer; to permit.—*v.i.* to endure grief, pain, etc.

Thole'-pin *n.* one of two pegs between which an oar works.

Thong *n.* a narrow strip of leather.

Thor'ax *n.* the part of the body between neck and belly.

Tho'rium *n.* a gray metallic element, used in the manufacture of incandescent gas mantles, filaments of thermionic valves, etc.

Thorn *n.* a prickle on a plant; a bush noted for its thorns.

Thor'ough (THur'a) *a.* complete, entire. — **thor'oughly** *adv.*—**thor'oughbred** *a.* of pure breed.—*n.* a pure-bred animal, *esp.* a horse.—**thor'-oughfare** *n.* a road or passage open at both ends; right of way.

Thorp, thorpe *n.* a hamlet; a village.

Those *pron. pl.* of *that*; noting, as a correlative of *these*, the former, as distinguished from the latter.

Thou (TH-) *pron.* the second person singular pronoun.

Though (THō) *conj.* in spite of the fact that.—*adv.* for all that.

Thought (thawt) *n.* the process of thinking; what one thinks; a product of thinking; meditation.—**thought'ful** *a.* engaged in meditation; considerate. — **thought'less** *a.* careless, heedless, inconsiderate.

Thou'sand (-z-) *a.* and *n.* a cardinal number, ten hundreds.

Thrall (-awl) *n.* a slave; slavery.—*v.t.* to enslave.—**thral'dom** *n.*

Thrash, thresh *v.t.* to beat out the grains of.—**thrash** *v.t.* to beat, whip.

Thread (-ed) *n.* a fine cord; yarn; the ridge cut spirally on a screw.—*v.t.* to put a thread into; to put on a thread; to pick (one's way, etc.).—**thread'bare** *a.* worn, with the nap rubbed off.

Threat (-et) *n.* an announcement of what the speaker intends to do if his orders or wishes are not complied with. —**threat'en** *v.t.* to utter threats against.

Three *n.* and *a.* a cardinal number, one more than two.

Thresh'old (-ōld) *n.* the bar of stone or wood forming the bottom of the framework of a door.

Thrice *adv.* three times.

Thrift *n.* saving, economy.—**thrift'y** *a.*—**thrift'ily** *adv.*—**thrift'less** *a.* *Syn.* frugality, parsimony, profit. *Ant.* extravagance, waste, prodigality.

Thrill *v.t.* to send a nervous tremor of emotion through. —*v.i.* to feel one.—*n.* such emotional tremor.—**thrill'ing** *a.* exciting.

Thrive *v.i.* to grow well; flourish, prosper.

Throat *n.* the front of the neck; either or both of the passages through it. — **throat'y** *a.* of voice, hoarse.

Throb *v.i.* to beat or quiver strongly.—*n.* a throbbing.

Throe *n.* a spasm or pang.

Thrombo'sis *n.* the coagulation of the blood in a blood-vessel, or in the heart, during life.

Throne *n.* a seat of state, *esp.* of a king.—*v.t.* to place on a throne.

Māte, mēte, mīte, mōte, mūte, bōōt.

Throng *n.*, *v.t.*, and *i.* crowd.

Thros'tle (-sl) *n.* a thrush.

Throt'tle *n.* the wind-pipe; in the internal-combustion engine, abbrev. for throttle-valve; in motoring, a lever controlling the throttle-valve. —*v.t.* to choke.—*v.i.* to suffocate; to open or close the throttle.—**throttle down**, to slow down by closing the throttle.

Through (thrōō) *prep.* from end to end of.—*adv.* from end to end; to the end.—**throughout'** *adv.* in every part.— *prep.* in every part of.

Throw *v.t.* to fling; bring down.—*n.* an act or distance of throwing.

Thrum *n.* the fringe of threads remaining attached to a loom when the web has been cut off; any loose thread.—*pl.* coarse yarn; waste yarn.—*a.* made of waste yarn.— **thrummy** *a.*

Thrush *n.* a song-bird.

Thrush *n.* a throat disease of children; a foot disease of horses.

Thrust *v.t.* to push, stab, drive. —*v.i.* to lunge, stab; push one's way.—*n.* a lunge or stab with a pointed weapon, etc.

Thud *n.* a dull heavy sound, as of a brick falling on earth.— *v.i.* to make a thud.

Thug *n.* one of a band of professional robbers and assassins formerly infesting India; a cut-throat; a ruffian.

Thu'lium *n.* a rare-earth metal.

Thumb (-m) *n.* the short thick finger, the one which can be opposed to the others.— *v.t.* to handle or dirty with the thumb.

Thump *v.t.* to strike heavily. —*n.* a dull heavy blow; the sound of one.

Thun'der *n.* the loud noise accompanying lightning.— *v.i.* of thunder, to sound.— *v.t.* to utter loudly.— **thun'derbolt** *n.* a lightning flash as an agent of destruction.—**thun'dery** *a.*—**thun'derous** *a.*

Thurs'day *n.* the fifth day of the week.

Thus (TH-) *adv.* in this way; therefore.

Thwack *v.t.* and *n.* whack.

Thwaite *n.* a piece of ground reclaimed for tillage.

Thwart *v.t.* to foil, frustrate.— *adv.* across.

Thwart *n.* seat for a rower across a boat.

Thy (THĪ) *pron.* or *a.* belonging to thee.

Thyme (tīm) *n.* an aromatic herb.

Thy'mus *n.* a small ductless gland in the upper part of the chest (corresponding to the sweetbread of calves and lambs).

Tiar'a *n.* a jewelled head-ornament.

Tib'ia *n.* the shin-bone.— **tib'ial** *a.*

Tic *n.* a spasmodic twitch in the muscles of the face.

Tick *n.* a mite in hair or fur.

Tick *n.* a mattress case.

Tick *n.* a slight tap, as of a watch-movement; a small mark (√).—*v.t.* to mark with a tick.—*v.i.* to make the sound.

Tick *n.* credit; trust.—*v.t.* to buy or sell on tick; to live on credit.—**tick-shop** *n.* a shop where goods may be had on credit.

Tick'et *n.* a card or paper entitling to admission, travel, etc.; a label.—*v.t.* to attach a label to.

Tickle *v.i.* to itch.—*v.t.* to make itch with light touches, etc.—**tick'lish** *a.* sensitive to tickling; requiring care or tact in handling.

Tide *n.* season or time; the rise and fall of the sea happening twice each lunar day; a stream.—*v.i.* **to tide over,** to get over or surmount.—*v.t.* to enable some one to do this.—**ti'dings** *n.* news.—**ti'dy** *a.* orderly, neat. —*v.t.* to put in order.—**ti'dal** *a.* of or resembling a tide.

Tie *v.t.* to fasten, bind; restrict.—*n.* that with which anything is bound; a cravat; a bond; a drawn game with equal points; a match. *Syn.* unite, join, secure, attach, knot, connect, link. *Ant.* untie, loosen, separate.

Ti'er (tē'ẹr) *n.* a row, rank, layer.

Tiff'in *n.* a lunch, or slight repast, between breakfast and dinner.

Ti'ger *n.* a large carnivorous animal with striped coat.— **ti'gress** *fem.*

Tight (tīt) *a.* firm; tense, taut; fitting close; not allowing the passage of water, etc.—

tights *n.pl.* tight-fitting elastic garments.—**tight'en** *v.t.* and *i.*—**tight'ly** *adv.*

Tile *n.* a slab of baked clay.— *v.t.* to cover with tiles.

Till *n.* a drawer for money in a shop.

Till *v.t.* to cultivate.—**till'er** *n.* —**till'age** *n.*—**tilth** *n.*

Till *prep.* up to the time of.— *conj* to the time that.

Till *n.* a stiff clay containing boulders; the boulder-clay.

Till'er *n.* a lever to move a rudder of a boat.

Tilt *n.* a cover for a wagon.

Tilt *v.t.* and *i.* to slope, slant. —*n.* slope.

Tilt *v.i.* to take part in a mediæval combat with lances.—*n.* a combat for mounted men with lances.

Timb'er *n.* wood for building, etc.—**tim'bered** *a.* made or partly made of wood.

Timbre (tam'br) *n.* quality of musical sound.

Time *n.* existence as a succession of states; hour; duration; period; a point in duration.—*v.t.* to choose or note the time of.—**time'ly** *a.* seasonable.—**time'-piece** *n.* a watch or clock. - **time'-honoured** *a.* respectable because old.—**time-server** *n.* an opportunist.—**Greenwich time,** time as settled by the passage of the sun over the meridian at Greenwich.— **mean time,** an average of apparent time.

Tim'id *a.* lacking courage.— **timid'ity** *n.*—**tim'idly** *adv.*— **tim'orous** *a.* timid.

Tin *n.* a malleable white metal;

a vessel of tin or tinned iron. —*v.t.* to coat with tin; to put in a tin, *esp.* for preserving (food).—**tinn'y** *a.* of sound, harsh or cracked.—**tin-hat**, soldier's name for a shrapnel-proof steel-helmet.

Tin'cal, tin'kal *n.* crude or unrefined borax.

Tinc'ture *n.* colour, stain; a solution of a medical substance.—*v.t.* to colour, imbue.

Tin'der *n.* dry easily-burning material used to catch a spark from flint and steel.

Tine *n.* the tooth or spike of a fork, an antler, a harrow, etc.

Ting *n.* a sharp sound, as of a bell; a tinkling.—*v.i.* to tinkle.

Tinge *v.t.* to colour or flavour slightly.—*n.* a slight trace.

Tin'gle (-ng-gl) *v.i.* to vibrate; thrill.

Tink'er *n.* a mender of pots and pans.—*v.i.* to work in clumsy or amateur fashion.

Tin'kle (-ng-kl) *v.* to give out a series of light sounds like a small bell.—*v.t.* to cause to do this.—*n.* the sound or action of this.

Tin'sel *n.* thin metal plates, cord, etc., for decoration; anything sham and showy.

Tint *n.* a colour; a tinge.—*v.t.* to dye, to give a tint to.

Tintinnabula'tion *n.* the sound of bells.

Tintom'eter *n.* a contrivance for measuring intensity of colour.

Ti'ny *a.* very small.

Tip *n.* the slender or pointed end of anything; a piece of metal, leather, etc., protecting or softening a tip.—*v.t.* to put a tip on.—**tip'staff** *n.* a sheriff's officer, who carried a tipped staff.—**tiptop'** *a.* of the best quality or highest degree.

Tip *n.* a small present of money; a piece of useful private information.—*v.t.* to give a tip to.—**tip'ster** *n.* one who sells tips about races.

Tip *v.t.* to upset.—*v.i.* to topple over.—*n.* a place for tipping carts, emptying out rubbish, etc.—**tip'-cat** *n.* a game in which a spindle of wood is struck into the air by hitting one of the pointed ends with a stick; the piece of wood struck.

Tip *v.t.* to touch lightly.—*n.* a children's game in which a pursuer touches one of the others pursued, who then becomes the pursuer.

Tipp'et *n.* a covering for the neck and shoulders.

Tip'ple *v.i.* to take strong drink habitually in considerable quantity.—*v.t.* to drink.—*n.* drink.—**tipp'ler** *n.*

Tip'sy *a.* drunk or partly drunk.

Tirade' *n.* a long speech, generally vigorous and hostile.

Tire *n.* and *v.* attire; (also **tyre** incorrectly) a rim of metal, rubber, etc., round a wheel.—*v.t.* to put one on.

Tire *v.i.* to become weary or fatigued.—*v.t.* to fatigue.—**tire'some** *a.* wearisome, irritating. *Syn.* harass, bore, fag. *Ant.* refresh, enliven, amuse.

Ti'ro *n.* (also tyro incorrectly) a beginner, novice.

Tiss'ue *n.* a fine woven fabric; the substance of an animal body, a plant, etc.—tiss'ue-paper *n.* a very thin paper.

Tit *n.* a small horse; varieties of small birds, usually in combination, e.g. *tomtit*, *blue-tit.*—tit'bit *n.* a toothsome morsel.

Titan'ic (tī-) *a.* huge.

Tita'nium *n.* a rare metal, of a deep blue colour, very light and brittle.

Tithe (-TH) *n.* a tenth part, *esp.* of agricultural produce paid as a tax.—*v.t.* to exact tithes from.

Tithon'ic *a.* pertaining to the chemical rays of light.—tithonicity *n.*

Tit'illate *v.t.* to tickle, stimulate agreeably. — titilla'tion *n.*

Titi'vate *v.t.* and *i.* to dress or smarten up.

Ti'tle *n.* a heading, name of a book; name, appellation; legal right or document proving it.

Tit'mouse *n.* a small bird.

Ti'trate *v.t.* to determine the amount of an ingredient in a solution by standard solution, as in volumetric analysis.

Titt'er *v.i.* to giggle or laugh in a suppressed way.—*n.* such laugh.

Tit'tle *n.* a whit, detail.

Tit'tle-tat'tle *n.* gossip.—*v.i.* to gossip.

Tit'ular *a.* so in name or title only; held by virtue of a title.—tit'ularly *adv.*

To *prep.* towards, in the direction of; as far as; *used* to introduce a comparison, ratio, indirect object, infinitive mood, etc.—*adv.* to the required or normal state or position.

Toad *n.* an animal like a frog. —toad'stool *n.* a fungus like a mushroom, but usually poisonous.—toad'y *n.* one who fawns or curries favour unworthily.—*v.i.* to do this. — toad-in-the-hole, beef baked in batter.

Toast *v.t.* to brown at the fire; to warm; to drink the health of.—*n.* a slice of bread browned at the fire; a health; a person toasted.—toast'-master *n.* one whose duty is to announce toasts at a public banquet.

Tobacc'o *n.* a plant of which the leaves are used for smoking; the prepared leaves.—tobacc'onist *n.* a dealer in tobacco.

Tobog'gan *n.* a sledge for sliding down a slope of snow or ice.—*v.i.* to slide on one.

Tob'y *n.* a small jug in the form of an old man with a three-cornered hat.

Toc'sin *n.* an alarm rung on a bell.

To-day' *n.* this day.—*adv.* on this day.

Tod'dle *v.i.* to walk with unsteady short steps.—*n.* a toddling.—todd'ler *n.* a little child.

Todd'y *n.* a sweetened mixture of whisky, hot water, etc.

Toe *n.* a digit of the foot.—*v.t.* to reach or touch with the toe.

Toff'ee *n.* a sweetmeat made of boiled sugar, etc.

To'ga *n.* the loose outer garment worn by the ancient Romans.

Togeth'er (-TH-) *adv.* in company, simultaneously.

Togg'ery *n.* clothes; garments.—**togs** *n.* garments; clothes.—**long togs**, shore-clothes.

Togg'le *n.* a small wooden pin, tapering both ends, with a groove round its centre; the cross-piece at the free end of a watch-chain. — **toggle-iron** *n.* a kind of harpoon having a movable blade instead of fixed barbs.—**toggle-joint**, an elbow or knee joint, consisting of two bars so connected that they may be brought into a straight line and made to produce great end-wise pressure.

Togt (toht) *n.* in South Africa, a trading journey; labour by the job.

Toil *v.i.* to labour.—*n.* heavy work or task.—**toil'some** *a.* *Syn.* of *n.* work, struggle, effort, travail, pains. *Ant.* ease, idleness, repose.

Toil'et *n.* the process of dressing; articles used in this manner of doing it, style of dress; a dressing-table; a cover for it.

Toils *n.pl.* nets for catching game.

Tokay' *n.* a kind of wine produced at *Tokay* in Hungary, made of white grapes, and having a remarkable aroma.

To'ken *n.* a sign or object used as evidence.

Tol'erate *v.t.* to put up with.—**tolera'tion** *n.*—**tol'erable** *a.*—**tol'erably** *adv.*—**tol'erant** *a.* disinclined to interfere with others' ways or opinions.—**tol'erance** *n.*—**tol'erantly** *adv.* *Syn.* allow, permit, admit, receive, abide, brook.

Toll (tōl) *n.* a tax, *esp.* for the use of a bridge or road.

Toll (tōl) *v.t.* to make (a bell) ring slowly at regular intervals; to announce a death thus.—*v.i.* to ring in this way.—*n.* the action or sound of tolling.

Tom'ahawk *n.* a fighting axe as used by Red Indians.—*v.t.* to strike or kill with one.

Toma'to (-à-) *n.* a plant with a bright red fruit; the fruit.

Tomb (tōōm) *n.* a grave or monument over one.

Tom'boy *n.* a romping boyish girl.

Tom'-cat *n.* a male cat.

Tome *n.* a volume or large book.

To-morr'ow (-ō) *n.* the day after to-day.—*adv.* on the next day after this one.

Ton (tun) *n.* a measure of weight, 20 cwt.; a unit of a ship's carrying capacity.—**tonn'age** *n.* carrying capacity; charge per ton; ships.

Tone *n.* quality of musical sound; quality of voice, colour, etc.; healthy condition.—*v.t.* to give a tone to.—**ton'ic** *a.* relating to tone; improving bodily tone or condition.—*n.* a medicine to do this.

Tongs (-z) *n.pl.* large pincers, *esp.* for handling coal, etc.

Tongue (tung) *n.* the muscular organ inside the mouth, used for speech, taste, etc.; various things shaped like this; language.

To-night' (-nīt) *n.* this night; the coming night.—*adv.* on this night.

Ton'ite (ton'-īt) *n.* an explosive of gun-cotton and barium nitrate.

Tonneau (ton-ō) *n.* a motor-car body open at the back.

Ton'sil *n.* a gland at the side of the throat.

Ton'sure *n.* the shaving of part of the head as a religious or monastic practice; the part shaved.—*v.t.* to shave thus.

Ton'tine (-ēn) *n.* an annuity paid to subscribers or the survivor(s).

Too *adv.* in addition; in excess, more than enough.

Tool *n.* an implement or appliance for mechanical operations.—*v.t.* to work on with a tool.

Toot *n.* the sound of a horn.—*v.t.* and *i.* to make it.

Tooth *n.*, **teeth** *pl.* an ivory process of the jaw; various pointed things like this.—**tooth'some** *a.* pleasant to eat.

Top *n.* the highest part; a platform on a ship's mast.—*v.t.* to cut off, put on, pass, or reach, a top.—**top'most** *a.*

Top *n.* a toy which spins on a point.

To'paz *n.* a precious stone of various colours.

Tope *v.i.* to drink to excess habitually.—**to'per** *n.*

Topee' *n.* the cork or pith helmet worn in the tropics.

To'piary *a.* shaped by cutting or pruning; made ornamental by trimming or training.

Top'ic *n.* a subject of a discourse or conversation.—**top'ical** *a.* of a topic; up-to-date, having news value.—**topog'raphy** *n.* the description of a place; its features.—**topograph'ic** *a.* — **topograph'ically** *adv.* — **topog'rapher** *n.*

Top'ple *v.t.* to fall over.

Topsy-tur'vy *a.* upside down.

Tor *n.* a pointed hill.

Torch *n.* a twist of hemp, etc., soaked in tar or oil to burn as a portable light.—**torch'light** *n.*—**torch'bearer** *n.*

Toreador' *n.* a bull-fighter.

Tor'ment *n.* suffering or agony of body or mind.—**torment'** *v.t.* to afflict; to tease.—**torment'or** *n.* *Syn.* agony, rack, torture, pang, throe, distress.

Torna'do *n.* a whirlwind; a violent storm.

Torpe'do *n.* a fish which gives out an electric discharge; a cigar-shaped missile filled with explosives and propelling itself by a compressed air engine through the water after discharge from a ship.—*v.t.* to strike or sink with a torpedo.—**torpe'do-boat** *n.*—**torpe'do-boat-destroy'er** *n.* (usually *destroyer*, or *T.B.D.*).

Tor'pid *a.* sluggish, dormant.—torpid'ity n.—tor'por n. torpid state.

Torque n. a collar, or similar ornament, of twisted gold or other metal; in mechanics, rotating or twisting forces.—torque-rod, in motoring, a rod fitted to live axle to prevent its twisting round with drive.—torque-tube, in motoring, tube enclosing propeller shaft, and acting as torque-rod.

Torr'ent n. a rushing stream.—torren'tial a.—torr'id a. hot, scorching.

Torr'id a. parched; dried with heat.—torr'idness n.—torrid'ity n.

Tor'sion n. twist.—tort n. a breach of legal duty.—tort'-oise (-us) n. a four-footed reptile covered with a shell of horny plates.—tort'uous a. winding, twisting; not straightforward.—tort'ure n. the infliction of severe pain.—v.t. to subject to torture.—tort'urer n. — torture chamber n.

Tor'so n., pl. torsos, the trunk of a statue mutilated of head and limbs.

Tort n. a wrong; a twist or wrench.—tor'tile a. twisted; coiled.—tor'tive a. twisted; wreathed.

Tor'y n. a political conservative or die-hard.

Toss v.t. to throw up or about.—v.i. to be thrown, or fling oneself, about.—n. an act of tossing.—toss'pot n. a toper.

Tot n. a very small thing; a small quantity, esp. of a drink; a tiny child.

Tot v.t. to add up.—v.i. (with up) to amount to.—n. an addition sum.—to'tal n. the whole amount.—a. complete, entire. — v.t. to add up; amount to. — total'ity n.—totalisa'tor n. a machine to operate mutual betting on a race-course.

Tote n. abbreviation from TOTALISATOR.

To'tem n. a tribal badge or emblem.

Tott'er v.i. to walk unsteadily, begin to fall.

Tou'can (tou-kan) n. a bird of tropical America remarkable for the large size of its bill.

Touch (tuch) v.t. to put the hand on, come into contact with; reach; move the feelings of.—v.i. to call; (with on) to refer to.—n. a touching; a slight blow, stroke, contact, amount, etc.—touch'wood n. tinder.—touch'stone n. a stone for testing gold or silver.—touch'-paper n. fuse for firing a charge.—touch'y a. irritable, sensitive.

Tough (tuf) a. strong and pliable, not brittle; sturdy; difficult; needing effort to bite.— tough'ness n.—tough'en v.t. and i.

Toupee', toupet' (-pē, -pā) n. a curl, or artificial lock of hair.

Tour (tōōr) n. a travelling round.—v.t. to travel through.—v.i. to travel.—tour'ist n. one who travels for pleasure.

Tour'nament n. a meeting for knightly contests; a meeting for games or athletic contests.—**tour'ney** *n.* a tournament.

Tour'niquet (-nē-kā) *n.* a bandage which can be tightened by twisting a crosspiece put through it.

Tou'sle *v.t.* disorder.

Tout *v.i.* to solicit custom (usually in an undesirable fashion).—*n.* one who does this.

Tow (tō) *n.* hemp or flax fibre.

Tow (tō) *v.t.* to drag at the end of a rope.—*n.* a towing or being towed; a vessel in tow.—**tow'age** *n.*

Tow'ard (tō'ard) *a.* docile (also **tow'ardly**). — **towards'** (tordz, to-wordz') *prep.* in the direction of.—(also **toward'**).

Tow'el *n.* a cloth for wiping off moisture after washing.—**tow'elling** *n.* material used for towels.

Tow'er *n.* a tall square or round building or part of a building; a fortress.—*v.i.* to rise aloft, to stand very high.

Town *n.* a collection of dwellings, etc., larger than a village. — **town'ship** *n.* a division of a large parish containing a village or town.

Tox'ic *a.* poisonous, due to poison.—**toxicol'ogy** *n.* the science of poisons.—**tox'in** *n.* a poisonous ptomaine.

Toxoph'ilite *n.* a student or lover of archery. — **toxophilit'ic** *a.*

Toy *n.* a plaything.—*v.i.* to act idly, trifle.

Trace *n.* the chain or strap by which a horse pulls a vehicle, a track left by anything; an indication; a minute quantity.—*v.t.* to follow the course or track of; to find out; to make a plan of, to draw.—**tra'cery** *n.* interlaced or network ornament.

Tracho'a (-kē-) *n.* the windpipe. — *pl.* **trache'æ.** — **trache'al** *a.*

Track *n.* a mark or line of marks, left by the passage of anything; a path; a course. —*v.t.* to follow up the track of, *esp.* in hunting.

Tract *n.* a space of land, etc., an area.

Tract *n.* a pamphlet, *esp.* a religious one.—**tract'ate** *n.* a treatise.—**tract'able** *a.* easy to manage, docile.

Trac'tion *n.* the action of drawing.—**trac'tion-engine** *n.* —**tract'or** *n.* an engine, *esp.* motor-driven, for drawing.

Trade *n.* commerce, traffic; the practice of buying and selling; any profitable pursuit; those engaged in a trade.—*v.i.* to engage in trade.—*v.t.* to buy and sell; to barter.—**trade'-mark** *n.* a distinctive mark on a maker's goods.—**tra'der** *n.*—**trade-u'nion** *n.* a society of workmen for protection of their interests.—**trade'-wind** *n.* a wind blowing constantly towards the equator in certain parts of the globe.

Tradi'tion *n.* a body of beliefs, facts, etc., handed down from generation to generation without being reduced to writing; the process of handing down.—**tradi'tional** *a.*—**tradi'tionally** *adv.*

Traduce' *v.t.* to slander. *Syn.* calumniate, vilify, disparage, detract, depreciate, decry.

Traff'ic *n.* the passing to and fro of vehicles, etc., in a road or street, etc.; trade.—*v.i.* to trade.—**traff'icker** *n.* a trader. (See illus. on p. 573.)

Trag'acanth (-kanth) *n.* leguminous plant of the genus *Astragalus* yielding an adhesive gum.

Trag'edy (-j-) *n.* a drama showing the ruin or downfall of the principal character, dealing with the sorrowful or terrible side of life; this type of drama.—**trag'ic** *a.* of, or in the manner of, tragedy; disastrous; appalling.—**trag'ically** *adv.*—**trage'dian** *n.* a player in tragedy.—**tragi-com'edy** *n.* a play with tragic and comic elements.

Tra'gus *n.* a prominence at the entrance of the outer ear.

Trail *v.t.* to drag behind one.—*v.i.* to be drawn behind; to hang loosely.—*n.* a thing that trails; the back end of a gun-carriage; a track or trace.—**trai'ler** *n.* a creeper; a vehicle attached to another vehicle; a trailing plant; a weight-carrying engineless vehicle designed to be towed by a heavy motor-car.—**trailing-axle**, in motoring, usually rear-axle of flexible six-wheeler.

Train *v.t.* to cause to grow in a particular way; to educate, instruct, exercise; to aim (a gun).—*v.i.* to follow a course of training, *esp.* to achieve physical fitness for athletics.—*n.* a trailing part of a dress; a body of attendants; a fuse or trail of powder to a mine; a line of railway vehicles joined to a locomotive; a collection of vehicles, etc., *esp.* in military use.—**train'-ing** *n.* the process of educating; education; the act of forming young trees or shrubs to grow in a particular way; the art of preparing men for athletic exercises, or horses for the race-course.

Train'-oil *n.* oil from the blubber of whales.

Trait (trā-) *n.* a characteristic.

Trait'or *n.* one who betrays or is guilty of treason.—**trait'-ress** *fem.*—**trait'orous** *a.*—**trait'orously** *adv.*

Trajec'tory *n.* the line of flight of a projectile.

Tram *n.* a mining wagon-road; a line of rails; a truck running on rails; a car for passengers running on rails laid through streets.—**tram'car** *n.*—**tram'way** *n.* rails for trams in a street.

Tramm'el *n.* a net; anything that restrains or holds captive; a beam compass.—*v.t.* to restrain.

Tramp *v.i.* to walk heavily; to travel on foot, *esp.* as a vagabond or for pleasure.—*v.t.* to cross on foot.—*n.* an act of tramping; a walk; a vagabond.—**tram'ple** *v.t.* to tread under foot.

Trance (-à-) *n.* a state of suspended consciousness, *esp.* of rapture or ecstasy.

Tran'quil (-ng-kw-) *a.* calm, quiet. — **tran'quilly** *adv.*—**tranquill'ity** *n.*—**tran'quillise** *v.t. Syn.* still, serene, unruffled, placid, peaceful, composed. *Ant.* restless, uneasy, nervy, jumpy.

Trans- *prefix,* across, through, beyond.—**transact'** *v.t.* to carry on or through; conduct (an affair, etc.).—**transac'tion** *n.* the performing of any business; that which is performed; a single sale or purchase.—*pl.* proceedings; reports of scientific or philosophical associations.—**transcend'** *v.t.* to exceed, surpass. —**transcend'ent** *a.* — **transcend'ence** *n.*—**transcendent'al** *a.* surpassing experience; supernatural; abstruse. — **transcendent'alism** *n.*—**transcribe'** *v.t.* to copy out.—**trans'cript** *n.* a copy.—**trans'ept** *n.* the transverse part of a cruciform church; either of its arms.—**transfer'** *v.t* t) make over; move from o'ie place to another.—**trans'fer** *n.* a transferring or being transferred.—**trans'ferable** *a.* —**trans'ference** *n.* — **transfig'ure** *v.t.* to alter the appearance of; glorify.—**transfigura'tion** *n.*—**transfix'** *v.t.* to pierce.—**transform'** *v.t.* to change the shape or character of. — **transforma'tion** *n.*—**transform'er** *n.* in electricity, apparatus for changing the voltage of an alternating-current without the use of moving parts. — **transfuse'** *v.t.* to convey from one vessel to another, *esp.* of blood from a healthy person to an ill one.—**transfu'sion** *n.* —**transgress'** *v.t.* to break (a law); to sin. — **transgres'sion** *n.* — **transgress'or** *n.* — **tranship** *v.t.* to move from one ship, train, etc., to another. —**tranship'ment** *n.* — **tran'sient** *a.* passing away.— **tran'sience** *n.* — **tran'sit** *n.* passage, crossing. — **transi'tion** *n.* change from one state to another. — **transitional** *a.*—**tran'sitory** *a.* transient.—**translate'** *v.t.* to move (a bishop) from one see to another; to turn from one language into another.— **transla'tion** *n.*—**transla'tor** *n.* —**translit'erate** *v.t.* to write in the letters of another a'phabet.—**translitera'tion** *n.* —**translu'cent** *a.* letting light pass, semi-transparent.— **translu'cence** *n.*—**trans'migrate** *v.i.* of the soul, to pass into another body.—**transmigra'tion** *n.*—**transmit'** *v.t.* to send or cause to pass to another place, person, etc.— **transmis'sion** *n.*—**transmute'** *v.t.* to change in form, properties, or nature.—**transmuta'tion** *n.*—**tran'som** *n.* a cross-piece; a lintel.—**transpar'ent** *a.* letting light pass without distortion, that can be seen through distinctly; obvious.—**transpar'ence** *n.*—**transpar'ency** *n.* transparence; a picture made visible by a light behind it.—**transpar'ently** *adv.*—**transpire'** *v.t.* to exhale.—*v.i.* to exhale; to come to be known.—transpira'tion *n.*—transplant' *v.t.* to move and plant again in another place.—transplanta'tion *n.*—transpon'tine *a.* situated across a bridge, as the Surrey side of London.—transport' *v.t.* to convey from one place to another; to carry into banishment; to enrapture. — trans'port *n.* means of conveyance; ships, vehicles, etc., used in transporting stores; a ship so used.—transpose' *v.t.* to change the order of, interchange; put music into a different key. — transpo'sal *n.*—transposi'tion *n.*—transubstantia'tion *n.* change in essence or substance.—transude' *v.i.* to pass through the pores of a substance.—trans'verse *a.* lying across, at right angles.

Trap *n.* a snare, a contrivance for catching game, etc.; *a* movable covering for an opening, *esp.* through a ceiling, etc.; a two-wheeled carriage; an arrangement of pipes to prevent escape of gas, etc.—*v.t.* to catch, entrap.—trap'door *n.* a door in a floor or roof.—trapp'er *n.*

Trap *v.t.* to caparison.—trapp'ings *n.pl.* a caparison; equipment, ornaments. *Syn.* of "trappings," decorations, accoutrements, equipments, paraphernalia, housings.

Trapan' *v.t.* to ensnare; to catch by stratagem. Also trepan.

Trape'zium *n.* a quadrilateral figure with two sides only parallel.—trape'zoid *n.* a quadrilateral with no parallel sides.—trapeze' *n.* a horizontal bar suspended from two ropes.

Trash *n.* a clog; an encumbrance.—*v.t.* to hold back; to encumber.

Trash *v.t.* to wear out; to beat down.—*v.i.* to tramp and shuffle about.

Trash *n.* rubbish; loppings of trees, bruised canes and the like; nonsense.—trash'y *a.*

Trav'ail *v.i.* to labour or be in labour.—*n.* toil; the pains of childbirth.

Trav'el *v.i.* to journey.—*v.t.* to journey through.—*n.* journeying.—*pl.* an account of travelling.—trave'ller *n.* —trav'elogue *n.* travel talk; a geographical film.

Trav'erse *v.t.* to cross, go through or over; oppose.—traverse-table, a table of differences of latitude and departure; a movable platform for shifting carriages, wagons, etc., from one set of rails to another.

Trav'esty *n.* a comic imitation. —*v.t.* to ridicule by a travesty.

Trawl *n.* a net dragged along the bottom of the sea.—*v.i.* to fish with one.—trawl'er *n.* a trawling vessel.

Tray *n.* a flat board, usually with a rim, for carrying things; any similar utensil.

Treach'ery (trech-) *n.* deceit, betrayal.—treach'erous *a.*—treach'erously *adv.*

Trea'cle n. unrefined molasses, a thick syrup.

Tread (tred) v.t. to set foot on.—v.i. to walk.—n. a treading; fashion of walking; the upper surface of a step.—**trea'dle** n. a lever worked by the foot to turn a wheel.

Trea'son n. the offence of attempting to overthrow the government to which the offender owes allegiance; treachery; breaking allegiance.—**trea'sonable** a. constituting treason.—**trea'sonous** a.

Treas'ure (trezh-) n. riches, stored wealth or valuables.—v.t. to prize; to store up.—**treas'urer** n. an official in charge of funds.—**treas'ury** n. a place for finds or treasure, esp. of a state.—**treas'ure-trove** n. treasure found hidden with no evidence of the ownership.

Treat v.t. to deal with, act towards.—v.i. to negotiate.—n. an entertainment, a pleasure given.—**treat'ise** n. a book discussing a subject.—**treat'ment** n.—**treat'y** n. a contract between states.

Tre'ble (treb'l) a. threefold.—n. a soprano voice; part of music for it; a singer with such a voice.—v.t. and i. to increase threefold.—**treb'ly** adv.

Tree n. a large perennial plant with a woody trunk; a beam.

Tre'foil n. a plant with leaves in three parts, like the clover.

Trek v.i. to draw a vehicle, as oxen; to travel by ox-wagon.

—n. a journey with a wagon; a march.—**trekk'er** n.

Trell'is n. a lattice or grating of light bars fixed crosswise.—v.t. to screen or supply with trellis.

Trem'ble v.i. to quiver, shake.—n. a trembling.—**tremen'dous** a. causing fear or awe; vast, immense.—**trem'or** n. a trembling.—**trem'ulous** a. quivering easily; timorous.

Trench v.t. to cut grooves or ditches in.—v.i. to infringe.—n. a long narrow ditch, esp. as a shelter in war.—**trench'ant** a. cutting, incisive.—**trench'er** n. a wooden plate.

Trend v.i. to have a general direction.—n. direction or tendency.

Trepan' n. a cylindrical saw for perforating the skull.—v.t. to perforate the skull with a trepan.

Trepida'tion n. alarm.

Tres'pass n. wrongdoing: wrongful entering on another's land.—v.i. to commit trespass. Syn. of v. transgress, encroach, infringe, trench, offend, sin; of n. misdemeanour, misdeed, sin, infringement, encroachment, invasion.

Tress n. a lock of hair.

Tres'tle (-sl) n. a bar fixed on pairs of spreading legs and used as a support.

Trews (trōoz) n.pl. trousers of soldiers in Highland regiments.

Tri- prefix three.—**tri'colour** a. three coloured.—n. a tricolour flag, esp. the French one.—tri′cycle *n.* a vehicle like a bicycle, but with three wheels.—tri′dent *n.* a three-pronged fork.—trienn′ial *a.* happening every, or lasting, three years.

Tri′angle *n.* a figure with three angles.—triang′ular *a.*

Tribe *n.* a race or subdivision of a race of people.—tri′bal *a.*

Tribula′tion *n.* misery, trouble.

Trib′une *n.* a popular leader; a speaker′s platform; a bishop′s throne. — tribu′nal *n.* a law-court.

Trib′ute *n.* a tax paid by one state to another.—trib′utary *a.* paying tribute; auxiliary. —*n.* a stream flowing into another.

Tri′car *n.* a three-wheeled motor-car with the single driving-wheel behind.

Trice *v.t.* to pull up and secure with a rope.—*n.* in a trice, in one pull, in an instant.

Trick *n.* a stratagem; a feat of skill or cunning; the cards played in one round.—*v.t.* to cheat; to attire.—trick′ery *n.*—trick′ster *n.*—trick′sy *a.* sportive; deceptive; crafty. —trick′y *a.* crafty; ticklish.

Tric′kle *v.i.* to flow slowly or in drops.

Tri′fle *n.* an insignificant thing or matter; a pudding of sponge-cake, whipped cream, etc. — *v.i.* to act or speak idly.—tri′fling *a.* — tri′fler *n.*

Trigg′er *n.* a catch which releases a spring, *esp.* to fire a gun, etc.

Trigonom′etry *n.* the branch of mathematics dealing with the relations of the sides and angles of triangles.—trigonomet′rical *a.*

Tri′graph *n.* three letters united in pronunciation so as to have but one sound, or to form but one syllable, as *ieu* in *adieu*.

Trihe′dron *n.* a figure having three equal sides.—trihe′dral *a.*

Trilat′eral *a.* having three sides.—trilaterally *adv.*

Tril′by *n.* a kind of soft felt hat.

Trill *v.i.* to sing with quavering voice; to sing lightly.— *n.* such singing.

Tril′ogy (-j-) *n.* a series of three related dramas or novels.

Trim *v.t.* to prune; to adjust, put in good order.—*v.i.* to shuffle, act as a time-server. —*n.* order, state of being trimmed.—*a.* neat, smart; in good order.

Trin′dle *n.* in bookbinding, a piece of wood or metal put between the cords and the cover of a book to flatten the edges before cutting.

Trin′ity *n.* the state of being threefold; the three persons of the Godhead.—trinitar′ian (-ér-) *n.* and *a.*

Trink′et *n.* a small ornament for the person.

Tri′ode *n.* in wireless, a three-electrode thermionic valve.

Trip *v.i.* to run lightly, skip; to stumble.—*v.t.* to cause to stumble.—*n.* a light step; a stumble; a journey, an excursion.

Tripe *n.* the stomach of a

ruminant animal prepared for food.

Tri'plane *n.* an aeroplane having three main supporting planes or wings.

Trip'le *a.* threefold.—*v.t.* and *i.* to treble.—**trip'ly** *adv.*—**trip'let** *n.* three of a kind.—**tri'o** *n.* a group of three; music for three performers, etc.—**tri'partite** *a.* having three parts.—**trip'licate** *a.* threefold. — *v.t.* to make threefold.—*n.* state of being triplicate; one of a set of three copies.—**triplica'tion** *n.* —**tri'pod** *n.* a stool or stand, etc., with three feet.—**tri'pos** *n.* an honours examination at Cambridge; list of the successful candidates in three classes.—**trip'tych** *n.* a carving or picture in three compartments.—**tri'reme** *n.* a three-banked galley.

Trip'oli *n.* an earthy substance, originally brought from *Tripoli*, used in polishing stones and metal.

Trite *a.* hackneyed.—**trit'urate** *v.t.* to rub to powder. —**tritura'tion** *n.*

Tri'umph *n.* great success, victory; exultation.—*v.i.* to achieve great success or victory; to exult.—**triumph'ant** *a.*—**triumph'al** *a.*

Tri'umvir *n.* one of three men joined equally in an office.—**trium'virate** *n.*

Tri'une *a.* three in one.

Triv'et *n.* an iron bracket or stand for putting a pot or kettle on.

Triv'ial *a.* commonplace, trifling.—**trivial'ity** *n.*

Tro'car (-kar) *n.* an instrument for withdrawing superfluous fluid from the body (used in dropsy, hydrocele, etc.).

Troche (trōch, trosh, trōk, trō'kĕ) *n.* a small circular cake or lozenge containing a drug.

Tro'chee (trō-kē) *n.* in verse, a foot of two syllables, the first accented and the second unaccented.

Trog'lodyte *n.* a cave-dweller.

Troll (-ō-) *v.t.* to pass (cup) round; to sing heartily.

Troll (-ō-) *n.* a diminutive supernatural being in Scandinavian mythology.

Troll'ey *n.* a truck; the pole and wheel by which a tram-car collects power from the wire.

Troll'op *n.* a woman loosely dressed; a slattern.

Trom'bone *n.* a large trumpet of which part slides in and out of the other.

Troop *n.* a crowd of persons or animals; a unit of cavalry. —*pl.* soldiers.—*v.i.* to move in a troop.—**troop'er** *n.* a cavalry soldier.

Trope *n.* a figure of speech.

Tro'phy *n.* a memorial of a victory, hunt, etc.

Trop'ic *n.* either of two circles in the heavens or round the earth where the sun seems to turn at a solstice.—*pl.* the hot regions between the tropics.—**trop'ical** *a.*

Trot *v.i.* of a horse, to move at a medium pace, lifting the feet in diagonal pairs; of a person, etc., to run easily with short strides.—*n.* the action of trotting.

Troth (-ō-) *n.* faith.

Trou'badour *n.* one of a class of early poets that first appeared in Provence.

Trou'ble (trub'l) *v.t.* to disturb, afflict.—*v.i.* to be agitated or disturbed.—*n.* disturbance, agitation; inconvenience; distress. — **troub'lous** *a.*—**troub'lesome** *a. Syn.* of *n.* affliction, suffering, calamity, misfortune, adversity, sorrow, misery, annoyance, vexation, embarrassment, plague, torment.

Trough (trof) *n.* a long open vessel; the hollow between two waves.

Trounce *v.t.* to beat thoroughly.

Trou'sers *n.pl.* a two-legged outer garment with legs reaching to the ankles.

Trou'sseau (trōō-) *n.* an outfit of clothing, *esp.* for a bride.

Trout *n.* a fresh-water fish esteemed as food.

Trow'el *n.* a small tool like a spade for spreading mortar, lifting plants, etc.

Troy-weight *n.* a system of weights used for gold and silver.

Tru'ant *n.* one absent from duty without leave, *esp.* a child so absenting himself (or herself) from school.

Truce *n.* a temporary cessation of fighting.

Truck *v.t.* and *i.* to barter.—*n.* barter; payment of workmen in goods; garden produce.— **truck farm** *n.* market garden.

Truck *n.* an open vehicle for heavy goods; a kind of barrow; a disc at a masthead.—**truc'kle-bed** *n.* a small bed on castors which could be pushed under a larger bed.—**truc'kle** *v.i.* to cringe, fawn.

Truc'ulent *a.* ferocious, inclined to fight. *Syn.* fell, barbarous, cruel, ruthless, bloodthirsty.

Trudge *v.i.* to walk laboriously. —*n.* a laborious walk.

Trudge'on (truj-) *n.* a racing stroke in swimming.

True (trōō) *a.* in accordance with facts; faithful; exact, correct.—**truth** (-ōō-) *n.* state of being true; something that is true.—**tru'ism** *n.* a self-evident truth. — **tru'ly** *adv.*—**truth'ful** *a.* — **truth'-fully** *adv. Syn.* real, actual, veritable, accurate, veracious, truthful, sincere, upright, honest, pure, constant, steady, loyal. *Ant.* untrue, false, inaccurate, lying, mendacious, two-faced, disloyal, wavering.

Truf'fle *n.* an eatable fungus growing underground.

Trull *n.* a drab; a trollop.

Trumeau' (-mō) *n.; pl.* **trumeaux'** (-mōz), a piece of wall between two openings.

Trump *n.* a trumpet. **trum'-pet** *n.* a metal wind instrument like a horn.—*v.i.* to blow a trumpet or make a sound like one.—*v.t.* to proclaim.

Trump *n.* a card of a suit temporarily ranking above the others.—*v.t.* to take with a trump.—*v.i.* to trump up, to get up, fabricate.

Trum'pery *a.* showy but worthless.—*n.* worthless finery.

Trunc'ate *v.t.* to cut short.

Trun'cheon *n.* a short thick club or baton; a staff of office.

Trun'dle *n.* any round, rolling thing; a low cart, with small wooden wheels; a wheel or pinion having its teeth formed of cylinders or spindles, as in mill-work.—*v.t.* to roll, as a thing on little wheels.—*v.i.* to roll, as on little wheels.—**trundle-bed**, a low bed that is moved on little wheels, so that it can be pushed under a higher bed.

Trunk *n.* the main stem of a tree; a person's body without or excluding the head and limbs; a box for clothes, etc.; an elephant's or other proboscis.

Truss *v.t.* to fasten up, tie up.—*n.* a support; a bundle (of hay, etc.).

Trust *n.* confidence, firm belief; property held for another; state of being relied on; a combination of producers to do away with competition and keep up prices.—*v.t.* to rely on, believe in.—**trustee'** *n.* one legally holding property on another's behalf. — **trustee'ship** *n.*—**trust'ful** *a.*—**trust'worthy** *a.*—**trust'y** *a.* trustworthy.

Truth *see* TRUE.

Try *v.t.* to test; investigate (a case); attempt.—*v.i.* to attempt something, endeavour.—**tri'al** *n.*

Tryst *n.* an appointment to meet.

Tset'se *n.* a fly found in South Africa the bite of which is often fatal to horses and cattle.

Tub *n.* an open wooden vessel like the bottom half of a barrel; a bath.—*v.t.* and *i.* to bathe.

Tube *n.* a pipe, a long narrow hollow cylinder.—**tu'bular** *a.*

Tu'ber *n.* a swelling on the roots of certain plants, e.g. a potato.—**tu'bercle** *n.* a granular small tumour in consumptive lungs, etc.—**tuber'cular** *a.*—**tuberculo'sis** *n.* a disease marked by the presence of tubercles and a characteristic bacillus, *esp.* consumption of the lungs.

Tuck *v.t.* to gather or stitch in folds; to draw or roll together.—*n.* a stitched fold; food, *esp.* dainties eaten by schoolboys.

Tues'day *n.* the third day of the week.

Tuft *n.* a bunch of feathers, threads, etc.

Tug *v.t.* to pull hard or violently.—*n.* a violent pull; a steamship used to tow other vessels.

Tui'tion *n.* teaching, instruction.

Tu'lip *n.* a plant with bright bell-shaped flowers.

Tulle (tōōl) *n.* a kind of fine thin silk, open network or lace.

Tum'ble *v.i.* to fall; turn somersaults.—*v.t.* to throw down; to rumple.—*n.* a fall; a somersault.—**tum'bler** *n.* an acrobat; a flat-bottomed drinking-glass.

Tu'mid *a.* swollen.—**tu'mour** *n.* a morbid swelling.—**tu'mult** *n.* uproar, commotion.—**tumult'uous** *a.*—**tu'mulus** *n.* a burial mound.—**tu'mular** *a.*

Tun *n.* a large cask.

Tun'dra *n.* the flat marshy plains in the north of Russia and Siberia.

Tune *n.* melody; concord; adjustment of a musical instrument.—*v.t.* to put in tune. — **tune'ful** *a.* — **tune'fully** *adv.*—**tu'ner** *n.*

Tung'sten *n.* a meta of a grayish-white colour and considerable lustre, used in the manufacture of steel and for electric lamp filaments.

Tu'nic *n.* a short military coat; a garment of similar shape.

Tunn'el *n.* an artificial underground passage.—*v.t.* to make a tunnel through.—**tunn'eller** *n.*

Tunn'y *n.* a fish.

Tur'ban *n.* an Oriental man's headdress made by coiling a length of material round a cap or the head.

Tur'bid *a.* muddy.—**turbid'ity** *n.*—**tur'bine** *n.* a kind of water-wheel; a rotary steam-engine.—**tur'bulent** *a.* riotous in commotion.

Tur'bot *n.* a large flat-fish.

Tureen' *n.* a dish for soup.

Turf *n.* short grass with the earth bound to it by the matted roots; a sod.—*v.t.* to lay with turf.

Tur'gid *a.* bombastic. — **turgid'ity** *n.* *Syn.* swollen, inflated, tumid, pompous, bombastic.

Tur'key *n.* a large bird reared for food.

Tur'moil *n.* confusion and bustle.

Turn *v.t.* to make move round or rotate; to shape on a lathe; to change, reverse, alter position of, etc.—*v.i.* to move round; to change; to become, etc.—*n.* act of turning; road; walk; rotation; part of a rotation; a performance; an inclination; etc.—**turn'er** *n.*—**turn'coat** *n.* one that forsakes his party or principles.—**turn'cock** *n.* a person in charge of public taps, etc.—**turn'key** *n.* a gaoler.—**turn'out** *n.* act of coming forth; a short side track on a railroad; an equipage; a strike, as of workmen; a crowd of spectators; the quantity of produce yielded.—**turn'over** *n.* act of turning over; the amount of money drawn in a business.—**turn'pike** *n.* a gate across a road where tolls are paid.—**turn'stile** *n.* a revolving gate for controlling admission of people.—**turn'table** *n.* a revolving platform, *esp.* to turn locomotives.—**turning circle**, in motoring, circle described by vehicle driven on full steering lock.

Turn'ip *n.* a plant with a round root used as a vegetable or fodder.

Turp'entine *n.* a resin got from certain trees; oil or spirit made from this.

Turp'itude *n.* baseness.

Tur'quoise *n.* a blue precious stone.

Turr'et *n.* a small tower; a revolving tower for a gun on a ship or fort.

Tur'tle *n.* a dove.

Tur'tle *n.* a sea-tortoise.

Tusk *n.* a long pointed tooth sticking out from a mouth.—**tusk'er** *n.* an animal with tusks fully developed.

Tus'sle *n.* a scuffle, struggle.

Tuss'ock *n.* a clump of grass.

Tu'tor *n.* a person giving lessons, privately, or to individuals in a college; a guardian.—**tutor'ial** *a.*—**tu'-telage** *n.* guardianship.—**tu'telary** *a.*

Twad'dle *n.* talk not worth listening to.—*v.t.* to utter twaddle.—**twadd'ler** *n.*

Twain *a.* two.—*n.* two persons or things.

Twang *n.* a ringing metallic sound.—*v.i.* and *t.* to make, or cause to make, such sound.

Tweak *v.t.* to pinch and twist or pull.—*n.* an act of tweaking.

Tweed *n.* a rough-surfaced cloth, usually of mixed colours.

Tweez'ers *n.pl.* small forceps or pincers.

Twelve *n.* and *a.* a cardinal number, two more than ten.—**twelfth** *a.* the ordinal number.

Twent'y *n.* and *a.* a cardinal number, twice ten.—**twent'ieth** *a.* the ordinal number.

Twice *adv.* two times.

Twid'dle *v.t.* to twirl.

Twig *n.* a small branch.

Twi'light *n.* the half light after sunset or before dawn.

Twill *n.* a fabric woven so as to have a surface of parallel ridges.—*v.t.* to weave thus.

Twin *n.* one of a pair, *esp.* of children born together.—*a.* being a twin.

Twine *v.t.* and *t.* to twist or coil round.—*n.* string.

Twinge *n.* a momentary sharp pain.

Twin'kle *v.i.* to shine with dancing or quivering light.—*n.* a twinkling; a flash; a gleam of amusement in eyes or face.

Twire *v.i.* to glance slyly; to look askance; to wink.

Twirl *v.t.* to turn or twist round quickly.

Twist *v.t.* and *i.* to make or become spiral, by turning with one end fast.—*n.* an act of twisting; something twisted.

Twit *v.t.* to taunt.

Twitch *v.i.* to give a momentary sharp pull; to jerk.—*v.t.* to pull at thus.—*n.* such pull or jerk; a spasmodic jerk.

Twitt'er *v.i.* of birds, to utter a succession of tremulous sounds. — *n.* such succession of notes.

Two (tōō) *n.* and *a.* a cardinal number, one more than one.—**two'fold** *adv.* and *a.*—**two-cycle**, in internal-combustion engine, to denote a two-stroke engine. — **two-decker**, in motoring, a bus having two decks for passengers.—**two-electrode valve**, in wireless, thermionic valve containing plates and filament only.—**two-stroke**, an internal-combustion engine making one explosion to every two strokes of piston.

Two-seat'er *n.* a motor-car designed to accomodate two persons.

Type *n.* a class; characteristic build; a specimen, a block bearing a letter used for printing; such pieces collectively; state of being set up for printing.—*v.t.* to print with a typewriter.—**type'writer** *n.* a keyed writing machine. — **ty'pist** *n.* —**typ'ical** *a.*—**typ'ically** *adv.* —**typ'ify** *v.t.* to serve as a type or model of.—**typog'raphy** *n.* the art of printing; style of printing.—**typograph'ical** *a.*

Ty'phoid *n.* a fever attacking the intestines.—**ty'phus** *n.* a contagious fever.

Typhoon' *n.* a violent hurricane

Ty'rant *n.* an oppressive or cruel ruler.—**tyrann'ical** *a.*—**tyrann'ically** *adv.*—**tyrann-icide.** *n.* the slayer of a tyrant; his deed.—**tyr'annise** *v.i.* — **tyr'annous** *a.* — **tyr'anny** *n.*

Tyre *n.* a ring, usually of inflated rubber, round the circumference of a wheel; a tire.

Tyro *see* TIRO.

U

Ubiq'uity (ū-bik'w-) *n.* a being everywhere.—**ubiq'uitous** *a.*

Udd'er *n.* the milk-bag of a cow, etc.

Ug'ly *a.* unpleasing or repulsive to the sight; ill-omened; threatening.—**ug'liness** *n.*

U'itlander (ōō-it-) *n.* an outlander or incomer in the Transvaal.

Ukele'le (ū-ke-lā-li) *n.* a small four-stringed instrument of Hawaiian origin, resembling a guitar.

Ul'cer *n.* an open sore.—**ul'cerate** *v.i.* to form an ulcer. —*v.t.* to make ulcerous.— **ul'cerous** *a.*—**ulcera'tion** *n.*

Ull'age *n.* that quantity which a cask wants of being full.

Ul'na *n.*; *pl.* **ul'næ**, the larger of the two bones of the fore-arm.

Ul'ster *n.* a long, loose overcoat originally made in *Ulster*.

Ulte'rior *a.* situated beyond; beyond what appears.

Ult'imate *a.* last, furthest.—**ult'imately** *adv.* — **ultima'tum** *n.* a final proposal the rejection of which causes war.—**ult'imo** *adv.* in last month.

Ultramarine' (-ēn) *a.* beyond the sea.—*n.* a blue pigment. —**ultramont'ane** *a.* south of or beyond the Alps; favourable to the absolute authority of the Pope.—**ul'tra-modern** *a.* very up-to-date.—**ul'tra-short waves,** in wireless, by international definition, waves below ten metres.—**ultravi'olet** *a.* beyond the violet (of rays of the spectrum).

Um'ber *n.* a dark brown pigment.

Umbili'cal *a.* of the navel.

Um'brage *n.* sense of injury, offence. — **umbrage'ous** *a.* shady.—**umbrell'a** *n.* a light folding circular cover of silk, etc., on a stick, carried in the hand to protect against rain.

Um'pire *n.* a person chosen to decide a question; a person chosen to decide disputes and enforce the rules in a game. —*v.t.* to act as umpire in.— *v.i.* to act as umpire.

Ump'teen *a. sl.* many; any number.

Un- *prefix*, makes compounds negativing the idea of the simple word, e.g. **unarmed'** *a.* not armed.—**unfast'en** *v.t.* to loosen or remove the fastening.—**untruth'** *n.* a lie. These are not given except where the meaning or derivation cannot easily be found from the simple word.

Unan'imous (ū-) *a.* of one mind, agreeing.—**unan'imously** *adv.*—**unanim'ity** *n.*

Unassu'ming (-sū-) *a.* not bold or forward.

Unavai'ling *a.* of no avail; ineffectual; useless.

Unbi'assed *a.* free from bias; impartial.

Uncann'y *a.* weird, mysterious; not canny.—**uncann'iness** *n.*

Un'cate *a.* hooked.

Unc'le (unk'l) *n.* the brother of a father or mother; the husband of an aunt.

Uncollec'tivised *a.* not working under a system of collectivisation.

Uncouth' (-ōōth) *a.* clumsy, without ease or polish.— **uncouth'ly** *adv.*

Unc'tion *n.* anointing; soothing words or thought; fervour of words or tone; imitation of this; affected enthusiasm.—**unc'tuous** *a.* full of unction; greasy.

Undamped' (-dampt) *a.* not moistened or wet; not depressed.—**undamped oscillations,** in electricity, continuous waves; waves persisting with undiminished amplitude.

Un'der *prep.* below, beneath; bound by, included in; in the time of.—*adv.* in a lower place or condition.—*a.* lower. —**underbred'** *a.* ill-bred.— **undercharge'** *v.t.* to charge less than the proper amount. —*n.* too low a charge.—**underhand'** *a.* unfair, sly.— **underhung'** *a.* with the lower part projecting beyond the upper.—**un'derling** *n.* a subordinate.—**underneath'** *adv.* below.—*prep.* under.—**un'dershot** *a.* moved by water passing under.—**un'dertow** *n.* a current beneath the surface moving in a different direction from the surface current; backwash; and numerous other compounds of *under* which need no explanation.

Undergrad'uate *n.* a student, or member of a university or college, who has not taken his first degree.

Und'erslung *a.* in motoring, of a car having frame or chassis below the axles.

Understand' *v.t.* to see the meaning of; infer; take for granted.—*v.i.* to be informed. —understand'ing *n.* intelligence.

Undertake' *v.t.* to make oneself responsible for; enter upon.—un'dertaker *n.* one who undertakes; one who manages funerals.

Un'derwrite *v.t.* to agree to pay, to take up shares in, e.g. in marine insurance.—un'derwriter *n.* an agent in marine insurance, etc.

Undistor'ted *a.* in wireless, without distortion.

Undo' *v.t.* to reverse what has been done; to annul; to unfasten.—undo'ing *n.*—undone' *a.* not performed; ruined.

Un'dulate (-dū-) *v.i.* to move in waves or like waves.—undula'tion *n.*—un'dulatory *a.*

Ungain'ly *a.* awkward, uncouth.

Un'guent *n.* an ointment.

Uni- *prefix,* one.

U'nicorn *n.* a fabulous animal with a single long horn.

U'niform *a.* not changing, unvarying; conforming to the same standard or rule.—*n.* uniform dress worn by members of the same body, e.g. soldiers, nurses, etc.—u'niformly *adv.*—uniform'ity *n.* —u'nify *v.t.* to bring to unity or uniformity.—unifica'tion *n.*—u'nion *n.* joining into one; state of being joined; the result of being joined; federation, combination of societies, etc.; a trade-union. —u'nionist *n.* a supporter of union.—Union Jack *n.* the national flag of the British

Empire. — u'nionism *n.*—unique' (-ēk) *a.* being the only one of its kind.—u'nison *n.* agreement, harmony; sounding at the same pitch.—unite' *v.t.* to join into one, connect.—*v.i.* to become one, combine.—u'nity *n.* the state of being one; harmony.—u'nit *n.* a single thing or person; a standard quantity. —unitar'ian(-ér-) *n.* a member of a Christian body that denies the doctrine of the Trinity.—unitar'ianism *n.*

U'niverse *n.* the whole of creation, all existing things.—univer'sal *a.* relating to all things or all men; applying to all members of a community.—univer'sally *adv.*—universal'ity *n.*—univer'sity *n.* an educational institution for study, examination and conferment of degrees in all or most of the important branches of learning.

Univ'ocal *a.* having but one meaning; having unison in sounds; sure; certain.—*n.* a word that has but one meaning.

Unkempt' *a.* of rough or uncared-for appearance.

Unleav'ened *a.* not raised by leaven or yeast.

Unless' *conj.* if not, except when.

Unnat'ural *a.* not natural; contrary to the laws of nature; acting without natural affections.

Unru'ly *a.* badly behaved, ungovernable.

Until' *prep.* up to the time of. —*conj.* to the time that;

with a negative, before.

Un'to *prep.* to.

Up *adv.* in or to a higher position, a source, an activity, etc.; quite.—*prep.* to or towards the source, etc.—**up'ward** *a.* and *adv.*—**up'wards** *adv.*

Up- as *prefix* makes compounds mostly of obvious meaning, e.g. **up'bringing** *n.* bringing up.—**uphold'** *v.t.* to hold up, support, etc.

Upbraid' *v.t.* to scold, reproach.

Upholst'erer (-ō-) *n.* one who provides carpets, hangings, or covers chairs, etc.—**upholst'er** *v.t.* to put coverings on, supply carpets, etc.—**upholst'ery** *n.*

Up'land *n.* high land; ground elevated above meadows and valleys.—*a.* rustic; rude.—**upland'ish** *a.*

Uplift' *v.t.* to raise aloft.—(**up'-**) *n.* an upheaval; exaltation of any kind.

Upon' *prep.* on.

Upp'er *a.* higher, situated above.—*n.* the upper part of a boot or shoe.—**upp'ish** *a.* self-assertive.

Up'right *a.* erect; honest, just.—*n.* a thing standing upright, e.g. a post in a framework.

Up'roar *n.* a tumult, disturbance.—**uproar'ious** *a.*—**uproar'iously** *adv.*

Upset' *v.t.* to overturn.—*a.* overturned.—*n.* an upsetting; trouble.

Up'shot *n.* outcome, end.

Up'start *n.* one suddenly raised to wealth, power, etc.

Urse'mia, ure'mia (ūr-ē-mi-a)

n. a morbid condition of the blood due to retention of waste products.

Urbane' *a.* polished, courteous.—**urban'ity** *n.*—**ur'ban** *a.* relating to a town or city.

Urch'in *n.* a hedgehog; a mischievous boy; a boy or youngster.

Urge *v.t.* to drive on; entreat or exhort earnestly.—**ur'gent** *a.* pressing; needing attention at once; importunate.—**ur'gently** *adv.*—**ur'gency** *n.*

U'rine *n.* the fluid secreted by the kidneys.—**u'ric** *a.*—**u'rinate** *v.t.* to discharge urine.—**u'rinal** *n.* a place for urinating.

Urn *n.* a vase with a foot and usually a rounded body.

Use (ūs) *n.* employment, application to a purpose; profit, serviceableness; need to employ; habit.—**use** (ūz) *v.t.* to employ, avail oneself of; accustom.—**u'sable** (-z-) *a.*—**u'sage** (-s-) *n.* act of using; custom; customary way of using.—**use'ful** (-s-) *a.*—**use'fully** *adv.*—**use'fulness** *n.*—**use'less** *a.*—**use'lessly** *adv.*—**use'lessness** *n.*—**u'sual** (-z-) *a.* habitual, ordinary.—**u'sually** *adv.*

Ush'er *n.* a doorkeeper, one showing people to seats, etc.; formerly an under-teacher.—*v.t.* to introduce, announce.

Us'quebaugh (-kwe-baw) *n.* whisky.

U'sufruct *n.* the right of using and enjoying the produce, benefit, or profits of a thing belonging to another, provided that it be without alienating or impairing the substance.

Usurp' (ū-) *v.t.* to seize wrongfully.—usurp'er *n.*—usurpa'tion *n.*

U'sury (-z-) *n.* lending of money at excessive interest; such interest.—u'surer *n.*—usu'rious *a.*

Uten'sil (ū-) *n.* a vessel or implement, *esp.* in domestic use.

Util'ity (ū-) *n.* usefulness; a useful thing.—utilita'rianism *n.* doctrine that the morality of actions is to be tested by their utility, *esp.* that the greatest good of the greatest number should be the sole end of public action.—utilita'rian (-ēr-) *a.*—u'tilise *v.t.* to make use of.—utilisa'tion *n. Syn.* advantageousness, benefit, profit, avail, service.

Ut'most *a.* extreme, furthest.

Uto'pia (ū-) *n.* an imaginary state with perfect political, social conditions or constitution.—Uto'pian *a.* visionary [title of Sir T. More's imaginary country (in book published 1516), fr. G. *ou*, not, and *topos*, place].

Utt'er *a.* complete, total.—utt'erly *adv.*

Utt'er *v.t.* express, emit audibly; put in circulation.—utt'erance *n.* uttering; expression in words; spoken words.

U'vula *n.* the pendent fleshy part of the soft palate.—u'vular *a.*

Uxor'ious *a.* excessively fond of one's wife.

V

Vacate' *v.t.* to quit, leave empty. — va'cant *a.* unoccupied; without thought, empty.—va'cantly *adv.*—va'cancy *n.*—vaca'tion *n.* act of vacating; holidays. — vac'uum *n.* a place devoid of matter; a place from which air has been practically exhausted.—vac'uous *a.* vacant.—vacu'ity *n.* — vacuum cleaner *n.* an apparatus for removing dust from carpets, etc., by suction.

Vac'cinate (-ks-) *v.t.* to inoculate with vaccine as a protection against smallpox. —vaccina'tion *n.*—vac'cinator *n.*—vac'cine *n.* a virus of cowpox.

Va'cillate (vas'-) *v.i.* to waver. —vacilla'tion *n.*

Va'de-me'cum *n.* a manual for ready reference; a pocket companion.

Vag'abond *a.* having no fixed dwelling.—*n.* a wanderer; an idle scamp.—vag'abondage *n.* —vagar'y (-ēr-) *n.* a freak; an unaccountable proceeding.—vague *a.* of indefinite or uncertain character or meaning.

Va'grant *n.* a tramp.—*a.* on tramp; wandering idly.—va'grancy *n.*

Vain *a.* worthless, useless; conceited; foolish.—vain'ly *adv.*

Val'ance *n.* a short curtain round a bedstead, etc.—val'anced *a.*

Vale *n.* valley.

Valedic'tion *n.* a farewell.—**valedic'tory** *a.*

Va'lence, va'lency *n.* in chemistry, the combining power of an element.

Valenci'ennes (-sĕ-enz) *n.* a rich kind of lace made at *Valenciennes*.

Val'entine *n.* a picture, set of verses, etc., sent to a sweetheart on the 14th February; a sweetheart chosen on that day.

Valer'ian (-ĕr-) *n.* a flowering herb.

Val'et (-ă, or -et) *n.* a manservant looking after his master's clothes, etc.

Valetu'dinary *a.* sickly.—**valetudina'rian** *n.* a person obliged or disposed to live the life of an invalid.

Valhall'a *n.* in Scandinavian mythology, the place of immortality.

Val'iant *a.* brave.

Val'id *a.* sound; of binding force in law.—**valid'ity** *n.*—**val'idate** *v.t.*

Val'ise (-ēs) *n.* a travelling bag.

Vall'ey *n.* a low area between hills.

Val'our (-ęr) *n.* bravery.—**val'orous** *a.*—**val'ue** *n.* worth, price; equivalent.—*v.t.* to estimate a value of; to care for.—**val'uable** *a.* capable of being valued; of great value.—*n.* a valuable thing.—**valua'tion** *n.*—**val'ueless** *a.*—**val'uer** *n.*

Valve *n.* a device to control the passage of a fluid through a pipe; a thermionic valve (*q.v.*).—**val'vular** *a.*

Vamoose' *v.t.* and *i.* in North America, to depart quickly; leave; decamp.

Vamp *n.* the upper leather of a shoe.—*v.t.* and *i.* to improvise.

Vamp'ire *n.* a blood-sucking ghost; (*slang*) a person who preys on others.—**vamp** *n.* (*slang*) a vampire.

Van *n.* a leading division of an army or fleet.—**van'guard** *n.*

Van *n.* a covered vehicle, *esp.* for goods.

Vana'dium *n.* a metallic element used in the manufacture of hard steel.

Van'dalism *n.* barbarous destruction of works of art.

Vane *n.* a weather-cock; part of a paravane; a fin on a bomb to prevent swerving when dropped from the air.

Vang *n.* a brace leading from the end of a gaff to the ship's side, to steady the gaff.

Vanill'a *n.* a plant of the orchid kind; an extract of this for flavouring.

Van'ish *v.i.* to disappear.

Van'ity *n.* empty display; vain or futile pride.

Van'quish *v.t.* to subdue in battle; to conquer; to refute. — **van'quishable** *a.* — **van'quisher** *n.*

Van'tage (vā-) *n.* advantage.

Vap'id *a.* flat, dull.—**vapid'ity** *n.*

Va'pour (-ĕr) *n.* a gaseous form of a substance more familiar as liquid or solid; steam or mist; invisible moisture in the air.—**va'porise** *a.*—**va'porous** *a.*—**va'poriser** *n.* in internal-combustion engine, device for reducing liquid to vapour.

Var'icose *a.* of a vein, morbidly dilated.

Var'nish *n.* a resinous solution put on a surface to make it hard and shiny.—*v.t.* to apply varnish to. *Syn.* lacquer, japan, glaze, polish, garnish, gild, gloss.

Var'y (vĕr'-i) *v.t.* to change.—*v.i.* to be changed; to become different.—var'iable *a.*—variabil'ity *n.*—var'iance *n.* state of discord.—var'iant *a.* different.—*n.* a difference in form.—varia'tion *n.*—var'iegate *v.t.* to diversify by patches of different colours.—variega'tion *n.*—vari'ety *n.* state of being varied or various; a varied assortment; a sort or kind.—var'ious *a.* manifold, diverse, of several kinds. *Syn.* modify, transform, metamorphose, variegate, deviate, depart, alternate.

Vase (vāz) *n.* a vessel, a jar.—vas'cular *a.* of, or having, vessels for conveying sap, blood, etc.

Vas'eline *n.* a substance obtained from petroleum, used as a salve, ointment, etc.

Vass'al *n.* a holder of land by feudal tenure; a dependant.—vass'alage *n.*

Vast (-à-) *a.* very large.—vast'ly *adv.*—vast'ness *n.*

Vat *n.* a large tub.

Vaude'ville (vōd-vil) *n.* a light gay song with a refrain; a theatrical piece with light satirical songs; in wireless, a variety concert.

Vault (volt) *n.* an arched roof; an arched apartment; a cellar.—*v.t.* to build with an arched roof.

Vault (volt) *v.i.* to spring or jump with the hands resting on something.—*v.t.* to jump over in this way.—*n.* such jump.

Vaunt *v.i.* to boast.—*v.t.* to boast of.—*n.* a boast.

Veal *n.* calf flesh.

Vedette' *n.* a mounted sentinel.

Veer *v.i.* to change direction; to change one's opinion.

Veer *v.t.* to slacken or let out (rope).

Veg'etable (-j-) *a.* of, from, or concerned with, plants.—*n.* a plant, *esp.* one used for food.—vegeta'rian *n.* one who does not eat meat.—vegeta'rianism *n.*—veg'etate *v.i.* to live the life of a plant.—vegeta'tion *n.* plants collectively; the plants growing in a place; the process of plant-growth.

Ve'hement (vĕ-im-) *a.* vigorous, impetuous. — ve'hemently *adv.*—ve'hemence *n. Syn.* furious, violent, passionate, hot, ardent, zealous, strong, intense, forcible, powerful.

Ve'hicle (vĕ-ikl) *n.* a carriage, cart, or other conveyance on land; a means of expression.—vehic'ular *a.*

Veil (vāl) *n.* a piece of material to cover the face or head; a pretext.—*v.t.* to cover with, or as with, a veil.

Vein (vān) *n.* tube in the body taking blood to the heart; a rib of a leaf or insect's wing; a fissure in rock filled with ore; a streak.—*v.t.* to mark with streaks.—ve'nous *a.*

Veldt, veld (velt) *n.* in South Africa, a grass country.—**veldt'schoen** *n.* a shoe made of untanned hide.

Vell'um *n.* parchment of calf skin prepared for writing on or bookbinding.

Velo'city (-os'-) *n.* speed, rate of speed.—**veloc'ipede** (-los-) *n.* the name originally given to the bicycle.

Vel'vet *n.* a silk fabric with a thick, short pile.—**vel'vety** *a.* —**velveteen'** *n.* a cotton fabric resembling velvet.

Ve'nal *a.* guilty of taking, prepared to take, bribes.—**venal'ity** *n.*

Ve'nary *n.* hunting; the chase. —**venat'ical** *a.* used in hunting; fond of hunting.

Vend *v.t.* to sell.—**vend'or** *n.*—**vend'ible** *a.*

Vendett'a *n.* a blood-feud.

Veneer' *v.t.* to cover with a thin layer of finer wood.—*n.* such covering.

Ven'erable *a.* worthy of reverence.—**ven'erate** *v.t.*—**venera'tion** *n.*

Vene'real *a.* from, or connected with, sexual intercourse.

Ven'ery *n.* hunting; sports of the chase.

Venesec'tion *n.* the act of opening a vein; blood letting.

Ven'geance *n.* revenge, retribution for wrong done.—**venge'ful** *a.*—**venge'fully** *adv.*

Ve'nial *a.* pardonable.

Ven'ison *n.* the flesh of deer.

Ven'om *n.* poison; spite.—**ven'omous** *a.*

Vent *n.* a small hole or outlet. —*v.t.* to give outlet to.

Vent'ilate *v.t.* to supply with fresh air; to bring into discussion.—**vent'ilator** *n.*—**ventila'tion** *n.*

Ven'tral *a.* abdominal.

Ven'tricle *n.* a cavity or hollow in the body, *esp.* in the heart or brain.—**ventric'ular** *a.*

Ventril'oquist *n.* one who can so speak that the sounds seem to come from some other person or place.—**ventril'oquism** *n.*—**ventrilo'quial** *a.*

Ven'ture *n.* an undertaking of a risk, a speculation.—*v.t.* to risk.—*v.i.* to dare; have courage to do something or go somewhere.—**ven'turesome** *a.*—**ven'turous** *a.*

Ven'ue *n.* district in which a case is tried; meeting place.

Vera'cious (-ā-) *a.* truthful.—**vera'city** (-as'-) *n. Syn.* of " veracity," credibility, honesty, consistency, accuracy. *Ant.* falseness, dishonesty, falsity, falsehood, untruth.

Veran'dah *n.* an open gallery or portico at the side of a house.

Verb *n.* the part of speech which asserts or declares.—**verb'al** *a.* of, by, or relating to, words.—**verb'ally** *adv.*—**verba'tim** *adv.* word for word. —**verb'iage** *n.* excess of words.—**verbose'** *a.* wordy. —**verbos'ity** *n.*

Verd'ant *a.* green.—**verd'ure** *n.* greenery.—**verd'urous** *a.*

Ver'derer *n.* an officer that has charge of the king's forests to preserve the vert and venison.

Ver'dict *n.* the decision of a jury; an opinion reached after examination of facts, etc.

Ver'digris *n.* green rust on copper.

Verd'ure *see* VERDANT.

Verein' (fer-ĭn) *n.* a voluntary and permanent association of persons or parties for some common purpose.

Verge *n.* edge, brink.—**ver'ger** *n.* a bearer of a wand of office; an usher in a church.

Verge *v.i.* to be on the border of, come close to.

Ver'ify (-fī) *v.t.* to prove or confirm the truth of.—**verifi'able** *a.*—**verifica'tion** *n.*—**ver'itable** *a.* true, genuine.—**ver'itably** *adv.*—**ver'ity** *n.* truth.—**ver'ily** *adv.* truly.—**verisimil'itude** *n.* appearance of truth, likelihood.

Ver'juice *n.* sour fruit juice.

Vermicell'i *n.* an Italian paste of flour, etc., made in long thin strings.—**verm'icide** *n.* a substance to destroy worms.—**verm'iform** *a.* shaped like a worm.—**verm'ifuge** *n.* a substance to drive out worms.—**vermil'ion** *n.* a bright red colour or pigment.—*a.* of this colour.—**ver'min** *n.* injurious animals, parasites, etc.—**ver'minous** *a.*—**ver'mouth** (-mōōth) *n.* a liqueur of wormwood.

Vernac'ular *a.* of language, of one's own country. — *n.* mother tongue; homely speech.

Vern'al *a.* of spring.

Vern'ier *n.* a small sliding scale for obtaining fractional parts of the subdivisions of a graduated scale.

Ver'onal *n.* the protected trade name of a colourless crystalline compound of malic acid, used extensively as hypnotic or sedative, dangerous in repeated doses.

Veron'ica *n.* a genus of plants including the speedwell.

Ver'satile *a.* capable of dealing with many subjects.—**versatil'ity** *n.*—**verse** *n.* a line or poetry; a short division of a poem or other composition.—**ver'sify** *v.t.* to turn into verse.—*v.i.* to write verses.—**versifica'tion** *n.*—**ver'sion** a translation; an account or description.—**ver'so** *n.* the back of an object; a left-hand page.—**versed** *a.* skilled. — **ver'sus** *prep.* against. **vert'ebra** *n.* a single section of a backbone.—**vert'ebrate** *a.* having a backbone.—**vert'ebral** *a.* — **vert'ex** *n.* **vert'ices** *pl.* summit.—**vert'ical** *a.* upright; overhead.—**verti'go** *n.* giddiness.—**verti'ginous** (-ij'-) *a.* dizzy.

Vers libre (vär-lĕbr) *n.* free verse.

Vert *n.* everything that bears a green leaf within the forest; liberty to cut green trees or wood.

Ver'vain *n.* a plant of the genus *Verbena.*

Verve *n.* enthusiasm; spirit; energy.

Ver'vet *n.* a South African monkey.

Ver'y *a.* true, real. — *adv.* extremely, to a great extent.

Ves'icle *n.* a small blister,

bubble, or cavity.—**versio′-
ular** *a.*

Ves′pers *n.pl.* an evening church service.

Vess′el *n.* any utensil or appliance for containing, *esp.* for liquids; a ship.

Vest *n.* a waistcoat; an undergarment for the trunk.—*v.t.* to endow.—*v.i.* to be in a person's authority.—**vest′-ment** *n.* a robe or official garment.—**vest′ry** *n.* a room attached to a church for keeping vestments, holding meetings, etc.; a parish meeting.—**vest′ure** *n.* clothing.

Ves′ta *n.* a small wax lucifer match; a small planet.—**ves′tal** *a.* pure; chaste.

Vest′ibule *n.* an entrance hall, passage, or space between outer and inner doors.

Vest′ige (-ij) *n.* trace or mark.

Vetch *n.* a plant of the bean family used for fodder.

Vet′eran *n.* a person who has served a long time, *esp.* a soldier with much service.

Vet′erinary *a.* of, or for, the diseases of domestic animals.—**vet′erinary sur′geon** *n.*—**vet** *v.t. sl.* for examine; check; audit.

Vet′iver *n.* the dried root of cuscus grass used for mats, fans, etc.

Ve′to *n.* the power of rejecting a piece of legislation, or preventing it from coming into effect; any prohibition.—*v.t.* to enforce a veto against; forbid with authority.

Vex *v.t.* to annoy or distress.—**vexa′tion** *n.*—**vexa′tious** *a.*—

vexed *a.* much discussed.

Vi′aduct *n.* a bridge over a valley for road or rail.

Vi′al, phi′al *n.* a small glass bottle.

Vi′ands *n.pl.* food.

Vi′brate *v.i.* to move to and fro rapidly and continuously, to oscillate, quiver.—*v.t.* to cause to do this.—**vibra′tion** *n.*—**vibra′tory** *a.*—**vi′brant** *a.*

Vic′ar *n.* a clergyman in charge of a parish; a deputy.—**vic′arage** *n.* a vicar's house.—**vicar′ial** (-ėr-) *a.*—**vicar′i-ous** *a.* done or suffered by one person on behalf of another.—**vicar′iously** *adv.*

Vice *n.* a fault or blemish; an evil or immoral habit or practice.—**vi′cious** (vish′us) *a.*—**vi′ciously** *adv.*

Vice *n.* an appliance with a screw jaw for holding things while working on them.

Viceger′ent (vīsj-) *n.* the holder of delegated authority.—**vice′roy** *n.* a ruler acting for a king in a province or dependency.—**vicere′gal** *a.*—**vice′reine** *n.fem.* a viceroy's wife.—**viceroy′alty** *n.*—**vi′ce** (-sē) **ver′sa** *adv.* the other way round.

Vic′enary (vis-) *a.* consisting of twenty.—**vi′cennial** *a.* happening once in twenty years.

Vicin′ity *n.* neighbourhood.

Viciss′itude *n.* change of fortune.—*pl.* ups and downs. *Syn.* interchange, mutation, revolution, variation.

Vic′tim *n.* a person or animal killed as a sacrifice; one killed or injured as an accident or so that an object may be gained by another.—vic'timise *v.t.* to make a victim of.—victimisa'tion *n.*

Vic'tor *n.* a conqueror or winner.—vic'tory *n.* the winning of a battle, etc.—victor'ious *a.*—victor'iously *adv.*

Victual (vit'l) *n.* (usually in *pl.*) food.*v.t.* to supply with food. —*v.i.* to obtain supplies.

Vicu'na (-kōō-) *n.* a South American animal of the camel kind.—vicuna cloth, a cloth made of a mixture of cotton and wool.

Vi'de *v.* see; refer to.

Videl'icet (-set) *adv.* to wit; namely; viz.

Vie (vī) *v.t.* to contend, enter into competition.

View (vū) *n.* a survey by eyes or mind; a picture; a scene; opinion; purpose.—*v.t.* to look at, examine, survey.—view'less *a.* invisible.

Vig'il (-j-) *n.* a keeping awake, a watch.—vig'ilant *a.*—vig'ilance *n.*

Vignette' (vin-yet') *n.* an illustration in a book not enclosed in a definite border; a portrait showing only head and shoulders with the background shaded off; a slight word-sketch.

Vig'our (-ger) *n.* force, strength, activity.—vig'orous *a.*—vig'orously *adv.*

Vi'king *n.* a Northern sea-rover of the eighth to tenth centuries.

Vile *a.* base, mean, bad.—vile'ness *n.*—vile'ly *adv.*—vil'ify *v.t.* to speak ill of.—

vilifica'tion *n.*—vil'ipend *v.t.* to vilify.

Vill'a *n.* a country or suburban house.—vill'age *n.* an assemblage of dwellings in the country.—vill'ager *n.* one who dwells in a village.—vill'ein (-en), vill'ain (-en) *n.* a feudal serf.—vill'ain *n.* a scoundrel.—vill'ainous *a.*—vill'ainy *n.*

Vim *n.* force, energy; vigour.

Vina'ceous *a.* belonging to grapes or wine; wine coloured.

Vinaigrette' *n.* a small bottle of smelling-salts.

Vin'dicate *v.t.* to establish the truth or merit of, to clear of charges.—vindica'tion *n.*—vin'dicator *n.*—vin'dicatory *a.*—vindic'tive *a.* revengeful; inspired by resentment. *Syn.* defend, justify, excuse, exonerate. *Ant.* condemn, accuse, incriminate.

Vine *n.* the climbing plant which bears grapes.—vine'yard (vin'-) *n.* a vine farm, or plantation of vines—vi'nery *n.* a greenhouse for grapes.—vi'nous *a.* of, or due, to wine.—vin'tage *n.* the gathering of the grapes; the yield; wine of a particular year.—vint'ner *n.* a dealer in wine.—vine'gar *n.* an acid liquid got from wine and other alcoholic liquors.

Vi'ol *n.* a mediæval instrument like a violin.—violin' *n.* a fiddle.—vi'ola *n.* a tenor fiddle.—violoncell'o (-chel'-) *n.* a large bass violin.—violin'ist *n.* — violoncell'ist *n.*

Vi'ola *n.* a single-coloured variety of pansy.

Vi'olate *v.t.* to outrage, desecrate; infringe.—**viola'tion** *n.*—**vi'olator** *n.*—**vi'olent** *a.* of great force; marked by, or due to, extreme force or passion or fierceness.—**vi'olence** *n.*—**vi'olently** *adv. Syn.* invade, ravish. *Ant.* obey, sanctify, treat well, respect.

Vi'clet *n.* a plant with a small bluish-purple flower; the flower; the colour of it.—*a.* of this colour.

Vi'per *n.* a venomous snake.

Vira'go *n.* an abusive woman.

Vir'gin *n.* a girl or woman who has not had sexual intercourse with a man.—*a.* without experience of sexual intercourse; unsullied; fresh, untilled (of land).—**vir'ginal** *a.*—**virgin'ity** *n.*

Virgin'ia (-jin-) *n.* a kind of tobacco so called from *Virginia*, the place of its growth.—**Virginia creeper**, a climbing vine whose leaves turn bright red in autumn.

Vir'ile *a.* manly; strong.—**viril'ity** *n.*

Vir'tue *n.* moral goodness; a good quality; inherent power.—**vir'tual** *a.* so in effect though not in name.—**vir'tually** *adv.*—**vir'tuous** *a.* morally good; chaste.—**vir'tuously** *adv.*—**virtu** *n.* artistic excellence; objects of art or antiquity taken collectively.—**virtuo'so** *n.* one with special skill in a fine art.

Vi'rus *n.* poison; a disease infection.—**vir'ulent** *a.* poison-ous; bitter, malignant.—**vir'ulently** *adv.* — **vir'ulence** *n.*

Vis *n.* force; power; energy.—**vis inertiæ**, inertia; sluggishness.

Vi'sa (vē-) *n.* an endorsement on a passport to show that it has been examined.

Vis'age (-z-) *n.* face.

Visc'era (vis-) *n.pl.* the contents of the great cavities of the body as of the abdomen, etc.—**visc'eral** *a.*

Vis'cid *a.* sticky, of a consistency like treacle.—**vis'cous** *a.* viscid.—**viscid'ity** *n.*—**viscos'ity** *n.*

Vis'count (vī-kownt) *n.* a peer of rank next above a baron.—**viscount'ess** *fem.*

Vis'ion (vizh'n) *n.* sight.—**vis'ionary** *a.* unpractical, dreamy.—*n.* one full of fancies.—**vis'ible** *a.* that can be seen.—**visibil'ity** *n.*—**vis'ibly** *adv.*—**vis'ta** *n.* a view, *esp.* between trees, etc.—**vis'ual** *a.* of sight.—**vis'ualise** *v.t.* to make visible; to form a mental image of.—**visualisa'tion** *n. Syn.* of *a.* discernible, perceptible, clear, conspicuous. *Ant.* indiscernible, imperceptible, obscure, inconspicuous.

Vis'it *v.t.* to go or come and see.—*n.* a visiting.—**vis'itor** *n.*—**vis'itant** *n.* a visitor.—**visita'tion** *n.* a formal visit or inspection; an affliction or plague.

Vi'sor, **vi'sard**, **viz'ard** *n.* the front part of a helmet made to move up and down before the face.

Vis′ta *n.* a view, *esp.* a distant view through trees.

Vi′ta-glass *n.* the protected trade name of a type of glass which ultra-violet rays can penetrate.

Vi′tal *a.* necessary to, or affecting l′fe.—vi′tally *adv.*—vital′ity *n.* life, vigour.—vi′talise *v.t.* give life to.

Vit′ianin *n.* a factor in certain foo l-stuffs regarded as essential to life and health.

Vi′tiate (vish′-) *v.t.* to spoil, deprive of efficacy.—vitia′tion *n.* [vines.

Vit′iculture *n.* the culture of

Vit′reous *a.* of glass; glassy.—vit′rify *v.t.* and *i.*—vitrifac′tion, vitrifica′tion *n.*—vit′riol *n.* sulphuric acid; caustic speech.—vitriol′ic *a.*

Vitu′perate (vī-) *v.t.* to abuse in words, revile.—vitupera′tion *n.*—vitu′perative *a.*

Viva′cious (vī-) *a.* lively.—viva′city (-as′-) *n.*—viv′id *a.* bright, intense; clear, lively, graphic.—viv′idly *adv.*—viv′ify *v.t.* to animate, inspire.—vivip′arous *a.* bringing forth young alive.—viv′isection *n.* dissection or experiment on living bodies of animals, etc.—viv′isector *n.*—viva′rium *n.* a place to keep living creatures.

Vi′va vo′co (vī-va vō-sē) *adv.* by word of mouth.

Vix′en *n.* a female fox; a spiteful woman.—vix′enish *a.*

Viz′ard *see* VISOR.

Viz′ier *n.* a minister of state in a Mohammedan country.

Vlei (vlĕ) *n.* in South Africa, a valley; a marshy place; a

depression where water stands; small lake.

Voc′able *n.* a word.—vocab′ulary *n.* a list of words; a stock of words used.

Vo′cal *a.* of, with, or giving out, voice.—vo′calist *n.* a singer.—vo′cally *adv.*—vo′calise *v.t.* to utter with the voice.—voca′tion *n.* a calling.—voc′ative *n.* in some languages, the case of nouns used in addressing a person.—vocif′erate *v.t.* to shout.—vocif′erous *a.* shouting, noisy.—vocifera′tion *n.*—voice *n.* the sound given out by a person in speaking or singing, etc.; the quality of the sound; expressed opinion; share in a discussion; the verbal forms proper to relation of subject and action.—*v.t.* give utterance to.—voice′less *a.*

Vod′ka *n.* a Russian whisky or brandy distilled from rye.

Vogue (vōg) *n.* fashion.

Void *a.* empty.—*n.* empty space.—*v.t.* to empty out.

Voile *n.* a thin woollen or silk material used in women's dresses.

Vol′atile *a.* evaporating quickly; lively.—volatil′ity *n.*—volat′ilise *v.t.* and *i.*

Volca′no *n.* a mountain with a hole through which lava, ashes, smoke, etc., are discharged.—volcan′ic *a.*

Voli′tion (-ish′-) *n.* act or power of willing.—voli′tional *a.*

Voll′ey *n.* a simultaneous discharge of weapons or missiles; a rush of oaths, questions, etc.—*v.t.* to discharge in a volley.—*v.i.* to fly in a volley.

Volt *n.* the practical unit of electro-motive force.—volt′age *n.* electrical potential difference expressed in volts. —volt′meter *n.* instrument for measuring force in volts.

Vol′uble *a.* with incessant or abundant speech.—volubil′ity *n.*—vol′ubly *adv.*—vol′ume *n.* a book, or part of a book, bound; a mass; bulk, space occupied.—volu′minous *a.* bulky, over ample. *Syn.* fluent, glib, loquacious. *Ant.* hesitant, slow of speech, taciturn, tongue-tied.

Volumet′ric, volumet′rical *a.* pertaining to measurement by volume.

Vol′untary *a.* having, or done by, free will.—*n.* an organ solo in a church service.—vol′untarily *adv.*—volunteer′ *n.* one who offers service, joins a force, etc., of his own free will.—*v.i.* to offer oneself.

Volup′tuous *a.* of or contributing to the pleasures of the senses.—volup′tuary *n.* one given to luxury and sensual pleasures.

Vom′it *v.t.* to eject from the stomach through the mouth. —*v.i.* to be sick.—*n.* matter vomited.

Voo′doo *n.* among the negroes of America, one who practises witchcraft, enchantments; an evil spirit.—*v.t.* to put a spell on.

Voor′trekker *n.* in South Africa, a pioneer.

Vora′cious *a.* greedy, raven-ous.—vora′city (-as′-) *n.*—vora′ciously *adv.* *Syn.* rapacious, insatiable. *Ant.* abstemious, generous, satiable.

Vor′tex *n.* vor′tices *pl.* a whirlpool; a whirling motion.

Vorticism′ *n.* modern movement in painting, which holds that the artist's aim is to create new realities, not copy nature.—vorticist′ *n.*

Vote *n.* the formal expression of a choice; an individual pronouncement, or right to give it, in a question or election; the result of voting; that which is given or allowed by vote.—*v.i.* to give a vote.—*v.t.* to grant or enact by vote.—vo′ter *n.*—vo′tary *n.* one vowed to a service or pursuit.—vo′taress *fem.*—vo′tive *a.* given or consecrated by vow.—vow *n.* a solemn promise, *esp.* a religious one.—*v.t.* to promise or threaten by vow.

Vouch *v.i.* to vouch for, to guarantee, make oneself responsible for.—vouch′er *n.* a document proving the correctness of an item in accounts.—vouchsafe′ *v.i.* to condescend to grant or do something.

Vow′el *n.* any of the sounds pronounced without stoppage or friction of the breath; a letter standing for such sound.

Voy′age *n.* a journey, *esp.* a long one, by water.—*v.i.* to make a voyage.

Vrille (vril) *n.* in aviation, a nose-dive with considerable spin.

Vul'canise *v.t.* to treat (rubber) with sulphur at a high temperature.—**vul'canite** *n.* rubber so hardened.—**vulcanisa'tion** *n.*—**vulcanol'ogy** *n.* the science of igneous phenomena, volcanoes, geysers, etc.

Vul'gar *a.* of the common people; common; coarse, not refined; offending against good taste.—**vulgar'ian** (-ér-) *n.* a vulgar fellow, *esp.* a rich one.—**vul'garly** *adv.*—**vul'garism** *n.* a word or construction used only by the uneducated.—**vulgar'ity** *n.*—**vul'garise** *v.t.* to make vulgar or too common.—**vulgarisa'tion** *n.*—**Vul'gate** *n.* the fourth century Latin version of the Bible. *Syn.* general, unrefined. *Ant.* particular, refined, exclusive, distinctive.

Vul'nerable *a.* not proof against wounds; offering an opening to criticism, etc.; in contract bridge, denoting a side which has won its first game in the rubber and is subject to increased honours and penalties.—**vulnerabil'ity** *n.*

Vul'nerary *a.* useful in healing wounds.— *n.* any plant, drug, or composition useful in the cure of wounds.

Vul'pine *a.* of foxes; foxy.

Vul'ture *n.* a large bird which feeds on carrion.

W

Wab'ble *see* WOBBLE.

Wad (wod) *n.* a small pad of fibrous material.—*v.t.* to line, pad, stuff, etc., with a wad.—**wadd'ing** *n.* stuffing.

Wad'dle (wod'l) *v.i.* to walk like a duck.

Waddy *n.* in Australia, a native wooden war-club or walking stick.

Wade *v.i.* to walk through something that hampers movement, *esp.* water.—**wa'der** *n.* a person or bird that wades; a high waterproof boot.

Wad'y, wad'i (wod-) *n.* the channel of a water-course which is dry, except in the wet season.

Wa'fer *n.* a thin cake or biscuit; a disc of paste for fastening papers.—*v.t.* to fasten with a wafer.—**waf'fle** *n.* a kind of pancake.

Waft (wà-) *v.t.* to convey smoothly through air or water.—*n.* a breath of wind, odour, etc.

Wag *v.t.* to cause to move to and fro.—*v.i.* to shake, swing. —*n.* a merry fellow.—**wagg'ery** *n.*—**wagg'ish** *a.*—**wag'tail** *n.* a small bird with a wagging tail.

Wage *n.* payment for work done (usually in *pl.*).—*v.t.* to carry on.—**wa'ger** *n.* and *v.t.* and *i.* bet.

Wag'gle *v.t.* to wag.

Wagg'on, wag'on *n.* a four-wheeled vehicle for heavy loads.—**wagg'oner, wag'oner** *n.*—**waggonette', wagonette'** *n.* a four-wheeled carriage with lengthwise seats drawn by horses.—**wagon lit** (vag-ön lē) *n.* an international term for a sleeping car on a train.

Waif n. a home ess person, esp. a child.

Wail n., v.t. and i. lament.

Wain n. a waggon, esp. in farm use.

Wains'cot n. wooden lining of the walls of a room.—v.t. to line thus.

Waist n. the part of the body between hips and ribs; various central parts.—waist'coat n. a sleeveless garment worn under a coat.

Wait v.t. to await.—v.i. to be expecting, to attend; to serve at table.—n. an act of waiting; a carol-singer.—wait'er n.—wait'ress fem.

Waive v.t. to forgo.

Wa'ke n. in New Zealand, a Maori canoe.

Wake v.i. to rouse from sleep. —v.t. to rouse from sleep; to stir up.—n. a watch by a dead person; a holiday. wa'ken v.t. to wake.—wake'-ful a.

Wake n. the track left by a ship; a track.

Wale, weal n. the streak left by the blow of a stick or whip.

Wa'ler n. a cavalry horse imported into India from New South Wales.

Walk (wawk) v.i. to move on the feet at an ordinary pace; to cross by walking; to cause to walk.—n. the slowest gait of animals; occupation or career; a path or other place for walking; a spell of walking for pleasure, etc.—walk'er n.

Wall (wawl) n. a structure of brick, stone, etc., serving as a fence, side of a building, etc.; the surface of one.—v.t. to supply with a wall; to block up with a wall.—wall'-flower n. a garden flower, often growing on walls.

Wall'a, wallah (wol'-) n. a merchant, an agent; a worker.—competition wallah, a member of the Indian Civil Service admitted by competitive examination.

Wall'aby (wol-) n. a small kangaroo.

Wallaroo' n. a large kangaroo.

Wall'et (wol-) n. a small bag; a pocket-book.

Wall'-eyed (wawl-īd) a. having eyes with pale irises.

Wall'op v.t. to beat soundly; to flog.—n. a stroke or blow. —wall'oper n.

Wall'ow (wol-ō) v.i. to roll (in a liquid).

Wal'nut (wawl-) n. a large nut with a crinkled shell splitting easily into two halves; the tree.

Wal'rus (wol-) n. a large sea-animal with long tusks.

Waltz (wawlts) n. a dance.— v.i. to dance it.

Wam'ble (wom-) v.i. to be disturbed with nausea; to move irregularly to and fro; to roll.

Wa'mmerah n. the Australian throwing stick.

Wam'pun n. small beads made of shells, used by North American Indians as money and for ornament.

Wan (won) a. pale, sickly-complexioned.

Wand (wond) n. a stick,

usually straight and slender.

Wand'er (won-) *v.i.* to roam; ramble.

Wane *v.i.* and *n.* decline.

Wang'le *v.t.* to manipulate, manage in a skilful way.

Want (wont) *n.* and *v.t.* and *i.* lack.

Want'on (won-) *a.* unrestrained; playful; dissolute; without motive.—*v.i.* to frolic.—*n.* a wanton person. *Syn.* loose, luxuriant, lewd. *Ant.* restrained, controlled, reserved, rigid, austere.

Wap'iti (wop-) *n.* a North American stag related to the red deer, erroneously called the elk.

War (wor) *n.* fighting between nations; state of hostility.— *v.i.* to make war.—**war'fare** *n.* hostilities —**war'like** *a.*— **warr'ior** *n.* a fighter.

War'atah *n.* an Australian shrub.

War'ble (wor-) *v.i.* to sing with trills.—**warb'ler** *n.*

Ward (word) *n.* guardianship; a minor under care of a guardian; a division of a city, or hospital, etc.—*pl.* the indentations of the head of a key or lock.—*v.t.* to guard.—**ward'er** *n.* a prison keeper. — **ward'ress** *fem.* — **ward'ship** *n.*—**ward'robe** *n.* a piece of furniture for hanging clothes in.—**ward'room** *n.* an officers' mess on a warship.— **ward'en** *n.* a president or governor.—**ward'enship** *n.*

Ware *n.* goods; articles collectively.—**ware'house** *n.* a store-house; a large commercial establishment.

Ware *a.* on guard.—*v.t.* to beware.

Warm (worm) *a.* moderately hot; ardent. — *v.t.* and *i.* to heat. — **warm'ly** *adv.*— **warm'th** *n.*

Warn (worn) *a.* to caution, put on guard.

Warp (worp) *n.* the lengthwise threads in a loom; a rope.— *v.t.* to twist; to move by a rope fastened to a buoy.— *v.i.* to become twisted.

Warr'ant (wor-) *a.* authority; a document giving authority. —*v.t.* to authorise; to guarantee.—**warr'anty** *n.*

Warr'en (wor-) *n.* ground occupied by rabbits.

Wart (wort) *n.* a hard growth on the skin.

War'y (wēr'i) *a.* cautious.— **war'ily** *adv.*

Wase *n.* a wisp of hay, straw, etc.; a pad worn on the head by porters, etc., to ease the pressure of a burden.

Wash (wosh) *v.t.* to clean with liquid; to carry along with a rush of water; to colour lightly.—*v.i.* to wash oneself; to stand washing.—*n.* an act of washing; clothes washed at one time; sweep of water, *esp.* set up by moving ship; a thin coat of colour. —**wash'er** *n.* one who or that which washes; a ring put under a nut.—**wash'y** *a.* dilute.—**wash'-out** *n.* *slang,* a failure; unsuccessful business or person.

Wasp (wosp) *n.* a striped stinging insect resembling a bee.—**wasp'ish** *a.* irritable.

Wass'ail (wos-l, was-l) *n.*

drinking-bout; liquor for it. —*v.i.* to carouse.

Waste (wåst) *v.t.* to expend uselessly, use extravagantly; lay desolate.—*v.i.* to dwindle; pine away.—*a.* wasted; desert.—*n.* what is wasted; act of wasting; a desert.—**wast'age** *n.*—**waste'ful** *a.*—**waste'fully** *adv.*—**wast'er** *n.*

Watch (wotsh) *n.* a state of being on the look-out; a spell of duty; a pocket clock.—*v.t.* to observe closely; guard. —*v.i.* to be on watch, be wakeful. — **watch'ful** *a.*—**watch'fully** *adv.*—**watch'man** *n.*—**watch'keeper** *n.* officer of the watch.—**watch'maker** *n.* —**watch'word** *n.* a rallying-cry. *Syn.* of "watchful," vigilant, heedful, attentive, cautious. *Ant.* careless, negligent, incautious, inattentive.

Wat'er (wawt'er) *n.* a transparent tasteless liquid, the substance of rain, rivers, etc.; the transparency of a gem.—*v.t.* to put water on or into; to cause to drink.—*v.i.* to take in or obtain water.— **wat'ery** *a.*—**wat'ertight** *a.*—**wat'erproof** *a.* not letting water through.—*n.* a waterproof garment.—**wat'ermark** *n.* a mark in paper made during manufacture and visible on holding the paper to the light.

Watt (wot) *n.* the unit of electric power.

Wat'tle (wot-) *n.* a hurdle of wicker.—*v.t.* to make into basket-work.

Waul, wawl *v.i.* to cry, as a cat; to squall.

Wave *v.i.* to move to and fro; to beckon; to have an undulating shape.—*v.t.* to move to and fro; to give the shape of waves; to express by waves.—*n.* an act or gesture of waving; a ridge and trough on water, etc.; a vibration.— **waves** *n.pl.* wireless disturbances, regular in nature, and consisting of electric and magnetic forces alternating in direction, set up in the ether by electrical oscillations radiated by a conductor. —**wa'vy** *a.*—**wa'vily** *adv.*

Wa'ver *v.i.* to hesitate, be irresolute.—**wa'verer** *n.* *Syn.* vacillate, fluctuate. *Ant.* decide, determine, remain steady.

Wax *v.i.* to grow, increase.

Wax *n.* a yellow plastic material made by bees; this or similar substance used for sealing, making candles, etc. —*v.t.* to put wax on.

Way *n.* track; direction; method.—**way'farer** *n.* a traveller, *esp.* on foot.—**waylay'** *v.t.* to lie in wait for.—**way'ward** *a.* capricious, perverse.— **way'wardly** *adv.*—**way'wardness** *n.*

Wayz'goose *n.* a fat goose; a printer's annual dinner.

We *pron.* the first person plural pronoun.

Weak *a.* lacking strength.— **weak'ly** *a.* weak; sickly.— **weak'ly** *adv.*—**weak'en** *v.t.* and *i.*—**weak'ling** *n.* a feeble creature.—**weak'ness** *n.*

Weal *n.* well-being.—**wealth** (welth) *n.* riches; abundance. —**wealth'y** *a.*

Weal *see* WALE.

Weald (wēld) *n* a forest; wold; any open country; a district in Kent.—**weald'en** *a.*

Wean *v.t.* to accustom to food other than mother's milk.—**wean'ling** *n.* a newly weaned child.

Weap'on (wep'n) *n.* an implement to fight with.

Wear (wēr) *v.t.* to carry on the body; show; consume.—*v.i.* to last; to become impaired by use.—*n.* act of wearing; impairment; things to wear. —**wear'er** *n.*

Wear'y *a.* tired.—*v.t.* and *i.* tire.—**wear'ily** *adv.*—**wear'iness** *n.*—**wear'isome** *a.*

Wea'sand *n.* the wind-pipe.

Weas'el (-z-) *n.* a small animal like a ferret.

Weath'er (weŦH) *n.* atmospheric conditions.—*a.* towards the wind.—*v.t.* to affect by weather; to sail to windward of; to come safely through.—**weath'er-cock** *n.* a revolving vane to show which way the wind blows.— **weather-proof,** to denote motor-car designed to bear exposure to all weathers without sensible depreciation. —**weather report,** a daily report of meteorological elements.

Weave *v.t.* to form in texture or fabric by interlacing.— **weav'er** *n.*

Web *n.* a woven fabric; the net spun by a spider; the membrane between the toes of waterfowl.

Wed *v.t.* to marry; to unite closely.—**wedd'ing** *n.* a mar-riage.—**wed'lock** *n.* marriage.

Wedge *n.* a piece of material sloping to an edge.—*v.t.* to fasten or split with a wedge; to stick by compression or crowding.

Wed'nesday (wenz'di) *n.* the fourth day of the week.

Wee *a.* small; little.—**Wee Frees,** those who refused to become members of the United Free Church (of Scotland) in 1900.

Weed *n.* a plant growing where it is not desired.—*v.t.* to free from weeds.—**weed'y** *a.*

Weeds *n. pl.* widow's mourning garments.

Week *n.* a period of seven days. —**week'ly** *a.* happening, done, etc., once a week.—**week'ly** *adv.* once a week.

Ween *v.i.* think.

Weep *v.i.* to shed tears.—*v.t.* to lament.

Wee'vil *n.* a beetle harmful to grain, etc.

Weft *n.* cross threads in weaving; woof.

Weigh (wā) *v.t.* to find the weight of; raise.—*v.i.* to have weight.—**weight** *n.* gravity as a property of bodies; a heavy mass; an object of known mass for weighing; importance.—*v.t.* to add a weight to.— **weight'y** *a.*—**weight'ily** *adv.*

Weir *n.* a dam across a river.

Weird *a.* unearthly.

Wel'come *a.* received gladly.— *n.* kindly greeting.—*v.t.* to receive gladly.

Weld *v.t.* to unite (hot metal) by hammering; to unite closely.—*n.* a welded joint.

Wel'fare *n.* well-being.

Wel'kin *n.* the sky.

Well *adv.* in good manner or degree.—*a.* in good health; suitable. *Syn.* healthy, hearty, sound, expedient. *Ant.* unhealthy, cold, unsound, inexpedient.

Well *n.* a deep hole for water; a spring.—*v.i.* to flow out or up.

Well'ington *n.* a rubber boot reaching to below the knee, and worn in wet weather.

Welsh *a.* of Wales.—*n.* the language of Wales, or the people.

Welsh, welch *v.t.* and *i.* to cheat, by running off from a race-course without paying one's debts. — **welsher, welcher** *n.*

Welt *n.* a seam; a leather rim put on a boot-upper for the sole to be attached to; a wale.—*v.t.* to provide a shoe with a welt; to thrash.

Welt'er *v.i.* to roll or tumble.—*n.* turmoil.

Wen *n.* a tumour forming a permanent swelling beneath the skin.

Wench *n.* a young woman.

Wend *v.i.* to go.

Werf, werft *n.* in South Africa, a meadow or paddock; a farmyard; a homestead.

Wer'wolf, were'wolf *n.* a human being turned into a wolf.

Wes'leyan (wes'-) *a.* of Wesley or the Church founded by him.—*n.* a member of that church.

West *n.* the part of the sky where the sun sets; a part of a country, etc., lying to this side.—*a.* that is toward this region.—*adv.* to the west.—**wes'terly** *a.*—**west'ward** *a.* and *adv.*—**west'wards** *adv.*—**west'ern** *a.*

West'inghouse brake' *n.* a brake for railway trains and motor-cars, worked by compressed air.

Wet *a.* having water or other liquid on a surface or being soaked in it; rainy.—*v.t.* to make wet.—*n.* moisture, rain.—**wet-battery**, in electricity, accumulator battery.

Weth'er (-TH-) *n.* a castrated ram.

Whack *v.t.* to hit, *esp.* with a stick.—*n.* such a blow.

Whale *n.* a large fish-shaped sea animal.—**whale'bone** *n.* a springy substance from the upper jaw of certain whales.—**wha'ler** *n.* a man or ship employed in hunting whales.—**whale-back**, a vessel with a covered-in and rounded deck, for rough seas.

Wha're (hwo-ri) *n.* in New Zealand, a dwelling.

Wharf (worf) *n.* a quay for loading and unloading ships.—**wharf'age** *n.* accommodation or dues at a wharf.—**wharf'inger** *n.* wharf owner.

What (hwot) *pron.* which thing?; that which.—*a.* which.—**whatev'er** *pron.* anything which; of what kind it may be.

What'not *n.* a piece of furniture having shelves for books, ornaments, etc.

Wheat *n.* the cereal plant with thick four-sided seed-spikes

---

thére, fáther, her; awl, oil, owl.

of which bread is chiefly made.—**wheat'en** a.

Wheat'ear n. a small bird.

Whee'dle v.t. to coax.

Wheel n. a circular frame or disc with spokes revolving on an axle.—v.t. to convey by wheeled apparatus or vehicles; to cause to turn or change direction.—v.i. to revolve; to change direction.—**wheel'barrow** n. a barrow with one wheel.—**wheel'-wright** n. a maker or repairer of wheels.—**wheel'-base,** in motoring, distance between front and rear hubs of vehicle.—**wheel'-bounce,** in motoring, bouncing of wheel permitted by uncontrolled spring.—**wheel'-spin,** revolution of wheels of motor-car without full grip of road.

Wheeze v.i. to breathe with difficulty and noise.—**wheez'y** a.

Whelk n. a shell-fish.

Whelm v.t. to submerge.

Whelp n. pup or cub.—v.i. and t. to produce whelps.

When adv. at what time.—conj. at the time that.—**whenev'er** adv. and conj. at whatever time.

Whence adv. from what place.

Where adv. and conj. at what place.—**whereas'** conj. considering that, while on the contrary.—**where'fore** adv. why.—conj. consequently.—**wherev'er** adv. at whatever place.

Wherr'y n. a light boat.

Whet v.t. to sharpen.—**whet'-stone** n. a stone for sharpening tools. Syn. incite, stimu-

late, provoke. Ant. make blunt, restrain, check, allay.

Wheth'er (-TH-) a. and pron. which of the two.—conj. introduces the first of two alternatives, of which the second may be expressed or implied.

Whey n. the watery part of milk.

Which a. asks for a selection from alternatives. — pron. which person or thing; the thing "who."

Whiff v.t. and i. and n. puff.

Whig n. a member of the political party that was more or less the ancestor of the Liberal Party.

While n. a space of time.—conj. in the time that.—v.t. to pass (time, usually idly).—**whilst** adv.

Whim n. a caprice, fancy.—**whim'sical** a.—**whimsical'ity** n.

Whim'per v.i. to cry or whine softly.—n. such cry.

Whin n. a plant with yellow flowers.—**whin-chat,** a small singing-bird which haunts whins.

Whine n. a long-drawn wail.—v.i. to make one.

Whinn'y v.i. to neigh joyfully.—n. such neigh.

Whip v.t. to apply a whip to; thrash; lash.—v.i. to dart.—n. a lash attached to a stick for urging or punishing.—**whip'cord** n. thin hard cord.—**whipp'er-snapper** n. a small child; an insignificant person.—**whipp'et** n. a coursing dog like a small greyhound.

Whip'-poor-will n. an American bird named from its note.

Whir v.i. to fly with a buzzing or whizzing sound.—n. a buzzing or whizzing sound.

Whirl v.t. and i. swing rapidly round.—n. a whirling movement.—**whirl'igig** n. a spinning toy.—**whirl'pool** n. a circular current. — **whirl'wind** n. a wind whirling round a forward-moving axis.

Whisk v.t. and i. brandish, sweep, or beat lightly.—n. a light brush; a flapper; an egg-beating implement. — **whisk'er** n. hair of a man's face.

Whisk'y, whisk'ey n. a spirit mainly distilled from barley.

Whisp'er v.t. and i. to speak with rustling breath instead of voice.—n. such speech.

Whist n. a card game.

Whis'tle (-sl) n. the sound made by forcing the breath through rounded and nearly closed lips; any similar sound; an instrument to make it.—v.i. to make such sound.—v.t. to utter or summon, etc., by whistle.—**whis'tler** n.

Whit n. a jot.

White a. of the colour of snow; pale; light in colour.—n. the colour of snow; white pigment; a white part.—**whi'ten** v.t. and i.—**white'ness** n.—**whi'tish** a.—**white'bait** n. a small eatable fish.—**white-line** n. a traffic sign; a safety line at a bend or corner of a road.—**white'smith** n. a tinsmith.—**white'wash** n. a liquid mixture for whitening.—v.t. to apply this; to clear of imputations.—**white drugs**, harmful narcotics; dope. — **whi'ting** n. dried chalk; a fish. *Syn.* hoar, clean, unblemished. *Ant.* black, dark, impure, stained, tarnished.

Whith'er (-TH-) adv. to what place.

Whit'low n. an inflamed swelling on a finger.

Whit'tle v.t. to cut or carve with a knife; to pare away.

Whiz n. a violent hissing sound.—v.i. to move with such sound, or make it.

Whizz-bang n. soldier's name for light German shell used in the war, the rush of the shell through the air and the explosion being heard almost simultaneously.

Who (hōō) *pron.* relative and interrogative pronoun, always referring to persons.—**whoev'er** *pron.* any one or everyone that.

Whole (h-) a. complete; healthy; all.—n. a complete thing or system.—**who'lly** adv.—**whole'meal** a. of or pertaining to flour which contains the whole of the grain.—**whole'sale** n. sale of goods by large quantities.—a. dealing by wholesale; extensive. — **whole'saler** n.—**whole'some** a. producing a good effect, physically or morally. *Syn.* perfect, intact, unbroken, good, strong, total, undivided. *Ant.* incomplete, imperfect, damaged, part.

Whoop (hōōp) v.t. and i. and n. shout.—**whoop'ing-cough**

n. a disease marked by a whooping breath.

Whop *v.t.* to beat severely.—**whopp'er** *n.* anything unusually large; a monstrous lie.

Whore (h-) *n.* a prostitute.

Whorl *n.* a turn of a spiral; a ring of leaves.

Whor'tleberry *n.* bilberry.

Why *adv.* and *conj.* for what cause.

Wick *n.* the strip or thread feeding the flame of a lamp or candle.

Wick *n.* a village; a jurisdiction.

Wick, wich (wik) *n.* a creek; a bay; a salt-pit.

Wick'ed *a.* evil, sinful.—**wick'edly** *adv.*—**wick'edness** *n.*

Wick'er *n.* plaited osiers, etc.

Wick'et *n.* a small gate; in cricket, a set of three stumps and bails.

Wide *a.* broad; far from the mark.—*n.* in cricket, a ball bowled wide of the wicket out of the batsman's reach.—**wi'den** *v.t.* and *i.*—**wide'ly** *adv.*—**width** *n.*

Wid'geon *n.* a wild duck.

Wid'ow (-ō) *n.* a woman whose husband is dead and who has not married again.—*v.t.* to make a widow of.—**wid'ower** *n.* a man whose wife has died and who has not married again.—**wid'owhood** *n.*

Wield *v.t.* to hold and use.

Wife *n.* wives *pl.* a woman married to a man.—**wife'ly** *a.*

Wig *n.* artificial hair for the head.

Wight (wit) *n.* a person.

Wig'wam *n.* a Red Indian's hut or tent.

Wild (wīld) *a.* not tamed or domesticated; savage; excited, rash.—**wild'ly** *adv.*—**wild'ness** *n.*—**wil'derness** *a.* desert.

Wil'debeest (wil-de-bēst) *n.* the gnu.

Wile *n.* a trick.—**wi'ly** *a.*

Will *v.aux.* forms moods and tenses indicating intention or conditional result.—*v.i.* to have a wish.—*v.t.* to wish; to intend, purpose; to leave as a legacy.—*n.* the faculty of deciding what one will do; purpose, wish; directions written for disposal of property after death.—**will'ing** *a.* ready or given cheerfully.—**will'ingly** *adv.*—**will'ingness** *n.*—**will'y-nill'y** *adv.* willing or unwilling.—**wil'ful** *a.* obstinate, refractory. *Syn.* of "wilful," perverse, stubborn, wayward, dogged, headstrong. *Ant.* obedient, submissive, unintentional.

Will'-o'-the-wisp *n.* a light flitting over marshes; an elusive person or hope.

Will'ow (-ō) *n.* a tree yielding osiers and wood for cricket-bats, etc.—**will'owy** *a.* lithe and slender.

Wi'lly-wi'lly *n.* in Australia, a heavy gale in the north-west coast.

Wilt *v.t.* to make flaccid, as a plant; to depress.—*v.i.* to fade; to droop.

Win *v.t.* to get by labour or effort; to reach; to allure; be successful in. — *v.i.* to be successful.—**winn'er** *n.*

Wince *v.i.* to flinch.—*n.* a flinching.

Win'cey *n.* a cotton and woollen cloth.

Winch *n.* a crank; a windlass.

Wind *n.* air in motion; breath. —(wind) *v.t.* to sound by blowing.—**wind'age** *n.* the difference between the diameter of the bore of a gun and that of the ball or shell. —**wind'fall** (-awl) *n.* a fallen fruit; a piece of good luck.— **wind'mill** *n.* a mill worked by sails.—**wind'pipe** *n.* the passage from throat to lungs.— **wind'y** *a.*—**wind'ward** (-ord) *n.* the side towards the wind.

Wind (wind) *v.i.* to twine; to vary from a direct course.— *v.t.* to twist round, wrap; to make ready for working by tightening a spring.—**wind'-lass** *n.* a machine which hauls or hoists by wrapping rope round an axle.

Win'dlestraw *n.* a stalk of grass, as dog's-tail.

Win'dow (-ō) *n.* a hole in a wall to admit light.

Wind'screen *n.* in motoring, a sheet of glass in front of the driver to protect him from the weather.

Wine *n.* the fermented juice of the grape.—**wine'press** *n.* —**wine'bibber** *n.* tippler.

Wing *n.* a limb a bird uses in flying; flight; a lateral extension.—*v.t.* to cross by flight; supply with wings; disable.—*v.i.* to fly.

Wink *v.i.* to close and open an eye; to connive.—*n.* an act of winking.

Win'kle *n.* a periwinkle.

Winn'ow (-ō) *v.t.* to blow free of chaff.

Win'some *a.* charming.

Win'ter *n.* the fourth season. —*v.i.* to pass the winter.— *v.t.* to tend during winter.— **win'try** *a.*

Wipe *v.t.* to rub so as to clean. —*n.* a wiping.—**wi'per** *n.* one that wipes; something that wipes; in motoring, an automatically operated arm to keep a part of the windscreen free from rain or dust; in electrical apparatus, a brush bearing on a wipe contact maker.

Wire *n.* metal drawn into the form of cord; a telegram.— *v.t.* to provide catch, fasten with, wire; send by telegraph.—**wi'ry** *a.* like wire, tough.—**wire'less** *n.*, *a.* and *v.t.* telegraphy or telephony without connecting wires.— **wire-pulling,** political, intrigue.

Wise *a.* sagacious; having intelligence and knowledge.— **wis'dom** *n.*—**wise'ly** *adv.* *Syn.* sensible, judicious, sage, erudite, politic, craft, prudent, sound. *Ant.* foolish, irrational, senseless, idiotic, unwise, absurd, indiscreet, preposterous.

Wise *n.* manner.

Wise'acre *n.* a foolish pretender to wisdom.

Wish *v.i.* to have a desire.— *v.t.* to desire.—*n.* a desire or thing desired.—**wish'ful** *a.*

Wisp *n.* a twisted handful, usually of straw, etc.

Wist'ful *a.* longing.—**wist'fully** *adv.*

Wit *n.* sense; intellect; ingenuity in connecting amus-ingly incongruous ideas; a person gifted with this power. — witt'y a. — witt'ily adv.—witt'icism n. a witty remark.—witt'ingly adv. on purpose.

Witch n. a woman supposed to be using magic.—witch'craft n.—witch'ery n.

Witch'-elm, wych'-elm n. a variety of elm.—witch'-hazel n.—witch'-alder n.

With prep. in company or possession of; against; in relation to; through. — withal' (-awl) adv. also, likewise.—withdraw' v.t. and i. to draw back, retire.—withdraw'al n.—within' prep. and adv. in, inside.—without' adv. outside. — prep. lacking.—withstand' v.t. to oppose.

Withe n. a tough, flexible twig.

With'er v.i. to fade.—v.t. to cause to fade; to blight.

With'ers n.pl. ridge between a horse's shoulder-blades.—withers unwrung, not galled.

Withhold' v.t. to restrain; to keep back.—withhold'er n.

With'y n. a willow; a withe.

Wit'ness n. testimony; one who sees something; one who gives testimony.—v.i. to give testimony.—v.t. to see; to attest; to see and sign as having seen.

Wiz'ard n. a sorcerer, magician.

Wiz'ened a. shrivelled.

Woad n. a blue dye.

Woe n. grief.—woe'begone a. sorrowful.—woe'ful a.—woe'fully adv.

Wold n. a down.

Wolf (woolf) n. wolves pl. a wild beast allied to the dog.—wolverine' n. a carnivorous mammal inhabiting the Arctic regions.

Wom'an (woo-) n. wom'en pl. an adult human female; the female sex.—wom'anhood n.—wom'anly a.—wom'anish a.—wom'ankind n.

Womb (wōōm) n. the female organ of conception and gestation.

Wom'bat n. a mammal with a pouch.

Won'der (wun-) n. a marvel; the emotion excited by an amazing or unusual thing.—v.i. to feel this emotion.—won'derful a.—won'derfully adv. — won'drous a. — won'drously adv.—won'derment n. Syn. of "wonderful," marvellous, surprising, astonishing, starting, miraculous. Ant. ordinary, commonplace, usual.

Wont (-ō) n. custom.—wont'ed a. habitual.

Woo v.t. to court, seek to marry.—woo'er n.

Wood n. a tract of land with growing trees; the substance of trees, timber.—wood'en a.—wood'y a.—wood'bine n. honeysuckle.—wood'cock n. a bird like a snipe.—wood'-cut n. engraving on wood, an impression from such an engraving. — wood'land n. woods, forest.—wood'pecker n. a bird which searches tree-trunks for insects.—woods'man n. a forester.—wood'craft n. knowledge of woodland conditions.

Māte, mēte, mīte, mōte, mūte, bōōt.

Woof *n.* the threads that cross the warp in weaving.

Wool *n.* soft hair of the sheep and certain other animals.—**wooll'en** *a.*—**wooll'y** *a.*—**wool'sack** *n.* a cushion stuffed with wool, *esp.* the Lord Chancellor's seat in the House of Lords.

Wootz *n.* a kind of Indian steel.

Word (wurd) *n.* a single symbol used in speaking or writing, a unit of speech; information; promise.—*v.t.* to express in words.—**word'y** *a.*—**word'ily** *adv.*

Work (wurk) *n.* labour; task; something made or accomplished.—*pl.* a factory.—*v.t.* to cause to operate; make, shape.—*v.i.* to apply effort; labour; operate; ferment; to be engaged in a trade, profession, etc.—**work'able** *a.*—**work'er** *n.*—**work'house** *n.* an institution for paupers.—**work'man** *n.* a manual worker. — **work'manship** *n.* skill of a workman; way a thing is finished, style.—**work'shop** *n.* a place where things are made.

World (wurld) *n.* the universe; sphere of existence; mankind; society.—**world'ling** *n.* one given up to affairs of this world.—**world'ly** *a.* engrossed in temporal pursuits.

Worm (wurm) *n.* a small limbless creeping creature, shaped like a snake; the thread of a screw; a gearwheel with teeth forming part of screw threads.—*v.i.* to crawl.—*v.t.* to work (oneself) in insidiously; to extract (a secret) craftily.—**worm-wheel,** a gear wheel with teeth cut to be driven by a worm.—**worm-drive,** in motoring, a system in which the power is communicated to the road wheels by means of a worm through a worm-wheel.

Worm'wood (wurm) *n.* a bitter herb.

Worr'y (wur'i) *v.t.* to seize or shake with teeth; to trouble, harass.—*v.i.* to be unduly concerned.—*n.* useless care or anxiety.

Worse (wurs) *a.* and *adv.* comparative of bad or badly.—**worst** *a.* and *adv.* superlative of bad or badly.—**wors'en** *v.t.* and *i.*

Wor'ship (wur-) *n.* reverence, adoration.—*v.t.* to adore; love and admire.—**wor'shipful** *a.*—**wor'shipper** *n.*

Wor'sted (wur-) *n.* woollen yarn.—*a.* made of woollen yarn; spun from wool.

Worth (wurth) *a.* having value specified; meriting.—*n.* merit, value.—**wor'thy** (-TH-) *a.*—**wor'thily** *adv.*—**wor'thiness** *n.*—**worth'less** *a.*

Wound (wōōnd) *n.* an injury, hurt by cut, stab, etc.—*v.t.* to inflict a wound on; to pain.

Wrack *n.* sea-weed; wreckage.

Wraith *n.* an apparition of a person seen shortly before or after death.

Wran'gle (-ng-gl) *v.i.* to quarrel noisily.—*n.*

Wrap *v.t.* to cover, *esp.* by putting something round; to put round.—*n.* a loose garment; a covering.—**wrapp'er** *n.*

Wrath (roth, rawth) *n.* anger. —**wrath'ful** *a.*—**wrath'fully** *adv.*

Wreak *v.t.* to inflict (vengeance, etc.).

Wreath *n.* something twisted into ring form; a garland.— **wreathe** *v.t.* to surround; to form into wreath; to wind round.

Wreck *n.* destruction of a ship by accident; a wrecked ship; ruin; something ruined. —*v.t.* to cause the wreck of. —**wreck'age** *n.*

Wren *n.* a very small bird.

Wrench *n.* a violent twist; a tool for twisting or screwing. —*v.t.* to twist; distort; seize forcibly.

Wrest *v.t.* to take by force; to twist violently.—*n.* a tool for tuning a harp, etc.— **wres'tle** (-sl) *v.i.* to contend by grappling and trying to throw down.—**wres'tler** *n.*

Wretch *n.* a miserable creature.—**wretch'ed** *a.* miserable; worthless.—**wretch'edness** *n.* —**wretch'edly** *adv.* *Syn.* of *a.* distressed, afflicted, forlorn, dejected, pitiable, contemptible. *Ant.* happy, prosperous, flourishing, worthy, excellent.

Wrig'gle *v.t.* and *i.* to move sinuously, like a worm.—*n.* a quick twisting movement.

Wright (rit) *n.* a workman, a maker.

Wring *v.t.* to twist; to extort; to pain.

Wrin'kle (-ng-kl) *n.* a slight ridge on a surface.—*v.t.* to make wrinkles in.—*v.i.* to become wrinkled.

Wrin'kle *n.* a valuable hint that may help one.

Wrist *n.* the joint between the hand and the arm.—**wrist'let** *n.* a band worn on the wrist.

Write *v.i.* to mark paper, etc., with the symbols which are used to represent words or sounds; compose; to send a letter.—*v.t.* to set down in words; to compose; to communicate in writing.—**writ'** *n.* a formal or legal document.—**wri'ter** *n.*

Writhe *v.i.* to twist or roll about.

Wrong *a.* not right or good or suitable.—*n.* that which is wrong; harm; evil.—*v.t.* to do wrong to.—**wrong'ly** *adv.* —**wrong'ful** *a.* — **wrong'fully** *adv.*

Wroth *a.* angry.

Wrought (rawt) *past tense* and *p.p.* of WORK.—**wrought-iron,** iron wrought by forging.

Wry *a.* turned to one side, distorted.—**wry'neck** *n.* a small bird. [fowls.

Wy'andotte *n.* a breed of

X

Xan'thein (zan'-the-in) *n.* the yellow colouring matter of flowers that is soluble in water.—**xan'thin** *n.* the yellow, insoluble, colouring matter contained in certain flowers.—**xan'thous** *a.* yellow; denoting the yellow tribes of mankind.

Xe′ma *n.* a genus of gulls, having forked tails.

Xen′on *n.* one of the inert constituents of the air.

Xenopho′bia (zen-o-fōb′-i-a) *n.* dislike, hatred, fear, of strangers or aliens.

Xy′lene *n.* a volatile inflammable liquid.

Xy′locarp (zī′-lō-kárp) *n.* a hard, woody fruit.—**xylocarp′ous** *a.* having fruit that becomes hard or woody.

Xy′lograph (zī′-lō-graf) *n.* a wood-engraving; impression from a wood-block.—**xylog′raphy** *n.* wood-engraving. **xylog′rapher** *n.* an engraver on wood.—**xylo′graphic** *a.* pert. to xylography.

Xy′loid *a.* pert. to wood; woody.

Xy′lol *n.* xylene.

Xy′lonite (zī) *n.* celluloid.

Xy′lophone (zī-) *n.* a musical instrument of wooden bars which vibrate when struck.

Xys′ter (zis′-ter) *n.* a surgeon's instrument for scraping bones.

Y

Yacht (yot) *n.* a light vessel for racing or pleasure.—*v.i.* to cruise or race in a yacht. —**yachts′man** *n.*

Yahoo′ *n.* a brute in human form.

Yak *n.* the wild ox of Central Asia.

Yam *n.* a large, esculent tuber.

Yank′ee *n.* an inhabitant of U.S.A., *esp.* of the New England states.—*a.* belonging to U.S.A.; smart.

Yap *n.* and *v.i.* bark (of small dog).

Yapp *n.* bookbinding with limp leather cover projecting over the edges.

Yard *n.* a unit of measure, 36 inches; that length of anything; a spar slung across a ship's mast to extend sails.

Yard *n.* a piece of enclosed ground, usually with hard floor.

Yarn *n.* spun thread; a tale. —*v.i.* to tell a tale.

Yaw *v.i.* to fall off from a course in steering a ship.

Yawl *n.* a small yacht or boat.

Yawn *v.i.* to gape; to open the mouth wide, *esp.* in sleepiness.—*n.* a yawning.

Ye *pron.* you.

Yea (yā) *interj.* yes.

Year *n.* a time taken by one revolution of the earth round the sun, about 365¼ days; twelve months.— **year′ling** *n.* an animal one year old.—**year′ly** *adv.* every year, once a year.—*a.* happening, etc., once a year.

Yearn (yern) *v.i.* to feel a longing or desire.

Yeast *n.* a substance used as a fermenting agent, *esp.* in raising bread.—**yeast′y** *a.* frothy, fermenting.

Yell *v.i.* to cry out in a loud shrill tone.—*n.* a loud, shrill cry.

Yell′ow (-ō) *a.* of the colour of lemons, gold, etc.—*n.* this colour. — **yell′ow-hammer** *n.* a yellow bunting.

Māte, mēte, mīte, mōte, mūte, bōōt.

Yelp v.i. to give a quick, shrill cry.-n. such cry.

Yen n. a gold or silver coin of Japan, valued about 4s. 2d.

Yeo'man (yo-) n. a man owning and farming a small estate.-yeo'manry n. yeomen collectively; a volunteer or territorial cavalry force.

Yes interj. affirms or consents, give, an affirmative answer.

Yes'terday n. the day before to-day.

Yet adv. now, still; hitherto; nevertheless.-conj. but, at the same time.

Yew n. an evergreen tree with dark leaves; its wood.

Yield v.t. to give or return as food; profit, or result; to give up, surrender.-v.i. to produce; to surrender, give way.-n. an amount produced. Syn. give way, assent, relinquish, resign, furnish, afford, allow, admit, relax. Ant. resist, retain, keep.

Yo'del, yo'dle v.i. to warble in a falsetto tone.-n. falsetto warbling as practised by Swiss mountaineers.

Yoke n. a wooden bar put across the necks of two animals to hold them together and to which a plough. etc., may be attached; various objects like a yoke in shape or use; a bond or tie.-v.t. to put a yoke on couple, unite.

Yo'kel n. a rustic.

Yolk (yok) n. the yellow part of an egg.

Yon a. that or those over there.-**yon'der** a. yon.-adv. over there, in that direction.

Yore n. the past.

You (u) pron. the plural of the second person pronoun, but used also as a singular.

Young (yung) a. not far advanced in growth, life or existence, not yet old; vigorus.-n. offspring.-young'-ster n. a child, esp. an active or lively boy.

Your (yawr) pron. belonging to you.-yours pron.-your-self pron.

Youth (uth) n. the state or time of being young; the state before adult age, a young person; young people. youth'ful a. Syn. of a juvenile, immature, vigorous, fresh. Ant. old, mature, senile, stale.

Yo'yo n. a child's toy, a king of top on a string (Protected trade name).

Yule (ul) n. the Christmas festival.

Z

Za'ny n. a clown.

Zeal n. fervour, keenness.-zeal'ous (zei'us) a.-zeal'-ously adv.-zeal'ot n. a fanatic. Syn. fervour, energy, keenness. Ant. apathy, indifference, unconcern.

Zèbra n. a striped animal like a horse.

Zena'na (-a-)n. the women's quarters in high-cast Indian houses.

Zen'ith n. a point of the heavens directly above an observer.

Zeph'yr (zef'er) n. the west wind; a gentle breeze.

Zepp'elin n. a German airship.

Ze'ro n. nothing; the figure O; a point on a graduated instrument from which positive and negative quantities are reckoned; in military operations, ze'ro hour, the time from which each item on the programme is at an interval stated.

Zesy n. relish.

Zig'zag n. a line bent by a series of angles, thus MM. -a. forming a zigzag.-adv. with a zigzag course.-v.i. to move along with a zigzag course.

Zinc n. a white metal.-v.t. to coat with it.

Zing'aro n. a gipsy.-pl. Zing'ari.

Zith'er, zith'ern n. a flat stringed instrument with 29 to 42 strings.

Zo'diac n. an imaginary belt of the heavens outside which the sun, moon, and the chief planets do not pass and divided crosswise into twelve equal areas, called signs of the zodiac, each named after a constellation.-zo'diacal a.

Zone n. a girdle; an encircling band; any of the five belts into each the tropics and the arctic and antarctic circles divide the earth.

Zool'ogy (zo-ol'-) the natural historcy of animals, zoolo'gical a. -zool'ogist.-zoo (zoo) n. short for zoo-lógical gardens, a place where wild animals are kept for show.-zo'ophyte n. a plant-like animal, e.g. a sponge.

Zouaye (zwaw, zoo-av) n. a. soldier of French-Algerian infantry, wearing a uniform of oriental type.

Zymot'ic a. of or caused by fermentation; of a disease, due to multiplication of germs introduced into the body from outside.